Contemporary Social Psychology
Representative Readings

CONTEMPORARY SOCIAL PSYCHOLOGY:

REPRESENTATIVE READINGS

thomas blass
UNIVERSITY OF MARYLAND BALTIMORE COUNTY

ITASCA, ILLINOIS
F. E. PEACOCK PUBLISHERS, INC.

In memory of
my father,
Cantor Sigmund Blass

Table of Contents

Preface

The seventeenth century English philosopher Sir Francis Bacon once said, "Some books are to be tasted, others to be swallowed, and some few to be chewed and digested." In order to help the reader assess what kind of food for thought this book will provide, I would like to share with him or her my goals in preparing this book and to describe its distinguishing features.

The purpose of this book is to provide the student of Social Psychology with direct contact with the major topics in the field through some of the best and most interesting work relating to each topical area.

The book is divided into nine chapters, each dealing with a well-defined area of current interest and investigation in social psychology. Each chapter begins with an introduction which provides an orientation and integrative framework for the selections to follow. Each article was chosen with several criteria in mind: that it deal with an important topic or issue that is the focus of current work in social psychology; that the article be intrinsically interesting; and that it be readable. The substantive chapter introductions as well as the comprehensive selection of readings and topical coverage make the book suitable for use with or without a text. Additionally, the large number of selections of varying levels of ease and difficulty allow the instructor a great deal of flexibility in tailoring a set of readings appropriate to the level of his students.

The reader will note that attribution processes are the foci of several articles. This I feel is in keeping with the degree of importance that the topic has currently attained: What dissonance theory was to the social psychology of the 1960s, attribution theory is to the seventies. The inclusion of the chapters titled "Personality and Social Behavior" and "Communication: Verbal and Nonverbal" was dictated by my evaluation of the increasing importance of these topics in recent years. The "Personality and Social Behavior" chapter reflects the fact that social psychologists have tended more and more to include in their studies conceptually relevant personality variables, in addition to situational manipulations, in attempts at making more precise predictions of social behavior. The chapter on verbal and nonverbal communication is meant to highlight the potential and empirically demonstrated value of sociolinguistic research, systematic observation of naturally occurring behaviors, and studies on nonverbal communication for understanding social interaction.

My appreciation is extended to the authors and publishers of the articles found in this book for permission to reprint their work; to William Taft Feldman, Jonathan C. Finkelstein, and David J. Jackson for reading and commenting on the manuscript; to M. Hirsh Goldberg, whose column in the *Baltimore Jewish Times* first brought the Solzhenitsyn quote reprinted in Chapter III to my attention; to my wife, Anne, who, through her encouragement and suggestions, made an important contribution to this book; to my children, Aviva and Noam, for inspiration; and to my mother, Maria, for her devotion, as always.

Thomas Blass
Baltimore, Maryland
November, 1975

Social Perception
and Attribution Processes

Whether Ann is good-looking or not depends upon your taste; also and perhaps chiefly on your age and sex. To Octavius she is an enchantingly beautiful woman, in whose presence the world becomes transfigured, and the puny limits of individual consciousness are suddenly made infinite by a mystic memory of the whole life of the race to its beginnings in the east, or even back to the paradise from which it fell. She is to him the reality of romance, the inner good sense of nonsense, the unveiling of his eyes, the freeing of his soul, the abolition of time, place, and circumstance, the etherealization of his blood into rapturous rivers of the very water of life itself, the revelation of all the mysteries and the sanctification of all the dogmas. To her mother she is, to put it as moderately as possible, nothing whatever of the kind. Not that Octavius's admiration is in any way ridiculous or discreditable. Ann is a well formed creature, as far as that goes; and she is perfectly ladylike, graceful, and comely, with ensnaring eyes and hair.

* * *

Violet appears at the door. She is as impenitent and self-possessed a young lady as one would desire to see among the best behaved of her sex. Her small head and tiny resolute mouth and chin; her haughty crispness of speech and trimness of carriage; the ruthless elegance of her equipment, which includes a very smart hat with a dead bird in it, mark a personality which is as formidable as it is exquisitely pretty. She is not a siren, like Ann: admiration comes to her without any compulsion or even interest on her part; besides, there is some fun in Ann, but in this woman none, perhaps no mercy either: if anything restrains her, it is intelligence and pride, not compassion. Her voice might be the voice of a schoolmistress addressing a class of girls who had disgraced themselves . . .

George Bernard Shaw, Man and Superman

Commentary

Social psychology is the study of the nature of the relationship between the individual and his social environment. Although the focus of the social psychologist's inquiry is primarily on observable behavior, he is guided by the assumption that a person's responses to his social environment cannot ultimately be understood without taking into account how the person perceives and interprets the social stimuli he encounters. That is, a person's behavior in relation to his social environment is assumed to be mediated by his perceptions of, and cognitions about, that environment. The study of the principles underlying the interdependence of perceptual processes and social and personal factors has been variously called social perception, person perception, or interpersonal perception. This is the focus of this chapter.

Historically, two related but nevertheless distinct categories of research have been encompassed by the term "social perception." In the first category are the earlier studies, which sought to determine the ways an individual's personal characteristics—be they products of his internal states (such as drives or needs) or externally derived through group or cultural influences—affect his perceptions of his physical environment. This body of research, some of which is summarized in Bruner (1958), came to be known as the "New Look" in perception.

The first selection in this chapter ("They Saw a Game: A Case Study," by Hastorf and Cantril) falls into this first category of social perception research. The authors set out to determine whether, in watching a football game, what the person brings into the situation (e.g., his devotion to his own team and the need to see the players as fair and sportsmanlike) would affect how he saw the behavior of the players in the game. The game studied was a highly important one, the last of the season, between Princeton and Dartmouth. Hastorf and Cantril were able to show that although only *one* game actually took place, the event Dartmouth students saw seemed to be quite different from the one seen by Princeton students. For example, when viewing a film of the game, Princeton undergraduates reported seeing more than twice as many infractions of the rules by the Dartmouth team than Dartmouth students did.

The second category of research embraced by the term "social perception" encompasses studies addressed to the question of how we perceive other people. Thus rather than studying the effects of personal and social variables on physical perception as did the earlier studies, in contemporary social perception the predominant concern is with the processes by which we come to make inferences about people's underlying characteristics, such as feelings, traits, abilities, and intentions. The rest of the readings in this chapter are addressed in various ways to this concern.

The dominant influence on contemporary work in social perception has been the writings of Fritz Heider (e.g., 1946, 1958a, 1958b). Gestalt psychologists had made a major contribution toward our understanding of the processes governing physical perception by demonstrating that perception follows certain principles of organization. For example the way we perceive the following series of *x*'s is in accord with the Gestalt principle of proximity:

$$x\,x \qquad x\,x \qquad x\,x$$
$$1\,2 \qquad 3\,4 \qquad 5\,6$$

We perceive the *x*'s in groupings of 1 and 2, 3 and 4, 5 and 6. We do not normally perceive 2 as going with 3, nor 4 with 5.

Heider felt that just as there are laws that govern physical perception, so too are there organizing principles—many of them analogues of Gestalt principles—which underlie person perception. Two fundamental sets of principles proposed by Heider to account for the way we perceive others are known as balance theory and attribution theory.

Balance theory refers to the assumption that our cognitions and feelings about others tend toward simplicity, uniformity, and harmony. Thus the situation is more harmonious and less stressful when we agree with a friend or disagree with an enemy than when the opposite is true. According to Heider, we prefer balance, and when we are confronted with imbalanced states we will experience stress and will tend to restructure the situation so that balance exists again. Most of the work on the balance principle has focused on the type of situation just exemplified: triadic situations involving a positive or negative relationship between two people (*P* and *O*) and a third entity (*X*)—a person or thing which forms a unit with *O*. A good illustration of this kind of study is found in Chapter II (Selection 2: "My Enemy's Enemy Is My Friend"), which discusses triadic balance as it relates to attraction.

A more basic consequence of the balance principle, however, is the tendency to perceive a high degree of homogeneity in the other person's traits. This tendency to see other people as having either all positive or all negative characteristics has been referred to as the "halo effect" in person perception (Bruner & Tagiuri, 1954). An everyday example of this balancing tendency in impression formation is the often-assumed link between physical beauty and other positive attributes of the individual. In the words of Heider: "The situation is balanced if external and internal characteristics correspond, if what looks good is also truly good" (1958b, p. 183).

The second selection in this chapter ("What Is Beautiful Is Good," by Dion, Berscheid, and Walster) provides concrete experimental evidence of the degree of influence physical beauty has on perceptions of other, more internal, attributes of the person. College students were asked to form impressions of other college students depicted in photographs who had been previously rated as physically attractive, of average attractiveness, or unattractive. The results indicated that attractive persons are ascribed more socially desirable personality traits than less attractive persons. Furthermore, subjects expected that the physically attractive person would attain a higher occupational status, was less likely to ever be divorced, and would generally be happier than the less attractive individuals. It is important to note that this study did not try to answer the question regarding the *actual* link between beauty and personality characteristics. Rather, it addressed itself to the question of the *perceived* co-occurrence of attractiveness and other characteristics of an individual. To the extent that our actions toward others are based on our impressions of them, it is important to determine the bases of those impressions, regardless of their accuracy. A recent article by Berscheid and Walster (1974) provides a review of social-psychological studies of physical attractiveness.

The other major theory (in addition to balance theory) that Heider has contributed toward our understanding of the perception of people is known as *attribution theory.* According to Heider, in order to understand and predict the behavior of others, we tend to trace the actions of others to the relatively stable underlying attributes of the person and the environment. That is, in our attempts at understanding other people's actions we are generally not satisfied to stay at the level of the observable act but find it necessary to *attribute* it to its underlying determinants. Heider (1958b) outlines the various patterns which the process of attribution can take. For example, the most basic attributional decision a perceiver makes is to infer to what extent another's action is due to personal causality, on the one hand, or to environmental factors, on the other hand. Thus if I get hit by a stick as I walk down the street, my reaction (and perhaps even my suffering) will differ depending on whether someone threw the stick at me or whether it was a branch blown off the tree by the wind. My interpretation of the event will depend on the kind of attribution I make. Once a perceiver attributes an event to personal factors, he makes further attributions to the person's ability and motivation. If, in the example above, I realize the stick was thrown at me by a person, the nature of further interactions with that person will be dependent on the extent to which his action was attributable to his ability or intent. If I decide, for example, that this person is a bad shot and, even though he intended to hit me, his success was only due to luck, I can discount him as a threat in future encounters.

Recently there have been two extensions and systematizations of Heider's attribution theory, by Jones and Davis (1965) and by Kelley (1967, 1971). The third selection in this chapter, by

Cialdini, Braver, and Lewis ("Attributional Bias and the Easily Persuaded Other"), presents a study to test an assumption concerning attributional processes that had been made by Kelley (1971). According to Kelley, a function of attributional processes is to create a sense of control in the perceiver. Thus the person tends to make attributions not merely as "a seeker after knowledge. His latent goal in gaining knowledge is that of effective management of himself and his environment. He is not a pure 'scientist,' then, but an applied one" (1971, p. 22).

In line with Kelley's notions, Cialdini and his colleagues reasoned that the inferences we make about another's characteristics on the basis of our interactions with them should be of the kind that enhance our own sense of competence. According to this reasoning, if I have succeeded in persuading someone to accept my point of view, I (relative to an observer) should perceive him as more intelligent than one whom I did not influence. This should occur because, by attributing greater intelligence to the person I have persuaded, I am increasing my own sense of control and effectiveness. The study reprinted here provides empirical support for this prediction.

In addition to the theory about attributional processes derived from Heider, there are two other important theories of attribution, represented by the last two articles in this chapter. They are Stanley Schachter's cognitive theory of emotions (Schachter & Singer, 1962) and Daryl Bem's (1965, 1967) self-perception theory. Schachter's theory states that the labeling of an emotional experience is "a function of a state of physiological arousal and of a cognition appropriate to this state of arousal. . . . Cognitions arising from the immediate situation as interpreted by past experience provide the framework within which one understands and labels his feelings" (p. 380). Thus in contrast to earlier theories which posited a one-to-one relationship between a state of physiological arousal and a specific emotional state, in Schachter's theory a given physiological state could be a correlate of a variety of subjective emotional states. The particular emotion experienced will depend on the person's cognitions about the possible causes for his state of arousal that are provided by his environment.

The fourth selection in this chapter ("Insomnia and the Attribution Process," by Storms and Nisbett) is an ingenious application of Schachter's theory to the possible alleviation of a real-life problem, insomnia. The authors assumed that a heightened emotional state is a cause of insomnia. They reasoned that insomniacs have difficulty going to sleep because they attribute their alertness and their state of arousal at bedtime to intense, emotion-laden thoughts and worries. If this is the case—that insomnia is caused by attributions to emotionally tinged cognitions—it should be possible to alleviate insomnia (have the person fall asleep faster) if his state of arousal could be misattributed to an emotionally neutral cause—that is, a placebo described as an arousal-producing drug. Conversely, subjects who are given a placebo pill with alleged relaxing properties should have a harder time falling asleep than usual, for the following reason: If the insomniac experiences arousal even with a pill that is supposed to lower his arousal, he will assume that his *actual* level of emotionality is higher than usual. The experiment confirmed their predictions. The discussion section of the article discusses the therapeutic implications of the technique, the relevance of the study to attribution processes, and possible alternate explanations of the phenomenon demonstrated. In particular, note how the authors reconcile their findings with a theory of suggestion effects which would predict results exactly opposite to what they found.

Daryl Bem's view of the attribution process, known as self-perception theory, is based on the assumption that the way we infer the existence of feelings and attitudes in ourselves is not different from the way others make inferences about our feelings and attitudes—that is, on the basis of our observable behaviors (Bem, 1965, 1967). The final selection in this chapter ("Self-Observation as a Source of Pain Perception," by Bandler, Madaras, and Bem) applies Bem's theory to a study in which subjects rated the intensity level of 30 electric shocks. Although for each subject the actual intensity level of the 30 shocks received was constant, subjects gave higher discomfort ratings to shocks administered during the "escape" condition, where the subject pressed a button which always terminated the shock, than in the "no escape" condition, where he did not terminate the shock. The discomfort ratings in the "escape" condition were also significantly higher than the ratings in a third condition, the "reaction time" condition, in which pressing the button terminated the shock only half of the time. Thus, in contrast to a more intuitive view which sees behavior as a consequence of subjective states (i.e., subjective experience of pain leading to escape from source of pain), the opposite conceptionalization—that a person's reported discomfort is a function of his behavior in the presence of a pain-producing stimulus—was supported in this study.

REFERENCES

Bem, D. J. An experimental analysis of self-persuasion. *Journal of Experimental Social Psychology*, 1965, *1*, 199-218.

Bem, D. J. Self-perception: An alternative interpretation of cognitive dissonance phenomena. *Psychological Review*, 1967, *74*, 183-200.

Berscheid, E., & Walster, E. Physical attractiveness. In L. Berkowitz (Ed.), *Advances in experimental social psychology* (Vol. 7). New York: Academic Press, 1974.

Bruner, J. S. Social psychology and perception. In E. E. Maccoby, T. M. Newcomb, & E. L. Hartley (Eds.), *Readings in social psychology* (3rd ed.). New York: Holt, Rinehart & Winston, 1958. Pp. 85-94.

Bruner, J. S., & Tagiuri, R. The perception of people. In G. Lindzey (Ed.), *Handbook of social psychology* (Vol. 2). Reading, Mass.: Addison-Wesley, 1954. Pp. 634-655.

Heider, F. Attitudes and cognitive organization. *Journal of Psychology*, 1946, *21*, 107-112.

Heider, F. Perceiving the other person. In R. Tagiuri & L. Petrullo (Eds.), *Person perception and interpersonal behavior.* Stanford, Calif.: Stanford University Press, 1958. Pp. 22-26. (a)

Heider, F. *The psychology of interpersonal relations.* New York: Wiley, 1958. (b)

Jones, E. E., & Davis, K. E. From acts to dispositions: The attribution process in person perception. In L. Berkowitz (Ed.), *Advances in experimental social psychology* (Vol. 2). New York: Academic Press, 1965. Pp. 219-266.

Kelley, H. H. Attribution theory in social psychology. In D. Levine (Ed.), *Nebraska Symposium of Motivation, 1967.* Lincoln: University of Nebraska Press, 1967. Pp. 192-238.

Kelley, H. H. *Attribution in social interaction.* Morristown, N.J.: General Learning Press, 1971.

Schachter, S., & Singer, J. E. Cognitive, social, and physiological determinants of emotional state. *Psychological Review*, 1962, *69*, 379-399.

1

ALBERT H. HASTORF and HADLEY CANTRIL

They Saw a Game: A Case Study

On a brisk Saturday afternoon, November 23, 1951, the Dartmouth
football team played Princeton in Princeton's Palmer Stadium. It was the
last game of the season for both teams and of rather special significance
because the Princeton team had won all its games so far and one of its
players, Kazmaier, was receiving All-American mention and had just
appeared as the cover man on *Time* magazine, and was playing his last
game.

A few minutes after the opening kick-off, it became apparent that the
game was going to be a rough one. The referees were kept busy blowing
their whistles and penalizing both sides. In the second quarter, Princeton's star left the game with a broken nose. In the third quarter, a
Dartmouth player was taken off the field with a broken leg. Tempers
flared both during and after the game. The official statistics of the game,
which Princeton won, showed that Dartmouth was penalized 70 yards,
Princeton 25, not counting more than a few plays in which both sides were
penalized.

Needless to say, accusations soon began to fly. The game immediately
became a matter of concern to players, students, coaches, and the administrative officials of the two institutions, as well as to alumni and the
general public who had not seen the game but had become sensitive to the
problem of big-time football through the recent exposures of subsidized
players, commercialism, etc. Discussion of the game continued for several
weeks.

One of the contributing factors to the extended discussion of the game
was the extensive space given to it by both campus and metropolitan newspapers. An indication of the fervor with which the discussions were carried
on is shown by a few excerpts from the campus dailies.

Source: Albert H. Hastorf and Hadley Cantril, "They Saw a Game: A Case Study,"
Journal of Abnormal and Social Psychology, 1954, *49,* 129-134. Copyright 1954 by the
American Psychological Association. Reprinted by permission.

For example, on November 27 (four days after the game), the *Daily Princetonian* (Princeton's student newspaper) said:

This observer has never seen quite such a disgusting exhibition of so-called "sport." Both teams were guilty but the blame must be laid primarily on Dartmouth's doorstep. Princeton, obviously the better team, had no reason to rough up Dartmouth. Looking at the situation rationally, we don't see why the Indians should make a deliberate attempt to cripple Dick Kazmaier or any other Princeton player. The Dartmouth psychology, however, is not rational itself.

The November 30th edition of the *Princeton Alumni Weekly* said:

But certain memories of what occurred will not be easily erased. Into the record books will go in indelible fashion the fact that the last game of Dick Kazmaier's career was cut short by more than half when he was forced out with a broken nose and a mild concussion, sustained from a tackle that came well after he had thrown a pass.

This second-period development was followed by a third quarter outbreak of roughness that was climaxed when a Dartmouth player deliberately kicked Brad Glass in the ribs while the latter was on his back. Throughout the often unpleasant afternoon, there was undeniable evidence that the losers' tactics were the result of an actual style of play, and reports on other games they have played this season substantiate this.

Dartmouth students were "seeing" an entirely different version of the game through the editorial eyes of the *Dartmouth* (Dartmouth's undergraduate newspaper). For example, on November 27 the *Dartmouth* said:

However, the Dartmouth-Princeton game set the stage for the other type of dirty football. A type which may be termed as an unjustifiable accusation.

Dick Kazmaier was injured early in the game. Kazmaier was the star, an All-American. Other stars have been injured before, but Kazmaier had been built to represent a Princeton idol. When an idol is hurt there is only one recourse—the tag of dirty football. So what did the Tiger Coach Charley Caldwell do? He announced to the world that the Big Green had been out to extinguish the Princeton star. His purpose was achieved.

After this incident, Caldwell instilled the old see-what-they-did-go-get-them attitude into his players. His talk got results. Gene Howard and Jim Miller were both injured. Both had dropped back to pass, had passed, and were standing unprotected in the backfield. Result: one bad leg and one leg broken.

The game was rough and did get a bit out of hand in the third quarter. Yet most of the roughing penalties were called against Princeton while Dartmouth received more of the illegal-use-of-the-hands variety.

On November 28 the *Dartmouth* said:

Dick Kazmaier of Princeton admittedly is an unusually able football player. Many Dartmouth men traveled to Princeton, not expecting to win—only hoping to see an All-American in action. Dick Kazmaier was hurt in the second period, and played only a token part in the remainder of the game. For this, spectators were sorry.

But there were no such feelings for Dick Kazmaier's health. Medical authorities have confirmed that as a relatively unprotected passing and running star in a contact sport, he is quite liable to injury. Also, his particular injuries—a broken nose and slight concussion—were no more serious than is experienced almost any day in any football practice, where there is no more serious stake than playing the following Saturday. Up to the Princeton game, Dartmouth players suffered about 10 known nose fractures and face injuries, not to mention several slight concussions.

Did Princeton players feel so badly about losing their star? They shouldn't have. During the past undefeated campaign they stopped several individual stars by a concentrated effort, including such mainstays as Frank Hauff of Navy, Glenn Adams of Pennsylvania and Rocco Calvo of Cornell.

In other words, the same brand of football condemned by the *Prince*—that of stopping the big man—is practiced quite successfully by the Tigers.

Basically, then, there was disagreement as to what had happened during the "game." Hence we took the opportunity presented by the occasion to make a "real life" study of a perceptual problem.[1]

PROCEDURE

Two steps were involved in gathering data. The first consisted of answers to a questionnaire designed to get reactions to the game and to learn something of the climate of opinion in each institution. This questionnaire was administered a week after the game to both Dartmouth and Princeton undergraduates who were taking introductory and intermediate psychology courses.

The second step consisted of showing the same motion picture of the game to a sample of undergraduates in each school and having them check on another questionnaire, as they watched the film, any infraction of the rules they saw and whether these infractions were "mild" or "flagrant."[2] At Dartmouth, members of two fraternities were asked to view the film on December 7; at Princeton, members of two undergraduate clubs saw the film early in January.

The answers to both questionnaires were carefully coded and transferred to punch cards.[3]

RESULTS

Table 1.1 shows the questions which received different replies from the two student populations on the first questionnaire.

TABLE 1.1
Data from First Questionnaire

Question	Dart-mouth Students [N = 163] %	Prince-ton Students [N = 161] %
1. Did you happen to see the actual game between Dart-mouth and Princeton in Palmer Stadium this year?		
Yes	33	71
No	67	29
2. Have you seen a movie of the game or seen it on television?		
Yes, movie	33	2
Yes, television	0	1
No, neither	67	97
3. (Asked of those who answered "yes" to either or both of above questions.) From your observations of what went on at the game, do you believe the game was clean and fairly played, or that it was unnecessarily rough and dirty?		
Clean and fair	6	0
Rough and dirty	24	69
Rough and fair[a]	25	2
No answer	45	29
4. (Asked of those who answered "no" on both of the first questions.) From what you have heard and read about the game, do you feel it was clean and fairly played, or that it was unnecessarily rough and dirty?		
Clean and fair	7	0
Rough and dirty	18	24
Rough and fair[a]	14	1
Don't know	6	4
No answer	55	71
(Combined answers to questions 3 and 4 above)		
Clean and fair	13	0
Rough and dirty	42	93
Rough and fair[a]	39	3
Don't know	6	4
5. From what you saw in the game or the movies, or from what you have read, which team do you feel started the rough play?		
Dartmouth started it	36	86
Princeton started it	2	0
Both started it	53	11
Neither	6	1
No answer	3	2
6. What is your understanding of the charges being made?[b]		
Dartmouth tried to get Kazmaier	71	47
Dartmouth intentionally dirty	52	44
Dartmouth unnecessarily rough	8	35

TABLE 1.1 (Continued)
Data from First Questionnaire

Question	Dart- mouth Students [N = 163] %	Prince- ton Students [N = 161] %
7. Do you feel there is any truth to these charges?		
Yes	10	55
No	57	4
Partly	29	35
Don't know	4	6
8. Why do you think the charges were made?		
Injury to Princeton star	70	23
To prevent repetition	2	46
No answer	28	31

aThis answer was not included on the checklist but was written in by the percentage of students indicated.

bReplies do not add to 100% since more than one charge could be given.

TABLE 1.2
Data from Second Questionnaire Checked while Seeing Film

Group	N	Total Number of Infractions Checked Against	
		Dartmouth Team (Mean SD)	Princeton Team (Mean SD)
Dartmouth students	48	4.3* 2.7	4.4 2.8
Princeton students	49	9.8* 5.7	4.2 3.5

*Significant at the .01 level.

Questions asking if the students had friends on the team, if they had ever played football themselves, if they felt they knew the rules of the game well, etc. showed no differences in either school and no relation to answers given to other questions. This is not surprising since the students in both schools come from essentially the same type of educational, economic, and ethnic background.

Summarizing the data of Tables 1.1 and 1.2, we find a marked contrast between the two student groups.

Nearly all *Princeton* students judged the game as "rough and dirty"— not one of them thought it "clean and fair." And almost nine-tenths of them thought the other side started the rough play. By and large they felt that the charges they understood were being made were true; most of them felt the charges were made in order to avoid similar situations in the future.

When Princeton students looked at the movie of the game, they saw the

Dartmouth team make over twice as many infractions as their own team made. And they saw the Dartmouth team make over twice as many infractions as were seen by Dartmouth students. When Princeton students judged these infractions as "flagrant" or "mild," the ratio was about two "flagrant" to one "mild" on the Dartmouth team, and about one "flagrant" to three "mild" on the Princeton team.

As for the *Dartmouth* students, while the plurality of answers fell in the "rough and dirty" category, over one-tenth thought the game was "clean and fair" and over a third introduced their own category of "rough and fair" to describe the action. Although a third of the Dartmouth students felt that Dartmouth was to blame for starting the rough play, the majority of Dartmouth students thought both sides were to blame. By and large, Dartmouth men felt that the charges they understood were being made were not true, and most of them thought the reason for the charges was Princeton's concern for its football star.

When Dartmouth students looked at the movie of the game they saw both teams make about the same number of infractions. And they saw their own team make only half the number of infractions the Princeton students saw them make. The ratio of "flagrant" to "mild" infractions was about one to one when Dartmouth students judged the Dartmouth team, and about one "flagrant" to two "mild" when Dartmouth students judged infractions made by the Princeton team.

It should be noted that Dartmouth and Princeton students were thinking of different charges in judging their validity and in assigning reasons as to why the charges were made. It should also be noted that whether or not students were spectators of the game in the stadium made little difference in their responses.

INTERPRETATION: THE NATURE OF A SOCIAL EVENT[4]

It seems clear that the "game" actually was many different games and that each version of the events that transpired was just as "real" to a particular person as other versions were to other people. A consideration of the experiential phenomena that constitute a "football game" for the spectator may help us both to account for the results obtained and illustrate something of the nature of any social event.

Like any other complex social occurrence, a "football game" consists of a whole host of happenings. Many different events are occurring simultaneously. Furthermore, each happening is a link in a chain of happenings, so that one follows another in sequence. The "football game," as well as other complex social situations, consists of a whole matrix of events. In the game situation, this matrix of events consists of the actions of all the players, together with the behavior of the referees and linesmen, the action on the sidelines, in the grandstands, over the loud-speaker, etc.

Of crucial importance is the fact that an "occurrence" on the football field or in any other social situation does not become an experiential "event" unless and until some significance is given to it: an "occurrence" becomes an *"event"* only when the happening has significance. And a happening generally has significance only if it reactivates learned significances already registered in what we have called a person's assumptive form-world (Cantril, 1950).

Hence the particular occurrences that different people experienced in the football game were a limited series of events from the total matrix of events *potentially* available to them. People experienced those occurrences that reactivated significances they brought to the occasion; they failed to experience those occurrences which did not reactivate past significances. We do not need to introduce "attention" as an "intervening third" (to paraphrase James on memory) to account for the selectivity of the experiential process.

In this particular study, one of the most interesting examples of this phenomenon was a telegram sent to an officer of Dartmouth College by a member of a Dartmouth alumni group in the Midwest. He had viewed the film which had been shipped to his alumni group from Princeton after its use with Princeton students, who saw, as we noted, an average of over nine infractions by Dartmouth players during the game. The alumnus, who couldn't see the infractions he had heard publicized, wired:

> Preview of Princeton movies indicates considerable cutting of important part, please wire explanation and possibly air mail missing part before showing scheduled for January 25 we have splicing equipment.

The "same" sensory impingements emanating from the football field, transmitted through the visual mechanism to the brain, also obviously gave rise to different experiences in different people. The significances assumed by different happenings for different people depend in large part on the purposes people bring to the occasion and the assumptions they have of the purposes and probable behavior of other people involved. This was amusingly pointed out by the New York *Herald Tribune's* sports columnist, Red Smith, in describing a prize fight between Chico Vejar and Carmine Fiore in his column of December 21, 1951. Among other things, he wrote:

> You see, Steve Ellis is the proprietor of Chico Vejar, who is a highly desirable tract of Stamford, Conn., welterweight. Steve is also a radio announcer. Ordinarily there is no conflict between Ellis the Brain and Ellis the Voice because Steve

is an uncommonly substantial lump of meat who can support both halves of a split personality and give away weight on each end without missing it.

This time, though, the two Ellises met head-on, with a sickening, rending crash. Steve the Manager sat at ringside in the guise of Steve the Announcer broadcasting a dispassionate, unbiased, objective report of Chico's adventures in the ring. . . .

Clear as mountain water, his words came through, winning big for Chico. Winning? Hell, Steve was slaughtering poor Fiore.

Watching and listening, you could see what a valiant effort the reporter was making to remain cool and detached. At the same time you had an illustration of the old, established truth that when anybody with a preference watches a fight, he sees only what he prefers to see.

That is always so. That is why, after any fight that doesn't end in a clean knock-out, there always are at least a few hoots when the decision is announced. A guy from, say, Billy Graham's neighborhood goes to see Billy fight and he watches Graham all the time. He sees all the punches Billy throws, and hardly any of the punches Billy catches. So it was with Steve.

"Fiore feints with a left," he would say, honestly believing that Fiore hadn't caught Chico full on the chops. "Fiore's knees buckle," he said, "and Chico backs away." Steve didn't see the hook that had driven Chico back. . . .

In brief, the data here indicate that there is no such "thing" as a "game" existing "out there" in its own right which people merely "observe." The "game" "exists" for a person and is experienced by him only in so far as certain happenings have significances in terms of his purpose. Out of all the occurrences going on in the environment, a person selects those that have some significance for him from his own egocentric position in the total matrix.

Obviously in the case of a football game, the value of the experience of watching the game is enhanced if the purpose of "your" team is accomplished, that is, if the happening of the desired consequence is experienced —i.e., if your team wins. But the value attribute of the experience can, of course, be spoiled if the desire to win crowds out behavior we value and have come to call sportsmanlike.

The sharing of significances provides the links except for which a "social" event would not be experienced and would not exist for anyone.

A "football game" would be impossible except for the rules of the game which we bring to the situation and which enable us to share with others the significances of various happenings. These rules make possible a certain repeatability of events such as first downs, touchdowns, etc. If a person is unfamiliar with the rules of the game, the behavior he sees lacks repeatability and consistent significance and hence "doesn't make sense."

And only because there is the possibility of repetition is there the possibility that a happening has a significance. For example, the balls used in games are designed to give a high degree of repeatability. While a football is about the only ball used in games which is not a sphere, the shape of the modern football has apparently evolved in order to achieve a higher degree of accuracy and speed in forward passing than would be obtained with a spherical ball, thus increasing the repeatability of an important phase of the game.

The rules of a football game, like laws, rituals, customs, and mores, are registered and preserved forms of sequential significances enabling people to share the significances of occurrences. The sharing of sequential significances which have value for us provides the links that operationally make social events possible. They are analogous to the forces of attraction that hold parts of an atom together, keeping each part from following its individual course.

From this point of view it is inaccurate and misleading to say that different people have different "attitudes" concerning the same "thing." For the "thing" simply is *not* the same for different people whether the "thing" is a football game, a presidential candidate, Communism, or spinach. We do not simply "react to" a happening or to some impingement from the environment in a determined way (except in behavior that has become reflexive or habitual). We behave according to what we bring to the occasion, and what each of us brings to the occasion is more or less unique. And except for these significances which we bring to the occasion, the happenings around us would be meaningless occurrences, would be "inconsequential."

From the transactional view, an attitude is not a predisposition to react in a certain way to an occurrence or stimulus "out there" that exists in its own right with certain fixed characteristics which we "color" according to our predisposition (Kilpatrick, 1952). That is, a subject does not simply "react to" an "object." An attitude would rather seem to be a complex of registered significances reactivated by some stimulus which assumes its own particular significance for us in terms of our purposes. That is, the object as experienced would not exist for us except for the reactivated aspects of the form-world which provide particular significance to the hieroglyphics of sensory impingements.

REFERENCES

Cantril, H. *The "why" of man's experience.* New York: Macmillan, 1950.
Kilpatrick, F. P. (Ed.). *Human behavior from the transactional point of view.* Hanover, N.H.: Institute for Associated Research, 1952.

NOTES

1. We are not concerned here with the problem of guilt or responsibility for infractions, and nothing here implies any judgment as to who was to blame.

2. The film shown was kindly loaned for the purpose of the experiment by the Dartmouth College Athletic Council. It should be pointed out that a movie of a football game follows the ball, is thus selective, and omits a good deal of the total action on the field. Also, of course, in viewing only a film of a game, the possibilities of participation as spectator are greatly limited.

3. We gratefully acknowledge the assistance of Virginia Zerega, Office of Public Opinion Research, and J. L. McCandless, Princeton University, and E. S. Horton, Dartmouth College, in the gathering and collation of the data.

4. The interpretation of the nature of a social event sketched here is in part based on discussions with Adelbert Ames, Jr., and is being elaborated in more detail elsewhere.

2

KAREN DION, ELLEN BERSCHEID, and ELAINE WALSTER

What Is Beautiful Is Good

A person's physical appearance, along with his sexual identity, is the personal characteristic that is most obvious and accessible to others in social interaction. The present experiment was designed to determine whether physically attractive stimulus persons, both male and female, are (a) assumed to possess more socially desirable personality traits than physically unattractive stimulus persons and (b) expected to lead better lives (e.g., be more competent husbands and wives, be more successful occupationally, etc.) than unattractive stimulus persons. Sex of Subject x Sex of Stimulus Person interactions along these dimensions also were investigated. The present results indicate a "what is beautiful is good" stereotype along the physical attractiveness dimension with no Sex of Judge x Sex of Stimulus interaction. The implications of such a stereotype on self-concept development and the course of social interaction are discussed.

A person's physical appearance, along with his sexual identity, is the personal characteristic most obvious and accessible to others in social interaction. It is perhaps for this reason that folk psychology has always

Source: Karen Dion, Ellen Berscheid, and Elaine Walster, "What Is Beautiful Is Good," *Journal of Personality and Social Psychology*, 1972, *24*, 285-290. Copyright 1972 by the American Psychological Association. Reprinted by permission.

This research was financed in part by National Institute of Mental Health Grants MH 16729 to Berscheid and MH 16661 to Walster.

contained a multitude of theorems which ostensibly permit the forecast of a person's character and personality simply from knowledge of his outward appearance. The line of deduction advanced by most physiognomic theories is simply that "What is beautiful is good . . . [Sappho, Fragments, No. 101]," and that "Physical beauty is the sign of an interior beauty, a spiritual and moral beauty . . . [Schiller, 1882]."

Several processes may operate to make the soothsayers' prophecies more logical and accurate than would appear at first glance. First, it is possible that a correlation between inward character and appearance exists because certain personality traits influence one's appearance. For example, a calm, relaxed person may develop fewer lines and wrinkles than a tense, irritable person. Second, cultural stereotypes about the kinds of personalities appropriate for beautiful or ugly people may mold the personalities of these individuals. If casual acquaintances invariably assume that attractive individuals are more sincere, noble, and honest than unattractive persons, then attractive individuals should be habitually regarded with more respect than unattractive persons. Many have noted that one's self-concept develops from observing what others think about oneself. Thus, if the physically attractive person is consistently treated as a virtuous person, he may become one.

The above considerations pose several questions: (a) Do individuals in fact have stereotyped notions of the personality traits possessed by individuals of varying attractiveness? (b) To what extent are these stereotypes accurate? (c) What is the cause of the correlation between beauty and personality if, in fact, such a correlation exists?

Some observers, of course, deny that such stereotyping exists, and thus render Questions b and c irrelevant. Chief among these are rehabilitation workers (cf. Wright, 1960) whose clients possess facial and other physical disabilities. These researchers, however, may have a vested interest in believing that physical beauty is a relatively unimportant determinant of the opportunities an individual has available to him.

Perhaps more interestingly, it has been asserted that other researchers also have had a vested interest in retaining the belief that beauty is a peripheral characteristic. Aronson (1969), for example, has suggested that the fear that investigation might prove this assumption wrong has generally caused this to be a taboo area for social psychologists:

As an aside, I might mention that physical attractiveness is rarely investigated as an antecedent of liking—even though a casual observation (even by us experimental social psychologists) would indicate that we seem to react differently to beautiful women than to homely women. It is difficult to be certain why the effects of physical beauty have not been studied more systematically. It may be that, at some levels, we would hate to find evidence indicating that beautiful women are better liked than homely women—somehow this seems undemocratic. In a democracy we like to feel that with hard work and a good deal of motivation, a person can accomplish almost anything. But, alas (most of us believe), hard work cannot make an ugly woman beautiful. Because of this suspicion perhaps most social psychologists implicitly prefer to believe that beauty is indeed only skin deep—and avoid the investigation of its social impact for fear they might learn otherwise [p. 160].

The present study was an attempt to determine if a physical attractiveness stereotype exists and, if so, to investigate the content of the stereotype along several dimensions. Specifically, it was designed to investigate (a) whether physically attractive stimulus persons, both male and female, are assumed to possess more *socially desirable personality traits* than unattractive persons and (b) whether they are expected to *lead better lives* than unattractive individuals. With respect to the latter, we wished to determine if physically attractive persons are generally expected to be better husbands and wives, better parents, and more successful socially and occupationally than less attractive persons.

Because it seemed possible that jealousy might attenuate these effects (if one is jealous of another, he may be reluctant to accord the other the status that he feels the other deserves), and since subjects might be expected to be more jealous of attractive stimulus persons of the same sex than of the opposite sex, we examined the Sex of Subject x Sex of Stimulus Person interactions along the dimensions described above.

METHOD

Subjects

Sixty students, 30 males and 30 females, who were enrolled in an introductory course in psychology at the University of Minnesota participated in this experiment. Each had agreed to participate in return for experimental points to be added to their final exam grade.

Procedure

When the subjects arrived at the designated rooms, they were introduced to the experiment as a study of accuracy in person perception. The experimenter stated that while psychological studies have shown that people do form detailed impressions of others on the basis of a very few cues, the variables determining the extent to which these early impressions are generally accurate have not yet been completely identified. The subjects were told that the purpose of the present study was to compare person perception accuracy of untrained college students with two other groups who had been trained in various interpersonal perception techniques, specifically graduate students in clinical psychology and clinical psychologists. The experimenter noted his belief that person perception accuracy is a general ability varying among people. Therefore, according to the experimenter, college students who are high on this ability may be as accurate as some professional clinicians when making first-impression judgments based on noninterview material.

The subjects were told that standard sets of photographs would be used as the basis for personality inferences. The individuals depicted in the photographs were said to be part of a group of college students currently enrolled at other universities who were participating in a longitudinal study of personality development scheduled to continue into adulthood. It would be possible, therefore, to assess the accuracy of each subject's judgments against information currently available on the stimulus persons and also against forthcoming information.

Stimulus Materials. Following the introduction, each subject was given three envelopes. Each envelope contained one photo of a stimulus person of approximately the subject's own age. One of the three envelopes that the subject received contained a photograph of a physically attractive stimulus person; another contained a photograph of a person of average attractiveness; and the final envelope contained a photograph of a relatively unattractive stimulus person.[1] Half of our subjects received three pictures of girls; the remainder received pictures of boys.

To increase the generalizability of our findings and to insure that the general dimension of attractiveness was the characteristic responded to (rather than unique characteristics such as hair color, etc.), 12 different sets of three pictures each were prepared. Each subject received and rated only 1 set. Which 1 of the 12 sets of pictures the subject received, the order in which each of the three envelopes in the set were presented, and the ratings made of the person depicted, were all randomly determined.

Dependent Variables. The subjects were requested to record their judgments of the three stimulus persons in several booklets.[2] The first page of each booklet cautioned the subjects that this study was an investigation of accuracy of person perception and that we were not interested in the subjects' tact, politeness, or other factors usually important in social situations. It was stressed that it was important for the subject to rate the stimulus persons frankly.

The booklets tapped impressions of the stimulus person along several dimensions. First, the subjects were asked to open the first envelope and then to rate the person depicted on 27 different *personality traits* (which were arranged in random order).[3] The subjects' ratings were made on

6-point scales, the ends of which were labeled by polar opposites (i.e., exciting-dull). When these ratings had been computed, the subject was asked to open the second envelope, make ratings, and then open the third envelope.

In a subsequent booklet, the subjects were asked to assess the stimulus persons on five additional personality traits.[4] These ratings were made on a slightly different scale. The subjects were asked to indicate which stimulus person possessed the "most" and "least" of a given trait. The stimulus person thought to best represent a positive trait was assigned a score of 3; the stimulus person thought to possess an intermediate amount of the trait was assigned a score of 2; and the stimulus person thought to least represent the trait was assigned a score of 1.

In a previous experiment (see Footnote 2), a subset of items was selected to comprise an index of the *social desirability* of the personality traits assigned to the stimulus person. The subjects' ratings of each stimulus person on the appropriate items were simply summed to determine the extent to which the subject perceived each stimulus person as socially desirable.

In order to assess whether or not attractive persons are expected to lead happier and more successful lives than unattractive persons, the subjects were asked to estimate which of the stimulus persons would be most likely, and which least likely, to have a number of different life experiences. The subjects were reminded again that their estimates would eventually be checked for accuracy as the lives of the various stimulus persons evolved. The subjects' estimates of the stimulus person's probable life experiences formed indexes of the stimulus person's future happiness in four areas: (a) marital happiness (Which stimulus person is most likely to ever be divorced?); (b) parental happiness (Which stimulus person is most likely to be a good parent?); (c) social and professional happiness (Which stimulus person is most likely to experience deep personal fulfillment?); and (d) total happiness (sum of Indexes a, b, and c).

A fifth index, an occupational success index, was also obtained for each stimulus person. The subjects were asked to indicate which of the three stimulus persons would be most likely to engage in 30 different occupations. (The order in which the occupations were presented and the estimates made was randomized.) The 30 occupations had been chosen such that three status levels of 10 different general occupations were represented, three examples of which follow: Army sergeant (low status); Army captain (average status); Army colonel (high status). Each time a high-status occupation was foreseen for a stimulus person, the stimulus person was assigned a score of 3; when a moderate status occupation was foreseen, the stimulus person was assigned a score of 2; when a low-status occupation was foreseen, a score of 1 was assigned. The average status of occupations that a subject ascribed to a stimulus person constituted the score for that stimulus person in the occupational status index.

RESULTS AND DISCUSSION

Manipulation Check

It is clear that our manipulation of the relative attractiveness of the stimulus persons depicted was effective. The six unattractive stimulus persons were seen as less attractive than the average stimulus persons, who, in turn, were seen as less attractive than the six attractive stimulus persons. The stimulus persons' mean rankings on the attractiveness dimension were 1.12, 2.02, and 2.87, respectively. These differences were statistically significant (F = 939.32).[5]

Test of Hypotheses

It will be recalled that it was predicted that the subjects would attribute more socially desirable personality traits to attractive individuals than to average or unattractive individuals. It also was anticipated that jealousy might attenuate these effects. Since the subjects might be expected to be more jealous of stimulus persons of the same sex than of the opposite sex, we blocked both on sex of subject and sex of stimulus person. If jealousy attenuated the predicted main effect, a significant Sex of Subject x Sex of Stimulus Person interaction should be secured in addition to the main effect.

TABLE 2.1
Traits Attributed to Various Stimulus Others

Trait Ascription[a]	Unattractive Stimulus Person	Average Stimulus Person	Attractive Stimulus Person
Social desirability of the stimulus person's personality	56.31	62.42	65.39
Occupational status of the stimulus person	1.70	2.02	2.25
Marital competence of the stimulus person	.37	.71	1.70
Parental competence of the stimulus person	3.91	4.55	3.54
Social and professional happiness of the stimulus person	5.28	6.34	6.37
Total happiness of the stimulus person	8.83	11.60	11.60
Likelihood of marriage	1.52	1.82	2.17

[a]The higher the number, the more socially desirable, the more prestigious an occupation, etc., the stimulus person is expected to possess.

All tests for detection of linear trend and interaction were conducted via a multivariate analysis of variance. (This procedure is outlined in Hays, 1963.)

The means relevant to the hypothesis that attractive individuals will be perceived to possess more socially desirable personalities than others are reported in Table 2.1. Analyses reveal that attractive individuals were indeed judged to be more socially desirable than are unattractive ($F = 29.61$) persons. The Sex of Subject x Sex of Stimulus Person interaction was insignificant (interaction $F = .00$). Whether the rater was of the same or the opposite sex as the stimulus person, attractive stimulus persons were judged as more socially desirable.[6]

Furthermore, it was also hypothesized that the subjects would assume that attractive stimulus persons are likely to secure more prestigious jobs than those of lesser attractiveness, as well as experiencing happier marriages, being better parents, and enjoying more fulfilling social and occupational lives.

The means relevant to these predictions concerning the estimated future life experiences of individuals of varying degrees of physical attractiveness are also depicted in Table 2.1. As shown in the table, there was strong support for all of the preceding hypotheses save one. Attractive men and women were expected to attain more prestigious occupations than were those of lesser attractiveness ($F = 42.30$), and this expectation was expressed equally by raters of the same or the opposite sex as the stimulus person (interaction $F = .25$).

The subjects also assumed that attractive individuals would be more competent spouses and have happier marriages than those of lesser attractiveness ($F = 62.54$). (It might be noted that there is some evidence that this may be a correct perception. Kirkpatrick and Cotton (1951) reported that "well-adjusted" wives were more physically attractive than "badly adjusted" wives. "Adjustment," however, was assessed by friends' perceptions, which may have been affected by the stereotype evident here.)

According to the means reported in Table 2.1., it is clear that attractive individuals were not expected to be better parents ($F = 1.47$). In fact, attractive persons were rated somewhat lower than any other group of stimulus persons as potential parents, although no statistically significant differences were apparent.

As predicted, attractive stimulus persons were assumed to have better prospects for happy social and professional lives ($F = 21.97$). All in all, the attractive stimulus persons were expected to have more total happiness in their lives than those of lesser attractiveness ($F = 24.20$).

The preceding results did not appear to be attenuated by a jealousy effect (Sex of Subject x Stimulus Person interaction Fs $= .01, .07, .21,$ and $.05$, respectively).

The subjects were also asked to estimate the likelihood that the various stimulus persons would marry early or marry at all. Responses were combined into a single index. It is evident that the subjects assumed that the attractive stimulus persons were more likely to find an acceptable partner than those of lesser attractiveness ($F = 35.84$). Attractive individuals were expected to marry earlier and to be less likely to remain single. Once again, these conclusions were reached by all subjects, regardless of whether they were of the same or opposite sex of the stimulus person (interaction $F = .01$).

The results suggest that a physical attractiveness stereotype exists and that its content is perfectly compatible with the "What is beautiful is good" thesis. Not only are physically attractive persons assumed to possess more socially desirable personalities than those of lesser attractiveness, but it is presumed that their lives will be happier and more successful.

The results also suggest that the physical attractiveness variable may have a number of implications for a variety of aspects of social interaction and influence. For example, it is clear that physically attractive individuals may have even more advantages in the dating market than has previously been assumed. In addition to an aesthetic advantage in marrying a beautiful spouse (cf. Josselin de Jong, 1952), potential marriage partners may also assume that the beautiful attract all of the world's material benefits and happiness. Thus, the lure of an attractive marriage partner should be strong indeed.

We do not know, of course, how well this stereotype stands up against contradictory information. Nor do we know the extent to which it determines the pattern of social interaction that develops with a person of a particular attractiveness level. Nevertheless, it would be odd if people did not behave toward others in accordance with this stereotype. Such behavior has been previously noted anecdotally. Monahan (1941) has observed that

Even social workers accustomed to dealing with all types often find it difficult to think of a normal, pretty girl as being guilty of a crime. Most people, for some inexplicable reason, think of crime in terms of abnormality in appearance, and I must say that beautiful women are not often convicted [p. 103].

A host of other familiar social psychological dependent variables also should be affected in predictable ways.

In the above connection, it might be noted that if standards of physical attractiveness vary widely, knowledge of the content of the physical attractiveness stereotype would be of limited usefulness in predicting its effect on social interaction and the development of the self-concept. The present study was not designed to investigate the degree of variance in perceived beauty. (The physical attractiveness ratings of the stimulus materials were made by college students of a similar background to those who participated in this study.) Preliminary evidence (Cross & Cross, 1971) suggests that such differences in perceived beauty may not be as severe as some observers have suggested.

REFERENCES

Aronson, E. Some antecedents of interpersonal attraction. In W. J. Arnold & D. Levine (Eds.), *Nebraska Symposium on Motivation,* 1969, *17,* 143-177.

Cross, J. F., & Cross, J. Age, sex, race, and the perception of facial beauty. *Developmental Psychology,* 1971, *5,* 433-439.

Hays, W. L. *Statistics for psychologists.* New York: Holt, Rinehart & Winston, 1963.

Josselin de Jong, J. P. B. *Lévi-Strauss' theory on kinship and marriage.* Leiden, Holland: Brill, 1952.

Kirkpatrick, C., & Cotton, J. Physical attractiveness, age, and marital adjustment. *American Sociological Review,* 1951, *16,* 81-86.

Monahan, F. *Women in crime.* New York: Ives Washburn, 1941.

Schiller, J. C. F. *Essays, esthetical and philosophical, including the dissertation on the "Connexions between the animal and the spiritual in man."* London: Bell, 1882.

Wright, B. A. *Physical disability—A psychological approach.* New York: Harper & Row, 1960.

NOTES

1. The physical attractiveness rating of each of the pictures was determined in a preliminary study. One hundred Minnesota undergraduates rated 50 yearbook pictures of persons of the opposite sex with respect to physical attractiveness. The criteria for choosing the 12 pictures to be used experimentally were (a) high-interrater agreement as to the physical attractiveness of the stimulus (the average interrater correlation for all of the pictures was .70); and (b) pictures chosen to represent the very attractive category and very unattractive category were not at the extreme ends of attractiveness.

2. A detailed report of the items included in these booklets is available. Order Document No. 01972 from the National Auxiliary Publication Service of the American Society for Information Science, c/o CCM Information Services, Inc., 909 3rd Avenue, New York, New York 10022. Remit in advance $5.00 for photocopies or $2.00 for microfiche and make checks payable to: Research and Microfilm Publications, Inc.

3. The subjects were asked how altruistic, conventional, self-assertive, exciting, stable, emotional, dependent, safe, interesting, genuine, sensitive, outgoing, sexually permissive, sincere, warm, sociable, competitive, obvious, kind, modest,

strong, serious, sexually warm, simple, poised, bold, and sophisticated each stimulus person was.

4. The subjects rated stimulus persons on the following traits: friendliness, enthusiasm, physical attractiveness, social poise, and trustworthiness.

5. Throughout this report, $df = 1/55$.

6. Before running the preliminary experiment to determine the identity of traits usually associated with a socially desirable person (see Footnote 5), we had assumed that an exciting date, a nurturant person, and a person of good character would be perceived as quite different personality types. Conceptually, for example, we expected that an exciting date would be seen to require a person who was unpredictable, challenging, etc., while a nurturant person would be seen to be predictable and unthreatening. It became clear, however, that these distinctions were not ones which made sense to the subjects. There was almost total overlap between the traits chosen as representative of an exciting date, of a nurturant person, and a person of good or ethical character. All were strongly correlated with social desirability. Thus, attractive stimulus persons are assumed to be more exciting dates ($F = 39.97$), more nurturant individuals ($F = 13.96$), and to have better character ($F = 19.57$) than persons of lesser attractiveness.

3

ROBERT B. CIALDINI, SANFORD L. BRAVER, and STEPHEN K. LEWIS

Attributional Bias and the Easily Persuaded Other

An experiment was conducted to test the hypothesis that a person positively biases his assessment of the intelligence of a person who he is able to persuade easily. In one condition, persuaders and observers saw a subject confederate easily convinced by the persuaders' arguments. In two other conditions, the confederate either was not convinced by the persuaders' arguments or did not indicate how he was affected by the arguments. According to prediction, it was found that relative to observers of the influence attempts, persuaders attributed higher levels of intelligence to yielders than to nonyielders. This effect resulted from a tendency of persuaders to enhance

Source: Robert B. Cialdini, Sanford L. Braver, and Stephen K. Lewis, "Attributional Bias and the Easily Persuaded Other," *Journal of Personality and Social Psychology,* 1974, *30,* 631-637. Copyright 1974 by the American Psychological Association. Reprinted by permission.

The authors would like to thank Harold H. Kelley for his helpful comments on an earlier version of this article. Thanks are also due George Thomas for his aid in the running of subjects.

the intelligence of yielders and a tendency of observers to derogate the intelligence of yielders. Thé findings were interpreted in terms of a desire to promote a sense of internal control.

In a recent article, Kelley (1971) has suggested that we may often bias our attributions about people and events in a way that serves to reinforce an "internal control" orientation: "attribution processes are to be understood, not only as a means of providing the individual with a veridical view of his world, but as a means of encouraging and maintaining his effective exercise of control in that world [p. 22]." A sense of competence (White, 1959), "originship" (deCharms, 1968), or internal control (Rotter, 1966) is seen as highly desirable from Kelley's perspective, and biased attribution is seen as a technique for perpetuating and promoting such an orientation to one's environment.

Support for this formulation can be seen in studies investigating locus of causality attributions under conditions of success and failure. Subjects tend to attribute causality to themselves when their efforts have produced favorable outcomes but attribute causality to other factors when the outcomes are unfavorable (e.g., Johnson, Feigenbaum, & Weiby, 1964; Jones, Gergen, & Davis, 1962; Streufert & Streufert, 1969). Kelley (1971) has contended that such data are consistent with his view of the function of attributional bias, since

the attribution to self of success and the attribution to external factors of failure provides the basis for the continuation of control attempts. If attributed to the self, success is a reason to exercise one's own causal powers again. Thus these attributional biases may reflect a system partially in support of an internal locus of control orientation [p. 23].

It seems likely that if attributional biases worked as Kelley has hypothesized, they would not be limited to attributions about locus of causality. For example, attributions about the personal traits of interacting others should also be affected. We ought to attribute to persons with whom we have dealt characteristics that are likely to enhance our sense of environmental competence. One situation in which such a bias might be seen to occur would be one involving an easily persuaded other. What level of intelligence would we attribute to someone whom we have easily convinced to our point of view? If the analysis of attributional bias as proposed by Kelley were correct, it might be expected that we would distort upward our perception of the intelligence of such a person. Certainly, the persuasion of a more intelligent person would better promote a sense of environmental effectiveness than the persuasion of a less intelligent person.

At first glance, however, the literature does not seem to support the prediction that a persuader biases his perception of the intelligence of an easily influenced other. The results of two studies (Cialdini, 1971; Lombardo, Weiss, & Buchanan, 1972) indicated that while persuaders rate yielders as more attractive than nonyielders, they do not rate yielders as any more or less intelligent than nonyielders. These findings do not, however, rule out the possibility of attributional bias on the part of the persuader. It may well be that an independent observer typically attributes low levels of intelligence to an easily convinced person. The influence agent, on the other hand, may bias his attributions against the perception of subnormal intelligence in someone he himself has convinced; in this way, a greater feeling of environmental control can be secured. In other words, the previous literature may fail to reveal evidence for attributional bias on the part of the persuader because of the lack of a comparison group of observers. If such a bias mechanism is operating, it follows that, relative to simple observers of the influence attempt, persuaders attribute higher levels of intelligence to yielders than to nonyielders.

An alternative explanation for this result could be offered, however. The earlier literature (Cialdini, 1971; Lombardo et al., 1972) has demonstrated that a series of successful influence attempts leads a persuader to like the yielder. It is possible that through the action of a halo effect, a successful persuader would tend to regard his target as more intelligent than would an observer. Such a process, then, could also work to produce the predicted result that, in comparison to observers, persuaders rate yielders as more intelligent than nonyielders. Thus any experiment that attempted to support the attributional bias interpretation would have to hold the liking factor constant for observers and persuaders.

A persuader's liking for a yielder could stem from two sources. First, since a yielder by definition has changed his view toward that of the persuader, the opinions of the two have become more similar; and opinion similarity has been reliably shown to enhance liking (Byrne, 1969). In the present experiment, an attempt was made to hold liking for the target person constant for persuaders and observers. Persuaders and observers always held the same opinions on the experimental issues so that any movement by the target person would have a comparable effect, in terms of opinion similarity, for the persuader and the observer. Second, Lombardo et al. (1972) have demonstrated that yielding has reinforcing properties. It was found that subjects would learn an instrumental response the only reinforcer for which was the yielding response of another person. Since we tend to like those who provide us with positive reinforcements, a persuader's liking for a yielder may derive also from the inherent reward properties of his yielding. Therefore, in the present experiment, the number of yielding instances was held to a minimum. A persuader was allowed to experience yielding only twice in the present study, while in the previous experiments showing liking for yielders (Cialdini, 1971; Lombardo et al., 1972), three times as many such experiences were provided for the persuader. It was hoped that by minimizing the reinforcement instances for the persuader, his liking for the yielder would not differ from the observer's.

An experiment was conducted, then, to test the hypothesis that in order to enhance the sense of his own environmental effectiveness, a persuader biases his attributions concerning the intelligence of someone whom he has easily persuaded. Pairs of subjects holding similar views on the experimental topics met with a target person who held opposing views. Within each pair, one subject (the persuader) attempted to change the target's opinions on the issues, while the other subject (the observer) simply looked on. In one condition, the target indicated that he had been swayed by the persuader's arguments; in a second condition, he indicated that he had not been swayed; and in a third condition, he gave no indication as to the influence of the persuader's arguments upon his opinions. It was predicted that while there would be no differential *liking* for the target, persuaders, relative to observers, would attribute more *intelligence* to a target who yielded to their influence attempts than to one who did not.

METHOD

Subjects

Subjects were 38 male and 38 female volunteers from an introductory psychology course. Their participation partially fulfilled a requirement for this course.

Procedure

Two same-sex subjects and a male confederate were present for each session. The experimenter introduced himself and asked each of the others to follow suit, with each explaining where he was from, his year in college, his major in college, and why he had chosen that major.

The subjects then completed questionnaires that asked for their opinion (pro or con) and degree of interest on nine attitude issues. Upon collecting the questionnaires, the experimenter excused himself in order to choose two issues on which the two subjects had similar attitudes and highest interest. When he returned, he explained that the study concerned "persuasion, attitude change, and attitude formation." Then, without further elaboration, he directed the subjects to another room, briefly explained the procedures that would be followed, and seated them around a table which was divided by a T-shaped wooden partition.

The confederate was always assigned, allegedly at random, the role of reader. He reread the statement of the first of the two selected attitude issues, then stated his "opinion" on that issue. The opinion he gave was, for all groups, the opposite of that held by the students. One of the two subjects, randomly assigned the role of persuader, next stated his opinion, then gave "at least a 30-second persuasive argument on the reasons for his opinion." The other subject was merely an "observer"; he did not publicly divulge his opinion, nor did he attempt to persuade.

At the conclusion of the persuasive argument, each of the participants indicated on a questionnaire the degree and direction of his own opinion change, if any. The confederate, in accordance with the instructions given by the experimenter, then stated aloud whether or not he had changed his attitude. The no-feedback control condition was an exception: Here the confederate was instructed simply to go on to the next attitude issue.

The identical procedures were followed again for the second of the two attitude issues. Then subjects were told that the experiment was over and were asked to complete "postexperimental" questionnaires, which included intelligence rating scales, liking scales, and probes for suspicion of deception.

Independent Variables

Three independent variables were used: sex of subject (both subjects in the session were either male or female), role of subject (one in each session was the persuader, the other was the observer), and reaction of the confederate reader (the target) to the persuader's argument. This last variable had three treatment levels: In the first, the yield condition, the confederate admitted after each of the two issues that on the basis of the persuader's arguments, he *had* changed his attitude somewhat, in the direction of the persuader's general position. The other two conditions were controls: In the no-change control condition, the confederate stated after each argument that his opinion had not changed at all from that before the persuader's argument. In the no-feedback control condition, the confederate was not asked, nor did he give, his final opinion on either issue.

Thus, the design was a 2 x 2 x 3 factorial. After elimination of the two males and two females who expressed suspicion, there remained six subjects in each cell of the design.[1]

Dependent Variables

Ratings of the intelligence of and liking for the confederate target were requested on the post-experimental questionnaire. This was administered following the second argument and the confederate's response to that argument. The rating scales consisted of 12 7-point semantic differentials, 7 for liking (likable-unlikable, personable-unpersonable, friendly-unfriendly, desirable as a friend-undesirable as a friend, attractive-unattractive, trustworthy-untrustworthy, pleasant-unpleasant) and 5 for intelligence (intelligent-unintelligent, knowledgeable of current events-unknowledgeable of current events, perceptive-unperceptive, intellectual-unintellectual, thoughtful-unthoughtful) randomly intermixed. The ratings for each subscale were averaged to produce a single mean score for each dependent variable. In addition, the questionnaire also requested (*a*) ratings of the "quality of the persuader's arguments" and (*b*) ratings of the other subjects in the room on the intelligence and liking scales.

RESULTS

The means for the two main dependent variables—rated liking for the target and rated intelligence of the target—are collapsed over the sex factor and presented in Table 3.1.

An analysis of variance was performed on all dependent variables in the following manner. The reaction of target factor was subdivided, for each component of variance, into two orthogonal contrasts (Hays, 1963, p. 466): (*a*) the yield condition as compared with the combined mean of two control conditions and (*b*) the no-feedback control as compared with the no-change control.

Liking for the Target

The purpose of including only two issues on which the confederate was persuaded or not persuaded was to minimize the effects of that variable on

TABLE 3.1
Mean Liking and Intelligence Ratings by Persuaders and
Observers Collapsed over Sex

Rating of the Target	Yield Condition		No-Change Control		No-Feedback Control	
	Persuader	Observer	Persuader	Observer	Persuader	Observer
Liking[a]	3.85	3.74	3.66	3.82	3.64	3.82
Intelligence[b]	3.67	3.25	3.04	3.73	3.02	3.72

Note: The scores represent an average rating on a series of 7-point scales, where 7 indicates very much of the quality and 1 indicates none of the quality.
For each condition, $n = 12$ persuaders and 12 observers.
[a] $MS_e = 1.10$, $df = 60$.
[b] $MS_e = .96$, $df = 60$.

attraction for the persuader and thereby permit a test of the attribution interpretation. The analysis of variance indicated that none of the main effects or interactions for liking were significant. The F ratios for the yield versus controls contrast on the main effect and the critical Role of Subject x Reaction of Target interaction were less than 1. Thus, the goal of keeping the liking for the target constant for persuaders and observers was achieved.

Intelligence of the Target

One problem this investigation had to surmount was to differentiate liking responses from respect (or intelligence) responses. While the two are analytically distinct, the halo effect problem makes it difficult to obtain empirical distinctions. Indeed, the correlation between the liking and intelligence scales was a very high .74.

Nonetheless, the experimental procedures produced a significant effect on only one of the measures, intelligence. The only significant effect ($F = 5.05$, $df = 1/60$, $p < .05$) in the analysis of this intelligence variable was the Role of Subject x Reaction of Target interaction.[2] Table 3.2 presents

TABLE 3.2
Mean Intelligence Ratings Collapsed over Sex and Control Conditions

Role of Subject	Yield	$\bar{X}$ Controls	F[a]
Persuader	3.67	3.03	3.371
Observer	3.25	3.72	1.806

Note: For the interaction term, $F = 5.05$, $df = 1/60$.
[a]For simple main effect, $df = 1/60$.

the mean intelligence ratings given by observers and persuaders in the yield condition as compared with the mean of the control conditions; simple main effect F ratios are also presented.

It can be observed that a yielding target had differential effects on the intelligence ratings of persuaders and observers. One who simply observes while another is easily persuaded, even to one's own point of view, has less (though not significantly less) respect for the other's intelligence. In contrast, the person doing the persuading enhances the intelligence of the target, though this simple main effect similarly is not reliable at conventional levels of significance. The latter effect is called significantly into focus only in the Role of Subject x Reaction of Target interaction, that is, only when this enhancement of intelligence attribution is contrasted with the diminution of respect exhibited by the observer.

Other Dependent Variables

Both the persuader and observer rated one another (but not themselves) on the liking and intelligence scales. Additionally, they each rated the "quality of the persuader's arguments" on each attitude issue. Analyses of variance on these dependent variables yielded no significant effects.

DISCUSSION

A number of conclusions appear warranted from the results of the present study. The first is that our major hypothesis was confirmed. Relative to witnesses to the influence attempt, persuaders attribute higher levels of intelligence to yielders than to nonyielders. Moreover, his effect seems mediated by the action of an attributional bias mechanism rather than that of a halo effect. The data clearly indicate that we were able to hold liking for the target constant across persuaders and observers. Further, the differences between persuaders' and observers' ratings of intelligence were approximately four times as large as those for liking. The differences in rated intelligence, then, can hardly be viewed as subsidiary effects of a liking halo. Finally, it can be concluded that the obtained effect derives from a combination of two smaller effects. As is evidenced in Table 3.2, an observer considers yielders to be less intelligent than nonyielders; a persuader, on the other hand, considers yielders to be more intelligent. Neither of these effects is significant by itself; it is only in combination that these effects produce the Role of Subject x Reaction of Target interaction which confirms our major prediction.

These findings fit quite well with Kelley's conception of attributional bias as a means for the fostering of an internal control orientation. It appears that when we have had a hand in the influence process, we resist the tendency to attribute low levels of intelligence to an easily convinced other; in fact, under these conditions we tend to enhance somewhat the intelligence of a yielder as compared with that of someone whose position is unchanged or unknown. Since the persuasion of a more intelligent other conveys a greater sense of environmental control, the implications of such a tack within the Kelley formulation are clear: To the extent that a successful persuader can resist the attribution of lower intelligence to his target and can make the attribution of higher intelligence, his sense of environmental mastery should increase. Our results are explained very nicely, then, by Kelley's conception of attributional bias as a means for strengthening a feeling of internal control.

However, there is another possible explanation for these results. In our experimental procedure the persuader always gave his *own* reasons for his position on the issue at hand, and these may not have been the observer's reasons. It is possible that a person sees his own reasons for holding a position as better than other reasons and thus attributes more intelligence to someone who is persuaded by his own reasons. It may have been, then, that the persuaders enhanced the intelligence of yielders because they saw the yielders as swayed by a more cogent set of arguments (i.e., their own) than did the observers; conversely, observers may have derogated the intelligence of yielders because they were seen as influenced by a less cogent set of arguments than the observers' own. The plausibility of such an interpretation is reduced considerably by an examination of our subjects' ratings of the quality of the persuaders' arguments. No main effects or interactions that even approached statistical significance occurred on this variable, which suggests that persuaders and observers did not differentially evaluate the goodness of the persuaders' arguments. Indeed, the comparison between persuaders and observers in the crucial yield condition showed identical quality ratings within these two groups ($\bar{X} = 3.58$). Further, if it had been the case that the obtained effect occurred because persuaders viewed yielders as more similar to themselves in opinion than did observers (since the target was influenced by the persuaders' own arguments), the effect should have appeared on the liking variable as well. Previous research (e.g., Byrne, 1969) provides strong evidence that the greater the perceived attitudinal agreement between two individuals, the greater the liking for one another.

A somewhat similar alternative account might suggest that reciprocation is the mediator of the obtained effect. That is, when the target yielded to the persuader's arguments, this implied his positive evaluation of the latter's intelligence. So as to reciprocate this evaluation, the persuader may have rated the intelligence of the target more highly. However, since the rating of the target's intelligence was a private one that would never be seen by the target himself, it seems unlikely that the basis for such reciprocation would be a calculated exchange of social favors. An intriguing alternative possibility is that a tendency to reciprocate intelligence evaluations might stem from the competence motive we have discussed in this article. Thus, if our persuaders felt the need to reciprocate the targets' positive evaluation of them, this need may have derived from the fact that it is enhancing to one's sense of competence to believe that a favorable estimate of one's intelligence has come from an intelligent other. Such an interpretation, of course, can be seen as quite similar to the one that we have proposed. Finally, it might be noted that while such a reciprocation mechanism is plausible, existing evidence supports only the notion that we like others who like us. It remains to be demonstrated by future research that we view as more intelligent those who see us as intelligent.

If we can assume that attributions are systematically biased to enhance a feeling of personal efficacy, it becomes an interesting question to ask, "Why is such a feeling so desirable?" One possibility is that general self-esteem is a direct function of the self-perception of competence; to maintain a sense of self-worth, one must maintain a sense of competence. Evidence in this regard can be seen in work suggesting that much of the variance in one's overall self-evaluation can be attributed to one's sense of competence (e.g., Murphy, 1962; Rosenberg, 1965). An alternative but not incompatible explanation for the desirability of a sense of personal control involves its adaptiveness (White, 1959). It appears from a large number of studies that an internal control orientation leads to the attainment of positive outcomes or to situations conducive to the attainment of such outcomes. For instance, Seeman (1963), controlling for such factors as level of education, reported that prisoners who believe that they can control their fates learn more about the requirements and operations of the parole process than prisoners who believe their fates to be determined by luck or chance factors; seemingly, the former group of inmates would be better able to make advantageous use of the parole system. Seeman and Evans (1962) have found a strikingly similar relationship among tuberculosis patients. Those patients with an internal control orientation knew more about the symptoms and properties of their disease than those with an external control orientation. In both of these examples, it can be seen that subjects holding an orientation similar to what might be called a sense of competence acted in a way that provided them with an adaptive advantage in their environments. [3]

If it can be assumed that interactants have knowledge of the biasing phenomenon demonstrated in the present study, some interesting implications follow. For example, there is evidence that persons strategically (though not necessarily consciously) change their opinions in order to facilitate the attainment of immediate situational goals (Cialdini, Levy, Herman, & Evenbeck, 1973; Cooper & Jones, 1969; Jones, 1965). It might be expected, then, that because of a desire to have one's intelligence favorably evaluated by others, persuasive appeals are more successful when delivered in private than in the presence of observers (who, the target knows, tend to derogate yielders). In addition, the extent to which a target person wishes to impress an initiator as opposed to an observer of an influence attempt might strongly affect the degree to which he is influenced.

REFERENCES

Byrne, D. Attitudes and attraction. In L. Berkowitz (Ed.), *Advances in experimental social psychology.* Vol. 4. New York: Academic Press, 1969.

Cialdini, R. B. Attitudinal advocacy in the verbal conditioner. *Journal of Personality and Social Psychology,* 1971, *17,* 350-358.
Cialdini, R. B., Levy, A., Herman, C. P., & Evenbeck, S. Attitudinal politics: The strategy of moderation. *Journal of Personality and Social Psychology,* 1973, *25,* 100-108.
Cooper, J., & Jones, E. E. Opinion divergence as a strategy to avoid being miscast. *Journal of Personality and Social Psychology,* 1969, *13,* 23-30.
deCharms, R. *Personal causation.* New York: Academic Press, 1968.
Hays, W. L. *Statistics for psychologists.* New York: Holt, Rinehart & Winston, 1963.
Johnson, T. J., Feigenbaum, R., & Weiby, M. Some determinants and consequences of the teacher's perception of causation. *Journal of Educational Psychology,* 1964, *55,* 237-246.
Jones, E. E. Conformity as a tactic of ingratiation. *Science,* 1965, *149,* 114-150.
Jones, E. E., Gergen, K. J., & Davis, K. E. Some determinants of reactions to being approved or disapproved as a person. *Psychological Monographs,* 1962, *76*(2, Whole No. 521).
Kelley, H. H. *Attribution in social interaction.* (*University Programs*) Morristown, N.J.: General Learning Press, 1971.
Lombardo, J. P., Weiss, R. F., & Buchanan, W. Reinforcing and attracting functions of yielding. *Journal of Personality and Social Psychology,* 1972, *21,* 359-368.
Murphy, L. *The widening world of childhood: Paths toward mastery.* New York: Basic Books, 1962.
Rosenberg, M. *Society and the adolescent self-image.* Princeton, N.J.: Princeton University Press, 1965.
Rotter, J. B. Generalized expectancies for internal versus external control of reinforcement. *Psychological Monographs,* 1966, *80*(1, Whole No. 609).
Seeman, M. Alienation and social learning in a reformatory. *American Journal of Sociology,* 1963, *69,* 270-284.
Seeman, M., & Evans, J. W. Alienation and learning in a hospital setting. *American Sociological Review,* 1962, *27,* 772-781.
Stotland, E., & Canon, L. K. *Social psychology: A cognitive approach.* Philadelphia, Pa.: Saunders, 1972.
Struefert, S., & Struefert, S. C. Effects of conceptual structure, failure, and success on attribution of causality and interpersonal attitudes. *Journal of Personality and Social Psychology,* 1969, *11,* 138-147.
White, R. W. Motivation reconsidered: The concept of competence. *Psychological Review,* 1959, *66,* 297-333.

NOTES

1. Inasmuch as the arguments heard in each session were unique to that session, but both the observer and the persuader heard the same arguments, the role of subject variable could be considered yoked, qualifying for repeated measures analysis. However, all significance levels obtained using this method of analysis were identical to those of the completely randomized design; hence, the analysis reported here is the more straightforward, completely randomized design.

2. There also was a near-significant ($F = 3.78$, $p < .06$) Sex x Reaction of the Target interaction for the yield versus control contrast which indicated that

females (persuaders and observers) tend generally to enhance the intelligence of a yielder, while males tend to derogate it. Inasmuch as the target was of the same sex as the males but the opposite sex of the female subjects, however, interpretation of this finding is unclear.

3. For a larger review of the relationship between perceived competence, self-esteem, and environmental effectiveness, see Stotland and Canon (1972).

4

MICHAEL D. STORMS and RICHARD E. NISBETT

Insomnia and the Attribution Process

Insomniac subjects were given placebo pills to take a few minutes before going to bed. Some subjects were told that the pills would cause arousal (arousal condition), and others were told that the pills would reduce arousal (relaxation condition). As predicted, arousal subjects got to sleep more quickly than they had on nights without the pills, presumably because they attributed their arousal to the pills rather than to their emotions, and as a consequence were less emotional. Also as predicted, relaxation subjects got to sleep less quickly than usual, presumably because they assumed that their emotions were unusually intense since their arousal level was high even after taking an arousal-reducing agent. The results have relevance for Schachter's theory of emotions and Kelley's attribution theory. Pragmatically, the findings suggest the feasibility of a therapy based on reattribution of symptoms, and indicate that traditional suggestion effect practices should be modified.

In an important experiment on emotion published in 1962, Schachter and Singer exposed subjects to situations designed to elicit either anger or euphoria. Prior to their exposure to these situations, subjects were injected with adrenalin, a drug which produces autonomic arousal. Some of the subjects were told that they were being injected with a drug which would cause autonomic arousal, while other subjects were given no information

Source: Michael D. Storms and Richard E. Nisbett, "Insomnia and the Attribution Process," *Journal of Personality and Social Psychology,* 1970, *16,* 319-328. Copyright 1970 by the American Psychological Association. Reprinted by permission.

This research was supported in part by a Yale University predissertation research fund and in part by National Science Foundation Research Grant GS 2585. The authors are indebted to Gerald Davison, Lee Ross, Stanley Schachter, and Stuart Valins for criticism of an earlier draft.

about the arousal effects which the injection would produce. The uninformed subjects were far more emotional—either euphoric or angry, depending on the experimental condition—than were informed subjects. The experiment has been taken as evidence of the emotional plasticity of the state of autonomic arousal. Individuals in a state of arousal may experience very disparate emotional states or no emotional state at all, depending on the cognitions which attend the arousal. A perhaps equally important implication of the experiment has received little attention. Not only were informed subjects less emotional than uninformed subjects, they were also less emotional than control subjects who received a placebo. This trend, though statistically not significant, suggests that informed subjects overcompensated for the injection. They perhaps attributed not only adrenalin-produced arousal to the injection, but naturally occurring arousal as well. As a consequence, informed subjects were less emotional than they "should" have been, given the emotion-eliciting situations in which they were placed.

In order to determine whether people can be induced to believe that part of their naturally occurring arousal is due to an artificial, external source, Nisbett and Schachter (1966) gave sugar pill placebos to subjects who were about to undergo a series of electric shocks. Some of their subjects were told that the pill would produce palpitation, breathing rate increase, and "butterflies in the stomach." Other subjects were told that the pill would produce a variety of symptoms which were not autonomic in nature. Those subjects who believed themselves to be in a state of drug-produced arousal found the shocks less painful than did other subjects, and were willing to tolerate higher shock intensities. Furthermore, an internal analysis revealed that toleration of shock was a direct function of the extent to which subjects ascribed their arousal to the pill. The experiment indicates that it is indeed possible to persuade subjects that their naturally occurring arousal has an external origin. As a consequence, such subjects lower their estimation of the intensity of the stimulus which actually produced the arousal.

It is useful to discuss this research in the context of the attribution theory of Kelley (1967) stemming from Heider's (1958) work. Briefly, Kelley proposes that many cognitive and motivational phenomena are the result of the individual's perception of causes for the psychological effects which he observes in himself. In this process of causal attribution, the individual can make mistakes, that is, attribute an effect to the wrong cause. Such errors may have pronounced effects on his subsequent motives and beliefs. Thus, the subjects in Schachter and Singer's (1962) experiment may be viewed as victims of an experimentally produced attribution error. Uninformed subjects in that experiment who were injected with adrenalin mistakenly attributed their arousal to the situation in which they found themselves, rather than to the injection. As a consequence, they became emotional. Similarly, subjects in Nisbett and Schachter's (1966) experiment, who were told that their placebo pills would produce arousal, mistakenly attributed shock-produced arousal to the pills, and as a consequence found the shock to be less aversive than it "really" was.

Ross, Rodin, and Zimbardo (1969) have proposed that the reattribution of arousal symptoms may be of use in alleviating maladaptive emotional states. Ross et al. conducted an experiment similar to that of Nisbett and Schachter. Their subjects were encouraged to attribute the arousal symptoms accompanying fear of electric shock to a loud noise piped in over a headset. Such subjects were shown to be less fearful than subjects who could only attribute their arousal symptoms to fear of electric shock. Following Valins' (Valins, 1966; Valins & Ray, 1967) suggestion that cognitive manipulations of perceived *level* of arousal may have therapeutic applications, Ross et al. proposed that manipulations of the perceived *source* of autonomic arousal may also have therapeutic uses. The present experiment was an attempt to produce such a therapeutic lessening of a maladaptive emotional state by means of a reattribution of arousal symptoms.

The state of insomnia seems a promising candidate for a first attempt at a therapeutic intervention using the reattribution technique. Emotionality at bedtime can be a chief proximal cause of insomnia. The high level of mental activity and the alertness produced by an emotion are incompatible with sleep and could delay sleep onset. The present line of theorizing would suggest that to the extent that an insomniac goes to bed in a state of autonomic arousal and associates that arousal with cognitions which are emotionally toned, he should become more emotional and have greater difficulty getting to sleep. However, if the insomniac were to take a "drug" which he believed to be capable of producing arousal symptoms, he might attribute part of his arousal to the drug, and might perceive the emotionally toned cognitions to be less intense. As a consequence, such a subject might become less emotional. Insomniac subjects given a placebo which they believe to be an arousal agent might therefore paradoxically get to sleep more quickly than usual.

Such an experiment also provides a framework within which to test a second hypothesis of theoretical and practical interest. If the belief that arousal has been produced by a drug leads to lowered emotionality, then the belief that arousal has been reduced by a drug should lead to increased emotionality. The subjects lead to increased emotionality. The subjects who mistakenly believe themselves to be under the influence of an arousal-decreasing agent should become highly emotional. Such subjects should say to themselves, in effect, "If I feel as aroused as I do now, when a drug is operating to lower my arousal, then I must be very aroused indeed." More formally, such subjects should perceive any arousal which they experience to be an underrepresentation of the intensity of their emotionally toned cognitions. If such a subject experiences normal arousal, but thinks it has been "drug reduced," he will infer that his cognitions are unusually powerful. Emotionality should thus be increased, and the state of insomnia should become worse for such subjects.

Thus, it was hypothesized that (a) insomniacs given placebo pills, which they believe capable of arousing them, will attribute their naturally occurring arousal to the pill, will therefore experience less intense emotions, and will fall asleep more quickly than usual; and (b) insomniacs given placebo pills, which they believe capable of calming them, will attribute more than their naturally occurring arousal to emotionally toned cognitions, will therefore experience more intense emotions, and will fall asleep less quickly than usual.

METHOD

The experimental test of the hypotheses required (a) recruiting subjects who suffer from insomnia; (b) leading some subjects to believe that a pill would increase their arousal at bedtime, and leading others to believe that a pill would decrease it; and (c) measuring changes in the delay of sleep onset.

Subjects

Forty-two subjects were recruited by signs posted on the campus of Yale University. The signs were headed "Insomniacs wanted for psychological research on dreams." Attached to the posters were cards which volunteers completed and mailed in. The experiment was described to volunteers over the telephone as one on dream-content analysis which would take two ½-hour sessions and pay $3.00. Subjects were told that "light sleepers" were being recruited because "they tend to have more dreams and to remember them better than deep sleepers."

Ages of the subjects ranged from 19 to 26 years, with a mean age of 22.1 years. Thirty-three of the 42 subjects were male, and all but 2 were undergraduates or graduate students. As a group, the subjects appeared to be people who had considerable difficulty in getting to sleep. They reported taking 42.56 minutes, on the average, to get to sleep on the 2 nights preceding the first experimental session. This is comparable to the 59.06 minutes characteristic of the "poor" sleepers in Monroe's (1967) study of insomnia and very much more than the 7.18 minutes reported by his "good" sleepers.

Procedure

Subjects were seen individually in two 30-minute sessions, the first session on a Wednesday and the second on Friday of the same week. On Wednesday, subjects answered questions about their sleep on the 2 previous nights, Monday and Tuesday. The experimenter then explained the alleged purpose of the study. "I am interested in the possible effects of level of bodily activity on dream content. I think there might be some relationship between how active your body is internally, during sleep, and what you dream about."

Subjects were then told that they would be given a drug in the experiment:

In order to find out the effects of bodily activity, I'm going to give you a drug to take tonight and tomorrow night. Of course, the drug is harmless; it's a non-prescription drug. It will have no effect on your ability to work or study.

Possible side effects of the drug, which constituted the experimental manipulation, were then described. While the experimenter excused himself to get the pills, subjects answered a bogus questionnaire about the frequency and type of dreams they usually experienced. When this was completed, subjects were given two sugar pill placebos, with instructions to take one that night, Wednesday, and the other on the next night, Thursday, about 15 minutes before going to bed. Subjects were instructed to continue taking any other medications as usual.[1] The drug side effects were then reiterated. To complete the cover story, subjects were given short dream-report forms which they were told to take home and complete whenever they awoke on the next 2 mornings. Finally, subjects answered a questionnaire designed to check whether they knew what symptoms the experimenter had told them to expect from the pill. The experimenter was prepared to correct any mistakes, but all subjects were aware of the appropriate side effects, and correction was never necessary.

Subjects returned on Friday of the same week for a session scheduled at the same time as the Wednesday session, and answered questions about their sleep on Wednesday and Thursday nights. Additional questions were asked about the experimental manipulation and the effects of the pills. Subjects were then interviewed, debriefed, and paid $3.

Manipulating Attribution

Arousal Condition. The subjects' attribution of arousal was manipulated by varying the described side effects of the placebo pills. The pill was described to one group of subjects, those in the arousal condition, as a drug which would increase their level of arousal.

This drug will increase your bodily activity. It works on the sympathetic nervous system, which is the system that arouses you and sends adrenalin through your system. The pill will increase your heart rate and it will increase your body temperature. You may feel a little like your mind is racing. In general it may arouse you.

These side effects were selected from arousal symptoms which pretest subjects reported as being typical of a night with insomnia. When subjects who have received this side-effect description go to bed, they should believe themselves to be under the influence of an arousal-producing drug. To the extent that they experience arousal symptoms, they should attribute them to the pill, rather than to emotional cues. This attribution should result in lowered emotionality, with a consequent decrease in the time needed to fall asleep.

Relaxation Condition. For subjects in the other experimental group, those in the relaxation condition, the pill was described as one which would decrease arousal.

This drug will lower your bodily activity. It works on the parasympathetic nervous system, which is the system that relaxes you. The pill will lower your heart rate. It will decrease your body temperature so that you will feel a little cooler. And it will calm down your mind. In general, it will relax you.

When subjects who have received this side-effect description go to bed, they should believe themselves to be under the influence of an arousal-reducing drug. Any arousal which they experience should be perceived as an underrepresentation of their true level of arousal. Such subjects should therefore attribute greater intensity to emotional cues than would otherwise be the case. This should result in heightened emotional states and a consequent increase in the time needed to fall asleep.

Control Condition. As a control on any possible variations in sleep behavior from the earlier to the later part of the week, and as a check on any possible effects of simply being in an experiment, a control group was included. These subjects were not given pills, and were asked just to report on their dreams. They were given the same cover story about the experimenter's interest in the relation between bodily activity and dream content, but were told: "You have been placed in a control group. We want to see what kind of dreams you report on your own, without me giving you a drug." The control group and each of the experimental groups contained 14 subjects.[2]

Measurement

Sleep Onset. In order to avoid possible suspicion as to the true nature of the experiment, the subjects were never directly asked how long it took them to fall asleep. Instead, subjects were asked to estimate for each of the 4 nights of the experiment, (*a*) when they went to bed and (*b*) when they fell asleep. The time it took each subject to fall asleep was computed by subtracting the time he reported going to bed from the time he reported falling asleep. This measure of sleep onset constituted the chief dependent variable.

Arousal Symptoms. In order to determine the extent to which arousal symptoms were experienced at bedtime and were attributed to the pills, subjects were asked to report on arousal symptoms for the 2 preexperimental nights and the 2 experimental nights. All questions were answered on either 5- or 7-point scales. In order to measure the level of experienced arousal, the following were asked: "How warm or cold did you feel?" and "How much did your mind race?" In order to determine the extent to which arousal was attributed to the pills, subjects were asked how much the pills affected their body temperature, mental activity, and alertness.

In addition, subjects were asked how much they suffered from insomnia on each night, what drug they thought the pills actually contained, and what medications they had taken during the week. Finally, subjects were asked in an open-ended interview how the manipulation had affected them and whether they had suspected the true purpose of the experiment.

RESULTS

Subjects who were encouraged to attribute their arousal to the placebo (arousal condition) should have attributed less arousal to emotional cues, should consequently have experienced less intense emotional states, and should have gotten to sleep more quickly than usual. Subjects who were encouraged to believe that the placebos had calming properties (relaxation condition) should have assumed that the arousal they experienced was an underrepresentation of that produced by emotional cues, should consequently have experienced more intense emotional states, and should have gotten to sleep less quickly than usual. If arousal subjects are to attribute less arousal to their cognitions than relaxation subjects, it is essential that they attribute more of their arousal to the pill. For preexperimental and experimental nights, subjects were asked how much arousal they experi-

TABLE 4.1
Mean Time to Get to Sleep per Night, in Minutes, as a
Function of Experimental Condition

Statistic	Arousal	Control	Sedation
Average of preexperimental nights	53.22	38.40	36.09
Average of experimental nights	41.52	36.96	51.24
Mean change	11.70	1.44	−15.15
t	2.25	.27	2.16
p	<.05	ns	<.05

Note: $n = 14$ in each condition.

enced (how much their minds raced and how warm or cold they felt); and for experimental nights, subjects were asked how much arousal the pill produced (how drowsy or alert the pills made them feel, how much the pills made their minds race, and how warm or cold the pill made them feel). Differences in reported arousal for preexperimental and experimental nights were slight and nonsignificant. Arousal subjects reported trivially more arousal on experimental than on preexperimental nights (+.25, on a 12-point scale consisting of the sum of the two arousal items), and relaxation subjects reported trivially less arousal (−.57, on the scale). Differences in attribution of arousal to the pill were quite marked, however. On each of the items which assessed beliefs about pill effects, arousal subjects reported more arousal as a consequence of having taken the pill than did relaxation subjects. The difference between the sum of the three items was highly significant ($t = 4.36$, $p < .001$).[3]

The differential attribution of arousal was associated with substantial differences in the time it took for subjects to fall asleep. Table 4.1 presents subjects' reports of the amount of time it took to fall asleep on preexperimental nights (Monday and Tuesday), and on experimental nights (Wednesday and Thursday), reported as mean number of minutes per night. It may be seen that changes were in the predicted direction. The analysis of variance of the changes in sleep-onset time was significant at the .02 level ($F = 5.03$, $df = 2/39$). Moreover, the individual treatment effects were significant. The change of nearly 12 minutes in time to get to sleep reported by subjects in the arousal condition was a significant improvement. The 15-minute change in time to get to sleep reported by subjects in the relaxation condition was a significant worsening. Subjects in the control condition reported only a trivial improvement of less than 2 minutes. Both of the hypotheses were therefore confirmed.

Examination of the sleep-onset means for the preexperimental nights showed that the arousal group took longer to get to sleep on those nights than the other groups. It therefore is important to demonstrate that the improvement shown by the arousal group was not simply due to regression. That the improvement was not due to regression is indicated by the following facts: (*a*) The difference in the highly variable sleep-onset times for preexperimental nights was not significant ($F = 1.45$, $df = 2/39$). (*b*) The elevated mean for the arousal group was entirely due to the presence in this group of two individuals who took an extremely long time to get to sleep on preexperimental nights. When these subjects were excluded from consideration, the experimental effect was still present. Eight of the remaining 12 subjects fell asleep more quickly on experimental nights, and only 2 fell asleep less quickly ($p = .05$). (*c*) Most importantly, an analysis of covariance of the change scores with preexperimental sleep onset as the covariate quite clearly indicated that regression did not account for the experimental effects. With all of the subjects included in this analysis, the F ratio was 5.38 ($df = 2/38$, $p < .01$). The fact that the covariance F was slightly higher than the F for the simple analysis of variance indicates that the experimental effects actually counteracted, to a degree, the effects of regression.

It is noteworthy that the experimental effects occurred only for subjects who believed the pill descriptions. In this first attempt at a therapeutic intervention, the experimenters were not uniformly successful in persuading the subjects that they were being given a real drug. At the final session, subjects were asked if they had believed that the pills they took were arousers, relaxers, or something else, such as a placebo. Two of the subjects in the arousal condition and six of the subjects in the relaxation condition indicated that they had not believed that either of their pills contained a drug with the properties described by the experimenter. Table 4.2 presents sleep-onset times for believing and disbelieving subjects in the arousal and relaxation conditions. It may be seen that disbelieving arousal subjects took slightly longer to get to sleep on experimental nights than on preexperimental nights, and disbelieving relaxation subjects fell asleep somewhat more quickly on experimental nights. This suggests that the experimental effects occurred only when subjects reinterpreted the meaning of their symptoms in lights of the "knowledge" that they had taken a drug with effects on arousal state.

TABLE 4.2

Change in Sleep-Onset Time, in Minutes, as a Function of Experimental Condition and Belief or Disbelief in Pill Descriptions

Group	Arousal	Relaxation
Believers	14.28	−29.40
	(12)	(8)
Disbelievers	−3.72	3.78
	(2)	(6)

Note: Numbers in parentheses indicate number of subjects.

It will be recalled that subjects were asked how much they suffered from insomnia on each of the preexperimental and experimental nights. The data for reported suffering do not at all resemble the data for sleep onset. Arousal subjects actually reported a trivial increase in suffering on experimental nights (.214 points on a 7-point scale), and relaxation subjects reported a trivial decrease (.071 points). Subjects apparently did not base their reports of suffering on the relative amount of time it took them to get to sleep. The correlation between the change in reported time to get to sleep and change in reported suffering was only .07.

Why is it that reports of suffering do not reflect the same patterns as reports of sleep onset? It may be that this result is merely another instance of a general, rather paradoxical finding common to studies employing cognitive manipulations of feeling states. Differences in verbal reports of feelings in these studies are usually much weaker than differences in physiological, behavioral, or behavioroid measures (Davison & Valins, 1969; Nisbett & Schachter, 1966; Valins & Ray, 1967; Zimbardo, 1966). This does not explain the present pattern of results, since the general pattern in studies of this type is itself unexplained. However, it is important to note that this is not the first study to obtain such a discrepancy.

Whatever the reason for the discrepancy, the data on reported suffering are comforting in one respect. They serve to reduce the likelihood that the data on sleep onset were produced by possible demand characteristics inherent in the design. Demand characteristics are at work if subjects, sensing what results the experimenter expects or would like to obtain, behave in such a way as to yield those results. Demand characteristics could have produced the data in the present experiment if subjects in the arousal condition sensed that the experimenter expected their insomnia to improve, and if subjects in the relaxation condition sensed that the experimenter expected their insomnia would become worse. If such biases were at work, it seems likely that they would have been reflected in subjects' answers to the straightforward question, "How much did you suffer from insomnia?" The fact that subjects did not respond in the predicted ways to such a direct question makes it appear unlikely that their reports of sleep onset were produced by a desire to please the experimenter.[4]

DISCUSSION

Therapeutic Applications

Insomniac subjects were led to believe that a pill produced their arousal symptoms at bedtime and were consequently able to fall asleep more quickly than usual. The goal of demonstrating the potential usefulness of reattribution therapy has therefore been realized. It would be premature, however, to propose that the reattribution technique has widespread therapeutic implications. The present study represents only a single therapeutic attempt, using only one technique, to achieve moderate improvement of unknown duration in a rather mild pathological condition. Moreover, the failure to obtain improvement in subjects' self-report of suffering must temper the authors' enthusiasm. One should demand of a therapeutic technique that it produce improvement in subjective state, not merely improvement of behavior. Nevertheless, the present findings are encouraging for a first attempt. It is hoped that the present investigation will prompt the study of other applications of the reattribution technique. To that end, the authors speculate briefly on extensions and improvements of the present method.

One undesirable aspect of the technique used in the present study, from the standpoint of producing lasting improvement, was the reliance on pills and deception. More permanent and less "gimmicky" techniques for achieving reattribution may be possible, however. For example, insomnia sufferers could be told that their arousal at bedtime is due to a general condition of high base-line autonomic arousal. (There is evidence that insomniacs do in fact have higher base-line arousal; Monroe, 1967.) Just as some people have high metabolic rates, insomniacs might be told, others have a high rate of autonomic functioning. This technique, like the pills, might offer a nonemotional attribution for naturally occurring bedtime arousal, yet at the same time would eliminate the need for the patient's continuing belief in placebos.

A second extrapolation of the present method might allow for temporary use of the pill technique. Let us consider what would happen to a patient whose condition improved through the use of placebos, and who then discovered that he had been hoaxed. An experimental model of such a situation has been examined by Davison and Valins (1969). Their subjects were given a series of electric shocks and were then given placebos which, they were told, might affect their sensitivity to shock. This was followed by a series of shocks surreptitiously decreased in intensity. At this point half of the subjects were told that their pills were really placebos, and the other half were told that the drug was wearing off. In a third set of shocks, "dehoaxed" subjects were able to tolerate shocks of greater intensity. This experiment suggests that dehoaxed subjects benefited from the belief that they themselves, instead of a drug, were responsible for their behavioral improvement. Similarly, insomniacs might also benefit from learning that a mere reattribution of arousal had caused improvement. This might make it apparent to such individuals that their suffering is not inevitable and that their attitudes toward their symptoms exert an influence on the symptoms.

The Attribution Process

In addition to demonstrating that reattribution techniques are of potential therapeutic value, the present study was concerned with shedding more light on the attribution process itself. It should be admitted at the outset of a discussion of process that we have no definitive means of showing that the sleep-onset changes were produced by the differential attribution of arousal symptoms to the pills. Sleep-onset changes may have been produced by a variety of processes which are theoretically less interesting. It is conceivable, for example, that before going to bed, the arousal subjects were worried about the possibility that the pill would make them uncomfortably aroused, and were relieved to find that it did not have this effect. This feeling of relief might have made it easier for arousal subjects to get to sleep. Similarly, relaxation subjects might have been happily anticipating a state of relaxation at bedtime. Their disappointment (and/or resentment) upon realizing that they were not in such a state might have prevented them from going to sleep. It is also possible that there were attention shifts which made it easier for arousal subjects to fall asleep and harder for relaxation subjects to fall asleep. For example, arousal subjects may have concentrated on their symptoms rather than their worries. Or it is possible that there were differences in behavior before bedtime which made it easier for arousal subjects to fall asleep and harder for relaxation subjects to fall asleep.

The scope of the present experiment was such as to make it impractical to control for all possible alternative explanations. Thus, there is little which can be said to counter these alternatives, except to point out that they detract little from the practical interest of the present research, and to note that there was nothing in the formal or informal comments of the subjects to lend plausibility to any of these alternatives. There is, however, a remaining alternative mechanism which is wholly consistent with the attribution-theory framework and highly plausible in view of some of the comments made by subjects.

Sleep-onset changes may have been produced not by an alteration in the perceived intensity of emotionally toned cognitions, as was proposed in the introduction, but by another consequence of the initial attribution error. Informal conversations with subjects revealed that many of them appeared to worry about the fact that they were insomniacs—about their inability to control such a basic function as sleep and about the state of insomnia as evidence of more general pathology. There is good reason to believe that the experimental manipulations would have had an effect on worries such as these. Arousal subjects were told, in effect, that on experimental nights their insomnia would be caused by a drug. On experimental nights, therefore, arousal subjects did not have to view their symptoms as evidence of inadequacy or pathology. They may have worried less about their condition and may have gotten to sleep more quickly for this reason. Similarly, relaxation subjects were told, in effect, that on experimental nights they should experience fewer insomnia symptoms than usual. On experimental nights, therefore, relaxation subjects would have had to view anything less than a noticeable reduction in their symptoms as evidence of a particularly bad bout with insomnia. Upon failing to experience such a reduction, they might have worried more than usual about their condition and consequently have gotten to sleep less quickly. The attribution error may not have resulted in a change in emotionality across the board, then, but only in a change in degree of worry about the condition of insomnia. To the extent that worry about insomnia further interferes with sleep, such changes could have produced the experimental results.

Whether or not such processes occurred in the present experiment, it seems likely that there are pathologies involving a vicious cycle of the following type: (a) occurrence of symptoms, (b) worry about symptoms, and (c) consequent exacerbation of symptoms. For example, males with problems of impotence probably respond with alarm to signs of detumescence in the sexual situation. Alarm, of course, would increase the likelihood of continued loss of erection. If it were possible to change the meaning which detumescence has for the individual, alarm and consequent impotence might be prevented. Such an individual might be given a drug, for example, and told that it might occasionally produce momentary detumescence; or he might be assured that occasional detumescence in the sexual situation was characteristic of most normal males, or even that it was characteristic of particularly virile males. A cycle of symptoms, worry about symptoms, and intensified symptoms might be expected to occur with a number of other behaviors as well, including perhaps stuttering, extreme shyness, and excessive awkwardness in athletic situations. With each such condition, an externalization of the symptoms or a reinterpretation of the symptoms in nonpathological terms might help to break the cycle.[5]

Suggestion and Attribution

A striking aspect of the present findings is their apparent contradiction of the body of thought and research dealing with the concept of suggestion effect. On the surface, the present experiment resembles a conventional study of suggestion or placebo effects, for example, an experiment showing that administration of a "pain killer" placebo produces a reduction of pain symptoms. Yet the predictions and the obtained results of the present study were exactly opposite to those which would be indicated by suggestion theory. Subjects given a "stimulant" actually got to sleep more quickly, and subjects given a "relaxant" got to sleep less quickly. How can the present results be reconciled with the characteristic findings in the area of suggestion effects? The answer probably lies in the fact that subjects in the present experiment were quite familiar with the symptoms of insomnia. Thus, subjects had two items of information, the first supplied by the experimenter's suggestion, and the second supplied by the subject's own past experience with insomnia symptoms: (a) Subjects knew that they had taken a drug which was supposed to affect insomnia symptoms, and (b) subjects knew that their actual experience of insomnia symptoms was about the same as it usually was. Subjects should have inferred from these facts that the arousal produced by their emotions was of a different magnitude than usual. Arousal subjects should have assumed that the magnitude of emotion-produced arousal was less than usual, and relaxation subjects should have assumed the magnitude was greater. Such an additional implication, stemming from an awareness of typical symptom level, is not characteristic of most suggestion experiments, with the following notable and very instructive exception.

Experiments designed to test the effectiveness of tranquilizers must have a control condition in which subjects are given placebos which they believe to be tranquilizers. Such a placebo control condition closely resembles the relaxation condition in the present experiment. The present line of reasoning leads to the expectation that such subjects would become more anxious upon realizing that their arousal level is still rather high, despite the "fact" that they are taking tranquilizers. Work done by Rickels and his colleagues (Rickels, Baumm, Raab, Taylor, & Moore, 1965; Rickels & Downing, 1967; Rickels, Lipman, & Raab, 1966) shows that this is often the case and indicates that the subjects who get worse are precisely those with the greatest awareness of typical symptom level.

A study by Rickels et al. (1966) shows that both prolonged experience with the anxiety state and extensive experience with tranquilizing drugs increase the likelihood that treatment with placebos will produce a worsening of anxiety state. Both experience with anxiety and experience with drugs would of course serve to give the patient a more accurate base line against which to judge the effectiveness of the placebo. Patients with a chronic, long-standing illness or patients who have previously experienced anxiety relief from drugs would readily perceive that the placebo is having little effect. If such patients infer from this fact that their symptoms are unusually severe, they should get worse. This is apparently the case. The results reported by Rickels et al. (1966) are particularly striking for patients whose experience both with drugs and with their illness is extensive. Whereas almost 80% of such patients improved when treated with tranquilizers, fewer than 30% improved on placebos. Although it is not completely clear from the presentation of the data, it seems likely that the majority of the placebo-treated patients got worse. In contrast, over 70% of the acutely ill patients with no previous experience with tranquilizers actually improved on placebo. Other work, by Rickels and Downing (1967) and Rickels et al. (1965), indicates that the higher the anxiety level of the patient, the more likely it is that his condition will worsen when placed on placebo. Patients with the highest anxiety levels would of course be expected to have the greatest awareness of their predrug symptom level. It should be particularly clear to these patients that the drug is having little effect, and they should therefore be particularly likely to infer that they are getting worse.

The findings of Rickels and his colleagues lend considerable support to the present theoretical framework. Their evidence indicates that some patients do indeed get worse when given placebo which they believe to be tranquilizers. The patients who get worse are precisely the ones who would be expected to do so in terms of the present framework. Rickels et al. (1966) professed themselves to be surprised at their findings, as well they might, since theory in the area of suggestion effects is not equipped to deal with the kinds of reversal effects which attribution theory leads us to expect. A clear implication of the present findings and framework is that clinical workers should beware the use of placebos and suggestion. Before resorting to placebos or suggestion, clinicians should probably ask themselves: "Is there a further implication of the suggestion I am making to the patient? If he fails to experience the effects I suggest, can he infer something damaging about himself?"

REFERENCES

Davison, G., & Valins, S. Maintenance of self-attributed and drug-attributed behavior change. *Journal of Personality and Social Psychology,* 1969, *11,* 25-33.

Heider, F. *The psychology of interpersonal relations.* New York: Wiley, 1958.

Kelley, H. Attribution theory in social psychology. *Nebraska Symposium on Motivation,* 1967, *15,* 192-240.

Monroe, L. J. Psychological and physiological differences between good and poor sleepers. *Journal of Abnormal Psychology,* 1967, *72,* 255-264.

Nisbett, R. E., & Schachter, S. Cognitive manipulation of pain. *Journal of Experimental Social Psychology,* 1966, *2,* 227-236.

Rickels, K., Baumm, C., Raab, E., Taylor, W., & Moore, E. A psychopharma-
cological evaluation of chlordiazepoxide, LA-1 and placebo, carried out with
anxious, neurotic medical clinic patients. *Medical Times,* 1965, *93,* 238-242.
Rickels, K., & Downing, R. Drug- and placebo-treated neurotic outpatients.
Archives of General Psychiatry, 1967, *16,* 369-372.
Rickels, K., Lipman, R., & Raab, E. Previous medication, duration of illness and
placebo response. *Journal of Nervous and Mental Disease,* 1966, *142,* 548-
554.
Ross, L., Rodin, J., & Zimbardo, P. G. Toward an attribution therapy: The re-
duction of fear through induced cognitive-emotional misattribution. *Journal
of Personality and Social Psychology,* 1969, *12,* 279-288.
Schachter, S., & Singer, J. E. Cognitive, social and physiological determinants of
emotional state. *Psychological Review,* 1962, *69,* 379-399.
Valins, S. Cognitive effects of false heart-rate feedback. *Journal of Personality
and Social Psychology,* 1966, *4,* 400-408.
Valins, S., & Ray, A. Effects of cognitive desensitization on avoidance behavior.
Journal of Personality and Social Psychology, 1967, *7,* 345-350.
Zimbardo, P. G. The cognitive control of motivation. *Transactions of the New
York Academy of Sciences,* 1966, *28,* 902-922.

NOTES

1. Only three subjects, all in the control condition, were taking sleeping pills, and they all took equal doses of their drug on each of the 4 nights of the experiment.

2. The first four subjects in the control condition were given pills "to change bodily activity level," but were told that they would not perceive any side effects. These subjects behaved like the other control subjects, and the two groups are combined for purposes of analysis.

3. All probability values are based on two-tailed tests.

4. One further artifactual possibility deserves some mention. It may have occurred to the reader that relaxation subjects might have gone to bed earlier than their usual bedtime, in the expectation that the pill would help to put them to sleep. If so, relaxation subjects might have been less tired than other subjects and might have gotten to sleep less quickly for this reason. Actually, there was a slightly greater tendency for relaxation subjects to go to bed earlier on experimental nights than there was for arousal subjects ($t = 1.57$, $p < .15$). However, the two groups reported almost identical degrees of tiredness at bedtime on experimental nights (5.32 for relaxation subjects; 5.31 for arousal subjects). Moreover, there was no correlation between the tendency to go to bed earlier on experimental nights and the tendency to take longer to get to sleep on experimental nights ($r = .12$ for relaxation subjects; $r = .04$ for arousal subjects). Thus, it seems unlikely that the tendency of relaxation subjects to go to bed earlier was responsible for the worsening in sleep-onset time.

5. The authors are indebted to Stanley Milgram for pointing out that this exacerbation cycle is probably characteristic of a number of pathologies.

5

RICHARD J. BANDLER, JR., GEORGE R. MADARAS, and DARYL J. BEM

Self-Observation as a Source of Pain Perception

The hypothesis was tested that an individual's perception of a stimulus as uncomfortable or painful is partially an inference from his own observation of his response to that stimulus. *S*s were required to observe themselves either escaping or enduring a series of electric shocks, all of the same physical intensity. As predicted, *S*s rated the felt discomfort produced by the shocks to be greater in the "escape" condition than in the "no-escape" condition. Appropriate controls and auxiliary data helped to rule out alternative explanations of the obtained difference, and the record of *S*s' galvanic skin responses suggested that actual physiological arousal was not serving as the basis for the *S*s' discomfort ratings.

An individual's perception of pain is only partially a function of the "pain producing" stimulus. This is apparent from the wide cultural differences in labeling stimuli as painful (e.g., childbirth; Melzack, 1961), from research on the long-familiar placebo effect (Beecher, 1959, 1960), and from the phenomena of hypnotic analgesia (Barber, 1959, 1963) and masochism (Brown, 1965). On what basis, then, does an individual infer that a particular stimulus is painful?

Recent research has indicated that the justification for enduring the aversive stimulation is one kind of information which may influence an individual's judgments of pain. Individuals who volunteered to participate in an experiment using painful electric shocks reported the shocks as less painful and were physiologically (GSR) less responsive than individuals who were forced to be in the experiment (Zimbardo, Cohen, Weisenberg, Dworkin, & Firestone, 1966). Other research on emotional states has indicated that situational cues (in addition to actual physiological arousal) provide a second type of information which may influence an individual's judgments of bodily states, including pain and discomfort (Schachter & Singer, 1962). In fact, it has been shown that both the intensity of shock-produced pain and the willingness to tolerate such pain can be manipu-

Source: Richard J. Bandler, Jr., George R. Madaras, and Daryl J. Bem, "Self-Observation as a Source of Pain Perception," *Journal of Personality and Social Psychology,* 1968, *9,* 205-209. Copyright 1968 by the American Psychological Association. Reprinted by permission.

This research was supported by National Science Foundation Grant GS 1452 awarded to the third author for the study of self-awareness and self-control.

lated by supplying the individual with an alternative explanation for the physiological arousal he is experiencing (Nisbett & Schachter, 1966).

A recent analysis of self-perception by Bem (1965, 1966, 1967) suggests a third kind of information which may influence an individual's self-judgments of pain or discomfort. Bem's experimental work demonstrates that individuals use their own overt behavior as a basis for inferring their attitudes, their beliefs about external events, and the truthfulness of their own confessions. Self-perceptions, according to Bem, may thus be viewed as inferences that are functionally similar to the inferences an outside observer would draw from observing the individual's behavior. This suggests the possibility that an individual may actually use his own overt behavior in response to an aversive stimulus as evidence for deciding that the stimulus was, in fact, uncomfortable or painful. For example, an affirmative reply to the question, "Was that last electric shock uncomfortable?," may be functionally equivalent to the individual's (or an outside observer's) saying, "It must have been; I (he) attempted to escape it as quickly as possible." In other words, an individual's behavioral response to an aversive stimulus, often treated as a dependent variable in pain research, may serve as an independent variable and partially control his perception of the stimulus as uncomfortable or painful.

The present experiment explored this hypothesis by requiring the subject to observe himself either escaping or enduring a series of electric shocks, all of the same physical intensity. The subject was then asked to rate the amount of discomfort he experienced from each shock. It was hypothesized that the discomfort should be greater for the shocks from which the individual escaped than for shocks which he endured, since this is the inference that an outside observer of his behavior would draw. Appropriate controls were included in an attempt to rule out alternative explanations of any obtained difference between conditions. The subject's galvanic skin response (GSR) was also monitored to assess the possibility that actual physiological arousal serves as the basis for the subject's self-judgments of discomfort.

METHOD

Twelve male college students were hired for individual experimental sessions "to help us determine shock levels for future research." Upon arrival each subject was seated in a comfortable chair in a small acoustically tiled room. A small rectangular box with a Plexiglas covering faced the subject. Contained within the box were three 25-watt light bulbs (red, green, and yellow), which could be controlled by the experimenter from a separate room. A 7-point shock rating scale, which ranged from "not uncomfortable" to "very uncomfortable," was displayed on the wall in front of the subject. Each subject was told that the experiment involved electric shock and that the upper and lower limits of the scale would be determined prior to the start of the experiment by a pretest. The shock electrodes were taped to the subject's left hand and connected to a Lafayette Instrument Company inductorium. The GSR electrodes (zinc), of the Lykken type (Lykken, 1959), were attached to the subject's right hand. A zinc-sulfate electrode paste was used. GSR was monitored by a Fels dermohmeter and recorded on a Esterline-Angus recorder.

After the subject's basal skin resistance was determined, a series of eight .5-second shocks, of varying physical intensities, was administered. The subject was asked to rate the discomfort produced by each shock in terms of the rating scale on the wall in front of him. A physical intensity of shock rated 6 in this pretest was used for all shocks during the ensuing experiment.

Following this pretest, the subject was instructed that there would be three different conditions during the experiment. He would feel a shock and .5 second later one of the three colored lights in the box in front of him would be illuminated, signaling the condition. The subject was told to hold the button on the left arm of the chair in his left hand. This button, at the experimenter's discretion, enabled the subject to terminate the shock. The subject was then told what to do in each of the three conditions.

Escape Condition

This is the red condition [turned on red light]. In the red condition you will be able to turn off the shock by pressing the button in your left hand. In this condition, the red condition, you *should* press the button and turn off the shock. However, if the shock is not uncomfortable you may elect to not depress the button. The choice is up to you.

No Escape Condition

This is the green condition [turned on green light]. In the green condition the button in your left hand will enable you to turn off the shock. In this condition, the green condition, you *should not* press the button and turn off the shock. However, if the shock is so uncomfortable that you feel you must turn it off, you may. Again, the choice is up to you.

Reaction-Time Condition

This is the yellow condition [turned on yellow light]. The yellow condition is a reaction time condition. We are interested in recording only the time that it takes you to press the button once the yellow light comes on. Therefore, please press the button as soon as the yellow light is illuminated. Your depression of the button *may* or *may not* turn off the shock.

Following each shock the subject was asked to rate the discomfort produced by each shock on the "shock rating scale." During the experiment each subject received 30 shocks of the physical intensity which he had rated 6 in the pretest.[1] If not terminated by the subject, duration of shock was 2 seconds. To ensure in all conditions that each subject received a minimum of shock which could not be avoided, .5 second elapsed between the onset of shock and the onset of the light. The "escape" and "no escape" lights were reversed for half of the subjects; green for "escape" and red for "no escape," and the order of lights was randomized for each subject.

Thus, for the 10 shocks paired with the "escape" light, the subject pressed a button and terminated the shock. For the 10 shocks paired with the "no escape" light, the subject did not press the button which would have allowed him to terminate the shock. For the 10 shocks paired with the "reaction time" light, the subject pressed the button as soon as the light was illuminated. For five of these trials pressing the button terminated the shock. For the remaining five "reaction time" trials, pressing the button had no effect on the shock.

It will be noted that the subject's overt behavior is the same in this reaction-time condition as it is in the escape condition; he presses the button when the light is illuminated. But, the subject is not given the implied choice of pressing or not pressing the button in the reaction-time condition, and, as the instructions make clear, pressing the button does not necessarily terminate the shock. Thus, the button press should no longer be seen by the subject as a self-determined "escape" response and he should not infer his discomfort from it. Discomfort ratings should therefore be significantly higher in the escape condition than in the reaction-time condition.

Demand Control Condition

It is conceivable that the predicted differences between conditions could arise in the present experiment as an artifact. That is, subjects may be led to entertain hypotheses about the purpose of the experiment which would lead them to anticipate more severe shocks in the escape condition than in the other conditions, thus producing a "demand characteristic" artifact of the type discussed by Orne (1962). To check on this possibility, an additional 10 subjects were employed who were treated the same as the experimental subjects except that they were not required to experience the 30 constant shocks. Instead, following the pretest and the instructions for the three conditions, they were asked to fill out a questionnaire about their anticipations concerning the experiment. The crucial questions were:

I expect to receive the following levels of shock during the course of the experiment (circle each expected level):

a. in the Red condition   1   2   3   4   5   6   7
b. in the Green condition   1   2   3   4   5   6   7
c. in the Yellow condition   1   2   3   4   5   6   7

During the course of the experiment I expect the average shock in the Red condition to be (circle answer):

>greater than
>equal to
>less than

the average shock in the Green condition.

A final question asked the subject to explain his answer to the latter item.

The total experiment, then, assesses the hypothesis that an individual's observation of his own behavior can serve as a source of evidence for his perception of pain or discomfort. The hypothesis predicts that discomfort ratings in the escape condition should be greater than those in the no escape and reaction-time conditions.

RESULTS AND DISCUSSION

The experimental test of the hypothesis required the successful manipulation of the subjects' escape and no escape behavior. Accordingly, two of the subjects were excluded from the analysis since they escaped on all trials in both the escape and no escape conditions. The remaining 10 subjects escaped on 96% of the escape trials and did not escape on 85% of the no escape trials. Removal of the few incorrect trials does not alter the

TABLE 5.1
Mean Shock-Discomfort Ratings and Comparison of Direction or Ratings for the Experimental Group

Condition	M Rating[b]	Direction of M Rating	No. S	Direction of M Rating	No. S
Escape (A)	5.14	Escape > No escape	8	Escape > Reaction time	8
No escape (B)	4.72	Escape = No escape	1	Escape = Reaction time	0
Reaction time (C)	4.66	Escape < No escape	1	Escape < Reaction time	2

	t		p		p
A vs. B.	3.88**	Exact probability[a]	.01	Exact probability	.01
A vs. C	2.40*				
B vs. C	0.30				

[a]Exact probability is defined as the probability of a distribution "at least as deviant as" the one considered.
[b]$n = 10$.
*$p < .05$, two-tailed.
**$p < .01$, two-tailed.

conclusions reached, and the analysis reported here includes them, providing a conservative test of the hypothesis.

The main prediction is that the ratings of discomfort produced by the shock in the escape condition will be greater than those in the no escape condition. It is seen in the first column of Table 5.1 that the mean ratings of discomfort in the escape condition are significantly higher than those in the no escape condition ($p < .01$, two tailed).

Table 5.1 further reveals that the button press must be seen as a self-determined "escape" response if it is to serve as the basis of inference for the individual's discomfort judgment. The reaction-time condition, which required the subject to push the button but did not permit him to interpret his response as a self-determined escape response, yields discomfort ratings significantly lower than those in the escape condition ($p < .05$, two tailed) and not significantly different from those found in the no escape condition.

Columns 2 and 3 reveal the consistency of the predicted effects: 8 of the 10 subjects rated "escape" shocks as more uncomfortable than either "no escape" or "reaction time" shocks. The exact probability of this distribution is less than .01 by a Chapanis (1962) multinomial significance test.

Although these results are consistent with our conceptual analysis, it is necessary to examine a number of alternative explanations that might account for the difference.

First, because the subject terminated all shocks in the escape condition, these shocks were necessarily of a shorter duration than those in the other conditions. It might be the case, then, that discomfort was simply a function of shock duration, with shorter shocks being perceived as more severe. This explanation is somewhat implausible, and is not supported by our other data. In the reaction time condition, the five nonterminated shocks were rated slightly more uncomfortable than the five terminated shocks (4.80 versus 4.52, $t = 2.14$). Shock duration would thus not seem to be able to account for the obtained differences between experimental conditions.

Second, a "demand characteristic" artifact may account for the observed rating difference. For some reason the subjects may have hypothesized that the experimenter would administer more intense shocks on those trials on which they were urged to escape. This possibility was checked, it will be recalled, by running a separate demand control condition, in which 10 additional subjects were asked to fill out a questionnaire about their anticipations concerning the experiment. In one question subjects were asked to circle the levels of shock expected in each condition. If a "demand" type of artifact were to account for the observed rating difference, it would be expected that the mean of the levels of shock

TABLE 5.2
**Mean Shock-Discomfort Ratings and Comparison of Direction of Ratings
for the Demand Control Group**

Condition	M Rating[a]	Direction of M Rating	No. S	Direction of M Rating	No. S
Escape (A)	3.93	Escape > No escape	4	Escape > Reaction time	4
No escape (B)	4.38	Escape = No escape	3	Escape = Reaction time	4
Reaction time (C)	4.10	Escape < No escape	3	Escape < Reaction time	2
	t		p		p
A vs. B	−0.82	Exact probability	.74	Exact probability	.53
A vs. C	−0.47				
B vs. C	0.85				

[a] $N = 10$.

circled in the escape condition would be greater than the mean of the levels circled in the other conditions. In fact, as seen in the first column of Table 5.2, the means show an insignificant reversal. In addition, when asked to circle whether the expected average level of shock in the escape condition was to be greater than, equal to, or less than the expected average level of shock in the no escape or reaction time condition, 6 of the 10 subjects reported the expected average shock in these two conditions to be equal to, or greater than, the expected average shock in the escape condition (Columns 2 and 3 of Table 5.2). Clearly, these results do not differ from chance expectation. Thus, these subjects' expectations would appear to run counter to the experimental hypothesis as often as they would confirm it artifactually. A "demand characteristic" artifact, then, does not appear to offer an alternative explanation of the results.

Finally, the research of Schachter and Singer (1962), Nisbett and Schachter (1966), and Valins (1966) suggests that subjects might use actual physiological arousal as a basis for self-judgments of discomfort. That is, if the subjects were more aroused in the escape condition than in the other conditions they might have rated the shocks as more painful for that reason. To assess this possibility subjects' GSR was monitored.[2] GSR was defined as a change in resistance occurring 1-4 seconds following shock onset. The mean GSR converted to change in log conductance x 1000 (Montagu & Coles, 1966) for the escape condition is 28.88; for the no escape condition it is 29.78; and for the reaction-time condition, 33.27. None of these differences is significant, and, further, the ordering of subjects' ratings of discomfort is the exact reverse of these. There is no evidence, then, that the subjects' ratings of discomfort were dependent on any internal cues that co-vary with changes in GSR. We conclude, then, that the obtained rating differences can be attributed to subjects' inferences from observation of their own response to the electric shock.

It may be that hypnotic analgesia and placebo "pain-relief" reflect the operation of the same process illustrated in this experiment. That is, through hypnosis or placebo suggestion the individual is led to suppress an avoidance or escape response to the aversive stimulus, and his perception of pain or discomfort is in turn predicated upon his observation of that response inhibition. Thus, in contrast with the usual interpretation of such phenomena, which argues that the perception of pain is directly affected by the suggestion, the present interpretation views the suggestion as merely a way of altering the individual's overt behavior, with the perception following as a self-judgment from his observation of that behavior.

REFERENCES

Barber, T. X. Toward a theory of pain: Relief of chronic pain by pre-frontal leucotomy, opiates, placebos, and hypnosis. *Psychological Bulletin,* 1959, *59,* 430-460.

Barber, T. X. The effects of hypnosis on pain. *Psychosomatic Medicine,* 1963, *25,* 303-333.

Beecher, H. K. *Measurement of subjective responses: Quantitative effects of drugs.* New York: Oxford University Press, 1959.

Beecher, H. K. Increased stress and effectiveness of placebos and "active" drugs. *Science,* 1960, *132,* 91-92.

Bem, D. J. An experimental analysis of self-persuasion. *Journal of Experimental Social Psychology,* 1965, *1,* 199-218.

Bem, D. J. Inducing belief in false confessions. *Journal of Personality and Social Psychology,* 1966, *3,* 707-710.

Bem, D. J. Self-perception: An alternative interpretation of cognitive dissonance phenomena. *Psychological Review,* 1967, *74,* 183-200.

Brown, J. S. A behavioral analysis of masochism. *Journal of Experimental Research in Personality,* 1965, *5,* 65-70.

Chapanis, A. An exact multinomial one-sample test of significance. *Psychological Bulletin,* 1962, *59,* 306-310.

Lykken, D. T. Properties of electrodes used in electrodermal measurement. *Journal of Comparative and Physiological Psychology,* 1959, *52,* 629-634.

Melzack, R. The perception of pain. *Scientific American,* 1961, *204,* 41-49.

Montagu, J. D., & Coles, E. M. Mechanism and measurement of the galvanic skin response. *Psychological Bulletin,* 1966, *65,* 261-279.

Nisbett, R. F., & Schachter, S. Cognitive manipulation of pain. *Journal of Experimental Social Psychology,* 1966, *2,* 227-236.

Orne, M. T. On the social psychology of the psychological experiment: With particular reference to demand characteristics and their implications. *American Psychologist,* 1962, *17,* 776-783.

Schachter, S. & Singer, J. Cognitive, social, and physiological determinants of emotional state. *Psychological Review,* 1962, *69,* 379-399.

Valins, S. Cognitive effects of false heart-rate feedback. *Journal of Personality and Social Psychology,* 1966, *4,* 400-408.

Zimbardo, P. G., Cohen, A. R., Weisenberg, M., Dworkin, L., & Firestone, I. Control of pain motivation by cognitive dissonance. *Science,* 1966, *151,* 217-219.

NOTES

1. Four shocks, all of a physical intensity rated 1 in the pretest, were also administered. These shocks serve to add credibility to the implication that different levels of shock were used during the experiment.

2. GSR data for one of the subjects could not be obtained owing to equipment failure.

CHAPTER II

Attraction and Prejudice

1. Susan Saegert, Walter Swap, and R. B. Zajonc, "Exposure, Context, and Interpersonal Attraction"
2. Elliot Aronson and Vernon Cope, "My Enemy's Enemy Is My Friend"
3. Elaine Walster, G. William Walster, Jane Piliavin, and Lynn Schmidt, "'Playing Hard to Get': Understanding an Elusive Phenomenon"
4. Bernie I. Silverman, "Consequences, Racial Discrimination, and the Principle of Belief Congruence"
5. Miriam A. Lewin, "Psychological Aspects of Minority Group Membership: The Concepts of Kurt Lewin"
6. F. K. Heussenstamm, "Bumper Stickers and the Cops"
7. John C. Touhey, "Effects of Additional Women Professionals on Ratings of Occupational Prestige and Desirability"

. . . Baltimore is not an easy city to get to know, and harder yet to come to admire. My own first two or three years here were not pleasant. I found oppressive the items I love most now . . . the rowhouses jammed together, the uneventful terrain of the rolling hills . . . in fact the seemingly uneventful nature of the city itself.

It was only after my third year here that I began to realize that Baltimore is a city that needs to be "discovered." I kept expecting to be hit in the face by dramatic landmarks like the Golden Gate Bridge or the Empire State Building. When one stops this vain search, he begins to discover what I believe to be Baltimore's hidden charms. It's like walking down the same street for the tenth time and suddenly seeing something you've always missed before.

William Bray, "The Hidden Charms of Baltimore,"
Baltimore Sunday Sun Magazine, June 15, 1975, p. 15.

When I'm not near the girl I love, I love the girl I'm near!

Finian's Rainbow

Commentary

The feelings we have about other people, whether positive or negative, are the basic elements of our interactions with them. Our likes and dislikes of other people are such a dominant feature of everyday social behavior that it would be hard to think of people we know without at the same time implicitly characterizing our relationship with them as either positive or negative. In spite of the pervasiveness and immediacy of interpersonal attraction, however, the topic has not lent itself readily to analysis. This is evidenced by the often-contradictory statements that characterize "commonsense" beliefs about interpersonal relations. "Absence makes the heart grow fonder" goes one well-known saying, but "Out of sight, out of mind" counters another. The saying "Familiarity breeds contempt" rings true, but so do the lyrics of a rock ballad of the late fifties, "To know him is to love him," which expresses the opposite belief. Recent systematic laboratory investigations of the factors influencing attraction have begun to place our knowledge about it on a firmer basis. The readings in this chapter explore some of the primary determinants of attraction and prejudice and their consequences.

In 1968, Robert Zajonc authored a monograph presenting evidence to support his hypothesis that "mere repeated exposure of the individual to a stimulus is a sufficient condition for the enhancement of his attitude toward it" (p. 1). This was a relatively novel idea because it does not invoke reinforcement principles to account for an individual's attraction to stimuli. Thus while the hypothesis does not deny the importance of reward or punishment, it says that repeated exposure of a person to an object is in and of itself sufficient to increase his attraction toward that object. Using a variety of stimuli—"Turkish" nonsense words, Chinese-like characters, and photographs of male graduating seniors at Michigan State University—Zajonc found essentially the same effect: Stimulus objects received more positive evaluations the more frequently they were exposed to subjects.

Although some reservations have been expressed about Zajonc's theory (e.g., Jakobovits, 1968; Maddi, 1968), experiments conducted since the 1968 monograph have tended to support the notion that attraction to objects increases with increasing exposure. From a social-psychological perspective, however, there has been a major limitation to the nature of the evidence so far. Studies on the exposure-affect relationship have so far used only nonsocial stimuli. Although a few studies have used photographs of individuals as stimuli, direct evidence for the validity of the mere-exposure hypothesis with actual people has been lacking. Does frequency of contact with people increase our liking for them? The first selection in this chapter ("Exposure, Context, and Interpersonal Attraction," by Saegert, Swap, and Zajonc) presents two studies conducted in an effort to answer that question. These studies also attempted to deal with some possible sources of error in earlier exposure studies, one of which may be the salience of the demand characteristics of the mere-exposure experiment. Demand characteristics refer to the "totality of cues which convey an experimental hypothesis to the subject" (Orne, 1962, p. 779). Thus when there is no attempt to disguise the true purpose of the experiment, subjects may be able to guess the hypothesis and act in a manner that will help confirm it. In order to counteract this possibility, Saegert and her colleagues disguised their experiments as studies on the psychophysics of taste, thereby hopefully shifting the subjects' focus away from those details of the experiment that dealt with the exposure-affect relationship.

Saegert and her colleagues were successful in demonstrating the validity of the exposure-liking relationship with social stimuli—the more frequently subjects shared a cubicle during a liquid-tasting task, the more likable each one rated the other. Now while this experiment establishes frequency of exposure as a determinant of attraction, most social situations provide opportunities for getting to know more about the other person than merely regarding him as a perceptual object. When the opportunity for social interaction is present, other factors come into play which may influence attraction. One of these is Heider's balance principle.

Fritz Heider's balance principle has already been encountered in the introduction to Chapter I as an explanation for our tendency to form unitary impressions—all good or all bad—of other persons. In our liking and disliking of others, we also prefer a balanced state, which Heider defines as "a situation in which the relations among the entities fit together harmoniously." Furthermore, "if a balanced state does not exist, then forces toward this state will arise. If a change is not possible, the state of imbalance will produce tension" (1958, p. 201). Thus, for example, "we tend to like people who have the same beliefs and attitudes we have, and when we like people, we want them to have the same attitudes we have" (p. 195).

An application of the balance principle to the prediction of interpersonal attraction is provided by the study reported in the second selection in this chapter ("My Enemy's Enemy Is My Friend," by Aronson and Cope). In this study subjects in an experiment were treated either harshly or pleasantly by an experimenter, and later they overheard the experimenter being either criticized or praised by the supervisor. As predicted by balance theory, subjects liked the supervisor more when subject and supervisor shared a dislike or a liking for the experimenter than when they did not have similar feelings about the experimenter. Furthermore, the study demonstrated that having a liking or dislike in common with a person leads to attraction toward that person, even when different reasons lead to that shared evaluation. Thus, for example, in one condition the subject disliked the experimenter for his quite severe criticism, whereas the supervisor disliked the experimenter because he thought poorly of the work being done by the experimenter. Regardless of what led to their respective feelings toward the experimenter, the subject liked the supervisor more when these feelings were perceived to be similar than when they were dissimilar.

The third selection in this chapter ("'Playing Hard to Get': Understanding an Elusive Phenomenon," by Walster et al.) reports a series of experiments which sought to determine if a woman who is hard to get is preferred to an easy-to-get woman. In spite of the fact that folklore, as well as several theories, suggests that the hard-to-get woman would be more desirable, five experiments failed to confirm that suggestion. Reexamining the matter, the authors realized that perhaps a girl would be most desirable when she was *selectively* hard to get. That is, a man would be most attracted to a woman who was generally considered as being hard to get but who was easy for him to get. The experiment confirmed this hypothesis—and the fact that social psychologists do not give up easily.

The remaining readings in this chapter shift focus somewhat. The articles so far have dealt with attraction toward individuals. The rest will examine some antecedents and consequences of extreme dislike for certain ethnic, racial, or other groups—in other words, prejudice.

Earlier in this introduction Heider was quoted on the effects of attitude and belief similarity on interpersonal attraction. It seems logical to expect that this factor would also play a role in prejudice. In fact, according to Rokeach, Smith, and Evans (1960), it does. They argue that a major determining factor in racial or ethnic prejudice is not the racial or ethnic difference per se but the factor of belief congruence. That is, our like or dislike for a member of another group is determined by similarity of beliefs; to the extent that we reject a person of another race, we do so because we assume that the other holds beliefs that are different from our own. Rokeach and his colleagues present evidence supporting this view in *The Open and Closed Mind* (1960). In one study, white college students were presented with brief descriptions of hypothetical persons which were systematically varied in terms of racial similarity and belief similarity. The subjects were to indicate the likelihood that they would be friends with such a person. The results showed that the subjects' friendship preferences were based on belief similarity rather than racial similarity.

While Rokeach's theory has not gone unchallenged (e.g., Triandis, 1961), most of the research on the race vs. belief similarity issue has supported his principle of belief congruence. However, almost all the studies on this topic (but see Rokeach and Mezei, 1966) have suffered from a major weakness: They have been primarily "as if" studies in which subjects are asked to imagine how they would react to hypothetical persons whose attitudinal and racial characteristics are systematically varied. What has been lacking is evidence that persons' actual behaviors—and not only their responses on a paper-and-pencil measure lacking any consequences for the individuals—are guided by belief similarity. The fourth selection in this chapter provides such evidence.

In the study ("Consequences, Racial Discrimination, and the Principle of Belief Congruence," by Silverman) a sample of incoming freshmen at a small college in Michigan (the experimental group) received a letter from the dean informing them that they would have a choice in selecting their roommates and containing a value and attitude questionnaire to be filled out. Later they received another mailing containing biographical sketches of eight different prospective roommates, each of which represented a different combination of the three variables of race, value, and attitude similarity. That is, some of the potential roommates were described as black, some white, and they were made to appear as having attitudes and values which were either similar to or different from those of the subjects. The subjects were to indicate how much they preferred each person as a roommate. It was stressed that their ratings would determine their actual roommate assignments. A control group of incoming freshmen also received similar mailings which differed from the first group's in one important respect: their mailings came from the psychology department of a university which was ostensibly doing a survey on student attitudes, and when they were sent the biographical sketches, they were asked to rate them *as if* they were selecting a roommate. Thus subjects in the experimental condition were led to believe that their choices had actual, real-life consequences, while the control subjects were not.

The findings supported the principle of belief congruence, but, at the same time, race was also found to be a significant, though weaker, determinant of roommate selection. In both experimental and control conditions subjects (all of whom were white) were much more likely to select a person with similar attitudes than one with different attitudes. This was by far the most powerful effect, accounting for 36 percent of the variance in subjects' responses. While subjects in both conditions also responded in terms of race (i.e., preferred the white roommate to the black), only 3 percent of the variance is attributable to this factor. Thus belief similarity was a much better predictor of preferences than racial similarity. At the same time Silverman found that the tendency to choose on the basis of race was greater in the experimental condition than in the control condition; Negroes were preferred significantly less in the experimental condition, where subjects thought roommate assignment would be based on their stated preference, than in the control condition, where they knew that their ratings had no such consequences.

Silverman's article throws light on some important determinants of prejudice. A more complete understanding of the dynamics of prejudice also requires an examination of its various behavioral consequences. The remaining three articles in this chapter deal with this issue, and each focuses on a different group which has been a target of prejudice and discrimination to varying degrees and at various times: Jews, blacks, and women.

Kurt Lewin was a Jewish psychologist who began his career in Germany but emigrated to the United States in 1933 when the Nazi persecution of Jews began (Marrow, 1969). His general approach to the study of social phenomena and his confidence that most questions of social importance can be answered through controlled experimentation have had a major impact on the scientific study of human behavior (Deutsch, 1968; Marrow, 1969), to the extent that "he may with some justice be considered the father of experimental social psychology, or at least of a major contemporary tradition of . . . hypothetico-deductive experimentation" (Jones & Gerard, 1967, p. 4). Although Lewin was a theorist who was interested in explaining basic processes of social behavior, he thought it important for the social scientist to try to apply his findings to the alleviation of social problems. As a Jew who had personally experienced anti-Jewish discrimination in Germany and who finally had to escape the Nazi terror, he was particularly sensitive to the problems of his co-religionists. Selection 5 ("Psychological Aspects of Minority Group Membership: The Concepts of Kurt Lewin," by Miriam A. Lewin) presents Lewin's insights on the psychological consequences of minority group membership and shows how he used his concepts of group processes to explain the reaction of Jews and members of other minority groups toward their minority status.

Selection 6 ("Bumper Stickers and the Cops," by Heussenstamm) is a field study which dramatically portrays the effects inflamed prejudices can have on perception and behavior. After a confrontation between the Black Panthers and the police, black students in Heussenstamm's class who belonged to the Black Panther party complained of harassment by police. She conducted the field study reported in this selection to determine the validity of her students' complaints.

The final selection in this chapter ("Effects of Additional Women Professionals on Ratings of Occupational Prestige and Desirability," by John Touhey) sheds light on some of the psychological concomitants of sex inequality in occupations. Most explanations why women occupy lower status positions than men in various professions point to admission and training practices that steer women toward less prestigious jobs. Touhey's study examines an intriguing alternate possibility: Perhaps women's poor representation in prestigious occupations is not so much due to their being kept out of them as it is to the fact that an occupation is no longer considered desirable or prestigious once women have entered it in large numbers.

REFERENCES

Deutsch, M. Field theory in social psychology. In G. Lindzey & E. Aronson (Eds.), *The handbook of social psychology* (2nd ed.; Vol. 1). Reading, Mass.: Addison-Wesley, 1968. Pp. 412-487.

Heider, F. *The psychology of interpersonal relations.* New York: Wiley, 1958.

Jakobovits, L. A. Effects of mere exposure: A comment. *Journal of Personality and Social Psychology Monograph Supplement,* 1968, *9* (2, Pt. 2), 30-32.

Jones, E. E., & Gerard, H. B. *Foundations of social psychology.* New York: Wiley, 1967.

Maddi, S. R. Meaning, novelty, and affect: Comments on Zajonc's paper. *Journal of Personality and Social Psychology Monography Supplement,* 1968, *9* (2, Pt. 2), 28-29.

Marrow, A. J. *The practical theorist: The life and work of Kurt Lewin.* New York: Basic Books, 1969.

Orne, M. T. On the social psychology of the psychological experiment: With particular reference to demand characteristics and their implications. *American Psychologist,* 1962, *17,* 776-783.

Rokeach, M., & Mezei, L. Race and shared belief as factors in social choice. *Science,* 1966, *151,* 167-172.

Rokeach, M., Smith, P. W., & Evans, R. I. Two kinds of prejudice or one? In M. Rokeach, *The open and closed mind.* New York: Basic Books, 1960. Pp. 132-168.

Triandis, H. C. A note on Rokeach's theory of prejudice. *Journal of Abnormal and Social Psychology,* 1961, *62,* 184-186.

Zajonc, R. B. Attitudinal effects of mere exposure. *Journal of Personality and Social Psychology Monograph Supplement,* 1968, *9* (2, Pt. 2), 1-27.

1

SUSAN SAEGERT, WALTER SWAP, and R. B. ZAJONC

Exposure, Context, and Interpersonal Attraction

Two experiments were performed to determine the effects of mere exposure and positive and negative contexts on interpersonal attraction. In both experiments, exposure was manipulated by varying the number of encounters among female subjects; context was varied by having subjects taste either pleasant or noxious solutions during the encounters. In both experiments, attraction varied as a direct function of number of encounters, in negative as well as positive contexts. The implications of these findings for the "mere exposure" hypothesis and for the "context," or association, hypothesis are discussed.

A number of recent studies investigated the hypothesis that the mere repeated exposure of a stimulus object is a sufficient condition for the enhancement of an individual's attraction to that object (Harrison, 1968, 1969; Matlin, 1970; Saegert & Jellison, 1970; Swap, 1970; Zajonc, 1968; Zajonc & Rajecki, 1969; Zajonc, Swap, Harrison, & Roberts, 1971). The basic experimental paradigm in these studies consisted of two phases—an exposure phase during which a number of stimuli, usually 12, are shown varying numbers of times in a random sequence and a subsequent test phase during which the subject makes evaluative ratings of the stimuli previously seen. While these studies have generally found an increase in attractiveness of the object with increasing frequency of exposure, two possible sources of error could cast doubt on their results. One source of error derives from the context within which the experiment takes place. Usually, it is carried out in agreeable surroundings, in a relaxed atmosphere designed to make the subject comfortable, not concealing the fact that the experimenter appreciates the subject's participation. These pleasant surroundings and atmosphere are present throughout every presentation of each stimulus, and it is conceivable that those stimuli that are exposed

Source: Susan Saegert, Walter Swap, and R. B. Zajonc, "Exposure, Context, and Interpersonal Attraction," *Journal of Personality and Social Psychology*, 1973, *25*, 234-242. Copyright 1973 by the American Psychological Association. Reprinted by permission.

This work was supported by National Science Foundation Grant GS 3119 to R. B. Zajonc.

more frequently may become more strongly associated with the pleasant context and thereby recruit more positive affect than stimuli exposed infrequently. Burgess and Sales (1971), in fact, reported that an increase in affect as a function of exposure was obtained by them only for subjects who claimed to have enjoyed taking part in the experiment. But it was not clear from their data whether the subjects' elation over taking part in a psychological experiment enhanced the attractiveness of the stimuli, or whether finding themselves liking the stimuli more at the end of the session than at the beginning, the subjects viewed their participation in retrospect to have been rather pleasant. Hence, Burgess and Sales carried out an experiment in which context was manipulated. To each presentation of a nonsense word, an associate was paired in the form of English words—positive, neutral, or negative in meaning. They found that nonsense words that were paired with positive associates were rated more positively with increasing frequency of exposure, while those that were paired with negative words were rated more negatively with increasing exposure.

The Burgess-Sales data demonstrate that it is possible, by association, to modify the rated affect of nonsense words, a finding previously reported by Staats and Staats (1958). However, the finding that a positive association increases positive affect and negative association negative affect is not contradictory to the mere exposure hypothesis. Neither classical and instrumental conditioning nor secondary reinforcement are preempted by the mere exposure hypothesis, which merely holds that exposure is *sufficient* for attitudinal enhancement. Showing that other variables can *also* produce changes in affect does not change the validity of that hypothesis: It only shows that they too are sufficient. The mere exposure hypothesis would be damaged if the exposure variable could not overcome negative affect, however moderate or weak. When the context associated with each stimulus presentation is positive, then both the context and frequency of exposure have enhancing effects on subsequent ratings. If the context is negative, however, exposure and context are in conflict. Results in this last case would support the exposure hypothesis if, in spite of the negative context, stimuli would increase in attractiveness with increasing exposure.

The second source of possible error in exposure studies is the ubiquitous demand characteristics of the experiment. Typically, the purposes of the exposure experiment are blatantly transparent. The subject is confronted with stimuli that differ in only one respect, and they differ in that respect quite conspicuously: Some are seen often, others, seldom. He is subsequently asked to rate these stimuli for their attractiveness. No superior intellectual effort is required to guess the experimenter's interest. The subject who undertakes this effort and is prone to please the experimenter simply orders his stimulus ratings according to frequency of exposure. But why would he order them in *increasing* attractiveness with increasing frequency? If he suspects the experimenter of entertaining an exposure hypothesis, and if he wishes to "help" him, his ratings would indeed be positively correlated with frequency of exposure. But if he suspects him of holding a satiation or a boredom hypothesis, the ratings would be negatively correlated with frequency of exposure. It is interesting in itself that subjects showing a negative correlation with frequency of exposure generally constitute a small minority in the past exposure studies. Nevertheless, the above possibility was examined in an unpublished experiment by Zajonc. An experiment in which frequency of exposure of Chinese ideographs was varied (Zajonc, 1968) was replicated in all respects, except that during the rating phase, the subjects were told that the ideographs stood for color names, all being combinations of green and blue—and one being pure green and one pure blue. Their task, following the exposure series, was to guess for each stimulus "how green" its meaning was. Given these ratings, there is no compelling reason for ordering the stimuli either in increasing "greenness" or in increasing "blueness." But, if frequency of exposure is all that is manipulated and if there are demand characteristics, then the subject population should be split into two sub-samples—one showing a positive correlation between "greenness" and frequency of exposure and another showing a negative correlation. The subjects in this experiment, however, could not be divided, the results being largely random, and only an occasional subject showing any correlation at all. Hence, no conclusions could be drawn—a reason why the experiment remained unpublished.

The present study reports two experiments in which both sources of error are hopefully eliminated. Stimulus frequency was manipulated against positive and negative context, but the manipulation was sufficiently subtle, in fact, entirely incidental, to escape the subjects' attention.

An additional purpose of these experiments was to extend the previous findings to social stimuli. That interpersonal attraction should vary with frequency of exposure is not a novel hypothesis. Homans (1950) hypothesized that "If the frequency of interaction between two or more persons increases, the degree of their liking for one another will increase [p. 112]." Newcomb (1956) related interpersonal attraction to the concept of "propinquity," and, while granting that attraction varies inversely with interpersonal distance and directly with frequency of interaction, he argued that the attraction results from a preponderance of rewards over punishments in most prolonged encounters. That is, propinquity and frequency of interaction, of themselves, are not sufficient conditions for attraction.

Rather, it is the *content* of the encounters that really matters, and decreasing distance and increasing frequency of interaction merely provide the opportunities for rewarding interactions. The exposure effect research, on the other hand, would argue that *mere* exposure, in the absence of "meaningful" or rewarding interaction, is a sufficient condition for interpersonal attraction.

In most earlier exposure studies, the exposure-affect relationship was confirmed for social stimuli only obliquely. Zajonc (1968) found an enhancement of liking for frequently exposed photographs of men's faces. Harrison (1969) used as stimuli names of public figures mentioned in national magazines during several years, and he found significant correlations between familiarity and popularity for four out of five samples of public figures.

Although just seeing actual persons frequently may also lead to increased liking for them, there is presently no evidence to corroborate this conjecture. For this reason the present investigations used actual persons met by subjects during the experiment as stimuli, whose frequency of exposure was manipulated in such a way as to appear incidental to the dramatic manipulations directly experienced by the subjects. This subtle manipulation of frequency also precludes the subjects' attributing their positive or negative experiences to the other subjects.

EXPERIMENT I

This experiment involved simultaneously manipulating frequency of the subjects' encounters with each other and the experimental context. Thus, the stimuli employed were the subjects themselves as seen by each other. Context was manipulated independently of exposure as a between-subjects factor. To accomplish this, the experiment was presented to the subjects as a study in the psychophysics of taste. Half of the subjects tasted pleasant substances, and half tasted unpleasant ones.

Method

Subjects. Forty-eight female undergraduates from the University of Michigan were paid $2 each for participating in the experiment.

Apparatus and Materials. Each of six cubicles affording visual and auditory privacy contained a taste rating form, a bottle of taste solution and one of water (both with siphons attached), a marked 50-millimeter measuring beaker, seven paper cups for tasting the solutions and the water, and a large covered beaker for expelling the solution. The taste rating forms as well as the paper cups were carried by the subjects as they changed cubicles. The pleasant taste solutions were three flavors of Kool-Aid. The noxious substances were weak solutions of vinegar, quinine, and citric acid.

The taste rating forms consisted of instructions and 25 numbered pages each containing 7-point rating scales for indicating the saltiness, sweetness, strength, pleasantness, bitterness, and sourness of that trial's taste solution. Each subject was rated for likeableness on a 7-point scale in a "general information" questionnaire administered at the end of the experiment. The questionnaire also asked the subject how enjoyable the experiment was, how much she liked the experimenter and the cubicles, and how upset she was at having to taste unknown solutions, all on 7-point scales, with anchor points at "extremely" and "not at all."

Procedure. The subjects were scheduled in groups of six. As each subject arrived, she was given a badge with a number from one to six on it, and she was shown to a cubicle. When all of the subjects had arrived, tape-recorded instructions were played over an intercom system to each cubicle. The subjects were told that the purpose of the experiment was to study their "perception of the tastes of substances that differ from each other in specific ways and which you will taste in different orders." The use of the rating forms and the procedure for tasting were then explained. At the end of each of the 25 tasting trials, some of the subjects were moved from one cubicle to another in such a way that the subjects spent 10, 5, 2, 1 or zero trials with every other subject. Each subject was escorted between cubicles individually to avoid encounters in the hallway. The fact that on some trials two subjects were tasting a solution in the same cubicle was explained as being a result of predetermined sequence of solutions to be tasted. The bottles of solutions were made unwieldy to justify their being stationary and necessitating the subjects' being moved. The subjects were instructed not to talk or make facial or other gestures that would distract the other subject. The shortest possible time (approximately 40 seconds, excluding room changes, determined by pretesting) was allotted for each trial in order to minimize verbal or nonverbal communication.

After the tasting trials were completed, the subjects were escorted to a large room where they sat in a circle facing each other. The "general information" questionnaires were administered, and the subjects were told to rate each other subject even if some had not been encountered before. Care was taken that the numbered badges were clearly visible. These and the other ratings were justified as being necessary since ratings of taste were believed to be sensitive to a variety of other influences. When the subjects had completed the forms, they were paid and debriefed.

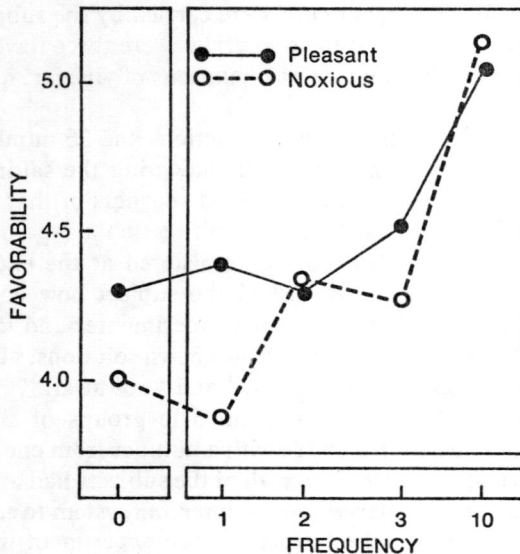

FIGURE 1.1
Favorability as a Function of Exposures and Pleasantness of Taste

Results and Conclusions

Figure 1.1 shows the frequency-liking curves obtained in the two conditions. In a three-factor analysis of variance for a repeated-measures design (groups, taste condition, and frequency) the main effect for frequency of exposure proved significant ($F = 6.10$, $df = 4/156$, $P < .001$). Neither the effect for taste condition nor for group approached significance. It appears, therefore, that the increased frequency of exposure to a person increases the person's popularity, regardless of the context within which exposure occurs.

The positive relationship between frequency of encounter and likability was confirmed at the individual subject level as well as at the group level. For each subject, the slope of the regression line on abscissa points 0, 1, 2, 5 and 10 was calculated. A positive slope would indicate that liking was enhanced for higher frequency stimuli—that is, the "frequency effect" was obtained. In the pleasant condition, positive slopes were obtained for 16 subjects and negative slopes for 3 ($p = .002$, by sign test); in the noxious condition, 17 subjects yielded positive and 4 negative slopes ($p = .004$). Across the two conditions, the probability of 33 slopes out of 40 being positive is less than .0001 (by sign test).

Although the manipulated pleasantness of the experiment was not a significant factor in the analysis of variance of liking ratings or the analysis of positive and negative slopes, two comparisons attest to the effectiveness of the manipulation of context. The mean rating of pleasantness of taste was 3.54 in the pleasant condition and 1.62 in the noxious condition ($t = 6.37$, $df = 23$, $p < .001$). Mean enjoyment of the experiment was 4.63 in the pleasant condition and 3.63 in the noxious condition ($t = 2.21$, $df = 23$, $p < .025$). Ratings of pleasantness of the taste substances correlate significantly ($p < .05$) but not strongly ($r = .26$) with liking for the experiment.

No support was obtained for the association (or secondary reinforcement) hypothesis. The pleasantness or unpleasantness of the experiment did not produce a significant effect on the slopes of the frequency effect or on liking. Furthermore, computing a correlation coefficient between each subject's exposure-liking slope and her liking for the experiment yielded a significant *negative* coefficient of —.27 ($p < .05$). The correlation of slope with mean taste rating for individual subjects ($r = .15$) was not significantly different from zero. Analysis of the subjects' liking ratings of the cubicle showed no significant difference between ratings of cubicles in the noxious condition ($\bar{X} = 3.79$) and in the pleasant condition ($\bar{X} = 4.39$; $t = .713$, $df = 23$). Thus, the data fail to support the Burgess and Sales (1971) prediction that the subjects who liked the experiment most would be the ones to show the strongest positive relationship between frequency of exposure and liking. The only significant correlation was in the opposite direction.

EXPERIMENT II

While the first experiment offers some evidence in favor of the hypothesis that the exposure effect is capable of overcoming the influence of context, a number of considerations led to the design of a second study. First, it seemed possible that during tasting trials the subjects exchanged meaningful gestures, sighs, and other communications. These communications, while probably minimized by instructing the subjects not to talk or gesture, could have removed the experiment from the mere exposure paradigm. In addition, while room changes were being made between trials, some combinations of subjects were left together for uncontrolled periods of time. That is, while *number* of interpersonal contacts was controlled, *duration* of the contact was not so tightly controlled. Finally, the fact that all of the subjects were engaging in a distinctive activity, tasting unknown substances, some with decidedly unpleasant odors and tastes, leads to an alternative interpretation of the results of the first experiment. A person might be attracted to another person perceived as similar to herself; in the context of the first experiment, subjects might perceive as most similar those people who have shared the tasting experience with them most frequently. The cause of the increased attraction would be a feeling of "shared fate," rather than exposure per se.

In an attempt to control for these factors, a second taste experiment was designed. Not only was frequency of contact varied, but duration of the contact was held constant and made briefer than in the first experiment. It was thus hoped to reduce further the incidence of nonverbal cues as well as to control for encounter duration. In a major modification of the first experiment, half of the subjects in each group of eight *tasted* the substances, while half simply *observed* the tasters during each trial. The manipulation of frequency occurred *across* these roles or tasks ("tasters" and "observers"); that is, the subjects were exposed only to people who did not share their "fate."

On the basis of the findings from the first experiment, it was hypothesized that interpersonal attraction would vary with number of encounters, independently of task. This relationship should obtain for both group data (means) and individual data (slopes). The experimental design also permitted another test of the context (or association) hypothesis. Specifically, if attitudinal enhancement is a function of the pleasantness of stimuli in the experimental session, then the exposure effect should not obtain (or be negative) for tasters in the noxious taste condition. Further, slopes of individual regression lines should vary positively with ratings of enjoyment of the experiment.

Method

Subjects. Sixty-four undergraduate women enrolled in psychology courses at the University of Michigan served as subjects as part of course requirements.

Apparatus and Materials. Each cubicle contained four beakers, each with a different taste solution, a beaker of water, five paper cups for tasting the solutions and the water, and a large covered beaker for expelling the solutions. In the pleasant condition, the solutions consisted of four flavors of Kool-Aid. Noxious solutions contained citric acid, vinegar, quinine, or soda salt.

Each taster was given a booklet with 18 rating scales—the booklets being essentially the same as those in Experiment I except somewhat shorter. The postexperimental questionnaire contained the critical dependent measures: ratings of the other subjects, the experiment, and the experimenter, all on 7-point scales. In addition, each subject was asked to rate, on 7-point scales, the pleasantness of each cubicle she had been in; tasters were asked to rate how upset they were at tasting the solutions; and observers rated how unpleasant or pleasant they guessed the solutions to be. Finally, each subject was asked to write down her guess as to the purpose of the experiment.

Procedure.   Each subject was randomly assigned to be either a taster or an observer and was given an adhesive badge (green for tasters, red for observers) with the word "taster" or "observer" and a number from 1 to 4. (This procedure was designed to facilitate recognition and to closely distinguish tasters from observers in the final rating stage of the experiment.) The subjects were seated in private rooms until all had arrived. Taped instructions similar to those in the first experiment were played over the intercom system. The tasting and observing procedures were described, and the tasters were given a practice trial. The observers were instructed to wait for the experimenter, who would escort them individually to the proper cubicle. Upon entering the cubicle, each observer was seated, facing the door, back-to-back with the taster, about 4 feet away from her. When all of the observers had been thus seated, a signal was given, and each observer moved to a chair directly facing the taster, and about 3 feet away from her. At the experimenter's signal, the actual tasting took place,

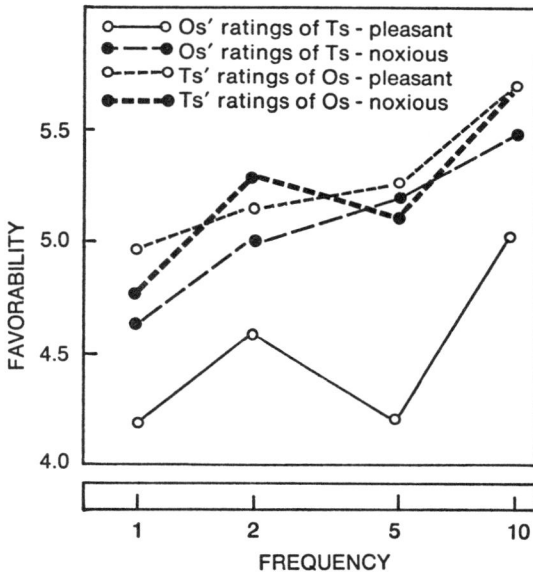

FIGURE 1.2
Favorability as a Function of Number of Exposures,
Task, and Pleasantness of Taste

while the observer watched the taster. When the signal was given ending
the taste trial, each observer returned to the chair facing the door. Thus,
the interval of actual face-to-face contact was firmly controlled and limited
to approximately 35 seconds per trial. Each observer was then conducted
individually to the next cubicle on the experimenter's change schedule. At
the end of the 18 taste trials, each observer had been exposed to each
taster either 1, 2, 5, or 10 times. After the eighteenth trial, all eight
subjects were escorted to a larger room where they were seated in a circle
to make their ratings on the postexperimental questionnaire.

Results

Figure 1.2 summarizes the mean liking for tasters and observers in both
the noxious and the pleasant taste conditions. An analysis of variance
demonstrated a significant effect for frequency of encounter ($F = 3.68$,
$df = 3/180$, $p < .025$). In addition, the tasters' ratings of the observers
were significantly more positive than were the observers' ratings of the
tasters ($F = 4.74$, $df = 1/48$, $p < .05$). No other effects or interactions
reached acceptable levels of significance.

A consideration of the individual subjects' frequency-affect slopes reveals a similar effect of frequency. As in the first experiment, the slope of
the regression line of liking on the abscissa points 1, 2, 5, and 10 was
calculated for each subject. A positive slope indicates that liking increased
with exposure. The distributions of positive and negative slopes for each of
the four Conditions x Task cells reveal a strikingly similar pattern. Of 14
nonzero slopes representing ratings of observers by tasters in the noxious
condition, 10 were positive ($p = .09$, by sign test); ratings of observers by
tasters in the pleasant condition also resulted in 10 positive slopes out of
14; for observers' ratings of tasters, the proportions of positive to total
nonzero slopes were, for the noxious condition, 10 out of 15 ($p = .16$),
and for the pleasant condition, 12 out of 15 ($p = .018$). Of 58 total nonzero slopes, 42 were positive ($p = .007$, by sign test).

As a check of the context hypothesis, a correlation was calculated between individual subjects' liking for the experiment and the slopes of their
frequency-liking curves. As in the first experiment, the correlation was
negative ($r = -.26$, $p < .05$, two-tailed). Yet, there can be little doubt
that context was successfully manipulated. Tasters rated noxious solutions
as significantly more unpleasant than the Kool-Aid solutions (1.73 versus
4.86; $t = 8.17$, $df = 30$, $p < .001$); tasters in the noxious condition liked
the experimenter less (3.75 versus 5.00; $t = 1.72$, $df = 30$, $p < .05$) and
enjoyed the experiment less (3.56 versus 5.00; $t = 2.70$, $df = 30$, $p < .01$)
than did tasters in the pleasant condition; and, while neither group of

tasters reported being particularly upset about tasting unknown sub-stances, tasters in the pleasant condition were less upset (6.63 versus 5.56; $t = 2.25$, $df = 30$, $p < .01$). Nonetheless, these two groups of subjects did not differ in their liking for the observers. What support the context hypothesis gains comes from a nonsignificant positive correlation ($r = .16$, $p < .30$) between mean ratings of pleasantness of the taste solutions and the slopes of the individual functions. There was also a small ($r = .17$) positive correlation between slope and liking for the experimenter.

Finally, as a check on the subtlety of the manipulation of the frequency variable, the subjects' comments on the possible purpose of the experiment were analyzed. None of the 64 subjects seemed to have any idea that attraction to the other subjects was of concern.

DISCUSSION

The results of the two studies reported here demonstrate that (a) even if the context is negative, frequency of stimuli exposed enhances their liking; and (b) this exposure effect is valid for interpersonal attitudes, as it was previously found to be true of attitudes toward inanimate objects. Both the analyses of variance and the slopes of the individual frequency-affect functions support the exposure effect. Even when the context surrounding the encounters was made fairly unpleasant, main effects for frequency were significant, and slopes were mostly positive. And positive correlations between pleasantness ratings of the experiment and the subjects' individual slopes of the frequency-affect functions were not found, as might have been predicted by the context hypothesis. In fact, in both experiments, these correlations were significantly *negative*. To be sure, the circumstances of the encounter between pairs of subjects were naturally never made so as to be painful for the participants. Yet, in both experiments, there were significant differences in the expected direction between the positive and negative groups in their ratings of the substances and their enjoyment of the experiment. In the second study, another measure —ratings of the subjects' liking for the experimenter—was included and also showed a significant difference in the predicted direction. To the extent that these ratings reflect differences in experienced context, and if exposure effects are merely context effects, negative slopes should have been found in a negative context.

Context is a very broad term, and in reference to interpersonal encounter, several meanings that have bearing on the exposure hypothesis can be distinguished. One meaning is simply that used in the present experiments: incidental stimuli, totally different from and independent of those used for exposure. In this case, the exposure effect was able to overcome the contrary effects of context. Another usage of the term "context" is that of incidental stimuli that are similar to and made to be associated with those whose frequency is being manipulated, and in the case of the Burgess and Sales (1971) experiment, these context effects were apparently sufficient to overcome exposure effects. Why the first type of context did not and the second did interfere with exposure is a question that cannot be answered at present, however, except perhaps by saying that there is more of an experimental demand characteristic in the Burgess and Sales study than one would at first expect. Or, since verbal stimuli were used in their study, the final ratings are those of meaning, and it is possible that evaluative ratings of meaning are more readily subject to associative effects than is interpersonal attraction.

A third meaning of context in exposure studies concerns not the presence but the nature of the association between the critical and the incidental stimuli. The context and the exposures may be confounded. That is, it is possible for the subject to interpret the differences in the frequency of stimulus occurrences as meaningful, informative, or even as determinative. Thus, for instance, seeing a stranger once in an implicating situation, let us say in handcuffs, may not lead one necessarily to categorize him as a criminal. It could after all be an error, or a minor offense. Seeing him in handcuffs on two different occasions may raise some doubts about him, while seeing him thus a dozen times leaves no doubts at all. Here the frequency effect and the attribution process (Jones & Davis, 1965; Kelley, 1967) are intertwined, which presents an interesting experimental problem. One would not expect, under these circumstances, that frequency would always result in enhanced attractiveness of the stimulus object. Thus, for instance, Perlman and Oskamp (1971) reported a study in which photographs of whites and blacks were shown different numbers of times in "good" and "bad" contexts. Men were photographed in clerical garb, for example, or in a police lineup. Hence, in fact, they were presented as "good" and "bad" individuals. Perlman and Oskamp found main effects for both frequency and context of the photographs. The large increase in liking for positive photographs accounted for most of the frequency effect. In addition, a Context x Frequency interaction was found because exposure to negative photographs resulted in less liking for more frequently exposed photographs. One is tempted to conclude from their data that exposure and context, or exposure and attribution, had joint effects on liking.

In addition to the context hypothesis, two other alternative explanations of the results reported in the present two experiments can be considered. These are the "shared fate" hypothesis and the "nonverbal communication" hypothesis.

In the first experiment, frequency of encounter and the sharing of identical experiences were confounded. This led to speculation that a subject might prefer a frequently encountered person only if the two were engaging in the same activity or sharing the same "fate." But since the exposure effect was obtained in the second experiment despite the fact that the subjects in the two "task" conditions did not share the same experiences (except in the very general sense of participating in the same experiment), the shared-fate hypothesis is not supported. In the second experiment, ratings were made by each subject of all other subjects, even those performing the same tasks, although these shared-fate subjects had not been encountered during the experiment itself. Tasters rated each other an average of 4.68 on a 7-point scale of liking, while observers received an average rating of 4.79 from other observers. If shared fate were to enhance liking, these points should lie above affective ratings of comparable subjects in different-fate conditions. However, since there was no zero-exposure condition in the second experiment, a direct comparison is not possible. An indirect comparison can be made between the above mean ratings (shared fate, zero exposures) and ratings after one exposure for non-shared-fate subjects. The above rating of 4.68 is somewhat lower than the 4.85 that tasters gave observers, while the rating of 4.79 is somewhat higher than the 4.42 that observers gave tasters. All in all, these figures do not suggest a significant effect of shared fate on favorability.

The nonverbal communication hypothesis would follow from Newcomb's (1956) contention that interpersonal attraction through propinquity is mediated by rewards and reinforcements dispensed during interaction. In the present investigations, great care was taken to minimize communication among subjects. In the verbal instructions, the subjects were asked not to communicate in any way with one another, and tasters were urged not to make facial expressions after tasting the solutions. Further, the amount of time spent in face-to-face encounter was kept down to about 35 seconds per trial in the second experiment. Nonetheless, some communication might still have occurred, and, if it did, it probably occurred more frequently between subjects encountering each other more often. Such communication might be experienced as rewarding in some way and could conceivably lead to enhanced attitudinal ratings. The only concrete evidence bearing on this problem comes from an analysis of ratings given by observers of their perception of the pleasantness of the taste solutions. Observers in the pleasant condition guessed that the solutions had a mean pleasantness of 4.20, while in the noxious condition the mean was 3.25 ($p < .05$, t test). This may indicate that the tasters communicated their distaste for the solutions; on the other hand, the difference could be attributed to color (the noxious solutions all being clear, the Kool-Aid, colored) or to odor. Further, if this possible source of communication were to result in enhanced ratings of the communicator, it would be expected that tasters, being more expressive, should receive more favorable ratings than observers. However, just the opposite was the case, tasters finding observers more likeable than observers found tasters.

The most parsimonious explanation of the results of the two experiments appears to be that the mere repeated exposure of people is a sufficient condition for enhancement of attraction, despite differences in favorability of context, and in the absence of any obvious rewards or punishments by these people.

REFERENCES

Burgess, T. D. G., & Sales, S. M. Attitudinal effects of mere exposure: A re-evaluation. *Journal of Experimental Social Psychology,* 1971, *7,* 461-472.

Harrison, A. A. Response competition, frequency, exploratory behavior, and liking. *Journal of Personality and Social Psychology,* 1968, *9,* 363-368.

Harrison, A. A. Exposure and popularity. *Journal of Personality,* 1969, *37,* 359-377.

Homans, G. C. *The human group.* New York: Harcourt, Brace, 1950.

Jones, E. E., & Davis, K. E. From acts to dispositions. In L. Berkowitz (Ed.), *Advances in experimental social psychology.* Vol. 2. New York: Academic Press, 1965.

Kelley, H. H. Attribution theory in social psychology. *Nebraska Symposium on Motivation,* 1967, *15,* 192-238.

Matlin, M. W. Response competition as a mediating factor in the frequency-affect relationship. *Journal of Personality and Social Psychology,* 1970, *16,* 536-552.

Newcomb, T. M. The prediction of interpersonal attraction. *American Psychologist,* 1956, *11,* 575-586.

Perlman, D., & Oskamp, S. The effects of picture content and exposure frequency on evaluations of Negroes and whites. *Journal of Experimental Social Psychology,* 1971, *7,* 503-514.

Saegert, S., & Jellison, J. The effects of initial level of response competition and frequency of exposure on liking and exploratory behavior. *Journal of Personality and Social Psychology,* 1970, *16,* 553-557.

Staats, A. W., & Staats, C. K. Attitudes established by classical conditioning. *Journal of Abnormal and Social Psychology,* 1958, *57,* 37-40.

Swap, W. C. *The effects of repeated exposure of meaningful stimuli on attitude formation and change.* Unpublished doctoral dissertation, University of Michigan, Ann Arbor, 1970.

Zajonc, R. B. Attitudinal effects of mere exposure. *Journal of Personality and Social Psychology Monograph Supplement,* 1968, *9* (2, Pt. 2) 2-27.

Zajonc, R. B., & Rajecki, D. W. Exposure and affect: A field experiment. *Psychonomic Science,* 1969, *17,* 216-217.

Zajonc, R. B., Swap, W. C., Harrison, A. A., & Roberts, P. Limiting conditions of the exposure effect: Satiation and relativity. *Journal of Personality and Social Psychology,* 1971, *18,* 386-391.

2

ELLIOT ARONSON and VERNON COPE

My Enemy's Enemy Is My Friend

An experiment was performed to explore the generality of the proposition that people like those who punish their enemies and reward their friends. Results indicated that the attractiveness of a person who punishes one's enemy or rewards one's friend is not limited to situations which provide indications of attitude similarity, gratitude, or social support. Specifically, the experiment was designed to show that this phenomenon occurs in spite of the fact that the situation was arranged so that: (a) The stimulus person's behavior in no way suggested that his attitudes were similar to those of S; (b) the stimulus person was clearly unaware of S's relationship to the latter's enemy or friend—thus he was not trying to help S; and (c) it was clear that S and the stimulus person would have no opportunity to meet and gain any social benefit from sharing a mutual friend or enemy. Methodologically, the possibility of bias was reduced by using separate Es, who were partially blinded as to treatment, and a 3rd person (similarly blinded) to collect the dependent-variable data.

It makes sense to assume that, all other things being equal, if two people discover that they share a common enemy, their mutual attractiveness will increase. This proposition is a simple derivation from balance theory (Heider, 1958). But such a situation may consist of one or more underlying factors. For example, if I know nothing about the reason why another person dislikes my enemy, I might assume that we dislike him for the same reasons and, therefore, that we share similar beliefs and attitudes. Thus, suppose that Person X's most outstanding characteristic is that he is a pompous ass, and I dislike him for it. If I learn that Person Y also dislikes X, I might assume that Y dislikes X for the same reason. A similarity of beliefs and attitudes has been shown to increase attractiveness (Byrne, 1961; Newcomb, 1961). Accordingly, I might like X because I feel that we both dislike people who exhibit "pompous assiness." Second, I might believe that this other person dislikes my enemy because he knows that I dislike him. This would suggest that my enemy's enemy likes me. Since people generally like those who like them (Aronson & Linder, 1965;

Source: Elliot Aronson and Vernon Cope, "My Enemy's Enemy Is My Friend," *Journal of Personality and Social Psychology,* 1968, *8,* 8-12. Copyright 1968 by the American Psychological Association. Reprinted by permission.

This experiment was supported by grants from the National Science Foundation (NSF GS 750) and the National Institute of Mental Health (MH 12357-01).

Backman & Secord, 1959), I might come to like him. Finally, this relationship may have certain concrete practical advantages. Specifically, if I dislike X and I discover that Y dislikes X also, I may feel that it is conceivable that Y and I might band together and beat X up or plot strategy against him or at least engage in some satisfying malicious gossip. Thus, I might like Y purely because he can do me some tangible good.

One may wonder whether the above criteria are essential for the phenomenon to occur. For example, suppose X behaved harshly to me. If Y behaved negatively to X, would I increase my liking for Y even if (a) he were unaware that X had behaved harshly toward me, (b) his nasty behavior toward X was inspired by a totally different set of events, and (c) there was no opportunity for us to socialize and commiserate? For example, if X had insulted me at a cocktail party, and 2 weeks later I noticed a police officer (Y) issuing a summons to X for a traffic violation, would that police officer become dear to my heart? The authors' guess is that he would. It is the authors' contention that Heider's proposition is a general one, not limited to such mediating events; that is, there is something good about seeing one's enemy punished—in and of itself. Consequently, it is predicted that individuals will like their enemy's punisher even if the two events are noncontingent and unrelated, that is, even if the punisher's behavior implies neither attitude similarity nor utility. By the same token, individuals will come to like a person who rewards someone who treated them kindly—even if the two events are noncontingent and unrelated.

METHOD

General Overview

The general procedure involved placing the subject in a situation in which he was treated either harshly or pleasantly by an experimenter and then allowing the subject to overhear the experimenter being treated either harshly or pleasantly by the latter's supervisor. The subject was then given an opportunity to express his feelings for the supervisor. It was obviously essential that the supervisor's evaluation of the experimenter be separate from and unrelated to the experimenter's evaluation of the subject.

Subjects and Design

The subjects were 40 male and 40 female introductory psychology students at the University of Texas. They were randomly assigned to one of four conditions designed to test the hypothesis: pleasant experimenter-

pleasant supervisor, pleasant-experimenter-harsh supervisor, harsh experimenter-pleasant supervisor, harsh experimenter-harsh supervisor.[1]

Procedure

The subjects volunteered for participation in a study of creativity. When
the subject arrived, the experimenter[2] led him into a cubicle and introduced himself as a graduate student who was assisting Dr. Cope in his
creativity project. The experimenter explained that the purpose of the
study was to determine the relationship between creativity and college performance. He informed the subject that he would present him with a series
of three pictures and that the subject's task would be to write a story about
each picture—what the situation is, what led to the situation, what the
people are thinking or feeling, and what they will do. The subjects were
told that they would have only 4 minutes to write each story.

After the subject had written a story, the experimenter silently read it and
marked it with various coded grading signals. During his reading of each
story and after the reading of all three stories, the manipulation of either
pleasant experimenter or harsh experimenter was put into effect. In order
to reduce opportunities for bias, the experimenter was kept ignorant of the
condition in which the subject was to be run until this point in the experiment. This was determined randomly. When it was essential to ensure
equal numbers of subjects per condition, the senior author determined the
condition of each subject in advance and handed the experimenter a
folded slip of paper before each subject was run. The slip contained the
word "harsh" or "pleasant." After delivering the initial instructions and
while the subject was writing the first story, the experimenter simply
reached into his pocket, unfolded the paper, and determined the subject's
condition. Thus, the initial instructions were delivered in ignorance of the
subject's condition. At this point the manipulation commenced.

Harsh Condition. While he read each story, the experimenter occasionally emitted a displeased and condescending grunt, sigh, or grumble.
After reading all three stories, the experimenter stated that although the
final scoring was not completed and would take more time he would give
the subject a tentative evaluation. He then proceeded to tell the subject
that his stories were unimaginative and uncreative. The evaluation was
given starkly and somewhat brutally, with no punches pulled. The experimenter acted as if he enjoyed making these negative statements.

Pleasant Condition. In this condition the evaluation was essentially
the same. The experimenter told the subject that although the final scoring was not completed and would take more time he would give the subject

a tentative evaluation. He then told the subject that his stories were uncreative and unimaginative. But in this condition the experimenter treated the subject very gently. Specifically, he told him not to be too worried about it—that although the test was a good measure of creativity, it *was* only one test. In short, although the experimenter told the subject that according to his analysis of the test results the subject was uncreative, he let the subject down gently rather than harshly; he allowed the subject to save face.

A few seconds before the experimenter finished his evaluation, he casually leaned against the door of the testing room and rubbed his foot against the air vent. This served as a signal to the "supervisor" who, although waiting some distance from the door, was able to see it move. After waiting a few seconds, the supervisor knocked on the door, entered, excused himself for interrupting, told the experimenter that he must talk to him for a moment, and asked the experimenter to step into the hall. The experimenter stood up and introduced the supervisor to the subject. The supervisor shook hands with the subject and escorted the experimenter into the corridor.

Although they were careful to close the door behind them (so as not to arouse the subject's suspicions), the situation was such that the subject could easily overhear their conversation through the air vent at the bottom of the door.

At this point the second variable was manipulated: the supervisor's treatment of the experimenter. Half of the subjects were randomly assigned to the pleasant-supervisor condition, half were randomly assigned to the harsh-supervisor condition. The conversations in each condition are presented in that order below:

I read that report you wrote for me, and, well, I think it's one of the finest analyses of the articles I've seen in a long, long time. In particular, I thought you made an excellent selection of references. I don't think I could have done a better job myself—and I know that area pretty well! Also, I think I'll make up another copy of your paper so I can show it to my other research assistants as an example of the sort of work I want from them and just as an example of good, creative work. Uh, I'm on my way to see the department chairman right now and, well, because I'm so impressed with the sort of work you've been doing here, I'm going to ask him if we can get you an increase in salary. Well, I have to run now so you can get back to your subject.

I read that report you wrote for me, and I think it's, well, virtually worthless. It's sloppy and somewhat stupid. I can see no logical reason for using the references you cited. They have absolutely no relevance to the topics you were supposed to write about. I have an idea you were just using those references as filler material. Well, there's a lot of irrelevant material, and the quality and the organization are both very poor. OK, I'm going to give you a couple of days to do it over. As a matter of fact, I'm on my way right now to see the department chairman, and I'm going to ask him if there's anyone else we have who could replace you if you continue to do bad work. OK, I've got to run now so you can get back to your subject.

After he had been "evaluated," the experimenter reentered the room with a gloomy face if he had been negatively evaluated and a smile if positively evaluated. He told the subject that that was all they had time for and instructed him to go upstairs to the psychology office where the secretary would give him credit for the experiment.

It should be noted that at the time the supervisor was acting either harshly or pleasantly to the experimenter, the supervisor was ignorant as to whether the experimenter had been pleasant or harsh to the subject. Similarly, while the experimenter was acting either pleasantly or harshly to the subject, the experimenter was unaware as to whether the supervisor was about to treat him pleasantly or harshly. Thus, since an interaction is being predicted, this technique of "partial ignorance" effectively guards against the systematic bias described by Rosenthal (1966). For a greater elaboration of the applicability of this partial ignorance technique, see Aronson and Carlsmith (1968).

Dependent Variable. The dependent variable was administered by the departmental secretary who was, of course, ignorant of the subject's experimental condition. As she prepared to give the subject credit for participation in the experiment, she said that she had a request to make on behalf of the supervisor of the experiment the subject had just participated in. After ascertaining that the subject recalled having met the supervisor, she proceeded to tell him that he (Dr. Cope) was spending 1 year at the University to do research for the National Science Foundation. In regard to a different project he was directing, she continued, the National Science Foundation had recently informed him that he must use a different body of subjects taken from the local community instead of the college students he had been using as subjects. The result was that the supervisor needed hundreds of nonuniversity people within the next 2 weeks and that the job of contacting people and convincing them to volunteer was enormous. She said that the supervisor did not have the staff to do this work, and he could not afford to pay for it; he was really desperate and needed a favor. Specifically, he had requested that she ask anyone to help him by making phone calls. She said that she had a long list of several thousand phone numbers randomly selected from the Austin telephone directory. She asked:

Would you be willing to help Dr. Cope by making some phone calls and asking people to serve as subjects? Other people have volunteered to call anywhere from 2 to 50 people—would you be willing to help him out?

The number of phone calls served as the dependent variable, being a reflection of the positive feelings the subjects held for the supervisor.

After the subject made his decision, the secretary thanked him. She then handed him a short questionnaire which she introduced as a departmental questionnaire designed to determine the effectiveness and viability of the departmental requirement that all introductory psychology students serve as subjects. The significant item on the questionnaire was an evaluation of the experimenter. The secretary was ignorant of the subject's experimental treatment while she was soliciting his aid in making phone calls and administering the questionnaire. Thus, the inevitable minor variations in her tone and manner could not have had a systematic effect on the results.

After the subject completed the questionnaire, Dr. Cope entered the office and debriefed him. Because all of the subjects had received a rather negative evaluation, they were delighted to learn that the evaluation was preprogrammed rather than an accurate reflection of their creative ability.

TABLE 2.1
Mean Number of Phone Calls Volunteered on Behalf of Supervisor

	Supervisor	
E	Harsh	Pleasant
Harsh	12.1	6.2
Pleasant	6.3	13.5

TABLE 2.2
Analysis of Variance

Source	MS	F
E's evaluation (A)	12.03	.12
Supervisor's evaluation (B)	8.53	.09
Sex of S (C)	122.00	1.26
Identity of E (D)	1.00	.01
AxB	816.40	8.42*
AxC	4.03	.04
AxD	140.83	1.45
BxC	48.13	.50
BxD	128.13	1.32
CxD	.40	.00
AxBxC	49.40	.51
AxBxD	25.20	.26
AxCxD	17.63	.18
BxCxD	.53	.00
AxBxCxD	143.00	1.47
Error	96.95	

*$p < .005$, $df = 1/64$.

RESULTS AND DISCUSSION

Before presenting the primary data, it is necessary to determine if the major manipulation worked: Did the subjects like the harsh experimenter less than the pleasant experimenter? Recall that the subjects were asked to complete a series of rating scales which were introduced as a departmental questionnaire aimed at determining their reaction to the experiment. Included in this questionnaire was a direct evaluation of the experimenter: "How much did you enjoy working with the experimenter?" The results indicate that the manipulation was effective. Subjects were more favorably disposed to the experimenter in the pleasant conditions than in the harsh conditions ($p < .005$).[3]

The hypothesis was that the subject would like his enemy's enemy more than his enemy's friend, and that he would like his friend's friend better than his friend's enemy. Specifically, it was predicted that the subject would volunteer to make the most phone calls as a favor to the supervisor if the latter had acted either harshly to the experimenter who treated the subject harshly or pleasantly to the experimenter who had treated the subject kindly. The results are presented in Table 2.1. Inspection of the table reveals that the subjects were willing to make more phone calls for a supervisor who was his enemy's enemy than for one who was his enemy's friend. Similarly, subjects were willing to make more phone calls for a friend's friend than for a friend's enemy. The data were analyzed by analysis of variance (Table 2.2). The prediction is reflected in the interaction between the experimenter's behavior toward the subject and the supervisor's behavior toward the experimenter. The interaction is highly significant ($p < .005$). Separate contrasts were performed between the harsh supervisor and the pleasant supervisor within the pleasant-experimenter condition and between the harsh supervisor and the pleasant supervisor within the harsh-experimenter condition. Both were significant ($p < .05$). As expected, there were no main effects due to the behavior of the experimenter or the behavior of the supervisor. Likewise, neither sex of the subject nor the identity of the person playing the role of experimenter affected the results to a significant degree.

The results, then, would seem to indicate that a person's hostility toward our enemy or pleasantness toward our friend is, in and of itself, sufficient to bring about an increase in our liking for him. In the present experiment, as far as the subject was concerned, the supervisor was unaware of the fact that the experimenter had been kind or unkind to the subject. Thus, the supervisor's treatment of the experimenter could in no way be construed as being caused by the experimenter's treatment of the subject. In addition, it was clear that the supervisor's reasons for being nice or nasty to the experimenter were unrelated to the subject's reasons for liking or disliking the experimenter. The subjects liked or disliked the experimenter because he was either kind or harsh during their encounter. On the other hand, the supervisor rewarded or punished the experimenter for his prior performance on a written report which had no relevance to the nature of the experimenter's behavior to the subject. Moreover, the vast difference in status between the subject and the supervisor made it extremely unlikely that the two would ever discuss their mutual feelings about the experimenter.

At the same time, it should be noted that all alternative explanations have not been ruled out. Although the subject and the supervisor clearly dislike the experimenter for different reasons, it is conceivable that the supervisor's negative evaluation of the experimenter could have had an effect on the impact of the experimenter's negative evaluation of the subject; that is, in the harsh-supervisor conditions, the supervisor told the experimenter that he wrote a poor report. This could imply that the experimenter is stupid and incompetent. If the subject had just received harsh criticism from a person, learning that he (that person) is stupid and incompetent could reduce the impact of this harsh treatment. Consequently, it is possible that the subject came to like the supervisor who treated the unpleasant experimenter harshly, not simply because we like people who punish our enemies, but, more specifically, because we like people who help us believe that a person who judged us harshly may be a stupid and incompetent person, and that, consequently, his harsh judgment may be erroneous. This alternative explanation is unlikely, however, because it is not symmetrical; that is, it does not apply in the pleasant experimenter-pleasant supervisor condition. Recall that, like the harsh experimenter, the pleasant experimenter rated the subject as uncreative— his manner was simply more pleasant as he made this negative evaluation of the subject. Consequently, when the pleasant supervisor implied that the pleasant experimenter was intelligent and competent, he was, in effect, offering support to the experimenter's evaluation of the subject as an uncreative person. In short, if we like someone because he questions the intelligence of someone who has recently judged us as uncreative, then we should have discovered a main effect due to the behavior of the supervisor. The fact that the data show a clear interaction and significant contrasts sharply reduces the plausibility of this alternative explanation.

The results suggest that balance theory applies in a behavioral context even in the absence of specific opinion similarity; that is, the data indicate that: (a) We like someone who likes someone that we like; (b) we like someone who dislikes someone we dislike; (c) we dislike someone who likes someone we dislike; and (d) we dislike someone who dislikes someone we like. This follows even though it is clear that the respective reasons for liking or disliking the target person are unrelated. The primary contribution of this experiment, then, is in the demonstration that the basic proposition of balance theory is true in a very general sense and is not limited to situations which are mediated by other phenomena, for example, by specific opinion similarity.

REFERENCES

Aronson, E., & Carlsmith, J. M. Experimentation in social psychology. In G. Lindzey & E. Aronson (Eds.), *Handbook of social psychology.* (Rev. ed.) Vol. 2. Reading, Mass.: Addison-Wesley, 1968.

Aronson, E., & Linder, D. Gain and loss of esteem as determinants of interpersonal attractiveness. *Journal of Experimental Social Psychology,* 1965, *1,* 156-171.

Backman, C. W., & Secord, P. F. The effect of perceived liking on interpersonal attraction. *Human Relations,* 1959, *12,* 379-384.

Byrne, D. Interpersonal attraction and attitude similarity. *Journal of Abnormal and Social Psychology,* 1961, *62,* 713-715.

Heider, F. *The psychology of interpersonal relations.* New York: Wiley, 1958.

Newcomb, T. M. *The acquaintance process.* New York: Holt, Rinehart & Winston, 1961.

Rosenthal, R. *Experimenter effects in behavioral research.* New York: Appleton-Century-Crofts, 1966.

NOTES

1. In actuality, 86 subjects were run. Because of suspiciousness, 2 subjects were discarded in each of Conditions 2, 3, and 4, respectively.

2. Two different experimenters were used in the experiment. They ran an equal proportion of subjects in all conditions; the results were not influenced by the identity of the experimenter.

3. A rather interesting serendipitous finding should be reported. Specifically, there was an interaction between the sex of the subject and the behavior of the supervisor as it affected the liking of the subject for the experimenter ($p < .005$). Generally, males tended to like the experimenter if he was pleasantly treated by the supervisor; females liked the experimenter better if he was harshly criticized by the supervisor, irrespective of how the experimenter behaved toward the subject. This may reflect a tendency for women to be more nurturant and/or less impressed by success than men.

3

ELAINE WALSTER, G. WILLIAM WALSTER, JANE PILIAVIN, and
LYNN SCHMIDT

"Playing Hard to Get": Understanding an Elusive Phenomenon

According to folklore, the woman who is hard to get is a more desirable catch the woman who is too eager for an alliance. Five experiments were conducted to demonstrate that individuals value hard-to-get dates more than easy-to-get ones. All five experiments failed. In Experiment VI, we finally gained an understanding of this elusive phenomenon. We proposed that two components contribute to a woman's desirability: (*a*) how hard the woman is for the subject to get and (*b*) how hard she is for other men to get. We predicted that the selectively hard-to-get woman (i.e., a woman who is easy for the subject to get but hard for all other men to get) would be preferred to either a uniformly hard-to-get woman, a uniformly easy-to-get woman, or a woman about which the subject has no information. This hypothesis received strong support. The reason for the popularity of the selective woman was evident. Men ascribe to her all of the assets of uniformly hard-to-get and the uniformly easy-to-get women and none of their liabilities.

According to folklore, the woman who is hard to get is a more desirable catch than is the woman who is overly eager for alliance. Socrates, Ovid, Terence, the *Kama Sutra,* and Dear Abby all agree that the person whose affection is easily won is unlikely to inspire passion in another. Ovid (1963), for example, argued:

Fool, if you feel no need to guard your girl for her own sake, see that you guard her for mine, so I may want her the more. Easy things nobody wants, but what is forbidden is tempting. . . . Anyone who can love the wife of an indolent cuckold, I should suppose, would steal buckets of sand from the shore [pp. 65-66].

When we first began our investigation, we accepted cultural lore. We assumed that men would prefer a hard-to-get woman. Thus, we began our research by interviewing college men as to why they preferred hard-to-get women. Predictably, the men responded to experimenter demands. They

Source: Elaine Walster, G. William Walster, Jane Piliavin, and Lynn Schmidt, " 'Playing Hard to Get': Understanding an Elusive Phenomenon," *Journal of Personality and Social Psychology,* 1973, *26,* 113-121. Copyright 1973 by the American Psychological Association. Reprinted by permission.

This research was supported in part by National Science Foundation Grants GS 2932 and GS 30822X and in part by National Institute for Mental Health Grant MH 16661.

explained that they preferred hard-to-get women because the elusive woman is almost inevitably a valuable woman. They pointed out that a woman can only afford to be "choosy" if she is popular—and a woman is popular for some reason. When a woman is hard to get, it is usually a tip-off that she is especially pretty, has a good personality, is sexy, etc. Men also were intrigued by the challenge that the elusive woman offered. One can spend a great deal of time fantasizing about what it would be like to date such a woman. Since the hard-to-get woman's desirability is well recognized, a man can gain prestige if he is seen with her.

An easy-to-get woman, on the other hand, spells trouble. She is probably desperate for a date. She is probably the kind of woman who will make too many demands on a person; she might want to get serious right away. Even worse, she might have a "disease."

In brief, nearly all interviewees agreed with our hypothesis that a hard-to-get woman is a valuable woman, and they could supply abundant justification for their prejudice. A few isolated men refused to cooperate. These dissenters noted that an elusive woman is not always more desirable than an available woman. Sometimes the hard-to-get woman is not only hard to get—she is *impossible* to get, because she is misanthropic and cold. Sometimes a woman is easy to get because she is a friendly, outgoing woman who boosts one's ego and insures that dates are "no hassle." We ignored the testimony of these deviant types.

We then conducted five experiments designed to demonstrate that an individual values a hard-to-get date more highly than an easy-to-get date. All five experiments failed.

THEORETICAL RATIONALE

Let us first review the theoretical rationale underlying these experiments.

In Walster, Walster, and Berscheid (1971) we argued that if playing hard to get does increase one's desirability, several psychological theories could account for this phenomenon:

1. Dissonance theory predicts that if one must expend great energy to attain a goal, he is unusually appreciative of the goal (see Aronson & Mills, 1959; Gerard & Mathewson, 1966; Zimbardo, 1965). The hard-to-get date requires a suitor to expend more effort in her pursuit than he would normally expend. One way for the suitor to justify such unusual effort is by aggrandizing her.

2. According to learning theory, an elusive person should have two distinct advantages: (a) Frustration may increase drive—by waiting until the suitor has achieved a high sexual drive state, heightening his drive level by introducing momentary frustration, and then finally rewarding

him, the hard-to-get woman can maximize the impact of the sexual reward she provides (see Kimball, 1961, for evidence that frustration does energize behavior and does increase the impact of appropriate rewards). (b) Elusiveness and value may be associated—individuals may have discovered through frequent experience that there is more competition for socially desirable dates than for undesirable partners. Thus, being "hard to get" comes to be associated with "value." As a consequence, the conditioned stimulus (CS) of being hard to get generates a fractional antedating goal response and a fractional goal response which leads to the conditioned response of liking.

3. In an extension of Schachterian theory, Walster (1971) argued that two components are necessary before an individual can experience passionate love: (a) He must be physiologically aroused; and (b) the setting must make it appropriate for him to conclude that his aroused feelings are due to love. On both counts, the person who plays hard to get might be expected to generate unusual passion. Frustration should increase the suitor's physiological arousal, and the association of "elusiveness" with "value" should increase the probability that the suitor will label his reaction to the other as "love."

From the preceding discussion, it is evident that several conceptually distinct variables may account for the hard-to-get phenomenon. In spite of the fact that we can suggest a plethora of reasons as to why playing hard-to-get strategy might be an effective strategy, all five studies failed to provide any support for the contention that an elusive woman is a desirable woman. Two experiments failed to demonstrate that outside observers perceive a hard-to-get individual as especially "valuable." Three experiments failed to demonstrate that a suitor perceives a hard-to-get date as especially valuable.

Walster, Walster, and Berscheid (1971) conducted two experiments to test the hypothesis that teenagers would deduce that a hard-to-get boy or girl was more socially desirable than was a teenager whose affection could be easily obtained. In these experiments high school juniors and seniors were told that we were interested in finding out what kind of first impression various teenagers made on others. They were shown pictures and biographies of a couple. They were told how romantically interested the stimulus person (a boy or girl) was in his partner after they had met only four times. The stimulus person was said to have liked the partner "extremely much," to have provided no information to us, or to like her "not particularly much." The teenagers were then asked how socially desirable both teenagers seemed (i.e., how likable, how physically attractive, etc., both teenagers seemed). Walster, Walster, and Berscheid, of course, predicted that the more romantic interest the stimulus person expressed in a slight acquaintance, the less socially desirable that stimulus person would appear to an outside observer. The results were diametrically opposed to those predicted. The more romantic interest the stimulus person expressed in an acquaintance, the *more* socially desirable teenagers judged him to be. Restraint does not appear to buy respect. Instead, it appears that "All the world *does* love a lover."

Lyons, Walster, and Walster (1971) conducted a field study and a laboratory experiment in an attempt to demonstrate that men prefer a date who plays hard to get. Both experiments were conducted in the context of a computer matching service. Experiment III was a field experiment. Women who signed up for the computer matching program were contacted and hired as experimenters. They were then given precise instructions as to how to respond when their computer match called them for a date. Half of the time they were told to pause and think for 3 seconds before accepting the date. (These women were labeled "hard to get.") Half of the time they were told to accept the date immediately. (These women were labeled "easy to get.") The data indicated that elusiveness had no impact on the man's liking for his computer date.

Experiment IV was a laboratory experiment. In this experiment, Lyons et al. hypothesized that the knowledge that a woman is elusive gives one indirect evidence that she is socially desirable. Such indirect evidence should have the biggest impact when a man has no way of acquiring *direct* evidence about a coed's value or when he has little confidence in his own ability to assess value. When direct evidence is available, and the man possesses supreme confidence in his ability to make correct judgments, information about a woman's elusiveness should have little impact on a man's reaction to her. Lyons et al. thus predicted that when men lacked direct evidence as to a woman's desirability, a man's self-esteem and the woman's elusiveness should interact in determining his respect and liking for her. Lyons et al. measured males' self-esteem via Rosenberg's (1965) measure of self-esteem, Rosenfeld's (1964) measure of fear or rejection, and Berger's (1952) measure of self-acceptance.

The dating counselor then told subjects that the computer had assigned them a date. They were asked to telephone her from the office phone, invite her out, and then report their first impression of her. Presumably the pair would then go out on a date, and eventually give us further information about how successful our computer matching techniques had been. Actually, all men were assigned a confederate as a date. Half of the time the woman played hard to get. When the man asked her out she replied:

Mmm [slight pause] No, I've got a date then. It seems like I signed up for that Date Match thing a long time ago and I've met more people since then—I'm really pretty busy all this week.

She paused again. If the subject suggested another time, the confederate hesitated only slightly, then accepted. If he did not suggest another time, the confederate would take the initiative of suggesting: "How about some time next week—or just meeting for coffee in the Union some afternoon?" And again, she accepted the next invitation. Half of the time, in the easy-to-get condition, the confederate eagerly accepted the man's offer of a date.

Lyons et al. predicted that since men in this blind date setting lacked direct evidence as to a woman's desirability, low-self-esteem men should be more receptive to the hard-to-get woman than were high-self-esteem men. Although Lyons et al.'s manipulation checks indicate that their manipulations were successful and their self-esteem measure was reliable, their hypothesis was not confirmed. Elusiveness had no impact on liking, regardless of subject's self-esteem level.

Did we give up our hypothesis? Heavens no. After all, it had only been disconfirmed four times.

By Experiment V, we had decided that perhaps the hard-to-get hypothesis must be tested in a sexual setting. After all, the first theorist who advised a woman to play hard to get was Socrates; his pupil was Theodota, a prostitute. He advised:

They will appreciate your favors most highly if you wait till they ask for them. The sweetest meats, you see, if served before they are wanted seem sour, and to those who had enough they are positively nauseating; but even poor fare is very welcome when offered to a hungry man. [Theodota inquired] And how can I make them hungry for my fare? [Socrates' reply] Why, in the first place, you must not offer it to them when they have had enough—but prompt them by behaving as a model of Propriety, by a show of reluctance to yield, and by holding back until they are as keen as can be; and then the same gifts are much more to the recipient than when they're offered before they are desired [see Xenophon, 1923, p. 48].

Walster, Walster, and Lambert (1971) thus proposed that a prostitute who states that she is selective in her choice of customers will be held in higher regard than will be the prostitute who admits that she is completely unselective in her choice of partners.

In this experiment, a prostitute served as the experimenter. When the customer arrived, she mixed a drink for him; then she delivered the experimental manipulation. Half of the time, in the hard-to-get condition, she stated, "Just because I see you this time it doesn't mean that you can have my phone number or see me again. I'm going to start school soon, so

I won't have much time, so I'll only be able to see the people that I like the best." Half of the time, in the easy-to-get condition, she did not communicate this information. From this point on, the prostitute and the customer interacted in conventional ways.

The client's liking for the prostitute was determined in two ways: First, the prostitute estimated how much the client had seemed to like her. (i.e., How much did he seem to like you? Did he make arrangements to return? How much did he pay you?) Second, the experimenter recorded how many times within the next 30 days the client arranged to have subsequent sexual relations with her.

Once again we failed to confirm the hard-to-get hypothesis. If anything, those clients who were told that the prostitute did not take just anyone were *less* likely to call back and liked the prostitute less than did other clients.

At this point, we ruefully decided that we had been on the wrong track. We decided that perhaps all those practitioners who advise women to play hard to get are wrong. Or perhaps it is only under very special circumstances that it will benefit one to play hard to get.

Thus, we began again. We reinterviewed students—this time with an open mind. This time we asked men to tell us about the advantages *and* disadvantages of hard-to-get *and* easy-to-get women. This time replies were more informative. According to reports, choosing between a hard-to-get woman and an easy-to-get woman was like choosing between Scylla and Charybdis—each woman was uniquely desirable and uniquely frightening.

Although the elusive woman was likely to be a popular prestige date, she presented certain problems. Since she was not particularly enthusiastic about you, she might stand you up or humiliate you in front of your friends. She was likely to be unfriendly, cold, and to possess inflexible standards.

The easy-to-get woman was certain to boost one's ego and to make a date a relaxing, enjoyable experience, but . . . . Unfortunately, dating an easy woman was a risky business. Such a woman might be easy to get, but hard to get rid of. She might "get serious." Perhaps she would be so oversexed or overaffectionate in public that she would embarrass you. Your buddies might snicker when they saw you together. After all, they would know perfectly well why you were dating *her.*

The interlocking assets and difficulties envisioned when they attempted to decide which was better—a hard-to-get or an easy-to-get woman—gave us a clue as to why our previous experiments had not worked out. The assets and liabilities of the elusive and the easy dates had evidently generally balanced out. On the average, then, both types of women tended to be equally well liked. When a slight difference in liking did appear, it favored the easy-to-get woman.

It finally impinged on us that there are *two* components that are important determinants of how much a man likes a woman: (*a*) How hard or easy she is for him to get; (*b*) how hard or easy she is for *other men* to get. So long as we were examining the desirability of women who were hard or easy for everyone to get, things balanced out. The minute we examined other possible configurations, it becomes evident that there is one type of woman who can transcend the limitations of the uniformly hard-to-get or the uniformly easy-to-get woman. If a woman has a reputation for being hard to get, but for some reason she is easy for the subject to get, she should be maximally appealing. Dating such a woman should insure one of great prestige; she is, after all, hard to get. Yet, since she is exceedingly available to the subject, the dating situation should be a relaxed, rewarding experience. Such a *selectively* hard-to-get woman possesses the assets of both the easy-to-get and the hard-to-get women, while avoiding all of their liabilities.

Thus, in Experiment VI, we hypothesized that a selectively hard-to-get woman (i.e., a woman who is easy for the subject to get but very hard for any other man to get) will be especially liked by her date. Women who are hard for everyone—including the subject—to get, or who are easy for everyone to get—or control women, about whom the subject had no information—will be liked a lesser amount.

METHOD

Subjects were 71 male summer students at the University of Wisconsin. They were recruited for a dating research project. This project was ostensibly designed to determine whether computer matching techniques are in fact more effective than is random matching. All participants were invited to come into the dating center in order to choose a date from a set of five potential dates.

When the subject arrived at the computer match office, he was handed folders containing background information on five women. Some of these women had supposedly been "randomly" matched with him; others had been "computer matched" with him. (He was not told which women were which.)

In reality, all five folders contained information about fictitious women. The first item in the folder was a "background questionnaire" on which the woman had presumably described herself. This questionnaire was similar to one the subject had completed when signing up for the match program. We attempted to make the five women's descriptions different enough to be believable, yet similar enough to minimize variance. There-fore, the way the five women described themselves was systematically varied. They claimed to be 18 or 19 years old; freshmen or sophomores; from a Wisconsin city, ranging in size from over 500,000 to under 50,000; 5 feet 2 inches to 5 feet 4 inches tall; Protestant, Catholic, Jewish, or had no preference; graduated in the upper 10%-50% of their high school class; and Caucasians who did not object to being matched with a person of another race. The women claimed to vary on a political spectrum from "left of center" through "moderate" to "near right of center"; to place little or no importance on politics and religion; and to like recent popular movies. Each woman listed four or five activities she liked to do on a first date (i.e., go to a movie, talk in a quiet place, etc.).

In addition to the background questionnaire, three of the five folders contained five "date selection forms." The experimenter explained that some of the women had already been able to come in, examine the back-ground information of their matches, and indicate their first impression of them. Two of the subject's matches had not yet come in. Three of the women had already come in and evaluated the subject along with her four other matches. These women would have five date selection forms in their folders. The subject was shown the forms, which consisted of a scale ranging from "definitely do *not* want to date" (—10) to "definitely want to date" (+10). A check appeared on each scale. Presumably the check indicated how much the woman had liked a given date. (At this point, the subject was told his identification dating number. Since all dates were identified by numbers on the forms, this identification number enabled him to ascertain how each date had evaluated both him and her four other matches.)

The date selection forms allowed us to manipulate the elusiveness of the woman. One woman appeared to be uniformly hard to get. She indicated that though she was willing to date any of the men assigned to her, she was not enthusiastic about any of them. She rated all five of her date choices from +1 to +2, including the subject (who was rated 1.75).

One woman appeared to be uniformly easy to get. She indicated that she was enthusiastic about dating all five of the men assigned to her. She rated her desire to date all five of her date choices +7 to +9. This included the subject, who was rated 8.

One woman appeared to be easy for the subject to get but hard for anyone else to get (i.e., the selectively hard-to-get woman). She indicated minimal enthusiasm for four of her date choices, rating them from +2 to +3, and extreme enthusiasm (+8) for the subject.

Two women had no date selection forms in their folders (i.e., no information women).

Naturally, each woman appears in each of the five conditions.

The experimenter asked the man to consider the folders, complete a "first impression questionnaire" for each woman, and then decide which *one* of the women he wished to date. (The subject's rating of the dates constitute our verbal measure of liking; his choice in a date constitutes our behavioral measure of liking.)

The experimenter explained that she was conducting a study of first impressions in conjunction with the dating research project. The study, she continued, was designed to learn more about how good people are at forming first impressions of others on the basis of rather limited information. She explained that filling out the forms would probably make it easier for the man to decide which one of the five women he wished to date.

The first impression questionnaire consisted of three sections:

1. *Liking for Various Dates.* Two questions assessed subject's liking for each woman: "If you went out with this girl, how well do you think you would get along?"—with possible responses ranging from "get along extremely well" (5) to "not get along at all" (1), and "What was your overall impression of the girl?"—with possible responses ranging from "extremely favorable" (7) to "extremely unfavorable" (1). Scores on these two questions were summed to form an index of expressed liking. This index enables us to compare subject's liking for each of the women.

2. *Assets and Liabilities Ascribed to Various Dates.* We predicted that subjects would prefer the selective woman, because they would expect her to possess the good qualities of both the uniformly hard-to-get and the uniformly easy-to-get woman, while avoiding the bad qualities of both her rivals. Thus, the second section was designed to determine the extent to which subjects imputed good and bad qualities to the various dates.

This section was comprised of 10 pairs of polar opposites. Subjects were asked to rate how friendly-unfriendly, cold-warm, attractive-unattractive, easy-going-rigid, exciting-boring, shy-outgoing, fun-loving-dull, popular-unpopular, aggressive-passive, selective-nonselective each woman was. Ratings were made on a 7-point scale. The more desirable the trait ascribed to a woman, the higher the score she was given.

3. *Liabilities Attributed to Easy-to-Get Women.* The third scale was designed to assess the extent to which subjects attributed selected negative attributes to each woman. The third scale consisted of six statements:

She would more than likely do something to embarrass me in public.
She probably would demand too much attention and affection from me.
She seems like the type who would be too dependent on me.
She might turn out to be too sexually promiscuous.
She probably would make me feel uneasy when I'm with her in a group.

She seems like the type who doesn't distinguish between the boys she dates. I probably would be "just another date."

Subjects were asked whether they anticipated any of the above difficulties in their relationship with each woman. They indicated their misgivings on a scale ranging from "certainly true of her" (1) to "certainly not true of her" (7).

The experimenter suggested that the subject carefully examine both the background questionnaires and the date selection forms of all potential dates in order to decide whom he wanted to date. Then she left the subject. (The experimenter was, of course, unaware of what date was in what folder.)

The experimenter did not return until the subject had completed the first impression questionnaires. Then she asked him which woman he had decided to date.

After his choice had been made, the experimenter questioned him as to what factors influenced his choice. Frequently men who chose the selectively easy-to-get woman said that "She chose me, and that made me feel really good" or "She seemed more selective than the others." The uniformly easy-to-get woman was often rejected by subjects who complained "She must be awfully hard up for a date—she really would take anyone." The uniformly hard-to-get woman was once described as a "challenge," but more often rejected as being "snotty" or "too picky."

At the end of the session, the experimenter debriefed the subject and then gave him the names of five actual dates who had been matched with him.

RESULTS

We predicted that the selectively hard-to-get woman (easy for me to get but hard for everyone else to get) would be liked more than women who were uniformly hard to get, uniformly easy to get, or neutral (the no information women). We had no prediction as to whether or not her three rivals would differ in attractiveness. The results strongly support our hypothesis.

TABLE 3.1
Men's Choices in a Date

Item	Selectively Hard to Get	Uniformly Hard to Get	Uniformly Easy to Get	No Information for No. 1	No Information for No. 2
Number of men choosing to date each woman	42	6	5	11	7

Dating Choices

When we examine the men's choices in dates, we see that the selective woman is far more popular than any of her rivals. (See Table 3.1.) We conducted a chi-square test to determine whether or not men's choices in dates were randomly distributed. They were not ($x^2 = 69.5$, $df = 4$, $p < .001$). Nearly all subjects preferred to date the selective woman. When we compare the frequency with which her four rivals (combined) are chosen, we see that the selective woman does get far more than her share of dates ($x^2 = 68.03$, $df = 1$, $p < .001$).

We also conducted an analysis to determine whether or not the women who are uniformly hard to get, uniformly easy to get, or whose popularity is unknown, differed in popularity. We see that they did not ($x^2 = 2.86$, $df = 3$).

Liking for the Various Dates

Two questions tapped the men's romantic liking for the various dates: (a) "If you went out with this woman, how well do you think you'd get along?" and (b) "What was your overall impression of the woman?" Scores on these two indexes were summed to form an index of liking. Possible scores ranged from 2 to 12.

A contrast was then set up to test our hypothesis that the selective woman will be preferred to her rivals. The contrast that tests this hypothesis is of the form $\Gamma_1 = 4\mu$ (selectively hard to get) $- 1\mu$ (uniformly hard to get) $- 2\mu$ (neutral). We tested the hypothesis $\Gamma_1 = 0$ against the

TABLE 3.2
Men's Reactions to Various Dates

Item	Type of Date			
	Selec-tively Hard to Get	Uni-formly Hard to Get	Uni-formly Easy to Get	No Infor-mation
Men's liking for dates	9.41[a]	7.90	8.53	8.58
Evaluation of women's assets and liabilities				
Selective[b]	5.23	4.39	2.85	4.30
Popular[b]	4.83	4.58	4.65	4.83
Friendly[c]	5.58	5.07	5.52	5.37
Warm[c]	5.15	4.51	4.99	4.79
Easy-going[c]	4.83	4.42	4.82	4.61
Problems expected in dating	5.23[d]	4.86	4.77	4.99

[a]The higher the number, the more liking the man is expressing for the date.
[b]Traits we expected to be ascribed to the selectively hard-to-get and the uniformly hard-to-get dates.
[c]Traits we expected to be ascribed to the selectively hard-to-get and the uniformly easy-to-get dates.
[d]The higher the number the *fewer* the problems the subject anticipates in dating.

alternative hypothesis $\Gamma_1 \neq 0$. An explanation of this basically simple procedure may be found in Hays (1963). If our hypothesis is true, the preceding contrast should be large. If our hypothesis is false, the resulting contrast should not differ significantly from 0. The data again provide strong support for the hypothesis that the selective woman is better liked than her rivals ($F = 23.92$, $df = 1/70$, $p < .001$).

Additional Data Snooping

We also conducted a second set of contrasts to determine whether the rivals (i.e., the uniformly hard-to-get woman, the uniformly easy-to-get woman, and the control woman) were differentially liked. Using the procedure presented by Morrison (1967) in Chapter 4, the data indicate that the rivals are differentially liked ($F = 4.43$, $df = 2/69$). As Table 3.2 indicates, the uniformly hard-to-get woman seems to be liked slightly less than the easy-to-get or control women.

In any attempt to explore data, one must account for the fact that observing the data permits the researcher to capitalize on chance. Thus, one must use simultaneous testing methods so as not to spuriously inflate the probability of attaining statistical significance. In the present situation, we are interested in comparing the mean of a number of dependent measures, namely the liking for the different women in the dating situation. To perform post hoc multiple comparisons in this situation, one can use a transformation of Hotelling's t^2 statistic which is distributed as F. The procedure is directly analogous to Scheffé's multiple-comparison procedure for independent groups, except where one compares means of a number of dependent measures.

To make it abundantly clear that the main result is that the discriminating woman is better liked than each of the other rivals, we performed an additional post hoc analysis, pitting each of the rivals separately against the discriminating woman. In these analyses, we see that the selective woman is better liked than the woman who is uniformly easy to get ($F = 3.99$, $df = 3/68$), than the woman who is uniformly hard to get ($F = 9.47$, $df = 3/68$), and finally, than the control women ($F = 4.93$, $df = 3/68$).

Thus, it is clear that although there are slight differences in the way rivals are liked, these differences are small, relative to the overwhelming attractiveness of the selective woman.

Assets and Liabilities Attributed to Dates

We can now attempt to ascertain *why* the selective woman is more popular than her rivals. Earlier, we argued that the selectively hard-to-get woman should occupy a unique position; she should be assumed to possess all of the virtues of her rivals, but none of their flaws.

The virtues and flaws that the subject ascribed to each woman were tapped by the polar-opposite scale. Subjects evaluated each woman on 10 characteristics.

We expected that subjects would associate two assets with a uniformly hard-to-get woman: Such a woman should be perceived to be both "selective" and "popular." Unfortunately, such a woman should also be assumed to possess three liabilities—she should be perceived to be "unfriendly," "cold," and "rigid." Subjects should ascribe exactly the opposite virtues and liabilities to the easy-to-get woman: Such a woman should possess the assets of "friendliness," "warmth," and "flexibility," and the liabilities of "unpopularity" and "lack of selectivity." The selective woman was expected to possess only assets: She should be perceived to be as "selective" and "popular" as the uniformly elusive woman, and as "friendly," "warm," and "easy-going" as the uniformly easy woman. A contrast was set up to test this specific hypothesis. (Once again, see Hays for the procedure.) This contrast indicates that our hypothesis is confirmed ($F = 62.43$, $df = 1/70$). The selective woman is rated most like the uniformly hard-to get woman on the first two positive characteristics; most like the uniformly easy-to-get woman on the last three characteristics.

For the reader's interest, the subjects' ratings of all five women's assets and liablities are presented in Table 3.2.

Comparing the Selective and the Easy Women

Scale 3 was designed to assess whether or not subjects anticipated fewer problems when they envisioned dating the selective woman than when they envisioned dating the uniformly easy-to-get woman. On the basis of pretest interviews, we compiled a list of many of the concerns men had about easy women (e.g., "She would more than likely do something to embarrass me in public.").

We, of course, predicted that subjects would experience more problems when contemplating dating the uniformly easy woman than when contemplating dating a woman who was easy for *them* to get, but hard for anyone else to get (i.e., the selective woman).

Men were asked to say whether or not they envisioned each of the difficulties were they to date each of the women. Possible replies varied from 1 (certainly true of her) to 7 (certainly not true of her). The subjects' evaluations of each woman were summed to form an index of anticipated difficulties. Possible scores ranged from 6 to 42.

A contrast was set up to determine whether the selective woman engendered less concern than the uniformly easy-to-get woman. The data indicate that she does ($F = 17.50$, $df = 1/70$). If the reader is interested in comparing concern engendered by each woman, these data are available in Table 3.2.

The data provide clear support for our hypotheses: The selective woman is strongly preferred to any of her rivals. The reason for her popularity is evident. Men ascribe to her all of the assets of the uniformly hard-to-get and the uniformly easy-to-get women, and none of their liabilities.

Thus, after five futile attempts to understand the "hard-to-get" phenomenon, it appears that we have finally gained an understanding of this process. It appears that a woman can intensify her desirability if she acquires a reputation for being hard-to-get and then, by her behavior, makes it clear to a selected romantic partner that she is attracted to him.

In retrospect, especially in view of the strongly supportive data, the logic underlying our predictions sounds compelling. In fact, after examining our data, a colleague who had helped design the five ill-fated experiments noted that, "That is exactly what I would have predicted" (given his economic view of man). Unfortunately, we are all better at postdiction than prediction.

REFERENCES

Aronson, E., & Mills, J. The effect of severity of initiation on liking for a group. *Journal of Abnormal and Social Psychology*, 1959, *67*, 31-36.

Berger, E. M. The relation between expressed acceptance of self and expressed acceptance of others. *Journal of Abnormal and Social Psychology*, 1952, *47*, 778-782.

Gerard, H. B., & Mathewson, G. C. The effects of severity of initiation and liking for a group: A replication. *Journal of Experimental Social Psychology*, 1966, *2*, 278-287.

Hays, W. L. *Statistics for psychologists*. New York: Holt, Rinehart, 1963.

Kimball, G. A. *Hilgard and Marquis' conditioning and learning*. New York: Appleton-Century-Crofts, 1961.

Lyons, J., Walster, E., & Walster, G. W. Playing hard-to-get: An elusive phenomenon. University of Wisconsin, Madison: Author, 1971. (Mimeo)

Morrison, D. F. *Multivariate statistical methods*. New York: McGraw-Hill, 1967.

Ovid. *The art of love*. Bloomington: University of Indiana Press, 1963.

Rosenberg, M. *Society and the adolescent self image*. Princeton, N.J.: Princeton University Press, 1965.

Rosenfeld, H. M. Social choice conceived as a level of aspiration. *Journal of Abnormal and Social Psychology*, 1964, *68*, 491-499.

Walster, E. Passionate love. In B. I. Murstein (Ed.), *Theories of attraction and love*. New York: Springer, 1971.

Walster, E., Walster, G. W., & Berscheid, E. The efficacy of playing hard-to-get. *Journal of Experimental Education*, 1971, *39*, 73-77.

Walster, E., Walster, G. W., & Lambert, P. Playing hard-to-get: A field study. University of Wisconsin, Madison: Author, 1971. (Mimeo)

Xenophon. *Memorabilia.* London: Heinemann, 1923.

Zimbardo, P. G. The effect of effort and improvisation on self persuasion produced by role-playing. *Journal of Experimental Social Psychology,* 1965, *1,*
103-120.

4

BERNIE I. SILVERMAN

Consequences, Racial Discrimination, and the Principle of Belief Congruence

The principle of belief congruence was tested with consequential and inconsequential behaviors. Subjects in the consequences condition were led to
believe that their roommate choices would actually determine who they
would be living with during their first year at college, while subjects in the
nonconsequences condition believed their choices had no bearing in determining their eventual roommates. Subjects in both groups chose roommates from among hypothetical persons who varied on race, attitude, and
value similarity. The findings showed (a) that discrimination against
Negroes increased as responses were invested with consequences, but (b)
that the principle of belief congruence yielded an accurate description of
consequential as well as inconsequential roommate choices, and (c) that
there was a very strong relationship between perceived social pressure for
racial discrimination and such discrimination in the consequences condition
but not in the nonconsequences condition. Possible explanations for these
and other findings are discussed.

According to the principle of belief congruence, belief similarity is a
more potent determinant of interpersonal attraction than is racial similarity (Rokeach, Smith, & Evans, 1960). Later, the principle was qualified

Source: Bernie I. Silverman, "Consequences, Racial Discrimination, and the Principle of
Belief Congruence," *Journal of Personality and Social Psychology,* 1974, *29,* 497-508. Copyright 1974 by the American Psychological Association. Reprinted by permission.

Thanks are especially due Dean Charles Marvin of Adrian College for his cooperation and
interest in the present study. Gratitude is also expressed to Raymond Cochrane, Larry
Messé, Frederick Wickert, and Milton Rokeach, who supervised the dissertation on which
this study was based.

so that it was required to accurately describe behavior only in the absence of perceived social pressure for racial discrimination (Rokeach & Mezei, 1966). While some have found data contrary to belief congruence (Triandis, 1961; Triandis & Davis, 1965; Triandis, Loh, & Levin, 1966) the principle has been supported by the weight of the evidence (Anderson & Cote, 1966; Byrne & McGrew, 1964; Byrne & Wong, 1962; Hendrick, Bixenstine, & Hawkins, 1971; Hendrick & Hawkins, 1969; Insko & Robinson, 1967; Mezei, 1971; Rokeach, 1961; Rokeach & Mezei, 1966; Rokeach et al., 1960; Silverman & Cochrane, 1972; Smith, Williams, & Willis, 1967; Stein, 1966; Stein, Hardyck, & Smith, 1965).

However, there are several reasons why the findings of these studies cannot be accepted at face value. In all the studies but one (Rokeach & Mezei, 1966), the subjects were required to imagine themselves in situations other than the one they were actually in and to respond as if they were in the imagined situations. For example, the subjects were asked to imagine working with, befriending, dating, living next to, and marrying both Caucasians and Negroes and to indicate how attracted they were to such persons in these situations. Data obtained in this fashion were interpreted as though they genuinely reflected the subjects' actual behavior. Freedman (1969), however, has pointed out that this interpretation is based on the untenable assumption that there is a close correspondence between subjects' opinions as to what they would do in a particular situation and their subsequent behavior in that situation. Though some have found a significant relationship between subjects' verbal expressions of behavioral intention and actual behavior (Silverman & Cochrane, 1971), for the most part there seems to be little relationship between what subjects say they will do in an imagined situation and what they in fact do (Kutner, Wilkens, & Yarrow, 1952; LaPiere, 1934; Linn, 1964; McGrew, 1967). Consideration of these results may have prompted Bem (1968) to write, "No 'as if' methodology . . . is an adequate substitute for intensive study of the actual situation being modeled [p. 273]."

One reason for the discrepancy between verbal expressions of behavioral intentions and actual behavior may be that the former are inordinately influenced by the tendency of subjects to make themselves look good in the eyes of the experimenter (Crowne & Marlowe, 1964; Edwards, 1957). Subjects can ignore their true feelings toward the hypothetical persons encountered in the situations conjured up by the experimenter because it is apparent that their responses have no real-life consequences other than to influence the experimenter's opinion of them. In contrast, subjects who believe they are actually in a situation may have their desire to respond in a socially desirable manner tempered by the knowledge that their responses may effect their future relationship with whatever stimuli are encountered. Cook and Selltiz (1964) emphasized this point when they wrote, "if responses are expected to have real-life consequences, the anticipation of such consequences may counter-balance the wish to make a good impression [p. 46]."

Unfortunately, most studies in which the principle of belief congruence was tested elicited inconsequential responses.[1] Therefore, these responses mainly may reflect subjects' conceptions of what is socially desirable rather than their own feelings towards the hypothetical persons. And in academic settings, socially desirable responses are clearly those that portray the subjects as "unprejudiced, rational, open-minded, and democratic [Cook & Selltiz, 1964, p. 39]." By inhibiting racial discrimination, the experimental situation provides built-in support for the principle of belief congruence. Viewed in this light, evidence for the principle is far less impressive than it might have first appeared.

The present study focused on the relationship between consequences and racial discrimination as manifested in verbal expressions of behavioral intentions. Consequential responses are those that are perceived by subjects as affecting their relationship with an attitude object. One group of subjects was led to believe that their evaluations of prospective roommates would actually determine whom they would be living with for the next academic year. Presumably this group of subjects viewed their responses as consequential. A second group of subjects performed the identical task but presumably realized their responses were inconsequential, as they were aware that they were participating in a psychological experiment. The first hypothesis tested was that consequences and racial discrimination are positively related. In other words, as responses are invested with consequences, discrimination against Negroes increases. Since previous research has indicated that the principle of belief congruence describes inconsequential behavior well, the second hypothesis tested was that subjects would discriminate significantly more on belief similarity than racial similarity when they perceived their responses to be of no consequence. Because it was expected that investing responses with consequences would enhance racial discrimination while not influencing belief discrimination, the third hypothesis tested was that belief discrimination would be no greater than racial discrimination when subjects believed they were actually choosing a roommate.

Up to now the methodological shortcomings of previous studies have been emphasized. But there is a logical problem as well. Silverman and Cochrane (1972) have pointed out that the failure of most investigators to employ an index of perceived social pressure has rendered the principle of belief congruence immune from falsification and therefore meaningless. In those studies where a large race effect was obtained in particular situations, it was attributed to social pressure towards racial discrimination. Yet the presence of these sanctions was inferred from subjects' discrimination on race. The reasoning is circular. Whenever results were in accord with it, social sanctions were not thought to be operating and the principle was supported. But when much of the variance in subjects' responses was due to the race of the hypothetical persons, social sanctions were invoked and the principle remained unscathed. Employing an independent measure of perceived social pressure toward racial discrimination would return the principle of belief congruence to the ranks of meaningful propositions by making it possible to obtain a situation in which there was racial discrimination but no detectable perceived social pressure.

Recent studies have used such a measure, making it possible to determine whether perceived social pressure for racial discrimination is related to racial discrimination and, thus, to the occasional failure of the principle of belief congruence to accurately describe subjects' responses. Both Mezei (1971) and Silverman and Cochrane (1972) found a positive correlation between racial discrimination and perceived social pressure to discriminate. Yet the import of these correlations is unclear because they describe relationships between racial discrimination, inferred from inconsequential expressions of preference, and perceived social pressure toward discrimination. For reasons given earlier, it is probable that the former does not correspond to discrimination outside the laboratory, and to the extent that it fails to, relationships based on it cannot be spoken of as though they describe real-life consequential behavior.

A measure of perceived social pressure was employed in the present study for two reasons: first, so that a fair test of the principle of belief congruence might be conducted and second, so that the relationship between societal sanctions and racial discrimination might be tested using consequential behavior from which to infer discrimination. Assuming that manifestations of racial discrimination vary depending on whether they are inferred from consequential or inconsequential behavior, it follows that relationships based on these manifestations may also differ. The fourth hypothesis tested was that relationships between perceived social pressure to discriminate on race and racial discrimination would significantly differ when racial discrimination was inferred from consequential as compared to inconsequential roommate choices.

The remainder of this study dealt with the relative importance of value similarity as compared to attitude similarity in determining interpersonal attraction. Several characteristics distinguish values from attitudes (Rokeach, 1968). Theoretically, a value consists of a single, deep-seated belief, whereas the several beliefs making up an attitude are thought to be less central to a belief system. Because of this difference in centrality, values are thought to determine attitudes although the reverse is not true. Finally, the influence of a value on behavior transcends specific situations, while the influence of an attitude is confined to a particular situation or object.

Those individuals seen as having a belief system most similar to one's own should be most favorably evaluated if belief congruence contributes to interpersonal attraction. From the distinction just drawn, it would seem that knowing something about an individual's values provides more insight into his belief system than knowing something about his attitudes. The perception of similar values in an individual should therefore result in the assumption of a more similar belief system than the perception of similar attitudes. Consequently, value similarity should prove to be a more important determinant of attraction than attitude similarity. Accordingly, the fifth hypothesis tested was that value similarity would account for more of the variance than attitude similarity in subjects' roommate selections.

METHOD

Fifteen universities and colleges were sent letters asking for their participation in the present study. Of these schools, only Adrian College agreed to provide complete cooperation, and thus it became the sole source of subjects. The college, with an enrollment of about 2,000, is located in southeastern Michigan and is nominally affiliated with the Methodist Church. Its students are drawn mainly from small towns in the Midwest.

The sampling frame consisted of all of the males who were accepted for admission to Adrian College as of April 10, 1970, for the academic year beginning September 1970. A systematic sample of 150 persons was chosen from this sampling frame, using a ½ sampling fraction. The same procedure was repeated with these persons, thereby selecting 75 persons to make up the experimental or consequences group while leaving an equal number to form the control or nonconsequences group.

Those assigned to the experimental group first received a letter from the Dean of Men at Adrian College in which it was explained that the college was initiating a program designed to give new students a greater voice in selecting their roommates. It was made clear that the students would receive descriptions of eight other new students from which they might choose their roommate for their first year at college. The Rokeach Value Survey (Kelly, Silverman, & Cochrane, 1972) and a student attitude survey were also included in the first mailing. The Rokeach Value Survey required the students to rank in order of importance, as guiding principles in their lives, two sets of 18 values, while the attitude survey gave students an opportunity to express their views toward four controversial issues. These issues were: (a) special college admission programs for blacks, (b) student protest demonstrations, (c) determination of course content by students, and (d) abolishing the draft. The students were asked not only to express their position on each issue but to explain why they felt the way they did. Those in the experimental group were led to believe that the descriptions, from which they would choose a roommate, would be based on the responses of other incoming freshmen to these same questionnaires.

Those assigned to the control group first received a letter from the experimenter who identified himself as a member of the Michigan State University psychology department. It was explained that the psychology department was conducting a survey designed to measure the attitudes and values of high school students before they entered college. This provided the rationale for returning the Rokeach Value Survey and attitude questionnaire which were enclosed along with the first letter. Further, those in the control group were informed that they would receive two more sets of questionnaires in the months to come so that more information about their attitudes might be gathered.

Of the 75 students in the experimental group, 43 (57%) filled out and returned the Rokeach Value Survey and the attitude questionnaire. The corresponding figure for the 75 students in the control group was 44 (59%). Having determined the attitudes and values of the subjects, the next task was to construct hypothetical persons for them to evaluate.

Each of eight hypothetical persons was designed to vary on three variables. The first variable was racial similarity. As all of the subjects were Caucasians, those hypothetical persons described as Caucasians manifested racial similarity, while those described as Negroes manifested racial dissimilarity. The second variable manipulated was that of attitude similarity. Each hypothetical person held attitudes towards the four issues to which subjects had previously given an opinion. Hypothetical persons who held four similar attitudes to those of the subject manifested attitude similarity, while those who held four dissimilar attitudes manifested attitude dissimilarity. The third variable manipulated was value similarity. Those hypothetical persons to whom similar values were attributed were described as considering important to their lives the three terminal values which the subject himself ranked first, second, and third, plus one other value that the subject ranked no lower than eighth. Hypothetical persons to whom dissimilar values were attributed were described as considering important in their lives the three terminal values which the subject ranked sixteenth, seventeenth, and eighteenth, plus one other value ranked no higher than eleventh. This procedure insured that each hypothetical person had one unique value. In addition, the order in which the values were listed for each hypothetical person was varied so as to reduce the probability that subjects would notice that two sets of four hypothetical persons each manifested almost identical values. Each hypothetical person, then, was described to the subject in a six-sentence paragraph. The first sentence contained the hypothetical person's name, race, and home town, the next four sentences his attitudes towards the issues mentioned earlier, and the final sentence conveyed his values. For example:

Raymond Dorsey is a Negro, 18 years old, and lives in Grand Rapids, Michigan. In response to the question should Negroes be given preferential treatment when applying for admission to college, Raymond answered, "By giving blacks special consideration when they apply to college more blacks will get into the mainstream of society, thus giving the black community a greater stake in America, so I'm all for it." Concerning the issue of student protest demonstrations, he writes, "I oppose all of those demonstrations as they only serve to take time away from studies and other important academic activities. As far as determination of course content goes, students know what they want to learn, so they should be allowed to determine course content. Abolishing the draft and having a volunteer army is a great idea and can be done if army wages are increased." The values Raymond considers to be most important as guiding principles in his life are A WORLD AT PEACE, EQUALITY, SELF RESPECT, and FREEDOM, which he ranked first to fourth respectively.

About two months after returning the Rokeach Value Survey and the Attitude questionnaire, subjects in both the experimental and control groups received descriptions of eight individuals to be evaluated. A cover letter from the Dean of Men at Adrian College explained to those subjects in the experimental group that the persons described in the accompanying booklet were, like themselves, high school students who planned to attend Adrian College in the fall. They were instructed to indicate how much they would like each person described as a roommate by circling a number from 1 to 9 on a scale that appeared directly below each description. By circling 1, subjects could indicate extreme preference for the person as a roommate. By circling 9, the opposite feeling could be expressed. It was explicitly spelled out to these subjects that their ratings would determine roommate assignments for the fall semester.

A cover letter from the psychology department at Michigan State University explained to those subjects in the control group that the persons described in the accompanying booklet were high school students who planned to attend Michigan State University in the fall. The control group subjects were instructed to imagine that they were being given an opportunity to select their roommates for the first year at college. They were then asked to respond *as if* they were actually choosing a roommate. As in the experimental group, the subjects could indicate their preferences on a scale from 1 to 9 that appeared below each description.

Of the 43 subjects in the experimental group, 39 (90%) returned their evaluations of the hypothetical persons as roommates. The corresponding figure for the 44 subjects in the control group was 42 (95%).

Although it would seem that those subjects in the experimental group should view their responses as consequential while those subjects in the control group should not, it was desirable to determine objectively that this crucial independent variable was in fact successfully manipulated. Perhaps those in the experimental group somehow guessed that they too were in a psychology experiment and realized roommate assignments would not be contingent on their responses. If the variable of consequences was not satisfactorily manipulated, testing hypotheses concerning its effects on racial discrimination and the principle of belief congruence would be illusory. To determine if the manipulation was successful, an attempt was made to find out if subjects had some idea as to whom they would be living with at Adrian College. Those who saw their roommate choices as consequential should have some idea as to whom they might be living with, whereas those who viewed their choices as inconsequential should not.

About two weeks after rating the hypothetical persons as roommates, all of the subjects received a cover letter and questionnaire from Alpha Tau Omega Fraternity at Adrian College. The letter explained that the fraternity was interested in discovering the aims and goals of the imminent freshman so that it might make its programs more appealing. To achieve this end, the subject was asked to complete and return the accompanying questionnaire. The questionnaire had but one question relevant to the study. It asked subjects to indicate if they had any idea who their roommate would be at college on a scale from 1 to 9, in which 1 signified subjects knew precisely who they would be living with, 5 indicated they had some idea of who they would be living with, and 9 indicated no knowledge of future roommates at all.

Of the 43 subjects in the experimental group, 22 (51%) returned the fraternity questionnaire. The corresponding figure for the 44 subjects in the control group was 24 (55%).

Twelve weeks after expressing their own attitudes and values, four weeks after rating the hypothetical persons as roommates, and one week after receiving the fraternity survey, subjects received the final mailing which again consisted of a letter and a questionnaire. Those in the experimental group received their materials from the Dean of Men at Adrian College, while those in the control group received theirs from the psychology department at Michigan State University. Both letters described the purpose of the questionnaire as being to find out something about the subjects' perception of friends' and parents' reactions to behaviors which the subjects might engage in. The significant-others questionnaire itself contained three relevant items. These items required subjects to indicate what they thought their best friends, parents, and the students at Adrian College would think of them if they shared a room with a Negro at college. Responses were given on three scales from 1 to 9, in which 1 represented extreme approval, 3 represented indifference, and 9 represented extreme disapproval on the part of significant others. These responses served to provide a measure of perceived social pressure for racial discrimination.

Of the 43 subjects in the experimental group, 36 (84%) returned the significant-others questionnaire. The corresponding figure for the 44 subjects in the control group was 42 (95%). An overview of the experimental procedure is shown in Table 4.1.

About September 1, the subjects in the experimental group, who had been deceived throughout the study, received a letter from the experi-

TABLE 4.1
The Experimental Design

Weeks from Begin- ning	Experimental Group	Response Rate[a]
0	Letter from Adrian College:	
	Rokeach Value Survey	43/75
	Student attitude survey	43/75
8	Letter from Adrian College:	
	Rating of hypothetical persons	39/43
10	Letter from Alpha Tau Omega:	
	Fraternity survey	22/43
12	Letter from Adrian College:	
	Significant-others questionnaire	36/43
16	Letter of explanation from Michigan State University	
22	Personal meeting with subjects	

	Control Group	Response Rate[a]
0	Letter from Michigan State University:	
	Rokeach Value Survey	44/75
	Student attitude survey	44/75
8	Letter from Michigan State University:	
	Rating of hypothetical persons	42/44
10	Letter from Alpha Tau Omega:	
	Fraternity survey	24/44
12	Letter from Michigan State University:	
	Significant-others questionnaire	42/44
22	Personal meeting with subjects	

[a]Subjects responding/total subjects.

menter explaining the deception and the purpose of the study. Further, the subjects were invited to meet with the experimenter later in the fall at Adrian so that their questions might be more completely answered. On October 15, the experimenter met with the subjects in both the experimental and control groups and reviewed the purpose, procedure, and results of the study.

RESULTS

To test the first hypothesis, that discrimination against Negroes increases as responses are invested with consequences, it was first necessary to ascertain whether those in the experimental group saw their responses to the hypothetical persons as determining their roommates for their first year at college while those in the control group did not. Experimental group subjects indicated that they had some idea of their roommate at

TABLE 4.2
Analysis of Variance of Subjects' Ratings of Hypothetical Persons

Source of Variance	SS	df	F	% Variance Accounted For
Consequences (A)	64.75	1	14.91*	1.4
Subjects within groups	330.51	76		
Race (B)	139.47	1	25.82*	3.0
A X B	84.03	1	15.56*	1.8
B X Subjects within groups	410.65	76		
Attitude (C)	1644.40	1	127.07*	36.0
A X C	3.57	1	.27*	—
C X Subjects within groups	983.61	76		
Values (D)	93.08	1	22.00*	2.0
A X D	.46	1	.10	—
D X Subjects within groups	321.61	76		
B X C	11.08	1	7.19*	—
A X B X C	3.22	1	2.09	—
B X C X Subjects within groups	117.31	76		
B X D	.85	1	.47	—
A X B X D	5.59	1	3.12	—
B X D X subjects within groups	136.67	76		
C X D	8.57	1	7.51*	—
A X C X D	.17	1	.14	—
C X D subjects within groups	86.88	76		
B X C X D	1.50	1	1.04	—
A X B X C X D	.48	1	.33	—
B X C X D X subjects within groups	109.65	76		
Total	4558.11	623		

*p < .01.

Adrian College ($\bar{X} = 5.22$, $N = 22$), whereas their control group counterparts indicated no knowledge about roommates ($\bar{X} = 8.95$, $N = 24$). A t test for independent samples revealed that the difference between the mean knowledge of roommate scores was significant ($t = 11.80$, $df = 44$, $p < .001$), leading to the conclusion that experimental group subjects

TABLE 4.3
Mean Evaluations of Hypothetical Persons

Effect	Levels	$\bar{X}$	Effects	Levels	$\bar{X}$
Consequences (A)	Consequence (A1)	5.02	A X B X D	A1-B1-D1	5.44
	No consequence			A1-B1-D2	6.28
	(A2)	4.38		A1-B2-D1	3.88
Race (B)	Negro (B1)	5.17		A1-B2-D2	4.48
	Caucasian (B2)	4.23		A2-B1-D1	4.20
Attitudes (C)	Similar (C1)	3.08		A2-B1-D2	4.76
	Dissimilar (D2)	6.32		A2-B2-D1	3.73
Values (D)	Similar (D1)	4.31		A2-B2-D2	4.82
	Dissimilar (D2)	5.08	A X C X D	A1-C1-D1	2.83
A X B	A1-B1	5.86		A1-C1-D2	3.82
	A1-B2	4.18		A1-C2-D1	6.50
	A2-B1	4.48		A1-C2-D2	6.94
	A2-B2	4.27		A2-C1-D1	2.32
A X C	A1-C1	3.32		A2-C1-D2	3.34
	A1-C2	6.72		A2-C2-D1	5.61
	A2-C1	2.83		A2-C2-D2	6.24
	A2-C2	5.92	B X C X D	B1-C1-D1	3.26
A X D	A1-D1	4.66		B1-C1-D2	4.10
	A1-D2	5.33		B1-C2-D1	6.38
	A2-D1	3.96		B1-C2-D2	6.94
	A2-D2	4.79		B2-C1-D1	1.88
B X C	B1-C1	3.68		B2-C1-D2	3.06
	B1-C2	6.66		B2-C2-D1	5.73
	B2-C1	2.47		B2-C2-D2	6.24
	B2-C2	5.98	A X B X C X D	A1-B1-C1-D1	3.89
B X D	B1-D1	4.82		A1-B1-C1-D2	4.84
	B1-D2	5.52		A1-B1-C2-D1	7.00
	B2-D1	3.80		A1-B1-C2-D2	7.71
	B2-D2	4.65		A1-B2-C1-D1	1.76
C X D	C1-D1	2.57		A1-B2-C1-D2	2.79
	C1-D2	3.58		A1-B2-C2-D1	6.00
	C2-D1	6.05		A1-B2-C2-D2	6.17
	C2-D2	6.59		A2-B1-C1-D1	2.64
A X B X C	A1-B1-C1	4.37		A2-B1-C1-D2	3.35
	A1-B1-C2	7.35		A2-B1-C2-D1	5.76
	A1-B2-C1	2.28		A2-B1-C2-D2	6.17
	A1-B2-C2	6.08		A2-B2-C1-D1	2.00
	A2-B1-C1	3.00		A2-B2-C1-D2	3.33
	A2-B1-C2	5.97		A2-B2-C2-D1	5.46
	A2-B2-C1	2.66		A2-B2-C2-D2	6.30
	A2-B2-C2	5.88			

Note: Smaller numbers indicate a more favorable evaluation.

perceived their choices as consequential while those in the control group did not.

Given that the consequences variable was adequately manipulated, its effects on racial discrimination may be examined. A 2 x 2 x 2 x 2 analysis of variance with repeated measures on three factors is shown in Table 4.2.[2] The finding of particular interest is the significant Consequences x Race interaction, for it reveals that the manipulation of consequences made a significant difference in subjects' reactions to the hypothetical persons' race. Table 4.3 shows the mean ratings assigned to the various attributes of the hypothetical persons by both experimental group subjects and control group subjects. Within the consequences condition, Caucasians ($\bar{X}$ = 4.18) were evaluated significantly more favorably than Negroes ($\bar{X}$ = 5.86, F = 40.81, df = 1/76, p < .01), but there was no difference in subjects' evaluation of Negroes ($\bar{X}$ = 4.48) and Caucasians ($\bar{X}$ = 4.27) when responses were perceived to be of no consequence (F = .55, df = 1/76, p > .05). Subjects' evaluations of Caucasians remained constant across levels of consequences (F = .14, df = 1/152, p > .05), while subjects' evaluations of Negroes grew significantly less favorable as responses came to be seen as consequential (F = 30.39, df = 1/152, p < .01). These findings strongly supported the hypothesis that discrimination against Negroes increases as responses are invested with consequences.

The second hypothesis held that subjects who perceive their responses to lack consequences discriminate more on belief similarity than race similarity. To test this hypothesis, Westie's (1953) Summated Differences Technique was used to calculate racial and belief discrimination scores for each control group subject. Racial discrimination scores were calculated by subtracting the ratings given the four Caucasian hypothetical persons from the sum of the ratings given the four Negro hypothetical persons. Belief discrimination scores were defined as the sum of attitude plus value discrimination scores. Attitude discrimination scores were calculated by subtracting the sum of the ratings given hypothetical persons expressing similar attitudes from the sum of the ratings given hypothetical persons expressing dissimilar attitudes. Value discrimination scores were calculated by subtracting the sum of the ratings given those expressing similar values from the sum of the ratings given those expressing dissimilar values. To remove negative values, a constant of 26 was added to both race and belief discrimination scores. Thus a racial discrimination score or a belief discrimination score of less than 26 indicated discrimination against Caucasians or hypothetical persons espousing similar beliefs, while scores greater than 26 meant subjects discriminated against Negroes or hypothetical persons with different beliefs. Control group subjects ($N = 39$) discriminated more on belief similarity ($\bar{X} = 39.94$) than racial similarity ($\bar{X} = 26.84$, $t = 5.02$, $df = 38$, $p < .01$). Therefore, the second hypothesis was confirmed.

The third hypothesis tested was that subjects who perceived their responses to be consequential would discriminate equally on race and belief similarity. As in the control group, both belief and race discrimination scores were calculated for each subject in the experimental group. Like their control group counterparts, experimental group subjects ($N = 39$) discriminated more on belief similarity ($\bar{X} = 41.83$) than on racial similarity ($\bar{X} = 32.71$, $t = 4.14$, $df = 38$, $p < .01$) when evaluating hypothetical persons as roommates. Thus, the principle of belief congruence accurately described subjects' roommate selections in the experimental group as well as the control group.

The fourth hypothesis tested was that the strength of the relationship between perceived social pressure and racial discrimination differs depending on whether racial discrimination is inferred from consequential or inconsequential responses. This hypothesis was supported as the correlation between perceived social pressure and racial discrimination was stronger in the experimental group ($r_{xy} = .77$, $N = 36$) than the control group ($r_{xy} = .30$, $N = 41$, $t = 3.04$, $df = 71$, $p < .01$).[3]

It is interesting to note that while a stronger relationship was obtained between perceived social pressure and discrimination when the latter was derived from consequential as compared to inconsequential responses, the manipulation of consequences did not affect average perceived social pressure. Perceived social pressure scores could range from 3 to 27 with scores greater than 9 reflecting varying degrees of perceived pressure for racial discrimination. The experimental ($\bar{X} = 11.25$) and control ($\bar{X} = 12.24$) groups perceived equally slight social pressure to discriminate against Negroes as roommates ($t = .80$, $df = 75$, $p > .05$).

The fifth hypothesis was that value similarity would prove to be a stronger determinant of subjects' evaluations of the hypothetical persons than attitude similarity. It can be seen by looking at Table 4.2 that while value similarity accounts for 2% of the variance in subjects' responses, 36% of the variance is accounted for by attitude similarity. Although both variables significantly affected subjects' evaluation of the hypothetical persons, attitude similarity was clearly the more important of the two.

DISCUSSION

One of the more interesting findings in need of explanation is the significant difference in correlations between perceived social pressure for racial discrimination and racial discrimination in the experimental and control groups. The subjects' perceived social pressure scores can be thought of as indicators of expected reinforcement or its withdrawal given their choosing of a Negro as a roommate. It is recalled that the subjects in both groups perceived equal social pressure against choosing a Negro roommate. But only experimental group subjects believed they were actually choosing a roommate and therefore only these subjects had to be concerned with the possible loss of rewards that might result from choosing a Negro roommate. And this concern may have been reflected in the significant correlation between perceived social pressure and racial discrimination found in the experimental group.

Control group subjects no doubt realized that while their friends and parents might object to their living with a Negro, they would object much less, if at all, to their saying they would live with a Negro. For control group subjects, then, the probability that parents and friends would withdraw rewards was equivalent to the probability that their choices would determine their roommate—about zero. Thus, there was much less reason for control group subjects to believe that their responses would lead to a gain or loss of reinforcement from parents and friends, and it is not surprising to find that their responses were only weakly correlated with an indicator of such reinforcement.

One plausible explanation of the greater racial discrimination shown by experimental group subjects follows directly from the previous discussion. Experimental group subjects, but not their control group counterparts, expected significant others to withhold rewards if they chose roommates in a nondiscriminatory manner. To avoid this loss of reinforcements, subjects in the experimental group may have been compelled to discriminate against Negroes. If this is in fact what happened, it constitutes a prime example of perceived social pressure causing racial discrimination and may be taken as evidence for Rokeach and Mezei's (1966) assertion that were it not for perceived social pressure, there would be no racial discrimination.

The significant and strong correlation between perceived social pressure and racial discrimination observed in the experimental group is a necessary, but not a sufficient, condition for claiming that the former causes the latter. It is not difficult to conceive of parents who, for whatever reason, expect few rewards from Negroes and inculcate the same expectancy in their children. The idea that children adopt the racial attitudes of their parents has received ample support in the literature (Epstein & Komorita, 1966; Horowitz, 1936; Mosher & Scodel, 1960), and the principle of belief congruence itself implies that persons choose as friends those who espouse similar attitudes. In general, then, subjects who have negative attitudes towards Negroes should have parents and friends who share these feelings, while subjects who have positive attitudes toward Negroes should have parents and friends who have similar feelings. These relationships, rather than the causal relationship suggested earlier, might be what is reflected in the significant correlation between perceived social pressure and racial discrimination. If so, another explanation for the difference in racial discrimination between the experimental and control groups needs to be found.

If subjects believe that interacting with Negroes will not be rewarding, they might reasonably be expected to discriminate against Negroes. It seems safe to assume that some subjects held the belief and that these subjects were equally distributed between the experimental and control groups. Accepting these assumptions changes the emphasis from trying to determine why experimental group subjects discriminated against Negroes to trying to determine why control group subjects did not.

Given the liberal stereotype of academic personnel, both experimental group subjects and control group subjects may have realized that they would receive a more positive evaluation from the Dean of Men and the experimenter, respectively, if they refrained from racial discrimination. Looking only at this source of reinforcement, no racial discrimination would be expected in either group. But experimental group subjects had to weigh the reinforcement value of a positive evaluation from the Dean of Men against potential reinforcements from their choice of roommate. And if some subjects expected few rewards from Negroes, the potentially greater reinforcements from a roommate of the same race might overcome the reinforcement value of a positive evaluation from the Dean, and significant racial discrimination might result.

Control group subjects would gain little by discriminating against Negroes even if they believed Negroes were less likely than Caucasians to provide them with reinforcement. Their only source of reinforcement for racial discrimination would lie in the avoidance of guilt that might result from responding in a manner not in accord with their underlying attitudes. And it is possible that the avoidance of guilt failed to constitute a large enough reward to balance the experimenter's approval that would accrue to subjects if they refrained from discrimination. The lack of racial discrimination among control group subjects can be understood in light of these reinforcement contingencies.

Up to now two distinct explanations have been advanced for the greater racial discrimination found in the experimental group as compared to the control group. The first explanation emphasized the effect of consequences on the probability that significant others would withdraw rewards from subjects if they refused to discriminate against Negroes, while the second explanation emphasized the effect of consequences on increasing the saliency of the hypothetical persons' reward potential and thereby reducing the relative importance of the experimenter (Dean of Men) as a source or reward. According to the first explanation, some subjects discriminated against Negroes not because they were prejudiced but because society's reward structure was such that racial discrimination was profitable. According to the second explanation, some subjects held negative attitudes toward Negroes and chose, and would choose again, Caucasians in preference to Negroes in the absence of pressure from significant others. These explanations are not mutually exclusive. It is not difficult to imagine subjects' own racial attitudes combining with perceived social pressure to determine racial discrimination in roommate choices.

The fact that attitude similarity accounted for so much more of the variance than value similarity in subjects' roommate selections is perhaps the most difficult finding to explain. Values are thought to be determinants of attitudes, but attitudes are not thought to be determinants of values. Evidence for these contentions is found in several studies in which attitude change resulted from experimental manipulation of values (Rokeach, 1968, 1971). Because of their greater centrality, values were expected to convey more about the hypothetical persons' belief systems to subjects than attitudes, and thus they were expected to be better indicators of potential reward. Perhaps this expectation was not realized because values are no more central than attitudes in belief systems and therefore no more revealing of cognitive structure. The preeminence of the attitude similarity variable in determining responses may be explained in another way. Although the number of attitudes and values manipulated was the same, a greater proportion of the hypothetical persons' descriptions pertained to attitudes than values. Thus, the way in which the attitude and value variables were operationalized, rather than their status in subjects' belief systems, may have contributed to attitude similarity being a significantly stronger determinant of roommate selections than value similarity.

Perhaps this study's most important finding was that the principle of belief congruence accurately described the responses of subjects in both the experimental and control groups. The experimental group subjects' roommate selections indicate that discrimination in the real world need not be along the lines of ethnic group affiliation as casual observation and some research suggests (Tajfel, 1970). Further, it suggests what sort of similarities might be emphasized in order to facilitate improved interracial relations.

A basic question raised by the principle's accurate description of roommate choices is, why does belief similarity constitute a stronger determinant of attraction than racial similarity? Evidence has been presented which suggests that belief similarity acquires its reinforcing properties from acting as an indicator of *approval* from others (Byrne & Griffitt, 1966; Ettinger, Nowiki, & Nelson, 1970). Racial similarity may acquire its reinforcing properties from acting as an indicator of belief similarity (Stein et al., 1965). Therefore, belief similarity might be thought of as a secondary reinforcer, whereas racial similarity might be thought of as a tertiary reinforcer. Belief similarity, then, should serve as a better cue for potential approval and should account for more of the variance in subjects' roommate choices.

Consequential Responses as Attitudinal

Although frequently used, the validity of questionnaire responses as indicators of attitudes and attitude change has been questioned (Festinger, 1964). Rokeach (1966) has suggested that overt behavior, either by itself or in conjunction with "paper-and-pencil" responses, might prove a more valid indicator of subjects' attitudes toward an object or situation. In adopting this outlook, social psychologists have become proponents of the maxim that actions speak louder than words.

Some overt behaviors, however, such as petition signing, may have only a small portion of their variance accounted for by the attitude they purportedly measure (Blake, Mouton, & Hain, 1956; Helson, Blake, & Mouton, 1958). It may be that in judging the quality of a behavior as an attitudinal indicator, the crucial factor is not whether a behavior is overt or verbal but whether it is consequential, that is, whether it is perceived by the subject as affecting his relationship with the attitude object.

As more or less intimate relationship may result from their behavior, subjects emitting consequential responses must take into account the reward value of the attitude object. This value is contingent in part on the subjects' own attitudes. Therefore, subjects must consider their attitudes toward the attitude object when emitting consequential responses. In contrast, subjects emitting inconsequential responses toward an attitude object can ignore the attitude object's potential reward value and thus need not seriously consider their own attitude toward the attitude object. For this reason, consequential responses should be better indicators of subjects' attitudes than their inconsequential counterparts.

This is not to say that consequential responses are necessarily pure indicators of attitudes. Making responses consequential may compel subjects to consider factors other than their own attitudes, such as the feelings of parents and friends, before issuing a response. If this happens, the response in question becomes less valuable as an attitudinal indicator.

Yet it may be assumed that one factor considered before a response is emitted is subjects' attitudes toward the attitude object if the response is consequential. The same assumption cannot be made if it is known simply that a behavior was overt or verbal. Therefore, it is suggested that whether or not a behavior is consequential is a more useful distinction than whether a behavior is verbal or overt when it comes to assessing the value of a behavior as an indicator of an attitude toward an object or situation.

REFERENCES

Anderson, C., & Cote, A. D. Belief dissonance as a source of disaffection between ethnic groups. *Journal of Personality and Social Psychology*, 1966, *4*, 447-453.

Bem, D. The epistemological status of interpersonal simulations. *Journal of Experimental Social Psychology*, 1968, *4*, 270-274.

Blake, R., Mouton, J., & Hain, J. Social forces in petition signing. *Southwestern Social Science Quarterly*, 1956, *36*, 385-390.

Byrne, D., & Griffitt, W. Similarity versus liking: A clarification. *Psychonomic Science*, 1966, *6*, 295-296.

Byrne, D., & McGrew, G. Interpersonal attraction towards Negroes. *Human Relations*, 1964, *17*, 201-213.

Byrne, D., & Wong, T. Racial prejudice, interpersonal attractions, and assumed dissimilarity of attitudes. *Journal of Abnormal and Social Psychology*, 1962, *65*, 246-253.

Cook, S., & Selltiz, C. Multiple indicator approach to attitude measurement. *Psychological Bulletin*, 1964, *62*, 36-55.

Crowne, D., & Marlowe, D. *The approval motive*. New York: Wiley, 1964.

Edwards, A. *The social desirability variable in personality assessment and research*. New York: Dryden, 1957.

Epstein, R., & Komorita, S. Childhood prejudice as a function of parental ethnocentrism and punitiveness. *Journal of Personality and Social Psychology*, 1966, *3*, 259-264.

Ettinger, R., Nowicki, S., & Nelson, D. Interpersonal attraction and the approval motive. *Journal of Experimental Research in Personality*, 1970, *4*, 95-99.

Festinger, L. Behavioral support for opinion change. *Public Opinion Quarterly*, 1964, *28*, 404-417.

Freedman, J. Role playing: Psychology by consensus. *Journal of Personality and Social Psychology*, 1969, *13*, 107-114.

Helson, H., Blake, R., & Mouton, J. Petition signing as adustment to situational and personal factors. *Journal of Social Psychology*, 1958, *48*, 3-10.

Hendrick, C., Bixenstine, V., & Hawkins, G. Race versus belief similarity as determinants of attraction. *Journal of Personality and Social Psychology*, 1971, *17*, 250-258.

Hendrick, C., & Hawkins, G. Race and belief similarity as determinants of attraction. *Perceptual and Motor Skills*, 1969, *29*, 710.

Horowitz, E. L. The development of attitudes toward the Negro. *Archives of Psychology*, 1936, No. 194.

Insko, C., & Robinson, J. Belief similarity versus race as determinants of reactions to Negroes by southern white adolescents. *Journal of Personality and Social Psychology*, 1967, *7*, 216-221.

Kelly, K., Silverman, B., & Cochrane, R. Social desirability and the Rokeach Value Survey. *Journal of Experimental Research in Personality,* 1972, *6,* 84-87.

Kutner, B., Wilkens, C., & Yarrow, P. R. Verbal attitudes and overt behavior involving prejudice. *Journal of Abnormal and Social Psychology,* 1952, *47,* 649-652.

LaPiere, R. Attitudes versus actions. *Social Forces,* 1934, *13,* 230-237.

Linn, L. Verbal attitudes and overt behavior: A study of racial discrimination. *Social Forces,* 1964, *43,* 353-364.

McGrew, J. How "open" are multiple-dwelling units. *Journal of Social Psychology,* 1967, *72,* 223-226.

Mezei, L. Perceived social pressure as an explanation of shifts in the relative influence of race and belief on prejudice across social interactions. *Journal of Personality and Social Psychology,* 1971, *19,* 69-81.

Mosher, D., & Scodel, A. Relationships between ethnocentrism in children and the ethnocentrism and authoritarian rearing practices of their mothers. *Child Development,* 1960, *31,* 369-376.

Rokeach, M. Belief versus race as determinants of social distance. *Journal of Abnormal and Social Psychology,* 1961, *62,* 187-188.

Rokeach, M. Attitude change and behavioral change. *Public Opinion Quarterly,* 1966, *30,* 529-550.

Rokeach, M. *Beliefs, attitudes, and values.* San Francisco: Jossey-Bass, 1968.

Rokeach, M. Long-range experimental manipulation of values, attitudes, and behavior. *American Psychologist,* 1971, *26,* 453-459.

Rokeach, M., & Mezei, L. Race and shared beliefs as factors in social choice. *Science,* 1966, *151,* 167-172.

Rokeach, M., Smith, P., & Evans, R. Two kinds of prejudice or one? In M. Rokeach (Ed.), *The open and closed mind.* New York: Basic Books, 1960.

Silverman, B., & Cochrane, R. The relationship between verbal expressions of behavioral intention and overt behavior. *Journal of Social Psychology,* 1971, *84,* 51-56.

Silverman, G., & Cochrane, R. The effect of the social context on the principle of belief congruence. *Journal of Personality and Social Psychology,* 1972, *22,* 259-268.

Smith, C., Williams, L., & Willis, R. H. Race, sex, and belief as determinants of friendship acceptance. *Journal of Personality and Social Psychology,* 1967, *5,* 127-137.

Stein, D. The influence of belief systems on interpersonal preference. *Psychological Monographs,* 1966, *80* (8, Whole No. 616).

Stein, D., Hardyck, J., & Smith, M. Race and belief: An open and shut case. *Journal of Personality and Social Psychology,* 1965, *1,* 281-289.

Tajfel, H. Experiments in intergroup discrimination. *Scientific American,* 1970, *223* (5), 96-102.

Triandis, H. A note on Rokeach's theory of prejudice. *Journal of Abnormal and Social Psychology,* 1961, *62,* 184-186.

Triandis, H., & Davis, E. Race and belief as determinants of behavioral intentions. *Journal of Personality and Social Psychology,* 1965, *2,* 715-725.

Triandis, H., Loh, W., & Levin, L. A. Race, status, quality of spoken English, and opinions about civil rights as determinants of interpersonal attitudes. *Journal of Personality and Social Psychology,* 1966, *3,* 468-472.

Westie, F. A technique for the measurement of race attitudes. *American Sociological Review*, 1953, *18*, 73-78.

NOTES

1. The single exception is the study by Rokeach and Mezei (1966). They emphasize that in contrast to previous studies in which subjects gave "paper-and-pencil" responses to "paper-and-pencil" stimuli, their subjects discriminated in real-life situations. Simply because a behavior is emitted in a real-life situation does not guarantee that it is consequential. For example, job applicants told to choose a work partner were in a real-life situation but were assured that their selections had nothing to do with their employment interviews. Considering that these men were uncertain of subsequent employment, it is difficult to imagine that they viewed their responses as consequential in the sense that they might determine with whom they might be working. In contrast, Rokeach and Mezei's student subjects no doubt believed their choices would determine whom they later joined for coffee and thus it may be assumed that they saw their responses as having consequences. Therefore, in only one of their tests of the principle of belief congruence did Rokeach and Mezei use consequential behavior.

2. Three subjects were randomly chosen for removal from the control group. This resulted in 39 subjects in both the experimental and control groups and served to facilitate the analysis.

3. Only subjects who returned both their roommate selections and their significant-others questionnaire could be included in this analysis.

5

MIRIAM A. LEWIN

Psychological Aspects of Minority Group Membership: The Concepts of Kurt Lewin

Kurt Lewin (1890-1947) began as a general rather than a social psychologist. He was intrigued by the challenge he perceived within the young field of psychology: to combine a high level of scientific rigor and conceptual sophistication with a meaningful approach to the individual and his behavior. Later in his professional life he became more interested in groups and in social action. This interest was stimulated by his own experiences with anti-Jewish prejudice, with emigration and with two cultures, the German and the American. These experiences made him think about the position of the Jewish community in a non-Jewish world.

They led him to ask, "What does it really mean to belong to a social group?" He decided that membership in a group is part of the "ground" upon which a person stands. Our every act depends partly on this background, although ordinarily we are barely aware of this fact. Therefore, Lewin began by postulating that *membership in a group is, psychologically, a background determinant of the individual's behavior* in a multitude of settings.

What happens if a person is not clear as to whether or not he belongs to a group? He no longer stands on stable ground. Therefore, his behavior becomes uncertain, like that of a person walking on quicksand, through a bog, or on thin ice. He is not firm, his decisions are vague and unclear, he is either inhibited or inclined to overact, and he feels self-conscious. Why might a person be uncertain as to his group belonging? Perhaps because membership in a group he wants to join is defined by others as incompatible with membership in his present group. In his 1935 article on the "Psycho-Sociological Problems of a Minority Group," Lewin writes:

Source: Reprinted from *Jewish Social Studies*, Vol. 36, No. 1, pp. 72-79 with the permission of the Conference on Jewish Social Studies, Inc.

Lewin was born in Germany and studied at the Universities of Freiburg, Munich, and Berlin. He was professor of psychology at the University of Berlin, until he came to the United States in 1932. He taught psychology at Stanford, Cornell, Harvard, the State University of Iowa, and at the Research Center for Group Dynamics, which he founded at M.I.T. shortly before his death. For additional information see Lewin, Kurt, *Field Theory in Social Science*, edited by Dorwin Cartwright (New York 1951); and Marrow, Alfred J., *The Practical Theorist, the Life and Work of Kurt Lewin* (New York 1969).

There are persons whose whole life-situation is characterized by such uncertainty about their belonging, resulting from standing near a margin of groups. This is typical, for instance. of the nouveaux riches or of other persons crossing the margin of social classes. It is typical furthermore of members of religious or national minority groups everywhere who try to enter the main group. . . .

It is one of the greatest theoretical and practical difficulties of the Jews, that Jewish people are often, in a high degree, uncertain of their relation to the Jewish group. They are uncertain whether they actually belong to the Jewish group, in what respect they belong to this group, and in what degree.

If an individual always acts as a member of the same specific group, it is usually symptomatic of the fact that he is somewhat out of balance, for he does not respond naturally and freely to the demands of the present situation. He feels too strongly his membership in a certain group, and this indicates that his personal relationship to this group is not sound.[1]

For example, recall the old jokes about the Jewish after-dinner speaker ready at a moment's notice to discuss such topics as "The trip to the moon and the Jewish Problem," or "Low-phosphate detergents and the Jew."

Lewin continues, "This *over*emphasis is only a different form of expression of the same kind of relationship which, in other individuals, leads to an *under*emphasis. There are persons who, in a situation in which it would be natural to respond as Jews, do not respond so; they repress or conceal their Jewishness."[2]

A second concept in Lewin's psychology is that of the psychological boundary, and of the nature of the *boundary of the social group.* How do the boundaries of the Jewish group in modern times compare with those of other periods in history? Lewin felt that this uncertainty about belonging to the group is a particular problem of the modern Jew. One must be reminded that he wrote before the establishment of Israel. In the period of the ghetto, there were firm boundaries between Jewish groups and other groups. For certain hours the ghetto wall with its locked gates literally cut off the Jewish group from communication with others.

Severe hardships, both material and psychological, were imposed by ghetto living. However, group membership was at least clear. Crossing the boundary, except superficially and temporarily, was virtually unthinkable and impossible. Any fantasies of doing so must have been recognized at once as daydreams, and to many, as unpleasant nightmares.

At this point Lewin introduces a third psychological concept, that of *space of free movement.* During the ghetto times the psychological space of free movement of Jews was severely limited. For example, many occupations were closed to them. This prison-like situation created a great deal of tension.

How did the ghetto situation compare with that of modern Jews in Germany in the early twentieth century? The boundary between the Jewish and other groups had grown weaker, less concrete, and, at least for some individuals, passable. The space of free movement in social action had greatly increased. Lewin felt that the Jewish group lived under less tension than in the ghetto period.

But strange as it may appear at first, the decrease of tension has brought no real relaxation to the life of the Jew, but instead has meant perhaps even higher tension in some respects. This paradoxical fact is not only a scientific problem, but one of the most disturbing elements in modern Jewish life. What this paradox means, and why it occurs, we shall best see if we now consider, not the Jewish group, but the individual Jew, and ask what forces are acting on him as an individual, and how the strength and the direction of the forces have been affected by a change in the position of his group.[3]

Earlier, the individual felt the pressure applied essentially to the Jewish group as a whole. Now he is much more exposed to pressure as an individual. His life is more separated from other Jews. He passes back and forth through the weaker boundary. Though in some ways less pressured when outside the ghetto, he has also lost an island of safety. The fact that the boundary, though *more* passable, is not necessarily *completely* passable, creates a new source of uncertainty: is there space of free movement in this particular direction or not? Is a particular criticism or rebuke "merited" or is it the result of prejudice? The person is deprived of standards by which to evaluate himself, and made unsure of his own worth.

In addition, the apparent possibility of reaching the goal of free movement in the wider social world *increases the strength of the desire* to reach the goal. This is a widespread psychological phenomenon. Experiments demonstrate that animals run faster as they approach a goal such as their food box. Prisoners show a disproportionate tendency to break out of jail shortly before they are due to be released. Emancipation, Lewin felt, placed the Jews in the tantalizing situation of almost but not quite being able to acquire the respect, status and prerogatives they had so long been denied. *Paradoxically, the price of increased freedom, for many Jews, was increased tension, conflict, and inner pressure.* Achad Haam called this situation "slavery within freedom."[4]

Today the confusingly shifting tides and fashions within the black community over the relative merits of integration and separatism reflect the fact that black Americans are now facing comparable problems. Their space of free movement increases; the boundary between the black and white communities is weakened, but it is still very much in existence. As the individual black person spends less time on the relatively safe segregated island and more in the wider world, tension and ambivalence will, according to this theory, rise. I think current events confirm the theory:

tension in the black individual is rising, even though the status of the black group has improved significantly.

Under these pressures some Jews became what sociologists call *marginal men*. These are often the most privileged within the lower status group. The youth especially feel the boundary to be weakest, and their identity to be the least fixed. "These marginal men and women," Lewin writes, "are in somewhat the same position as an adolescent who is no longer a child and certainly does not want to be a child any longer, but who knows at the same time that he is not really accepted as a grown-up. This uncertainty about the ground on which he stands and the group to which he belongs often makes the adolescent loud and restless, at once timid and aggressive, over-sensitive, and tending to extremes—overcritical of others and himself.

"The marginal Jew is condemned for his lifetime to remain in a similar situation. . . . He is . . . in a rather vague and uncertain but permanent inner conflict. He is the 'eternal adolescent.' He shows the same unhappiness and lack of adjustment." Lewin concludes "Not *belonging to many groups* is the cause of the difficulty, but an *uncertainty* of belongingness."[5]

Lewin discussed a related issue in a 1941 article called "Self-Hatred Among Jews." "Hatred" is an ugly word and perhaps you feel the phrase "self-hatred"[6] is too strong. But Lewin argues that the members of any minority group are subject to this tendency. He gives examples such as the summer camp which in fact accommodates only Jewish children, but hires only non-Jewish counselors, holds a Christian service, but has no Jewish activities.[7] Some German and Austrian Jews complained in the 1930s, Lewin reports, that all their troubles were due to the bad conduct of East European Jews. Other Jews were prejudiced against rich Jews, or poor Jews, or Jews from here, or there, or wherever.

Because of the psychological impact of the state of Israel one suspects that self-hatred is considerably reduced today, but it has hardly vanished. For example, in a recent letter to *The New York Times Magazine,* Frumess[8] argues that antisemitism today is the fault of Zionists. He adds various fantastic charges holding Zionists responsible for every fault in American life. The author of this letter seems to be a self-hating Jew, as are the Jewish defenders of Al-Fatah terrorism. On a milder level, a touch of self-hatred that seems to go beyond justifiable and healthy self-criticism is not uncommon among Jewish comedians and writers, who find Jewish audiences generally responsive to this attitude.

Examples of the same tendency toward self-hatred seem to be found in all lower status groups. For reports on the attitudes of black people toward their ethnic identity see the works by Kenneth Clark,[9] Kardiner and Ovesey,[10] Grier and Cobbs,[11] and Lee Rainwater.[12] Father Andrew

Greeley has written on self-hatred within the Irish Catholic group. He suggests that the novel *Studs Lonigan* by Farrell,[13] was a 1925 Irish "Portnoy."[14] According to Lambert,[15] French Canadians rate the identical bilingual actor as "more attractive" and "intelligent" when he records prose in English rather than in French! Women have been known to say "Isn't that just like a woman?" when a member of their own sex displeases them.

But why, you may well wonder, should anyone hate his own identity? Lewin offers the following analysis. Ordinarily a person will leave a group, if he can, if the positive attractions of group membership are significantly less than the negative aspects. In any lower status minority group pressure to leave is generated by the desire for the respect and rewards of higher status. However, free mobility across the boundary is limited or entirely prevented by the majority group.

The person who would like to leave the group will tend to move as far away from the center of his group as the outside majority permits. He will stay on the boundary of the group and may be psychologically more frustrated than those members who keep well inside the group. Frustration, psychologists find, often leads to aggression. In this case, aggression should, logically, be directed toward the majority who prevent the person from leaving the lower status group. However, the person who most wishes to leave the group is precisely the one who most admires the majority for its higher status. He believes the majority group to be too powerful to attack. Its power is part of its attraction. He has internalized the negative stereotypes held by the majority group about the lower status group. For all these reasons he deflects his aggressive feelings from their realistic target and turns against his own group and himself. Thus he develops self-hatred.

In view of his ideas, it is not surprising that Lewin believed that a firm understanding of one's Jewish identity is important to the psychological well-being of the person born into the Jewish ethnic group.

What, then, *is* Jewish identity? In the 1930s and 1940s, when Lewin met with Hillel and Avukah groups at Harvard, Cornell, and the State University of Iowa, the students asked him how they should understand their identity. Iowa students asked: "Why, if I am Jewish, do I sometimes feel more alike, more *similar* to non-Jewish Midwesterners than I do to the New York City Jewish students at the University?" "Who am I?" asks an eastern college co-ed, described by Lewin. "I am on the fence. . . . As a Jew I don't amount to much . . . yet I'm always conscious that I am Jewish, whether I hide it or try to impress it on others . . . I'm wrong, utterly wrong in being that way. . . ."[16] Compare these words, now over thirty-five years old, with the following quotations from a 1971 *New York Times* article: "There's something Jewish that keeps us all together, but I couldn't say what it is," remarked the 22 year old managing editor of a Boston Jewish student paper. A contributor to another student quarterly writes: "I am not quite sure what it means to be a woman. I am equally unclear about what it means to be a Jew."[17]

What did Lewin reply to these heartfelt questions? ". . . It is not similarity or dissimilarity of individuals that constitutes a group but *interdependence of fate.*"[18] The bewildered Jewish youth is not necessarily reached, Lewin says, by a religious, or a national, or a cultural definition of Jewish identity. Instead he or she must understand that a "group is best defined as a *dynamic whole based on interdependence rather than similarity.* . . . A husband, wife, and baby are less similar to each other, in spite of their being a strong natural group, than the baby is to other babies, the husband to other men, and the wife to other women."[19]

"It is easy enough to see that the common fate of all Jews makes them a group in reality. One who has grasped this simple idea will not feel that he has to break away from Judaism altogether whenever he changes his attitude toward a fundamental Jewish issue."[20] "Young American Jews may abhor Jewish national mysticism; they may not be willing to suffer for cultural or religious values they do not fully understand, or perhaps even dislike; but they must be sufficiently factminded to see clearly their interdependence of fate with the rest of the American Jews, and indeed with the Jews all over the world."[21] "A realistic sociological understanding of interdependence would, I think, go a long way toward a proper balance in Jewish action."[22] With this understanding people will be ready to accept the variety of opinions and beliefs within the Jewish group as quite natural. They will also be ready and even eager to take their fair share of responsibility for the welfare of the group. The fog of uncertainty and conflicting feelings which paralyzes action will be much reduced.

Today similar bewilderment about group identity plagues many black, Puerto Rican American, Chicano, and other minority group members. They ask themselves: "If my ideas, beliefs, and values are so different from, or even completely opposed to, those of another member of my ethnic group, is something wrong with me, or with the other person? Am I a traitor to my group, or is he? Why do I have to feel "black" (or Chicano, etc.) at all? And where are the boundaries of my group identity? Are we all one Third World group? Or is it wrong for blacks to identify with Puerto Ricans and vice versa?" An example of this dilemma is the recent decision of a Latin American group of students on a U.S. college campus to bifurcate into two separate groups: the Brown Group and the Latin American Student Association.

Lewin's analysis, which indicates that membership may be defined by interdependence of fate rather than similarity of opinions, might provide a psychological basis for some feelings of common identity while legitimizing diversity of opinion with the group.

In his interesting recent book *Israelis and Jews: The Continuity of an Identity* Professor Simon N. Herman traces the impact of the Six-Day War upon Israeli-Jewish identity. Herman, who studied with Lewin, is a social psychologist at the Hebrew University. He found that the Six-Day War made Israelis and Jews in the Diaspora more keenly aware of their interdependence. Positively, the outpouring of concern, of support, and of volunteers heightened the sense of community between Israelis and other Jews. Negative interdependence of fate was also demonstrated. Professor Herman summarizes the impact on Israelis of the antisemitism occurring in Poland, and France, and of the treatment of Jews in Egypt, Syria, and Iraq. After doing a comprehensive study of Israeli high school students and their parents, he concludes: "The sense of interdependence rather than similarity is the basis of Jewish cohesiveness in the world today."[23]

In another recent report, a woman reared to be "just" a Soviet citizen describes the discovery of her Jewish identity in a Russian prison camp. She says: "In 1956 in Moscow, antisemitism was thick, deep—it was everywhere. Wherever you turned, you heard it and saw it. . . . The Six-Day War changed everything. [She does not mean that antisemitism ended, but rather that the relationship between bully and victim underwent a most significant change.] Suddenly you saw young men and women openly wearing the Star of David. . . . Once I saw a man walking around and around a huge square holding the hand of a little girl. . . . Her dress was pinned all over with big Stars of David. . . . A policeman chased him away finally."[24]

Lewin, who died the year before the establishment of the state of Israel, felt that Zionism made possible a more effective response by Jews to their problems. In introducing his ideas about the psychological concepts *time perspective* and *morale,* Lewin describes the German Zionists at the time of Hitler's rise to power. "They had a time perspective which included a psychological past of surviving adverse conditions for thousands of years and a meaningful and inspiring goal for the future. As the result of such a time perspective, this group showed high morale—initiative and organized planning. . . . Whatever one's opinion about Zionism . . . no one who has observed closely the German Jews during the fateful first weeks after Hitler's rise to power will deny that thousands of German Jews were saved from suicide only by the famous article of the *Jüdische Rundschau* with its headlines, *'Jasagen zum Judentum'* (Saying Yes to Being a Jew)"[25]—or, as we would put it today, Jewish Is Beautiful.

Lewin here helps us to understand the psychological rationale for the current desires of lower-status group members for Black Studies, Puerto Rican Studies, Woman's Studies, etc. Sound and informative history curricula in these areas should have the goal of enlarging the student's time perspective, assisting him or her in developing an accurately positive identity, heightening self-respect, and decreasing self-pity, by placing the problem in a wider perspective.

A second psychological benefit of Zionism, Lewin felt, grew out of the change in the Israeli's psychological *life space*. The restlessness and other characteristics described as typical of the adolescent and of the marginal man are not innate to Jews or to other minority group members. They are not deep-rooted products of long cultural traditions. Rather, they are determined by the current psychological situation of the minority group member. The crucial determinant of the destructive tension is the *degree of inner conflict*, not the degree of external danger. As early as 1935 Lewin felt that one of the outstanding characteristics of Jews in what was then "Palestine" was the absence of this restlessness.

Lewin was hopeful that Israel would create a better socio-psychological situation for Jews everywhere. It is in accord with his thinking to suggest that it would, for the first time in centuries, offer Jews a genuine choice: are they willing to accept the status of minority group membership in the nation within which they live, or not? It is a psychological truism that both for oneself and for others, the mere existence of a choice alters the psychological situation enormously, even if one does not, in fact, exercise certain available options. The existence of the state of Israel makes it psychologically possible for a Jew to freely choose to remain an American, not as a second-class recipient of America's charity, but as a person who has, himself, made a choice, and who accepts a positive identity as both Jewish and American.

Similarly, the availability of free access by all American subgroups to either relatively homogeneous or heterogeneous residential, occupational, educational, and other settings would give the individual American greater space of free movement and, according to this theory, reduce tension within the individual.

We could, if time permitted, explore other areas of Kurt Lewin's social psychology related to the psychology of minority group membership, such as his ideas about the special problems of leadership in minority groups (the phenomenon he called the *leader from the periphery*, which in another context, has been called the problem of the white Negro), or his concept of *action research*, and his dictum "There is nothing so practical as a good theory." He was convinced that research in the social sciences must be closely linked to action for improvement. Among the specific efforts in which he was involved to improve intergroup relations was the

Commission on Community Interrelations of the American Jewish Congress.[26]

Six of Lewin's concepts have been discussed:

1. *Group membership as ground* for the individual's actions, and certainty or uncertainty of group membership as an important dimension.
2. The psychological characteristics of the *boundary* of the group, such as its permeability.
3. The individual's *space of free movement* within his total life space.
4. *Self-hatred* among lower-status group members.
5. *Interdependence* (rather than similarity) of members as a defining characteristic of group membership.
6. *Time perspective* and its effect on *identity* and *morale.*

They illustrate how the psychological analysis of minority group membership served Lewin in his endeavor to "begin the transformation of social psychology into an intellectually challenging endeavor, in vital touch with human experience and social action."[27]

NOTES

1. Lewin, Kurt, *Resolving Social Conflicts,* edited by Gertrud W. Lewin (New York 1948), pp. 147-48.
2. *Ibid.,* p. 149.
3. *Ibid.,* p. 153.
4. *Ibid.,* p. 157.
5. *Ibid.,* pp. 179-92. See also Sanua, Victor, "Differences in Personality Adjustment Among Different Generations of Jews and Non-Jews," unpublished doctoral dissertation, Michigan State University (East Lansing, Michigan 1956).
6. An early use of the expression "Jewish self-hatred" was by the German philosopher Theodor Lessing, born 1872. Originally Jewish, he converted to Christianity, and returned to Judaism in 1900. He resigned his academic post around 1927 under antisemitic student protest. *Judisches Lexicon,* vol. iii (Berlin 1929), p. 237. Translation courtesy of Gertrud Lewin.
7. *Op. cit.,* p. 186.
8. Frumess, Richard, *The New York Times Magazine* (March 14, 1971), p. 16.
9. Clark, Kenneth B., *Dark Ghetto* (New York 1965).
10. Kardiner and Ovesey, *The Mark of Oppression* (New York 1951).
11. Grier, William, and Price Cobbs, *Black Rage* (New York 1968).
12. Rainwater, Lee, "Crucible of Identity: The Negro Lower Class Family" in Wechsler, Henry, L. Solomon, and B. Kramer, *Social Psychology and Mental Health* (New York 1970), pp. 652-82.
13. Farrell, James T., *Studs Lonigan* (New York 1925).
14. Greeley, Andrew, "The Last of the American Irish Fade Away," *The New York Times Magazine* (March 14, 1971).
15. Lambert, W. E., R. C. Hodgson, R. C. Gardner, and S. Fillenbaum, "Evaluational Reactions to Spoken Languages," *Journal of Abnormal and Social*

Psychology, 1960, pp. 44-51. Cited in Krech, D., R. Crutchfield, and N. Livson, *Elements of Psychology* (New York 1969), p. 810.

16. *Op. cit.*, pp. 178-79.
17. *The New York Times* (March 13, 1971), pp. 31, 33.
18. *Op. cit.*, p. 165.
19. *Ibid.*, p. 184.
20. *Ibid.*, p. 166.
21. *Ibid.*, p. 184.
22. *Ibid.*, p. 185.
23. Herman, Simon N., *Israelis and Jews: The Continuity of an Identity* (New York 1970), p. 208.
24. Vocse, Trudie, "Twenty-Four Years in the Life of Lyuba Bershadskaya," *The New York Times Magazine* (March 14, 1971), pp. 27, 86, 88.
25. *Op. cit.*, pp. 104-5, 198.
26. Lippett, Ronald, *Training in Community Relations* (New York 1949).
27. Smith, M. Brewster, *Social Psychology and Human Values* (Chicago 1969), p. 3.

6

F. K. HEUSSENSTAMM

Bumper Stickers and the Cops

A series of violent, bloody encounters between police and Black Panther Party members punctuated the early summer days of 1969. Soon after, a group of black students I taught at California State College, Los Angeles, who were members of the Panther Party, began to complain of continuous harassment by law enforcement officers. Among their many grievances, they complained about receiving so many traffic citations that some were in danger of losing their driving privileges. During one lengthy discussion, we realized that all of them drove automobiles with Panther Party signs glued to their bumpers. This is a report of a study that I undertook to assess the seriousness of their charges and to determine whether we were hearing the voice of paranoia or reality.

Recruitment advertising for subjects to participate in the research elicited 45 possible subjects from the student body. Careful screening

Source: Published by permission of Transaction, Inc. from Transaction, Vol. 8, #4, February, 1971, 32-33. Copyright © 1971, by Transaction, Inc.

thinned the ranks to 15—five black, five white, and five of Mexican descent. Each group included three males and two females. Although the college enrolls more than 20,000 students (largest minority group numbers on the west coast), it provides no residential facilities; all participants, of necessity then, traveled to campus daily on freeways or surface streets. The average round trip was roughly ten miles, but some drove as far as 18 miles. Eleven of the 15 had part-time jobs which involved driving to and from work after class as well.

All participants in the study had exemplary driving records, attested to by a sworn statement that each driver had received no "moving" traffic violations in the preceding twelve months. In addition, each promised to continue to drive in accordance with all in-force Department of Motor Vehicles regulations. Each student signed another statement, to the effect that he would do nothing to "attract the attention" of either police, sheriff's deputies or highway patrolmen—all of whom survey traffic in Los Angeles county. The participants declared that their cars, which ranged from a "flower child" hippie van to standard American makes of all types, had no defective equipment. Lights, horns, brakes and tires were duly inspected and pronounced satisfactory.

The appearance of the drivers was varied. There were three blacks with processed hair and two with exaggerated naturals, two white-shirt-and-necktie, straight Caucasians and a shoulder-length-maned hippie, and two mustache-and-sideburn-sporting Mexican-Americans. All wore typical campus dress, with the exception of the resident hippie and the militant blacks, who sometimes wore dashikis.

A fund of $500 was obtained from a private source to pay fines for any citations received by the driving pool and students were briefed on the purposes of the study. After a review of lawful operation of motor vehicles, all agreed on the seriousness of receiving excessive moving traffic violations. In California, four citations within a twelve-month period precipitates automatic examination of driving records, with a year of probation likely, or, depending on the seriousness of the offenses, suspension of the driver's license for varying lengths of time. Probation or suspension is usually accompanied by commensurate increases in insurance premiums. Thus, the students knew they were accepting considerable personal jeopardy as a condition of involvement in the study.

Bumper stickers in lurid day-glo orange and black, depicting a menacing panther with large BLACK PANTHER lettering were attached to the rear bumper of each subject car and the study began. The first student received a ticket for making an "incorrect lane change" on the freeway less than two hours after heading home in the rush hour traffic. Five more tickets were received by others on the second day for "following too closely," "failing to yield the right of way," "driving too slowly in the high-speed lane of the freeway," "failure to make a proper signal before turning right at an intersection," and "failure to observe proper safety of pedestrians using a crosswalk." On day three, students were cited for "excessive speed," "making unsafe lane changes" and "driving erratically." And so it went every day.

One student was forced to drop out of the study by day four, because he had already received three citations. Three others reached what we had agreed was the maximum limit—three citations—within the first week. Altogether, the participants received 33 citations in 17 days, and the violations fund was exhausted.

Drivers reported that their encounters with the intercepting officers ranged from affable and "standard polite" to surly, accompanied by search of the vehicle. Five cars were thoroughly gone over and their drivers were shaken down. One white girl, a striking blonde and a member of a leading campus sorority, was questioned at length about her reasons for supporting the "criminal activity" of the Black Panther Party. This was the only time that an actual reference to the bumper stickers was made during any of the ticketings. Students, by prior agreement, made no effort to dissuade officers from giving citations, once the vehicle had been halted.

PLEDGES TO DRIVE SAFELY

Students received citations equally, regardless of race or sex or ethnicity or personal appearance. Being in jeopardy made them "nervous" and "edgy" and they reported being very uncomfortable whenever they were in their automobiles. After the first few days, black students stopped saying "I told you so," and showed a sober, demoralized air of futility. Continuous pledges to safe driving were made daily, and all expressed increasing incredulity as the totals mounted. They paid their fines in person immediately after receiving a citation. One student received his second ticket on the way to pay his fine for the first one.

No student requested a court appearance to protest a citation, regardless of the circumstances surrounding a ticketing incident. When the investigator announced the end of the study on the eighteenth day, the remaining drivers expressed relief, and went straight to their cars to remove the stickers.

Some citations were undoubtedly deserved. How many, we cannot be sure. A tightly designed replication of this study would involve control of make and year of cars through the use of standard rented vehicles of low-intensity color. A driving pool of individuals who represented an equal number of both extreme-left and straight-looking appearance with matched age-range could be developed. Drivers could be assigned at random to pre-selected, alternate routes of a set length. Both left-wing and right-wing bumper stickers could also be attached at random after drivers were seated in their assigned vehicles and the doors sealed. In this way, no subject would know in advance whether he was driving around with "Black Panther Party" or "America Love It Or Leave It" on his auto. This would permit us to check actual driving behavior in a more reliable way. We might also wish to include a tape recorder in each car to preserve the dialogue at citation incidents.

NO MORE STICKERS

It is possible, of course, that the subject's bias influenced his driving, making it less circumspect than usual. But it is statistically unlikely that this number of previously "safe" drivers could amass such a collection of tickets without assuming real bias by police against drivers with Black Panther bumper stickers.

The reactions of the traffic officers might have been influenced, and we hypothesize that they were, by the recent deaths of police in collision with Black Panther Party members. But whatever the provocation, unwarranted traffic citations are a clear violation of the civil rights of citizens, and cannot be tolerated. Unattended, the legitimate grievances of the black community against individuals who represent agencies of the dominant society contribute to the climate of hostility between the races at all levels, and predispose victims to acts of violent retaliation.

As a footnote to this study, I should mention that Black Panther bumper stickers are not seen in Los Angeles these days, although the party has considerable local strength. Apparently members discovered for themselves the danger of blatantly announcing their politics on their bumpers, and have long since removed the "incriminating" evidence.

7

JOHN C. TOUHEY

Effects of Additional Women Professionals on Ratings of Occupational Prestige and Desirability

To examine the effects of increased occupational participation by women, male and female college students were led to believe that five high-status professions would sustain increasing proportions of female practitioners. Findings showed that ratings of occupational prestige and desirability decreased when subjects anticipated increased proportions of women in four of five professions and that the decrease did not differ for ratings by male and female subjects. Ratings on adjective pairs taken from the semantic differential suggested that reductions in prestige and desirability were accompanied by attributions of increased passiveness, insecurity and uselessness, and decreased success to occupations admitting increased proportions of women.

Increased participation of women in the labor force has occasioned numerous studies designed to explore the effects of increased employment among women in diverse areas of social interaction. Patterns of marital interaction among working wives, for example, have been extensively studied (e.g., Hoffman, 1960; Nye, 1963; Powell, 1961), as have the scholastic performances and juvenile delinquencies among children of working mothers (e.g., Douvan & Adelson, 1966; Hartley, 1960; Hoffman, 1963). Surprisingly, then, few psychologists and fewer sociologists have sought to examine the impact of increasing proportions of women on the very occupations that women have entered, although there is some evidence to suggest that the consequences may not benefit either the prestige or the desirability of the occupation itself.

In one recent study, Gross (1967) examined the proportions of women in the higher and lower status specialties within the professions of the United States. In medicine, for example, women were most frequently found among the ranks of pediatricians, psychiatrists, and dermatologists and seldom appeared in neurology, internal medicine, and the surgical specialties. A similar pattern of placement was obtained for law, with women appearing in lower status practices involving divorce, juvenile, and welfare cases while relatively absent from practices of higher status

Source: John C. Touhey, "Effects of Additional Women Professionals on Ratings of Occupational Prestige and Desirability," *Journal of Personality and Social Psychology,* 1974, *29,* 86-89. Copyright 1974 by the American Psychological Association. Reprinted by permission.

specialties involving tax law and corporate litigation. Finally, the academic community itself showed a similar pattern of stratification with women comprising 42% of the faculties of state teachers colleges and less than 10% of the faculties of the schools with the highest prestige and endowments.

One common explanation of these discrepancies points to admission policies and many other aspects of professional training that tend to discourage female applicants and that secure less prestigious placements for women who do complete their training. However, a second interpretation, not inconsistent with the first, raises the possibility that professions and specialties within a single profession may lose occupational prestige and desirability as a consequence of increased proportions of women practitioners. Thus, while relatively impersonal forces may conspire to place women in lower status occupations and professional specialties, it is equally plausible to suggest that the mere presence of women in an occupation or specialty may have social psychological consequences, particularly on the ratings of occupational prestige and desirability obtained from observers who are considering entry into the same occupations.

The present study, then, examines the hypothesis that the expectation of an increased proportion of women practitioners reduces the prestige and desirability of a profession. Specifically, males and females rated the prestige and desirability of five high-status occupations after they were led to believe that each profession would show a sharply increased proportion of women practitioners. Control subjects rated the occupations with no expectations concerning changing sex ratios.

METHOD

The subjects were 200 students (114 males, 86 females) enrolled in introductory psychology classes at the University of Tulsa. Since the experimental design required each subject to rate the prestige and desirability of one of five professions after receiving information that the proportion of women practitioners was increasing or unchanging, 20 subjects were randomly assigned to each of 10 treatment conditions.

Professions

Five professions rated highly in occupational prestige (National Opinion Research Center ratings, 1963; see Hodge, Siegel, & Rossi, 1964) were selected for further study. These were architect, college professor, lawyer, physician, and scientist. The decision to study professions rather than other occupations was based on a concern that the occupations represent realistic vocational aspirations for the subjects.

Each profession was described on an information sheet that had been abstracted from the appropriate entry in the 1970-1971 edition of the *Occupational Outlook Handbook* (U.S. Department of Labor, 1971). The information sheet described each occupation in terms of the nature of the work, places of employment, training and other qualifications, employment outlook, earnings and working conditions, and additional opportunities. To provide one abbreviated example, the information sheet for physician included the following:

Occupation: Physician

Nature of the Work: Physicians diagnose diseases and treat people who are ill or in poor health. Most physicians examine and treat patients in their own offices and in hospitals. Others hold fulltime research or teaching positions or perform administrative work in hospitals, professional associations and other organizations.

Places of Employment: Of nearly 300,000 physicians, about 190,000 are engaged in private practice. The remainder are employed in hospitals, private industry, state and other local health departments, medical schools, research foundations, and professional organizations.

Training and Other Qualifications: The first 2 years of medical training are spent learning basic medical sciences and during the last 2 years, students spend most of their time in hospitals and clinics under the supervision of experienced physicians.

Employment Outlook: Excellent opportunities are anticipated for physicians through the next few decades. The expected increase in demand for physicians' services will result from such factors as the anticipated population growth, the rising health consciousness of the public, and the trend toward higher standards of medical care.

Earnings and Working Conditions: The net income of private physicians in general practice is between $25,000 and $35,000, according to the limited information available.

Additional Opportunities: Approximately 7% of the physicians in the United States are women. Current patterns of recruitment indicate that the percentage of women physicians will stabilize at between 6 and 8% during the next 25 to 30 years.

Control subjects received this information sheet or a similar description of approximately 400 words for the profession of architect, college professor, lawyer, or scientist. It should be emphasized that the information sheets for all of the control subjects indicated that the proportion of women in the profession had stabilized and was likely to remain unchanged over the next 30 years.

The experimental subjects received the same information sheets except that the narrative under the heading, Additional Opportunities, predicted a sharply increasing proportion of women practitioners over the next 30 years. For example, experimental subjects who received the information for physicians read the following:

Approximately 7% of the physicians in the United States are women. However, current patterns of recruitment indicate that the percentage of women physicians will increase to 35% during the next 15 years, and that women will comprise a majority of physicians in 25 to 30 years.

Dependent Variables

The subjects were given 10 minutes to study the information sheets, after which it announced that the study was concerned with the way people evaluate different occupations. The subjects were then asked to rate the profession about which they had read. The ratings of prestige were obtained on a 61-point scale labeled at 10-point intervals from 0, very low prestige, to 60, very high prestige. Next, the subjects rated the desirability of the profession they had read about on a similar 61-point

TABLE 7.1
Ratings of Occupational Prestige for Five Professions with Two Sex Ratios

	Sex Ratio		
Profession	No Change	Increasing Number of Women	t
Architect			
X	48.4	44.9	2.55*
s	3.8	4.6	
Female subjects per cell	8	9	
College professor			
X	54.0	50.2	2.94*
s	3.9	4.1	
Female subjects per cell	8	9	
Lawyer			
X	50.1	48.2	1.33
s	4.0	4.8	
Female subjects per cell	8	9	
Physician			
X	56.2	51.7	3.26*
s	3.2	5.1	
Female subjects per cell	8	9	
Scientist			
X	53.4	50.3	2.23*
s	3.6	4.8	
Female subjects per cell	9	9	

Note: n = 20 per cell.
*p .05.

scale labeled at 10-point intervals from 0, very undesirable, to 60, very desirable. Finally, the subjects rated the profession on 12 pairs of polar adjectives from the semantic differential for which Gusfield and Schwartz (1963) had obtained significant correlations with occupational status. The polar adjectives were evaluated on a 7-point scale, and they were included in the present study in order to identify attributions that accompanied the hypothesized treatment effects. The adjective pairs were as follows: dirty-clean, passive-active, successful-unsuccessful, middle class-working class, Democrat-Republican, poor-rich, sober-drunk, insecure-secure, useful-useless, honest-dishonest, rural-urban, and Negro-white.

RESULTS AND DISCUSSION

Table 7.1 shows the mean ratings of occupational prestige for the five professions with changing and unchanging sex ratios. As seen in the first column of Table 7.1, all of the professions except architect received scores above 50 (high prestige) when rated with the expectation of unchanging sex ratios. Examination of the second column of Table 7.1 reveals a consistent tendency for each profession to show reduced prestige when subjects expected an increasing proportion of women practitioners. When ratings are compared between treatments, the medical profession sustains the largest decline in prestige, 4.5 points, and law shows the smallest decline, 1.9 points.

The third column of Table 7.1 shows the results of t tests between the two treatments for each occupation (all $dfs = 38$).[1] Comparisons for physicians and college professors fell beyond the .01 level of significance, and differences for architects and scientists attained the .02 and .05 levels of significance, respectively. However, the difference for ratings of lawyers was not significant.

The second primary dependent variable rated the subjects' estimates of the desirability of each profession. Overall desirability ratings followed the same pattern as the prestige ratings. For all five professions, expectations of increasing proportions of women practitioners yielded lower ratings than the expectations of unchanging sex ratios. Differences for physicians and college professors again reached the .01 level of significance. Treatment effects for architects and scientists were significant at the .05 level, and the difference for lawyers, which was not significant for the prestige ratings, reached borderline significance ($p < .10$) for the ratings of occupational desirability.

In sum, the general findings provide some support for the hypothesis that increased proportions of women may reduce the prestige and desirability of a high-status profession. The remaining analyses are concerned with sex differences and other variables which mediated this effect.

Additional Analyses

Compared to an average decline in prestige of 3.16 points for all of the subjects, decreases in the prestige ratings were 3.07 and 3.28 points for male and female subjects, respectively, and the difference was not significant. The corresponding analysis for sex differences on the ratings of occupational desirability was also nonsignificant. The average decline in the desirability ratings was 3.04 points, and decreases of 3.10 and 2.97 points for males and females, respectively, did not differ from each other.

Analysis of the semantic differential scales yielded significant differences on 4 of the 12 adjective pairs. When the professions were expected to show increased proportions of women, they were rated as more passive on the passive-active scale ($t = 2.81$, $p < .01$), less successful on the successful-unsuccessful scale ($t = 5.14$, $p < .001$), more insecure on the insecure-secure scale ($t = 2.19$, $p < .05$), and less useful on the useful-useless scale ($t = 4.67$, $p < .001$) than under control conditions (all $dfs = 198$). It should be recalled that all 12 adjective scales had previously been identified as correlates of occupational prestige (Gusfield & Schwartz, 1963) and that the 4 significant scales in the present study suggest that losses in prestige and desirability were accompanied by fairly specific expectations.

When the subjects were led to believe that a high-status occupation was expected to increase its proportion of female practitioners, both the prestige and the desirability of the occupation declined. This finding was consistent for four out of five professions and was evident for the ratings by female subjects as it was for the ratings by males. Moreover, evidence from the semantic differential items was also consistent across occupations and sexes.

Gross (1967) has noted that demographic findings concerning changing sex structures of occupations may be interpreted to indicate that whenever large numbers of women enter an occupation, men begin to seek employment elsewhere. The present findings, then, may provide an experimental analogue of Gross's interpretation, insofar as ratings of prestige and desirability are related to the decision to enter a high-status profession. At the same time, several limitations on the generalizability of the findings might be noted.

First, the nature of the manipulation raises the possibility that changing sex ratios were made unduly salient for the experimental subjects. For example, ascriptions of insecurity, lack of success, passiveness, and usefulness frequently characterize sex role stereotypes of women in general. Consequently, the subjects may have responded principally to stereotypes and perhaps little else. The second characteristic of the differentiating scales is that they load largely on the evaluative rather than descriptive dimension of the semantic differential. Adjective pairs which failed to accompany losses in status appear to refer primarily to descriptive categories (e.g., race, place of residence), while the differentiating adjectives seem to emphasize more evaluative consequences (e.g., attitudes, feelings) entailed by increased proportions of women professionals.

In conclusion, the results lend some credence to the hypothesis that increasing proportions of women professionals may reduce the prestige and desirability of high-status occupations. However, the present study does not attain the complexity commonly found in communications in the everyday world. It is suggested, then, that further research might be pursued at two somewhat different levels of analysis: one involving evaluations of specific women professionals in occupational settings and the second consisting of additional experimental studies which directly vary the parameters of occupational status.

REFERENCES

Douvan, E., & Adelson, J. *The adolescent experience.* New York: Wiley, 1966.

Gross, E. The sexual structure of occupations over time. Paper presented at the meeting of the American Sociological Association, San Francisco, August 1967.

Gusfield, J. R. & Schwartz, M. The meanings of occupational prestige. *American Sociological Review,* 1963, *28,* 265-271.

Hartley, R. E. Children's concepts of male and female roles. *Merrill-Palmer Quarterly,* 1960, *6,* 83-91.

Hodge, R. W., Siegel, P. M., & Rossi, P. Occupational prestige in the United States, 1925-63. *American Journal of Sociology,* 1964, *70,* 286-302.

Hoffman, L. W. Parental power relations and the division of household tasks. *Marriage and Family Living,* 1960, *22,* 27-35.

Hoffman, L. W. Effects on children: Summary and discussion. In F. I. Nye & L. W. Hoffman (Eds.), *The employed mother in America.* Chicago: Rand McNally, 1963.

Nye, F. I. Marital interaction. In F. I. Nye & L. W. Hoffman (Eds.), *The employed mother in America.* Chicago: Rand McNally, 1963.

Powell, K. S. Maternal employment in relation to family life. *Marriage and Family Living,* 1961, *23,* 350-355.

United States Department of Labor. *Occupational outlook handbook.* (1970-1971 edition) Washington, D.C.: U.S. Government Printing Office, 1971.

NOTE
1. All probability values are based on two-tailed tests.

Conformity,
Compliance, and Obedience

A district Party conference was under way in Moscow Province. It was presided over by a new secretary of the District Party Committee, replacing one recently *arrested*. At the conclusion of the conference, a tribute to Comrade Stalin was called for. Of course, everyone stood up (just as everyone had leaped to his feet during the conference at every mention of his name). The small hall echoed with "stormy applause, rising to an ovation." For three minutes, four minutes, five minutes, the "stormy applause, rising to an ovation," continued. But palms were getting sore and raised arms were already aching. And the older people were panting from exhaustion. It was becoming insufferably silly even to those who really adored Stalin. However, who would dare be the *first* to stop? The secretary of the District

Party Committee could have done it. He was standing on the platform, and it was he who had just called for the ovation. But he was a newcomer. He had taken the place of a man who'd been arrested. He was afraid! After all, NKVD men were standing in the hall applauding and watching to see *who* quit first! And in that obscure, small hall, unknown to the Leader, the applause went on—six, seven, eight minutes! They were done for! Their goose was cooked! They couldn't stop now till they collapsed with heart attacks! At the rear of the hall, which was crowded, they could of course cheat a bit, clap less frequently, less vigorously, not so eagerly—but up there with the presidium where everyone could see them? The director of the local paper factory, an independent and strong-minded man, stood with the presidium. Aware of all the falsity and all the impossibility of the situation, he still kept on applauding! Nine minutes! Ten! In anguish he watched the secretary of the District Party Committee, but the latter dared not stop. Insanity! To the last man! With make-believe enthusiasm on their faces, looking at each other with faint hope, the district leaders were just going to go on and on applauding till they fell where they stood, till they were carried out of the hall on stretchers! And even then those who were left would not falter. . . . Then, after eleven minutes, the director of the paper factory assumed a businesslike expression and sat down in his seat. And, oh, a miracle took place! Where had the universal, uninhibited, indescribable enthusiasm gone? To a man, everyone else stopped dead and sat down. They had been saved! The squirrel had been smart enough to jump off his revolving wheel.

That, however, was how they discovered who the independent people were. And that was how they went about eliminating them. That same night the factory director was arrested. They easily pasted ten years on him on the pretext of something quite different. But after he had signed Form 206, the final document of the interrogation, his interrogator reminded him:

"Don't ever be the first to stop applauding!"

Commentary

The four selections in this chapter deal with various forms of social influence. The terms "conformity," "compliance," and "obedience" refer to different forms of social influence distinguishable from one another by the degree of directness and immediacy of the pressures exerted on the individual. *Conformity* refers to a person's acquiescence to group pressure. As the definition implies, the term encompasses a lot of territory, from adherence to societal norms (such as crossing at the green and not in between) to modifying one's opinion during jury deliberations. A defining characteristic of conforming behavior is that it can occur even in response to group pressure which is neither explicit nor directed specifically at the person but is only subjectively felt. Thus, descriptively, although not necessarily experientially, it is the least direct of the types of social influence considered in this chapter.

Compliance, as distinct from conformity, refers to behavioral acquiescence elicited in a more direct manner via a request, force, or some other form of pressure. *Obedience* refers to compliance at its most extreme. In the social-psychological literature the term almost always is associated with the work of Stanley Milgram (see Selection 4), where obedience refers to total compliance with an experimenter's orders which apparently result in the suffering of another person.

The classic experimental procedure for studying the effects of group pressure on individual judgments was developed by Asch (1958). The Asch conformity paradigm "employed the procedure of placing an individual in a relation of radical conflict with all the other members of a group, of measuring its effect upon him in quantitative terms, and of describing its psychological consequences" (p. 175). Specifically, the subject in Asch's experiments would participate in what was ostensibly a line judgment task in a group setting. The task was to match the length of a line with one of a set of three lines of differing lengths. On each trial each person in the group gave his judgments publicly. All persons in the group, with the exception of the subject, were confederates of the experimenter who were instructed to respond unanimously with incorrect judgments on certain trials. Thus the subject found himself a minority of one, pitted against a unanimous majority. In the words of Asch: "He faced, possibly for the first time in his life, a situation in which a group unanimously contradicted the evidence of his senses" (p. 175). In the basic experiment subjects yielded to the majority on one third of their estimates, on the average.

One of the persisting ambiguities in conformity research is whether or not the subject's yielding to group pressure reflects an actual acceptance of the validity of the majority's judgments or is merely an overt expression of his agreement, although he does not actually believe that his judgment is wrong. On the basis of postexperimental interviews with his subjects, Asch distinguished three categories of yielding: The first category, which he calls distortion of perception, describes subjects who reported perceiving the majority estimates as the correct ones and who were not aware that the judgments of the majority distorted their own. Only a few subjects were in this category. The second category, distortion of judgment, was comprised of subjects who came to believe that their perceptions were not accurate and the majority's were. Most subjects who yielded were in this category. Thus, subjects in both of these categories not only expressed agreement with the majority but also privately believed in the correctness of the majority judgment. Subjects in the third category, distortion of action, privately believed they were right and only appeared to accept the majority's estimates as correct. One limitation in Asch's data bearing on the question of private vs. public acceptance of the majority's judgments is that they were based on subjects' reports or interpretations of what they did, elicited during the postexperimental interview.

One of the major purposes of the study reported in the first selection ("Canned Laughter and Public and Private Conformity," by Nosanchuk and Lightstone) was to provide a more direct determination of the underlying dynamics of yielding by obtaining measures of both public and private conformity within the experiment itself. The subject's task in this experiment was to rate the humorousness of ten anecdotes. The subject sat in a curtained booth and heard the anecdotes through earphones, believing that there were four other subjects in the adjacent booths. In actuality, no other subjects were there, but their presence was simulated through "canned" laughter coming over the intercom during the reading of half of the anecdotes. The subject's written ratings of the anecdotes represented the measure of private conformity, while his audible reactions (picked up by a microphone) defined public conformity. Nosanchuk and Lightstone compared subjects' reactions to the anecdotes when they were accompanied by canned laughter and when they were not. The general finding was that public conformity was much greater than private conformity. Although the written ratings (the private conformity measure) indicated that anecdotes accompanied by a laughter tape tended to be judged as funnier than those not accompanied by canned laughter, this difference was only marginally significant statistically. On the other hand, the audible responses (the public conformity measure) in the "canned laughter" condition were significantly louder than were the ones in the "no laughter" condition.

Assuming that we can generalize from this study to the kinds of conformity pressures encountered in daily life, does the relatively weak effect of group pressure on private conformity minimize the potential importance of that pressure? Not necessarily. Kiesler (1969), using the example of parents teaching children acceptable social behaviors, points out that most parents prefer that their children believe in the validity of their wishes, but they will settle for overt behavioral conformity even without inner acceptance by the child. Thus it is important to know about the factors influencing public conformity even when it is not accompanied by private conformity.[1]

A defining characteristic of conformity pressures on an individual in a group is that they are rarely directly applied; that is, a person is not usually explicitly requested to go along with the group. The rest of the selections in this chapter move to more direct, one-to-one types of social influence, characterized by one person's attempt to elicit behavioral compliance in another through some form of direct request. Each of the articles is addressed to different techniques for eliciting compliance, and they are arranged sequentially to correspond to the increasing magnitude of the situational forces confronting the individual.

The paper by Pliner et al. (Selection 2, "Compliance without Pressure: Some Further Data on the Foot-in-the-Door Technique") describes a study which attempted to replicate a technique for inducing compliance which was first demonstrated by Freedman and Fraser (1966). Freedman and Fraser demonstrated that a person who first complies with a small request is more likely to agree to a larger request later than would a person who had not first complied with a small request. The study by Pliner et al. reprinted here tried to replicate the foot-in-the-door effect, but with some differences designed to elucidate the effect. For example, Pliner et al. used a measure of actual compliance (donation of money) to test the effect rather than verbal intention to comply, as had Freedman and Fraser. What is the explanation for the foot-in-the-door phenomenon? After ruling out other explanations, Freedman and Fraser had suggested that the mediating mechanism may be a change in self-image. That is, once the person has complied with the small request, "he may become, in his own eyes, the kind of person who does this sort of thing, who agrees to requests made by strangers, who takes action on things he believes in, who cooperates with good causes" (p. 201). The findings of Pliner and her colleagues are in line with this explanation, which, they point out, is very much akin to Bem's self-perception theory (one of the attribution theories presented in Chapter I). Bem's theory states that we make inferences about ourselves on the basis of observations of our own actions. Further evidence for the self-perception explanation of the foot-in-the-door effect has recently been provided by Snyder and Cunningham (1975).

The hypnotized subject has long epitomized the maximally compliant person. Most of us have seen stage hypnotists getting volunteers to comply with a variety of posthypnotic suggestions such as scratching the head on hearing a cue word or reporting that a sweet drink is bitter. Scientific investigators of hypnosis are in disagreement about how to conceptualize hypnotic phenomena. One view holds that it is meaningful to consider hypnosis as an altered state or trance that is qualitatively distinct from the usual states of wakefulness or sleep. Others, the nonstate theorists, hold that the findings of hypnosis research "can be more parsimoniously conceptualized in terms of constructs that are already an integral part of contemporary social psychology" (Spanos & Barber, 1974, p. 500). Specifically, "the guiding assumption of the nonstate theorists [is] that the good hypnotic subject is not fundamentally different from the normal individual who is cooperating in a social situation in which he is asked to experience suggested effects" (p. 509).

The findings reported in Selection 3 ("Effects of 'Hypnosis' and Task Motivational Instructions in Attempting to Influence the 'Voluntary' Self-Deprivation of Money," by Wickramasekera) provide some input for this controversy. In this study subjects preselected for superior hypnotic ability were assigned either to an experimental group which received a standard hypnotic induction or to a control group which was not hypnotized but was given instructions intended to heighten task motivation. Subjects in both groups received a posthypnotic suggestion telling them not to collect the $5 they had been promised for their participation. Although no subject in either condition requested payment immediately after the experiment, subjects in the hypnosis group waited significantly longer before calling in for their money than did the control subjects. The study provided no evidence for the qualitative distinctiveness of the hypnotic state, but it did show that there is a distinction in terms of behavioral consequences between the hypnotized subject and one who is merely highly motivated to carry out the experimenter's instructions.

The last selection in this chapter ("Obedience to Criminal Orders: The Compulsion to Do Evil," by Milgram) examines the dynamics of the most extreme kind of compliance: obedience by a person to an authority who tells him to administer shocks of increasing intensity to another person. Milgram's laboratory experiments on obedience, first reported by him in the early 1960s, continue to evoke the interest of both layman and professional. In a recent book about his work, Milgram (1974) states the basic question to which his studies were addressed: "If an experimenter tells a subject to act with increasing severity against another person, under what conditions will the subject comply, and under what conditions will he disobey?" (p. xii). The article reprinted here describes Milgram's studies and the thought-provoking conclusions he derives from them.

REFERENCES

Asch, S. E. Effects of group pressure upon the modification and distortion of judgments. In E. E. Maccoby, T. M. Newcomb, & E. L. Hartley (Eds.), *Readings in social psychology* (3rd ed.). New York: Holt, Rinehart & Winston, 1958. Pp. 174-183.

Freedman, J. L., & Fraser, S. C. Compliance without pressure: The foot-in-the-door technique. *Journal of Personality and Social Psychology,* 1966, *4,* 195-202.

Kiesler, C. A. Group pressure and conformity. In J. Mills (Ed.), *Experimental social psychology.* New York: Macmillan, 1969. Pp. 233-306.

Milgram, S. *Obedience to authority.* New York: Harper & Row, 1974.

Snyder, M., & Cunningham, M. R. To comply or not comply: Testing the self-perception explanation of the "foot-in-the-door" phenomenon. *Journal of Personality and Social Psychology,* 1975, *31,* 64-67.

Spanos, N. P., & Barber, T. X. Toward a convergence in hypnosis research. *American Psychologist,* 1974, *29,* 500-511.

NOTE

1. The distinction between overt action and private beliefs will be encountered again in the chapter on attitudes and attitude change (Chapter VII). As we shall see, according to the theory of cognitive dissonance the discrepancy between beliefs and actions can often lead to attitude change.

1

T. A. NOSANCHUK and JACK LIGHTSTONE

Canned Laughter and Public and Private Conformity

In order to examine conformity pressures in everyday situations while simultaneously avoiding the pressures placed on subjects by the Asch-type paradigm, subjects judged jokes, and the authors used "canned" laughter to provide conformity pressure. Each of 40 university undergraduates (20 males, 20 females), randomly assigned to one of four experimental groups, judged the quality of 10 short anecdotes while in a curtained booth. Each believed himself to be one of five subjects in booths similar to his own. A laughter tape was used to make the subject believe that he was hearing the reactions of his fellow subjects and was also being heard by them. Experimental conditions included positive stimuli with poor anecdotes, negative stimuli with good anecdotes, and perceived complete privacy with the belief that the microphones in the booths were turned off. The various experimental groups were so constituted that each was a control for the others. Data included the privately recorded judgments of the subject under the various experimental conditions (enabling the measurements of private conformity) and a record of any of the subject's oral reactions during the experiment (a measurement of his public conformity). Substantial differences in public relative to private conformity were found.

The present study on conformity is the product of three separate concerns: The first is theoretical, in that when using "standard" conformity paradigms (e.g., Asch, 1958; Crutchfield, 1955), it is very difficult to distinguish between purely verbal public utterances which the subject consciously believes erroneous and private conformity in which the subject comes to believe that the judgments made by the majority are the correct ones. This determination has typically been made during the debriefing (e.g., see Asch, 1958), and, as a result, it is likely to be in error.

Source: T. A. Nosanchuk and Jack Lightstone, "Canned Laughter and Public and Private Conformity," *Journal of Personality and Social Psychology,* 1974, *29,* 153-156. Copyright 1974 by the American Psychological Association. Reprinted by permission.

This article was presented at the Canadian Sociology and Anthropology Association meetings in Montreal, May 31, 1972. The research was supported by a departmental seed grant.

The second concern relates to the ethics of conformity research. Subjects typically have found participation in such studies extremely painful. This should not surprise us when we realize that for perhaps the first time in a subject's life, his own sense impressions and verbal reports of others are in sharp disagreement. Without going too deeply into ethical issues, most researchers would probably agree that such painful paradigms are more nearly justifiable when they are likely to yield new and important findings. Since students, in the course of training, are likely to want to replicate one of these studies, implying little chance of such findings, this issue becomes rather more important.

The third concern is what Aronson and Carlsmith (1968) referred to as the problems of experimental and mundane realism. The usual conformity paradigm, perhaps because of its almost Kafkaesque quality, tends to be extremely compelling for the subject, making it high on experimental realism. But this unreal quality renders it low on mundane realism making generalizations difficult. Berger (1963) argued that if we can so extract conformity in cases where objective truth can be verified by use of objective measuring devices, such as a ruler in the case of the relative length of line segments,

it should not surprise us, consequently, that our group opinions in political, ethical, aesthetic matters should exercise even greater force, since the individual thus pressured cannot have desperate recourse to a political, ethical, or aesthetic measure [p. 120].

However, it may be due to the unusual setting for disagreement that causes conformity to be so easily obtained; that is, people are accustomed to disagreeing about politics and ethics but not about measurable objective issues.

The present authors take the view that having subjects make judgments of the funniness of anecdotes while hearing the laughter (i.e., judgments) of other putative subjects provide a paradigm capable of coping with the three concerns. It would be difficult to deny the applicability of an experiment based on this situation to the real world in the light of the television industry's use of such a stimulus in its liberal use of "canned laughter." Sitting in our living rooms, then, we are subjected to a stimulus which is subtle (for so we experience it) yet believed to be capable of exacting "conformity" (as indeed the industry vows by its continued use), with practically no cognitive pressure being felt on the part of the "victim," even in the absence of any real group at all.

Furthermore, the experimenter using such a paradigm can make a comparison which the television industry cannot: By obtaining the subject's written judgments as well as his audible reactions to the stimulus, it appears possible to measure separately both private and public conformity.

Generally, the present experiment consisted of playing a tape containing 10 jokes to each subject and having him give a written rating of each, as well as, unknown to the subject, recording a written judgment of any of his audible reactions or responses. More precisely the 10 jokes were made up of two matched sets of 5 (Set A and Set B), the matching being based on 20 judges' evaluations in a pilot study. The jokes ranged from quite funny to extremely unfunny and pointless. Since the pilot study also found an order effect, that is, latter jokes tend to be evaluated more funny than early ones, half of the groups received Set A first and half, Set B first.

In addition, the subjects were led to believe that for half of the jokes the intercom system linking them to the four other (putative) subjects was live and that they were hearing the audible reactions of these subjects (and, reciprocally, that they were being heard by them). Half of the subjects heard this "laughter tape" (conformity pressure) with the first set of jokes presented to them, and half with the second set. Thus we have four experimental groups: (a) Set A—laughter tape, Set B—no tape; (b) Set A—no tape, Set B—tape; (c) Set B—tape, Set A, no tape; and (d) Set B—no tape, Set A—tape.

METHOD

Each of 40 university undergraduates (20 males, and 20 females) recruited from students studying in the Carleton University library was randomly assigned to one of the four treatments. Each was placed in a curtained booth believing that four other subjects occupied the adjacent enclosures. The subject found before him a set of headphones, a microphone, and an evaluation form on which he was to record his judgments. He was instructed to put on the headphones as soon as he was seated. The following instructions were then read to all of the subjects:

You are about to take part in a short experiment—a study on the judgment of humor being done by members of the sociology department. Ten short, pretaped anecdotes will be played into the intercommunications system connecting the five booths. After each anecdote you are asked simply to record your judgment on the answer sheet in front of you.

The subjects in Groups 1 and 3 then listened to the first set of five anecdotes believing that the intercom system linking the booths was open and that they were hearing the audible reactions (i.e., laughter) of four other subjects. At this point the experimenter appeared and apologized for his mistake of leaving the intercom open. He then ostensibly turned off the intercom, and the second set of anecdotes was then read to the subject without the laughter tape. For Groups 2 and 4 the procedure was reversed;

that is, after the first set of jokes was read, the experimenter explained that the intercom system was not supposed to be closed in this condition and apologized for his mistake, and then the second set of anecdotes was heard accompanied by the tape.

We therefore obtained a written record of each subject's judgment (our measure of private conformity) as well as, by means of the very sensitive microphone in the booth, an accurate record of any of the subject's audible reactions during the experiment for both stimulated and unstimulated conditions.

There was one additional complication in the design. The two joke sets, A and B, were each composed of three moderately funny jokes, one very funny joke, and one pointless and unfunny joke. Moreover, the canned laughter was at a moderate (i.e., appropriate) level for the moderate jokes, an inappropriately high level for the unfunny joke, and an equally inappropriately low level for the very funny joke. Thus, we provided analogues of the differential discrepancies in the usual conformity experiment.

The data were scored as follows: The written responses were scored from 0 (not funny at all) to 4 (extremely funny), and the audible reactions were also scored from 0 (no noticeable sound) to 4 (loud laughter). Intercoder reliability for the audible responses was .90.

TABLE 1.1
Means of the Written Responses

Condition (jokes)	Group			
	1	2	3	4
First half	1.58[a]	1.64	1.36[a]	1.38
Second half	1.48	2.20[a]	1.38	1.46[a]
Total	1.53	1.92	1.37	1.42

Note: For the tape conditions, $\bar{X} = 1.65$; for the no-tape conditions, $\bar{X} = 1.47$; $t = 1.567$, $df = 398$, $.05 < p < .10$.
[a]Laughter tape sessions.

TABLE 1.2
Means of Audible Responses

Condition (jokes)	Group			
	1	2	3	4
First half	1.18[a]	.64	1.18[a]	.36
Second half	.44	1.10[a]	.62	1.16[a]
Total	.81	.87	.90	.76

Note: For the tape conditions, $\bar{X} = 1.16$; for the no-tape conditions, $\bar{X} = .52$; $t = 5.732$, $df = 398$, $p < .01$.
[a]Laughter tape sessions.

RESULTS AND DISCUSSION

Table 1.1 gives the means for the written responses for the first half and the second half of the jokes. While the difference is in the predicted direction and is fairly consistent within the body of Table 1.1, it is quite small and of only moderate significance. It appears, then, that overall the level of private conformity as we have defined it here is rather low.

The means for the audible reactions are presented in Table 1.2. Compared to the means for private conformity, these differences are almost startlingly large. Although the overall audible response rate was rarely large and averaged less than 1.0, it was consistently and substantially greater for subjects in the stimulated conditions.

It may be possible to take the view that for three of the five jokes at least in the stimulated condition, we are not really obtaining conformity which is defined by Wheeler (1968) as a conflict produced in the subject

by the judgments of other individuals. The conflict is between making the subjectively and objectively veridical but socially rejected judgment and making the subjectively . . . counter-factual but socially-accepted judgment. . . . The actions of the other individuals create the conflict and do not aid in the resolution of the conflict [p. 191].

After all, for the three moderately funny jokes, the level of laughter was at an appropriate level. We might argue that people laugh at jokes if they are funny and if laughter is facilitated, as in the present study by laughter tape. This interpretation is consistent with Thorpe's (as quoted in Wheeler, 1968) definition of facilitation which is said to occur when "the performance of a more or less instinctive pattern of behaviour by one

TABLE 1.3
Means of Written and Audible Responses for Poor and Good Jokes

Response	$\bar{X}$	t
Written		
Poor joke		
Tape	1.3	3.318*
No tape	.7	
Good joke		
Tape	1.5	.854
No tape	1.7	
Audible		
Poor joke		
Tape	1.2	4.843*
No tape	.2	
Good joke		
Tape	1.2	2.350*
No tape	.6	

*$p < .01$.

member of a species will tend to act as a release for the same behaviour in another or others . . . [p. 192]."

If this argument were correct, we would expect our two inappropriately stimulated anecdotes to be accurately evaluated privately (e.g., no conformity), to generate little audible response in the unstimulated condition, and to generate an appropriate level of audible response in the stimulated condition. The means for the written responses to these two joke types are presented in Table 1.3. The effect of the inappropriately low level of laughter was a slight depression in the rating of the good jokes, while too much laughter on the tape substantially increased the rating of the poor jokes, both results being in the direction predicted by the conformity view.

The audible responses similarly supported the conformity view. There was some audible response in the unstimulated conditions and an inappropriate amount in the stimulated conditions. (The observed responses might have been appropriate to one pair of the jokes; they could have scarely been appropriate to both.) In short, on this evidence, we would reject the facilitation argument in favor of the conformity view.

In examining the individual response patterns of subjects, two emerged as most prevalent. The most common pattern, visible in the responses of about 40% of the subjects, was one in which the audible response was almost completely absent during the unstimulated condition and appeared at a more or less stable level all the way through the stimulated condition. This pattern was observed regardless of whether the unstimulated preceded the stimulated or vice versa. About 28% of the subjects showed a similar audible pattern, but unlike the first group which occasionally conformed privately, these subjects never conformed privately. Approximately 10% of the subjects seemed, in contrast to those mentioned above, to be conforming privately but without any audible responses at all. Lastly, about 7% of the subjects showed patterns definite enough to suspect that they conformed to the stimuli both publicly and privately, while the remaining 15% exhibited diverse behaviors.

Debriefing was a particularly pleasant and easy task for this study. Because subjects felt neither intimidated nor emotionally strained they were curious and friendly. Most subjects were interested enough to ask about the study's place in the general framework of theory, and as such the whole relationship of the study to the Asch paradigm had to be explained countless times. Conspicuously absent were questions by the subject as to how he had done, whether he had conformed, and other signs of anxiety exhibited by subjects of conformity studies. The television industry's use of canned laughter was often the perspective from which the subjects approached his experience.

The subject was then thanked, and more often than not the experimenter was thanked in return for an interesting time and for a pleasant and welcome diversion from work. No complaints as to the ethics of the experiment were registered, although each subject was asked, and each was told that his opinion in this matter was of vital importance to the study.

In summary, then, we believe that we have accomplished our objective: Our paradigm for studying conformity appears to be high in mundane as well as in experimental realism, appears to distinguish between public and private conformity, and seems to be quite painless for the subjects. In addition, it is quite easy to run, making it a suitable paradigm for students interested in conceptually replicating the various conformity studies.

REFERENCES

Aronson, E., & Carlsmith, J. M. Experimentation in social psychology. In G. Lindzey & E. Aronson (Eds.), *Handbook of social psychology.* (2nd ed.) Vol. 2. Cambridge, Mass.: Addison-Wesley, 1968.

Asch, S. E. Effects of group pressures upon modification and distortion of judgments. In E. E. Maccoby, T. M. Newcomb, & E. L. Hartley (Eds.), *Readings in social psychology.* (3rd ed.) New York: Holt, Rinehart & Winston, 1958.

Berger, P. L. *Invitation to sociology.* Garden City, N.Y.: Anchor Books, 1963.

Crutchfield, R. S. Conformity and character. *American Psychologist,* 1955, *10,* 191-198.

Wheeler, L. Behavioral contagion: Theory and research. In E. C. Simmel, R. A. Hoppe, & G. A. Milton (Eds.), *Social facilitation and imitative behavior.* Boston: Allyn & Bacon, 1968.

2

PATRICIA PLINER, HEATHER HART, JOANNE KOHL, and DORY SAARI

Compliance without Pressure: Some Further Data on the Foot-in-the-Door Technique

A replication of the Freedman and Fraser (1966) "foot-in-the-door" technique was attempted in which subjects were exposed to one of two prior requests and were then asked to comply with a larger request. The results showed that subjects receiving prior requests complied with the larger request significantly more often than did control subjects. The mechanism by which the technique operates was discussed.

As a part of a recent series of studies designed to investigate methods for obtaining behavioral compliance with minimal pressure, Freedman and Fraser (1966) have described a procedure known as the foot-in-the-door technique. This technique is based on the notion that "once a person has been induced to comply with a small request, he is more likely to comply with a larger demand" (Freedman & Fraser, 1966). In an experiment designed to demonstrate this technique, Freedman and Fraser asked a group of women to answer a few questions about the household products they used. Subsequently, these women were more likely than appropriate controls to report themselves willing to comply with a larger request involving the examination of the products in their cupboards and closets by a survey team. In a second study, homeowners who had received a request to sign a petition or to place a small sign in the front windows of their houses were more likely than controls to agree to the placement of a large, unattractive sign in their yards.

Freedman and Fraser suggested that the mechanism underlying these increases in compliance is based on a person's feelings about getting involved or taking action. When an individual agrees to perform the small prior request, he begins to think of himself as the "kind of person who does this sort of thing . . . who cooperates with good causes." It is this self-perception that increases the likelihood that he will comply with a larger request. This hypothesis is closely related to Bem's (1970) theory of self-perception which asserts that an individual infers his attitudes and beliefs from self-observation of his behavior. Thus in Bem's terms, com-

Source: *Journal of Experimental Social Psychology*, 1974, *10*, 17–22. Copyright © 1974 by Academic Press, Inc. All rights reserved.

pliance with a small request causes the subject to infer that he has a positive attitude toward cooperating with good causes; in turn, this positive attitude leads to compliance with the larger request.

The present investigation was designed as a conceptual replication of the Freedman and Fraser studies; however, a few differences were built into the study in an attempt to shed some additional light on the foot-in-the-door phenomenon.

1. In the Freedman and Fraser studies the dependent variable was discrete; subjects agreed or not to the large request, while in the present experiment the dependent variable could be treated either as a continuous or a discrete one. Subjects were asked to make a monetary contribution to charity; therefore, it was possible either to look at whether or not subjects donated or to look at the amounts of money donated. Such a dependent variable makes it possible to determine whether the foot-in-the-door technique operates to produce a change in the likelihood of compliance or to modulate the amount of compliance in those already inclined to comply, or both.
2. In order to determine whether the size of the prior request had any effect on compliance with the large request, the present study manipulated the size of the prior request; in one condition it was small and in a second condition, it was of moderate size.
3. In the present study, the dependent variable was subjects' actual compliance with the large request rather than their reported willingness to comply. This modification was included because of the frequently noted lack of correspondence between what subjects say they will do and what they actually do (e.g., LaPiere, 1934).

METHOD

Overview

The experiment was conducted in the context of canvassing for funds for a charitable organization. The prior requests consisted of asking the subject (and a member of his family, in one condition) to wear a pin publicizing the fund drive. The large request consisted of asking the subject to donate money to the charitable organization.

Subjects

Subjects were 88 householders living in suburban Toronto. An individual was automatically considered to be a subject if he opened the door of his home to a canvasser for the Cancer Society. Subjects were approximately evenly divided into males and females, and their estimated ages ranged from 17 to 60.

Procedure

Establishment of Experimental Conditions. The area assigned to be canvassed contained a total of 108 houses; each house was randomly assigned to one of three experimental conditions.

1. Small Prior Request. The evening before the experimenter canvassed for donations, another young woman rang the door bell, explained that she was from the Cancer Society, and asked the person answering the door if he would wear a plastic daffodil lapel pin the next day to publicize the fund drive. When the individual answering the door agreed (and all did), he or she was thanked and given a lapel pin to wear.
2. Moderate Prior Request. This condition was exactly the same as the preceding condition except that the person answering the door was asked if he would wear a lapel pin himself the next day and persuade another member of his family to do the same. Again, all subjects complied with the request.
3. No Prior Request. Subjects in this condition were not contacted at all before the experimenter canvassed for donations.

Houses which had originally been assigned to either the Small or Moderate Prior Request conditions but at which no one answered the door on the evening on which the experimental conditions were established were eliminated from the experiment. There were two such houses in each of the Prior Request conditions. In addition, 16 houses were eliminated because no one answered the door on the evening on which canvassing took place. The final number of houses in each of the conditions was: No Prior Request, 35; Small Prior Request, 27; Moderate Prior Request, 26.

Large Request. On the evening following the establishment of the Prior Request conditions the experimenter, who was blind to the experimental conditions, went to each of the houses to collect donations. At each house she gave a standard speech to whomever answered the door:

"Hello, my name is _____, and I'm canvassing for the Cancer Society. Would you like to make a contribution?"

RESULTS

Table 2.1 shows the number of subjects in each condition who compiled with the large request to donate money. Only 45.7% of subjects in the No Prior Request condition made donations as compared with 74.1%

TABLE 2.1
Number of Subjects in Each Experimental Condition Complying
with Request to Donate Money

	No Request	Small Request	Moderate Request
Complies	16	20	21
Does not comply	19	7	5
Total	35	27	26

and 80.8% of subjects in the Small and Moderate Prior request conditions, respectively. Subjects in both the Small ($x^2 = 3.94$, corrected for continuity, $p < .05$) and Moderate ($x = 6.28$ corrected for continuity, $p < .02$). Prior Request conditions were significantly more likely to make a donation than No Prior Request subjects.[1] There was no significant difference between the Small and Moderate Prior Request conditions.

If the data are analyzed in terms of the amounts of money donated by subjects in each of the experimental conditions, the results are similar. Subjects in the No Prior Request condition donated on the average $.58 while Small and Moderate Prior Request subjects donated $.98 and $.87, respectively. Subjects in the conditions in which prior requests were made donated significantly more than did subjects in the No Prior Request condition ($F = (1.85) = 5.15$, $p < .05$) but the Small and Moderate Prior Request conditions did not differ from one another.

A greater number of subjects in the Small and Moderate Prior Request conditions donated money than in the No Prior Request condition. In addition, subjects in the Small and Moderate Prior Request conditions donated more money on the average than those in the No Prior Request condition. This raises the issue of whether the differences in average amounts donated in the various conditions are accounted for entirely by the differences in number of donors or at least in part by varying degrees of generosity per donor from condition to condition. In order to resolve this question, nondonors were eliminated from the analysis and the contributions of donors were compared. When this was done, the three groups did not differ at all in mean contribution. Thus the Prior Request seemed to have an all-or-none effect on the probability of a donation rather than a moderating effect on the size of a donation once a subject decided to contribute.

DISCUSSION

In the present study, subjects who complied with a previous request were clearly more likely to comply with a subsequent larger request.[2] Thus the outcome of the experiment confirms the Freedman and Fraser (1966) results and extends them in two respects. First, subjects did not simply offer a promise of compliance with a larger request, but actually were more likely to donate money. Thus, the prior requests had a measurable effect on action and not just on verbal behavior. Second, the use of a continuous dependent variable permitted a conclusion about the operation of the mechanism mediating the compliance phenomenon. Subjects in the various conditions did not differ significantly in the magnitude of their generosity but in the likelihood that they would manifest generosity. This suggests that the prior requests operated to produce a quantal shift in the threshold for giving rather than to modulate existing degrees of generosity. Such a result is consistent with the hypothesis that compliance with a small request shifts an individual's self-perception to one of "the kind of person who does this sort of thing," thereby changing the probability of compliance. Had the experimental manipulation also affected the amount of money donated, this "change of self-image" explanation would be less appropriate since its implication is one of a qualitative rather than quantitative change in self-perception.

If the "self-perception" hypothesis is correct, our data suggest that a comparatively trivial behavior is sufficient to generate the self-perception that one is "in favor of cooperating with good causes." The small and moderate prior requests were equally effective in eliciting donating behavior, and according to the present analysis, must have been equally effective in inducing such self-perceptions. Evidently, the relatively minor behavior of agreeing to wear a daffodil pin was sufficient to have a substantial effect on the process mediating later giving behavior. Because of this there may have been a ceiling effect which militated against finding an effect of size of prior request.

REFERENCES

Bem, D. J. *Beliefs, attitudes and human affairs.* Belmont, Cal.: Brooks/Cole, 1970.

Freedman, J. L., & Fraser, S. C. Compliance without pressure: The foot-in-the-door technique. *Journal of Personality and Social Psychology,* 1966, *4,* 195-202.

LaPiere, R. T. Attitudes vs. actions. *Social Forces,* 1934, *13,* 230-237.

NOTES

1. It may have occurred to the reader that some subjects in the conditions in which prior requests were made may not, in fact, have received them since another member of the household could have answered the door during the prior request manipulation. In an attempt to identify cases in which this may have happened,

the experimenter, after making the large request and receiving a donation or not, asked at all houses "Did someone else from the Cancer Society come by last night and ask you to wear a daffodil today?" With reasonable confidence it may be assumed that those who responded in the negative were never exposed to the request. There were five such subjects in the Small Prior Request condition and three in the Large Prior Request condition. If these subjects are eliminated from the analysis, the data improve slightly with 77.2% and 82.6% of subjects in the Small and Moderate Request conditions making donations. The experimenter also asked subjects who reported receiving the prior requests whether or not they had complied. Two in each of the prior request conditions admitted that they had not. If these subjects, too, are eliminated, the data improve still further with 85.0% and 85.7% of subjects in the Small and Moderate Prior Request conditions making donations.

2. An alternative explanation which must be considered is that the prior requests were effective simply because they increased the salience of the Cancer Society fund drive. Two sources tend to rule out such an explanation. First, heavy media publicity for the drive had already given it a great deal of salience; an informal survey conducted during the week of the fund drive indicated that 11 of 13 people were aware of it. Consequently, it is likely that salience was also quite high for subjects in all three experimental conditions. Second, when Freedman and Fraser (1966) actually manipulated salience without a prior request, they found that it had no effect on later compliance.

3

IAN WICKRAMASEKERA

Effects of "Hypnosis" and Task Motivational Instructions in Attempting to Influence the "Voluntary" Self-Deprivation of Money

Excellent hypnotic subjects, similarly selected and treated, were given a posthypnotic suggestion under two apparently different conditions. Subjects in the experimental condition were administered the suggestion after a standardized "hypnotic" induction. Subjects in the control condition received the same suggestion after a set of task motivational instructions. The suggestion given within the context of the procedure labeled "hypnosis" appeared to be more effective.

"A post hypnotic suggestion refers to a suggestion given to a hypnotized person to behave in a specified manner after the termination of the trance [Barber, 1962, p. 321]." Erickson and Erickson (1941) have described posthypnotic behavior as being involuntary, quasi-automatic, and compulsive. Barber (1969) has challenged the above view and stated: "A hypnotic induction (and presumed "hypnotic trance state") is not necessary to elicit compliance with a suggestion to perform specified acts, post-experimentally [p. 205]."

Two hypotheses can be derived from the above empirical generalization. The first hypothesis stated by Barber (1969) was: "It can be hypothesized that hypnotic and nonhypnotic subjects will not comply with suggestions to carry out post-experimental acts if they are led to believe that the experimenter will not know whether or not they complied [p. 205]." A study by Orne, Sheehan, and Evans (1968) claims to have demonstrated that the posthypnotic behavior of excellent hypnotic subjects is independent of the knowledge or presence of the experimenter. In the Orne et al. study, the posthypnotic test was administered by the experimenter's secretary. Hence, the subjects had reason to believe that she would report

Source: Ian Wickramasekera, "Effects of 'Hypnosis' and Task Motivational Instructions in Attempting to Influence the 'Voluntary' Self-Deprivation of Money," *Journal of Personality and Social Psychology*, 1971, *19*, 311-314. Copyright 1971 by the American Psychological Association. Reprinted by permission.

The author would like to acknowledge his appreciation to C. H. Patterson for his critical reactions to this study and to Christie Drockelman for typing the manuscript.

their responses to the experimenter. It appears therefore that Barber's (1969) hypothesis was not adequately tested by the Orne et al. study.

A second hypothesis is that there will be no statistically significant difference between hypnotized and nonhypnotized excellent hypnotic subjects on a postexperimental act if they are similarly selected and treated. The present study tested this second hypothesis.

METHOD

Subjects

The subjects in this study were undergraduate college students, white females, between the ages of 18 and 20, who agreed to participate in a "hypnosis-imagination emotional arousal study" for the payment of $5. Subjects were told specifically that they would not be paid for the group screening on the Harvard scale (used as a preliminary test to select subjects with superior hypnotic ability) and that the author intended to measure with the galvanic skin response the degree of emotional arousal when certain events were imagined. From the large pool of subjects who offered themselves for group screening, the first 20 subjects who scored between 10 and 12 on the Harvard scale were selected for the study. The 20 subjects were randomly assigned equally to control and experimental groups. All 20 subjects were told: "You will be paid $5 for your participation in this emotional arousal study, immediately after your individual session with me." All procedures were administered by the author.

The subjects assigned to the hypnosis group were "induced" individually with the Barber (1969) hypnotic induction procedure and then given the following suggestions from the Stanford Hypnotic Susceptibility

TABLE 3.1
Number of Hours that Elapsed since Delivery of the Suggestion and Request for the Payment Check in the Hypnosis and Task Motivational Groups

Subject	Hypnosis Group	Task Motivational Group
1	312	22
2	172	200
3	196	29
4	213	30
5	288	46
6	129	38
7	330	112
8	312	143
9	240	21
10	360	6

Scale (Form C and Profile Scale) and the Barber Suggestibility Scale: (*a*) thirst hallucination (1 minute), (*b*) taste hallucination (2½ minutes), (*c*) hand analgesia (1½ minutes), (*d*) heat hallucination (2 minutes), and (*e*) a posthypnotic suggestion.

Subjects in the control group were individually administered the Barber task motivation instructions (Barber, 1969, p. 46) and told: "Please close your eyes, and imagine what I ask you to, without being hypnotized. It is important that you do not become hypnotized." Control subjects were asked to imagine the following scenes: (*a*) drinking their favorite beverage (1 minute), (*b*) eating their favorite food (2½ minutes), (*c*) putting on their favorite clothes (1½ minutes), (*d*) taking a warm shower (2 minutes), and (*e*) posthypnotic suggestion.

The following posthypnotic suggestion was read to both the control and experimental subjects:

Please pay close attention to what I am going to say to you now. In a few minutes I will ask you to open your eyes. You will then have the opportunity to collect $5 for your participation in this study. After you open your eyes you will start to feel something very interesting. You will notice no desire to accept payment for your participation in this pleasant and unusual study. In fact, you will even feel a certain pride in giving freely of your time for the advancement of science. You will not want to cheapen what you have done today by placing a price on it. You will find it much easier and more personally satisfying to ignore entirely the fact that you previously agreed to take money for the privilege of participating in this study. You will feel a certain pride in your inner freedom to refuse money for your participation in this test of your imagination.

All subjects were connected to a galvanic skin response machine (LaFayette Model 760C) before the induction procedure. The following instructions were read to both the control and experimental subjects after they had opened their eyes:

Thank you for your participation in this study. Your $5 is in an envelope with your name on it on the table in the next room. You may pick it up on your way out or you can have it mailed to you by calling this number (they were handed the experimenter's telephone number at his home) any time of the night or day. If you have not called me within 15 days, I will assume that you do not want the money, and I will dispose of it.

RESULTS

The data analyzed in this study consisted of the *number of hours* elapsed between the delivery of the posthypnotic suggestion and the receipt of the telephone call from the subject requesting that her check be mailed (see Table 3.1). This type of data can be regarded as interval scale data, but to avoid the restrictive assumptions associated with parametric statistical procedures and because of the very small size of the present sample, the data were analyzed with the Wilcoxon matched-pairs signed-ranks test. The test indicated a statistically significant difference between the data for the hypnotic group and the "task motivational" group. Since the direction of the difference was predicted beforehand, the null hypothesis was rejected at the .005 level for a one-tailed test. No checks were picked up on the way out, immediately after the experimental or control procedures. One subject did not request payment at the end of the experimental period and refused payment even afterward.

DISCUSSION

Currently, there appears to be no objective independent means of inferring the existence of an altered hypnotic state of consciousness. A small number of imaginative experiments (Bower & Pribram;[1] Deckert, 1964; Parrish, Lundy, & Leibowitz, 1969) suggest a direction from which this kind of independent specification may come. It appears, however, that recent reviews do not mention these studies in the above specific context.

From the point of view of controlling and predicting the behavior of the subjects in this study, the determination of whether or not they were hypnotized does not seem important, but what appears to be demonstrated is that there is a difference in the degree of subject compliance with verbal instructions when such instructions are given within the context of a procedure labeled hypnosis, as compared with the same instructions given within the context of a procedure not labeled hypnosis.

It may be argued that this study simply illustrates compliant behavior. This is specifically what the author was attempting to demonstrate and measure. Future studies can test the strength of similarly developed compliant behaviors by manipulating upward the quantity of money or the quantity of time associated with the verbal suggestions (i.e., $100 and a 30-day deadline, etc.). The voluntary-involuntary dimension formulation, although an intellectually interesting one, does not seem to have much relevance to the practical problems of the stimulus control of behavior.

It may also be argued that the procedure used with control subjects reduced their motivation to comply with the posthypnotic suggestion. For example, screening the controls with a hypnotic procedure, but failing to test them with it, may have been a "letdown" for them. On the other hand, it may be argued that it made the experiment more interesting to them because they were exposed to a variety of procedures (hypnotic instructions plus task motivational instructions). If the experience of the control subject was more interesting, it was better fitted to the common rationale (e.g., since this was an interesting experience, you should not accept payment for participating in it) which the subjects were offered for complying with the posthypnotic suggestion. Hence, it may be argued that rather than being let down, they had a motivational advantage over the hypnotic subjects.

It has been empirically demonstrated (Barber, 1969) that task motivational instructions can elicit a degree of compliance equal to hypnotic instructions. In the present study, such task motivational instructions were used to elicit posthypnotic compliance. Hence, the control subjects were treated with a procedure that has appeared to be equally powerful. The speculation that changing motivational procedures (hypnotic screening to task motivational instructions) reduces the probability of compliance remains to be empirically demonstrated.

It may also be argued that since the control subjects were not hypnotized, they were not led to believe that the experimenter expected them to comply with the posthypnotic suggestion. For example, telling the control subjects not to become hypnotized may have implied that they were not expected to comply with the posthypnotic suggestion. Also, the control subjects were given tests that were similar to but different from those that were given to the hypnotic subjects. It may be argued that these tests were less pleasant than those that were given to the hypnotic subjects. If they were experienced as less pleasant, this may have implied to the control subjects that the rationale for complying with the posthypnotic suggestion was not intended to apply to them. From the above rationale, it may be inferred that the experimenter was covertly telling the control subjects in at least two ways that he did not expect them to comply with his posthypnotic suggestion.

First, it is a matter of empirical fact that all of the control subjects complied to some degree with the posthypnotic suggestion. Second, it is also a fact that three of the control subjects complied almost as well as those exposed to hypnotic instructions. Hence, the data suggest that all control subjects knew that they were expected to comply with the posthypnotic suggestion.

Third, an attempt was made to disguise the purpose of this experiment by presenting it as a test of "hypnosis, imagination, and emotional arousal." But there is no indication of how effective a disguise it was. When informally questioned after the 15-day deadline, only one subject (in the experimental group) stated that she believed that the experiment was primarily intended to test the strength of a posthypnotic suggestion. The posthypnotic suggestion was carefully worded to avoid any implication that compliance with it was contingent on the experience of hypnosis.

Compliance was related implicitly to the satisfaction derived from participation in a pleasant and interesting experience, and not necessarily a
hypnotic one. But there appear to be no independent objective means of
determining how the subjects interpreted these instructions. Apart from
all the above possible inferences and speculations, the empirical observation was that the verbal suggestion given within the context of a procedure
labeled hypnosis appears to have been more effective than within the
context of the control procedure.

This study suggests that it may be empirically more productive to think
of hypnosis as a socially learned type of cognitive set about hypnotic
behavior, and that this cognitive set can be the starting point for some
subjects for profound psychophysiological and motivational alterations.
Hence, even if the belief in hypnosis as an "altered state" turns out to be a
delusion (e.g., like certain religious and scientific beliefs), it may be a
useful delusion, in that it may be used to provide some people with a
rationale for extending themselves in ways in which they would not
usually. Beliefs that can have profound physical and motivational consequences are clearly powerful tools for behavioral engineers and
clinicians.

It would appear that the major role of money in the posthypnotic
suggestion gives the suggestion a peculiarly relevant and "life-like" quality
insofar as the behavior of the college undergraduate is concerned.
Requesting subjects to "voluntarily" deprive themselves of a generalized
reinforcer (Skinner, 1953), in this case, money, makes provision for the
demonstration of the effectiveness of verbal stimulus control over a wide
range of alternative behaviors and motivational contingencies. The apparent demonstration of the continued effectiveness of verbal instructions
after the subject had returned to his natural habitat and the artifacts and
props of the experimental situation were "faded" seems to suggest that
verbal instructions given within the context of an operation labeled
hypnosis become peculiarly effective.

A very important result of this study is that, with one exception, the
desire to be paid eventually became stronger than the desire to comply
with the posthypnotic suggestion. This result illustrates the limits of a
single cognitive structuring procedure conducted within the context of a
broader procedure labeled hypnosis. It also suggests ways (e.g., individualized rationales and reinforcement schedules) in which more durable
cognitive sets may be programmed and measured objectively after the
individual has returned to his natural habitat. It would be interesting to
know how long such "self-deprivation" or "self-control" can be maintained with individualized reinforcement schedules or boosters.

After the termination of the experimental period, a check was mailed to

the subject who had not received payment for participation. The check
was returned by the experimental subject and had to be mailed to her
several times before she finally accepted it.

REFERENCES

Barber, T. X. Toward a theory of hypnosis: Posthypnotic behavior. *Archives of
    General Psychiatry,* 1962, *7,* 321-342.
Barber, T. X. *Hypnosis: A scientific approach.* New York: Von Nostrand Rein-
    hold, 1969.
Deckert, G. H. Pursuit eye movements on the absence of a moving visual stimu-
    lus. *Science,* 1964, *143,* 1192-1193.
Erickson, M. H., & Erickson, E. M. Concerning the nature and character of
    posthypnotic behavior. *Journal of General Psychology,* 1941, *24,* 95-133.
Orne, M. T., Sheehan, P. W., & Evans, F. J. Occurrence of posthypnotic be-
    havior outside the experimental setting. *Journal of Personality and Social
    Psychology,* 1968, *9,* 189-196.
Parrish, M., Lundy, R. M., & Leibowitz, H. W. Effect of hypnotic regression on
    the magnitude of the Ponzo and Poggendorff illusions. *Journal of Abnormal
    Psychology.* 1969, *74,* 693-698.
Skinner, B. F. *Science and human behavior.* New York: Macmillan, 1953.

NOTE

1. G. Bower and K. Pribam. Unpublished manuscript. Cited by E. Hilgard,
Hypnotic Susceptibility. New York: Harcourt, Brace & World, 1965.

4

STANLEY MILGRAM

Obedience to Criminal Orders: The Compulsion to Do Evil

The destruction of European Jewry in 1933-45 did not take place as the
result of the deeds of one man acting by himself. No person is omnipotent
in this direct sense. Rather, power, including the power to destroy individuals, comes about through the control of social organisations in which

Source: *Patterns of prejudice.* 1967, *1*(6), 3-7.
A more complete account of these experiment is available in: S. Milgram, *Obedience to
Authority.* Harper & Row Publishers, 1974.

numerous individuals participate. Among these organisations are the
political party, the administrative bureaucracy, and the police and
military branches of government. What binds each of these units into a
monolithic force capable of carrying out the directives issued from the top
is the reliable obedience of the participants. Obedience links individual
men to systems of authority, cements individual action to political
purpose.

And it is to the phenomenon of obedience that several commentators
have directed attention in seeking to explain the Nazi holocaust. Thousands of ordinary Germans, they note, took part in the Devil's work, and
many did so out of a compelling sense of duty. The propensity to obey
authority without limit or question, William Shirer asserts, is the basic
characterological flaw of the German people, and is chiefly responsible for
the complicity of large numbers of them in the terror of Auschwitz and
Belsen. C. P. Snow asserts that more horrible crimes have been committed
in the name of obedience than for any other cause or ideology.

The Nazi extermination of European Jews is the most extreme instance
of abhorrent immoral acts carried out by thousands of people in the name
of obedience. It is the most extreme case because of (1) the numbers of
victims involved, (2) the non-combatant status of the victims, (3) the
inclusion of women, children, and the aged in the slaughter, (4) the innocent nature of the victims by any accepted standard of justice, (5) the prolonged and calculated nature of the programme: it was not an impulsive
massacre, but a solidly designed programme, requiring organisation, and
the employment of many intelligent persons possessing technical and
managerial skills, and (6) the overall level of brutality and callousness
shown towards the victims.

Yet in lesser degree, this type of thing is constantly recurring: ordinary
citizens are ordered to destroy other people, and they do it because they see
it as their duty to obey orders. Thus obedience to authority, a characteristic long praised as a virtue, takes on a new aspect when it serves a
malevolent cause: far from standing as a virtue it is transformed into a
heinous sin. Or is it?

The moral question of whether one should obey when commands
conflict with conscience was argued by Plato, dramatised in Antigone, and
treated to philosophical analysis in every historical epoch. Conservative
philosophers argue that the very fabric of society is threatened by disobedience, and even when the act prescribed by an authority is an evil one, it is
better to carry out the act than to wrench at the structure of authority.
Hobbes stated further that an act so executed is in no sense the
responsibility of the person who carries it out, but only of the authority
that orders it. But humanists argue for the primacy of individual

conscience in such matters, insisting that the moral judgments of the individual must override authority when the two are in conflict.

The legal and philosophical aspects of obedience are of enormous import, but an empirically grounded scientist eventually comes to the point where he wishes to move from the realm of abstract discourse to the careful observation of concrete instances. In order to take a close look at the act of obeying, I set up a simple experiment at Yale University. Eventually, the experiment was to involve more than a thousand participants and would be repeated at several universities, but at the beginning, the conception was simple. A person comes to a psychological laboratory and is told to carry out a series of acts that come increasingly into conflict with conscience. The main question is how far the participant will comply with the experimenter's instructions before refusing to carry out the actions required of him.

But the reader needs to know a little more detail about the experiment. In this situation two people come to a psychology laboratory to take part in a study of memory and learning. One of them is designated as a "teacher" and the other a "learner." The experimenter explains that the study is concerned with the effects of "negative reinforcement" on learning. The learner is conducted into a room, seated in a chair, his arms strapped to prevent excessive movement, and an electrode attached to his wrist. He is told that he is to learn a list of word pairs; whenever he makes an error, he will receive "negative reinforcement." The civilised quality of the language masks the simple fact that the man is going to receive painful electric shocks.

The real focus of the experiment is the teacher. After watching the learner being strapped into place, he is taken into the main experimental room and seated before an impressive shock generator. Its main feature is a horizontal line of thirty switches, ranging from 15 volts to 450 volts, in 15-volt increments. There are also verbal designations which range from "Slight Shock" to "Danger—Severe Shock." The teacher is told that he is to administer the learning test to the man in the other room by reading the first word of each of a set of word pairs. When the learner responds correctly, with the second word of the pair, the teacher moves on to the next item; when the other man gives an incorrect answer, the teacher is to give him an electric shock. He is to start at the lowest shock level (15 volts) and to increase the level each time the man makes an error, going through 30 volts, 45 volts and so on.

The "teacher" is a genuinely naive subject who has come to the laboratory to participate in an experiment. The learner, or victim, is an actor who actually receives no shock at all. The point of the experiment is simply to see how far a person will proceed in a concrete and measurable situation in which he is ordered to inflict increasing pain on a protesting victim. At what point will the subject refuse to obey the experimenter?

Conflict arises when the man receiving the shock begins to indicate that he is experiencing discomfort. Until the 75-volt shock, there is no protesting response. At 75 volts, the learner grunts. At 120 volts he complains verbally; at 150 he demands to be released from the experiment. His protests continue as the shocks escalate, growing increasingly vehement and emotional. At 285 volts his response can only be described as an agonised scream.

Observers of the experiment agree that its gripping quality is somewhat obscured in print. For the subject, the situation is not a game; conflict is intense and obvious. On one hand, the manifest suffering of the learner presses him to quit. On the other, the experimenter, a legitimate authority to whom the subject feels some commitment, enjoins him to continue. Each time the teacher hesitates to administer shock, the experimenter applies, in order, four verbal prods: "Please continue"; "The experiment requires that you continue"; "It is absolutely essential that you go on"; or, finally, "You have no choice but to go on."

In order to extricate himself from the situation, the subject must make a clear break with authority. The aim of this investigation was to find when and how people would defy authority in the face of a clear moral imperative.

It is true that between carrying out the orders of a commanding officer during times of war, and carrying out the orders of an experimenter, there are enormous differences. Yet the essence of certain relationships remains, for one may ask in a general way: how does a man behave when he is told by a legitimate authority to act against a third individual? If anything, we may expect the experimenter's power to be considerably less than that of the general, since he has no power to enforce his imperatives, and participation in a psychological experiment scarcely evokes the sense of urgency *and* dedication engendered in war. Despite these limitations, I thought it would be worthwhile to start careful observation of obedience in this modest situation, in the hope that it would stimulate insights and yield general propositions that can be applied to a variety of circumstances.

The initial reaction a reader might have to the experiment is: why would anyone in his right mind even bother to administer the first shocks at all? Why would he not simply get up and walk out of the laboratory? But the fact is that no one ever does. Since the subject has come to the laboratory to aid the experimenter, he is quite willing to start off with the procedure. There is nothing very extraordinary in this, particularly since the person who is to receive the shocks seems initially cooperative, if somewhat apprehensive. What is surprising is how far ordinary individuals will go in complying with the experimenter's instructions. Indeed, the results of the experiment were both surprising and dismaying. Despite the fact that many subjects experience stress, despite the fact that many protest to the experimenter, a substantial proportion continue to the last shock on the generator.

Many subjects will obey the experimenter no matter how vehement or insistent are the demands of the person being shocked, no matter how painful the shocks to him, and no matter how he pleads, yells, or begs to be let out. This was seen time and again in our studies, and has been observed in several universities where the experiment was repeated. It is the extreme willingness of adults to go to almost any lengths on the command of an authority that constitutes the chief finding of the study and the fact most urgently demanding explanation.

A commonly offered explanation is that those who shocked the victim at the most severe level were monsters, the sadistic fringe of society. But if one considers that almost two thirds of the participants fall into the category of "obedient" subjects, and that they represented ordinary people drawn from working, managerial, and professional classes, the argument becomes very shaky. Indeed, it is highly reminiscent of the issue that arose in connection with Hannah Arendt's book, *Eichmann in Jerusalem*. Arendt contended that the prosecution's effort to depict Eichmann as a sadistic monster was fundamentally wrong, that he came closer to being an uninspired bureaucrat who simply sat at his desk and did his job. For asserting these views, Arendt became the object of considerable scorn, even calumny. Somehow, it was felt that the monstrous deeds carried out by Eichmann required a brutal, twisted, and sadistic personality, evil incarnate. After witnessing hundreds of ordinary persons submit to the authority in our own experiments, I must conclude that Arendt's conception of the *banality of evil* comes closer to the truth than one might dare imagine. The ordinary person who shocked the victim did so out of a sense of obligation, a conception of his duties as a subject and not from any peculiarly aggressive tendencies.

This is, perhaps, the most fundamental lesson of our study: that ordinary people, simply doing their jobs, and without any particular hostility on their part, can become agents in a terrible destructive process. Moreover, even when the destructive effects of their work become patently clear, and they are asked to carry out actions incompatible with fundamental standards of morality, relatively few people have the resources needed to resist authority. A great variety of inhibitions against disobeying authority come into play and successfully keep the person in his place.

Sitting back in one's armchair, it is easy to condemn the actions of the obedient subjects. Those who condemn the subjects measure them against the standard of their own ability to formulate high-minded moral prescriptions. But that is hardly a fair standard. Many of the subjects, at the level of stated opinion, feel quite as strongly as any of us about the moral requirement of refraining from action against a helpless victim. They too in general terms know what ought to be done, and can state their values when the occasion arises. This has little, if anything, to do with actual behaviour under the pressure of circumstances.

If people are asked to render a moral judgment on what constitutes appropriate behaviour in this situation, they unfailingly see disobedience as proper. But values are not the only forces at work in an actual situation. They are but one narrow band of causes on the total spectrum of forces impinging on a person. Many people are unable to realise their values in action, and find themselves continuing in the experiment even though they protest what they are doing.

The causal force exerted by the moral sense of the individual is less effective than social myth would have us believe. To be sure, it has an effect, but it takes its place in a broad field of determinants of human action. Though such prescriptions as "Thou shalt not kill" occupy a pre-eminent place in the moral order, they do not occupy a correspondingly intractable position in human psychic structure. A few changes in newspaper headlines, a call from the draft board, orders from a man with epaulets, and men are led to kill with little difficulty. Even the forces mustered in a psychology experiment will go a long way towards removing the individual from moral controls. Moral factors can be shunted aside with relative ease by a calculated restructuring of the informational and social field.

What, then, keeps the person obeying the experimenter? The answer consists of two parts. First, there are a set of "binding factors" that lock the subject into the situation. They include such factors as politeness on his part, his desire to uphold his initial promise of aid to the experimenter, and the awkwardness of withdrawal. Second, a number of adjustments in the subject's thinking occur that undermine his resolve to break with the authority. The adjustments help the subject maintain his relationship with the experimenter, while at the same time reducing the strain brought about by the experimental conflict. They are typical of thinking that comes about in obedient persons when they are instructed by authority to act against helpless individuals.

One such mechanism is the tendency of the individual to become so absorbed in the narrow technical performance of the task that he loses sight of the broader consequences of his action. The film "Dr. Strangelove" brilliantly satirised the absorption of a bomber crew with the precise and exacting technical procedure of dropping nuclear weapons on a country. Similarly, in this experiment, subjects become immersed in the apparatus, reading the word pairs with exquisite articulation and pressing the switches with great care. They want to put on a competent performance, but they show an accompanying narrowing of moral concern. The technician is a person who has the necessary competence and skill to carry out an action successfully, but he is not concerned with its broader human consequences. Similarly, the subject entrusts the broader tasks of setting goals and assessing morality to the experimental authority he is serving.

The most common adjustment of thought in the obedient subject is merely to see himself as not responsible for his own actions. He divests himself of responsibility by attributing all initiative to the experimenter, to a legitimate authority. He sees himself not as a full person acting in a morally accountable way but as the agent of an external authority. In the postexperimental interview, subjects, asked why they went on, typically reply: "I wouldn't have done it by myself. I was just doing what I was told." Unable to defy the authority of the experimenter, they attribute all responsibility to him. It is the old story of "just doing one's duty," that was heard time and again in the defence statement of the accused at Nuremberg. But it would be wrong to think of it as a thin alibi concocted for the occasion. Rather, it is a fundamental mode of thinking for a great many people once they are locked into a subordinate position in a structure of authority. The disappearance of a sense of responsibility is the most far-reaching consequence of submission to a system of authority.

Persons under authority perform actions that seem to violate standards of conscience, but it would not be true to say that a moral sense has really disappeared. Instead, it acquires a radically different focus. Once a person has entered an authority system, he does not respond with a moral sentiment to the actions he performs. Rather, his moral concern now shifts to a consideration of how well or how poorly he is living up to the expectations that the authority has of him. In wartime, a soldier does not ask whether it is a good thing or a bad thing to bomb a hamlet; he does not experience shame or guilt in destruction of a village; rather he feels pride or shame depending on how well he has performed the mission assigned to him.

Another psychological force at work in this situation may be termed "counter-anthropomorphism." For decades psychologists have discussed the primitive tendency among men to attribute to inanimate objects and forces the qualities of the human species. A countervailing tendency, however, is that of attributing an impersonal quality to forces that are essentially human in origin and maintenance. For some individuals systems of human origin are treated as if they existed above and beyond any human agent, beyond the control of whim or human feeling. The human element behind agencies and institutions is denied. Thus, when the experimenter says "The experiment requires that you continue," the subject feels an imperative that goes beyond human desire. He does not ask the seemingly obvious question "Whose experiment? Why should the designer be served while the victim suffers?" The wishes of a man—the designer of the experiment—become embodied in a schema which exerts a force on the subject's mind that transcends the personal. "It's *got* to go on. It's *got* to go on," repeats one subject. He fails to realise that a man like himself wants it to go on. For him the human agent has faded from the picture, and "The Experiment" acquires an impersonal momentum of its own.

Context Dominates Meaning.   No action of itself has an unchangeable psychological quality. The meaning of any act can be altered by placing it in the appropriate context. An American newspaper recently quoted a pilot who conceded that Americans were bombing Vietnamese men, women, and children but felt that the bombing was for a "noble cause" and thus was justified. Similarly, most subjects in the experiment see their behaviour in a larger context that is benevolent, and useful to society, namely, the pursuit of scientific truth. By virtue of its articulation with the larger society, the psychological laboratory has a strong claim to legitimacy, and evokes trust and confidence in those who come to perform there. An action, such as shocking a victim, which in isolation appears evil, acquires a totally different meaning when placed in this setting. But allowing an act to be dominated by context, without giving due consideration to the essential qualities of the act one is performing, can be dangerous in the extreme.

At least one essential feature of the situation in Germany was not studied here, namely, the intense devaluation of the victim prior to action against him. For a decade and more, vehement anti-Jewish propaganda systematically prepared the German population to accept the destruction of the Jews. Step by step the Jews were excluded from the category of citizen, national, and finally were denied the status of human beings. Systematic devaluation of the victim provides a measure of psychological justification for brutal treatment of the victim, and has been the constant accompaniment of massacres, pogroms, and wars. In all likelihood, our subjects would have experienced greater ease in shocking the victim, had he been convincingly portrayed as a brutal criminal or pervert.

Of considerable interest, however, is the fact that many subjects harshly devalue the victim *as a consequence* of acting against the victim. Such comments as: "He was so stupid and stubborn he deserved to get shocked," were common. Once having acted against the victim, it seems to be necessary for many persons to view him as an unworthy individual, whose punishment was made inevitable by his own deficiencies of intellect and character.

Many of the people studied in the experiment were, in some sense, against what they did to the learner, and many protested even while they obeyed. But between thoughts, words, and the critical step of disobeying a malevolent authority lies another ingredient, that is, the capacity for transforming beliefs and values into action. Some subjects were totally convinced of the wrongness of what they were doing but could not bring themselves to an open break with authority. Some derived satisfaction from their thoughts and felt that, within themselves at least, they had been on the side of the angels. What they failed to realise is that subjective feelings are largely irrelevant so long as they are not transformed into action. Political control is effected through action. The attitudes of the guards at a concentration camp are of no consequence when in fact they are allowing the slaughter of innocent men to take place before them. Similarly, so-called "intellectual resistance" in occupied Europe—in which persons by a twist of thought felt that they had defied the invader—was merely indulgence in a consoling psychological mechanism. Tyrannies are perpetuated by diffident men who do not possess the courage to act on their beliefs. Time and again in the experiment people disvalued what they were doing but could not muster the inner resources to translate their values into action.

One further experimental situation depicts a dilemma which is more common than the one outlined above: In this condition there are three "teachers" at the shock generator giving shocks to the protesting victim. Two are confederates of the experimenter. The naive subject does not actually push the trigger that shocks the victim; he performs the subsidiary act of pulling a master switch before one of the others actually delivers the shock. In this situation, thirty-seven out of forty adults from the New Haven area continued to the highest shock level on the generator. Predictably, subjects excused their behaviour by saying that the responsibility belonged to the man who actually pulled the switch. This may illustrate a dangerously typical situation in complex society: It is psychologically easy to ignore responsibility when one is involved in a chain of evil action but is far from the final consequences of the action. Even Eichmann was sickened when he toured the concentration camps, but, in order to participate in mass murder he had only to sit at a desk and shuffle papers. At the same time the man in the camp who actually dropped Cyclon-B into the gas chambers is able to justify *his* behaviour on the grounds that he is only following orders from above. Thus there is fragmentation of the total human act; no one man decides to carry out the evil act and is confronted with its consequences. The person who assumes full responsibility for the act has evaporated. Perhaps this is the most common characteristic of socially organised evil in modern society.

The problem of obedience, therefore, is not wholly psychological. The form and shape of society and the way it is developing have much to do with it. There was a time, perhaps, when men were able to give a fully human response to any situation because they were fully absorbed in it as human beings. But as soon as there was a division of labour among men, things changed. Beyond a certain point, the breaking up of society into people carrying out narrow and very special jobs takes away from the human quality of work and life. A person does not get to see the whole situation, but only knows a small part of it, and because of this, cannot possibly act without some kind of overall direction. Yet for important moral choices, I believe, the individual must insist on reserving for himself the final right of decision.

Of course, the military is one area where obedience is expected. Yet even here there are growing signs that obedience cannot be the ultimate rule of life. There are two armies in the world in which a soldier is obligated by law to disobey immoral orders. They are the West German and Israeli armies. Perhaps Jews and Germans, above all, have had the chance to learn that men are doomed if they act only within the alternatives handed down to them.

CHAPTER IV

Aggression

1. Leonard Berkowitz, "The Case for Bottling Up Rage"
2. Anthony N. Doob and Lorraine E. Wood, "Catharsis and Aggression: Effects of Annoyance and Retaliation on Aggressive Behavior"
3. Richard E. Goranson, "The Impact of TV Violence"

. . . how were people selected and trained to carry out the murder of 11 million people, and how did they keep their secrets so well that they were not known for years after the end of the war? Obviously, men assigned to the gas chambers, who had to watch the deaths of tens of thousands of people day after day and week after week, would have to be trained technically *and* psychologically, otherwise they might collapse under the continuous stress.

. . . We knew that at the Wannsee Conference in January 1942, the Nazis had determined upon the methodical extermination of 11 million Jews in Europe, and that various methods of genocide had been tried out. We knew that there had been mechanical breakdowns. Once Himmler was present when experiments using the exhaust gases of submarine engines for extermination had proved highly unsatisfactory. Himmler had been furious, and there had been draconic punishment. Machines broke down, but the people handling them never did. How could it be that the people operating the gas chambers and ovens were more reliable than the machines? Had they been trained mechanically *and* psychologically to stand the terrific strain? The question bothered me for years. The Nazis had known that time was running out for them. Plans already existed for the annihilation of the Gypsies, the Poles, the Russians. That meant the machinery of genocide had to be kept running at high speed. All facts pointed toward the conclusion that special cadres of technically skilled and emotionally hardened executioners were trained somewhere. Castle Hartheim and the other euthanasia centers were the answer.

Hartheim was organized like a medical school—except that the "students" were not taught to save human life but to destroy it as efficiently as possible. The deaths of the victims were clinically studied, precisely photographed, scientifically perfected. (At later trials in Germany it was proven that at the death camps of Belzec, Sobibor, and Treblinka special photographers also made pictures of people being killed.) Various mixtures of gases were tried out to find the most effective one. Doctors with stopwatches would observe the dying patients through the peephole in the cellar door of Castle Hartheim, and the length of the death struggle was clocked down to one tenth of a second. Slow-motion pictures were made and studied by the experts. Victims' brains were photographed to see exactly when death had occurred. Nothing was left to chance.

The "students" first watched the experiments; later they carried them out themselves.

* * *

Hartheim graduates later became teachers of future cadres of scientifically trained killers. After some practice, the "students" became insensible to the cries of the victims. The "teachers" would watch the reaction of their "students." It was a brilliant psychological touch to use Germans and Austrians as victims in the basic training for mass murder. If a "student" did not break when he had to kill his own people, he would have no moral scruple about exterminating thousands of *Untermenschen* ["subhumans"]. A "student" who couldn't take it was sent to the front, where his commander would assign him to a *Himmelfahrtskommando*—suicide squad.

The Murderers Among Us: The Simon Wiesenthal Memoirs,
ed. Joseph Wechsberg, McGraw-Hill Book Company, 1967

Commentary

The study of aggression occupies a unique position in social psychology in that developments in this area are followed closely both by the social scientist interested in basic research and by the one with more applied interests. The basic scientist's interest in aggression stems from the relevance of findings in this area to the broader questions concerning the determinants of social behavior. That is, much of the current work on aggression can be viewed in terms of whether it provides evidence for a predispositional view of behavior or one that stresses situational determinants. For the applied scientist aggression research has the potential for providing empirically based input for social policy decisions.

The three readings in this chapter are addressed in various ways to the following basic question: What are the consequences of direct or indirect aggressive experiences on subsequent behavior? Does behaving aggressively or viewing violence in others increase subsequent aggression, or does it decrease the likelihood of its occurrence?

Some theorists, such as Freud and Lorenz, have regarded aggression as a form of energy. This view of aggression has often been referred to as a "hydraulic model" of aggression because it assumes that, like fluid under pressure, aggressive energy needs to be discharged. A release of energy—catharsis—is assumed to occur as a result of either direct or indirect expression of aggression. An important aspect of this view is the assumption that the catharsis produced by participation in aggressive activity will lead to the reduction of subsequent aggressive behavior.

The first selection ("The Case for Bottling Up Rage," by Leonard Berkowitz) questions the validity of the catharsis point of view. Most of the evidence from laboratory experimentation suggests that aggressive actions have consequences opposite to what would be predicted by a catharsis model. Berkowitz's article presents some of this experimental evidence and brings it to bear on current therapies which assume that there are beneficial effects of expressing hostility.

Although most studies have not supported a catharsis approach, there is evidence that in certain specific situations catharsis effects can occur. Selection 2 ("Catharsis and Aggression: Effects of Annoyance and Retaliation on Aggressive Behavior," by Doob and Wood) describes such a situation. In their experiment, half of the subjects were annoyed by a confederate of the experimenter, while the other half were not bothered by her. Then the confederate was either shocked by the subject or the experimenter or received no shock. Subsequently, all subjects had an opportunity to administer shocks to the confederate. Doob and Wood found that subjects who had been annoyed administered fewer shocks when the confederate had been shocked previously than when she had not received shocks. This catharsis effect did not occur, however, for subjects who had not been initially annoyed by the confederate.

The current concern with the behavioral consequences of the expression or observation of aggression is due, at least in part, to the virtual inundation of television programming and film content with depictions of violence. Concern with this violence led the U.S. government in 1969 to sponsor an ambitious research program to collect data on the effects of TV violence on aggressive behavior. This effort yielded 60 reports and resulted in the publication of a book summarizing the findings of the research program (Surgeon General's Scientific Advisory Committee on Television and Social Behavior, 1971) as well as five separate volumes of technical reports. Selection 3 ("The Impact of TV Violence," by Goranson) is a review and brief summary of the Surgeon General's report. A more detailed summary of the report and a fascinating history of the project can be found in Bogart (1972-73), which also includes the following quote from Jesse L. Steinfeld, the former Surgeon General, regarding the report:

While the committee report is carefully phrased and qualified in language acceptable to social scientists, it is clear to me that the causal relationship between televised violence and antisocial behavior is sufficient to warrant appropriate and immediate remedial action. The data on social phenomena such as television and violence and/or aggressive behavior will never be clear enough for all social scientists to agree on the formulation of a succinct statement of causality. But there comes a time when the data are sufficient to justify action. That time has come (p. 521).

An unsystematic sampling of an evening's television fare or a night at the movies will reveal that neither the networks nor the film studios seem to have taken any action to reduce the level of violence portrayed in the media. Nor have dramatic demonstrations of the media's direct influence on behavior diminished. For example, a recent escape by helicopter of a prisoner at the State Prison of Southern Michigan was clearly modeled after a similar escape portrayed in the film "Breakout," which in turn was based on an actual incident of a helicopter escape of an American from a Mexican prison in 1971 (*Time,* June 16, 1975, p. 8). That violence in real life can create a contagion effect has been demonstrated by Berkowitz and Macaulay (1971). Using data compiled by the FBI, they compared the incidence of violent crimes in 40 cities following President Kennedy's assassination in November 1963 and the murder of eight nurses by Richard Speck in Chicago in July 1966 with the overall trend of violent crimes from 1960 to 1966. Both of these sensational crimes were followed by unusual jumps in the total violent crime rate. An analysis of the specific categories of violent crimes, however, revealed statistically significant effects only for aggravated assault and robbery, but not for rape nor, surprisingly, for murder. The authors explain the lack of statistically significant increases for murder as probably due to the unreliability of the homicide data; normally, there are large fluctuations in the number of homicides from month to month.

Despite the weight of the accumulating evidence from laboratory experiments which points to the facilitative effects of film violence on aggressive behavior (Goranson, 1970), the matter is not closed, and this chapter introduction must end on an inconclusive note. This is because two major field experiments attempting to determine the impact of televised violence failed to find increased aggression among those watching violent TV content as compared to those watching nonviolent programming. In one (Feshbach & Singer, 1971), boys at seven residential schools and institutions in Southern California and New York City were randomly assigned to a six-week diet of either aggressive TV programs or nonaggressive programs. Three of the schools were private schools, and four were boys' homes. Each boy was required to watch at least six hours of television a week during that period. The list of aggressive programs contained fare such as "Bonanza," "Combat," "FBI," and "Outer Limits," while subjects in the nonaggressive condition saw programs such as "American Bandstand," "Dick Van Dyke Show," "Grand Ole Opry," and "Petticoat Junction."

Ratings of the boys' behavior showed that those exposed to the nonaggressive programs were significantly more aggressive toward their peers and toward authority figures than those who had viewed the aggressive programs. Further analysis showed that these overall effects were due primarily to the differential impact of the two kinds of programs among the residents of the boys' homes, who were primarily from lower socioeconomic backgrounds. The experimental treatments did not have a differential effect among the boys from the private schools, who were primarily from middle-class backgrounds. On the basis of these and other findings, Feshback and Singer concluded:

Within the restrictions of sample characteristics, range of stimuli utilized, and duration of the experiment, two major conclusions are indicated by the experimental findings: First, exposure to aggressive content in television does not lead to an increase in aggressive behavior. Second, exposure to aggressive content in television seems to reduce or control the expression of aggression in aggressive boys from relatively low socioeconomic backgrounds (p. 145).

There were methodological shortcomings in this study, however, which do not permit a clear-cut interpretation of the findings. For example, subjects were permitted to drop out of the study, and some did. Also, although the program "Batman" was in the list of aggressive programs, boys in the control group at three of the schools were permitted to watch it after they complained. A more detailed criticism of the study can be found in Bandura (1973).

Recently, a more ambitious and more tightly controlled series of field experiments by Milgram and Shotland (1973) also failed to find any evidence that TV violence increases aggressive behavior. Three versions of an episode of the TV program "Medical Center" were created for the purposes of the study. The episode dealt with Tom Desmond, a young man who has been hit by a series of misfortunes. First, he impulsively quits his job as an attendant at the medical center, and when he wants it back, it is already taken. Then his wife becomes ill, and finally his boat, which he relied on as a source of income, is repossessed because he cannot meet payments on it. In the two antisocial behavior versions, Tom goes on a looting rampage, breaking into five charity boxes the Medical Center had distributed throughout the city in a fund-raising drive. In one antisocial version Tom is caught by the police and jailed. In the other he eludes punishment by escaping to Mexico. In the prosocial version Tom considers smashing into a collection box, thinks of his wife and child, and, as a result, refrains from doing it. Instead, as the story ends, he drops a coin into one of the charity boxes. A fourth program, the neutral program, was an episode unrelated to the previous one.

The first six studies by Milgram and Shotland were variations of the following basic design: Subjects viewed one of the versions of the program and were then provided with the opportunity to break into a charity box. A seventh study assessed the effects of exposure to the program on the imitation of another antisocial act—an abusive telephone call—embedded in the antisocial versions of the Medical Center sequence. An eighth study differed from the others in that the antisocial act—robbing a charity box—was presented as an actual occurrence as part of a newscast. Some of the studies presented the programs in a preview theater, some used closed-circuit TV formats, and in others subjects saw the program on their home TV sets as part of their usual viewing routine. In none of the studies did viewing an antisocial act produce significantly more antisocial behaviors than the prosocial or neutral programs.

As with any experiment in which no differences are found among treatments, a variety of factors that might explain the lack of an effect could be involved. At the same time the fact that TV violence had no discernible impact on viewers watching it in situations approximating, or identical to, their usual viewing conditions suggests caution in extrapolating from laboratory studies on the effects of filmed aggression. In assessing their studies, Milgram and Shotland see the need for further study, but they add:

It is possible that people have been entirely too glib in discussing the negative social consequences of the depiction of television violence. Personally, the investigators find the constant depiction of violence on television repugnant. But that is quite different from saying it leads to antisocial behavior among its viewers. We have not been able to find evidence for this; for if television is on trial, the judgment of this investigation must be the Scottish verdict: Not proven (p. 68).

REFERENCES

Bandura, A. *Aggression: A social learning analysis.* Englewood Cliffs, N.J.: Prentice-Hall, 1973.

Berkowitz, L., & Macaulay, J. The contagion of criminal violence. *Sociometry,* 1971, *34,* 238-260.

Bogart, L. Warning: The Surgeon General has determined that TV violence is moderately dangerous to your child's mental health. *Public Opinion Quarterly,* 1972-73, *36,* 491-521.

Feshbach, S., & Singer, R. D. *Television and aggression.* San Francisco: Jossey-Bass, 1971.

Goranson, R. E. Media violence and aggressive behavior: A review of experimental research. In L. Berkowitz (Ed.), *Advances in experimental social psychology* (Vol. 5). New York: Academic Press, 1970. Pp. 1-31.

Milgram, S., & Shotland, R. L. *Television and antisocial behavior: Field experiments.* New York: Academic Press, 1973.

Surgeon General's Scientific Advisory Committee on Television and Social Behavior, U.S. Public Health Service. *Television and growing up: The impact of televised violence.* Rockville, Md.: U.S. Department of Health, Education & Welfare, 1971.

1

LEONARD BERKOWITZ

The Case for Bottling Up Rage

Dear Ann: I was shocked at your advice to the mother whose three-year-old had
temper tantrums. You suggested that the child be taught to kick the furniture and
"get the anger out of his system." I always thought you were a little cuckoo. Now
I'm sure.

My younger brother used to kick the furniture when he got mad. Mother called
it, "Letting off steam." Well, he's 32 years old now and still kicking the furniture
—what's left of it, that is. He is also kicking his wife, the cat, the kids, and anything else that gets in his way. Last October he threw the TV set out of the window
when his favorite team failed to score and lost the game. (The window was closed
at the time.)

Why don't you tell mothers that children must be taught to control their anger?
This is what separates civilized human beings from savages, Dummy.

—Star Witness.

Dear Star: You, like some others who wrote to criticize, ignored the most important part of my answer. I did not condone destroying furniture. I suggested
that a punching bag or an old chair, specifically set aside for the purpose, be the
object of the child's hostility. And P.S.—the most important part of my answer
went like this: "Youngsters should be taught to vent their anger against things—
not people."

—from an Ann Landers column[1]

"If a person suppresses aggression (which is thus not at his disposal) . . . if he
bottles up his rage, we have to find an outlet. We have to give him an opportunity
of letting off steam. Punching a ball, chopping wood, or any kind of aggressive
sport, such as football, will sometimes work wonders."

—from Fritz Perls, *Ego, Hunger and Aggression*[2]

"So-called polar disease, also known as expedition choler, attacks small groups
of men who are completely dependent on one another and are thus prevented from

Source: Reprinted from *Psychology Today* Magazine, July 1973, *7*, 24-31. Copyright ©
1973. Ziff-Davis Publishing Company. All rights reserved.

quarreling with strangers or people outside their own circle of friends. From this it will be clear that the damming up of aggression will be the more dangerous, the better the members of the group know, understand and like each other . . . The man of perception finds an outlet by creeping out of the barracks (tent, igloo) and smashing a not too expensive object with as resounding a crash as the occasion merits."

—from Konrad Lorenz, *On Aggression*[3]

These three quotations illustrate a widely shared belief: that it is desirable and necessary to let out one's aggressive feelings. A popular newspaper columnist, a very influential psychiatrist, and an eminent ethologist urge us to express our emotions freely, to discharge our pent-up anger (or our accumulating aggressive drive) by displaying our feelings, or by attacking someone or something.

I call advocates of this popular view "ventilationists," because they insist that it is unhealthy to bottle up feelings. Many go further and argue that if we could overcome our inhibitions and show our emotions, we would eliminate disturbing tensions, conquer nagging aches and pains, and promote "deeper" and "more meaningful" relationships with others.

I have put the various ventilationists into a single camp even though there are important differences among them. For example, they don't always trace aggression to the same roots. Some writers—such as Konrad Lorenz, Alexander Lowen, and Fritz Perls—believe that emotional display releases one's accumulating instinctive energy, although they disagree about the exact nature of this conjectured instinct. Other ventilationists, who are closer to the American psychological tradition, such as Arthur Janov and George Bach, think that anger stems from earlier frustrating or painful experiences. Nor do these theorists propose the same way of discharging the "damned-up" emotional state. Still, there is sufficient commonality among the ventilationists so that we can view them, for present purposes, as a single culture. There are even geographic similarities. Although there are small colonies scattered throughout the United States, most ventilationists are located on the East and West Coasts, but particularly in California; I regard them as part of California's contribution to the American Dream, along with Hollywood and Disneyland.

MATTER OVER MIND

One notable feature of this culture is its rejection of the intellect. Most of the ventilationists contend that our society has overemphasized intelligence and planning and neglected feelings and spontaneity. They deny that intelligence is the culmination of human development and the major characteristic that separates man from other animals. Indeed many of the movement's leading voices tend to go to the opposite extreme, deriding the intellect as they exalt emotion and sensual experience. Fritz Perls, founder of Gestalt therapy, has stated this attitude quite explicitly in *Gestalt Therapy Verbatim:*

"Each time you use the question *why,* you diminish in stature. You bother yourself with false, unnecessary information. You only feed the computer, the intellect. And the intellect is the whore of intelligence. It's a drag on your life."

Many ventilationists also extol the overriding importance of the present, the "here-and-now." "Now," they say, "is all that exists. The past is over and the future is not yet." So they encourage the individual to become more aware of his present sensations, to show his immediate feelings. As participants in the therapy, encounter or sensitivity groups confront each other, they neglect much of the past (their occupations, statuses and roles, family backgrounds) and minimize the future (what will happen outside the group, their responsibilities to others, and the like).

This emphasis on the here-and-now deflects attention from the question of transfer effects—i.e., how the individual acts in situations outside the therapy or encounter setting. I think this question is particularly important in the case of aggressive behavior. Expressing anger or acting out aggression might have one set of consequences in the immediate therapy situation, but very different outcomes at later times and in other places. But many therapists and trainers do not consider possible long-term effects.

HOW TO LET GO

Ventilationists use a variety of techniques in their attempts to purge the individual's emotions. Sometimes they encourage him to fantasize his aggression. Perls gives us one example of how this might be done. According to Perls, the drive to destroy originally gratified our need to eat, and found "its natural biological outlet in the use of the teeth." This being so, the best way to discharge aggressive energy is supposedly through biting or imagined biting:

"If you are afraid to hurt people, to attack them, to say 'no' when the situation demands it, you should attend to the following exercise: imagine yourself biting a piece of flesh out of someone's body. . . . If, in your imagination, you are able to bite right through, can you experience the proper 'feel' of the flesh in your teeth? You might condemn such an exercise as vicious and cruel, but this cruelty is just as much part and parcel of your organism as it is the animal's in its struggle for life."

Other ventilationists recommend slightly more realistic behavior. In his "bioenergetic" approach, Lowen maintains that dammed-up energy resulting in chronic muscular tensions is best released through overt action. For example:

"A woman subject is given a tennis racket and directed to beat the bed. While doing this she is asked to make an appropriate verbal statement such as 'I hate you,' 'You bitch,' 'Son of a bitch,' or 'I'll kill you.' The group observing the subject's actions, interacts with her in the following ways. One, it encourages her to be more aggressive, to let go, to let it out. Two, it comments on any disparity between the words used and the expression of the subject's face . . ."

There are a number of theoretical and empirical approaches that stand in opposition to the ventilationist's view. Even contemporary psychoanalysis generally sees little value in emotional release per se, even though much of the ventilation therapies' current popularity can be traced to the influence of the early Freud. For example, psychoanalyst Edward Bibring argues that any benefits that derive from the emotional reliving of earlier experiences stem from the objective insights the patient attains.

THE SKEPTICS' VIEW

But most of the opposition comes from experimental research, a culture that provides an entirely different point of view. Here we have a questioning, intellectual approach, and one that sees potential danger in the unrestricted show of aggression.

Experimental psychologists, by and large, are skeptical of the energy theory that underlies the ventilation therapies. More and more investigators of animal and human motivation—such as R. A. Hinde, R. C. Bolles, and C. N. Cofer—believe that traditional energy notions don't hold up under close scrutiny and, as a matter of fact, that they often lead to incorrect predictions. Ventilationists invoke the idea of energy as a kind of descriptive shorthand when they don't know enough about the behavior in question to specify the controlling factors. Most systematic analyses of aggression, on the other hand, rest upon a general behavior theory that encompasses associative, cognitive, reinforcement and incentive concepts.

For example, while here-and-now therapists ignore the long-term effects of the individual's expressive actions, behavior theory indicates what may happen. Depending upon the circumstances, a person's inhibitions might be lowered or his aggressive behavior might be reinforced, increasing the chances that the person will again act aggressively outside the therapy situation.

Seymour Feshbach demonstrated this clearly in an experiment years ago. Young boys who were initially low in aggressive behavior significantly increased their overt hostility after a series of freeplay experiences with aggressive toys. Instead of "draining" pent-up anger, the aggressive make-believe evidently lowered the youngsters' restraints against aggression. They might have felt better, much as Lowen's bioenergetically treated patients presumably feel better, because their disturbing anxieties were extinguished. But the boys were also more aggressive afterwards. S. K. Mallick and B. R. McCandless found similar results in a better controlled study.

In addition to reducing inhibitions and anxieties, ventilative therapies typically reward aggression. The therapist or group members usually approve the patient's display of aggression. As a number of researchers have shown, these rewards heighten the likelihood of subsequent violence. R. H. Walters and Murray Brown gave seven-year-old boys intermittent rewards for punching a Bobo doll. When the boys competed against peers several days later, they proved to be more aggressive than control-group boys. The occasional rewards had done more than strengthen the playful punching; they had also strengthened a broad variety of aggressive responses.

REWARDING RAGE

Extreme ventilative therapies ask patients to attack someone or something physically with everything from tennis rackets or teeth to styrofoam swords. A more common procedure calls only for verbal "discharge," urging the patient to scream and curse, with or without a specific target. Here too, the other persons in the room approve the patient and spur him on to more intense outbursts of anger. R. D. Parke, William Ewall and R. G. Slaby, and C. A. Loew before them, have demonstrated that rewarding the use of aggressive words encourages an individual to attack available targets later.

Onlookers aren't the only source of reinforcements for aggression. Angry persons who want and expect to attack someone are frequently gratified to learn that their intended victim has been injured. If they think the individual they wanted to "get" has been hurt, whether by themselves or through someone else's action, there is a fairly good chance that they will experience a pleasant reduction of tension and even a lessened desire to attack the victim further. Many experiments have demonstrated this in the laboratory. But there are later consequences too. The information that one's enemy has suffered is rewarding, and acts in the long run to strengthen the angry person's aggressive habits. G. R. Patterson, R. A. Littman and William Bricker found that children who see their victim's defeat and submission are *more* likely to act aggressively again, not less so.

Most of my own research has focused on the associative determinants of impulsive violence. That is, stimuli that are associated with aggression (the deliberate injury of others) are capable of evoking hostile reactions from a person who, for one reason or another, is ready to attack someone. Such stimuli can evoke associated words—curses, perhaps, or threats—as well as aggressive acts. Whatever else it may do, violence on the movie and television screen often stimulates reactions that facilitate aggression. I have spent more than a decade doing careful laboratory research, which consistently has shown that a person who watches violence is much more apt to become aggressive himself, whether he is angry at the time or not. He is not purged of angry impulses.

PROVOKING THE PASSIVE

Further, this heightened stimulation to violence occurs whether the individual passively observes the aggressive stimuli or actually constructs these stimuli in his thoughts and fantasies. Leigh Minturn and her associates have obtained direct evidence to support this point. In one of their studies they asked undergraduates to write stories in response to pictures of aggressive exchanges. Afterwards, the students evaluated the experimenter. The subjects were significantly more hostile to the experimenter after they had written stories about verbal aggression than after writing emotionally neutral stories. This difference existed both for subjects whom the experimenter had previously angered and for those whom the experimenter had treated in a neutral manner. In a later experiment the subjects read stories with violent themes and then rated them. Here too, subjects who had been provoked into anger and who read aggressive stories became more hostile toward the experimenter than were similarly provoked students who had read neutral stories.

One may argue that aggressive fantasies can also arouse anxiety or even moral repugnance, and that these feelings might restrain violent tendencies. But the safe, accepting, nonjudgmental atmosphere of the therapy situation is apt to lessen or even eliminate such anxiety and guilt. As a result, one learns to act on aggressive fantasies without fear.

CURSES VS. COMMENTS

Let me speculate. The stimulus-response model suggests an important distinction between *verbal aggression* and *talking about one's feelings*. When a person attacks someone verbally (for example, when he curses "you bitch," or screams "I'll kill you," as Lowen recommends for his patients) he provides aggressive stimuli to himself and to his listeners. These stimuli, in turn, can evoke further aggressive reactions. However, if he merely describes his own emotion (saying, for example, "I'm boiling mad"), his remarks constitute somewhat less of an attack upon the other, except through implication, and might therefore be less likely to stimulate other aggressive acts.

Telling someone that one is angry can be informative and perhaps beneficial. You let the other person know how he has affected you, and this might cause him to make amends or change his behavior. You give him *cognitive* feedback so that he is less likely to hurt you inadvertently again. With this knowledge, or better, with learning that he hadn't meant to attack you, you might even feel happier yourself. In the Mallick and McCandless experiment, angry children who learned that the person who frustrated them hadn't wanted to hurt them became less aggressive later, whereas expressive play with toy guns had no such beneficial effect. Cognitive learning of this sort is important in human interaction. It is very different to vent one's anger and to attack an annoying person.

I have suggested that the individual should report his feelings to others. Frequently, however, especially in therapeutic situations, others tell the person what emotion he is supposedly displaying. (Lowen notes that "often group members describe the subject's feelings more accurately" than he or she senses it.) This kind of interpretation has a way of making the diagnosis come true. As Stanley Schachter found, an emotionally aroused person doesn't necessarily have any "real" underlying emotion. He can act in very different ways, showing either fight or flight, euphoria or anger, depending on what those around him are doing and how they define his arousal. If his group insists he is "really" angry and he accepts this interpretation, he may well become more inclined to act aggressively in conformity with this view.

FEARS OF FEELING

Do the ventilative procedures produce any benefits? Expressive therapies are undoubtedly popular because many persons are highly anxious about their aggressive inclinations. According to R. D. Palmer's survey of over 500 hospitalized psychiatric and nonpsychiatric patients, the feature most characteristic of the psychiatric group was conflict "involving a fear and inhibition of aggressive feelings." These persons apparently often want to lash out at others but feel guilty or anxious about their anger. It is not that they walk around with rage boiling constantly within them.

Rather, they are easily provoked for one reason or another, and *when stirred up* they become anxious and tense with internal conflict. Because of this anxiety, they may even deny that others anger them.

Ventilative therapies can have positive benefits in treating such neurotic conflicts over anger. When the therapist encourages a person to vent his feelings, he helps reduce the tension-producing guilt—or anxiety. The patient learns that he isn't going to be punished for showing his hatred or for making hostile remarks. He can now admit to himself that certain persons make him angry, and he is no longer bothered by this awareness. In the course of expressing his emotions, he might also gain insight into the effects he has on others; he understands how and why they respond to him. With this knowledge he can steer his behavior more effectively. He might even learn to be more assertive and drop the submissive, retiring manner that contributed to his frustrations.

But I do not think it is necessary to *act out* one's hostility to achieve these benefits, which probably arise from the display of feeling rather than the show of aggression. We can talk about our feelings and describe our emotional reactions without attacking others verbally or physically, directly or in fantasy.

Stanley Schachter, and others who have studied the psychology of affiliation, clearly demonstrated that individuals are frequently drawn to others who undergo the same emotional experiences, even when aggression isn't involved. Human beings don't have to divert "aggressive energy" into emotional bonds, as Lorenz claimed, for ties of friendship and affection to develop.

THE BEST INTENTIONS

Ventilationists believe that their patients, who are overly inhibited to begin with, can "loosen up" in therapy without being indiscriminately aggressive in other settings. But can we be sure that aggression will always be kept within "proper" bounds? Violence has a way of getting out of hand and breeding still more violence. And even if many patients can keep themselves from attacking inappropriately, surely there are many others who require stronger rather than weaker inhibitions. In general, as we encourage aggression, we increase the chances that more and more persons, the attacker as well as his victims, will be hurt.

In the long run, our social and human problems can be solved only with intelligence. If society hasn't recognized that there is a time and a place for emotion, it is because we aren't smart enough. If untrammeled technology brings pollution and mechanization, it is because we weren't wise enough to anticipate these difficulties. The evidence dictates now that it is unintelligent to encourage persons to be aggressive, even if, with the best of intentions, we want to limit such behavior to the confines of psychotherapy.

NOTES

1. From the Ann Landers column, April 8, 1969, as published in the *Wisconsin State Journal.* Copyright© by Publishers-Hall Syndicate.
2. From Fritz Perls, *Ego, Hunger and Aggression.* Copyright © 1969, 1947 by F. S. Perls. Reprinted by permission from Random House, Inc.
3. From *On Aggression* by Konrad Lorenz, Harcourt, Brace Jovanovich, Inc.

2

ANTHONY N. DOOB and LORRAINE E. WOOD

Catharsis and Aggression: Effects of Annoyance and Retaliation on Aggressive Behavior

Subjects were either annoyed by a confederate or left alone. One-third of the subjects then gave electric shocks to the confederate; another third watched the experimenter give identical shocks; and for the rest of the subjects the confederate was not hurt by anyone. All subjects were than given an opportunity to give electric shocks to the confederate. It was found that when subjects were annoyed, having the confederate get hurt decreased the number of electric shocks that he was subsequently given, whereas when the subject was not annoyed, hurting the confederate increased the number of shocks he was subsequently given. The results are discussed in terms of a very specific form of the catharsis hypothesis as well as other alternative interpretations such as retaliation.

The catharsis hypothesis of aggression usually refers to a decrease in aggression after the expression of aggression. The assumption as stated by Freud is that there is a certain amount of aggression that has to be

Source: Anthony N. Doob and Lorraine E. Wood, "Catharsis and Aggression: Effects of Annoyance and Retaliation on Aggressive Behavior," *Journal of Personality and Social Psychology.* 1972, *22,* 156-162. Copyright 1972 by the American Psychological Association. Reprinted by permission.

This research was supported by a grant from the Canada Council. We wish to thank Stanley Heshka for being the experimenter for a substantial number of subjects.

expressed, and that once this has happened, there is less left to be expressed later on. In war, for example, Freud (1959) stated that "Killing an enemy satisfies an instinctual inclination [p. 275]." This instinct, he goes on, "is at work in every living being and is striving to bring it to ruin and to reduce life to its original condition of inanimate matter [p. 282]." Dollard, Doob, Miller, Mowrer, and Sears (1939) pictured aggression very much as Freud did, stating that "the occurrence of any act of aggression is assumed to reduce the instigation to aggression [p. 50]." On the other hand, they admit the possibility of opposite effects when they say that "the repetition of a mode of release may produce learning of it [p. 50]."

Although these would seem to be quite straightforward statements of the catharsis hypothesis, social psychologists have not treated the hypothesis that simply. In the first place, the Aristotelian notion of catharsis is definitely a vicarious one—that one's emotions are drained through the vicarious experience of that emotion. And this notion, when applied to the catharsis of aggression, suggests a very different kind of experiment from that suggested by the Freudian or the Dollard et al. statement of the hypothesis.

For reasons that are not clear, experimental social psychologists seem to have taken the position that either the catharsis hypothesis is true (under specified conditions) or it is not true at all. Disconfirmations of the hypothesis under certain conditions have been taken as nonreplications of previous experiments, rather than as experiments done with very different research paradigms testing very different hypotheses.

As outlined previously (Doob, 1970), tests of the loosely defined catharsis hypothesis have involved measures of aggressive behavior (e.g., Doob, 1970; Hartmann, 1969; Mallick & McCandless, 1966), feelings of general hostility or arousal (e.g., Berkowitz, Green, & Macaulay, 1962; Feshbach, 1955; Worchel, 1957), physiological arousal (e.g., Hokanson & Burgess, 1962; Hokanson & Shetler, 1961), or feelings of hostility toward an annoying person (e.g., Bramel, Taub, & Blum, 1968; Kahn, 1966). There is no good theoretical reason why all of these should be considered to be equivalent forms of "aggression," unless one automatically assumes a perfect correspondence between cognitive, conative, and affective aspects of aggression.

The problems involved in the "tests" of the catharsis hypothesis would be fairly simple if the only problem were that different measures were used. Unfortunately, not only are different measures used in these tests, but very different things seem to happen to the subjects, and, once again, there is no good reason why all of these things should be considered to be cathartic. The catharsis hypothesis states that the "expression" of aggression is supposed to be cathartic. In tests of the catharsis hypothesis, this expression has consisted of a variety of things such as watching a video-tape of a person having an unpleasant drug experience (Bramel et al., 1968), watching a movie of a fight at a basketball game (Hartmann, 1969), writing Thematic Apperception Test stories (Feshbach, 1955), saying nasty things about an obnoxious person (Kahn, 1966), writing notes to a person who was insulting (Thibaut & Coules, 1952), helping the experimenter take money away from another person (Doob, 1970), and a variety of other things.

Moreover, there seems to be at least some difference in opinion as to whether the subject must be annoyed in order to show a catharsis effect or whether the state of the subject makes no difference. Feshbach (1961), Buss (1961), and Bramel et al. (1968) all appear to believe that it is important that subjects be annoyed, whereas Hartmann (1969), Walters and Llewellyn Thomas (1963), and others do not appear to feel that this is an important variable.

It is clear, then, that when these three sources of differences are combined, there are a large number of things that could qualify as "tests" of the catharsis hypothesis. It is no wonder, then, that there have been contradictory results from the tests.

The experiments that tend to support the catharsis hypothesis can be divided into two categories. In the first place, there are those experiments in which aggressive feelings have been measured, rather than aggressive behavior. Thus, for example, Hokanson and Shetler (1961), using systolic blood pressure as a measure of physiological arousal, found that when subjects had been frustrated and were then given an opportunity to aggress against a relatively low-status annoyer, there was a decrease in the monitored level of physiological arousal. Similarly, Worchel (1957) found that expressing hostility when annoyed reduced drive (as measured by per-formance on a digit-symbol task). Thus, it would seem that at least in some situations, giving an annoyed person a chance to aggress will reduce drive levels.

A second set of situations which produces decreased levels of aggression are those in which a person sees the person who annoyed him getting hurt. Bramel et al. (1968) found that annoyed subjects who watched a videotape of their annoyer suffering (even though they knew that this tape had been made some time in the past) subsequently rated him as more competent and courteous than did subjects who had watched either of two other tapes. The opposite effect was shown for subjects who had not been annoyed. Doob (1970) showed that subjects who had had a chance to hurt the person who annoyed them subsequently gave shorter shocks to the annoying person than did subjects who had not had a chance to hurt the annoying person. Once again, there was no such effect for subjects who were not annoyed.

It is clear then that there is no such thing as a "test" of the catharsis hypothesis. It is perhaps better to put such tests into the framework of experiments designed to delineate the conditions in which aggression is followed by a reduction of hostility or by aggressive behavior.

The present experiment is a replication and extension of the Doob (1970) experiment. It is clear from previous work that the state (annoyed or not) of the subject is a critical variable. Also, it appears that a decrease in aggressive behavior is more likely to be found when the annoying person is actually hurt in some way. However, it is unclear from previous work whether it is necessary to have the subject himself involved in this hurting. This experiment attempts to compare the effect of having the annoying person get hurt by the subject or by another person. In addition, it compares these effects for subjects who have been annoyed and for those who have not been annoyed.

The experiment, then, is a 2 x 3 factorial design: half of the subjects were annoyed by a confederate; half were not. One-third of the subjects in each of these groups were then given a chance to hurt the confederate; one-third watched the confederate being hurt by the experimenter; and for one-third of the subjects, the confederate did not get hurt. All subjects then had a chance to give electric shocks to the confederate.

It is predicted that in the annoy conditions, having the confederate get hurt (either by the subject or the experimenter) would decrease the number of shocks that the subject gave. In the no-annoy conditions, it was predicted that watching the experimenter hurt the confederate would, if anything, increase the number of shocks that the subject gives the confederate. It was expected that having the subject hurt the confederate in the catharsis session when the subject was not annoyed would, if anything, increase the number of shocks that the confederate was given.

METHOD

Subjects were run individually with a confederate. The subject was given a card-sorting task and left alone with the confederate. For the next 10 minutes, the confederate either annoyed the subject or sat quietly watching the subject. When the experimenter returned, the confederate was given the task of learning a list of paired associates. The confederate was then tested by the subject alone or by the experimenter in the presence of the subject. In two of the three conditions, the confederate was supposedly shocked for incorrect responses either by the subject or by the experimenter. In a third condition, no shock was given in this second stage. The confederate was then given the task of giving creative associations in a free association task. All subjects judged these responses and supposedly delivered a shock if he evaluated the confederate's responses as "uncreative." The number of shocks given during this last phase was used as the main dependent variable.

Procedure

The subjects were 99 male and female first-year university and high school students of a minimum age of 16 years. The university students participated to fulfill a requirement for their introductory psychology course, while the high school students were paid $1.50.

The confederate, a female, and the subject arrived at approximately the same time and were shown to the experimental lab. This lab consisted of two small rooms separated by a door and a wall with a large glassless window. For the experiment, this window was covered by a black curtain which prevented visual, but not auditory, contact between the two rooms. A large table was placed against this wall in the first room. A small metal box with a button was placed at the edge of the table. A wire ran from this box under the curtain to an event recorder in the second room. A detachable electric buzzer was connected to the recorder. When the buzzer was connected to the recorder, and the button on the metal box was depressed, the buzzer sounded for approximately 2 seconds.

After the subject and the confederate were seated at the table in the first room, the experimenter told them that they would be participating in a number of different learning experiments. He stated:

The usual learning experiment consists of one person coming in, the experimenter giving him some task to learn, and later testing him. Today, however, we will be doing something slightly different. For this first task, a concept-formation task, one of you will be the teacher and the other the learner. I guess for this task you [pointing to the subject] might as well be the learner and you [pointing to the confederate] the teacher. I have here a stack of white index cards, 125 of them in all. On each card, there is a different number of colored figures. There are either 1, 2, 3, 4, or 5 figures per card, and these figures are either triangles, squares, rectangles, circles, or diamonds of five different colors. For this task, you [to the subject] are to sort these 125 cards into 25 sets of 5 cards each. In each of these 5-card sets, you must have each of the five numbers, colors, and shapes represented. There can be no repetitions of any of these three dimensions in a set. For example, a set that is a valid set might be one red triangle, two green squares, three yellow circles, four blue rectangles, and five orange diamonds. You [to the subject] will have 10 minutes to make up as many sets as you can. Your job [to the confederate] will be to check that each set that he makes is a valid one, to write down on this sheet what each set consists of, that is, one red triangle, two green squares, etc., and also to time with this stopwatch how long it takes to make up each set.

The experimenter then answered any questions the subject asked by repeating the appropriate section of the instructions, and then left the room. At this point the annoy manipulation was begun for subjects who had been randomly assigned to the annoy conditions.

Annoy Manipulation

Approximately 2 minutes after the experimenter had left the room, the confederate began sarcastically to attack the subject's "obvious lack of intelligence." The confederate used a variety of derogatory remarks and reacted with disgust to any comments or questions the subject made. The confederate attacked any personal characteristic that the subject might be sensitive to, that is, dress, the subject's major, etc.

Obviously, this procedure was not exactly the same for every subject. In order to get all subjects annoyed, the confederate used a number of different techniques which varied slightly from one subject to the next. However, at this point the experimenter did not know what condition the subject was in, nor did the confederate know whether or not shock would be given on the second task. In the no-annoy conditions, the confederate acted like a normal subject, and sat relatively quietly for this first task until the experimenter returned.

Shock-No-Shock Manipulation

When the experimenter returned after 10 minutes, he was careful not to comment on the subject's performance, but indicated that it would be best to continue with the rest of the experiment. The instructions for the next part went as follows:

The next task is called a paired-associate learning task. Let's see, you [to the confederate] will be the learner for this task. You will have to learn the number that goes with each of these words. On the testing, the word will be read, and you will give the correct number. You'll have 4 minutes to study this list.

At this point, the instructions varied slightly for each of the shock conditions.

In the no-shock conditions, the experimenter stated:

During the testing, you [to the confederate] will be seated in the next room, and I will do the testing. I will read the word on the list, and you will give the number that goes with it. You [to the subject] won't have anything to do for the next few minutes.

In the conditions where the subject shocked the confederate, the experimenter stated:

Now, during the testing, you [to the confederate] will be seated in the next room. You [to the subject] will read each word aloud, and you [to the confederate] will give the number that goes with it. If the number is correct, then nothing will happen on that trial. If the number is incorrect, you [to the subject] will give her a medium intensity, fixed-duration electric shock. Medium intensity means that it is an uncomfortable shock, but it is not extremely painful or dangerous.

Moving the metal box in front of the subject, the experimenter then stated: "When this button is pressed, a buzzer will sound, and the fixed-duration shock will be automatically delivered. Do either of you have any questions?" He then answered any questions by repeating the instructions. In the conditions where the experimenter shocked the confederate, the instructions were the same as when the subject gave the shocks except that the experimenter referred to himself as the tester.

After the 4-minute learning period, the confederate was seated in a metal chair in front of the apparatus in the second room. For the conditions in which the subject gave shocks, the experimenter gave the subject the list of paired associates and the instructions:

If she gives the correct response, go on to read the next word. If she gives an incorrect response, mark an X beside the word and press the button. A buzzer will sound when the button is depressed, and the fixed-length shock will be automatically delivered.

In the conditions in which the experimenter delivered the shock, he said: "I'll read the list in order once. If you make a mistake, a buzzer will sound, and a shock will automatically be delivered."

In the two shock conditions, the experimenter attached the electrodes to the confederate and turned on the recorder. He instructed the confederate not to make comments or noises if a shock was delivered. He then closed the door to the second room and either left the first room or proceeded with the testing (depending on experimental condition). During the testing, the confederate made eight intentional errors and ostensibly received eight shocks. In the no-shock conditions, the experimenter simply read the words to the confederate, and the confederate answered with the same responses as he did in the two shock conditions. When the testing was complete, the experimenter turned off the recorder and disconnected the buzzer.

Dependent Measure

The last part was the same for all subjects and went as follows:

The last thing that we will be doing is what is known as a free association task. In this type of task what usually happens is that one person reads a word, and the other person gives the first word that comes to mind. Today, we will be doing something slightly different. For this task, you [turning to the subject] will be reading a list of words, and you [to the confederate] will be giving a response to each word. However, instead of necessarily giving the first word that comes to mind, you should try to give a creative response, perhaps an unusual response, to the word that is read. Your job [to the subject] will be to write down the word that she gives and to judge whether or not you think her response is a creative one. If you think it is a creative response, then nothing will happen on that trial. If you think that it is not a creative response, then you will be giving her a medium intensity shock. The length of the shock is to be determined by how bad a response you think the one she gives is. If you think that it is a very bad response, then you hold the button down a longer time. If you think it is only slightly uncreative, then hold the button down a shorter time. If you think her response is a good response, then there will be no shock at all. Now, obviously, I cannot give you any strict set of criteria about what is creative and what is not creative. That's for you to decide. Use your own judgment.

In the two shock conditions, the experimenter explained that there would be no buzzer on this last test. He then turned on the recorder, closed the door to the second room (after attaching the electrodes in the no-shock conditions), and instructed the confederate not to comment if a shock was delivered. He then left the room. In all of the conditions, the confederate gave the same set of responses. Obviously, at no point in the experiment did the confederate actually receive any electric shocks.

When the testing was completed, the experimenter returned, turned off the recorder, detached the electrodes, and asked the confederate to wait in another room. He then gave the subject a questionnaire designed to evaluate his opinions of the confederate. When the subject had finished the questionnaire, the experiment was completely explained to him.

RESULTS

Nine subjects' data were not included in the analysis: 3 had heard about the experiment from their friends; 3, because of language difficulties, did not understand that they were supposed to be delivering shocks; 2 terminated the experiment before the end, having read one of the popularized versions of Milgram (1963) and thinking that that was what the experiment was all about; 1 was color blind and could not perform the first part of the experiment. This left 90 subjects for analysis (15 per cell).

From looking at the results of the ratings that the subjects made of the confederate, it is clear that the annoy manipulation was successful. Annoyed subjects liked the confederate significantly less than did the subjects who had not been annoyed; they thought that it was less likely that they could ever be good friends; they rated her as more aggressive, colder, less likable, more emotional, less friendly, less interesting, more dishonest, and stronger. There were no differences in the ratings attributable to the shock variable.

TABLE 2.1
**Mean Number of Shocks Delivered on the "Creative Association"
Task by Experimental Condition**

Condition	Subject Shocks	Experimenter Shocks	No Shock
Annoy	6.80	7.60	10.67
No annoy	8.07	9.73	6.60

The major results of the experiment are presented in Table 2.1. All analyses are reported in terms of the number of shocks delivered. The number and average length of the shocks were slightly correlated (average r for the six experimental conditions $= .39$). However, perhaps because of some confusion between the "fixed length" shocks in the "catharsis" session, and the high variance on the length of shocks delivered (since the subjects had no stated range given to them), the results are clearest for the number of shocks delivered. The interaction between the annoy variable and the catharsis activity was significant ($F = 4.54$, $df = 2/84$, $p < .05$), and the two main effects were not ($Fs < 1$). The major hypothesis is that in the annoy conditions having a chance to hurt the annoying person should be cathartic. Clearly, this is so: the difference between the annoy-subject-shocks cell and the annoy-no-shock cell is significant ($F = 6.03$, $p < .05$). The difference between the annoy-no shock and annoy-experimenter shocks is in the same direction, but is not significant ($F = 3.79$, $p < .10$). Subjects in the no-shock conditions gave significantly more shocks when they had been annoyed ($F = 6.69$, $p < .05$).

As indicated by the significant interaction, the catharsis activity had different effects for the subjects who were not annoyed as compared to the effects on the annoyed subjects. Having the confederate get hurt (either by the subject himself or by the experimenter) when the subject was annoyed reduced the number of shocks that the confederate subsequently was given, whereas having the experimenter hurt the confederate when the subject was not annoyed at him tended to increase the amount of shock he was given (no annoy-no shock versus no annoy-experimenter shocks, $F = 3.94$, $p < .07$; no annoy-no shock versus no annoy-subject shocks, *ns*).

DISCUSSION

The Doob (1970) experiment showed that angered subjects who participated in the hurting of their annoyer subsequently hurt him less than did annoyed subjects who were given no chance to hurt their annoyer. No such decrease in aggressive behavior occurred for subjects who were not annoyed. The present experiment extends these results somewhat by showing that this decrease will occur when either the subject or someone else hurts the annoying person.

It is difficult to interpret these data in terms of the subjects' feeling guilty in the shock conditions. Berkowitz (1962) suggested that this is a major problem with many experiments in the area of catharsis of aggression. In this experiment, if one is to postulate that the decrease in aggression after aggression in the annoy conditions is due to guilt, it would seem reasonable to postulate the same effect for the no-annoy conditions. Obviously, however, the results do not support this notion, since subjects who were not annoyed tended to give more shocks after the confederate had been hurt than when he had not been hurt.

These data are entirely consistent with those reported by Bramel et al. (1968) in which subjects who had just been annoyed by someone rated him less negatively if they had just finished watching a videotape of him suffering than if they had watched him having a neutral or happy experience. In that experiment, an opposite effect was found for people who were not annoyed. In many ways that experiment is analogous to the no-shock and experimenter-shocks conditions of this experiment, in that in neither case did the subject actually do the hurting.

At first glance, it would seem that these results were exactly opposite from those of Kahn (1966), where annoyed subjects were either encouraged to express their hostile feelings toward an obnoxious experimenter or were given no such opportunity. Subjects who had been induced to say nasty things about the experimenter in the "catharsis" session once again rated the experimenter on the negative ends of the rating scales. Subjects who had had no such initial opportunity did not rate the experimenter so negatively. Kahn (1966) explained these results in terms of dissonance theory:

Once the subject has counteraggressed and gotten [the obnoxious experimenter] into trouble, the cognition of this action would seem dissonant with the thought that the experimenter was not such a bad guy and that the subject was not really angry with him [p. 285].

In other words, the subject in this experiment was simply acting in a consistent manner—after aggressing once, when given an additional opportunity, he aggressed again. The experiment reported here minimizes the similarities between the catharsis activity and the dependent measure. Thus, the subject who aggresses in the catharsis session is not under the same sort of consistency pressure as is the subject in Kahn's experiment.

It might be tempting to describe the results of this experiment simply in terms of a successful "test" of the catharsis hypothesis. However, as pointed out above, there are so many things that might be considered to be "tests" of the catharsis hypothesis that it is futile to consider any single experiment as a test. One alternative way of looking at these results is in terms of retaliation that occurs in the subject-shocks and experimenter-shocks conditions. As Berkowitz (1970) pointed out: "We evidently feel better when we see that the person who had angered us has been hurt. . . . We do not have to hurt the frustrator ourselves to experience this pleasure [p. 6]." However, this does not mean that some sort of diminution of aggressive impluses has necessarily occurred. All that it implies in the context of the present study is that the angered person who has hurt his annoyer (or seen his annoyer hurt) has "evened the score." Thus, the annoyed person whose annoyer has been hurt will feel less of a need to retaliate further than the annoyed person whose annoyer has not been hurt in some way.

Although these results are different from the experiments on observed film aggression (cf. Bandura, 1965; Berkowitz, 1965; Hartmann, 1969; Walters & Llewellyn Thomas, 1963), they do not in any way contradict those findings. As Berkowitz (1970) has pointed out, the last 10 years of research have demonstrated quite thoroughly that observing the aggressive behavior of others in situations such as movies tends to increase the level of aggression rather than decrease it. This tends to be the case when the aggressive response is the same as that which was observed (e.g., Bandura, Ross, & Ross, 1963) or when it is different (e.g., Hartmann, 1969). However, in the experiments on the effects of film violence, the subject (either angry or not) is typically exposed to a film where the aggression is unrelated to the setting in which the subject finds himself. In the present experiment, the person being hurt (in either the subject-shocks or experimenter-shocks conditions) is the person with whom the subject interacted in the first part of the experiment. It would seem that the paradigms are different enough so that there would be no good reason to expect the experience of aggression to have the same effect in these two very different situations.

REFERENCES

Bandura, A. Vicarious processes: A case of no-trial learning. In L. Berkowitz (Ed.), *Advances in experimental social psychology.* Vol. 2. New York: Academic Press, 1965.

Bandura, A., Ross, D., & Ross, S. A. Imitation of film-mediated aggressive models. *Journal of Abnormal and Social Psychology,* 1963, *66,* 3-11.

Berkowitz, L. *Aggression: A social psychological analysis.* New York: McGraw-Hill, 1962.

Berkowitz, L. Some aspects of observed aggression. *Journal of Personality and Social Psychology,* 1965, *2,* 359-369.

Berkowitz, L. Experimental investigations of hostility catharsis. *Journal of Consulting and Clinical Psychology,* 1970, *35,* 1-7.

Berkowitz, L., Green, J. A., & Macaulay, J. R. Hostility catharsis as the reduction of emotional tension. *Psychiatry,* 1962, *25,* 23-31.

Bramel, D., Taub, B., & Blum, B. An observer's reaction to the suffering of his enemy. *Journal of Personality and Social Psychology,* 1968, *8,* 384-392.

Buss, A. H. *The psychology of aggression.* New York: Wiley, 1961.

Dollard, J., Doob, L. W., Miller, N. E., Mowrer, O. H., & Sears, R. R. *Frustration and aggression.* New Haven: Yale University Press, 1939.

Doob, A. N. Catharsis and aggression: The effect of hurting one's enemy. *Journal of Experimental Research in Personality,* 1970, *4,* 291-296.

Feshbach, S. The drive-reduction function of fantasy behavior. *Journal of Abnormal and Social Psychology,* 1955, *50,* 3-11.

Feshbach, S. The stimulating vs. cathartic effects of a vicarious aggressive activity. *Journal of Abnormal and Social Psychology,* 1961, *63,* 381-385.

Freud, S. Why war? Letter to Professor Albert Einstein, 1932. In *Collected papers.* Vol. 5. New York: Basic Books, 1959.

Hartmann, D. T. Influence of symbolically modeled instrumental aggression and pain cues on aggressive behavior. *Journal of Personality and Social Psychology,* 1969, *11,* 280-288.

Hokanson, J. E., & Burgess, M. The effects of status, type of frustration, and aggression on vascular processes. *Journal of Abnormal and Social Psychology,* 1962, *65,* 232-237.

Hokanson, J. E., & Shetler, S. The effect of overt aggression on physiological arousal level. *Journal of Abnormal and Social Psychology,* 1961, *63,* 446-448.

Kahn, M. The physiology of catharsis. *Journal of Personality and Social Psychology,* 1966, *3,* 278-286.

Mallick, S., & McCandless, B. R. A study of catharsis of aggression. *Journal of Personality and Social Psychology,* 1966, *4,* 591-596.

Milgram, S. Behavioral study of obedience. *Journal of Abnormal and Social Psychology,* 1963, *67,* 371-378.

Thibaut, J. W., & Coules, J. The role of communication in the reduction of interpersonal hostility. *Journal of Abnormal and Social Psychology,* 1952, *47,* 770-777.

Walters, R. H., & Llewellyn Thomas, E. Enhancement of punitiveness by visual and audiovisual displays. *Canadian Journal of Psychology,* 1963, *17,* 244-255.

Worchel, P. Catharsis and the relief of hostility. *Journal of Abnormal and Social Psychology,* 1957, *55,* 238-243.

3

RICHARD E. GORANSON

The Impact of TV Violence

The Surgeon General's Scientific Advisory Committee on Television and Social Behavior was established in 1969 to examine the effects of TV violence. Over the next two years, 23 independent research projects were funded, resulting in a total of 60 reports and papers. Late in 1971 the Advisory Committee released its summary report reviewing the findings of the commissioned research. Early the following year the five volumes of detailed research reports were released.

The summary volume (*Television and Growing Up: The Impact of Televised Violence*) is especially disappointing in one respect. It fails to conclude the obvious. There is strong evidence that TV violence contributes to aggression in children and violence in society. The five supporting volumes of detailed research reports amply justify this statement, yet the summary report fails to come to this simple conclusion. The impact of the report is lost in excessive qualification. The strongest conclusion that the authors of the report could agree upon is preceded by several

Source: Richard E. Goranson, "The Impact of TV Violence," *Contemporary Psychology,* 1975, *20*(4), 291-292. Copyright 1975 by the American Psychological Association. Reprinted by permission.

This is a review (slightly abridged), in *Contemporary Psychology,* of the following books: Surgeon General's Scientific Advisory Committee on Television and Social Behavior, U.S. Public Health Service, *Television and Growing Up: The Impact of Televised Violence* (Rockville, Md.: U.S. Department of Health, Education, and Welfare, 1971).

G. A. Comstock and E. A. Rubinstein (Eds.), *Television and Social Behavior,* Vol. I: *Media Content and Control* (Rockville, Md.: U.S. Department of Health, Education, and Welfare, 1971).

J. P. Murray, E. A. Rubinstein, and G. A. Comstock (Eds.), *Television and Social Behavior,* Vol. II: *Television and Social Learning* (Rockville, Md.: U.S. Department of Health, Education, and Welfare, 1971).

G. A. Comstock and E. A. Rubinstein (Eds.), *Television and Social Behavior,* Vol. III: *Television and Adolescent Aggressiveness* (Rockville, Md.: U.S. Department of Health, Education, and Welfare, 1971).

E. A. Rubinstein, G. A. Comstock, and J. P. Murray (Eds.), *Television and Social Behavior,* Vol. IV: *Television in Day-to-Day Life: Patterns of Use* (Rockville, Md.: U.S. Department of Health, Education, and Welfare, 1971).

G. A. Comstock, E. A. Rubinstein, and J. P. Murray (Eds.), *Television and Social Behavior,* Vol. V: *Television's Effects: Further Explorations* (Rockville, Md.: U.S. Department of Health, Education, and Welfare, 1971).

cautionary paragraphs stressing the difficulties of interpreting research data:

Thus, there is a convergence of the fairly substantial experimental evidence for *short-run* causation of aggression among some children by viewing violence on the screen and the much less certain evidence from field studies that extensive violence viewing precedes some *long-run* manifestations of aggressive behavior. This convergence of the two types of evidence constitutes some preliminary indication of a causal relationship, but a good deal of research remains to be done before one can have confidence in these conclusions.

Throughout the summary report there are statements that downgrade or negate the importance of the research findings. After reviewing several controlled studies demonstrating heightened aggressiveness in children following exposure to TV violence, this comment is added:

The accumulated evidence, however, does not warrant the conclusion that televised violence has a uniformly adverse effect nor the conclusion that it has an adverse effect on the majority of children.

A quick or careless reading of this sentence gives the impression that the evidence is weak or uncertain. A more careful reading shows that the sentence means only that half or fewer of the children are adversely affected. There are many other examples of this sort of cautionary zeal. Several large scale studies are summarized showing a significant positive correlation between watching TV violence and aggressive actions and attitudes. The authors point out that this correlation does not necessarily mean that TV violence is the cause of the aggression since some third variable could account for the covariation. This is a valid point, but the same point is made again and again in one form or another for a total of 13 separate times!

What is the explanation for the diffident tone of this awkward and sometimes contradictory report? A clue can be found in the history and composition of the Advisory Committee that prepared it. *Science* magazine (May 22, 1970) carried an account of the black-balling procedure by which the three major TV networks and the National Association of Broadcasters were able to prevent seven distinguished researchers from serving on the Committee. They were apparently blackballed for previously expressing opinions or reporting research on harmful effects of TV violence. Finally the committee was composed of two broadcast network employers, three researchers closely associated with the networks, and seven additional social scientists. It is not surprising then that the final report is so uncertainly phrased. In working out the compromise wording of the final report, the Advisory Committee combined the caution of the social scientists and the concerns of the broadcast industry. The product was the guarded and inconclusive report that has since had such little influence on policy and practice in TV programming.

While the summary report is disappointing, the five volumes of supporting research are excellent. Since these have already been given a thorough and intelligent review by Leo Bogart (*Public Opinion Quarterly,* Winter 1972-73), the contents will be only briefly described here.

Volume I (*Media Content and Control*) documents the prevalence of TV viewing and TV violence. Here are a few of the findings: Over 96 percent of U.S. homes have TV. The set is turned on for an average of six hours a day. Both children and adults watch television for an average of two hours a day. During the research period the rate of violent episodes remained fairly stable at about eight per hour, with children's cartoons being the single most violent type of programming. In one study, about 30% of the dramatic sequences were saturated with violence and almost 70% had at least one violent incident. Going beyond these statistics, several valuable papers in this volume explain the reason for the inclusion of so much violent TV material. Program producers and network officials see violence as a cheap and easy means of sparking viewer interest. This in turn is believed to increase audience size, program ratings, and, ultimately, advertising revenue. Thus the inclusion of violent material is not so much an artistic decision on the part of the writers as it is part of a production formula geared to maximizing commercial profits.

Volume II (*Television and Social Behavior*) reports a number of controlled laboratory studies of the effects of TV violence on children's behavior and attitudes. Previous research has clearly established that children can imitate novel acts of aggression seen on television. The studies in this volume focus on the conditions that prompt children to actually perform these acts of imitative aggression. The complex design and analysis of these studies provide a rich variety of results that cannot be briefly summarized with justice. At the risk of oversimplifying, the results show that TV violence is most likely to result in heightened aggression when the violence is depicted realistically, when there is a large amount of violence in the program, when the violence is presented as being justified, and when the viewer is male.

Volume III (*Television and Adolescent Aggressiveness*) is devoted to field studies correlating various measures of TV violence viewing and aggressiveness. In a longitudinal study that has attracted a good deal of public interest, the preference for TV violence among third grade boys was found to be positively and significantly related to their aggressive behavior 10 years later. Detailed statistical analysis indicates that this correlation is consistent with the interpretation that early viewing of TV violence is a direct cause of later aggression. This interpretation has been the source of a good deal of controversy, and the complete data reported in this volume will not resolve the conflict. Other studies in this volume support the conclusion that viewing TV violence is reliably associated with adolescent aggressiveness, but here too the pattern of causation remains elusive. The most that can be said is that the correlations are about what one would expect if TV violence were in fact a substantial contributor to aggressive behavior.

Volume IV (*Television in Day-to-Day Life: Patterns of Use*) is not directly related to the effects of TV violence. However the volume does contain some fascinating results on what people choose to watch and how they watch it. One study, for example, actually filmed a number of families as they watched television. These viewers spent almost half of their time talking, reading, looking away, or moving around inside and outside the viewing area. Another study found that over half of the viewers rarely or never watched national news programs. From yet another study we learn that it is principally the children who control the family TV set in the early evening; in fact, parents often ask their children for advice on program selection. The preceding haphazard selection of surprising findings does not reflect the systematic nature of the almost two dozen projects reported in this volume. Taken together they represent a large advance in our knowledge of TV viewing behavior.

Volume V (*Television's Effects: Further Explorations*) deals with a variety of papers that do not fit in with the themes of the previous volumes. These include experiments on the effects of television on emotional arousal, dream content, racial awareness, and sensitivity to violence. The reports contain a wealth of intriguing findings and provocative interpretations.

The major portion of the research reported in these five volumes is concerned with harmful effects of TV violence. But one may ask, What good effects does TV violence have? How does it benefit the individual viewer or society in general? The results of this massive project give little evidence for any positive effects of TV violence, but the probable harmful effects are described and documented to a point well beyond the evidence available in the 1960's.

Prosocial Behavior

Rabbi Levi bar Chama says in the name of Rabbi Shimon ben Lakish: A man should always incite the good impulse (in his soul) to fight against the evil impulse. . . .

Babylonian Talmud, Tractate B'rachot, 5a
(Soncino translation)

He [Hillel] used to say, "If I am not for myself, who will be for me? And if I am only for myself, what am I? And if not now, when?"

Ethics of the Fathers, I:14
(Hertz translation)

The only thing necessary for the triumph of evil is for good men to do nothing.

Edmund Burke

Commentary

The view that man is capable of positive actions toward his fellow man has been expressed by many writers throughout history. Yet until very recently much of modern psychology has pictured mankind as self-centered, "constantly oriented toward reducing their own tensions, and . . . persistently on the defensive" (Berkowitz & Daniels, 1963, p. 429). Since the early 1960s, however, increasing numbers of social psychologists have turned to the study of altruism. By the early 1970s the topic had attained such a degree of popularity and recognition as a well-defined subject of study that it began appearing in chapter headings of social psychology textbooks (e.g., Freedman, Carlsmith, & Sears, 1970).

Wispé (1972) suggests three reasons for the current interest in positive forms of social behavior: (1) the appearance of writings on the topic by several major behavioral scientists, (2) a changing social climate, and (3) the tragic incident involving Kitty Genovese, who in 1964 was brutally stabbed to death while 38 of her neighbors did nothing. Not only did this incident shock the public, it served as the impetus for a series of classic laboratory studies on bystander intervention conducted by Latané and Darley (to be discussed later in relation to the first selection in this chapter). Incidents such as the Kitty Genovese case shock us not only because of their cold-blooded brutality but also because their occurrence violates one of the working assumptions we hold about the nature of social existence. Our everyday activities are predicated on the cooperativeness and helpfulness of others. We take the routine benignity of others so much for granted that positive, helpful acts do not normally make the newspapers. It is only when helpfulness involves self-sacrifice of heroic proportions that we take notice.

This chapter focuses on the positive aspects of human dispositions which can manifest themselves, at one extreme, in altruistic behavior entailing some degree of self-sacrifice and, at the other extreme, in the everyday social courtesies that require little cost or effort. Whatever their degree or manifestation, concern for others is an important topic in social psychology because it challenges the assumption, held in several major psychological theories, that man is self-centered. As Krebs (1970) puts it:

. . . the study of altruism raises important questions about the ability of several influential theories to account for the apparently altruistic aspects of general human behavior. Reinforcement theory, psychoanalytic theory, and the theory of evolution seem to suggest that human behavior is essentially egoistic. Yet, behavior that seems quite altruistic is apparent in everyday life (pp. 258-259).

As with other kinds of behavior, the study of prosocial behavior can be approached from two directions. Altruism can be viewed as a relatively stable personality disposition or as a less durable inclination whose expression varies as a function of the situation. Although some studies have taken the first approach and have looked at helpfulness as a function of personality differences (Gergen, Gergen, & Meter, 1972; London, 1970; Zuckerman, 1975), most current research on altruism has taken the second approach, focusing primarily on situational determinants. The four selections in this chapter examine the role of several situational factors which have received attention in the literature as determinants of altruistic actions: (1) the number of people present and their reactions, (2) the presence of a helping model, (3) the nature of attributions, and (4) the potential helper's mood.

While "classic" may be inappropriate to describe work that is not even ten years old, there is no question that the studies of Latané and Darley (1970) on bystander intervention have been among the most important and imaginative in the area of prosocial behavior. The public outcry that followed the revelation that several dozen people did nothing to save Kitty Genovese from her attacker one March night in 1964 attributed the bystanders' inaction to apathy and indifference. Latané and Darley did not accept this view. Rather than viewing the large size of the group of nonintervening bystanders as an indication of the magnitude of public apathy, they saw in the number of people present a possible explanation for the inaction of the individual bystander. They reasoned that the bystander in a crowd witnessing an emergency may be reluctant to help not because of callousness or indifference but because action is inhibited by the presence of other bystanders, in the following ways. First, in order for a person to help in an emergency, the situation must first be defined as one. Many emergency situations are ambiguous (e.g., Is that man lying in the doorway just sleeping it off, or is he ill?). Thus, the inaction of others leads to inaction in the individual by interpreting the situation for him as one not requiring intervention. The second way a group inhibits intervention is that even after an individual recognizes that what he is witnessing is an emergency, the presence of others may work against his intervening by allowing a diffusion of responsibility. On the basis of these considerations, Latané and Darley predicted that a person would be more likely to help in an emergency when he is alone than when he is with others. They confirmed the prediction in a series of experiments in which the subject was confronted with a staged emergency, either alone or with others.

The first selection in this chapter, by Darley, Teger, and Lewis, addresses itself to the question stated in its title: "Do Groups Always Inhibit Individuals' Responses to Potential Emergencies?" Their experiment demonstrated that the answer is no. Darley and his associates found that when subjects in groups of two could see each other's startled reactions during an emergency, they were as likely to respond as subjects who were alone, and they were more likely to respond than subjects in groups of two who could not see each other's reactions.

The second selection ("Models and Helping: Naturalistic Studies in Aiding Behavior," by Bryan and Test) presents three studies which demonstrated that helping models can increase helping among observers, as well as a fourth study which tested the effect on donations of the race of the solicitor. The selection is interesting because it shows how an investigator can unobtrusively superimpose the structural features of an experiment (e.g., creation of different treatments, random assignment of subjects) on ongoing behavior in a field setting. In addition, a reading of the first three experiments provides a demonstration of the converging nature of scientific inquiry.

Each of the first three studies focused on the impact of a model's altruistic behavior on the behavior of passersby. Each subsequent demonstration of the model's effect on helping not only increased the external validity or generality of the phenomenon, it also ruled out factors other than the altruistic behavior of the model that could account for the observer's altruism. Thus the first study showed that drivers who observed a stranded motorist receiving help changing a tire were more likely to aid another stranded motorist than subjects who had not observed a helping model. However, rather than demonstrating that observing another's helpfulness increases one's own, the study could simply have shown that a model's initiative may have reduced the other motorists' inhibitions about picking up girls. The plausibility of this alternate explanation is enhanced by the fact that the stranded motorist was a girl and almost all the motorists who stopped to help were males, some of whom insisted on helping even after being told that help was already on the way.

In order to rule out this possibility—as well as some other alternative explanations—the second experiment was conducted. In this experiment it was found that more people donated money to a Salvation Army kettle when preceded by a donating model than when no model preceded them. After conducting this experiment, the experimenter realized that the results may have been due not to the altruistic behavior of the model per se but rather to the reinforcing behavior of the person manning the kettle which occurred when the model deposited money. To rule out this alternative explanation, a third experiment was conducted which differed from the second in that the solicitors were instructed not to acknowledge the model's contribution. In spite of this change, significantly more contributions still occurred in the "model" condition than in the "no model" condition. The discussion section of Selection 2 explores several possible mechanisms that may account for a model's effectiveness in increasing helping in the observer.

The third selection ("Helping and Self-Attributions: A Field Experiment," by Uranowitz) attempts to apply Bem's self-perception theory (see introduction to Chapter I) to the prediction of helping behavior in a field setting. On the basis of Bem's theory, which states that we make inferences about our feelings and characteristics by observing our own behaviors, Uranowitz predicted and found that a person who complied with a request to help under low justification would be more likely to help subsequently on a second occasion than a person who initially helped under high justification or one whose help had not been requested initially. The person who had only minimal justification for helping is assmed to infer more strongly that she is a helpful person than one who initially helped because there was a lot of justification for doing so. These differences in self-attributed helpfulness were seen as mediating differences in subsequent helping behaviors.

The final selection in this chapter ("Further Studies on the Effect of Feeling Good on Helping," by Levin and Isen) is a follow-up of earlier work by Isen and Levin (1972) which demonstrated that a positive mood could lead to increased helping. In the second study reported in that paper, some subjects found a dime in designated phone booths, while others did not. After leaving the phone booth, all subjects were confronted with an opportunity to help a confederate of the experimenter who "accidentally" dropped a manila folder full of papers. Isen and Levin found that significantly more subjects helped if they were in the "dime" condition rather than the "no dime" condition. According to the authors, the positive mood subjects found themselves in as a result of their unexpected good fortune led them to be more helpful than subjects who had not found a dime.

One purpose of the studies reprinted here was to determine whether or not the positive affect-helping relationship is limited to situations in which helping involves interaction with another person, as was the case in the previously mentioned study by Isen and Levin. Would a positive affective state increase the likelihood of helping, even when the measure of helping did not involve interaction with another person? On the basis of the evidence provided in the two studies reported in Selection 4, the answer is yes. As in the previous "dime" study in Isen and Levin, some subjects in these studies found a dime in the coin returns of designated phone booths, and others did not. Unlike the previous study, however, here the measure of helping was whether or not the subjects mailed an addressed letter left in the phone booth. Regardless of whether the letter was stamped or unstamped, subjects who found a dime were more likely to mail it than those who did not, thereby extending the generality of the link between feeling good and helping found in earlier studies.

REFERENCES

Berkowitz, L., & Daniels, L. R. Responsibility and dependency. *Journal of Abnormal and Social Psychology,* 1963, *66,* 429-436.

Freedman, J. L., Carlsmith, J. M., & Sears, D. O. *Social psychology.* Englewood Cliffs, N.J.: Prentice-Hall, 1970.

Gergen, K. J., Gergen, M. M., & Meter, K. Individual orientations to prosocial behavior. *Journal of Social Issues,* 1972, *28* (3), 105-130.

Isen, A. M., & Levin, P. F. The effect of feeling good on helping: Cookies and kindness. *Journal of Personality and Social Psychology,* 1972, *21,* 384-388.

Krebs, D. L. Altruism—An examination of the concept and a review of the literature. *Psychological Bulletin,* 1970, *73,* 258-302.

Latané, B., & Darley, J. M. Some determinants of bystander intervention in emergencies. In J. Macaulay & L. Berkowitz (Eds.), *Altruism and helping behavior: Social psychological studies of some antecedents and consequences.* New York: Academic Press, 1970. Pp. 13-27.

London, P. The rescuers: Motivational hypotheses about Christians who saved Jews from the Nazis. In J. Macaulay & L. Berkowitz (Eds.), *Altruism and helping behavior: Social psychological studies of some antecedents and consequences.* New York: Academic Press, 1970. Pp. 241-250.

Wispé, L. G. Positive forms of social behavior: An overview. *Journal of Social Issues,* 1972, *28* (3), 1-19.

Zuckerman, M. Belief in a just world and altruistic behavior. *Journal of Personality and Social Psychology,* 1975, *31,* 972-976.

1

JOHN M. DARLEY, ALLAN I. TEGER, and LAWRENCE D. LEWIS

Do Groups Always Inhibit Individuals' Responses to Potential Emergencies?

Previous studies of bystander intervention in emergencies have found that an individual is more likely to intervene if he witnesses the emergency alone than as a member of a group. The present study qualifies this general finding in the framework of group communication processes. Pairs of subjects working on a task overheard a loud crash in an adjoining room. Some pairs of subjects were seated in a pattern that facilitated the visual communication exchanges that naturally occur when a noisy event takes place and others were seated so as to block these communications. When the emergency occurred, groups which could exchange reactions were not reliably less likely to respond than were a third group of subjects who faced the emergency alone. The blocked communications groups tended not to respond and responded significantly less than the other two conditions. These results were interpreted as supporting the hypothesis that a group of people who witness an ambiguous event interact to arrive at a definition or interpretation of it, which then guides each member's reactions to the event.

From studies of bystander intervention in emergencies, one empirical generalization emerges: An individual who witnesses a potential emergency alone is more likely to intervene than one who witnesses it as a member of a group. This has been found whether the emergency involves smoke pouring into a waiting room (Latané & Darley, 1968), a noisy accident to a girl in a nearby room (Latané & Rodin, 1969), a person stealing a case of beer from a liquor store (Latané & Darley, 1970), or a child crying in another room (Staub, 1970, true of older children but not younger ones).

Source: John M. Darley, Allan I. Teger and Lawrence D. Lewis, "Do Groups Always Inhibit Individuals' Responses to Potential Emergencies?" *Journal of Personality and Social Psychology.* 1973, *26,* 395-399. Copyright 1973 by the American Psychological Association. Reprinted by permission.
This research was supported by National Science Foundation Grant 2293.

One explanation for this effect postulates a decision process on the part of the individual bystander which is itself the result of two other processes. First, in our culture, "it is considered desirable to appear poised and collected in times of stress [Latané & Darley, 1969, p. 249]." Second, when an ambiguous event occurs, an individual bystander will be considerably influenced by the ways in which other bystanders are reacting to the event.

Therefore when a bystander is faced with the calm reactions of other bystanders, he may infer that they do not define the event as an emergency, and so he begins to define it himself as no emergency. Thus a state of "pluralistic ignorance" may develop (Latané & Darley, 1969). Although the bystander apparently conforms to the passive, nonhelping behavior of the other people, he does so because he has decided nothing serious is taking place, so that it would be inconsistent with his own thinking to intervene. He has been influenced by the other people, but influenced to accept a particular cognitive definition of the event. This is similar to the process which Asch has labeled, "a change in the object of judgment" rather than a change in the judgment of the object. Inaction, then, is a rational response to a situation that is reinterpreted to require no intervention, rather than an irrational compliance with others' inaction. This explanation might be called the "definition of the situation" hypothesis and can also account for the increase in helping behavior that other investigators have found when an individual observes another person helping (Bryan & Test, 1967; Ross, 1970).

This suggests that, as in the case of conformity research (Allen & Levine, 1968; Asch, 1952), any signals which break the uniformity of the group's apparent unanimous indifference to the emergency may free the individual to consider the possibility that the event is in fact an emergency and act accordingly. One set of signals which may work in this manner is the group of signals which we might call "startle responses" (orienting toward the noise, jumping, facial expressions of concern, etc.). In previously mentioned experiments, in which many subjects apparently defined the event as a nonemergency and offered no help, the subjects were either engaged in tasks which made observing each other's startle responses unlikely (Latané & Darley, 1969; Latané & Rodin, 1969; Staub, 1970) or the nature of the emergency was such as not to provoke visible startle responses.

There is some reason to believe that the startle response of an individual, if it is visible, might be taken as particularly revealing of his true thoughts. Goffman (1969) and others have suggested that we tend to place more faith in information from others which is spontaneous and apparently out of their control. Thus facial expressions are often seen as a more valid indication of the feelings of others than is their overt behavior, for the former are thought to be more spontaneous and less subject to control than the latter.

The startle response, then, is a naturally occurring response that signals some break in the unanimity of the group's passive reactions to a potential emergency, and thus provides a mechanism for testing the definition of the situation explanation for the typical lack of response of groups witnessing emergencies. An emergency was staged in a room adjacent to one in which two subjects were working on a visual perception task. The emergency was a noisy crash which signaled that some precariously balanced construction equipment had fallen on a workman. Some of the groups overheard the emergency while facing each other, and thus were in a position to see each other's startle response. Other groups were oriented away from each other. In a third condition, subjects faced the emergency alone.

The predictions were that the subjects who overheard the crash while alone would intervene, while the nonfacing groups would redefine the event as no emergency and therefore fail to intervene. These experimental conditions replicate those of previous experiments, and the predicted findings would replicate these results. The orientation hypothesis predicts that the subjects from the facing groups will be more likely to define the event as an emergency, and thus more likely to offer help than the subjects from the nonfacing groups.

METHOD

Subjects

Fifty male Princeton University undergraduates served as subjects. All were volunteers who were paid for their participation.

Procedure

Subjects, either in pairs or alone, arrived at the experimenter's office where they were given a short printed paragraph explaining the two types of activities in which they would be participating. The first activity centered around various tests of vision while the second involved an artist-like sketching situation. They then accompanied the experimenter and his assistant down the corridor to a room where the vision testing was conducted. Here they took several vision tests, while the assistant recorded their responses.

After the vision tests had been completed, the experimenter explained that he had arranged to borrow a room from another research team for the sketching task which would take up the remainder of the session. Subjects then followed the experimenter upstairs to the sketching room where the door was found to be locked. The experimenter, expressing consternation over the fact that the door was "supposed to be left open" for him, muttered something about checking to see if there was anyone around who had the key. He knocked next door and after a short delay a workman (actually a confederate of the experimenter) with screwdriver in hand opened the door. The experimenter pointed down the hall to the sketching room and asked if the workman had a key that would open the door. The workman replied that he didn't but speculated that they could get in through a closed but unlocked floor-to-ceiling partition which separated the two rooms. The experimenter asked the subjects to follow him through the workman's room as he pulled open the sliding partition, admitted the subjects and himself into the sketching room, thanked the workman, and pulled the partition shut.

Both rooms were filled with an array of electronic equipment and construction materials, apparently being used by the other investigators from whom the room had been borrowed. Part of the construction materials included several large, heavy wooden-framed metal screens balanced against a wall, which the subjects had to step around in order to enter the sketching room through the partition.

When the subjects had been seated, the experimenter read a prepared set of instructions which directed them to make a sketch of a model horse that was in front of them. They were told not to be concerned about how *artistic* the sketches were but the experimenter merely wanted a rough idea of *perspective* in sketching from a real model as compared to other groups who would do their sketching from a photograph of the model. Subjects were instructed not to talk and to do their sketches independently. The experimenter then announced that he was going back downstairs to correlate the results of their vision tests and would be back in about 10 minutes. (Actually the experimenter joined the experimental assistant in an observation room to observe and record the session through a one-way mirror which was disguised by drawings which were hanging in front of it.)

Experimental Conditions

In the facing condition pairs of subjects were seated face-to-face across a table on which there was a large plastic model of a horse along with sketching pads and drawing pencils. For the alone condition, single subjects were seated in one of these same two positions 50% of the time on one side of the table and the remaining 50% on the opposite side. In the nonfacing condition pairs of subjects were seated back to back, and each subject had his own horse model in front of him on a small stand. Ten subjects were run in the alone condition and 10 pairs of subjects in each of the other two conditions. The experimenter was blind as to which of the two group conditions was being run until, of course, he entered the sketching room and could see the arrangement of the chairs.

The Emergency Incident

Four minutes after the experimenter had left, the workman staged the emergency incident. Pushing over the heavy screens that had been balanced against the wall on his side of the partition produced a resounding crash which was immediately followed by an exclamation of "Oh, my leg!" and a series of painful groans lasting for 3 seconds, which were actually emanating from a concealed tape recorder. After an interval of 5 seconds there was another shorter set of groans heard for 1.5 seconds followed by complete silence. The confederate positioned himself on the floor next to the fallen screens, holding his leg.

Dependent Measures and Debriefing

Subjects' reactions to the incident were recorded and timed. The reaction time was measured from the moment of the crash until the occurrence of some overt helping response. For most subjects who helped, the measure of response latency terminated when they grasped the handle of the partition and began to slide it back to investigate the situation in the other room. The shouting of an inquiry through the partition was also considered a helping response and the reaction time measure was ended as soon as the subject called out loudly enough to be heard and acknowledged by the confederate.

After 6 minutes of observation the experimenter returned to the sketching room and inquired how things were going. If there was no spontaneous report of the incident, the experimenter commented that a secretary had mentioned that she had passed by the room several minutes before and had heard some sort of "commotion." After listening to the subjects' replies, the experimenter carefully explained the nature and necessity of the experimental deception and assured the subjects that the other person was uninjured. He then administered a short questionnaire to obtain subjects' impressions of the incident and its perceived seriousness, previous experience with emergencies, and possible suspicion about the experimental procedure.

TABLE 1.1
Likelihood and Speed of Helping Responses

Condition	Percent Responding ($N = 10$)	Average Time of Responders in Seconds	Average Time of all Subjects in Seconds
Alone	90	11.9 (9 individuals)	46.7
Facing	80	16.6 (8 groups)	85.3
Nonfacing	20	17.0 (2 groups)	291.4
M	63.3	14.4	141.1

RESULTS AND DISCUSSION

The results supported the experimental hypothesis: As Table 1.1 indicates, 80% of the groups in a face-to-face orientation responded to the crash with the offer of some kind of help whereas only 20% of those groups not facing each other reacted when the incident occurred. (Fisher's exact test, $p < .01$.) Ninety percent of subjects reacted to the crash when alone. Therefore 99% of a set of two-person groups could be expected to contain at least one individual who responds $(1 - .10^2)$. If the effect of the group on helping behavior is due to anything other than a simple increase in number of people over the alone condition, then the rate of helping in a group should be significantly different from 99%. The 80% response rate of the face-to-face groups was not significantly different from the value[1] ($p = .24$) while the 20% response rate of the nonfacing condition was significantly smaller (Fisher's exact test, $p < .01$).[2]

Helping rate was thus affected not simply by the presence of other bystanders, but by their physical orientation vis-à-vis each other; groups in a facing orientation were more likely to respond than nonfacing groups. In fact, the facing groups were not significantly slower or less likely to respond than were individuals who were alone when the incident occurred.

What happens in the face-to-face situation which increases the level of helping over the nonfacing situation? There are a number of processes which may be involved—all of which are related to the definition of the situation. First, the observer receives contradictory information (the other observer does not give help, indicating that the situation is *not* an emergency; the other observer also shows a startle response or worried expression, indicating that the situation *is* an emergency). Since all the available information from the other person does not support any single interpretation, the first observer feels free to respond as do the subjects in the alone condition—that is, as though it were an emergency. Second, the startle response is a spontaneous communication and as such it is given greater weight (following Goffman) than the more controllable and less spontaneous decision to refrain from helping. Third, the individual not only observed the startle response sequence of the bystander, but also produced one himself. Realizing that the other observer in the face-to-face situation has observed his response, he may feel that he had communicated that he defined the situation as an emergency. He might then feel obligated to behave in a manner consistent with his definiton.

There are several other aspects of the subject's behavior which support the idea that the definition of the situation process is a crucial determinant of the subjects' response (but not uniquely predicted by it). First, all of the information that signaled the possibility that the event was an emergency (the crash, groans, and whatever startle responses were given) occurred almost immediately. If the subject were to adopt an emergency definition, therefore, one would expect him to do it early or not at all, since all later information—the other person's inaction—mitigated against the emergency definition. All subjects who were to respond did so within the first 30 seconds of the 6-minute interval (that is, within 20 seconds of the final groan). Those subjects who responded did so in an average of 14.4 seconds (and did not differ by condition; Table 1.1, Column 3). Second, subjects in the two-group conditions reported different definitions of the event. Nineteen out of the 20 subjects in the facing condition indicated on the postexperimental questionnaire that the crash had signaled that something was *wrong*, while only 11 of the nonfacing subjects did so. (The definitions of pairs of subjects are not statistically independent, therefore they were combined, and a test between the average definition of the 10 facing and the 10 nonfacing pairs was run, $t = 2.72$, $df = 18$, $p < .05$.) Subjects in the facing condition consistently emphasized that some equipment had fallen *on* the workman and frequently used adjectives such as "injured" or "hurt" to describe his fate, while subjects in the nonfacing condition tended to report that some equipment had merely fallen down.

To conceptualize the defining process in the face-to-face groups a single exchange of signals may underrate its complexity. An observer kept a record of events throughout the experiment, and these impressions emerged from the protocols: Generally in all conditions, subjects individually showed similar degrees of initial startle response and facial expressions indicating concern or arousal. In the facing condition, a subject could see the other person's startle response and apparently also looked for confirmatory expressions of concern from the other. Usually he got them, but, in the two nonresponding facing groups, it was the observer's judgment that one of the dyad members initiated helping but terminated his efforts when he did not observe any signs of concomitant concern on the part of the other subject. In the nonfacing condition, subjects also sought defining cues from the other person. Unable to see the visual cues, many subjects appeared to be listening for possible auditory cues produced by their partner in order to learn how he was reacting. In 8 out of the 10 groups the absence of such cues signaled inaction. In both of the groups which responded, when one subject got up to investigate the incident, the remaining subject, upon hearing indications of his partner's action, helped also.

The findings of the current study may help to explain some of the inconsistencies in the early research on bystander intervention. Darley and Latané (1968) found that the rate of helping was reduced as the number of bystanders increased. However, Piliavin, Rodin, and Piliavin (1969), in a field experiment staged in a subway car, found that rate of helping was unaffected by the number of bystanders present. In subways, however, the seating arrangement is similar to that in the face-to-face condition of the present study. The seats are oriented across from or at right angles to one another—placing the passengers in a facing or semifacing situation. Present results indicate that other bystanders will not decrease the rate of helping in such a situation.

Current results also suggest that when the diffusion and definition processes are both possible, the definition process tends to dominate. The diffusion of personal responsibility felt by a subject in the facing or nonfacing condition of the present study was presumably equal since in each case there was one other person available to help. However, markedly different response rates in fact occurred, caused by processes leading to different definitions of the situation.

Our characterization of the process as one in which the observer arrives at an immediate definition of the situation may also be an oversimplification. It is possible that the process may be extended by various means so that the subject *redefines* the situation at various points, after observing his own behavior or the behavior of the other subject. The present data, however, do not permit us to choose definitely among these alternative explanations.

Despite the problems presented by the competing explanations mentioned above, this study indicates that it may be productive to pay greater attention to the nonverbal aspects of those social influence processes which are operative during the time when a situation is being defined.

REFERENCES

Allen, V., & Levine, J. Social support, dissent, and conformity. *Sociometry,* 1968, *31,* 138-149.

Asch, S. *Social psychology.* New York: Prentice-Hall, 1952.

232   PROSOCIAL BEHAVIOR

Bryan, J., & Test, M. A. Models and helping: Naturalistic studies in aiding behavior. *Journal of Personality and Social Psychology,* 1967, *6,* 400-407.
Darley, J. M., & Latané, B. Bystander intervention in emergencies: Diffusion of responsibility. *Journal of Personality and Social Psychology,* 1968, *8,* 377-383.
Goffman, E. *Strategic interaction.* Philadelphia: University of Pennsylvania Press, 1969.
Latané, B., & Darley, J. M. Group inhibition of bystander intervention in emergencies. *Journal of Personality and Social Psychology,* 1968, *10,* 215-221.
Latané, B., & Darley, J. M. Bystander "apathy." *American Scientist,* 1969, *57,* 244-268.
Latané, B., & Darley, J. M. *The unresponsive bystander: Why doesn't he help?* New York: Appleton-Century-Crofts, 1970.
Latané, B., & Rodin, J. A lady in distress: Inhibiting effects of friends and strangers on bystander intervention. *Journal of Experimental Social Psychology,* 1969, *5,* 189-202.
Piliavin, J. M., Rodin, J., & Piliavin, J. A. Good Samaritanism: An underground phenomenon? *Journal of Personality and Social Psychology,* 1969, *13,* 289-299.
Ross, A. S. The effect of observing a helpful model on helping behavior. *Journal of Social Psychology,* 1970, *81,* 131-132.
Staub, E. A child in distress: The influence of age and number of witnesses on children's attempts to help. *Journal of Personality and Psychology,* 1970, *14,* 130-140.

NOTES

1. For simplicity these calculations were made, assuring an expected response rate of 100% rather than 99%.

2. If the *speed of response* results are analyzed by analysis of variance procedures and multiple comparisons (on the time scores), the above results emerge more strongly ($F = 9.60$, $p < .01$). However, this method of analysis is questionable since the data are essentially dichotomous between quick responders and nonresponders. No usual transformation eliminates this bimodality.

2

JAMES H. BRYAN and MARY ANN TEST

Models and Helping: Naturalistic Studies in Aiding Behavior

Four experiments concerned with helping behavior were conducted. Three were addressed to the effects of altruistic models upon helping, while 1 was concerned with the impact of the solicitor's race upon donations. Three investigations employed as a site parking lots of 2 large department stores in New Jersey, and indexed helping by contributions to the Salvation Army. A 4th experiment indexed helping by offers of aid by passing motorists to a woman with a disabled vehicle. Whether one employed motorists in California or shoppers in New Jersey, the results were quite consistent. The presence of a helping model significantly increased helping behavior. As race of the Salvation Army solicitor did affect the percentage of donors willing to contribute money, it was concluded that interpersonal attraction is a relevant variable affecting donations.

Recently, concern has been evidenced regarding the determinants and correlates of altruistic behavior, those acts wherein individuals share or sacrifice a presumed positive reinforcer for no apparent social or material gain. Studies addressed to these behaviors have explored both individual differences in the tendency to be altruistic and the situational determinants of such responses. Gore and Rotter (1963) found that students at a southern Negro college were more likely to volunteer for a social protest movement if they perceived sources of reinforcement as internally rather than externally guided. Subjects high on internal control were more likely

Source: James H. Bryan and Mary Ann Test, "Models and Helping: Naturalistic Studies in Aiding Behavior," *Journal of Personality and Social Psychology*, 1967, 6, 400-407. Copyright 1967 by the American Psychological Association. Reprinted by permission.

While Mary Ann Test collaborated with the senior author on Experiment I, the remaining work is the latter's sole responsibility.

Thanks are due to Cheryl Dellhoussay, Betty Umann, Joe McNair, and Frank Siri who served as the experimenters and stooges for Experiment I, and to Edward Nystrom, Alice Anderson, Katherine Moore, and Irene Paramoure who served as the models, observers, and solicitors in studies II, III, and IV. Studies II, III, and IV were carried out while the author was affiliated with Educational Testing Service and were supported by the National Institute of Child Health and Human Development, under Research Grant 1 PO1 HD1762-01. The authors are especially grateful to the Salvation Army of Trenton, New Jersey, and specifically to George H. Gibb, whose cooperation made these experiments possible. Thanks are also due to Perry London, David Rosenhan, Ladd Wheeler, Lawrence Stricker, and Bruce K. Eckland for the many helpful comments upon various portions of the manuscript.

to volunteer as freedom riders, marchers, or petition signers than subjects who perceived others as primary agents of reinforcement. Experimental evidence has been generated supporting the often-made assumption that guilt may serve as a stimulus to altruistic activity. Darlington and Macker (1966) found that subjects led to believe that they had harmed another through incompetent performances on the experimental tasks (three paper-and-pencil tests) were more willing than control subjects to donate blood to a local hospital. Aronfreed and Paskal[1] and Midlarsky and Bryan (1967) found that children exposed to treatment conditions designed to produce empathy were more willing to donate M&M candies than subjects given control conditions, while Handlon and Gross (1959), Ugurel-Semin (1952), Wright (1942), and Midlarsky and Bryan have found sharing to be positively correlated with age among school-age children. Lastly, Berkowitz and Friedman (1967) have demonstrated that adolescents of the working class are less affected in their helping behaviors by interpersonal attraction than adolescents of the entrepreneur middle class.

Three hypotheses have emerged regarding the situational determinants of self-sacrificing behaviors. One suggests that individuals behave in an altruistic fashion because of compliance to a norm of reciprocity. That is, individuals are aware of the social debts and credits established between them, and expect that ultimately the mutual exchange of goods and services will balance (Gouldner, 1960). Berkowitz and Daniels (1964) have suggested that individuals might show a generalization of such obligatory feelings and thus aid others who had not previously assisted them.

A second hypothesis was put forth by Berkowitz and his colleagues (Berkowitz, 1966; Berkowitz & Daniels, 1963; Berkowitz, Klanderman, & Harris, 1964; Daniels & Berkowitz, 1963) who have postulated the social responsibility norm. They have contended that dependency on others evokes helping responses even under conditions where the possibility of external rewards for the helper are remote. Using supervisor's ratings of an unknown and absent other to produce dependency, and a box-construction task as the dependent variable, considerable support has been generated for the suggestion that dependency increases helping.

A third major determinant of helping may be the presence of helping (or nonhelping) models. While attention to the effects of models has generally been directed toward antisocial behaviors (cf. Bandura & Walters, 1963; Freed, Chandler, Mouton, & Blake, 1955; Lefkowitz, Blake, & Mouton, 1955), some recent evidence suggests that observation of self-sacrificing models may lead to subsequent succorant behavior by children. For example, Rosenhan and White (1967) have demonstrated that children are more likely to donate highly valued gift certificates to residents of a fictitious orphanage if they have seen an adult do so. Hartup and Coates[2] found that nursery school children who have been exposed to a self-sacrificing peer were more likely to be altruistic than children not so exposed. Test and Bryan[3] found that female college students were more likely to render aid to another in computing arithmetic problems if they saw other people so doing.

The present series of experiments was designed to test the effects of models in natural settings on subject samples other than college or high school students, and in contexts other than a school room or university setting. The first three experiments reported are concerned with the impact of observing helping models upon subsequent helping behaviors, while the fourth is addressed to the influence of interpersonal attraction upon donation behavior.

EXPERIMENT I: LADY IN DISTRESS: A FLAT TIRE STUDY

Few studies have been concerned with the effects of models upon *adults*, and fewer still with the impact of *prosocial* models upon them (Wheeler, 1966). Those that have been concerned with such behaviors have invariably employed college students as subjects. For example, Rosenbaum and Blake (1955) and Rosenbaum (1956) have found that college students exposed to a model who volunteered, upon the personal request of the experimenter, to participate in an experiment would be more likely to consent than subjects not exposed to such a model or than subjects who observed a model refuse to cooperate. Pressures toward conformity in these experiments were great, however, as the request was made directly by the experimenter and in the presence of a large number of other students.

Test and Bryan found that the observation of helping models significantly increased the subsequent offers of aid by observers. However, in that study, subjects were given the task of solving arithmetic problems and then rating their difficulty, a task ordinarily requiring autonomous efforts. Furthermore, the experiment was conducted within a university setting, a context where independence of thought is often stressed. The effects of the model may have been simply to increase the subjects' faith that assisting others was allowed. While questionnaire data of the study did not support this interpretation, such effects could not be ruled out entirely. Thus, it is possible that the model impact was simply a propriety-defining activity which reduced the inhibitions associated with such helping behavior.

In general, then, investigations of modeling that employ adults as subjects and that demand self-sacrifice on the part of subjects are limited in number, exploit strong pressures toward conformity, and rely upon college students as subjects. The present experiment was designed to assess the impact of models upon subsequent spontaneous offers of help in other than a university setting.

Method

The standard condition consisted of an undergraduate female stationed by a 1964 Ford Mustang (control car) with a flat left-rear tire. An inflated tire was leaned upon the left side of the auto. The girl, the flat tire, and the inflated tire were conspicuous to the passing traffic.

In the model condition, a 1965 Oldsmobile was located approximately ¼ mile from the control car. The car was raised by jack under the left rear bumper, and a girl was watching a male changing the flat tire.

In the no-model condition, the model was absent; thus, only the control car was visible to the passing traffic.

The cars were located in a predominantly residential section in Los Angeles, California. They were placed in such a manner that no intersection separated the model from the control car. No turnoffs were thus available to the passing traffic. Further, opposite flows of traffic were divided by a separator such that the first U turn available to the traffic going in the opposite direction of the control car would be after exposure to the model condition.

The experiment was conducted on two successive Saturdays between the hours of 1:45 and 5:50 P.M. Each treatment condition lasted for the time required for 1000 vehicles to pass the control car. While private automobiles and trucks, motorscooters, and motorcycles were tallied as vehicles, commercial trucks, taxis, and buses were not. Vehicle count was made by a fourth member of the experiment who stood approximately 100 feet from the control car hidden from the passing motorists. On the first Saturday, the model condition was run first and lasted from 1:45 to 3:15 P.M. In order to exploit changing traffic patterns and to keep the time intervals equal across treatment conditions, the control car was moved several blocks and placed on the opposite side of the street for the no-model condition. The time of the no-model treatment was 4:00 to 5:00 P.M. On the following Saturday, counterbalancing the order and the location of treatment conditions was accomplished. That is, the no-model condition was run initially and the control car was placed in the same location that it had been placed on the previous Saturday during the model condition. The time of the no-model condition was 2:00 to 3:30 P.M. For the model condition, the control car was placed in that locale where it had been previously during the no-model condition. The time of the model condition was 4:30 to 5:30 P.M.

Individuals who had stopped to offer help were told by the young lady that she had already phoned an auto club and that help was imminent. Those who nonetheless insisted on helping her were told the nature of the experiment.

Results

The dependent variable was the number of cars that stopped and from which at least one individual offered help to the stooge by the control car. Of the 4000 passing vehicles, 93 stopped. With the model car absent, 35 vehicles stopped; with the model present, 58 halted. The difference between the conditions was statistically significant ($x^2 = 5.53$, corrected for continuity, $df = 1$, $p < .02$, two-tailed). Virtually all offers of aid were from men rather than woman drivers.

The time of day had little impact upon the offering of aid. Fifty vehicles stopped during the early part of the afternoon; 43 during the later hours. Likewise, differences in help offers were not great between successive Saturdays, as 45 offers of aid were made on the first Saturday, 48 on the second Saturday.

The results of the present study support the hypothesis that helping behaviors can be significantly increased through the observation of others' helpfulness. However, other plausible hypotheses exist which may account for the findings. It is possible to account for the differences in treatment effects by differences in sympathy arousal. That is, in the model condition, the motorist observed a woman who had had some difficulty. Such observations may have elicited sympathy and may have served as a reminder to the driver of his own social responsibilities.

Another explanation of the findings revolves around traffic slowdown. It is possible that the imposition of the model condition served to reduce traffic speed, thus making subsequent stopping to help a less hazardous undertaking. While the time taken for 1000 autos to pass the control car was virtually identical in the model and no-model condition and thus not supportive of such an explanation, the "slowdown" hypothesis cannot be eliminated. Assuming the model effect to be real, one might still argue that it was not a norm of helping that was facilitated by the model, but rather that inhibitions against picking up helpless young ladies were reduced. That is, within the model condition, the passing motorists may have observed a tempted other and thus felt less constrained themselves regarding similar efforts. Indeed, the insistence of some people to help in spite of the imminent arrival of other aiders suggested the operation of motives other than simply helping. Indeed, while the authors did not index the frequency of pick-up attempts, it was clear that a rather large number were evidenced.

Because of the number of alternative explanations, the evidence supporting the hypothesis that the observation of helpers per se will increase subsequent aiding is weak. Experiment II was designed to test further the prediction that the perception of another's altruistic activity would elicit similar behavior on the part of the observer.

EXPERIMENT II: COINS IN THE KETTLE

The investigation was conducted on December 14th between the hours of 10:00 A.M. and 5:00 P.M. The subjects were shoppers at a large department store in Princeton, New Jersey. Observations made on the previous day indicated that the shoppers were overwhelmingly Caucasian females.

A Salvation Army kettle was placed on the side-walk in front of the main entrance to the store. Two females, both in experimenter's employ, alternatively manned the kettle for periods of 25 minutes. One solicitor was a Negro, the other a Caucasion. Each wore a Salvation Army cape and hat. Although allowed to ring the Salvation Army bell, they were not permitted to make any verbal plea or to maintain eye contact with the passing shoppers, except to thank any contributor for his donation.

The model condition (M) was produced as follows: Once every minute on the minute, a male dressed as a white-collar worker would approach the kettle from within the store and contribute 5 cents. As the model donated, he started a stopwatch and walked from the kettle toward a parking lot as if searching for someone. He then returned to the store. The following 20-second period constituted the duration of the treatment condition.

Following a subsequent lapse of 20 seconds, the next 20-second period defined the no-model condition (NM). Within any one minute, therefore, both M and NM treatments occurred. There were 365 occasions of each treatment.

It should be noted that it was possible that some subjects in the NM condition observed the contribution of the model or a donor affected by the model. If that hypothesis is correct, however, the effects of such incidents would be to reduce rather than enhance the differences between treatments.

Results

The dependent variable was the number of people who independently donated to the Salvation Army. People obviously acquainted, as for example, man and wife, were construed as one potential donating unit. In such conditions, if both members of a couple contributed, they were counted as a single donor.

Since there were no differences in model effects for the Negro or Caucasian solicitor, data obtained from each were combined. The total number of contributors under the NM condition was 43; under the M condition, 69. Assuming that the chance distribution of donations would be equal across the two conditions, a chi-square analysis was performed. The chi-square equaled 6.01 ($p < .01$).[4]

In spite of precautions concerning the elimination of correlated observations within a treatment condition, it was possible for subjects in any one observational period to influence one another. Such influence may have been mediated through acquaintances not eliminated by our procedures or the observations of others as well as the model donating. A more conservative analysis of the data, insuring independent observation, was therefore made. Instead of comparing treatments by analyzing the number of donors, the analysis used, as the dependent variable, the number of observation periods in which there was a contribution, that is, those periods in which more than one donation occurred were scored identically to those in which only a single contribution was received. Occasions of donations equaled 60 in the M treatment, 43 in the NM condition. The chi-square equaled 2.89 ($p < .05$).

The results of Experiment II further support the hypothesis that observation of altruistic activity will increase such behavior among observers. But the matter is not yet entirely clear, for when the observer saw the model donate he saw two things: first, the actual donation, and second, the polite and potentially reinforcing interaction that occurred between the donor and solicitor. Conceivably, the observation of an altruistic model, per se, who was not socially reinforced for his behavior, would have little or no effect on an observer. The third experiment was designed to examine this possibility.

EXPERIMENT III: COINS IN THE KETTLE II

The experiment was conducted at a Trenton, New Jersey, shopping center from the hours of 10:00 A.M. to 5:00 P.M. Again, the majority of the patrons were Caucasian females. It is likely, however, that these shoppers were of a lower socioeconomic status than those in the Princeton group.

Salvation Army kettles were placed before the main entrance of a large department store (Kettle 1) and a large food center (Kettle 2). The kettles were separated by more than 200 yards. During the first 120 observations (10:00 A.M. to 12:00 P.M.), two male college students, employed by the Salvation Army and wearing its uniform, manned the kettles. The site of the experiment was Kettle 1, except on those occasions where the worker took his "coffee break." At those times, data collection was centered at Kettle 2. An equal number of M and NM conditions were run at each site, although approximately two-thirds of the observational time was spent at Kettle 1. During the remaining 240 observation periods (1:00 P.M. to 5:00 P.M.) the same male worker and his spouse alternately manned Kettle 1. The wife was stationed by the kettle for 136 minutes, the male for 104 minutes. The experiment was conducted only at Kettle 1 during the afternoon period.

Solicitors were told to make no verbal appeals for donations or responses to the model upon his contribution. While they were not informed of the hypothesis underlying the experiment, they may well have deduced it. The model was the same as in Experiment II, and again was dressed as a white-collar worker.

The imposition of the treatment conditions were identical to those described in Experiment I with the following exceptions. Since the kettle was more visible at this site than at the previous one, 30-second rather than 20-second periods were used for each treatment. To simplify the procedures, no waiting periods between treatments occurred. Additionally, after donating, the model would return to the parking lot. There were a total of 360 occasions of each of the M and NM conditions.

Results

The criteria defining a donor were identical to those outlined in Experiment I. Under the M condition, 84 donors were tallied; under the NM treatment, 56. The chi-square value was 4.86 ($p < .025$).

Since it was possible that one donor might have seen a donor other than the model receive social approval from the solicitor, the more conservative comparison of the treatments as outlined in Experiment II was made. That is, treatments were compared by noting the number of observational periods in which any donation occurred. Therefore, those donors who may have been influenced by a contributor receiving the solicitor's thanks were excluded. Of the 360 observational periods under the M condition, there were 75 in which some donation was made. Of the 360 NM periods, 51 were marked by contributions. Chi-square yielded a value of 5.09 ($p < .025$).

EXPERIMENT IV: ETHNOCENTRISM AND DONATION BEHAVIOR

While Experiment III was conducted to eliminate the solicitor's explicit social approval as a mechanism underlying donation behavior, it is possible that the model's impact was due to the information communicated to the observer regarding the consequence of donations. Work by Bandura, Ross, and Ross (1963), for example, found that children observing a model rewarded for aggression would be more aggressive than children who had observed a model being punished for such behavior. Additionally, considerable data have been gathered within the university laboratory suggesting that interpersonal attraction may greatly influence the helping response. Berkowitz and Friedman (1967), Daniels and Berkowitz (1963), and Goranson and Berkowitz (1966) have suggested that positive affect increases the probability of low payoff helping behavior.

The present experiment was designed to assess the impact of the solicitor's race upon the donation behavior of shoppers. It was assumed that a Negro solicitor would be held in less esteem by Caucasian shoppers than a solicitor of their same race, and that such attitudes would affect contributions. While the applicability of the "consequence to the model" hypothesis in accounting for the model's effect was not tested directly, the study assesses the importance of interpersonal attraction in eliciting charitable behavior.

Method

The experiment was conducted on December 2 and 3 between the hours of 10 A.M. and 6 P.M. at the Trenton area site. The subjects were Caucasian shoppers at a large department store.[5] Three thousand seven hundred and three shoppers were observed; 2,154 females and 1,549 males. In order to reduce the possibility of including the same subject in the experiment on more than one occasion, tallies were made only of exiting shoppers.

Two Salvation Army kettles were placed at two store exits, their location being separated by approximately 75 yards. Two female solicitors, a Negro and a Caucasian, manned the kettles. Both were in their early twenties, wore the uniform of the Salvation Army, and were in the employ of the experimenter. Each was instructed to make no verbal appeals for donations and to avoid eye contact with the shoppers. After a period of 25 minutes, the girls rotated kettle assignments, and during the last 10 minutes of the hour were allowed to take a coffee break. Hence, during a single hour, each solicitor manned both kettles. Each solicitor manned each kettle on seven occasions per day. Thus, each solicitor was observed for a total of 28 observational periods; 14 on each day (seven on each kettle) over a period of two days.

Two observers, each assigned to a particular kettle, tallied the number and sex of the exiting shoppers and contributors during each of the 25-minute periods. In addition, records were kept of the amount of money donated within any period, although it was impossible on this measure to separate those donations made by incoming from outgoing customers.

Results

The dependent variable was the percentage of donors contibuting to the kettle within an observational period. That is, observational periods were assigned a percentage donor score. Shoppers within an observational period were treated as a single group, with differences between groups on percentage donor score forming the critical comparisons. The total N of the study was then the 56 observational periods, rather than the 3,703 shoppers. Since the mean group size for the Negro solicitor was 70.32 and for the Caucasian 61.93 (standard deviations equal to 53.33 and 42.98, respectively), it was assumed that the percentage score was relatively stable.

The effects of race, kettle location, and day and their interactions were analyzed by analysis of variance.

As can be seen from Table 2.1, both the main effect of race and of day were significant. As predicted, the Negro solicitor elicited a statistically significant lower percentage of donors than did the Caucasian. For the

TABLE 2.1
Analysis of Variance of Percentage Donor Scores

	df	MS	F
Race (A)	1	38.778	4.84*
Day (B)	1	98.315	12.28**
Kettle (C)	1	.018	
A X B	1	1.511	
A X C	1	11.340	
B X C	1	1.031	
A X B X C	1	3.206	
Error	48	8.009	

*$p < .05$ (2-tailed).
**$p < .01$ (2-tailed).

Negro solicitor, the average percentage donor score for observational periods was 2.22 ($SD = 2.36$), while for the Caucasian solicitor the average percentage donor score was 3.89 ($SD = 3.60$). Additionally, Saturday shoppers were by and large less generous than Friday customers. The average percentage donor score of the group was 1.73 ($SD = 1.97$) for the Saturday shopper, and 4.38 for the Friday shopper ($SD = 3.52$).

A second dependent variable was the amount of money donated during each time period. No significant differences were found for race, day, or kettle location.

The present investigation does support, albeit equivocally, the notion that interpersonal attraction may affect donations even when the solicitors are not the eventual recipients of such contributions. While it is possible that race differences simply fail to remind observers of their social responsibilities, it is also feasible that the subjects wanted to avoid interpersonal contact with a minority group member. If this is true, then it is interesting to note that interpersonal attraction may play an important role even in those situations where personal anonymity is high and escape from unpleasant situations easy.

DISCUSSION

The results of the first three experiments clearly replicate those of Test and Bryan and extend the findings over a variety of subject populations, settings, and tasks. The results hold for college students, motorists, and shoppers; in the university laboratory, city streets, and shopping centers; and when helping is indexed by aiding others solve arithmetic problems, changing flat tires, or donating money to the Salvation Army. The findings then are quite consistent: the presence of helping models significantly increases subsequent altruistic behavior.

That generosity breeds generosity is interesting in light of the recent concern with helping behaviors in emergency contexts. Darley and Latané[6] and Latané and Darley[7] have found that subjects are less inclined to act quickly in emergency situations when in the presence of other potential helpers. Whether faced with a medical emergency (a simulated epileptic seizure) or a dangerous natural event (simulated fire), the rapidity with which students sought to aid was reduced by the presence of others. These findings have been interpreted in three ways: as reflecting the subjects' willingness to diffuse responsibility (others will aid); as reflecting their diffusion of blame (others didn't aid either); or as reflecting conformity to the nonpanicked stooges. It is clear that the results of the first three experiments in the present series do not follow that which might be predicted by the diffusion concepts. A giving model apparently does not lend credibility to the belief that others than the self will make the necessary sacrifices. The helping other did not strengthen the observer's willingness to diffuse his social obligations, but rather stimulated greater social responsibility. In light of these results, the delayed reaction exhibited by the subjects tested by Darley and Latané might be best attributable to conformity behavior. As they have suggested, subjects faced with a unique and stressful situation may have been either reassured by the presence of calm others or fearful of acting stupidly or cowardly. Additionally, it is possible that diffusion of responsibility is only associated with anxiety-inducing situations. The current data fail to indicate that such diffusion occurs in nonstressful situations which demand fulfillment of social obligations.

While it appears clear that the behavior of the motorists and shoppers was not dictated by a variety of situational and social pressures usually associated with the study of modeling in adults or experiment in academic settings (Orne, 1962), the mechanisms underlying the effects are not obvious. While the presence of the model in the flat-tire study may have reminded the motorists as to the social responsibility norm, such a hypothesis does not appear reasonable in accounting for the results in the coins-in-the-kettle series. The bell-ringing Salvation Army worker, with kettle and self placed squarely in the pathway of the oncoming pedestrian, would seem to be reminder enough of one's obligation toward charity. A priori, it would not appear necessary to superimpose upon that scene the donating other for purposes of cognitive cueing (Wheeler, 1966).

One hypothesis to account for the model effect is that the observer is given more information regarding the consequences of such donation behavior. Experiment IV suggested that solicitor status or personal attraction might operate on donation behaviors even under conditions of personal anonymity and few social constraints. It is possible that the model serves to communicate to the potential donor relevant information concerning the consequences of his act. That is, the model may demonstrate that an approach to the solicitor does not involve an unwanted interpersonal interaction (e.g., lectures on religion).

A second hypothesis to account for the data pertains to the shame-provoking capacities of the model. It is reasonable to assume that most people feel that they are, by and large, benevolent and charitable. Furthermore, it is likely that such a self-image is rarely challenged: first because charitable acts are not frequently required; second, at least in the street scenes employed in the current series of studies, solicitations are made in the context of many nongiving others. That is, a multitude of negative models—of noncharitable others—surround the solicitations in the current series of studies. Indeed, the contexts are such that most people are not helping; many more cars pass than stop to offer aid to the lady in distress; and there are many more people who refuse to put coins in the kettle than those who do. However, the witnessing of a donor, an individual who not only recognizes his social responsibility but in fact acts upon it, may produce a greater challenge to the good-self image of the observer. Acts rather than thoughts may be required of the observer in order to maintain the self-image of benevolence and charity. If such is the case, then the model characteristics most effective in producing prosocial behavior by socialized adults would be those directed toward shame or guilt production (e.g., donations from the poor), rather than those reflecting potential reinforcement power (e.g., donations from the high status).

Whatever the mechanism underlying the model effect, it does appear quite clear that prosocial behavior can be elicited through the observation of benign others.

REFERENCES

Bandura, A., Ross, D., & Ross, S. Vicarious reinforcement and imitative learning. *Journal of Abnormal and Social Psychology,* 1963, *66,* 601-607.

Bandura, A., & Walters, R. H. *Social learning and personality development.* New York: Holt, Rinehart & Winston, 1963.

Berkowitz, L. A laboratory investigation of social class and national differences in helping behavior. *International Journal of Psychology,* 1966, *1,* 231-240.

Berkowitz, L., & Daniels, L. Responsibility and dependency. *Journal of Abnormal and Social Psychology,* 1963, *66,* 429-436.

Berkowitz, L., & Daniels, L. Affecting the salience of the social responsibility norm: Effects of past help on the response to dependency relationships. *Journal of Abnormal and Social Psychology,* 1964, *68,* 275-281.

Berkowitz, L., & Friedman, P. Some social class differences in helping behavior. *Journal of Personality and Social Psychology,* 1967, *5,* 217-225.

Berkowitz, L., Klanderman, S. B., & Harris, R. Effects of experimenter awareness and sex of subject and experimenter on reactions to dependency relationships. *Sociometry,* 1964, *27,* 327-337.

Daniels, L., & Berkowitz, L. Liking and response to dependency relationships. *Human Relations,* 1963, *16,* 141-148.

Darlington, R. B., & Macker, C. E. Displacement of guilt-produced altruistic behavior. *Journal of Personality and Social Psychology,* 1966, *4,* 442-443.

Freed, A., Chandler, P., Mouton, J., & Blake, R. Stimulus and background factors in sign violation. *Journal of Personality,* 1955, *23,* 499.

Goranson, R., & Berkowitz, L. Reciprocity and responsibility reactions to prior help. *Journal of Personality and Social Psychology,* 1966, *3,* 227-232.

Gore, P. M., & Rotter, J. B. A personality correlate of social action. *Journal of Personality,* 1963, *31,* 58-64.

Gouldner, A. The norm of reciprocity: A preliminary statement. *American Sociological Review,* 1960, *25,* 161-178.

Handlon, B. J., & Gross, P. The development of sharing behavior. *Journal of Abnormal and Social Psychology,* 1959, *59,* 425-428.

Lefkowitz, M., Blake, R., & Mouton, J. Status factors in pedestrian violation of traffic signals. *Journal of Abnormal and Social Psychology,* 1955, *51,* 704-706.

Midlarsky, E., & Bryan, J. H. Training charity in children. *Journal of Personality and Social Psychology,* 1967, *5,* 408-415.

Orne, M. On the social psychology of the psychological experiment: With particular reference to demand characteristics and their implications. *American Psychologist,* 1962, *17,* 776-783.

Rosenbaum, M. The effect of stimulus and background factors on the volunteering response. *Journal of Abnormal and Social Psychology,* 1956, *53,* 118-121.

Rosenbaum, M., & Blake, R. Volunteering as a function of field structure. *Journal of Abnormal and Social Psychology,* 1955, *50,* 193-196.

Rosenhan, D., & White, G. M. Observation and rehearsal as determinants of prosocial behavior. *Journal of Personality and Social Psychology,* 1967, *5,* 424-431.

Ugurel-Semin, R. Moral behavior and moral judgment of children. *Journal of Abnormal and Social Psychology,* 1952, *47,* 463-474.

Wheeler, L. Toward a theory of behavioral contagion. *Psychological Review,* 1966, *73,* 179-192.

Wright, B. A. Altruism in children and perceived conduct of others. *Journal of Abnormal and Social Psychology,* 1942, *37,* 218-233.

NOTES

1. J. Aronfreed & V. Paskal. Altruism, empathy and the conditioning of positive affect. Unpublished manuscript, 1965.

2. W. W. Hartup & B. Coates. Imitation of peers as a function of reinforcement from the peer group and rewardingness of the model. Unpublished manuscript, 1966.

3. M. A. Test & J. H. Bryan. Dependency, models and reciprocity. Unpublished manuscript, 1966.

4. All chi-square analyses were corrected for continuity and all tests of significance were one-tailed.

5. As there were very few Negro donors ($N = 7$), analysis was confined to the behavior of Caucasian shoppers.

6. J. Darley & B. Latané. Diffusion of responsibility in emergency situations. Unpublished manuscript, 1966.

7. B. Latané & J. Darley. Group inhibition of bystander intervention in emergencies. Unpublished manuscript, 1966.

3

SEYMOUR W. URANOWITZ

Helping and Self-Attributions: A Field Experiment

A field experiment was conducted to test the derivations of Bem's self-perception theory as described by Lepper, who investigated the behavioral effects of self-attributions formed as a result of previous behavior. Women in a shopping center were asked by an experimenter to watch his packages while he retrieved either his wallet (high justification) or a dollar (low justification). It was hypothesized that low justification subjects would make self-attributions of "helpfulness," while high justification subjects would attribute their behavior to external factors and would thereby make no such self-attribution. To test this hypothesis, subjects were given the opportunity to help a second experimenter, who crossed the subjects' path and dropped a package, apparently unnoticed. The prediction was that low justification subjects would show more subsequent helping behavior than high justification subjects or control subjects, who had no initial contact. This prediction was confirmed, thereby lending additional support to the self-perception analysis.

Lepper (1973) has recently attempted to broaden the scope of Bem's (1967, 1972) self-perception theory to include behavioral consequences of self-attributions, a phenomenon largely unexplored except for an intriguing finding by Freedman and Fraser (1966). The authors demonstrated what they called the "foot-in-the-door" phenomenon, by which they meant that a person's initial compliance with a small, inconsequential request would increase the likelihood that he would comply with a later, more substantial request, possibly because he identifies himself as a "doer." Lepper (1973) attempted to systematically explore behavioral consequences of self-attributions. He found that children who initially resisted the temptation to play with a toy under mild threat showed more

Source: Seymour W. Uranowitz, "Helping and Self-Attributions: A Field Experiment," *Journal of Personality and Social Psychology*, 1975, *31*, 852-854. Copyright by the American Psychological Association. Reprinted by permission.

This article is based on a senior thesis submitted in partial fulfillment of the honors program at the University of California, Berkeley under the sponsorship of Thomas J. Crawford, whose guidance, support, and encouragement is gratefully acknowledged. The author also wishes to thank Daryl J. Bem, Mark R. Lepper, and Christina Maslach, for their insightful and instructive comments, and Pamela Crozat for her role as the second experimenter.

resistance to cheat in a game to obtain prizes 3 weeks later, presumably due to the self-attribution of honesty.

The purpose of the present study was to bring Lepper's paradigm back into the field, where Freedman and Fraser had first obtained the foot-in-the-door result confirmed in Lepper's study. If the precision of a laboratory setting could be maintained in the field, using an important social behavior of widespread interest, significant results would have clear implications both for the problem of the effects of self-attributions upon subsequent behavior and in interpreting relevant areas of the behavior itself. The behavior thus chosen for study was helpful behavior, and the presumed mediating self-attribution would be helpfulness or altruism. The hypothesis is that subjects who comply with an innocuous request under conditions of minimal justification show more helpful behavior in a subsequent encounter than either subjects in the high justification or control conditions, the latter involving no initial contact. The basic rationale is that under low justification, subjects are more likely to make self-attributions of "helpfulness," in accordance with the insufficient justification studies by Lepper (1973) and (through inference) Freedman and Fraser (1966).

METHOD

Subjects

The subjects were 60 women aged from about mid-20s to mid-60s who were approached in a shopping center in Concord, California. There were 20 subjects in each justification condition and 20 control subjects, who received only the dependent measure.

Procedure

Justification Variation. Women walking alone out of a shopping center department store who did not appear to be in a great hurry were approached by the first experimenter, a college-aged male, who was carrying five bulky grocery bags in a very awkward manner. He asked the subject if she would watch his bags for a moment while he went back into the store from which they had both just emerged to retrieve something he claimed to have lost while shopping in the store. In the high justification condition, he appeared to be in a highly agitated state with a worried look on his face and hurriedly explained that he had lost his wallet, which contained "a lot of money." In the low justification condition, he appeared calm and seemed to be in no great hurry as he explained that he had dropped a dollar bill in the store. All 40 experimental subjects (as well as 4 who were lost because of inadvertent path changes between experimenters) complied with this request. Upon the subject's compliance with the request, the experimenter placed his bags on the ground near the subject's feet and ran back into the store, taking the same route each time to a far corner of the store. This procedure standardized the amount of time each subject waited alone with the experimenter's packages, a period of approximately 1 minute. In both experimental conditions, the experimenter returned with a smile on his face and reported that he had found what he had lost.

Dependent Measure. The dependent measure was adapted from a field experiment by Regan, Williams, and Sparling (1972), in which the dependent variable was whether subjects informed a confederate that candy was dropping unnoticed from a torn bag. In the present study, after thanking the subject, the first experimenter spent several minutes retrieving the grocery bags from the ground and arranging them in his arms in order to enable him to continue without dropping them. The subject continued on her way as he was engaged in this activity, and in fact the first experimenter did not leave the scene of the encounter until the subject could no longer see him. This was done in order to prevent any confounding of the subject's subsequent behavior due to the notion that she was being observed by an individual when she had just helped.

A few stores away, at a distance of about 50 feet from the initial encounter and in the direction the subject was walking, the second experimenter, a college-aged female, waited in an inconspicuous manner, ostensibly looking in a store window. A fairly heavily traveled area was used for the encounter between the second experimenter and the subject, as it has been shown that the likelihood of a victim receiving help from a bystander is inversely related to the number of onlookers (cf. Darley & Latané, 1968; Korte, 1969).

The second experimenter observed the encounter between the first experimenter and the subject, but remained blind at all times to the conditions of all experimental subjects. She held a large grocery bag in her arms, as well as a small flat bag, measuring about 4 x 6 inches (10.16 x 15.24 cm), which was wedged between her body and the large bag in her arms. As the subject approached, she left her vantage point and crossed the subject's path at a point where it was assured that she would be seen by the subject (about 8-10 feet or 2.44-3.05 m). She then released pressure on the large bag imperceptibly, allowing the small bag which was wedged next to her body to drop, apparently unnoticed, and continued on her way. The measure of helpfulness was whether the subject stopped the second experimenter to return the dropped package or to inform her that she had dropped it.

TABLE 3.1
Number of Subjects Who Helped the Second Experimenter

	Justification		
Variable	Low	High	Control
Helped	16	9	7
Did not help	4	11	13

RESULTS

Justification Manipulation

The observed effects of justification are clear-cut. It can be seen in Table 3.1 that a much greater number of low justification subjects helped the second experimenter than did subjects in either the high justification or control conditions. The differences are significant by the chi-square test (Siegel, 1956), indicating the significant effect the minimum justification manipulation had on subsequent behavior, $x^2(2) = 9.2$, $p < .02$. Additional chi-square analyses demonstrated that the number of helping subjects in the low justification condition differed significantly from those in both the high justification condition, $x^2(1) = 3.84$, $p < .05$, using Yates' correction for continuity, and the control condition, $x^2(1) = 6.55$, $p < .02$, using the correction for continuity. No significant difference was found between high justification and control subjects, $x^2(1) = .104$, *ns*.

DISCUSSION

The major hypothesis that compliance with an initial request under minimal justification conditions produces greater compliance with a later more substantial task was strongly supported by the present results, thus providing further experimental evidence of a "foot-in-the-door" effect. The disparate paradigm and setting used here which yielded results consistent with those of other studies in this area attest further to the apparent robustness of the effect and also provide a new direction for field research in helping behavior. The results obtained here, when combined with the others, provide firm ground from which new self-perception and "foot-in-the-door" effects can be explored not only in the laboratory, but also in the field, as was done here. What is now clearly needed is self-report data which yields evidence of the hypothesized changes in self-attributions. Although previous attempts have not been fruitful (e.g., Lepper, 1973), further exploration is certainly called for in light of the significant results obtained using this paradigm.

REFERENCES

Bem, D. J. Self-perception: An alternative interpretation of cognitive dissonance phenomena. *Psychological Review,* 1967, *74,* 183-200.

Bem, D. J. Self-perception theory. In L. Berkowitz (Ed.), *Advances in experimental social psychology* (Vol. 6). New York: Academic Press, 1972.

Darley, J. M., & Latané, B. Bystander intervention in emergencies: Diffusion of responsibility. *Journal of Personality and Social Psychology,* 1968, *8,* 377-383.

Freedman, J. L., & Fraser, S. C. Compliance without pressure: The foot-in-the-door technique. *Journal of Personality and Social Psychology,* 1966, *4,* 195-202.

Korte, C. Group effects on help-giving in an emergency. *Proceedings of the 77th Annual Convention of the American Psychological Association,* 1969, *4,* 383-384. (Summary)

Lepper, M. R. Dissonance, self-perception, and honesty in children. *Journal of Personality and Social Psychology,* 1973, *25,* 65-74.

Regan, D. T., Williams, M., & Sparling, S. Voluntary expiation of guilt: A field experiment. *Journal of Personality and Social Psychology,* 1972, *24,* 42-45.

Siegel, S. *Nonparametric statistics for the behavioral sciences.* New York: McGraw-Hill, 1956.

4

PAULA F. LEVIN and ALICE M. ISEN

Further Studies on the Effect of Feeling Good on Helping

In an attempt to clarify and extend the findings of an earlier study (Isen and Levin, 1972), two experiments investigated the effects of a person's positive affective state on his or her subsequent helpfulness to others. The studies were conducted in divergent locations of a large eastern city, and the subjects differed in ethnic and socio-economic characteristics. As in the earlier investigation, "good mood" was induced by the discovery of a dime in the coin return of a public telephone. The dependent measure in the present experiments, however, was willingness to mail a sealed and addressed letter

Source: *Sociometry,* 1975, *38,* 141-147.

This research was supported by a grant to the second author from the Grants Committee of Franklin and Marshall College.

The authors thank Shel Feldman and Kenneth Gergen for their many helpful suggestions, and Paul Gold for his help in conducting Study II. Thanks are also due to Charles Egli, Peter Fairchild and Timothy Fluck (all alias Michael Ross) for their assistance in the experiment.

which had been left at the telephone, apparently by accident. Both stamped and unstamped letters were used. This measure of helping was designed to demonstrate the existence of a relationship between feeling good and helping in situations which do not involve interaction with a person, and to rule out an interpretation of the earlier findings in terms of differential attention to the person in need. Results supported the prediction that those finding a dime would be more helpful, even though all subjects saw the letter and even though the help did not involve interpersonal interaction.

A recent study (Isen & Levin, 1972) investigating the relationship between "feeling good" and helping found that experimental subjects who had unexpectedly received a dime in the coin return of a public telephone more often spontaneously helped a confederate pick up papers than did control subjects whose telephone had not been "stocked." An accompanying experiment, and a growing body of literature on the effects of mood on helping, allowed the authors tentatively to conclude that the determinant of helping in this case had been positive affective state. However, an alternate interpretation remained. An explanation in terms of differential reinforcement of attention suggested that the experimental group had received reinforcement (in the form of a dime) for attentiveness and might therefore have paid more attention to the surroundings (Feldman, personal communication). Thus their increased helpfulness could be seen as a reflection of their having been more likely to notice the person in need, rather than as a function of their mood state.

The present experiment was conducted in order to determine whether, in a situation where the minimal necessary attention to the helping situation was guaranteed, mood state as manipulated in the earlier study would still affect spontaneous helping as it had before.

A second aim of this study was to begin to clarify the relationship between feeling good and helping. Now that this relationship has been demonstrated in a variety of ways (Aderman, 1972; Aderman & Berkowitz, 1970; Berkowitz & Connor, 1966; Isen, 1970; Isen & Levin, 1972), it becomes necessary to distinguish among the several possible mediators of this association: some of the proposed mediators may be absolutely necessary for the observed relationship, while others may only enhance the association or may even be unrelated to it.

One possibility is that good feeling leads to a desire to interact with others, and that helping follows because it is one of the few ways of initiating contact with strangers. In all of the studies which have attempted to manipulate mood state and which have had as the dependent measure some non-solicited helpful behavior, that measure has always involved helping another person directly. Thus, it may be that feeling good results in helpfulness but only because the helpful act is a way to initiate interaction with another person. Several studies have indicated such association between good mood and a high desire to interact with others (e.g., Isen, 1970). Nonetheless, it is not clear whether desire for interaction plays any role in the association between feeling good and helping, and if it does, whether this actually produces the relationship or merely enhances it. If the desire to interact after the induction of positive affect is the primary motivation for helping, then one might expect to find that good mood and helping are related only if the helpful acts involve an opportunity to interact.

In the present experiment the dependent measure—rather than requiring direct aid to another individual—involved picking up and/or mailing an unstamped, but addressed and sealed letter which had apparently been left behind accidentally by the sender. In an attempt to deal with the differential attention interpretation of the Isen and Levin "dime" study (1972), the amount of attention necessary for helping to occur was minimized in this experiment. That is, the letter was left on the ledge in a telephone booth where it was plainly in sight to anyone who used the booth. Preliminary observations revealed that subjects looked at the letter almost immediately upon entering the booth and certainly before checking the coin return slot. Thus, dime-induced differential awareness of the presence of the letter could not be a factor in differential helping.

Since we conceive of the relationship between feeling good and helping as a more pervasive one than that implied by the interaction hypothesis, and following from Isen and Levin's findings and the "warm glow" hypothesis, we predicted that those subjects who found the dime would be more likely to help (that is, to take the letter with them and mail it), than those who found no money. If this manipulation were to result in increased helping of the kind under investigation here, then one might be able to conclude that (1) minimal attention (awareness of another's need) is not, in and of itself, sufficient to produce helping, and (2) the prospect of interpersonal interaction is not necessary in order for feeling good to result in helpfulness.

STUDY I

Method

Subjects. Subjects were male and female adults who were alone and who happened to make telephone calls at designated telephone booths at Suburban Station of the Penn-Central Railroad and International Airport in Philadelphia. All but a few of these subjects were Caucasian. Excluded as subjects were: people who were not alone; official personnel, such as conductors and policemen, who took the letter without making a phone call; and other persons who checked the coin return without making a phone call. One potential subject was not included in the study because he failed to check the coin slot.

Procedure. Telephone booths were "set up" in the following manner. The experimenter entered an empty booth, put her belongings on the shelf under the phone, and made an incomplete call. She then ostensibly took her dime from the return slot, gathered up her books and papers, and left. What actually happened was that in both conditions a letter was left behind face down on the shelf, and in the experimental condition the dime was really left in the coin slot. The experimenter then unobtrusively waited near the phone booth. When a subject arrived to make a telephone call at the designated booth, the experimenter recorded whether the subject was in the experimental or control condition, whether and when the subject checked the coin return slot, and whether the subject took the letter with him. The letter left in the booths was sealed and addressed, but unstamped. Other than the address there were no marks on the letter. As the envelope was translucent, a short letter was enclosed. The name of the addressee—Michael Ross—was fictitious, chosen in order to be ethnically ambiguous; and the street address was one in Lancaster, Pa., where the experimenters could receive those letters actually sent. Each letter was numbered on the inside, and the observer kept an account of the numbers which corresponded to the two conditions. This was done to provide a check as to whether or not those who took the letter did mail it, and if so, whether they stamped the letter or sent it postage-due.

Results

Table 4.1 presents a summary of the findings. Fisher Exact Tests revealed that Ss who unexpectedly received a dime were more likely to take and mail the letter than were control Ss ($p < .02$).

TABLE 4.1
Experiment I: Behavior of Subjects in Each Condition

Condition	Mailed Letter	Did Not Mail Letter
Found dime	6	3
Did not find dime	1	9

In every case the subject noticed the letter and did handle it sometime before checking the coin return slot.

Discussion

The results of the present experiment indicate that, as predicted, subjects who discovered money in the telephone were significantly more likely to take and mail a letter which seemed to have been accidentally left behind. Differential helping occurred, even though only a minimal amount of attention was required for noticing the lost letter, and even though the helping did not entail social interaction. This lends credence to the hypothesis that there are additional mechanisms which mediate the relationship between good mood and helpfulness.

Since the letter was unstamped, however, an alternative interpretation of the results is plausible. It could be argued that subjects who received the dime might simply be better able to afford the $.08 postage, and that this difference in money accounted for the difference between conditions in number of people who mailed the letter. (Of interest here may be the fact that only one letter arrived postage-due; it was sent by someone in the dime condition.) Thus, we performed a second study which replicated Study I and added conditions using stamped envelopes. This was done in order to demonstrate that the effect was not due to an attempt on the part of experimental subjects to "return" the found money, or merely to their being financially better able to afford the postage. The use of stamped letters eliminated the issue of postage cost. We would like to suggest that increased helping when in a positive mood state is not due to an actually increased ability to afford the helpful act, but to an increased optimism, an altered *perception* of the costs and rewards of helping. Study II, we felt, would be a first step in allowing such an interpretation.

Second, Study II gave us the opportunity to extend the generality of our findings, through the use of a new experimental location.

STUDY

Method

Subjects and Locale.   As before, subjects were male and female adults who were alone and who made telephone calls at designated telephone booths. However, while Study I had been conducted at an airport and at a train station which served predominantly suburban commuters, Study II was conducted at the city's main station of the Penn-Central Railroad (30th Street Station). Eighty percent of the subjects of Study II were black.

Design and Procedure.   The design and procedure of Experiment II were identical with those described above for Experiment I, except that there were four conditions in all: two in which subjects found unstamped envelopes, and two in which each letter bore a stamp.

TABLE 4.2
Experiment 2: For Stamped and Unstamped Letter,
Behavior of Subjects in Each Condition

	Unstamped Letter		Stamped Letter	
Condition	Mailed Letter	Left Letter	Mailed Letter	Left Letter
Found dime				
Males	4	1	6	1
Females	3	0	4	0
Total	7	1	10	1
Did not find dime				
Males	0	6	4	4
Females	1	3	0	5
Total	1	9	4	9

Results

Table 4.2 presents a summary of the findings. Although there were no differences between the sexes on this measure, the data are presented by sex for your interest. A Fisher Exact Test revealed that, as in Study I subjects who had unexpectedly received a dime took the unstamped letter with them significantly more often than did Control subjects ($p < .005$). In addition, it can be seen from Table 4.2 that the same effect held when the letter already bore a stamp ($p < .005$).

Discussion

The addition of Study II allows us to say that the results obtained in the first experiment were not due solely to a greater ability on the part of the "dime" subjects to afford the cost of postage. Moreover, Study II revealed that the effect appears in both the predominantly black and predominantly white samples. Recently, there have been several interesting studies involving racial, socioeconomic, or ethnic identification as a variable in helping (Bryan & Test, 1967; Feldman, 1968; Gaertner & Bickman, 1971; Hornstein, Fisch, & Holmes, 1968; Piliavin, Rodin, & Piliavin, 1969; Wispé & Freshley, 1971). The present study does not make such comparisons directly, but it broadens the base of the observed effect of feeling good on helping. It indicates that the relationship holds true in divergent locations and for both whites and blacks. We feel that these subject sources do provide, in general, socioeconomically different populations, but at the same time represent a restricted range of economic subcultures. The same study conducted at other locations might well yield different findings.

The results of the two studies, taken together, provide evidence that the connection between feeling good and helping obtained in the earlier "dime" study (Isen & Levin, 1972) cannot be accounted for solely in terms of differential awareness of the need for help, since all subjects were aware of the lost letter. The results also suggest that the opportunity for social interaction need not be present in order for good mood to lead to helping. This implies that desire for social contact is not the only mediator of the observed relationship. However, it does not rule out the possibility that variables such as desire for social contact may affect the association between feeling good and helping in a secondary, possibly cumulative, manner.

REFERENCES

Aderman, D. "Elation, depression and helping behavior." *Journal of Personality and Social Psychology,* 1972, *24,* 91-101.

Aderman, D., & L. Berkowitz. "Observational set, empathy, and helping." *Journal of Personality and Social Psychology,* 1970, *14,* 141-148.

Berkowitz, L., & W. H. Connor. "Success, failure, and social responsibility." *Journal of Personality and Social Psychology,* 1966, *4,* 664-669.

Bryan, J. H., & M. A. Test. "Models and helping: Naturalistic studies in aiding behavior." *Journal of Personality and Social Psychology,* 1967, *6,* 400-407.

Feldman, R. E. "Response to compatriot and foreigner who seek assistance," *Journal of Personality and Social Psychology,* 1968, *10,* 202-214.

Gaertner, S., & L. Bickman. "Effects of race on the elicitation of helping behavior: The wrong number technique." *Journal of Personality and Social Psychology,* 1971, *20,* 218-222.

Hornstein, H. A., E. Fisch, & M. Holmes. "Influence of a model's feeling about his behavior and his relevance as a comparison other on observers' helping behavior." *Journal of Personality and Social Psychology,* 1968, *10,* 222-226.

Isen, A. M. "Success, failure, attention, and reactions to others: The warm glow of success." *Journal of Personality and Social Psychology,* 1970, *15,* 294-301.

Isen, A. M., & P. F. Levin. "The effect of feeling good on helping: Cookies and kindness." *Journal of Personality and Social Psychology,* 1972, *21,* 384-388.

Piliavin, I. M., J. Rodin, & J. A. Piliavin. "Good Samaritanism: An underground phenomenon?" *Journal of Personality and Social Psychology,* 1969, *13,* 289-299.

Wispé, L. G., & H. B. Freshley. "Race, sex, and sympathetic helping behavior: The broken bag caper." *Journal of Personality and Social Psychology,* 1971, *17,* 59-65.

Dyadic and Group Behavior

. . . once we'd got our wings we couldn't play a note wrong. I thought, this isn't right because the music we're playing is useless. OK, it has its moments but it's not what they deserve. They're paying too much, they're applauding too much and it makes me feel like a con man. I don't want to feel like a con man. I want to feel that I've earned what I've got. You see, it got to the point where we were playing so badly and the audience was still going raving mad—they thought it was a gas. But I thought, we're cheating them. . . .

Interview with blues-rock guitarist Eric Clapton, by Steve Turner, from *Rolling Stone,* Issue 165, July 18, 1974. Copyright © 1975 by Rolling Stone. All rights reserved. Reprinted by permission.

Commentary

The focus of this chapter is on the characteristics and consequences of face-to-face, direct social interaction as it occurs in dyads, or two-person entities, as well as in social units involving more than two people. A common thread running through both dyadic and small-group interaction is that the nature of social influence to be found within them is usually not unidirectional. That is, while the other member of the dyad, or other members of the group, influence the individual, he in turn exerts influence on the other(s) in the dyad or group. This mutuality of influence is what distinguishes the behaviors that are considered in this chapter from the primarily unidirectional nature of the social influence process which characterizes the work on conformity, compliance, and obedience discussed in Chapter III.

Nevertheless, it is necessary to distinguish between a dyad and a group. The form of dyadic interaction which is characterized by the mutual influence of its members has been described by Jones and Gerard (1967) as having the characteristic of mutual contingency, "in which each response is partially determined by the preceding responses of the other and partly by the individual's own planned or internal stimulation" (p. 511). A social entity, be it two-person or larger, is considered to have the psychological properties of a group when it is characterized not only by the occurrence of social interaction but also by the interdependence of its members in the pursuit of a common goal.

The first selection in this chapter deals with dyadic interaction, while the others focus on aspects of group process. A theoretical approach that is highly relevant to an understanding of dyadic interaction is *equity theory* (Adams, 1963, 1965; Walster, Berscheid, & Walster, 1973). This theory assumes that social relationships are guided by a motive to maintain equity. Adams (1965) defines a state of inequity as follows: "Inequity exists for Person whenever he perceives that the ratio of his outcomes to inputs and the ratio of Other's outcomes to Other's inputs are unequal" (p. 280). Very much as in the state of cognitive dissonance (see the introduction to Chapter VII), a state of inequity is assumed to create tension which will lead the person involved in an inequitable relationship to attempt to reduce the tension by restoring equity.

In the study reported in the first selection in this chapter

("Equity, Reciprocity, and Reallocating Rewards in the Dyad"), Leventhal, Weiss, and Long attempted to distinguish experimentally the condition under which equity motivation operates from one in which a motivation to reciprocate is aroused. They proposed that equity motivation is aroused whenever a person experiences a discrepancy between inputs and outcomes, whatever the cause of this discrepancy. That is, a person's motivation to restore equity will be aroused whether inequity has occurred by chance or through the deliberate actions of the other person in a dyad. Reciprocity motivation, on the other hand, is assumed to be aroused only when the person sees the other person in the dyad as having intentionally caused the disproportionality between inputs and outputs. On the basis of these considerations, they predicted that, when a person in a dyad is confronted with an uneven distribution of rewards, he should make a stronger effort at reallocating rewards when the inequity was intentionally caused by his partner than when it was chance determined. This should occur because, when inequity is deliberately caused by the partner, two motives are aroused—equity as well as reciprocity—while a disproportionality that is solely due to chance arouses only one motive, the equity motive. A further prediction was that a difference in the strength of reallocation attempts as a function of the source of inequity would occur only when the subject was overrewarded. When the subject is underrewarded intentionally, however, he will be inhibited from reallocating a larger share of the reward to himself because of fear of social disapproval. Subjects in this condition were, therefore, not expected to take a larger share of the reward for themselves than subjects who were underrewarded by chance. The study reprinted here provides an experimental test of these predictions.

An early, and continuing, interest of social psychologists has concerned the effects of others on an individual's performance. In fact, the first social-psychological experiment—conducted by Norman Triplett at Indiana University—dealt with this question. Triplett (1897) tested the relative superiority of competition over individual performance by having 40 children wind a fishing reel apparatus alone on three trials and in competition on another three trials. Twenty of the subjects wound the reel faster under competition, ten were adversely affected by competition, and the speed of the remaining ten did not differ between conditions. Triplett concluded that "the bodily presence of another contestant participating simultaneously in the race serves to liberate latent energy not ordinarily available" (p. 533).

While the studies of Triplett and others have demonstrated that the *mere presence* of others can have a facilitating effect on an individual's performance, other studies have concerned themselves with the effects of *group interaction* on performance. A recent example is the second selection in this chapter ("Group Problem Solving Effectiveness under Conditions of Pooling vs. Interaction," by Hall, Mouton, and Blake), in which subjects were asked to solve a problem derived from the film classic "Twelve Angry Men." The film focuses on a jury which is deliberating the fate of a teen-ager who has been accused of murder. A first poll of the jurors reveals that all but one are ready to find the accused guilty. The remainder of the film depicts how the rest of the jurors, one by one, come around to the "not-guilty" verdict. After viewing a portion of the film which allows the viewer to become acquainted with the jurors, subjects were asked to determine, first individually and then as part of a group, the order of capitulation of the 11 jurors. One main finding was that the group prediction was significantly more accurate than the average of the individual judgments.

A phenomenon of group interaction that has captured the interest of a large number of investigators since the early 1960s—187 investigators, according to a recent count (Cartwright, 1973)—is the "risky shift." They have generally found that when persons are asked to make decisions about a set of life dilemmas known as the Choice Dilemmas Questionnaire, first as individuals and again after group discussion, there is a shift toward riskier decisions. An example of a hypothetical dilemma a subject is given is as follows: An engineer is assured of a lifetime job at a modest salary with his present firm. He now has an offer to join a new company with an uncertain future but which will yield him more lucrative benefits than his present job, should the company survive (Kogan & Wallach, 1964). Although the phenomenon is not as general as had been originally thought (i.e., some choice dilemmas result in shifts toward caution rather than risk), it continues to interest social psychologists (Pruitt, 1971a). One evidence of this interest is in the fact that a special issue of the *Journal of Personality and Social Psychology* (Pruitt, 1971b) was devoted to the topic. Why has it been such a popular topic? Among other reasons, the risky-shift effect seems to contradict commonsense assumptions as well as previous findings on the effects of groups, and it has generated a lot of theoretical controversy about the explanation for the effect (Cartwright, 1971).

The study reported in the third selection in this chapter ("The Group Risky-Shift Effect as a Function of Emotional Bonds, Actual Consequences, and Extent of Responsibility," by Runyan) is addressed to a number of theoretical and methodological issues raised by previous research on decisions concerning choice dilemmas in groups. One of the goals of Runyan's study was to test a prediction derived from Brown's (1965) theory about the tendency toward risk in groups. According to Brown, being risky in some situations is a personal attribute that is valued in American society. A shift to risk occurs when the person realizes that the level of risk he has chosen as an individual deviates from the group mean of riskiness. As Brown (1974) states:

. . . in arriving at a group consensus, or at new individual recommendations, those who have in fact been exceptionally conservative or just average, but who *meant* to be audacious, will feel inclined to favor a new recommendation riskier than their first recommendations. It should also be true that those whose first recommendations turn out to be absurdly or wildly risky would feel some inclination to get closer to the central tendency, though still above it. The net result with just the right story problems and action options will be a shift to increased risk from the central tendency of initial private recommendations to the recommendation on which the group agrees or which is obtained a second time, from each person alone. The basic idea is that knowledge of a distribution of opinions, taken for a completely new situation, teaches one how to *realize* or make manifest the value he held all along (p. 469).

Runyan reasoned that group values are more salient in a group in which members share the emotional bonds of friendship than among a group of strangers. Thus he predicted and found that there would be a greater shift toward risk in groups composed of friends than of strangers.

This chapter ends with a qualitatively different aspect of social interaction and group process than that seen in the selections so far. "Pathology of Imprisonment" describes a study conducted by Philip G. Zimbardo and his colleagues in which the conditions of a prison were simulated in the basement of a building at Stanford University. Paid college student volunteers were randomly assigned to roles of prisoners or guards, and their behavior was observed. The study had to be terminated at the end of six days because the assigned roles created such dramatic and frightening behavioral changes that it was hard to determine what was real and what was role-played. As Zimbardo says, "We were horrified because we saw some boys (guards) treat others as if they were despicable animals, taking pleasure in cruelty, while other boys (prisoners) became servile, dehumanized robots who thought only of escape, of their own individual survival and of their mounting hatred for the guards."

As you read the article, note the inferences the author draws from his findings concerning the powerful impact of assigned roles and the prison environment, in particular, and situational forces, in general, on individual behavior. While unquestionably the Stanford Prison Experiment was valuable in dramatizing an important social problem, the conclusions Zimbardo and his colleagues have drawn from it have been questioned. In a recent article, Banuazizi and Movahedi (1975) argue that, rather than being overcome by the prison environment, subjects in the experiment may have simply been responding to the demand characteristics of the situation and acting on the basis of their stereotypes of what it means to be a prisoner or guard. Regardless of the explanation one accepts, however, there is no question that the Stanford Prison Experiment has been valuable in focusing the public's attention on the need for prison reform.

REFERENCES

Adams, J. S. Toward an understanding of inequity. *Journal of Abnormal and Social Psychology,* 1963, *67,* 422-436.

Adams, J. S. Inequity in social exchange. In L. Berkowitz (Ed.), *Advances in experimental social psychology* (Vol. 2). New York: Academic Press, 1965. Pp. 267-299.

Banuazizi, A., & Movahedi, S. Interpersonal dynamics in a simulated prison: A methodological analysis. *American Psychologist,* 1975, *30,* 152-160.

Brown, R. *Social psychology.* New York: Free Press, 1965.

Brown, R. Further comment on the risky shift. *American Psychologist,* 1974, *29,* 468-470.

Cartwright, D. Risk taking by individuals and groups: An assessment of research employing choice dilemmas. *Journal of Personality and Social Psychology,* 1971, *20,* 361-378.

Cartwright, D. Determinants of scientific progress: The case of research on the risky shift. *American Psychologist,* 1973, *28,* 222-231.

Jones, E. E., & Gerard, H. B. *Foundations of social psychology.* New York: Wiley, 1967.

Kogan, N., & Wallach, M. A. *Risk taking: A study in cognition and personality.* New York: Holt, Rinehart & Winston, 1964.

Pruitt, D. G. Choice shifts in group discussion: An introductory review. *Journal of Personality and Social Psychology,* 1971, *20,* 339-360. (a)

Pruitt, D. G. (guest editor). Special issue on the risky shift. *Journal of Personality and Social Psychology,* 1971, *20,* 339-510. (b)

Triplett, N. The dynamogenic factors in pacemaking and competition. *American Journal of Psychology,* 1897, *9,* 507-533.

Walster, E., Berscheid, E., & Walster, G. W. New directions in equity research. *Journal of Personality and Social Psychology,* 1973, *25,* 151-176.

1

GERALD S. LEVENTHAL, THOMAS WEISS, and GARY LONG

Equity, Reciprocity, and Reallocating Rewards in the Dyad

It is proposed that a member of a dyad who is underrewarded or over-rewarded by his partner will be motivated both to reciprocate and to restore equity. However, if the member is underrewarded or overrewarded by chance, he will be motivated only to restore equity. Consequently, an inequitable division of reward which is intentionally produced by the member's partner will arouse a stronger reallocation response than an inequitable division which occurs by chance. As expected, intentionally over-rewarded subjects decrease their own share of reward to a greater extent than subjects overrewarded by chance. Varying the cause of inequity does not affect the extent to which underrewarded subjects increase their share of reward. The latter finding suggests the presence of forces which inhibit overt retaliatory reciprocation.

The members of a dyad often work together to obtain rewards from their group's external environment. Given successful performance, the dyad is confronted with the problem of dividing the rewards earned. The equity model (Adams, 1965) allows one to predict the manner in which a given number of the dyad, P, will divide available rewards between himself and the second member of the dyad, O. The basic proposition of the equity model is that P will attempt to reward each member of the dyad in accordance with the member's contribution to the group effort. In theoretical terms, P will attempt to maintain proportionality between inputs and outcomes. Inputs are the traits and behaviors for which P believes a given member of the dyad ought to be rewarded, particularly those traits and behaviors which are instrumental to effective performance. Outcomes are the rewards and satisfactions which P believes are being received by either member of the dyad. When P's outcomes are too

Source: Gerald S. Leventhal, Thomas Weiss, and Gary Long, "Equity, Reciprocity, and Reallocating Rewards in the Dyad," *Journal of Personality and Social Psychology,* 1969, *13,* 300-305. Copyright 1969 by the American Psychological Association. Reprinted by permission.

This research was supported by Grant GS-1821 from the National Science Foundation to the first author. The authors wish to thank Frank Weyer for his help.

large relative to his inputs, a state of *profitable* inequity exists and P will be motivated to decrease his own share of reward and increase that of O. When P's outcomes are too small relative to his inputs, a state of *unprofitable* inequity exists and P will be motivated to increase his own share of reward and decrease that of O.

A recent study by Leventhal, Allen, and Kemelgor (1969) investigated subjects' response to profitable and unprofitable inequity. A dyad was rewarded for performing a task in which the members' work inputs were highly similar. Subjects who were given more than half the reward by their partner subsequently increased their partner's share while those who were given less than half the reward subsequently decreased their partner's share. These results are consistent with equity theory but can also be explained by the assumption that subjects were attempting to reciprocate their partner's behavior. The work of a number of investigators suggests that P will attempt to treat O as O has treated him (Berkowitz & Friedman, 1967; Goranson & Berkowitz, 1966; Gouldner, 1960; Pruitt, 1968; Schopler & Thompson, 1968). Thus, subjects given more than half the reward may have been attempting to repay their partner's generosity while subjects given less than half the reward may have been attempting to retaliate against a partner who had taken advantage of them. Although the findings of Leventhal et al. (1969) can be attributed either to reciprocity or equity motivation, there is no reason to assume that the arousal of equity motivation precludes the arousal of reciprocity motivation or vice versa. Consequently, subjects in that study may have been motivated both to reciprocate and to restore equity. The two motives may have summated to produce a relatively strong tendency to reallocate rewards.

The present study attempts to clarify the findings of Leventhal et al. with procedures which make it possible to distinguish the effects of reciprocity from those of equity on subjects' response to being over-rewarded or underrewarded. The need to determine the relative influence of the two motives on subjects' reallocation of reward is especially important because the results of other studies generated by the equity model are also open to alternative explanation with the reciprocity construct. For example, Adams and his associates (Adams, 1963a, 1963b; Adams & Jacobsen, 1964; Adams & Rosenbaum, 1962) have shown that subjects who believe they are unqualified to receive a normal wage will subsequently improve their performance. Equity theory suggests that such subjects are attempting to eliminate profitable inequity by increasing their inputs. However, it is also possible that these subjects are reciprocating the generosity of an employer who hired them in spite of the fact that they were not fully qualified.

A basic assumption of the present analysis is that equity and reciprocity motivation differ with respect to the conditions which arouse them. Equity motivation will be aroused whenever outcomes are disproportionate to inputs, irrespective of the reasons for the disproportionality. P's level of equity motivation is solely a function of the magnitude of the disproportionality. Since the cause of the disparity between inputs and outcomes is irrelevant, the magnitude of equity motivation will be the same whether the imbalance between work and rewards has come about by chance or through the intentional actions of one of the members of the dyad. On the other hand, the magnitude of reciprocity motivation will be greatly influenced by the perceived cause of the disparity between inputs and outcomes. P will be motivated to reciprocate only when he believes O is directly responsible for benefiting or harming him. Thus, if P believes O has intentionally underrewarded or overrewarded him, reciprocity motivation directed toward O will be aroused. However, if the inequitable division of reward results from circumstances beyond O's control, P will not be motivated to reciprocate because O has done nothing to him. It is further proposed that an inequity which is intentionally caused by O will motivate P both to reciprocate and to restore equity. Consequently, an intentionally created inequitable division of reward will arouse two independent motives which summate and increase the strength of P's reallocation response. When inequity is chance produced, only one motive will be aroused, the need to restore equity. Consequently, P's reallocation response will be weaker.

To test the preceding propositions, subjects in the present study worked with a partner on a task in which the members' inputs were highly similar. The dyad was awarded a sum of money which was to be divided in either of two ways. Half the subjects believed the reward was divided by a chance procedure over which their partner had little control. The remaining subjects believed their partner had complete control over the division of reward. The profitableness of inequity for subjects was also manipulated. Subjects received more than half or less than half the reward. They were then permitted to make a substantial change in the division of reward. The preceding analysis suggests the prediction that intentionally overrewarded subjects will decrease their own share of reward more than subjects overrewarded by chance. Similarly, intentionally underrewarded subjects will increase their own share more than subjects underrewarded by chance.

Preliminary investigations by Long (1968) and Weiss (1969) suggest an important qualification to the preceding predictions. Their results suggest that the effect of varying the cause of a disparity between inputs and outcomes is greater among overrewarded than among underrewarded

subjects. The intentionally underrewarded subject who wishes to reciprocate must engage in highly assertive behavior which is likely to be
considered aggressive by himself, by O, or by observers of the P-O
relationship. Since aggressive acts often elicit social disapproval and P
himself may feel guilty or anxious about retaliating, intentionally underrewarded subjects may hesitate to reciprocate openly. To the extent that
overt retaliatory reciprocation is inhibited, they will take no greater a
share of reward than subjects who have been underrewarded by chance.
Among intentionally overrewarded subjects, comparable inhibition of
reciprocity is not expected. Reciprocation of a favor is unlikely to be
inhibited by fear of social disapproval. Consequently, intentionally overrewarded subjects should not hesitate to reciprocate and give a greater
share of reward to their partner than subjects who have been overrewarded
by chance.

METHOD

Subjects

The subjects were 55 male students drawn from lower level psychology,
education, economics, sociology, geography, and mathematics classes at
Campbell College. Participation was entirely voluntary and students did
not receive extra course credit for agreeing to take part. The data from one
subject who detected the deception have been deleted.

Procedure

A 2 x 2 factorial design was employed in which the independent
variables were cause of inequity and profitableness of inequity. Subjects
were tested by a male experimenter and were told they were participating
in a study of the effects of motivation on clerical performance. They would
work with and compete against another male student who was being tested
by another experimenter in a room nearby. The other male student was
actually fictitious. The subject was told that he and his partner would
work on an identical task, the "California Proofreading Test," for which
they would receive a monetary reward of $2. The member of the dyad who
obtained the higher score would earn the privilege of dividing the money
between his partner and himself, while the low-scoring member would be
allowed to modify the division made by his high-scoring partner. However,
the experimenter also indicated that if the two members tied by performing at the same level, a coin would be tossed to determine the manner in
which the money would be divided. Subjects were then instructed to begin

work and the experimenter left the room, ostensibly to obtain the performance score of the subject's fictitious partner. The bogus proofreading test consisted of five pages of single-spaced printed material. The subject's task was to draw diagonal lines through the letters *a* and *e* each time they appeared in the text. He had been told that his score on the task would be calculated by subtracting the number of correct responses and then multiplying the obtained difference score by a number which took into account the total number of lines of text he had completed.

After the experimenter left the testing room, he randomly assigned the subject to one of four conditions. After 7½ minutes had passed, he returned and pretended to score the subject's performance on the proofreading task. All subjects then received false information about their own score and that of their fictitious partner. They were not given exact scores but were told the 10-point interval, of eight such intervals, into which each member's score had fallen. They were told they and their partner had both obtained scores in the 30-39 interval and had therefore performed at the same level. Because of the alleged tie, the experimenter indicated he would toss a coin to determine which member would be responsible for dividing the reward. Cause of inequity was then manipulated. Half the subjects were told that the winner of the toss would be permitted to choose freely one of 21 possible divisions of the $2 reward. The remaining subjects were told that the winner of the coin toss would randomly draw one slip from among 21 slips which listed the same 21 possible divisions of the $2 reward. In the chance-inequity group it was emphasized that the winner of the toss would have no control over the division of money because he would blindly draw a slip at random and would have to divide the money in accordance with the amounts listed on the slip. In the intentional inequity group it was emphasized that the winner of the toss would have complete control over the division of money and would be free to choose any one of the 21 possible divisions of reward. In all instances the subject was asked to make a call and subsequently lost the coin toss. The experimenter then left the room, ostensibly to give the subject's partner an opportunity to make his decision or draw the chance division slip. The experimenter returned in 3 minutes and showed the subject a printed form on which 21 possible divisions of the $2 reward were listed. The divisions ranged in $.10 steps from "$2 for Member 1, $.00 for Member 2" to "$.00 for Member 1, $2 for Member 2." Profitableness of inequity was manipulated by presenting subjects with either of two divisions. In profitable-inequity conditions, subjects received $1.40 while their partner received $.60. In unprofitable-inequity conditions, subjects received $.60 while their partner received $1.40. Subjects were then permitted to modify the division of reward by as much as $.70 in either direction. They were

TABLE 1.1
**Mean Number of Cents by Which Subjects Change Their Share of Reward
as a Function of Profitableness and Cause of Inequity**

	Profitableness of Inequity for S	
Cause of Inequity	Profitable	Unprofitable
Chance	−17.14	42.31
Intentional	−42.86	43.85

Note: In each profitable condition, $n = 14$. In each unprofitable condition, $n = 13$.

required to check one of eight statements which ranged in $.20 steps from
"add $.70 to my share and subtract $.70 from my partner's share" to
"subtract $.70 from my share and add $.70 to my partner's share." It was
impossible for subjects to divide the reward evenly because they were
unable to make an exact change of $.40.

After subjects had altered the division of reward, a postexperimental
questionnaire was administered. An interview was then conducted to
determine whether the subject had detected the deception. Then the true
purpose of the experiment was revealed and subjects were pledged to
maintain secrecy. They were also asked whether they would be willing to
forfeit the money they had been awarded. All subjects readily agreed to
forego payment, probably because they had come to the experiment
without expecting to be paid.

RESULTS

The mean number of cents by which subjects increased or decreased
their share of reward is shown in Table 1.1. The data were analyzed with
an unweighted means analysis of variance. There are significant main
effects of profitableness of inequity $(F = 159.92, p < .001)$ and cause of
inequity $(F = 4.38, p < .05)$. Subjects given more than half the reward
subsequently decreased their share while those given less than half the
reward subsequently increased their share. The significant main effect of
cause of inequity is due entirely to differences between the chance-profitable and intentional-profitable conditions. The interaction term is significant at the .05 level $(F = 5.56)$, and a specific comparison between the two
profitable-inequity conditions is also significant $(F = 10.28, p < .01)$. The
comparable difference between the two unprofitable-inequity conditions
does not approach significance. The pattern of response in the chance-
and intentional-unprofitable conditions was nearly identical. These results
clearly indicate that varying the cause of inequity has much greater impact
among overrewarded subjects than among underrewarded subjects.

The data reported in Table 1.1 can also be described in terms of the
total amount of money which subjects have in their possession at the close

of the experiment. Subjects in the chance-profitable group had approximately $1.23 from a total reward of $2 while subjects in the remaining three conditions had approximately $1. Two-tailed t tests were used to determine whether there was significant change toward equity (i.e., toward an even division of reward) in each condition. The mean change in the division of reward exceeded zero at beyond the .01 level in all conditions but the chance-profitable condition, for which a t of 2.07 ($p < .07$) was obtained. In addition, the absolute magnitude of change toward an equal division of reward was significantly greater in the chance-unprofitable than in the chance-profitable condition ($t = 2.51$, $p < .05$).

Data from each questionnaire item were analyzed with an unweighted-means analysis of variance. Only items which help clarify the motivational state of subjects in unprofitable-inequity conditions are discussed here. There were clear differences between chance and intentionally under-rewarded subjects in evaluations of the fictitious partner. Subjects in the intentional-unprofitable condition judged their partner to be less fair-minded ($F = 9.35$, $p < .01$) and less generous ($F = 11.16$, $p < .01$) than subjects in the chance-unprofitable condition. In addition, there was some indication that intentionally underrewarded subjects covertly desired to reciprocate their partner's behavior. In response to a question which asked whether they had desired to alter their partner's share, subjects in the intentional-unprofitable condition tended to express greater desire to decrease their partner's share than subjects in the chance-unprofitable condition. However, the significance of the difference for this comparison only reaches the .10 level of confidence ($F = 3.15$).

DISCUSSION

This study has attempted to assess the relative influence of equity and reciprocity motivation on P's response to a division of reward disparate with the inputs of P and O. It was suggested that an inequitable division of reward intentionally created by O will arouse both equity and reciprocity motivation in P. A chance-produced inequitable division of reward, on the other hand, will arouse only equity motivation. It was therefore hypothesized that intentionally produced inequity would generate a stronger reallocation response than chance-produced inequity because, under intentional inequity, the simultaneously aroused equity and reciprocity motives would summate to produce a reallocation response of relatively high strength. This prediction was qualified with the proviso that intentionally underrewarded subjects might inhibit overt retaliatory reciprocation because they fear censure from O or from observers of the P-O relationship or because of feelings of guilt and anxiety about behaving aggressively. Comparable inhibition of the tendency to reciprocate beneficial acts was not expected to occur. Consequently, it was suggested that varying the cause of inequity would have a greater effect on overrewarded than on underrewarded subjects. The results were generally consistent with these expectations. Cause of inequity interacted with profitableness of inequity. Intentionally overrewarded subjects decreased their share of reward to a greater extent than subjects overrewarded by chance. Among underrewarded subjects, cause of inequity had little effect on the magnitude of subjects' reallocation response. Another important aspect of the findings is that while both chance-overrewarded and chance-underrewarded subjects tend to reduce inequity by moving toward an equal division of reward, the chance-underrewarded group showed a much stronger tendency to move toward equity than the chance-overrewarded group. At the close of the experiment, subjects in the chance-unprofitable condition were closer to the point of exact mathematical equity, $1 for each member, than subjects in the chance-profitable condition. This result is consistent with Adams' (1965) suggestion that there is a higher threshold of response for profitable disparities between inputs and outcomes than for unprofitable disparities.

Although the manipulation of cause of inequity was expected to have less impact under unprofitable than under profitable inequity, it is surprising that there was virtually no tendency for intentionally underrewarded subjects to take more money than chance-underrewarded subjects. Although this finding could provide a basis for claiming that intentional underreward does not arouse retaliatory reciprocity, the authors prefer to attribute the result to forces which inhibit overt retaliatory reciprocity. The questionnaire data provide some support for the claim that reciprocity motivation was aroused in intentionally underrewarded subjects but was denied expression in their overt behavior. Compared to chance-underrewarded subjects, intentionally underrewarded subjects evaluated their partner less favorably and displayed a near-significantly stronger desire to decrease their partner's share of reward. While these questionnaire data are far from conclusive, they are consistent with the assumption that intentionally underrewarded subjects desired to retaliate against their partner but avoided doing so. Clearly, further studies are needed to test the proposition that there are forces which actively inhibit the expression of retaliatory reciprocity in the present investigation. Such studies might establish conditions designed to weaken such inhibitions. If fear of censure and internal constraints against aggressive behavior could be reduced, one would expect intentionally underrewarded subjects to increase their share of reward to a greater extent than chance-underrewarded subjects. However, future investigations will also have to take account of an additional factor which could inhibit reciprocation responses, namely, subjects' concern about creating a new state of inequity. A strong reciprocation response could shift the division of reward *past* the exact point of mathematical equity and thereby create a state of inequity opposite to that which existed initially.

REFERENCES

Adams, J. S. Toward an understanding of inequity. *Journal of Abnormal and Social Psychology,* 1963, *67,* 422-436. (a)

Adams, J. S. Wage inequities, productivity, and work quality. *Industrial relations,* 1963, *3,* 9-16. (b)

Adams, J. S. Inequity in social exchange. In L. Berkowitz (Ed.), *Advances in experimental social psychology.* Vol. 2. New York: Academic Press, 1965.

Adams, J. S., & Jacobsen, P. R. Effects of wage inequities on work quality. *Journal of Abnormal and Social Psychology,* 1964, *69,* 19-25.

Adams, J. S., & Rosenbaum, W. B. The relationship of worker productivity to cognitive dissonance about wage inequities. *Journal of Applied Psychology,* 1962, *46,* 161-164.

Berkowitz, L., & Friedman, P. Some social class differences in helping behavior. *Journal of Personality and Social Psychology,* 1967, *5,* 217-225.

Goranson, R. E., & Berkowitz, L. Reciprocity and responsibility reactions to prior help. *Journal of Personality and Social Psychology,* 1966, *3,* 227-232.

Gouldner, A. W. The norm of reciprocity: A preliminary statement. *American Sociological Review,* 1960, *25,* 161-178.

Leventhal, G. S., Allen, J., & Kemelgor, B. Reducing inequity by reallocating rewards. *Psychonomic Science,* 1969, *14,* 295-296.

Long, G. T. Prior resources, source of inequity, and the response to underpayment. Unpublished master's thesis, North Carolina State University, 1968.

Pruitt, D. G. Reciprocity and credit building in a laboratory dyad. *Journal of Personality and Social Psychology,* 1968, *8,* 143-147.

Schopler, J., & Thompson, V. D. Role of attribution processes in mediating amount of reciprocity for a favor. *Journal of Personality and Social Psychology,* 1968, *10,* 243-250.

Weiss, T. Prior resources, source of inequity, and the response to overpayment. Unpublished master's thesis, North Carolina State University, 1969.

2

ERNEST J. HALL, JANE S. MOUTON, and ROBERT R. BLAKE

Group Problem Solving Effectiveness under Conditions of Pooling vs. Interaction

A. INTRODUCTION AND PURPOSE

Why groups should produce qualitatively superior decisions, as compared with individuals working alone, has never been fully explored. A decision superior to the majority of individual judgments represented in the group can be obtained by a statistical pooling of individual estimates. Thus, group superiority may reflect an average of the individual contributions and be, not a function of interaction phenomena, but a statistical matter in which pooled contributions tend to cancel out individual errors. The question remains as to whether such a decision is significantly different from one obtained through interaction of individuals in a face-to-face group. The present investigation tests the hypothesis that decisions made by groups after interaction are better than decisions based on the statistical pooling of individual judgments.

B. HISTORICAL POSITIONS

There are at least three distinct positions represented in the literature concerning the quality of group vs. individual decision-making.

1. Pooled Products

One is that the group decision is superior to decisions made by individuals because of the effects of pooling. In a number of investigations, groups have been created statistically, *i.e.*, by pooling the judgments of several non face-to-face, non-interacting individuals, to obtain the average of individual judgments to represent the group decision. This average of individual judgments has been found to be superior or equal to a majority of individual judgments which contributed to the group product (6, 7, 11, 17, 18). The only way in which the average judgment can be better than or equal to the majority of individual judgments is for the distribution of individual estimates to be skewed in a direction away from the correct

Source: *Journal of Social Psychology*, 1963, *59*, 147-157.

response. The studies demonstrated that a more correct judgment is likely to be had if the average of individual judgments is used rather than the evaluation of any one person.

2. Emergent Product

Other investigations, however, suggest that group superiority over the average individual cannot be explained entirely by the statistical pooling of individual judgments (4, 14, 16). The product which emerges after interaction is different than that which would have been obtained by pooling or majority effect. Moore (13), Wheeler and Jordan (22), Marple, (12), and Jenness (9) demonstrated that there is a strong tendency for individuals to conform to majority opinions and that judgments subscribed to by the majority will, in the absence of a constant bias, tend to be correct. Thorndike (19) attempted to determine whether, when the effects of averaging and of majority influence were allowed for, discussion in a group carried the group toward a correct rather than an incorrect decision. He concluded that discussion moves a group toward the correct solution although he provided no actual tests of his statement.

Other writers such as Timmons (20) support Thorndike's position by suggesting that the wider range and variety of facts, interpretations, proposed solutions, suggestions and criticisms which can result from the interaction of several persons may account for unexplainable differences associated with interaction. He found that the average of individual rank ordering of items after a period of group discussion was significantly closer to expert opinion than the average of other individual judgments pooled after an equal period of time of individual restudy. Preston (14), who found group decisions to be better than decisions made by individuals, concluded that the group superiority was directly attributable to the psychological factors of interaction inherent in group process. These latter studies support the position of interaction-based group superiority, but do not test *directly* the superiority of interacting groups with statistically concocted groups.

3. Compromise Product

A position opposite to the two given above is represented by those who reject altogether the validity of group decisions for types of problems which require more than a simple perceptual judgment or the solution to a factually correct problem. Particularly conspicuous among these are managerial theorists who employ the term "committee" in place of group in their discussion. For example, Davis (5) observes that a committee's decision may represent merely a compromise achieved by a bargaining process, rather than an integration of the best ideas of its members, especially when the topic under consideration is personal or departmental.

The latter position, in effect, argues against the probability that a group produced decision arising from interaction among members of the group can be as valid as a pooled average of their individual judgments. The argument becomes one, then, of methodology unless evidence can be offered supporting either statistically or interaction produced decisions. Evidence of both theoretical and practical import has been found in the literature which supports the validity of non-interacting groups' solution, *i.e.*, the combined solutions of individuals working alone. Similarly, research evidence is available which supports an interaction hypothesis in explaining group superiority. Needed are experiments specifically designed to assess the question of whether or not, and under what conditions, emergent group decisions are more or less valid than the pooled individual decisions or compromise position.

4. Hypotheses

The specific hypotheses tested in the present study are:

Hypothesis 1.   Under conditions requiring complex judgments, emergent group decisions are significantly superior to those represented by the averaging of individuals' judgments made under alone conditions.

Hypothesis 2.   Decisions resulting from group interaction approximate or equal the *best* individual judgment rather than the worst individual judgment.

C.   EXPERIMENTAL DESIGN

1. Setting and Subjects

The study was conducted in connection with seven human relations training laboratory programs (15) with laboratory populations ranging from 24 to 54 people each. The 158 adult Ss comprising 22 groups ranging in size from six to eight members, represented the ages from 25 to 55 and ranks in the management hierarchy of organizations from shift foreman to department or division head to general manager or president. Groups were matched for education, occupation, and levels within their home organizations. Forty college S participating in a university training laboratory program were composed into five groups, with 12 Ss working as individuals to provide a control condition. The purpose of meeting was to study the group decision-making process under autonomous conditions (2), and the groups devoted from 26 to 50 hours to ingroup activity over a period of seven to nine days up until the time when the experiment took place.

2. Task

Ss viewed a presentation of the film *12 Angry Men*[1] and made predictions concerning the behavior of the film's 12 characters as a test of their understanding of social events against those actually occurring in the film. No Ss who had previously seen the film were used in the experiment.

Twelve Angry Men is the story of a jury in which, on a preliminary vote, all the jurors, save one, think the defendant guilty and wish to render that verdict without discussion. The one juror voting "not guilty" influences the 11 others to his point of view until, one by one, they capitulate to a like verdict. The task was for each S under *alone* conditions to predict the order in which each of the jurors would capitulate to the "not guilty" position. Then, under conditions of interaction, a unanimous group prediction was made. Such a prediction involves a complex judgment upon which a number of points of view can be brought to bear.

3. Procedure

Participants were assembled to view the film. Ss were instructed to pay particular attention to the characters in the film; their occupations, mannerisms, apparent biases, modes of response, etc. They were not informed prior to the beginning of the film that all jurors eventually would accept the logic of the "not guilty" argument nor that they, the Ss, would be asked to predict on the basis of their observations the order in which the film's characters would change their vote to "not guilty."

a. *Individual Predictions.* Thirty-eight minutes after the beginning of the film, the occasion arose for a second, written ballot. It was at this point that the film was interrupted for Ss to make individual predictions as to the order in which each of the jurors would shift to "not guilty." Each S recorded his predictions on a seating chart of the jury. Ss were given ample time to arrive at their decisions, thus eliminating the variable of pressure resulting from time restrictions. The original forms were collected at this time and a carbon copy of his prediction order was retained by each S as a guide in the group discussion which followed the individual prediction session.

b. *Group Predictions.* When all the Ss had completed their individual predictions, they joined their respective groups. The groups were asked to produce a unanimous decision regarding the sequence of shifting to "not guilty." Once again no time limit was exercised. Groups operated under autonomous conditions during the decision-making process, taking from 65 to 80 minutes to reach their decisions.

c. *Individual Predictions after Alone Study.* Twelve Ss spent an additional hour in private reconstruction of the film and in assessing the validity of their initial judgments in order to provide a control for the *amount* of additional time spent by the groups of Ss in arriving at a group decision.

4. Criterion of Measurement

Since Ss rank ordered the capitulation of the jurors, it was possible to compare individual prediction order with the actual order of shifting to "not guilty," as subsequently occurred in the movie. An accuracy score was obtained by summing the deviation in rank order from the actual order of S's prediction for each juror. Therefore, prediction accuracy and deviation score were inversely related.

Under the procedure described, comparisons were made of: (a) the accuracy of the average of individual scores with the accuracy of an order produced through group interaction, as a test of the first hypothesis; (b) the accuracy of the group decision with that of the most accurate and least accurate individual judgment as a basis for evaluating the second hypothesis; and (c) individual scores before and after an additional hour of individual decision-making time.

D.   RESULTS

1. Prediction Accuracy as a Function of Individual and Group Performance

In studying the absolute accuracy of individuals as compared with the accuracy of groups, the hypothesis was that the prediction resulting from group interaction would approach the literal order in which the jurors shifted their votes more closely than would the average of individual judgments. The results confirm this hypothesis.

The average score for the 22 adult groups, as represented by the average of all individual contributions, was 20.5 points away from absolute accuracy. Group averages of individual judgments ranged from 13 to 29 and approached a normal distribution. Under conditions of interaction, the 22 groups had an average of 12.72 away from absolute accuracy. Scores ranged from four to 26. The groups performed under autonomous conditions and required an average of 70 minutes in reaching a consensus. Length of time was not correlated with accuracy.

While group performance was far superior to that of the average of individual rank order judgments, the hypothesis specifically tested was that a judgment reached through interaction would be superior to that acquired from a statistical averaging of individual contributions.

The data demonstrate that group effort produced a more accurate score than the average of pooled individual scores. The t of 17.72 (21 df, $p < .001$) provides confirmation of the hypothesis of greater validity of group decisions under the present conditions. The average of individual scores produced by college Ss was 18.48, while the mean deviation of group produced orders was 11.2. The average gain of 7.28 points of groups over the average of individuals was significant beyond the .001 level ($t = 7.21$, 4 df). The data demonstrate conclusively that experienced decision-making groups can produce decisions of a higher validity than is obtainable from pooling individual judgments.

2. A Comparison of the Effects of Individual Judgments upon the Group Decision

Had the group products been the result of averaging it would be expected that extreme predictions would tend to cancel out, thus producing, in effect, a compromise decision. The results, however, support the second hypothesis. The group decision moves in the correct direction, *i.e.*, towards the most accurate prediction possible, regardless of individual attempts to influence the group decision.

a. *Most Accurate Individual Predictions.* In 17 of the 22 adult cases, the highest individual prediction was superior or equal to the group prediction. For all cases the mean absolute difference of the best individual prediction within a group from the group's decision was 3.45. It appears that interaction can produce conditions that lead to improved group accuracy. However, a surplus of individual accuracy *over* group accuracy remains unused. The question arises as to whether such a surplus constitutes a loss, *i.e.*, is this a significant surplus of individual wisdom that the group is unable to use? An analysis was made of the mean *surplus* of 2.18 points rather than of the absolute difference of 3.45 cited above and the t of 1.65 failed to reach significance. Scores of the most accurate college Ss did not differ significantly from their group products, with the mean absolute deviation of group from best individual score being equal to 2.4 and the mean *surplus* deviation equal to 1.2.

b. *Most Inaccurate Individual Predictions.* There were no instances in which the least accurate individual prediction either equalled or surpassed that of the group. The mean difference of poorest individual predictions from group predictions was 21.9 for adult groups and 14.2 for college Ss. A comparison of the group scores and least accurate individual scores lends support to the actuality that a group decision is not "leveled" to the quality of its least skilled member. The results for adult groups, which are significant beyond the .001 level ($t = 9.81$, 21 df), are in the expected direction. Similarly, the scores of least accurate college Ss differ significantly from their group scores ($t = 4.66$, 4 df, $p < .01$). Results of this sort would seem to refute Davis' contention that group or "committee" produced decisions are often significantly affected by the group's least skilled members.

The results indicate that the group decision moved significantly in the direction of the best individual product. The t of 7.88 (21 df, $p < .001$) obtained from the comparison of most accurate individual means and least accurate individual means confirms the hypothesis that the group approaches or equals the best rather than the worst individual judgments of its members.

3. Effect of Increased Individual Decision-Making Time

Of the 12 Ss spending an additional hour for reconsideration of their initial predictions, seven either improved upon or equalled their initial predictions. The mean improvement was 2.0, while the remaining five Ss produced scores an average of 4.6 inferior to their original predictions. A comparison of initial with reconstructed scores yielded a t of .65 which is insignificant. Additional time for restudy is insufficient to account for the gain experienced by groups.

E. DISCUSSION

There are three distinct positions with respect to the question of whether group decisions are significantly superior to individual decisions. One is that group decisions are superior to decisions made by individuals because of the effects of pooling. Another suggests that group superiority over individuals working alone is a function of interaction which allows a product to emerge. The third position rejects both the statistical and interaction explanations and holds, in fact, that group decisions may represent only a compromise of individual contributions.

Results demonstrated that: (a) it is possible to obtain a "group" score which is superior or equal to the majority of individual contributions by pooling; (b) this pooled score is, in turn, significantly inferior to one produced by a group through interaction; and (c) the group judgment approaches the best individual judgment rather than the worst as would be expected. Two hypotheses were specifically tested: first, it was predicted that under conditions requiring complex judgments, group decisions would be more valid than those represented by the averaging of individuals' judgments made under alone conditions; and secondly, it was hypothesized that decisions emerging from interaction would approximate or equal the *best* individual judgment rather than the worst individual judgment. Both hypotheses were confirmed by the results obtained, with the level of significance in each case being well beyond .001.

It seems appropriate to give some consideration to the reasons for differences which have been obtained in this study. Previous experimental work indicates that there exists a particular analytic parallel between the individual and the group problem-solving processes. Dashiell (1935), commenting on Carr's (1929) analysis of the interactions in committee work, said "Qualitatively . . . group discussion seems to be adequately characterized by the traditional analyses of individual thinking, as *e.g.*, stated by Dewey as: (*a*) motivation by some felt difficulty, (*b*) its analysis and diagnosis, (*c*) suggestions of possible solutions and consequences, and perhaps, (*d*) an experimental trying out, before (*e*) accepting or rejecting the suggestions."

Kelly and Thibaut (10), in discussing the effect of group size on process, graphically point out a significant difference in the two processes, however. While the group process (as viewed in terms of a person working as a group member) proceeds from: (*a*) independent thought and the formation of an initial private opinion; through (*b*) group discussion to a final private opinion; and culminates in (*c*) an overt vote for the group solution; a person working as an individual merely moves from independent thought or interspersed activity to a final private opinion.

The question arises as to whether the deletion of the interaction phase, as experienced by groups, is sufficient reason for individual products to be, by and large, inferior to those of groups. Experimental evidence is divided on the answer. Gurnee (8), Knight (11), Gordon (7) and others support the interpretation that group superiority is due to a statistical pooling of individual judgments with uncorrelated error. The data of Timmons (20, 21) suggests that group discussion contributes something over and beyond the effects of statistical pooling, and Thorndike (19), and Dashiell (4) support the validity of this hypothesis.

If the assumption of group superiority as a function of social interaction can be accepted, it then becomes important to consider the nature of the interaction occurring in groups. Is there a unique pattern of interaction common only to successful groups, or do all groups proceed in much the same fashion, attaining success as a matter of chance? Bales and Strodtbeck (1) conclude that there is a pattern of interaction which facilitates the attainment of success, but qualify their conclusions by observing that in the absence of cohesiveness interaction proves less effective. It becomes fairly obvious, therefore, that many sources of variance exist which may significantly affect group performance as opposed to individual. Cohesiveness, interaction, task requirements, social setting, and the like have all been demonstrated to have some bearing on the final product.

The present study indicates that interaction *per se* contributes something to group performance over and above the effects obtainable from bringing several individual judgments to bear on a common problem. Grouping of individual judgments improves the chances of success statistically due to the simple cancellation of individual errors, but the addition of interaction apparently further improves the success trend due to the objective *evaluation* of individual judgments which it fosters. The decision which results from group interaction may be considered *emergent* since it represents more than either a simple combination of member contributions or a reflection of the best member effort. Such an emergent product seemed characteristic of group efforts in the present study.

F. SUMMARY

The present investigation is concerned with differences between group decisions based on interaction of members and those produced through statistical pooling of individual judgments. Two hypotheses were tested. The first hypothesis predicted that under conditions requiring complex judgments, emergent group decisions would be significantly superior to those represented by the averaging of individuals' judgments made under alone conditions. The second hypothesis stated that decisions resulting from group interaction would approximate or equal the best individual judgment rather than the worst individual judgment.

The 198 Ss were assigned to 27 groups on the basis of education, occupation, and sex. Groups had devoted from 26 to 50 hours to ingroup activity at the time the experiment took place. Twelve Ss worked as individuals. Ss viewed a presentation of the film *12 Angry Men* and made predictions as to the order in which each of the film's 12 characters would, in their role as jurors, change their vote from "guilty" to "not guilty." The Ss were asked to make two predictions: first, as individuals working alone, and, secondly, as members of a group whose goal was the production of a unanimous decision regarding the order of juror capitulation. The 12 Ss working alone made a second prediction after an hour of individual decision-making time.

Under the procedure described, comparisons were made of (*a*) the accuracy of the average individual score with the accuracy of an order produced through group interaction; (*b*) the accuracy of the group decision with that of the most accurate and the least accurate individual judgment in each group; and (c) shifts in individual scores after an hour.

REFERENCES

1. Bales, R. F., & Strodtbeck, F. L. Phases in group problem solving. *Journal of Abnormal and Social Psychology,* 1951, *46,* 485-495.
2. Blake, R. R., & Mouton, J. S. *Training for Decision-Making in Groups.* New York: Putnam, 1961.
3. Carr, L. J. Experimental sociology: A preliminary note on theory and method. *Social Forces,* 1929, *8,* 63-74.
4. Dashiell, J. F. Experimental studies of the influence of social situations on the behavior of individual human adults. *In* Murchison, C. (*Ed.*), *Handbook of Social Psychology.* Worcester: Clark Univ. Press, 1935. Pp. 1097-1158.
5. Davis, R. C. *The Fundamentals of Top Management.* New York: Harper, 1951. Pp. 482-484.
6. Eysenck, H. J. The validity and reliability of group judgments. *Journal of Experimental Psychology,* 1941, *29,* 427-434.
7. Gordon, K. A study of aesthetic judgments. *Journal of Experimental Psychology,* 1923, *6,* 36-42.
8. Gurnee, H. A comparison of collective and individual judgments of fact. *Journal of Experimental Psychology,* 1937, *21,* 106-112.
9. Jenness, A. The role of discussion in changing opinion regarding a matter of fact. *Journal of Abnormal and Social Psychology,* 1932, *27,* 279-296.
10. Kelly, H. H., & Thibaut, J. W. Experimental studies of group problem solving and process. *In* Lindzey, G. (*Ed.*), *Handbook of Social Psychology.* Cambridge, Mass.: Addison-Wesley, 1954. Pp. 746-747.
11. Knight, H. C. A comparison of the reliability of group and individual judgments. Unpublished master's thesis, Columbia Univ., 1921.
12. Marple, C. H. The comparative susceptibility of three age levels to the suggestion of group versus expert opinion. *Journal of Social Psychology,* 1933, *4,* 176-186.
13. Moore, H. T. The comparative influence of majority and expert opinion. *American Journal of Psychology,* 1921, *32,* 16-20.
14. Preston, M. Note on the reliablity and validity of the group judgment. *Journal of Experimental Psychology,* 1938, *22,* 462-471.
15. *Proceedings,* Austin, Texas: The Human Relations Training Laboratory 1960.
16. Smith, B. The validity and reliability of group judgments. *Journal of Experimental Psychology,* 1941, *29,* 420-426.
17. Smith, M. Group judgments in the field of personality traits. *Journal of Experimental Psychology,* 1931, *14,* 562-565.
18. Stroop, J. B. Is the judgment of the group better than that of the average member of the group? *Journal of Experimental Psychology,* 1932, *15,* 550-560.
19. Thorndike, R. L. The effects of discussion upon the correctness of group decision when the factor of majority influence is allowed for. *Journal of Social Psychology,* 1938, *9,* 343-362.
20. Timmons, W. M. Decisions and attitudes as outcomes of the discussion of a social problem. Teachers Coll., Contrib. Educ., No. 777, Columbia Univer., Bureau of Publications, 1939.

21. _____. Can the product superiority of discussers be attributed to averaging and majority influences? *Journal of Social Psychology,* 1942, *15,* 23-32.
22. Wheeler, D., & Jordan, H. Change of individual opinion to accord with group opinion. *Journal of Abnormal and Social Psychology,* 1929, *24,* 203-206.

NOTES

1. Fonda-Cobb Production released through United Artists Studios, New York, April, 1957. Rental for the film was provided by The University of Texas Research Institute, Austin, Texas, through the grant Project #099-SRF, Account 21375, Evaluation of An Individual's Diagnostic Skill Predicting the Behavior of Others.

3

DAVID L. RUNYAN

The Group Risky-Shift Effect as a Function of Emotional Bonds, Actual Consequences, and Extent of Responsibility

Emotional bonds were hypothesized to increase risk taking following group decision concerning a realistic gambling task designed to be analogous to the Kogan and Wallach Choice Dilemma Questionnaires. Forty-eight groups of 3-5 subjects were assigned to one of eight different conditions. All groups were instructed to reach consensus on a suitable gamble involving an "outside" person. Groups were composed of either friends or strangers, decisions were either binding or advisory, and the outside person was either real or hypothetical. Results supported the hypothesis in that friends, and groups reaching advisory decisions, were significantly riskier than their counterparts. Real and hypothetical situations did not differ with respect to risk level, suggesting that generalization from hypothetical choice dilemma

Source: David L. Runyan, "The Group Risky-Shift Effect as a Function of Emotional Bonds, Actual Consequences, and Extent of Responsibility," *Journal of Personality and Social Psychology,* 1974, *29,* 670-676. Copyright 1974 by the American Psychological Association. Reprinted by permission.

The research reported in this article was supported by USAFOSR Grant 44620-69-C-0114 from the Cooperation/Conflict Research Group of the Computer Institute for Social Science Research. The author wishes to thank Clint Tarkoe for his help in running subjects and Lawrence A. Messé, whose insightful comments were always invaluable.

problems to more consequential situations is not as potentially invalid as previously believed.

During the past decade, an increasing number of studies have examined the differences in choice behavior for persons who make decisions as individuals or as members of a group. Results from some of these studies, including the original research performed by Stoner (1961), indicate that persons tend to make riskier decisions within a group situation on many task items than when they decide as individuals (Lamm & Kogan, 1970; Marquis, 1962; Wallach, Kogan, & Bem, 1962). On the other hand, other findings, using different task items, indicate that persons deciding collectively as members of a group tend to make more conservative decisions than those made by the individuals (Brown, 1965; Pruitt & Teger, 1967; Stoner, 1968).

Because of the ambiguous research findings, recently several authors (e.g., Cartwright, 1971; Dion, Baron, & Miller, 1970; Pruitt, 1971) have raised a number of theoretical and methodological issues. It seems obvious that these issues must be resolved before a valid evaluation of the utility of the construct risky shift (Stoner, 1961) or, more generally, choice shift (Pruitt, 1971) can be made. The present research addressed itself to three points that have been noted as controversial by the above researchers but relevant to the understanding of individual-versus-group-member choice behavior as a real psychological phenomenon.

EMOTIONAL BONDS

Brown (1965) postulated that the willingness to take risks is a value that has general acceptance in our culture. In a more conservative statement, Pruitt (1971) argued that a strong case can be made that the value or values underlying risks are more compelling than those underlying caution. Jellison and Riskind (1970) provide evidence that ego ideals and the association between risk taking and general competency underlie the value toward risk taking. From this theoretical framework, it follows that positive emotional bonds and high group cohesion would increase members' identification with the group and therefore increase the saliency of the values or ego ideals operating within the group. Personal identification and commitment to the group would be less intense with a group of strangers, and it would be less important to each group member that the group live up to his values or ego ideals. He would perceive greater disparity between himself and the others in initial risk orientation and feel less possibility of influencing them. Many researchers (Levinger & Schneider, 1969; Pruitt & Teger, 1967; Wallach & Wing, 1968) noted that generally each group member felt initially that he was the riskiest group member. These findings were elicited from groups of strangers. Identification and cohesion would lead all group members to perceive the others to be more nearly as risk oriented as himself and to be more amenable to influence.

An early theoretical orientation emphasized the role of affective bonds in groups which permit members to diffuse responsibility for risky decisions (Kogan & Wallach, 1967a, 1967b). Pruitt (1971), however, has suggested that the emotional bonds hypothesis should be viewed as distinct from diffusion of responsibility since as noted above, the effect of emotional ties may be explained as well by other theoretical orientations. Given that the emotional bonds hypothesis is congruent with at least two explanations of choice shifts, it seemed reasonable to attempt a direct test of its validity. Several studies provided correlational support for the emotional bonds hypothesis of increased group risk taking (Kogan & Wallach, 1967c; Pruitt & Teger, 1969; Teger & Pruitt, 1967), but none have presented evidence based on a prior manipulation of emotional bonds. One study (Dion, Miller, & Magnan, 1971) did attempt to manipulate at least the probability that different levels of emotional bonds would be generated by arbitrarily telling groups of strangers that their scores on previously administered personality scales (actually discarded) indicated that their group should be either highly compatible or very incompatible. They concluded that high perceived compatibility inhibited group risk taking because the more intense emotional bonds interfered with the diffusion of personal responsibility onto other group members. Results of one study can only be considered tentative. A possibly more compelling procedure would be to use groups of friends or co-workers with strong collective emotional bonds already established.

The present research used groups of friends in comparison with groups of strangers to examine the effect of high and low levels of emotional bonds on group choice taking. Based on the theoretical position outlined above, it was predicted that high levels of emotional bonds would lead to greater risk taking than low levels of emotional bonds.

ACTUAL CONSEQUENCES

A second purpose of the present study was to assess some properties of the Choice Dilemma Questionnaires which could inhibit the generalization of results discovered in the laboratory. Dion et al. (1970) report that 80% of all of the research on the risky-shift phenomenon used the Choice Dilemma Questionnaires created by Kogan and Wallach (1964). Dion et al. (1970) and Cartwright (1971) have criticized the "unnatural" properties of the Choice Dilemma Questionnaire. Each choice-dilemma problem requires the group to reach an advisory decision concerning a hypothetical problem confronting a fictitious person. Group members are never confronted with the consequences of their decisions.

Some research in the risky shift has used situations with actual consequences. Wallach, Kogan, and Bem (1964) gave subjects increasing monetary reward for correct answers to College Board Entrance Examination problems of commensurate difficulty and still obtained a risky shift. However, in studies involving other experimental situations, Flanders (1970) and Clement and Sullivan (1970) demonstrated a conservative orientation with actual consequences. A few studies have used pure gambling situations with actual payoffs and produced heterogeneous results (Lonergan & McClintock, 1961; Pruitt & Teger, 1969; Zajonc, Wolosin, Wolosin, & Sherman, 1968, 1969). Sometimes groups are riskier than individuals, sometimes more cautious, and sometimes there is no difference.

The present research attempted to create a realistic situation (in the Aronson & Carlsmith, 1969, sense of "experimental realism"), yet one that was still analogous to the situations created by the widely used Choice Dilemma Questionnaires. The situation used was similar to that employed by Pruitt and Teger (1969) and Zaleska and Kogan (1971), who examined the effect on risk of gambling for oneself versus gambling for another person. The present situation, on the other hand, examined the effect of gambling for a real or hypothetical other. In this way, the effect on risk of actual consequences (real other) versus hypothetical consequences (fictitious other) was examined directly, and since choices always affected a party outside the group, the situation was analogous to the choice dilemmas. If the risky shift occurs primarily when decisions are hypothetical because there is little cost attached to this choice, there should be smaller shifts when decisions have actual consequences. On the other hand, if persons can "role play" effectively, then hypothetical decisions should accurately reflect "actual" behavior, and there should be no difference in shift between real and hypothetical choices.

EXTENT OF RESPONSIBILITY

Another idiosyncratic property of the Choice Dilemma Questionnaires is that the group is asked simply to give advice. It is conceivable that since the group is reaching only an advisory decision, the prospect of success and reward seems closer to realization than the possibility of failure, as the ultimate decision is not the responsibility of the group but must be made later by the person actually involved in the dilemma. In this typical approach-avoidance situation (Lewin, 1935), where a distant goal has both positive and negative valences, the positive valences of success seem stronger. On the other hand, if the group decision was known to be binding on the outside person, the final outcome would be much closer because now the group is ultimately responsible for the decision and the negative valence of failure would become stronger—which should result in a smaller risky shift with binding group decisions.

Dion et al. (1971) varied group decisions for a hypothetical other only on the binding–nonbinding dimension. Obtaining differences which approached significance, they argued that low social responsibility (nonbinding decisions) increased group risk taking and that high social responsibility (binding decisions), inhibited group risk taking. Here, social responsibility referred to the group's sense of liability for a group decision affecting a hypothetical person outside of the group.

In summary, the present research examined the effect of differences in (a) level of emotional bonds (friends versus strangers), (b) degree of consequences (real versus hypothetical decisions), and (c) extent of responsibility (binding versus advisory decisions) on changes in risk-taking behavior as a function of group discussion. An experimental procedure analogous to the Choice Dilemma Questionnaires was used; however, the present procedure generated conditions in which group members knew that their behavior had actual consequences for the reward of another person.

METHOD

Subjects

One hundred and seventy-three students at Michigan State University were randomly assigned to 48 homogeneous groups of 3 to 5 male or female students. For half of the groups (strangers), the subjects were randomly selected from a group of 500 respondents to an advertisement in the school newspaper asking for volunteers to participate in "motivational" research for pay. Groups of friends were recruited by contacting

TABLE 3.1
Probabilities of Success and Corresponding Rewards

Probability of Success					
.1	.3	.5	.7	.9	1.0 (no bet)
Corresponding Reward					
$20.00	$7.00	$4.00	$3.00	$2.25	$2.00

one member of the subject pool and requesting him to bring 2-4 mutual friends of the same sex to the experimental sessions. All subjects were Michigan State University students. Some subjects in the friend condition were not originally part of the motivational-research subject pool, but agreed to do the experiment for pay at the request of their friends.

Choice-Dilemma Situation

A single modified choice-dilemma problem was used as the group task. Each group was to decide whether or not to gamble with the $2 earned by a person outside of the group whom they knew had written a one-hour essay giving pro and con arguments concerning the legalization of marijuana. As in the procedure used in the actual choice-dilemma problems, the group was given six different alternatives from which to choose (see Table 3.1). Each alternative associated a different probability of success with a monetary reward. The greater the risk, the greater the reward if successful.

Once the group reached a decision, 10 slips of paper, marked either win or lose according to the probability of success of the gamble chosen, were placed face down in a box. One slip was picked up by the person who wrote the essay. If it was a win slip he was paid accordingly; if it was a lose slip he was paid only $1. All group members knew that they were going to be paid $2 each for participating.

Design and Procedure

Groups were run in one of eight different conditions. Each group was composed of either friends or strangers, making either a binding or advisory decision, for either a real or fictitious outside worker (real-consequence or hypothetical-consequence conditions, respectively).

The procedure in the real-consequence conditions had a group enter the experimental room together. Once in the room, they were shown, through a window to a second room, another subject (actually a confederate) seated at a table with his back to them. After the group was seated and each member had a copy of Table 3.1, they were told that the "outside worker" was also a part of the study. Each person was to decide individually the minimum probability of success they would require before advising him to gamble with his pay for a more rewarding alternative. Later, they were asked to reach a group consensus on the same problem. They were told that the previous individual decisions were preliminary steps to acquaint them with the problem. After consensus was reached, the outside worker was brought in and the final decision was implemented. The group was detained a few minutes to allow the outside worker to depart, and then they also were allowed to leave.

There were several procedural variations depending on the different conditions. If the group decision was not binding, the outside worker was only advised of the group decision, but he actually made his own decision. In practice, the confederate chose "no bet" in the advisory conditions. If the decision was binding, he was forced to implement the group decision. In the hypothetical-consequence conditions, the group was simply asked to imagine that the outside worker existed.

RESULTS

Individual Decisions

The individual decisions were classified by the experimental conditions (i.e., emotional bonds, consequences and responsibility) and subjected to an unweighted-means analysis of variance.[1] Cell means are presented in Table 3.2. The analysis revealed a highly significant difference in the predilection for risk taking between subjects in the binding decision and advisory decision conditions ($F = 11.83$, $df = 1/40$, $p < .01$). Subjects who made binding decisions were less risky than subjects whose decisions were advisory.

TABLE 3.2
Mean Individual Decision Scores

Emotional Bond	Responsibility	Consequence	
		Real	Hypothetical
Friends	Binding	.43	.58
	Not binding	.41	.45
Strangers	Binding	.56	.53
	Not binding	.39	.42

TABLE 3.3
Mean Group Decision Scores

Emotional Bond	Responsibility	Consequence	
		Real	Hypothetical
Friends	Binding	.43	.53
	Not binding	.18	.30
Strangers	Binding	.58	.60
	Not binding	.33	.38

Group Decisions

An unweighted-means analysis of variance of the group shift following decisions revealed significant main effects for the emotional bonds factor and nearly main effects for the responsibility factor ($F = 5.27$, $df = 1/40$, $p < .05$ and $F = 3.22$, $df = 1/40$, $p < .10$, respectively).[2] Cell means for the group decision scores are presented in Table 3.3. As predicted by the emotional bonds hypothesis, there was a greater shift in groups of friends than in groups of strangers. However, there was no difference as a function of real versus hypothetical consequences. Thus, the present study yielded no evidence that the risky shift is tempered when subjects' decisions have real consequences than when they are merely the result of role playing. Groups in the advisory conditions exhibited a greater risky shift than those making binding decisions, but this difference did not quite reach significance.

Since subjects in the binding-decision condition were significantly less risky in their original, individual choices than were subjects in the non-binding, advisory condition, the amount of shift that groups could manifest was different as a function of differences in this factor. Perhaps this situation affected the magnitude of shift possible following group decisions and artificially reduced the amount of shift.

DISCUSSION

The results provide strong support for the hypothesis that high levels of emotional bonds existing among group members enhance the risky shift effect in comparison to groups with low levels of emotional bonds. These results have relevance to several value approaches to the choice-shift phenomenon.

One of the assumptions made by social comparison theorists (Brown, 1965; Jellison & Riskind, 1970) and also by pluralistic ignorance theorists (Levinger & Schneider, 1969) is that ego ideals and concerns of general competency underlie the value towards risk. Release theorists (Pruitt, 1971) suggest that the riskiest group member releases other members from social restraints that hold them to more cautious alternatives. Relevant argument theorists (Nordhoy, 1962; Teger & Pruitt, 1967) hypothesize that pervasive arguments toward risk convince group members to move further towards these values. Relevant arguments concerning the merits of a risky position (or a cautious position in a different situation) may be more easily accepted when made by a friend than when made by a stranger. Research dealing with cohesion and group productivity (Berkowitz, 1954; Schachter, Ellertson, McBride, & Gregory, 1951; Seashore, 1954) indicate that highly cohesive groups are more likely to be high or low in terms of work productivity, whereas more indifferent groups tend to conform toward average productivity. Considering the present research situation, the emotional bonds of friendship strengthen each member's personal identification with the group and therefore increase the saliency of the ego ideals behind the positive value on risk taking, thus leading the friendship groups to greater risk taking. The real strength and influence of emotional bonds become readily apparent when one considers that the risky shift in risk-oriented situations has been demonstrated again and again with groups of strangers, yet in the present study the risky shift in friendship groups was significantly greater than for groups of strangers.

These results are exactly the opposite of those obtained by Dion et al. (1971). However, Dion et al.'s statement to the subjects that personality test scores (actually discarded) indicated high compatibility for a group of strangers is probably not the psychological equivalent of the compatibility obtained by friends from everyday social contact.

It is possible that the present manipulation of the friends-strangers variable caused confounding differences between the groups. However, all groups used, whether friends or strangers, consisted of college students enrolled at Michigan State University and, therefore, it is unlikely that members in the two types of groups differed substantially and consistently on potentially relevant variables other than emotional bonds.

One of the findings of applied humanistic psychology is that self-disclosure in a group leads to feelings of trust and warmth for other group members (Jourard, 1964). Trust and warmth inevitably lead group members to be riskier with their own behavior in the group and outside of the group (Rogers, 1970). These results have typically been obtained with people in therapy or sensitivity groups, but perhaps the variables of warmth and trust between group members, so far unexamined in choice-shift research, might be important in determining the direction of group shifts. The present findings concerning the emotional bonds hypothesis suggest that further research along these lines might be profitable.

Another purpose of the present study was to explore some of the unique properties of the choice-dilemma problems used in most risky-shift studies that would inhibit generalization of these results. In particular, using a problem analogous to the choice-dilemma problems with a risky orientation, no difference in risk taking was observed when groups made decisions with real consequences or with hypothetical consequences. These data indicate that speculation regarding the invalidity of generalizing form hypothetical to real-life situations was not supported. Subjects can role play very well what their actual behavior would be, and there is no evidence that they cannot do so for even more important decisions.

Another unique feature of the choice-dilemma problems involves the advisory nature of the group decisions. The results of this study indicate that both individuals and groups are riskier when asked to make advisory decisions than when asked to make binding decisions for another person. Dion et al. (1971) have argued that high social responsibility inhibits risk taking and low social responsibility enhances risk taking. The results of the present study provide even stronger support for the Dion et al. hypothesis, as these results were confirmed for group decisions involving real as well as hypothetical others.

There are other problems associated with the use of the Choice Dilemma Questionnaires in choice-shift research that were not directly dealt with in this study. A major concern is an explanation for the many cautious shifts documented by researchers using other task problems (Nordhoy, 1962; Stoner, 1968) and the consistent finding that 2 of the 14 Kogan and Wallach (1964) choice-dilemma problems consistently elicit cautious shifts (Brown, 1965; Pruitt & Teger, 1967). The task problem in this study, however, consistently elicited an attraction towards risk taking, and thus, variables relevant to the cautious shift could not be examined.

In conclusion, the present study shows that real groups of friends and advisory decisions increased the risky shift and that there is no difference in shift using real or hypothetical situations. The present study attempted to bridge some of the gaps between laboratory and "real life," but clearly even closer approximations are needed before a satisfactory explanation of complex choice behavior can be attained.

REFERENCES

Aronson, E., & Carlsmith, J. M. Experimentation in social psychology. In G. Lindzey & E. Aronson (Eds.), *The handbook of social psychology.* (2nd ed.) Vol. 4. Reading, Mass.: Addison-Wesley, 1969.

Berkowitz, L. Group standards, cohesiveness, and productivity. *Human Relations,* 1954, *7,* 509-519.

Brown, R. *Social psychology.* New York: Free Press, 1965.

Cartwright, D. Risk taking by individuals and groups: An assessment of research employing choice dilemmas. *Journal of Personality and Social Psychology,* 1971, *20,* 361-378.

Clement, D., & Sullivan, D. W. No risky shift effect with real groups and real risks. *Psychonomic Science,* 1970, *18,* 243-245.

Dion, K. L., Baron, R. S., & Miller, N. Why do groups make riskier decisions than individuals? In L. Berkowitz (Ed.), *Advances in experimental social psychology,* 1970, Vol. 5. New York: Academic Press.

Dion, K. L., Miller, N., & Magnan, M. A. Group cohesiveness and social responsibility as determinants of the risky shift. *Journal of Personality and Social Psychology,* 1971, *20,* 400-406.

Flanders, J. P. Does the risky shift generalize to a task with demonstrably non-trivial decision consequences? *Proceedings of the 78th Annual Convention of the American Psychological Association,* 1970, *5,* 331-332. (Summary)

Jellison, J. M., & Riskind, S. A. A social comparison of abilities interpretation of risk taking behavior. *Journal of Personality and Social Psychology,* 1970, *15,* 375-390.

Jourard, S. M. *The transparent self.* New York: Van Nostrand, 1964.

Kogan, N., & Wallach, M. A. Effects of physical separation of group members New York: Holt, 1964.

Kogan, N., & Wallach, M. A. Effects of physical separation of group members upon risk taking. *Human Relations,* 1967, *20,* 41-48. (a)

Kogan, N., & Wallach, M. A. Group risk taking as a function of members' anxiety and defensiveness levels. *Journal of Personality,* 1967, *35,* 57-63. (b)

Kogan, N., & Wallach, M. A. The risky-shift phenomenon in small decision making groups: A test of the information exchange hypothesis. *Journal of Experimental Social Psychology,* 1967, *3,* 75-85. (c)

Lamm, H., & Kogan, N. Risk taking in the context of intergroup negotiation. *Journal of Experimental Social Psychology,* 1970, *6,* 351-363.

Levinger, G., & Schneider, D. J. Test of the "risk as a value" hypothesis. *Journal of Personality and Social Psychology,* 1969, *11,* 165-170.

Lewin, K. A dynamic theory of personality. (Trans. by D. K. Adams & K. Zener) New York: McGraw-Hill, 1935.

Lonergan, S. G., & McClintock, C. G. Effects of group membership on risk taking behavior. *Psychological Reports,* 1961, *8,* 447-455.

Marquis, D. G. Individual responsibility and group decision involving risk. *Industrial Management Review,* 1962, *3,* 8-23.

Nordhoy, F. Group interaction in decision-making under risk. Unpublished master's thesis, School of Industrial Management, Massachusetts Institute of Technology, 1962.

Pruitt, D. G. Choice shifts in group discussion: An introductory review. *Journal of Personality and Social Psychology,* 1971, *20,* 330-361.

Pruitt, D. G., & Teger, A. I. Is there a shift toward risk in group discussion? If so, is it a group phenomenon? If so, what causes it? Paper presented at the meeting of the American Psychological Association, Washington, D.C., September 1967.

Pruitt, D. G., & Teger, A. I. The risky shift in betting. *Journal of Experimental and Social Psychology,* 1969, *5,* 115-126.

Rogers, C. *Encounter groups.* New York: Harper & Row, 1970.

Schachter, S., Ellertson, N., McBride, D., & Gregory, D. An experimental study of cohesiveness and productivity. *Human Relations,* 1951, *4,* 229-238.

Seashore, S. E. *Group cohesiveness in the industrial work group.* Ann Arbor: University of Michigan, Institute for Social Research, 1954.

Stoner, J. A. F. A comparison of individual and group decisions including risk. Unpublished master's thesis, School of Industrial Management, Massachusetts Institute of Technology, 1961.

Stoner, J. A. F. Risky and cautious shifts in group decisions: The influence of widely held values. *Journal of Experimental Social Psychology,* 1968, *4,* 442-459.

Teger, A. I., & Pruitt, D. G. Components of group risk taking. *Journal of Experimental Social Psychology,* 1967, *3,* 189-205.

Wallach, M. A., Kogan, N., & Bem, D. J. Group influence on individual risk taking. *Journal of Abnormal Social Psychology,* 1962, *65,* 75-86.

Wallach, M. A., Kogan, N., & Bem, D. J. Diffusion of responsibility and level of risk taking in groups. *Journal of Abnormal and Social Psychology,* 1964, *68,* 263-274.

Wallach, M. A., & Wing, C. W., Jr. To risk a value? *Journal of Personality and Social Psychology,* 1968, *9,* 101-107.

Zajonc, R. B., Wolosin, R. J., Wolosin, M. A., & Sherman, S. J. Individual and group risk-taking in a two-choice situation. *Journal of Experimental Social Psychology,* 1968, *4,* 89-107.

Zajonc, R. B., Wolosin, R. J., Wolosin, M. A., & Sherman, S. J. Group risk-taking in a two-choice situation: Replication, extension, and a model. *Journal of Experimental Social Psychology,* 1969, *5,* 127-140.

Zaleska, M., & Kogan, N. Level of risk selected by individuals and groups when deciding for self and for others. *Sociometry,* 1971, *34,* 198-213.

NOTES

1. Preliminary inspection of the data indicated that there were no differences as a function of sex; therefore, this variable was disregarded in subsequent analyses. Also, groups within conditions were included as a nested factor in the analysis. However, since a preliminary test indicated that the effect of this variable was not significant, a pooled error term was used for subsequent tests.

2. Since a preliminary test revealed that the effect of the groups within conditions nested factor was significant ($p < .05$), it was used as the error term for subsequent tests.

4

PHILIP G. ZIMBARDO

Pathology of Imprisonment

I was recently released from solitary confinement after being held therein for 37 months [months!]. A silent system was imposed upon me and to even whisper to the man in the next cell resulted in being beaten by guards, sprayed with chemical mace, blackjacked, stomped and thrown into a strip-cell naked to sleep on a concrete floor without bedding, covering, wash basin or

Source: Published by permission of Transaction, Inc. from *Society,* Vol. 9, # 6, April, 1972, 4,6,8. Copyright © 1972 by Transaction, Inc.

even a toilet. The floor served as toilet and bed, and even there the silent system was enforced. To let a moan escape your lips because of the pain and discomfort . . . resulted in another beating. I spent not days, but months there during my 37 months in solitary. . . . I have filed every writ possible against the administrative acts of brutality. The state courts have all denied the petitions. Because of my refusal to let the things die down and forget all that happened during my 37 months in solitary . . . I am the most hated prisoner in [this] penitentiary, and called a "hard-core incorrigible."

Maybe I am an incorrigible, but if true, it's because I would rather die than to accept being treated as less than a human being. I have never complained of my prison sentence as being unjustified except through legal means of appeals. I have never put a knife on a guard's throat and demanded my release. I know that thieves must be punished and I don't justify stealing, even though I am a thief myself. But now I don't think I will be a thief when I am released. No, I'm not rehabilitated. It's just that I no longer think of becoming wealthy by stealing. I now only think of killing—killing those who have beaten me and treated me as if I were a dog. I hope and pray for the sake of my own soul and future life of freedom that I am able to overcome the bitterness and hatred which eats daily at my soul, but I know to overcome it will not be easy.

This eloquent plea for prison reform—for humane treatment of human beings, for the basic dignity that is the right of every American—came to me secretly in a letter from a prisoner who cannot be identified because he is still in a state correctional institution. He sent it to me because he read of an experiment I recently conducted at Stanford University. In an attempt to understand just what it means psychologically to be a prisoner or a prison guard, Craig Haney, Curt Banks, Dave Jaffe and I created our own prison. We carefully screened over 70 volunteers who answered an ad in a Palo Alto city newspaper and ended up with about two dozen young men who were selected to be part of this study. They were mature, emotionally stable, normal, intelligent college students from middle-class homes throughout the United States and Canada. They appeared to represent the cream of the crop of this generation. None had any criminal record and all were relatively homogeneous on many dimensions initially.

Half were arbitrarily designated as prisoners by a flip of a coin, the others as guards. These were the roles they were to play in our simulated prison. The guards were made aware of the potential seriousness and danger of the situation and their own vulnerability. They made up their own formal rules for maintaining law, order and respect, and were generally free to improvise new ones during their eight-hour, three-man shifts. The prisoners were unexpectedly picked up at their homes by a city policeman in a squad car, searched, handcuffed, fingerprinted, booked at the Palo Alto station house and taken blindfolded to our jail. There they were stripped, deloused, put into a uniform, given a number and put into a cell with two other prisoners where they expected to live for the next two weeks. The pay was good ($15 a day) and their motivation was to make money.

We observed and recorded on videotape the events that occurred in the prison, and we interviewed and tested the prisoners and guards at various points throughout the study. Some of the videotapes of the actual encounters between the prisoners and guards were seen on the NBC News feature "Chronolog" on November 26, 1971.

At the end of only six days we had to close down our mock prison because what we saw was frightening. It was no longer apparent to most of the subjects (or to us) where reality ended and their roles began. The majority had indeed become prisoners or guards, no longer able to clearly differentiate between role playing and self. There were dramatic changes in virtually every aspect of their behavior, thinking and feeling. In less than a week the experience of imprisonment undid (temporarily) a lifetime of learning; human values were suspended, self-concepts were challenged and the ugliest, most base, pathological side of human nature surfaced. We were horrified because we saw some boys (guards) treat others as if they were despicable animals, taking pleasure in cruelty, while other boys (prisoners) became servile, dehumanized robots who thought only of escape, of their own individual survival and of their mounting hatred for the guards.

We had to release three prisoners in the first four days because they had such acute situational traumatic reactions as hysterical crying, confusion in thinking and severe depression. Others begged to be paroled, and all but three were willing to forfeit all the money they had earned if they could be paroled. By then (the fifth day) they had been so programmed to think of themselves as prisoners that when their request for parole was denied, they returned docilely to their cells. Now, had they been thinking as college students acting in an oppressive experiment, they would have quit once they no longer wanted the $15 a day we used as our only incentive. However, the reality was not quitting an experiment but "being paroled by the parole board from the Stanford County Jail." By the last days, the earlier solidarity among the prisoners (systematically broken by the guards) dissolved into "each man for himself." Finally, when one of their fellows was put in solitary confinement (a small closet) for refusing to eat, the prisoners were given a choice by one of the guards: give up their blankets and the incorrigible prisoner would be let out, or keep their blankets and he would be kept in all night. They voted to keep their blankets and to abandon their brother.

About a third of the guards became tyrannical in their arbitrary use of power, in enjoying their control over other people. They were corrupted by the power of their roles and became quite inventive in their techniques of breaking the spirit of the prisoners and making them feel they were worthless. Some of the guards merely did their jobs as tough but fair correctional officers, and several were good guards from the prisoners' point of view since they did them small favors and were friendly. However, no good guard ever interfered with a command by any of the bad guards; they never intervened on the side of the prisoners, they never told the others to ease off because it was only an experiment, and they never even came to me as prison superintendent or experimenter in charge to complain. In part, they were good because the others were bad; they needed the others to help establish their own egos in a positive light. In a sense, the good guards perpetuated the prison more than the other guards because their own needs to be liked prevented them from disobeying or violating the implicit guards' code. At the same time, the act of befriending the prisoners created a social reality which made the prisoners less likely to rebel.

By the end of the week the experiment had become a reality, as if it were a Pirandello play directed by Kafka that just keeps going after the audience has left. The consultant for our prison, Carlo Prescott, an ex-convict with 16 years of imprisonment in California's jails, would get so depressed and furious each time he visited our prison, because of its psychological similarity to his experiences, that he would have to leave. A Catholic priest who was a former prison chaplain in Washington, D.C. talked to our prisoners after four days and said they were just like the other first-timers he had seen.

But in the end, I called off the experiment not because of the horror I saw out there in the prison yard, but because of the horror of realizing that *I* could have easily traded places with the most brutal guard or become the weakest prisoner full of hatred at being so powerless that I could not eat, sleep or go to the toilet without permission of the authorities. *I* could have become Calley at My Lai, George Jackson at San Quentin, one of the men at Attica or the prisoner quoted at the beginning of this article.

Individual behavior is largely under the control of social forces and environmental contingencies rather than personality traits, character, will power or other empirically unvalidated constructs. Thus we create an illusion of freedom by attributing more internal control to ourselves, to the individual, than actually exists. We thus underestimate the power and pervasiveness of situational controls over behavior because: (a) they are often non-obvious and subtle, (b) we can often avoid entering situations where we might be so controlled, (c) we label as "weak" or "deviant" people in those situations who do behave differently from how we believe we would.

Each of us carries around in our heads a favorable self-image in which we are essentially just, fair, humane and understanding. For example, we could not imagine inflicting pain on others without much provocation or hurting people who had done nothing to us, who in fact were even liked by us. However, there is a growing body of social psychological research which underscores the conclusion derived from this prison study. Many people, perhaps the majority, can be made to do almost anything when put into psychologically compelling situations—regardless of their morals, ethics, values, attitudes, beliefs or personal convictions. My colleague, Stanley Milgram, has shown that more than 60 percent of the population will deliver what they think is a series of painful electric shocks to another person even after the victim cries for mercy, begs them to stop and then apparently passes out. The subjects complained that they did not want to inflict more pain but blindly obeyed the command of the authority figure (the experimenter) who said that they must go on. In my own research on violence, I have seen mild-mannered co-eds repeatedly give shocks (which they thought were causing pain) to another girl, a stranger whom they had rated very favorably, simply by being made to feel anonymous and put in a situation where they were expected to engage in this activity.

Observers of these and similar experimental situations never predict their outcomes and estimate that it is unlikely that they themselves would behave similarly. They can be so confident only when they were outside the situation. However, since the majority of people in these studies do act in non-rational, non-obvious ways, it follows that the majority of observers would also succumb to the social psychological forces in the situation.

With regard to prisons, we can state that the mere act of assigning labels to people and putting them into a situation where those labels acquire validity and meaning is sufficient to elicit pathological behavior. This pathology is not predictable from any available diagnostic indicators we have in the social sciences, and is extreme enough to modify in very significant ways fundamental attitudes and behavior. The prison situation, as presently arranged, is guaranteed to generate severe enough pathological reactions in both guards and prisoners as to debase their humanity, lower their feelings of self-worth and make it difficult for them to be part of a society outside of their prison.

For years our national leaders have been pointing to the enemies of freedom, to the fascist or communist threat to the American way of life. In so doing they have overlooked the threat of social anarchy that is building within our own country without any outside agitation. As soon as a person comes to the realization that he is being imprisoned by his society or individuals in it, then, in the best American tradition, he demands liberty and rebels, accepting death as an alternative. The third alternative, however, is to allow oneself to become a good prisoner—docile, cooperative, uncomplaining, conforming in thought and complying in deed.

Our prison authorities now point to the militant agitators who are still vaguely referred to as part of some communist plot, as the irresponsible, incorrigible troublemakers. They imply that there would be no trouble, riots, hostages or deaths if it weren't for this small band of bad prisoners. In other words, then, everything would return to "normal" again in the life of our nation's prisons if they could break these men.

The riots in prison are coming from within—from within every man and woman who refuses to let the system turn them into an object, a number, a thing or a no-thing. It is not communist inspired, but inspired by the spirit of American freedom. No man wants to be enslaved. To be powerless, to be subject to the arbitrary exercise of power, to not be recognized as a human being is to be a slave.

To be a militant prisoner is to become aware that the physical jails are but more blatant extensions of the forms of social and psychological oppression experienced daily in the nation's ghettos. They are trying to awaken the conscience of the nation to the ways in which the American ideals are being perverted, apparently in the name of justice but actually under the banner of apathy, fear and hatred. If we do not listen to the pleas of the prisoners at Attica to be treated like human beings, then we have all become brutalized by our priorities for property rights over human rights. The consequence will not only be more prison riots but a loss of all those ideals on which this country was founded.

The public should be aware that they own the prisons and that their business is failing. The 70 percent recidivism rate and the escalation in severity of crimes committed by graduates of our prisons are evidence that current prisons fail to rehabilitate the inmates in any positive way. Rather, they are breeding grounds for hatred of the establishment, a hatred that makes every citizen a target of violent assault. Prisons are a bad investment for us taxpayers. Until now we have not cared, we have turned over to wardens and prison authorities the unpleasant job of keeping people who threaten us out of our sight. Now we are shocked to learn that their management practices have failed to improve the product and instead turn petty thieves into murderers. We must insist upon new management or improved operating procedures.

The cloak of secrecy should be removed from the prisons. Prisoners claim they are brutalized by the guards, guards say it is a lie. Where is the impartial test of the truth in such a situation? Prison officials have forgotten that they work for us, that they are only public servants whose salaries are paid by our taxes. They act as if it is their prison, like a child with a toy he won't share. Neither lawyers, judges, the legislature nor the public is allowed into prisons to ascertain the truth unless the visit is sanctioned by authorities and until all is prepared for their visit. I was shocked to learn that my request to join a congressional investigating committee's tour of San Quentin and Soledad was refused, as was that of the news media.

There should be an ombudsman in every prison, not under the pay or control of the prison authority, and responsible only to the courts, state legislature and the public. Such a person could report on violations of constitutional and human rights.

Guards must be given better training than they now receive for the difficult job society imposes upon them. To be a prison guard as now constituted is to be put in a situation of constant threat from within the prison, with no social recognition from the society at large. As was shown graphically at Attica, prison guards are also prisoners of the system who can be sacrificed to the demands of the public to be punitive and the needs of politicians to preserve an image. Social scientists and business administrators should be called upon to design and help carry out this training.

The relationship between the individual (who is sentenced by the courts to a prison term) and his community must be maintained. How can a prisoner return to a dynamically changing society that most of us cannot cope with after being out of it for a number of years? There should be more community involvement in these rehabilitation centers, more ties encouraged and promoted between the trainees and promoted between the trainees and family and friends, more educational opportunities to prepare them for returning to their communities as more valuable members of it than they were before they left.

Finally, the main ingredient necessary to effect any change at all in prison reform, in the rehabilitation of a single prisoner or even in the optimal development of a child is caring. Reform must start with people—especially people with power—caring about the well-being of others. Underneath the toughest, society-hating convict, rebel or anarchist is a human being who wants his existence to be recognized by his fellows and who wants someone else to care about whether he lives or dies and to grieve if he lives imprisoned rather than lives free.

CHAPTER VII

Attitudes and Attitude Change

1. Russell H. Weigel, David T. A. Vernon, and Louis N. Tognacci, "Specificity of the Attitude as a Determinant of Attitude-Behavior Congruence"
2. Clyde Hendrick and B. A. Seyfried, "Assessing the Validity of Laboratory-Produced Attitude Change"
3. Mark P. Zanna and Joel Cooper, "Dissonance and the Pill: An Attribution Approach to Studying the Arousal Properties of Dissonance"
4. Robert E. Knox and James A. Inkster, "Postdecision Dissonance at Post Time"

An attitude is a mental and neural state of readiness, organized through experience, exerting a directive or dynamic influence upon the individual's response to all objects and situations with which it is related.

Gordon W. Allport (1935/1967, p. 810)

Commentary

The study of attitudes and attitude change has continued to occupy an important role in social psychology (Kelman, 1974), in spite of the fact that from time to time questions have been raised about the usefulness and meaningfulness of the attitude concept. Although there are many different definitions of attitude, most theorists would agree with Gordon Allport's conception of attitude (quoted above) as having a directive influence on behavior (Calder & Ross, 1973). If attitudes do, indeed, have this steering function and do predispose individuals to act in certain ways, a good deal of consistency between attitudes and behavior would be expected. That is, attitudes should be fairly good predictors of behavior. In actuality, the evidence for attitude-behavior consistency has been rather weak. In fact, a classic study by R. T. LaPiere (1934) failed to find any relationship between attitudes and behavior.

For a period of two years beginning in 1930, LaPiere traveled around the United States with a young Chinese couple. He began his trip with some apprehension because of what he knew the attitude surveys of the time indicated about Americans' attitudes toward the Chinese. Yet, when they first approached a hotel clerk in an exclusive hotel in a small town reputed to be bigoted against Chinese, they were given accommodations without any problem. Two months later, when they passed through that town again, they decided to stay at the same hotel. This time, however, LaPiere called ahead and asked if they would accommodate "an important Chinese gentleman." The answer was no. The apparent contradiction between these two incidents aroused LaPiere's curiosity and led him to do his systematic study (1934). He kept records of the service rendered to him and his Chinese companions during 10,000 miles of travel. In 251 requests for food or lodging, they were only refused once. Six months later, LaPiere sent out a questionnaire to each of the places they had been to, asking whether they would "accept members of the Chinese race as guests of your establishment?" (p. 233). He received replies from 128 of them, over 90 percent replying no. LaPiere received only one yes reply, from an owner of an auto camp who described a pleasant visit she had recently had from a nice Chinese couple. LaPiere concluded that it is worthless to obtain a verbal assessment of a person's attitudes, since it is not likely to predict what he will do in an actual situation. As he summed up in his article, "it would seem far more worth while to make a shrewd guess regarding that which is essential than to accurately measure that which is likely to prove quite irrelevant" (p. 237).

Although LaPiere's study is regularly cited in textbooks as evidence for attitude-behavior discrepancy, a recent article by Dillehay (1973) argues that the study by LaPiere—and two other oft-cited studies—cannot provide evidence for or against the relationship between attitudes and behavior. Among the reasons he presents for the inappropriateness of the LaPiere study as evidence against the attitude-behavior relationship is the probability that measures of behavior and attitude were elicited from different people. That is, the persons who served LaPiere and the couple may not have been the ones who answered the questionnaire. The argument against the ability of attitudes to predict behavior, however, does not have to rely for evidence solely on such early studies as LaPiere's. In a recent article Wicker (1969), after reviewing the results of studies attempting to relate attitudes to behavior, reached a conclusion very similar to one reached by LaPiere in 1934: "Taken as a whole, these studies suggest that it is considerably more likely that attitudes will be unrelated or only slightly related to overt behaviors than that attitudes will be closely related to actions" (Wicker, 1969, p. 65).

Many attitude theorists take a more optimistic view, however. For example, Kelman (1974) does not regard the low correlations that are often found between attitudes and actions as evidence against the validity of the attitude concept itself. Rather,

They merely confirm the view that the use of attitude in the prediction of action requires a refined and detailed assessment of attitudes, as well as a thorough analysis of the action situation to which we hope to predict, including the social constraints that govern that situation and the variety of attitudes that are aroused within it (p. 314).

As studies in this chapter show, there is cause for optimism: Given the existence of certain conditions, consistency between attitudes and behavior does exist.

The four selections in this chapter point in various ways to the meaningfulness of the attitude concept. The first two demonstrate that attitudes can predict behavior, while the last two, based on the theory of cognitive dissonance (Festinger, 1957), show that behavior can affect attitudes.

One of the factors that has been assumed to affect the strength of the attitude-behavior relationship is the specificity of the attitude being measured relative to the behavior to be predicted. That is, attitude-behavior inconsistency may often be due to the fact that the attitude tapped by a verbal measure is very general, while the behavior it is meant to predict is very specific. An implication of this is that if both the attitude and the behavior are made highly specific, the predictive power of the attitude measure should be increased. The validity of these notions was tested by the study reported in the first selection in this chapter ("Specificity of the Attitude as a Determinant of Attitude-Behavior Congruence," by Weigel, Vernon, and Tognacci). Subjects were first asked to complete an attitude survey concerned with environmental issues. In the survey were four measures varying in degree of specificity in relation to the criterion behavior—participation in Sierra Club activities. The authors found that the more specific the attitude measure, the better a predictor it was of a subject's degree of commitment to work for the Sierra Club.

Most current attitude research has focused primarily on processes of attitude change rather than on the nature of the attitudes the person already holds. In the area of attitude change the issue of attitude-behavior consistency can be examined by asking to what extent a change in attitude results in a corresponding change in behavior. That is, does a change in attitude created in the laboratory have any meaning beyond the mark on the scale by which attitude change is defined?

The experiment described in Selection 2 ("Assessing the Validity of Laboratory-Produced Attitude Change," by Hendrick and Seyfried) provides evidence that it does. The point of departure for this study was the well-established relationship between similarity and attraction demonstrated by Byrne (1969). Subjects with identical or highly similar response patterns on a pretest attitude measure were paired, one in each pair being randomly assigned to the experimental condition, the other to the control condition. Then, only the experimental subjects read a counterattitudinal essay, and their attitudes were assessed again by means of a posttest. Subsequently, both experimental and control subjects were presented with two completed attitude questionnaires, allegedly filled out by two strangers, and were asked to form impressions of them. The pattern of responses of the first stranger was made identical to the subjects' pretest scores, while the responses of the second stranger were identical to the experimental subject's posttest attitude scores. Control subjects, not having had their attitudes changed, liked the first stranger more than the second stranger, while experimental subjects whose attitudes, as a result of the persuasive communication, were identical to the second stranger's, were more attracted to him than to the first one.

Unquestionably, the most influential theory in contemporary social psychology has been the theory of cognitive dissonance formulated by Leon Festinger (1957). According to this theory, when a person holds two cognitions that are psychologically inconsistent with each other, he experiences a state of cognitive dissonance. A state of dissonance is assumed to be uncomfortable and, therefore, dissonance arousal is expected to lead to attempts to reduce the dissonance. One of the most controversial aspects of the theory has been its predictions regarding the effects of counterattitudinal behavior on the person's subsequent attitudes. According to the theory, the less the amount of external pressure, incentive, or justification that is brought to bear on the person to act contrary to his private beliefs, the greater the amount of attitude change in the direction of his actions is expected to occur.

A test of this prediction was provided by a classic experiment by Festinger and Carlsmith (1959), in which subjects first participated in an extremely boring task and later were asked by the experimenter to tell another subject, a confederate of the experimenter, that the task was enjoyable. Subjects were paid either $1 or $20 to tell the lie. Subsequently, those subjects who had been paid only $1 indicated greater enjoyment of the task than those who received the $20. The latter did not differ significantly in reported enjoyment from subjects in the control group, who had not been asked to lie to a confederate. According to dissonance theory, a subject in the experimental groups is confronted with two conflicting cognitions: One, that he participated in a boring task; and, two, that he told someone that it was enjoyable. When dissonance is aroused, it can be reduced by changing one of the two conflicting cognitions in the situation. In this case this can be accomplished by changing the initially negative attitude toward the task to a positive one. This explains the positive shift in attitude found among the $1 subjects. The $20 subjects experienced little dissonance, and hence little attitude change, since receiving $20 was enough justification for behavior contrary to their actual beliefs.

This study spawned one of the most enduring controversies in contemporary social psychology. Since Festinger and Carlsmith's experiment, scores of studies have been conducted using their "forced compliance" paradigm to test competing explanations for their paradoxical finding that a smaller incentive to behave counterattitudinally leads to greater attitude change than a larger incentive. Current perspectives on the controversy can be found in Calder, Ross, and Insko (1973) and Collins and Hoyt (1972). An annotated bibliography of the relevant literature through 1972 has been prepared by Tate (1973). The third selection in this chapter ("Dissonance and the Pill: An Attribution Approach to Studying the Arousal Properties of Dissonance," by Zanna and Cooper) provides recent input for the controversy involving the forced-compliance paradigm.

Dissonance theory assumes that dissonance is experienced as a state of tension or arousal. One aspect of the controversy derives from the claim of self-perception theory (Bem, 1965, 1967) that one can explain dissonancelike effects of counterattitudinal behavior without the necessity of postulating the existence of dissonance arousal. The experiment reported in Selection 3 provides evidence for the arousal properties of dissonance by means of an attribution procedure similar to the one used in Storms and Nisbett's study on insomnia (reprinted in Chapter I, Selection 4). Subjects were given a pill as part of a procedure in an experiment on short-term memory. They were then asked to write essays arguing that inflammatory speakers should not be permitted on campus. In the low-dissonance or low-choice condition, subjects were simply asked to write the essay. In the high-choice (high-dissonance) condition, subjects were given the choice of whether or not to write the essay. Cutting across this choice variable was the nature of the expectation given to subjects regarding the effects of the pill. Subjects in the arousal condition were told that they would become tense, another group was given the expectation that they would feel relaxed from the pill, while a third group was told that there would be no side effects. Subsequently, a measure of subjects' attitude about banning inflammatory speakers was obtained. An additional group of subjects, the control group, was given a measure of attitude only, but no experimental treatments. The results were in line with expectations based on the assumption that dissonance has arousal properties. In the words of the authors:

High-dissonance subjects who could attribute their arousal to a pill showed less of a tendency to change their attitudes, while subjects in the high-dissonance-relaxation condition showed an increased need to deal with their arousal by changing their opinions. Under the low-dissonance conditions, the various side effects made virtually no difference.

The applications of dissonance theory have tended to concentrate on several well-defined behavioral domains. One area of application, which we have just discussed, has been in the prediction of the consequences of actions which are inconsistent with beliefs. Another application of dissonance theory has been in the prediction of the effects of having made a choice. According to the theory, a person who decides between two (or more) attractive alternatives experiences dissonance. Postdecision dissonance is assumed to occur because of the inconsistency between the cognition that one alternative has been rejected and the cognition that the rejected alternative had attractive features. The theory states that one way to reduce dissonance is for the person to increase the perceived attractiveness of the chosen alternative relative to the rejected alternative. The last selection in this chapter examines the operation of postdecision dissonance among bettors at a race track. In two studies reported in "Postdecision Dissonance at Post Time," by Knox and Inkster, bettors were approached either right before they placed a bet on a horse or immediately after. In one study, subjects were asked to rate the horse's chance of winning the race, while in the other the subjects' degree of confidence about having picked the winner was elicited. In line with expectations from dissonance theory, bettors approached after they had placed bets gave their horse a higher rating than patrons questioned before placing their bets.

REFERENCES

Allport, G. W. Attitudes. In C. Murchison (Ed.), *Handbook of social psychology* (Vol. 2). New York: Russell & Russell, 1967. Pp. 798-884. (Originally published, 1935.)

Bem, D. J. An experimental analysis of self-persuasion. *Journal of Experimental Social Psychology,* 1965, *1,* 199-218.

Bem, D. J. Self-perception: An alternative interpretation of cognitive dissonance phenomena. *Psychological Review,* 1967, *74,* 183-200.

Byrne, D. Attitudes and attraction. In L. Berkowitz (Ed.), *Advances in experimental social psychology* (Vol. 4). New York: Academic Press, 1969.

Calder, B. J., & Ross, M. *Attitudes and behavior.* Morristown, N.J.: General Learning Press, 1973.

Calder, B. J., Ross, M., & Insko, C. A. Attitude change and attitude attribution: Effects of incentive, choice, and consequences. *Journal of Personality and Social Psychology,* 1973, *25,* 84-99.

Collins, B. E., & Hoyt, M. F. Personal responsibility-for-consequences: An integration and extension of the "forced compliance" literature. *Journal of Experimental Social Psychology,* 1972, *8,* 558-593.

Dillehay, R. C. On the irrelevance of the classical negative evidence concerning the effect of attitudes on behavior. *American Psychologist,* 1973, *28,* 887-891.

Festinger, L. *A theory of cognitive dissonance.* Stanford, Calif.: Stanford University Press, 1957.

Festinger, L., & Carlsmith, J. M. Cognitive consequences of forced compliance. *Journal of Abnormal and Social Psychology,* 1959, *58,* 203-211.

Kelman, H. C. Attitudes are alive and well and gainfully employed in the sphere of action. *American Psychologist,* 1974, *29,* 310-324.

LaPiere, R. T. Attitudes vs. actions. *Social Forces,* 1934, *13,* 230-237.

Tate, E. *An annotated bibliography of studies on counterattitudinal advocacy.* Saskatoon, Saskatchewan: St. Thomas Moore College, University of Saskatchewan, 1973.

Wicker, A. W. Attitudes versus actions: The relationship of verbal and overt behavioral responses to attitude objects. *Journal of Social Issues,* 1969, *25* (4), 41-78.

1

RUSSELL H. WEIGEL, DAVID T. A. VERNON, and LOUIS N. TOGNACCI

Specificity of the Attitude as a Determinant of Attitude-Behavior Congruence

Persons who had reported varying degrees of ecological concern in a survey about environmental problems were contacted five months later by representatives of the Sierra Club. Respondents' subsequent level of behavioral commitment to the Sierra Club was compared to the scores that they had previously attained on four different attitude scales. Results lend support to the proposition that attitude-behavior congruence improves when the attitude measured is highly specific to the behavioral criterion. Implications of these findings for attitude research are discussed.

Attitudes have generally been conceptualized as underlying dispositions which enter, along with other influences, into the determination of a variety of behaviors toward an object (Allport, 1954; Campbell, 1963; Cook & Selltiz, 1964; DeFleur & Westie, 1963). In this view, attitudes are seen as influencing statements of beliefs and feelings about the object and approach-avoidance actions with respect to it. Although supporters of this position have been careful to emphasize that personal and situational factors tend to inhibit the degree to which verbally expressed attitudes and behavior covary, they generally assert that attitudes are "precursors of behavior . . . determinants of how a person will actually behave in his daily affairs [Cohen, 1964, pp. 137-138]." It is also clear, however, that past research has been literally riddled with evidence of inconsistencies between attitudes and observed behaviors (see Wicker, 1969). Indeed, some investigators (McClelland & Winter, 1969; Wicker, 1969) have argued

Source: Russell H. Weigel, David T. A. Vernon, and Louis N. Tognacci, "Specificity of the Attitude as a Determinant of Attitude-Behavior Congruence," *Journal of Personality and Social Psychology*, 1974, *30*, 724-728. Copyright 1974 by the American Psychological Association.

The authors are indebted to Stuart W. Cook and John R. Forward for their very helpful suggestions about an earlier draft of this article.

that the demonstrated relationship between verbal-attitude measures and overt behavior is essentially zero.

In the midst of the controversy, several issues have been raised. A number of writers (Chein, 1949; Cook & Selltiz, 1964; Crespi, 1971; Fishbein, 1966) have pointed out that many instances of attitude-behavior inconsistency may be due to the fact that the stimulus in the verbal-response situation tends to be very general, while the stimulus in the overt-response situation tends to be highly specific. For example, in many cases the subject's general attitudes toward a given social group are measured, and then attempts are made to predict his behavior with respect to a *particular member* of that group on the basis of his more general attitude. The problem is that the subject's beliefs about the particular group member he comes in contact with may not be at all similar to his beliefs about the group in general (Fishbein, 1966). Recognizing this difficulty Crespi (1971) has suggested that attitude-behavior congruency is enhanced when both the attitude measured and the behavior observed are highly specific. Conversely, when the attitude is general and the behavior specific, the predictive capacity of the attitude measure should be poor.

The present study emerged from a concern with the attitude-behavior controversy and an interest in exploring the degree to which the specificity of the attitude acted as a determinant of congruence between verbally expressed attitudes and subsequent actions. The investigation was designed to assess whether subjects' self-reported attitudes about a variety of contemporary ecological issues corresponded to their willingness to actually participate in the activities of an organization engaged in seeking solutions to environmental problems at the local and national levels. On the basis of the specificity notion discussed above, it was hypothesized that attitudes which were most specific to the organization's activities would yield better predictions of the degree of later participation than would more general measures of ecological concern.

METHOD

Subjects

A survey of attitudes toward a variety of environmental issues, including attitudes about particular organizations such as the Sierra Club, was administered to 141 randomly selected residents of a medium-sized western city (see Tognacci, Weigel, Wideen, & Vernon, 1972). After answering the questions incorporated into this initial survey, the respondents were asked to sign a consent slip indicating their willingness to have their names and opinions forwarded to the Sierra Club. Eighty of the 141 respondents signed the consent form.

The original plan was to have members of the local Sierra Club chapter seek out all 80 of these respondents in an attempt to solicit help for the organization's activities. However, it soon became clear that the Sierra Club volunteers had less time to devote to the project than had been previously anticipated. Consequently, a subsample of 60 of the original 80 consenting subjects was drawn on a random basis. The five-month interval between the administration of the initial survey and the follow-up contact generated some further attrition: Six persons could not be contacted because they had moved away from the area during the interim, and two other subjects were not contacted because they were on vacation during the period in which the Sierra Club representatives were available to work on this research.

The final subject pool, then, consisted of 113 persons including 61 individuals who refused at the outset to have anything to do with the Sierra Club and 52 others who had agreed to have their names turned over to the organization. These 113 subjects were comprised of 58 males and 55 females with an average age of 37 years ($SD = 13.6$). Using the Coleman (1959) index of socioeconomic status, 60% of these subjects were in the upper-middle-class and middle-class categories with the remaining 40% in the lower-middle class or below.

Procedures

Ten members of the Rocky Mountain Chapter of the Sierra Club agreed to systematically contact and solicit help for their organization from the designated, consenting respondents. These 10 Sierra Club representatives participated in a two-hour training session detailing the interviewing techniques to be employed. Each representative was then provided with a list of names of persons to contact. In order to preclude confounding the persuasiveness of the individual representatives and initial attitude of the interviewee, each list was balanced in the sense that each contained some respondents who had previously expressed minimal interest in the Sierra Club and others who had reported more favorable attitudes toward that organization.[1] The representatives were not given any information as to how their interviewees had responded to the initial survey and were instructed not to probe for the level of previously expressed interest in or approval of the Sierra Club. Instead, they were given a detailed standardized outline describing what to say during the interview and were cautioned repeatedly about the necessity of approaching each individual on their list in the same manner.

The Attitude Measures

Included in the initial survey were four measures of environmental attitudes designed to vary in terms of their specificity to the behavioral criterion as follows:

High-Specificity Measure. The measure which was most directly related to the behavior under consideration was the attitude toward the Sierra Club scale. This six-item measure was developed to assess the respondent's interest in participating at some level in the activities of the club. Answers could range from a very mild interest in the Sierra Club (willing to read information about conservation issues provided by the Sierra Club) to a much more pronounced verbal commitment to the organization (willing to offer my house for a meeting of the local Sierra Club and interested neighbors). Subjects responded with a yes or a no to each item in the scale. An individual's score could vary from 6 to 12 with a high score indicating a more marked interest in the club. The internal consistency of the scale was quite satisfactory: Cronbach's (1951) alpha was .81, and Scott's (1968) homogeneity ratio was .42.

Moderate-Specificity Measures. Two measures were included which focused on areas of special concern and action for the Sierra Club: conservation of natural resources and pollution control. The club continues to be outspoken and politically active in both these areas of public concern. Nearly all of the local chapter's subcommittees directed their attention to one of these two issues. Concern about conservation and concern about pollution, then, were considered to represent attitudes which were moderately specific to the criterion behavior. Consequently, two 15-item Likert-type scales were developed to gauge the extent to which respondents considered conservation and pollution control important. Each item in both scales was rated along a 5-point continuum ranging from strongly agree to strongly disagree with a high score reflecting high attitudinal concern. Both scales exhibited good internal consistency. Alphas were .84 for the conservation scale and .88 for the pollution scale; homogeneity ratios were .27 and .32, respectively.

Low-Specificity Measures. The importance of a pure environment scale was designed to assess the individual's more general environmental concerns. The content of the eight items included in the Likert-type scale ranged across such issues as the importance of clean air and water, ability to live in harmony with nature, city and landscape beautification, and freedom from overcrowding. Respondents were asked to rate each of these environmental goals in terms of how satisfying it would be to them personally if the country were to realize the goal. Ratings were made along a dimension extending from maximum satisfaction to maximum dissatisfaction. Each item was scored on a 1-5 basis with a high score indicating

TABLE 1.1
Intercorrelations among the Four Attitude Measures

Scale	Attitude toward the Sierra Club Scale	Conservation Scale	Pollution Scale	Importance of a Pure Environment Scale
Attitude toward the Sierra Club		.58**	.56**	.28*
Conservation			.81**	.50**
Pollution				.45**
Importance of a pure environment				

Note: $N = 113$.
*$p < .01$.
**$p < .001$.

endorsement of these general environmentalist objectives. Although Cronbach's alpha at .72 was slightly lower here than on the previously described measures, the homogeneity ratio of .28 attained by the importance of a pure environment scale demonstrated that the measure had quite an adequate degree of interitem consistency.

The four attitude measures were intercorrelated to determine the degree to which they mapped out a common domain of environmental concern. These intercorrelations are presented in Table 1.1.

Inspection of these data reveals that all four attitude measures displayed positive intercorrelations, significant at $p < .01$ or better. The various measures, then, appear to be mutually complementary indexes of the subject's level of concern about environmental quality. As expected, the lowest correlation coefficient characterizes the relationship between the attitude toward the Sierra Club scale (the high-specificity measure) and the importance of a pure environment scale (the low-specificity measure), while the highest correlation value is observed between the two moderate specificity measures focusing on concerns about conservation and pollution.

The Criterion Behavior

Each subject's level of behavioral commitment to the Sierra Club was categorized according to the following procedure.

No Consent. This category represented the low end of the action continuum. Included in this group were the 61 individuals who refused to sign the consent form in the original survey which would have allowed their names to be given to the local Sierra Club chapter. Although it seems reasonable to argue that refusal to sign the consent form represents the ultimate in behavioral rejection of further contact with the organization, it is also true that none of these 61 subjects were interviewed later. The objection could be raised, therefore, that these individuals might have agreed to offer assistance if they had been exposed to a subsequent interview. In response to this potential criticism, parallel analyses are reported using first the data derived from all 113 subjects and second only the data from the 52 subjects who were actually interviewed.

Low Commitment. This classification included subjects who made any of three types of responses when contacted by a Sierra Club representative. Subjects who refused to make an appointment for a personal interview were placed in this category as were individuals who were interviewed in person but who declined to offer any help to the organization. Also placed in this group were subjects whose interest in further association with the Sierra Club extended only so far as a willingness to be put on the organization's mailing list.

Moderate Commitment. Subjects who agreed to write a letter to an elected official about either a national or a local environmental issue were put in this category. In terms of actual behavior, persons who agreed to write were given a preaddressed envelope and required to take notes on an outline of a letter dictated by the interviewer. Also included under the classification of moderate commitment were subjects who actually mailed a financial contribution to the treasurer of the local Sierra Club chapter.

High Commitment. Persons who indicated that they wanted to do volunteer work on a particular subcommittee of the club (Conservation Education, Wildlife, Water Pollution, etc.) were informed that the appropriate chairman would contact them so that they could attend future meetings. Only if the subject reaffirmed his intention to work on the subcommittee when later approached by the chairman was he placed in the high-commitment category. Individuals who became club members by filling out the Sierra Club membership application and sending the $17 annual dues to the treasurer were also included in this category.

A subject received a score of 0 on the behavioral commitment index if he was in the no-consent category, 1 if in the low-commitment category, 2 if in the moderate-commitment category, and 3 if in the high-commitment category. Evidence for evaluating the research hypothesis was sought by examining the relationship of variation on this behavioral commitment index to variation on each of the four attitude measures.

RESULTS

The hypothesis may now be stated in more precise terms. It was anticipated that the individual's level of behavioral commitment would be best predicted by his responses to the attitude toward the Sierra Club scale because this measure was most specifically related to the criterion

TABLE 1.2
Correlations between Scores on the Attitude Measures and Scores on the Behavioral Commitment Index

Index	Attitude toward the Sierra Club Scale	Conservation Scale	Pollution Scale	Importance of a Pure Environment Scale
Behavioral commitment[a]				
($n = 113$)	.60***	.37**	.38**	.16
Behavioral commitment				
($n = 52$)	.68***	.24	.32*	.06

[a] Non-consent group included in analysis as the low end of the action continuum.
* $p < .05$.
** $p < .01$.
*** $p < .001$.

behavior. Subjects' participation in Sierra Club activities was expected to bear a more moderate positive relationship to scores on the measures gauging concerns about conservation and pollution—concerns shared by already established subcommittees of the club. Finally, it was hypothesized that our low-specificity instrument measuring more general ecological concerns (importance of a pure environment scale) would yield the weakest prediction of the level of subsequent participation in the organization.

In order to examine the relationship between the specificity of the attitude and the behavioral criterion, scores on each of the four attitude measures were correlated with scores on the index of behavioral commitment. These data are presented in Table 1.2.

Examination of the data reported in Table 1.2 indicates that the hypothesized pattern of attitude-behavior relationships was obtained both for the larger sample, including the 61 no-consent subjects, and for the subsample comprised of only those subjects who were actually interviewed by Sierra Club representatives. The attitude toward the Sierra Club scale was the best predictor of subsequent behavioral commitment, with more modest positive correlations characterizing the relationships observed between the two moderate-specificity measures and the behavioral criterion. Only the importance of a pure environment scale, assessing more general ecological concern, consistently yielded nonsignificant correlations with subjects' behavioral responsiveness to the Sierra Club.

Tests of the significance of the differences observed between these correlation coefficients revealed that, for the larger sample, the predictive power of the high-, moderate-, and low-specificity measures differed significantly from one another with $p < .05$ in all comparisons. For the smaller sample including only the 52 subjects who were interviewed, the predictive power of the attitude toward the Sierra Club scale was again significantly greater than any of the other three measures ($p < .01$). Although the magnitude of the differences among the attitude-behavior correlations for the moderate- and low-specificity measures paralleled those found for the larger sample, these differences were not significant when the number of subjects was reduced to 52.

DISCUSSION

The findings of this investigation support the hypothesis that attitudes exhibit increased power to predict behavior when the content of the attitude measure is highly specific to the behavioral criterion. It might be argued that the observed variation in the predictive capacity of the three attitude measures resulted merely from variation in the quality of the scales employed. However, such an interpretation does not seem plausible because while the scales did vary in length, all three measures displayed quite similar levels of internal consistency. Differences in the degree to which a given attitude measure implied a specific behavior rather than differences in the inherent quality of the scales themselves, then, seem to best explain the results obtained.

Although the findings of the present study are not surprising, they do underscore an important question for attitude research: To what extent should attitude measures be expected to predict behavior? It is clear that attitudes do not fully determine the course that behavior will take. Rather, the determinants of any action include a host of personal and situational variables which are operative at a given point in time. One important determinant of attitude-behavior congruence would seem to be the degree to which the attitude measured specifies the behavioral criterion employed.

Our results indicate that attitude measures which vary in their specificity of relation to a behavioral criterion exhibit differential power to predict that criterion. We would *not* argue that this suggests the wisdom of abandoning the concept of attitudes as underlying dispositions in favor of a descriptive concept which equates attitudes and behaviors under specified situational circumstances. We would argue, instead, that attitude measures should be expected to predict only behaviors that are appropriate to or specified by the attitude under consideration. It would follow that when the attitude object is a general or comprehensive one, for example, the environment, then the behavioral criterion should be equally general or comprehensive. To achieve the latter would imply the necessity of using multiple indexes designed to adequately sample the universe of pro- and antienvironmental activities.

318 ATTITUDES AND ATTITUDE CHANGE

REFERENCES

Allport, G. W. The historical background of modern social psychology. In G. Lindzey (Ed.), *Handbook of social psychology.* Vol. 1. *Theory and method.* Cambridge, Mass.: Addison-Wesley, 1954.

Campbell, D. T. Social attitudes and other acquired behavioral dispositions. In S. Koch (Ed.), *Psychology: A study of a science.* Vol. 6. *Investigations of man as socius: Their place in psychology and the social sciences.* New York: McGraw-Hill, 1963.

Chein, I. The problems of inconsistency: A restatement. *Journal of Social Issues,* 1949, *5,* 52-61.

Cohen, A. R. *Attitude change and social influence.* New York: Basic Books, 1964.

Coleman, R. P. Social class in Kansas City. Unpublished doctoral dissertation, University of Chicago, 1959.

Cook, S. W., & Selltiz, C. A multiple-indicator approach to attitude measurement. *Psychological Bulletin,* 1964, *62,* 36-65.

Crespi, I. What kinds of attitude measures are predictive of behavior? *Public Opinion Quarterly,* 1971, *35,* 327-334.

Cronbach, L. J. Coefficient alpha and the internal structure of tests. *Psychometrika,* 1951, *16,* 297-334.

DeFleur, M. L., & Westie, F. R. Attitude as a scientific concept. *Social Forces,* 1963, *42,* 17-31.

Fishbein, M. The relationships between beliefs, attitudes, and behavior. In S. Feldman (Ed.), *Cognitive consistency.* New York: Academic Press, 1966.

McClelland, D. C., & Winter, D. G. *Motivating economic achievement.* New York: Free Press, 1969.

Scott, W. A. Attitude measurement. In G. Lindzey & E. Aronson (Eds.), *Handbook of social psychology.* (Rev. ed.) Vol. 2. Reading, Mass.: Addison-Wesley, 1968.

Tognacci, L. N., Weigel, R. H., Wideen, M. F., & Vernon, D. T. A. Environmental quality: How universal is public concern? *Environment and Behavior,* 1972, *4,* 73-86.

Wicker, A. W. Attitudes versus actions: The relationship of verbal and overt behavioral responses to attitude objects. *Journal of Social Issues,* 1969, *25,* 41-78.

NOTES

1. To assess the degree of variation among the representatives in the level of commitment obtained, a one-way analysis of variance was carried out using interviewee commitments as the dependent variable. This analysis resulted in an F ratio of 1.06 ($df = 9/42$, ns). Thus, variation in the behavioral commitment levels of the subjects cannot be attributed to variation in interviewing skill or individual differences in persuasiveness.

2

CLYDE HENDRICK and B. A. SEYFRIED

Assessing the Validity of Laboratory-Produced Attitude Change

The validity of attitude change produced in the laboratory is one of the major problems for attitude research. The results of many attitude change studies may be attributed rather easily to demand characteristics. One great difficulty has been the lack of a suitable method for assessing validity. The present experiment solved this problem by the use of a well-known experimental paradigm that could demonstrate implications of attitude change for another conceptually relevant behavior. Subjects were pretested on an issue and were then divided into matched pairs based on identical attitude response patterns. One subject in each pair was randomly assigned to an experimental condition, and the second, to a control condition. Experimental subjects read a persuasive communication and completed an attitude posttest. Later, subjects in both conditions served in an experiment on interpersonal attraction. Each experimental subject and his matched control examined two complete attitude questionnaires attributed to two strangers and rated their attraction toward them. One stranger had a pattern of attitude responses identical to the subjects' attitude pretest responses, and the second stranger had a pattern of attitude responses identical to the experimental subject's attitude posttest responses. Results showed that experimental subjects liked their attitude posttest stranger better than their pretest stranger, but just the reverse was true for control subjects. Thus the results showed that attitude change strongly affected attraction responses, demonstrating that changing an attitude has real consequences for another conceptually related behavior.

The present study was concerned with the question of the validity of attitude change as produced and measured in a standard laboratory experiment. This issue is of considerable importance in view of the massive amount of work devoted to the study of attitude change. Recent reviews (e.g., Abelson, 1972; Fishbein & Ajzen, 1972) have been pessimistic about a variety of problems, ranging from definitional and measurement issues to the relationship between attitude change and behavior change. Rokeach (1968) has been particularly critical of the

Source: Clyde Hendrick and B. A. Seyfried, "Assessing the Validity of Laboratory-Produced Attitude Change," *Journal of Personality and Social Psychology*, 1974, *29*, 865-870. Copyright 1974 by the American Psychological Association. Reprinted by permission.

attitude change literature. Rokeach has made a theoretical distinction between expressed opinion and the underlying attitude. True attitude change requires engagement of two attitudes, one toward the object in question and one toward the situation existing for that object. Measured opinion change may represent only differential activation of the attitude toward object in two situations (e.g., precommunication-postcommunication exposure) without any real attitude change at all. As Rokeach (1968, p. 150) had correctly noted, most experiments use only a single posttest measure, and thus the relation of expressed opinion change to actual attitude change is ambiguous.

The possibility that measured opinion change is only superficial scale change, in conjunction with the fact of the temporary nature of most laboratory-produced attitude change, plus the ever present possibility that subjects change their rating responses as a result of demand characteristics suggest that the question of validity of attitude change is a real one. Establishment of validity of attitude change is a difficult problem, partly because of problems of definition of an attitude and partly because of the difficulty in establishing a suitable external criterion. One type of criterion is other kinds of conceptually relevant behavior to which an attitude score can be related. However, some authors define attitude so as to preclude any necessary consistent relation between attitude and other behaviors, thus rendering such a search for validity meaningless (De Fleur & Westie, 1963, p. 27). Others might assume an intrinsic positive relation between attitude and various criterion behaviors, but one that is usually obscured by interfering variables (Kiesler, 1971, p. 10).

The literature relating attitudes to various other behavioral indexes is disappointing. In a comprehensive review Wicker (1969) concluded that there is "little evidence to support the postulated existence of stable, underlying attitudes within the individual which influence both his verbal expressions and his actions [p. 75]." A few studies have been able to relate attitude change to behavior change under circumscribed conditions (e.g., Greenwald, 1966), but little research on this specific problem has been done (Cohen, 1964), and most studies have found no relationship (e.g., Festinger, 1964).

The approach of the present study was to view an attitude as a latent variable (De Fleur & Westie, 1963) that is expressed in a variety of related effects, beliefs, and overt behaviors. If change on a rating scale as a result of a persuasive message represents true change in the latent variable, as opposed to superficial scale movement, then such change ought to be reflected in a powerful way in another situation conceptually relevant to the attitude change situation. The problem lay in finding such a conceptually relevant situation.

A suitable solution to that problem seemed to be the attraction paradigm developed by Byrne (1971) and his students. Byrne has shown that attraction toward a stimulus stranger is a positive function of similarity on several attributes, including similarity in attitudes, personality dimensions, and economic background. Since the similarity-attraction relation is well-established, the paradigm may be used as a suitable transfer test for implications of attitude change, and hence a measure of the validity of attitude change. Predicted changes in the similarity-attraction relation as a function of attitude change could be deduced that, if confirmed, would provide firm evidence for the validity of attitude change.

Implications between the two paradigms were deduced and tested by the following experimental arrangements. Subjects' attitudes on an issue were initially pretested on a multiple-item attitude scale. Subjects were divided into yoked pairs based on an identical pretest response pattern. One member of each pair was randomly assigned to an experimental condition and the second, to a control condition. Subjects in the experimental condition were exposed to a persuasive communication, and an attitude posttest was administered. Both experimental and control subjects then participated in an experiment on interpersonal attraction. Subjects examined two completed attitude questionnaires attributed to two strangers and rated their attraction toward each stranger. The strangers' response patterns were prepared so that for each yoked pair of subjects, one pattern was identical to the experimental subject's (and hence the control subject's) pretest attitude pattern, and the second was identical to the experimental subject's posttest attitude pattern. Each experimental subject's yoked control rated the same two stimulus questionnaires as did his experimental counterpart.

The basic question of interest was which stranger the experimental subjects would like best. According to Byrne (1971), they should like the most similar stranger best. But which stranger was the most similar to the experimental subjects, the stranger expressing the same pretest attitudes or the stranger expressing the same posttest attitudes? If, as Rokeach (1967) suggested, the typical experiment manipulates superficial opinion and leaves the basic attitude unchanged, then experimental subjects should find the pretest stranger more similar, and hence more likable, than the posttest stranger. Control subjects would be expected to show the same results. However, if the attitude change of the experimental subjects was real change, then they should find the posttest stranger more similar, and hence more likable, than the pretest stranger. Control subjects, since they were not exposed to a communication, should still prefer the pretest stranger.

Thus the implication of attitude change was a relative change in attraction toward two strangers. The basic design of the experiment was a 2 x 2 factorial. One variable consisted of exposure (experimental group) versus no exposure (control group) to a persuasive communication. The second variable was the stimulus strangers' attitudes, either the same as the subjects' pretest attitudes or the same as the experimental subjects' posttest attitudes. A main effect of pretest-posttest strangers, with greater attraction toward the pretest stranger, would indicate lack of a transfer of attitude change to attraction. An interaction between the two variables with control subjects preferring the pretest stranger and experimental subjects preferring the posttest stranger would be positive evidence of evaluative transfer and therefore evidence for the basic validity of attitude change.

METHOD

Subject Selection and Overview

Students in an introductory psychology course completed several questionnaires in a large testing session early in the quarter. One was a five-item Likert-type scale called Student Opinion Survey, which assessed student attitudes toward voting in local elections. Two questions were phrased in a pro and three in a con direction. There were five response alternatives for each item: strongly disagree, disagree, uncertain, agree, and strongly agree. Subjects were selected who responded favorably toward student voting in local elections on at least four of the items and responded no less than uncertain on the fifth item. Insofar as possible, pairs of subjects of the same sex were matched in terms of an identical response pattern on the pretest. Perfect matching was possible for most pairs, but a deviation of one response alternative on a single item was required to obtain a match for a few pairs. Within each pair of subjects one was randomly assigned to an experimental condition and one, to a control condition. There were 29 subjects assigned to each condition, or a total of 58, who served in the experiment. There were 12 pairs of males and 17 pairs of females.

Subjects were contacted by telephone to serve in the experiment. Subjects in the experimental condition served in two sessions. In the first session they read a three-page counterattitudinal essay attributed to a student in an English class, rated their attraction toward and impressions of the student, and completed an attitude posttest identical in format to the pretest. In the second session the next day experimental subjects rated their attraction toward two stimulus strangers after examining completed attitude scales attributed to the strangers. The response pattern of one stranger was identical to the experimental subjects' pretest attitude pattern, and the response pattern of the second stranger was identical to the experimental subjects' posttest attitude pattern.

Control subjects participated in only one session, which was held the day following the second session for experimental subjects. These subjects completed the attitude scale and then evaluated two stimulus strangers who purportedly had completed the same scale. Each control subject actually evaluated the same two strangers that his yoked experimental counterpart evaluated.

Procedure

Experimental Group. Subjects were told the experiment was concerned with person perception and that "in today's session, you will form impressions based on one type of information, and tomorrow you will do the same thing with a different type of information." Subjects then read a three-page essay attributed to a student in an English class that argued forcefully against students voting in local elections. Subjects then rated their impressions of and attraction toward the student on a form attached to the end of the essay. After these ratings were completed, the five-item attitude scale was administered with the explanation that knowledge of the subjects' own personal reactions was necessary, because "your attitudes can influence your responses to the person who wrote the essay."

The subjects returned the next day and were told, "Yesterday, you formed an impression of a person based on an essay he wrote. Today, we wish you to form an impression of two more people based on the attitudes they express." Booklets were distributed that contained two completed attitude scales. For all of the subjects one scale was identical to their pretest attitudes, and the second was identical to the postessay attitudes they had expressed the previous day. The subjects examined both attitude response patterns of the two strangers and then evaluated each stranger on a dependent variable form identical to the one used the previous day to evaluate the essay stranger. The order in which the two strangers was presented was counterbalanced across subjects.

After the ratings were completed, subjects were asked to write a brief paragraph giving their conception of what the experiment was about.[1] Data were collected from small groups of subjects, usually two to four in number.

Control Group. The control group subjects participated in only one session. These subjects always participated the day following the second session for their yoked experimental counterparts. They first completed the attitude scale to "familiarize them with the issues." The person perception experiment was then introduced, and the procedures from that point on were identical to those for the experimental group.

Dependent Variables

The dependent variable form for each stimulus person consisted of one page of rating items. The person was rated on the attributes of intelligence, knowledge of current events, morality, and adjustment. Two items assessed attraction: "How much do you think you would like this person?" and "How much would you enjoy working with this person?" Two other items measured perceived similarity in attitudes and perceived similarity in other attributes. Each measure was rated on a 7-point scale with endpoints appropriately labeled.

RESULTS

Attitude Change

The mean attitude scores are shown in the first row of Table 2.1. These scores are based on the sum of the five items for each subject, and the scores could range from 5 to 25. The pretest scores were virtually identical for the two groups (21.2 and 21.1), as they should be because of the matching. The mean posttest score of the control group was identical to the pretest score, indicating overall stability of the control subjects' attitudes. However, the experimental group was strongly influenced by the persuasive communication. For this group, the mean posttest attitude score was 16.3. All three effects from the analysis of variance were significant ($F = 14.2$, 34.6, and 34.6, respectively, $df = 1/56$, $p < .001$ for all cases).

Two points require comment. First, the experimental subjects varied considerably in how much they shifted as a result of the communication. However, for generality of the results, all subjects were retained for the analyses. This decision in effect provided a conservative test for the transfer of attitude change to the attraction paradigm. The two stimulus strangers differed from each other in direct proportion to the amount of attitude change that occurred for a given subject in the experimental condition. When there was little attitude change, the two strangers differed only slightly; hence there was less chance of finding differences on the dependent variables.

Second, although the mean attitude change was zero for the control group, perfect stability for individual attitude items should not be expected. The control group might vary considerably in response pattern even though the net change was zero. Consequently, the control attitude data were carefully inspected for each subject. There was some slight fluctuation, but only two control subjects showed both pro and con changes within the five attitude items. Nine control subjects showed zero change on any item, 12 subjects shifted an average of 1.82 units in the direction advocated for the experimental group, 7 subjects became on the average 2.71 units more extreme in their initial attitude, and 1 subject showed an average change of zero.

Perhaps the best measure of stability for the control group is to consider each of the 29 subjects as contributing five attitude responses. A 5×29 matrix constructed to represent pre- to postchange indicated zero shift in 101 of the 145 cells. It may be concluded that the control group subjects were adequately stable in their attitude scores.[2]

Dependent Measures

The two attraction items were correlated .83 and .85, respectively, for the two stimulus strangers; therefore the responses to these two items were summed to form a single attraction index. The two items assessing similarity were also summed since the correlations were .72 and .86, respectively. The attraction and similarity scores could vary from 2 to 14, while scores on the other measures could vary from 1 to 7.

For each of the six measures shown in Table 2.1, as expected, the control group rated their posttest stranger less favorably than their pretest

TABLE 2.1
Mean Attitude, Attraction, Similarity, and Evaluation Scores

Item	Experimental Condition		Control Condition	
	Pretest	*Posttest*	*Pretest*	*Posttest*
Attitude	21.2_a	16.3_b	21.1_a	21.1_a
	Pretest Stranger	Posttest Stranger	Pretest Stranger	Posttest Stranger
Dependent variable				
Attraction	9.3_a	11.3_b	11.6_b	8.9_a
Similarity	8.3_a	12.1_b	11.7_b	8.0_a
Intelligence	4.8_a	5.4_b	5.6_b	4.9_a
Knowledge of				
current events	4.9_a	$5.2_{a, b}$	5.6_b	4.5_c
Morality	4.4_a	5.3_b	5.4_b	5.0_b
Adustment	4.8_a	5.4_b	5.7_b	4.4_a

Note: Within each of the 2X2 analyses, for orthogonal comparisons means with no subscripts in common differed at the .05 level by the Newman-Keuls test.

stranger. This result indicated that the posttest stranger was perceived by control subjects as different in attitudes relative to their own pretest attitudes, with consequent lower evaluations. However, the results for the experimental group showed a different pattern. Subjects in the experimental condition rated the posttest stranger more favorably, perceiving him as more attractive, similar, intelligent, moral, better adjusted, and knowledgeable of current events than the pretest stranger.

These results indicated that after the experimental group subjects' attitudes were changed, they were highly attracted to a stranger represented by their new attitude responses and relatively unattracted to a stranger represented by their old pretest attitudes. In fact, members of the experimental group were just as negative in evaluations of their pretest stranger as the control group subjects were in evaluations of their posttest stranger. Thus, the shift in attraction as a function of changed attitude was almost entirely complete.

These results were strongly confirmed by the analyses of variance. The interaction was significant for all six measures: (for attraction, $F = 33.4$; for similarity, $F = 51.8$; for intelligence, $F = 16.0$; for current events, $F = 14.1$; for morality, $F = 13.7$; for adjustment, $F = 21.9$; $df = 1/56$, $p < .05$, for each measure). Only one measure showed a significant main effect. For knowledge of current events, the pretest stranger received slightly higher ratings than did the posttest stranger ($F = 4.4$, $df = 1/56$, $p < .03$).

The symmetry of the interaction effect is shown by the Newman-Keuls comparisons in Table 2.1. The direction of the differences was consistent in all cases, and on four measures the posttest stranger was rated significantly more favorably than the pretest stranger by the experimental group, but the reverse was true for the control group.

DISCUSSION

The results of the experiment were highly successful in demonstrating that attitude change does have implications for other conceptually relevant behavior. These results should provide considerable comfort for the attitude researcher concerned with whether attitude change has any meaning beyond a minor cognitive realignment expressed as a verbal rating score. The present results show unequivocally that attitude change does have consequences beyond the mere fact of the attitude change score. If this were not the case, then the mean ratings of the pretest and posttest strangers for the experimental group would have been identical to the comparable ratings for the control group. However, the pattern of the means was almost exactly reversed for the experimental group, indicating strong consequences on attraction and related responses of changing the attitude of the experimental group.

In one sense this complete reversal of attraction and related ratings by the experimental subjects was something of an anomaly. Experimental subjects, after attitude change, relatively "disowned" a stranger represented by their pretest attitudes to the same extent that control subjects disowned an equally dissimilar posttest stranger. This much of a shift would not be expected unless subjects had largely forgotten their original prepersuasion attitudes. Indeed, there is evidence that subjects are unable to recall a significant portion of their premanipulation attitudes after a manipulation is introduced (Bem & McConnell, 1970). No measure of recall of initial attitude was obtained in the present study, but it seems likely that such recall for the experimental group would have yielded a mean closer to the posttest than to the initial pretest attitude.

The results of the present study provide considerable evidence supporting the validity of attitude change produced in the laboratory. Choice of Byrne's (1971) attraction paradigm as a tool to assess validity seemed appropriate on theoretical grounds, and the results justified that choice. These data provide the initial basis for the study of the generalizability of attitude change to other types of behavioral change situations. The present study was concerned primarily with the transfer of the evaluative component of an attitude to an evaluatively laden situation (i.e., interpersonal attraction). Prior research (e.g., Wicker, 1969) showing low attitude-behavior correlations may have often assessed behaviors that were unrelated to evaluation. One suggestion from the present study is that firm attitude-behavior linkages (including verbal as well as motor behavior) may be found only when the test behavior is affect related in some fairly direct way. Many behaviors may be intuitively relevant to a given attitude but affectively neutral. Perhaps only that subset of relevant behaviors that are evaluatively loaded will be consistently related to the attitude.

REFERENCES

Abelson, R. P. Are attitudes necessary? In B. T. King & E. McGinnies (Eds.), *Attitudes, conflict, and social change.* New York: Academic Press, 1972.

Bem, D. J., & McConnell, K. Testing the self-perception explanation of dissonance phenomena: On the salience of premanipulation attitudes. *Journal of Personality and Social Psychology,* 1970, *14,* 23-31.

Byrne, D. *The attraction paradigm.* New York: Academic Press, 1971.

Cohen, A. R. *Attitude change and social influence.* New York: Basic Books, 1964.

De Fleur, M. L., & Westie, F. R. Attitude as a scientific concept. *Social Forces,* 1963, *42,* 17-31.

Festinger, L. Behavioral support for opinion change. *Public Opinion Quarterly,*
1964, *28,* 404-417.

Fishbein, M., & Ajzen, I.   Attitudes and opinions. *Annual Review of Psychology,*
1972, *23,* 487-544.

Greenwald, A. G. Effects of prior commitment on behavior change after a persuasive communication. *Public Opinion Quarterly,* 1966, *29,* 595-601.

Kiesler, C. A. *The psychology of commitment.* New York: Academic Press, 1971.

Rokeach, M. Attitude change and behavior change. *Public Opinion Quarterly,*
1967, *30,* 529-550.

Rokeach, M. *Beliefs, attitudes, and values.* San Francisco: Jossey-Bass, 1968.

Wicker, A. W. Attitudes versus actions: The relationship of verbal and overt behavioral responses to attitude objects. *Journal of Social Issues,* 1969, *25,*
41-78.

NOTE

1. Subjects' comments indicated a wide variety of hypotheses concerning the
nature of the experiment. Only one experimental subject suggested we might be
interested in attraction as a function of attitude change. One other subject indicated some suspicion that the stimulus strangers might have been fabricated. Both
subjects were retained in the data analyses.

2. An argument could be made that the particular type of control group used
was not optimal. Control subjects might have participated in two sessions. In the
first session, they would have read an extraneous communication, and as an incidental measure, completed the attitude posttest. During the second session the
next day, they would have evaluated strangers identical to their *own* pretest and
posttest strangers. The relevant comparison question would then have been
whether the difference in attraction between posttest and pretest strangers was significantly greater for the experimental than for the control group. Such a control
group would have been more elegant in terms of exact comparability of procedures. It was not used because we felt that the "incidental" measure of the
relevant attitude for control subjects during the first session would have cued off
strong suspicion during the second session the following day. In addition, more
robust interaction effects would have been expected for the dependent variables (if
attitude change had had true transfer effects) with the design actually used. For
these reasons literal procedural comparability between the two groups was not
used in toto, and this fact may pose some limitation on the data. However, the
magnitude of the effects for the dependent variables suggests that such limitation
in interpretation is minor.

3

MARK P. ZANNA and JOEL COOPER

Dissonance and the Pill: An Attribution Approach to Studying the Arousal Properties of Dissonance

A study was designed to test the notion that dissonance has arousal properties. In a 2 x 3 design, experimental subjects were induced to write counterattitudinal essays under either high- or low-choice conditions. One third of
the subjects were led to believe that a pill, which they had just taken in the
context of a separate experiment, would lead them to feel tense. Another
third were led to believe that the pill would cause them to feel relaxed. The
final third expected the pill to have no side effects whatsoever. In this last
condition, the results yielded the usual dissonance effect: High choice
produced more attitude change in the direction of the essay than low choice.
When subjects could attribute their arousal to the pill, this effect was virtually eliminated; when subjects felt they should have been relaxed by the pill,
this effect was significantly enhanced. The implications of these results for
Festinger's original statement that dissonance is a drivelike state were
discussed.

In most investigations on the effects of cognitive dissonance, one can
generally find terms like dissonance arousal, dissonance reduction, and
tensions due to dissonance. These follow directly from Festinger's (1957)
original statement of dissonance theory which indicated that dissonance
has drivelike properties and is experienced as psychological discomfort or
tension. Yet very few investigations have addressed themselves to the
question of whether there actually is any arousal attached to the observed
fact that inconsistency among cognitions often leads to efforts to reduce
that inconsistency.

Perhaps spurred on by Bem's (1965) behavioristic explanation of
dissonance results, Waterman and Katkin (1967) devised an ingenious
paradigm to obtain some evidence for arousal. They argued that if
dissonance is truly a drivelike state, then it should have energizing effects

Source: Mark P. Zanna and Joel Cooper, "Dissonance and the Pill: An Attribution Ap-
proach to Studying the Arousal Properties of Dissonance," *Journal of Personality and Social
Psychology*, 1974, *29*, 703-709. Copyright 1974 by the American Psychological Association.
Reprinted by permission.

This research was supported by National Institutes of Health Biomedical Research Grants
5 S05 FR07057-04 and 5 S05 RR07057-07. The authors are indebted to Charles A. Kiesler
for his valuable suggestions and to Susan A. Darley for her helpful comments.

similar to other drive states such as hunger. Therefore, they first aroused dissonance by inducing subjects to write counterattitudinal essays and then had subjects learn either a simple or a complex assignment. Since Spence, Farber, and McFann (1956) had shown that high-drive states have an energizing effect upon dominant, well learned responses, Waterman and Katkin predicted enhanced learning of the simple task and diminished learning of the complex task by dissonance-aroused subjects. The results, however, provided only partial support for the hypotheses. Enhancement of simple learning was obtained, but there was no obtained interference with complex learning on the part of subjects who had gone through the dissonance procedure.

Subsequent experiments using this paradigm (Cottrell & Wack, 1967; Waterman, 1969) have tended to support the arousal notion—but not unequivocally. Moreover, as Pallak and Pittman (1972) have aptly pointed out, none of the earlier studies have obtained evidence that their dissonance-provoking procedures ever produced dissonance. That is, there is no evidence of dissonance-produced attitude change in any of those experiments. Of all of the research using this paradigm, only one of two recent experiments reported by Pallak and Pittman demonstrated both the attitude-change and learning-interference effects and then only in a complex learning situation.

In the present research, we would like to suggest a new approach to the study of arousal in dissonance. We take our lead from the work of Schachter and Singer (1962) who investigated the labeling of emotion. Those investigators reasoned that emotion was a combination of physiological arousal and cognitive labeling. They demonstrated that subjects who were aroused with epinephrine, but did not know the reason for that arousal, used external cues to label it as either anger or euphoria. Several years later, Ross, Rodin, and Zimbardo (1969) reasoned that subjects who were aroused by a given stimulus could reduce that arousal if they were able to attribute it to a different external cause. Specifically, they found that subjects who were frightened of electric shocks could reduce their fear and tolerate more shocks if they were able to attribute their naturally occurring arousal to the effects of a loud noise.

Finally, Storms and Nisbett (1970) suggested that subjects who were suffering from the arousal state of insomnia might find it easier to fall asleep if they were able to attribute their physiological arousal to some external agent—such as a pill. The investigators told a group of insomniacs that they were participating in a "drug and fantasy" experiment. They were instructed to take a pill prior to bedtime and were warned that the pill might cause them to feel tense, aroused, etc. Another group of insomniacs was told that the pill would have no side effects, while a third group believed that the pill would make them calm and relaxed. Storms and Nisbett reasoned that if insomniacs could attribute their arousal to the pill, they would find it easier to fall asleep, while subjects who believed they should experience relaxation might become more upset than ever when they found themselves as aroused as usual at bedtime. The results indicated that subjects given the "tension due to pill" label for their arousal actually fell asleep more quickly than control subjects who, in turn, fell asleep more quickly than subjects who believed they should be relaxed.

Now, if dissonance is arousing, it should be affected by the use of external labels in the same way as fear was for the Ross et al. (1969) subjects and insomnia was for Storms and Nisbett's (1970) subjects. If we can allow subjects, who have been aroused by dissonance, to attribute their arousal to an external agent, they should show less of a need to change their attitudes as a means of reducing dissonance.

Suppose that an individual is aroused by choosing to write an essay contrary to his belief. Festinger's theory leads us to believe that he will be in an uncomfortable tension state and will look for some means to reduce that tension; for example, he can change his opinion so as to eliminate the inconsistency. But suppose this individual had just taken a pill which he knew would cause tension and arousal. Then, after writing his essay, he would have an adequate (albeit, false) explanation for his tension. Attributing his tension to the pill, he would not have a need to change his opinion. Consequently, we would expect less opinion change from subjects exposed to a high dissonance manipulation if they could attribute their arousal to a pill than subjects who had no pill to which to attribute their arousal. Similarly, we would expect subjects whose inconsistent essay writing led to arousal *despite* their taking a pill which they believed would relax them to show more of a need to alter their opinion (cf. Storms & Nisbett, 1970).

To test these hypotheses, we established a 2 x 3 factorial design. Subjects wrote counter-attitudinal essays under either high- or low-choice conditions. One third of all subjects were led to believe that a pill which they had just taken in the context of a separate experiment would lead them to feel tense. Another third were led to believe that the pill would cause them to feel relaxed. The final third expected that their pill would have no side effects whatsoever. A control condition, in which subjects simply indicated their attitude toward the experimental issue, was also run. If dissonance is truly arousing, then we predicted (a) a standard dissonance effect (i.e., more attitude change under high- than low-choice conditions) when the pill had no side effects, (b) a diminished dissonance effect when the pill provided a "tense" label, and (c) an enhanced dissonance effect when a "relaxed" label was provided.

METHOD

Subjects

Seventy-seven freshmen males at Princeton University participated in a study on memory. They were each promised $1.50. Subjects were usually run in groups of 3 or 4. Seven subjects were not used in the analyses. Of these, 6 (comprising two groups) were omitted because at least 1 member of each group refused to take the drug. In addition, 1 subject indicated suspicion as a result of auditing a psychology course and having heard a description of a similar experiment.

Procedure

Subjects arrived at a common experimental room where the experimenter began by explaining the alleged purpose of the experiment.* She indicated that subjects were "asked to come here today to participate in an experiment on memory processes . . ." and that they would be given a drug in order to investigate its effects on short-term memory. After assuring subjects that "the drug is perfectly safe," the experimenter outlined the supposed design of the study by stating, "you will have two memory tasks to do: one prior to taking the drug, and the second one after its total absorption."

Subjects were then taken to separate experimental cubicles where they performed the first memory task. A straightforward free-recall task was employed. Twelve nonsense words were presented consecutively on a common screen. Immediately after the last presentation, the subjects were asked to recall (in writing) as many words as they could.

Manipulation of Drug Side Effect. Next, the experimenter entered each cubicle and gave each subject in turn a capsule and a glass of water. The capsule, in fact, contained powdered milk. In order to manipulate the potential side effect of the drug, the experimenter, blind to condition, gave each subject one of three drug consent forms to sign. In the arousal condition, the form stated:

This M.C. 5771 capsule contains chemical elements that are more soluble than other parts of the compound. In this form of the drug these elements may produce

---

*The authors wish to thank Marie-Claire Kamin for her skillful assistance as the experimenter.

a reaction of tenseness prior to the total absorption of the drug, 5 minutes after ingestion. This side effect will disappear within 30 minutes.

In the relaxation condition, the form was identical, except that "tenseness" was replaced with "relaxation." In the no-information condition the form merely stated that "the total absorption time of the drug is 30 minutes" and that "there are no side effects." Each group always contained at least one subject in each of the three drug side-effect conditions.

Manipulation of Dissonance. After subjects had signed their consent forms and had ingested their capsules, the experimenter explained that "we now have 30 minutes before the second memory task" and that she had "another study going on, not about memory, but about opinion research."

Dissonance was manipulated by varying the degree of decision freedom which subjects were given to write an attitude-discrepant essay (Linder, Cooper, & Jones, 1967). In the high-choice (or high-dissonance) condition, therefore, the experimenter continued:

"I will leave it entirely up to you to decide if you would like to participate in it, but I would be very grateful if you would . . . ."

In the low-choice (or low-dissonance) condition, she simply stated:

"During this wait, I am going to ask you to do a small task for this opinion research experiment."

In both conditions the experimenter continued by indicating that

The issue of whether inflammatory speakers should be allowed to speak on a college campus often becomes a problem. . . . The Ivy League Administrators Association is trying to formulate a standard policy on whether or not, and in what circumstances, inflammatory speakers should be allowed to speak on campus. . . . Past experience has indicated that one of the best ways to understand what the relevant arguments are on both sides of any issue is to ask people to write essays favoring one side of the issue. Therefore, what we would like you to do is to write the strongest, the most forceful essay that you can taking the position that inflammatory speakers should be banned from college campuses.

In the high-choice condition, the experimenter then secured each subject's verbal consent, adding after compliance, "Remember, you are under no obligation." All of the subjects agreed to write the essay.

In the control condition, subjects were recruited in an identical way as the experimental subjects but were not exposed to the experimental procedures. Instead, control subjects merely indicated their opinions on the attitudinal dependent measure to be described below.

Dependent Measures. Subjects were given 10 minutes to complete the essay after which the experimenter collected the dependent measures. Subjects were first asked to indicate how they felt "right now" on a

31-point scale with endpoints labeled calm (1) and tense (31). Next, presumably for the Ivy League Administrators Association, subjects described their present feeling "about the adoption of a ban against inflammatory speakers on campus" on a 31-point scale with endpoints labeled strongly opposed (1) and strongly in favor (31). This served as the major dependent measure. Finally, to assess the effectiveness of the decision-freedom manipulation, subjects indicated "how free [they] felt to decline to participate in this Ivy League Administrators research project" on a 31-point scale with endpoints labeled not free at all (1) and extremely free (31).

After subjects completed these questions, they returned to the common experimental room and were debriefed with special emphasis placed on the fact that the ingested capsule was, in reality, a placebo.

RESULTS

Decision Freedom

Responses to the question designed to tap perceived freedom in writing the essay revealed that high-choice subjects reported more choice than low-choice subjects ($\bar{X} = 24.23$ versus 11.33, respectively; $F = 43.05$, $df = 1/54$, $p < .001$). No other effects on the choice measure were significant. Apparently the decision-freedom manipulation was successful.

Reported Tension

Subjects were also asked to indicate how tense or relaxed they felt immediately after having written their essays. The mean responses are presented in Table 3.1.

Analysis of variance indicated that only the main effect for the drug side effect ($F = 10.32$, $df = 2/54$, $p < .001$) and the interaction ($F = 4.08$, $df = 2/54$, $p < .05$) were significant. Subjects in the arousal condition reported being *more* tense than subjects in the no-information condition ($\bar{X} = 20.80$ versus 13.45, respectively; $F = 10.63$, $df = 1/54$, $p < .01$), while subjects in the relaxation condition reported being *less* tense than

TABLE 3.1
Mean of Subjects' Reported Tension

Decision Freedom	Potential Side Effect of the Drug		
	Arousal	None	Relaxation
High	19.60	17.90	9.90
Low	22.00	9.00	12.00

Note: Cell $n = 10$. The larger the mean, the more tense the response.

subjects in the no-information condition ($\bar{X} = 10.95$ versus 13.45, respectively; $F = 4.92$, $df = 1/54$, $p < .05$). While this main effect may indicate real differences, it seems as reasonable to conclude that it was a result of the demand characteristics of the situation.

More interesting is the interaction which can best be described as follows: High-choice subjects reported more tension than low-choice subjects ($t = 2.79$, $p < .01$), but only in the no-information condition; in the arousal and relaxation conditions, high-choice subjects reported trivially less tension than low-choice subjects ($t < 1$, in both cases).

This interaction is evidence in favor of viewing dissonance as an arousing state. When information was provided about the alleged side effect of the drug, subjects' self-reports tended to parrot the information provided. But when no information was provided, subjects reported being considerably more tense when dissonance was high rather than low.

Attitude toward the Speaker Ban

The mean attitudes toward banning speakers on campus are presented in Table 3.2. Before describing the results in the experimental conditions, it should be noted that the mean attitude reported by the control subjects indicated that the essays which experimental subjects were induced to write were clearly attitude discrepant.

A 2x3 analysis of variance presented in Table 3.3 reveals that the predicted main effects and interaction were highly significant ($p < .001$,

TABLE 3.2
Mean of Subjects' Opinions toward Banning Speakers on Campus

	Potential Side Effect of the Drug		
Decision Freedom	Arousal	None	Relaxation
High	3.40_a	9.10_b	13.40_c
Low	3.50_a	4.50_a	4.70_a

Note: Cell $n = 10$. The larger the mean, the more agreement with the attitude-discrepant essay (Control group $\bar{X} = 2.30_a$). Cells not sharing a common subscript differ at the the .01 level by the Newman-Keuls procedure; cells showing a common subscript do not differ at the .05 level.

TABLE 3.3
Summary of the Analysis of Variance of Subjects' Opinions toward Banning Speakers on Campus

Source	df	MS	F
Decision freedom (A)	1	290.40	40.73*
Side effect (B)	2	158.82	22.29*
A X B	2	96.95	13.60*
Error	54	7.13	

*$p < .001$.

in each case). This overall analysis of variance, however, does not provide an exact test of the hypotheses. Comparison of individual conditions by the Newman-Keuls procedure indicated that the pattern of results conformed exactly to expectation. In the no-information condition, the standard dissonance effect was replicated: High-choice subjects agreed more with the position taken in their counterattitudinal essays than did low-choice subjects. In the arousal condition, this dissonance effect was virtually eliminated; in the relaxation condition, the effect was magnified.

Intracell correlations between the degree of attitude change and the magnitude of reported tension were also informative. All conditions revealed a positive correlation between tension and attitudes. However, the correlations were not significant in the four conditions in which information was provided regarding the alleged side effect of the pill. As we suggested previously, at least one factor in subjects' reports of tension in these conditions was probably the demand characteristic of parroting back the information that was just given to them. In the no-side-effects-low-choice condition, the reported tension was, as expected, quite low and the correlation with attitude change did not reach significance. However, when dissonance was high and no demand characteristics were present (no-side-effects–high-choice condition), the correlation between the magnitude of tension and the degree of opinion change was highly reliable ($r = .69$, $p < .05$).

Finally, two independent raters were asked to rate each essay in order to assess the possibility that differences in essay performance mediated the final attitude scores. The judges were asked to rate the essays on a 7-point scale according to their degree of "convincingness." The interjudge reliability was quite high ($r = .88$). No differences were found among conditions on the convincingness dimension nor were any differences revealed when the length of each essay was considered.

DISCUSSION

The results of the experiment provide support for the notion that dissonance does indeed have arousal properties as Festinger (1957) originally suggested. High-dissonance subjects who could attribute their arousal to a pill showed less of a tendency to change their attitudes, while subjects in the high-dissonance–relaxation condition showed an increased need to deal with their arousal by changing their opinions. Under the low-dissonance conditions, the various side effects made virtually no difference.

Since previous dissonance research had focused mainly on the attitudinal effects which the drive state was supposed to produce, the way was paved for the appearance of alternative models of attitude change which could predict identical attitudinal results. First, Bem (1965) proposed that the results of previous dissonance experiments could be understood in terms of the mand-tact (Skinner, 1957) quality of the stimulus situation. Kelley (1967) then presented an attributional analysis that incorporated Bem's interpretation within a more general model of information processing. Like Bem, he proposed that dissonance results could be accounted for without recourse to assumptions about arousal or drives within the person. Rather, he viewed attitude change within the dissonance paradigm as a special case of an individual observing his own behavior and logically attributing an attitude to himself.

Research critical of Bem's analysis (Jones, Linder, Kiesler, Zanna, & Brehm, 1968) suggested that the way in which the behavioristic reinterpretation of dissonance theory was stated could not account for all of the data predicted and obtained in dissonance experiments. Similarly, Cooper, Jones, and Tuller (1972) provided evidence which is at variance with Kelley's alternative based upon attribution theory. But because such criticisms do not provide data that bear on the internal process of dissonance arousal, they do not get at the heart of the argument.

However, the present results do combine with the earlier research using the Waterman and Katkin (1967) paradigm to provide support for the internal process of dissonance arousal. The results of the present investigation could only have been obtained if inconsistent cognitions produced at least the perception of arousal. While Bem's and Kelley's models may be considered useful heuristic devices and while they may accurately reflect the processes employed by observer subjects, the present results suggest that involved subjects do indeed perceive themselves to be aroused when participating in a counter-attitudinal role-playing situation.

In our analysis of arousal in forced-compliance situations, we are not arguing against the veridicality of general attribution phenomena. To the contrary, attribution notions generated the present experiment. Following Storms and Nisbett (1970), for example, our arousal condition was intended to manipulate the perceived source of arousal; our relaxation condition, the perceived level of arousal. We have argued that subjects in the arousal condition mistakenly attributed their dissonance-produced arousal to a nonemotional, external agent (i.e., the pill) and, therefore, experienced less dissonance. Relaxation condition subjects, on the other hand, were assumed to make the mistaken attribution that they were more aroused than they really were and, therefore, to experience more dissonance.

We might speculate on a slightly different attributional process in accounting for the pattern of results. Just as insomniacs appear to "worry about their insomnia," individuals who have freely performed counterattitudinal behavior might be said to "worry about their dissonant cognitions." In this view, the tension pill essentially told the subject not to worry about his inconsistency. The pill which was supposed to produce relaxation, on the other hand, indicated that he should be more worried than usual about his inconsistency. To paraphrase Storms and Nisbett (1970), the subject may have said to himself: "The pill relaxes me X amount, and the discrepant behavior arouses me Y amount. If it weren't for the pill, the inconsistency would have bothered me X + Y amount." Therefore, the subject is more upset by his arousal in the relaxation condition than he would be in the no-information condition in which one only has to worry about Y amount of arousal.

Whether arousal is due to inconsistency per se or to worry about inconsistency, the present analysis implies that the amount of arousal which a person must deal with is arrived at by a process of attribution. That is, it seems that once arousal (due to inconsistent behavior) exists, the person begins a series of attributional processes designed toward understanding and possibly eliminating the arousal.

When no external agent exists, the process is straightforward. The arousal is chalked up to the inconsistency between cognitions and is reduced by a change of cognitions. When a tension pill has been taken, the arousal is attributed to the pill and there is less of a need for action directed at the true cause of the arousal (i.e., the inconsistent cognitions). But in the case of relaxation, the subject must deduce the amount of arousal he has by adding the amount he actually experiences to the amount which the pill has supposedly reduced. He then continues his logical deduction toward deciding (perhaps at some unaware level) on the amount of attitude change that is necessary in the situation.

Another interpretation for the results in the relaxation condition deserves comment. Recently, Zanna, Lepper, and Abelson (1973) have demonstrated that focusing a subject's attention on dissonant cognitions apparently increases the dissonance, as indicated by a greater amount of dissonance reduction. In this present case, it is possible that the unexpected arousal in the relaxation condition had the effect of focusing subjects' attention on their cognitive dilemma more than usual. Such focused attention, then, may have increased dissonance and subsequent dissonance reduction.

The results of our study have undoubtedly provoked questions which can only be answered by future research. One question revolves about the awareness that subjects had regarding their arousal and the attributional processes that they undertook to handle that arousal. We have spoken as though subjects were deliberate, logical, and certainly conscious of their attempts to handle arousal. But this has been primarily a heuristic device;

the study provides no direct evidence regarding the subjects' degree of awareness. Indeed, Brock (1968) has discussed evidence which suggests that dissonance processes may take place beyond the subjects' awareness.

In addition, the term arousal needs further clarification. The present results require, at the very least, the perception on the part of the subjects that they were aroused. But were they actually aroused? Would physiological measurement find evidence of heightened autonomic responses? Moreover, if subjects were aroused, was the arousal of a "drivelike" nature, as Festinger suggested, or was it more of the nature of worry or anxiety? Now that we have evidence that dissonance does involve the activation of internal processes involving perceived arousal, future investigations can be directed toward resolving these cloudy but significant issues.

REFERENCES

Bem, D. J. An experimental analysis of self-persuasion. *Journal of Experimental Social Psychology,* 1965, *1,* 199-218.

Brock, T. C. Dissonance without awareness. In R. P. Abelson et al., *Theories of cognitive consistency.* Chicago: Rand McNally, 1968.

Cooper, J., Jones, E. E., & Tuller, S. M. Attribution, dissonance, and the illusion of uniqueness. *Journal of Experimental Social Psychology,* 1972, *8,* 45-57.

Cottrell, N. B., & Wack, D. L. The energizing effect of cognitive dissonance on dominant and subordinate responses. *Journal of Personality and Social Psychology,* 1967, *6,* 132-138.

Festinger, L. A theory of cognitive dissonance. Stanford, Calif.: Stanford University Press, 1957.

Jones, R. A., Linder, D. E., Kiesler, C. A., Zanna, M., & Brehm, J. W. Internal states or external stimuli: Observers' attitude judgments and the dissonance-self-persuasion controversy. *Journal of Experimental Social Psychology,* 1968, *4,* 247-269.

Kelley, H. H. Attribution theory in social psychology. In D. Levine (Ed.), *Nebraska Symposium on Motivation: 1967.* Lincoln: University of Nebraska Press, 1967.

Linder, D. E., Cooper, J., & Jones, E. E. Decision freedom as a determinant of the role of incentive magnitude in attitude change. *Journal of Personality and Social Psychology,* 1967, *6,* 245-254.

Pallak, M. S., & Pittman, T. S. General motivational effects of dissonance arousal. *Journal of Personality and Social Psychology,* 1972, *21,* 349-358.

Ross, L., Rodin, J., & Zimbardo, P. G. Toward an attribution therapy: The reduction of fear through induced cognitive-emotional misattribution. *Journal of Personality and Social Psychology,* 1969, *12,* 279-288.

Schachter, S., & Singer, J. E. Cognitive, social, and physiological determinants of emotional state. *Psychological Review,* 1962, *69,* 379-399.

Skinner, B. F. *Verbal behavior.* New York: Appleton-Century-Crofts, 1957.

Spence, K. W., Farber, I. E., & McFann, H. H. The relation of anxiety (drive) level to performance in competitional paired-associates learning. *Journal of Experimental Psychology,* 1956, *52,* 296-305.

Storms, M. D., & Nisbett, R. E. Insomnia and the attribution process. *Journal of Personality and Social Psychology,* 1970, *2,* 319-328.

Waterman, C. K. The facilitating and interfering effects of cognitive dissonance on simple and complex paired-associate learning tasks. *Journal of Experimental Social Psychology,* 1969, *5,* 31-42.

Waterman, C. K., & Katkin, E. S. The energizing (dynamogenic) effect of cognitive dissonance on task performance. *Journal of Personality and Social Psychology,* 1967, *6,* 126-131.

Zanna, M. P., Lepper, M. R., & Abelson, R. P. Attentional mechanisms in children's devaluation of a forbidden activity in a forced-compliance situation. *Journal of Personality and Social Psychology,* 1973, *28,* 355-359.

4

ROBERT E. KNOX and JAMES A. INKSTER

Postdecision Dissonance at Post Time

Two experiments were conducted to investigate postdecisional dissonance reduction processes following a commitment to bet on a horse in the natural and uncontrived setting of a race track. In the 1st study, 69 $2 Win bettors rated the chance that the horse they had selected would win the forthcoming race and 72 other bettors provided ratings immediately after making a $2 Win bet. On the 7-point rating scale employed, prebet subjects gave a median rating of 3.48, which corresponded to a "fair chance of winning"; postbet subjects gave a median rating of 4.81, which corresponded to a "good chance of winning." This difference was significant beyond the .01 level. The general findings were replicated in a 2nd study in which harness-race patrons rated how confident they felt about their selected horse either just before or just after betting. Results from both studies provide support for Festinger's theory in a real life setting and indicate that dissonance-

Source: Robert E. Knox and James A. Inkster, "Postdecision Dissonance at Post Time," *Journal of Personality and Social Psychology,* 1968, *8,* 319-323. Copyright 1968 by the American Psychological Association. Reprinted by permission.

This study was supported by a grant from the Faculty of Graduate Studies, University of British Columbia. The cooperation of the British Columbia Jockey Club and the management of the Delta Raceways Limited is gratefully acknowledged. The authors also gratefully acknowledge the assistance of Herbert Kee, Ronald Douglas, and Warren Thorngate during the data-collection phases of these studies.

reducing processes may occur very rapidly following commitment to a decision.

In the last decade there have been numerous laboratory experiments conducted to test various implications of Festinger's (1957) theory of cognitive dissonance. In spite of sometimes serious methodological faults (cf. Chapanis & Chapanis, 1964), the laboratory evidence as a whole has tended to support Festinger's notions. Confidence in the theory, as Brehm and Cohen (1962) have previously suggested, can now be further strengthened by extending empirical tests from lifelike to real life situations. The present study investigates the effects of postdecision dissonance on bettors in their natural habitat, the race track.

Festinger (1957) had originally contended that due to the lingering cognitions about the favorable characteristics of the rejected alternative(s), dissonance was an inevitable consequence of a decision. Subsequently, however, Festinger (1964) accepted the qualification that in order for dissonance to occur, the decision must also have the effect of committing the person. A favorite technique for reducing postdecisional dissonance, according to the theory, is to change cognitions in such a manner as to increase the attractiveness of the chosen alternative relative to the unchosen alternative(s). At the race track a bettor becomes financially committed to his decision when he purchases a parimutuel ticket on a particular horse. Once this occurs, postdecisional processes should operate to reduce dissonance by increasing the attractiveness of the chosen horse relative to the unchosen horses in the race. These processes would be reflected by the bettor's expression of greater confidence in his having picked a winner after his bet had been made than before.

In order to test this notion, one need only go to a race track, acquire a prebet and postbet sample, and ask members of each how confident they are that they have selected the winning horse in the forthcoming race. The two samples should be independent since the same subjects in a before-after design could contravene the observed effects of dissonance reduction by carrying over consistent responses in the brief interval between pre- and postmeasurements. In essence, this was the approach employed in the two natural experiments reported here. More formally, the experimental hypothesis in both experiments was that bettors would be more confident of their selected horse just after betting $2 than just before betting.

EXPERIMENT I

Subjects

Subjects were 141 bettors at the Exhibition Park Race Track in Vancouver, British Columbia. Sixty-nine of these subjects, the prebet group, were interviewed less than 30 seconds *before* making a $2 Win bet. Seventy-two subjects, the postbet group, were interviewed a few seconds after making a $2 Win bet. Fifty-one subjects, interviewed before the fourth and fifth races, were obtained in the exclusive Clubhouse section. Data from the remaining 90 bettors were collected prior to the second, third, sixth, and seventh races at various betting locations in the General Admission or grandstand area.

No formal rituals were performed to guarantee random sampling, but instead, every person approaching or leaving a $2 Win window at a time when the experimenters were not already engaged in an interview was contacted. Of those contacted, approximately 15% refused to cooperate further because they could not speak English, refused to talk to "race touts," never discussed their racing information with strangers, or because of some unexpressed other reason. The final sample consisted of white, Negro, and Oriental men and women ranging in estimated age from the early twenties to late sixties and ranging in style from ladies in fur to shabby old men. The final sample was felt to be reasonably representative of the Vancouver race-track crowd.

Procedure

The two experimenters were stationed in the immediate vicinity of the "Sellers" window during the 25-minute betting interval between races. For any given race, one experimenter intercepted bettors as they approached a $2 Win window and the other experimenter intercepted different bettors as they left these windows. Prebet and postbet interview roles were alternated with each race between the two experimenters.

The introductory appeal to subjects and instructions for their ratings were as follows:

I beg your pardon. I am a member of a University of British Columbia research team studying risk-taking behavior. Are you about to place a $2 Win bet? [Have you just made a $2 Win bet?] Have we already talked to you today? I wonder if you would mind looking at this card and telling me what chance you think the horse your are going to bet on [have just bet on] has of winning this race. The scale goes from 1, a slight chance, to 7, an excellent chance. Just tell me the number from 1 to 7 that best describes the chance that you think your horse has of winning. Never mind now what the tote board or professional handicappers say; what chance do *you* think your horse has?

It was, of course, sometimes necessary to give some of the subjects further explanation of the task or to elaborate further on the cover story for the study.

FIGURE 4.1
Rating Scale Shown to Subjects in the Study

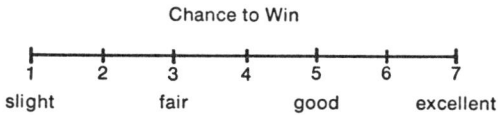

Chance to Win

| | | | | | | |
|1|2|3|4|5|6|7|
|slight| |fair| |good| |excellent|

The scale, reproduced here in Figure 4.1, was prepared on 8½ x 11-inch posterboard. The subjects responded verbally with a number or, in some cases, with the corresponding descriptive word from the scale.

After each prebet rating the experimenter visually confirmed that his subject proceeded directly to a $2 Win window. In the few instances that subjects did wander elsewhere, their data were discarded. No effort was made to collect data in the 3 frantic minutes of betting just prior to post time.

Results

Since no stronger than ordinal properties may be safely assumed for the rating scale, nonparametric statistics were employed in the analysis. Several x^2 approximations of the Kolmogorov-Smirnov test (Siegel, 1956) were first performed to test for distributional differences between the ratings collected by the two experimenters. For prebet ratings ($x^2 = .274$, $df = 2$, $p > .80$) and for the combined pre-and postbet ratings ($x^2 = 2.16$, $df = 2$, $p > .30$) the differences in the two distributions may be considered negligible according to these tests. Distributional differences on postbet ratings ($x^2 = 3.14$, $df = 2$, $p > .20$) were greater but still did not meet even the .20 probability level.[1] On the basis of these tests the two experimenters were assumed to have collected sufficiently comparable ratings to justify pooling of their data for the subsequent test of the major hypothesis of the study.

The median for the 69 subjects in the prebet group was 3.48. In qualitative terms they gave their horses little better than a "fair" chance of winning its race. The median for the 72 subjects in the postbet group, on the other hand, was 4.81. They gave their horse close to a "good" chance in the race. The median test for the data summarized in Table 4.1 produced a x^2 of 8.70, ($df = 1$), significant beyond the .01 level.

TABLE 4.1
Division of Subjects with Respect to the Overall Median for the
Prebet and Postbet Groups: Experiment I

	Prebet Group	Postbet Group
Above the median	25	45
Below the median	44	27

These results, in accord with our predictions from dissonance theory, might also have arisen, however, had a substantial number of bettors simply made last-minute switches from relative long shots to favorites in these races. Although this possibility was not pursued with the above sample of subjects, two follow-up inquiries on another day at the same race track indicated that the "switch to favorites" explanation was unlikely. The first of these inquiries involved 38 $2 bettors who were contacted prior to the first race and merely asked if they ever changed their mind about which horse to bet on in the last minute or so before actually reaching a Sellers window. Nine of the 38 indicated that they sometimes changed, but among the 9 occasional changers a clear tendency to switch to long shots rather than to favorites was reported. Additional evidence against a "switch to favorites" explanation was obtained from a sample of 46 bettors for whom the prebet procedure of Experiment I was repeated. Each of these bettors was then contacted by a second interviewer just as he was leaving the $2 Win window and asked if he had changed to a different horse since talking to the first interviewer. All 46 responded that they had not changed horses in midinterviews.

In order to investigate the robustness of the findings in Experiment I a second study was undertaken which was like the first study in its essentials but employed different experimenters, a different response scale, and a different population of subjects. It also provided for a test of the "switch to favorites" explanation among subjects in a postbet group.

EXPERIMENT II

Subjects and Procedure

Ninety-four subjects were interviewed at the Patterson Park Harness Raceway in Ladner, British Columbia. Forty-eight of these subjects, the prebet group, were interviewed prior to the first six races as they approached one of the track's four $2 Win windows. This contact was usually completed just a few seconds before the subject actually reached the window to make his bet, but occasionally, when the betting lines were long, up to ¾ minute elapsed between interview and bet. Forty-six subjects, the postbet group, were interviewed a few seconds after leaving one of the $2 Win windows. As in Experiment I, all persons approaching or leaving a $2 Win window at a time when the experimenters were not already engaged were contacted. Of those contacted, fewer than 10% refused to cooperate, thus producing a heterogeneous and, presumably, representative sample of $2 Win bettors.

The overall design was the same as in the first study. Two experimenters, different from those who interviewed bettors in Experiment I, were located in the immediate area of the Sellers windows. One of these experimenters would intercept bettors as they approached a $2 Win window and the other intercepted different bettors as they left a $2 Win window. The prebet and postbet interview roles were alternated between the two experimenters as in the first study.

After a brief introductory preamble, the experimenter established whether a bettor was about to make a $2 Win bet (or had just made such a bet) and whether he had been previously interviewed. The experimenters proceeded only with those $2 bettors who had not already provided data. These subjects were then asked to indicate on a 23-centimeter scale how confident they felt that they had picked the winning horse. The mimeo-graphed response scales were labeled with the words "No confidence" at the extreme left and "Complete confidence" at the extreme right. Although no other labels were printed on the scale, the experimenters made explicit that mild confidence would fall in the middle of the scale and ". . . the more confident that a person felt, the further along he should put his mark on the scale." When subjects indicated understanding, they were handed a pencil and a mimeographed scale and directed to ". . . just draw a line across the point in the scale that best corresponds to your own confidence." All bettors in the postbet sample were also asked if they changed their mind about which horse to bet on while waiting in line or while on the way to the window.

Within the limits permitted by extremely crowded conditions, the prebet experimenter visually confirmed that subjects in his sample proceeded to a $2 Win window. Data collection was suspended during the last minute before post time.

Confidence scores for each subject were determined by laying a ruler along the 23-centimeter scale and measuring his response to the nearest millimeter.

Results

On the strength of insignificant Kolmogorov-Smirnov tests for dis-tributional differences between ratings collected by the two experimenters, data from the two experimenters were combined to test the major hy-pothesis of the study. The median rating for the 48 subjects in the prebet

TABLE 4.2
Division of Subjects with Respect to the Overall Median for the Prebet and Postbet Groups: Experiment II

	Prebet group	Postbet group
Above the median	19	28
Below the median	29	18

group was 14.60, and for the postbet group it was 19.30. The median test for these data, summarized in Table 4.2, produced a x^2 of 4.26 ($df = 1$), significant at less than the .05 level.

Since data in Experiment II might reasonably be assumed to satisfy interval scale assumptions, a t test between pre- and postbet means was also performed. The difference between the prebet mean of 14.73 and the postbet mean of 17.47 was also significant ($t = 2.31$, $p < .05$).

No subject in the postbet sample indicated that he had changed horses while waiting in line or, if there were no line, just before reaching the window.

DISCUSSION

These studies have examined the effects of real life postdecisional dissonance in the uncontrived setting of a race track. The data furnished by two relatively heterogeneous samples of bettors strongly support our hypothesis derived from Festinger's theory. The reaction of one bettor in Experiment I well illustrates the overall effect observed in the data. This particular bettor had been a subject in the prebet sample and had then proceeded to the pari-mutuel window to place his bet. Following that transaction, he approached the postbet experimenter and volunteered the following:

Are you working with that other fellow there? [indicating the prebet experimenter who was by then engaged in another interview] Well, I just told him that my horse had a fair chance of winning. Will you have him change that to a good chance? No, by God, make that an excellent chance.

It might reasonably be conjectured that, at least until the finish of the race, this bettor felt more comfortable about his decision to wager on a horse with an excellent chance than he could have felt about a decision to wager on a horse with only a fair chance. In the human race, dissonance had won again.

The results also bear upon the issue of rapidity of onset of dissonance-reducing processes discussed by Festinger (1964). On the basis of an experiment by Davidson described in that work, Festinger argued that predecisional cognitive familiarity with the characteristics of alternatives facilitated the onset of dissonance reduction. It is reasonable to assume that most bettors in the present studies were informed, to some extent, about the virtues and liabilities of all the horses in a race before making a $2 commitment on one. Since never more than 30 seconds elapsed between the time of commitment at the window and confrontation with the rating task, the present results are consistent with the notion that the effects of dissonance reduction can, indeed, be observed very soon after a commitment is made to one alternative, providing that some information about the unchosen alternatives is already possessed. Furthermore, the exceedingly short time span here suggests that the cognitive reevaluation process could hardly have been very explicit or as deliberate as conscious rationalization.

Finally, these studies, like the earlier Ehrlich, Guttman, Schonbach, and Mills (1957) study which showed that recent new car buyers preferred to read automobile advertisements that were consonant with their purchase, demonstrate that meaningful tests of dissonance theory can be made in the context of real life situations. Insofar as real life studies are unaffected by contrived circumstances, improbable events, and credibility gaps, they may offer stronger and less contentious support for dissonance theory than their laboratory counterparts. It is also clear that such studies will help to define the range of applicability of the theory in natural settings.

REFERENCES

Brehm, J. W., & Cohen, A. R. *Explorations in cognitive dissonance.* New York: Wiley, 1962.

Chapanis, N. P., & Chapanis, A. Cognitive dissonance: Five years later. *Psychological Bulletin,* 1964, *61,* 1-22.

Ehrlich, D. Guttman, I., Schonbach, P., & Mills, J. Postdecision exposure to relevant information. *Journal of Abnormal and Social Psychology,* 1957, *54,* 98-102.

Festinger, L. *A theory of cognitive dissonance.* Evanston, Ill.: Row, Peterson, 1957.

Festinger, L. *Conflict, decision, and dissonance.* Stanford, Calif.: Stanford University Press, 1964.

Siegel, S. *Nonparametric statistics for the behavioral sciences.* New York: McGraw-Hill, 1956.

NOTE

1. The x^2 approximation for Kolmogorov-Smirnov is designed for one-tailed tests, whereas the hypothesis tested here is nondirectional. However, since the differences were insignificant by a one-tailed test, they would necessarily be insignificant by the two-tailed test.

CHAPTER VIII

Personality and Social Behavior

1. Herman E. Mitchell and Donn Byrne, "The Defendant's Dilemma: Effects of Jurors' Attitudes and Authoritarianism on Judicial Decisions"
2. Paul D. Cherulnik and Murray M. Citrin, "Individual Difference in Psychological Reactance: The Interaction between Locus of Control and Mode of Elimination of Freedom"
3. Henry L. Kaplowitz, "Machiavellianism and Forming Impressions of Others"
4. Ronald Goldman, Melvyn Jaffa, and Stanley Schachter, "Yom Kippur, Air France, Dormitory Food, and the Eating Behavior of Obese and Normal Persons"

Every man is in certain respects
a. like all other men,
b. like some other men,
c. like no other man.

Kluckhohn and Murray (1967, p. 53)

Commentary

Social psychologists have tended to focus on situational variables rather then predispositional factors in testing hypotheses about the determinants of social behavior. Even a cursory look at the journals in the field will reveal that in most studies the primary independent variable is operationalized by means of differential experimental treatments rather than by measured individual differences. No doubt the social psychologist's tendency to look at the situation rather than at the personality characteristics brought by the individual into the situation can be at least partially attributed to the criticisms that have been leveled periodically at the concept of transsituational personality dispositions or traits (e.g., Mischel, 1969; Wallace, 1966). There are, however, more practical reasons for looking at behavior as a function of the situation rather than as a function of some stable personality attribute of the individual.

When a person's behavior is found to be significantly affected by an experimentally created situational intervention, we can say with a good degree of confidence that the behavior was caused by the situational characteristic that was varied. Effects obtained by means of experimental manipulations allow causal inferences to be made because random assignment of subjects to treatments eliminates any systematic differences among them on any dimensions other than the one tapped by the experimental treatments. On the other hand, when we look at behavior as a function of some relatively stable dimension of personality, we cannot make causal inferences with any degree of confidence. This is because attempts to link behaviors to characteristics of the individual usually involve correlating some measured attribute of the person with some aspect of behavior. Even if a personality variable is found to be significantly correlated with some behavior, we cannot be sure about the ultimate cause of that behavior. While it is possible that it is our measured personality dimension, it is also possible that the observed behavior was caused by some more fundamental individual difference characteristic of which we may not be aware.

The practical advantage of causal inference inherent in experimental, in contrast to correlational, data has made the preference of the social psychologist for situational manipulations an understandable one. At the same time, this powerful aspect of the experimental method has tended to obscure the usefulness of correlational data in enabling us to make predictive connections between variables. Although understanding of behavior is maximally attained by determining its underlying causes, in many cases it is very useful to be able to predict behavior even in the absence of knowledge about its causal determinants. While knowledge that variable A correlates significantly with variable B may not enable us to pinpoint the cause of this relationship, it does allow us to predict with varying degrees of confidence that, given A, B is likely to occur. The ability to predict behavior thus does not necessarily require an understanding of the causes of behavior, and one can make valuable use of predictive knowledge even in the absence of causal knowledge. For example, if the proverbial calm usually precedes the storm, it would be a good idea to pack up regardless of whether or not the storm was caused by the calm or, in fact, both the calm and the storm are the consequences of some underlying third factor. More seriously, if airplane hijackers are found to be distinguishable by their behavioral characteristics (see Dailey & Pickrel, 1975), this information would be valuable even if such behavioral characteristics are only correlates, but not necessarily causes, of hijacking behavior.

There is evidence, however, that social psychologists are becoming increasingly aware of the importance of taking individual differences into account and are tending more and more to design experiments that permit the determination of the effects of both personality variables and situational factors. A recent analysis of social psychology journals by Sarason, Smith, and Diener (in press) found that a majority of studies appearing in the 1971 volumes of the *Journal of Personality and Social Psychology* and the *Journal of Personality* used only situational independent variables. Nevertheless, from 1950 to 1970 there was an increase in the percentage of studies in which the interaction between individual-difference variables and situational variables could be determined.

Looking at behavior as a function of both the situation and what the person brings into the situation agrees with the phenomenology of our interaction with others. What we remember most about another person is the set of attributes that makes him uniquely distinguishable from other people, rather than the behavioral characteristics that make him similar to others. A conceptualization of behavior as a function of both individual differences and situational factors is also in line with the dictum of Kurt Lewin, who left a legacy of confidence in the experiment for gaining knowledge about social behavior. He said: ". . . *the dynamics of environmental influences* can be investigated *only simultaneously with the determination of individual differences* and with *general psychological laws"* (1935, p. 73).

The four selections in this chapter demonstrate in various ways the usefulness of taking individual differences as well as situational factors into account in increasing the precision of our understanding about the determinants of social behavior. The first three studies involve well-developed personality constructs—authoritarianism, locus of control, and Machiavellianism, respectively—while the fourth looks at some behavioral differences between obese and normal-weight persons.

One of the most durable personality constructs of interest to the social psychologist is authoritarianism, measured by the F scale first developed by Adorno, Frenkel-Brunswik, Levinson, and Sanford (1950). Authoritarianism refers to a constellation of personality characteristics that are associated with antidemocratic, intolerant tendencies. The first selection in this chapter ("The Defendant's Dilemma: Effects of Jurors' Attitudes and Authoritarianism on Judicial Decisions," by Mitchell and Byrne) presents a study which tried to assess the role of some extralegal factors in jury decisions. Specifically, the study determined the manner in which a subject's reactions toward a defendant would be affected by the former's degree of authoritarianism and by the similarity or dissimilarity between the attitudes of the subject and the defendant.

The second selection ("Individual Difference in Psychological Reactance: The Interaction between Locus of Control and Mode of Elimination of Freedom," by Cherulnik and Citrin) provides an interesting integration of two important contemporary theoretical ideas, locus of control and psychological reactance. Locus of control refers to a personality dimension, developed by Rotter (1966), which taps the nature of a person's beliefs regarding the consequences of his actions. A person with a belief in external control regards the reinforcements he receives as due to fate or luck and not to his own efforts. The person with a belief in internal control of reinforcement perceives the rewards he receives as being due to his own actions rather than forces beyond his control. A great deal of research has been done on this personality variable. A recent estimate (Rotter, 1975) is that there are over 600 published articles relating to the topic of internal vs. external control of reinforcement.

The theory of psychological reactance is a formulation pro-

posed by Brehm (1966) regarding the consequences of the elimination of a person's freedom. According to the theory,

for a given individual at a given time, there is a set of behaviors
in which he believes he is free to engage. Any reduction or
threat of reduction in that set of free behaviors arouses a motivational state, "reactance," which is directed toward reestablish-
ment of the lost or threatened freedom (Brehm & Cole, 1966, p.
420).

Cherulnik and Citrin argued that there is a conceptual parallel
between the dichotomy of internal versus external control of
reinforcement, on the one hand, and the distinction between a
personal and an impersonal mode of elimination of freedom, on
the other. On the basis of that parallel, they predicted that
internals would be more likely to experience reactance if they
were deprived of a freedom because of some personal characteristic rather than on an impersonal basis, while the reverse would
hold for externals. Their experiment reprinted here tested and
confirmed their prediction.

The third selection ("Machiavellianism and Forming Impressions of Others," by Kaplowitz) describes a study demonstrating that the nature of our social perceptions can be influenced
by a stable personality characteristic. In the study reported
here, Kaplowitz related a person's score on the Machiavellianism scale, a measure of manipulative tendencies developed by
Christie and Geis (1970), to the nature of his impressions of
another person who behaves in either a "warm" or "cold"
manner.

The last selection in this chapter ("Yom Kippur, Air France,
Dormitory Food, and the Eating Behavior of Obese and Normal
Persons," by Goldman, Jaffa, and Schachter) presents three
field studies testing Schachter's theory concerning the differing
antecedents of eating behavior among obese and normal individuals. According to Schachter, an obese person's hunger is
triggered primarily by external cues (such as the sight, smell,
and taste of food), while the normal individual relies on internal,
physiological cues to tell him when he is hungry. In the report
reprinted here support was found for the theory with three
widely different behaviors: fasting on Yom Kippur, eating dormitory food, and reacting to time-zone changes on trans-Atlantic
flights.

Current theoretical perspectives on, and reviews of, major
personality variables that have relevance for social behavior can

be found in Blass's forthcoming book entitled *Personality Variables in Social Behavior.*

REFERENCES

Adorno, T. W., Frenkel-Brunswik, E., Levinson, D. J., & Sanford, R. N. *The authoritarian personality.* New York: Norton, 1969. (Originally published 1950.)

Blass, T. (Ed.). *Personality variables in social behavior.* Hilldale, N.J.: Lawrence Erlbaum Associates, in preparation.

Brehm, J. W. *A Theory of Psychological Reactance.* New York: Academic Press, 1966.

Brehm, J. W., & Cole, A. H. Effects of a favor which reduces freedom. *Journal of Personality and Social Psychology,* 1966, *3,* 420-426.

Christie, R., & Geis, F. L. *Studies in Machiavellianism.* New York: Academic Press, 1970.

Dailey, J. T., & Pickrel, E. W. Some psychological contributions to defenses against hijackers. *American Psychologist,* 1975, *30,* 161-165.

Kluckhohn, C., & Murray, H. A. Personality formation: The determinants. In C. Kluckhohn, H. A. Murray, & D. M. Schneider (Eds.), *Personality in nature, society, and culture.* New York: Knopf, 1967.

Lewin, K. [*A dynamic theory of personality: Selected papers.*] (Donald K. Adams & Karl E. Zener, trans.). New York: McGraw-Hill, 1935.

Mischel, W. Continuity and change in personality. *American Psychologist,* 1969, *24,* 1012-1018.

Rotter, J. B. Generalized expectancies for internal versus external control of reinforcement. *Psychological Monographs,* 1966, *80* (1, Whole No. 609).

Rotter, J. B. Some problems and misconceptions related to the construct of internal versus external control of reinforcement. *Journal of Consulting and Clinical Psychology,* 1975, *43,* 56-67.

Sarason, I. G., Smith, R. E., & Diener, E. Personality research: Components of variance attributable to the person and the situation. *Journal of Personality and Social Psychology,* in press.

Wallace, J. An abilities conception of personality: Some implications for personality measurement. *American Psychologist,* 1966, *21,* 132-138.

1

HERMAN E. MITCHELL and DONN BYRNE

The Defendant's Dilemma: Effects of Jurors' Attitudes and Authoritarianism on Judicial Decisions

This study was undertaken to test the hypotheses that (a) attitude similarity between defendant and juror is positively related to judicial decisions favoring the defendant and that (b) juror authoritarianism is negatively related to judicial decisions favoring the defendant. In a simulated jury situation, 139 subjects who were either high or low in authoritarianism responded to an accused defendant whose attitudes were either similar to or dissimilar from their own on five issues irrelevant to the case. Analysis of variance indicated a significant interaction between authoritarianism and attitude similarity on certainty of the defendant's guilt ($p < .004$) and recommended severity of punishment ($p < .02$). It appears that attraction influences the judicial decisions of authoritarians but not of egalitarians.

Legal practitioners have long been aware of the influence of psychological variables on judicial decisions. In 1933, Clarence Darrow declared that

Jurymen seldom convict a person they like, or acquit one they dislike. The main work of the trial lawyer is to make a jury like his client, or at least to feel sympathy for him; facts regarding the crime are relatively unimportant [as quoted in Sutherland, 1966, p. 442].

Jerome Frank (1950) labeled prejudice "the thirteenth juror [p. 122]." Lake (1954) instructs the lawyer that

casual reference to things people like, and avoidance of what they dislike, is always a safe policy. Deep seated prejudices that are unknown to you can be raised if a policy of caution is not followed [p. 33].

Source: Herman E. Mitchell and Donn Byrne, "The Defendant's Dilemma: Effects of Jurors' Attitudes and Authoritarianism on Judicial Decisions," *Journal of Personality and Social Psychology,* 1973, *25,* 123-129. Copyright 1973 by the American Psychological Association. Reprinted by permission.

This research was supported in part by Research Fellowship Grant 710-0259 from the Ford Foundation to the first author, while he held Graduate Fellowship NI 71-083-GF7 from the National Institute of Law Enforcement and Criminal Justice, United States Department of Justice, and also Research Grant GS-2752, National Science Foundation, Donn Byrne, principal investigator.

It may be a truism, but when such extralegal and irrelevant variables affect judicial decisions, the objectivity and impartiality of the legal system are jeopardized.

Despite a long history of anecdotal and experimental evidence, only recently have systematic investigations of evaluative factors in the jury system been undertaken. In a landmark study involving 3,576 cases, Kalven and Zeisel (1966) found that the jury disagreed with the judge on almost one-third of the cases; disagreements in part were attributed to juror's sentiments about the defendant. Among the specific variables that have been found to influence jury decisions are the defendant's race, sex, income, education, family status, and the prestige of his attorney (Broeder, 1965; Bullock, 1961; Nagel, 1969; Weld & Danzig, 1940). Behavioral studies of the jury system have dealt with variables such as severity of the crime (Walster, 1966), familiar versus novel arguments (Sears & Freedman, 1965), peer consensus about the law (Berkowitz & Walker, 1967), and the character of the defendant and the victim (Landy & Aronson, 1969). These various lines of investigation strongly suggest that evaluative variables do, in fact, influence the decisions of jurors.

One general framework for the study of evaluative responses has been the reinforcement model developed in a paradigmatic program of research on interpersonal attraction (Byrne, 1969, 1971; Byrne & Clore, 1970). Evaluative responses directed toward any stimulus are conceptualized to vary as a function of the amount of positive and negative affect asociated with that stimulus. Among the stimuli used to manipulate affect have been similar and dissimilar attitudes (Byrne, 1961), temperature (Griffitt, 1970), movies (Byrne & Clore, 1967; Gouaux, 1971), ratings of the subject's creativity (Griffitt & Guay, 1969), personal evaluations (Byrne & Ervin, 1969), overcrowding (Griffitt & Veitch, 1971), and erotic stimuli (Byrne & Lamberth, 1971). Among the evaluative responses found to be influenced by such manipulations are interpersonal attraction and ratings of intelligence, knowledge, morality, and adjustment (Byrne, 1961); desirability as a date (Byrne, Ervin, & Lamberth, 1970); votes for a political candidate (Byrne, Bond, & Diamond, 1969); hiring decisions (Griffitt & Jackson, 1970; Merritt, 1970); and decisions about pornography and its legal restrictions (Byrne & Lamberth, 1971). This body of research suggests that the attraction of a juror toward a defendant would be influenced by any variable that influences affect—including the attitudes of the defendant. It would be expected that attraction would, in turn, influence decisions concerning guilt and innocence. If the defendant is judged to be guilty, decisions concerning the severity of punishment should reflect these same influences.

In addition to the proposed relationship between the juror's liking for the defendant and subsequent decisions about him, previous research suggests the importance of personality variables in the courtroom situation (Hatton, Snortum, & Oskamp, 1971; Kalven & Zeisel, 1966; Lipsitt & Strodtbeck, 1967; Strodtbeck, James, & Hawkins, 1957). One personality variable that would seem to be especially relevant is authoritarianism (Adorno, Frenkel-Brunswik, Levinson, & Sanford, 1950). Individuals scoring high on the *F* scale are described as being rigid and intolerant and as having the tendency to condemn, reject, and punish those who violate conventional values. The prejudicial aggression and punitiveness of authoritarians has been well documented (Epstein, 1965, 1966; Roberts & Jessor, 1958; Sherwood, 1966; Thibaut & Riecken, 1955). On the basis of these theoretical and empirical considerations, it would be expected that individuals high in authoritarianism would be more likely to find a defendant guilty and would sentence a guilty defendant more severely than would individuals low in authoritarianism.

Specifically, then, the present experiment was designed to test the hypotheses that (*a*) the similarity of attitudes between a juror and a defendant is positively related to judicial decisions favoring the defendant and that (*b*) the authoritarianism of a juror is negatively related to judicial decisions favoring the defendant.

METHOD

The subjects for the experiment were 139 introductory psychology students (64 males, 75 females) at Purdue University. Early in the semester, a 32-item attitude survey was administered in order to assess the subjects' views on a series of topics. Each item was arranged in a 6-point format, and the topics covered a wide variety of issues from the necessity of war to attitudes about gardening. From the pool of items, five topics were selected for use in the jury simulation experiment. These five topics were attitudes concerning the college fraternity system, college students' drinking, emphasis on the social aspects of college life, belief in God, and the American way of life.

Each experimental session was conducted in class sections of 20-30 subjects each. Each student was given a six-page booklet containing instructions, a description of the case, and a questionnaire dealing with the subject's opinions concerning the case and the defendant involved. The cover page of the booklet contained the following instructions:

This study is concerned with the nature of decision making and its relationship to an appeals system for students charged with violations of university regulations. The first part of this study entails reading a summary of an actual case taken from the files of the Dean of Men's office of the University of Toledo. The summary contains a complete description of the violation committed and of the student involved. Names of the participants have been changed. Similarly, several transcripts have been retyped to leave out confidential information. The second part of this study requires completion of a questionnaire (attached) concerning your opinions about this case.

The defendant was described as a junior in the College of Arts and Sciences, who was charged with the theft of an examination from a departmental duplicating office. The following description of the incident was recorded in the booklet:

On Tuesday, November 12, 1969, Mrs. Sarah Dinesmore, a secretary in the Department of English, was working in room 247 of Kinsleen Hall. This room, commonly referred to as the duplicating room, is used almost exclusively for the preparation of course materials, such as handouts and tests. On this particular day Mrs. Dinesmore was mimeographing copies of an English 212 examination which was to be administered the following morning. At 2:30 that afternoon she took her regular coffee break with several other secretaries. Room 247 was left unattended and unlocked for approximately 15 minutes. As she returned to the room, she observed a student (later identified as William Davidson) walk out of the room, place a number of folded papers in his pocket, and begin walking rapidly rapidly toward a stairway. Suspecting that copies of the examination may have been taken, Mrs. Dinesmore ran to the office of Dr. Robert Hossenger, assistant chairman of the department, and reported the incident to him. Together, they pursued the student and overtook him just outside the building. A copy of the English 212 examination was found in his possession. It was later determined that he was enrolled in the course.

This description of the incident leading to the Dean of Men's hearing was followed by a "personal data" description of the defendant. This description of the defendant contained information about the defendant's position on the five attitudinal topics that were manipulated in this study. The actual statements concerning these attitudes were changed for each subject, so that the subject jurors were presented with a defendant with whom they were in complete agreement or in complete disagreement on all five attitudinal topics. In order to accomplish the necessary conditions of attitude similarity (0% or 100%) with each subject, 44 different combinations of specific statements about these topics were employed in the experiment. An example of these descriptions is given below:

William Davidson is a junior in the College of Arts and Sciences, and currently holds a grade point average of 2.68 (4.00 = A). His academic records show that he has never been placed on academic probation. When questioned about Bill's activities, his dormitory counselor stated that Bill is not a member of a fraternity, nor did he seem to be enthusiastic about the fraternity system in general. He also stated that Bill did not seem to emphasize the social aspects of college and is not in favor of college students' drinking. He was described by his roommate in the dormitory as a person with a firm belief in God, and a negative opinion concerning the American way of life. His records show no evidence of past disciplinary problems.

Following the personal description of the defendant was the following statement made by the defendant at the hearing:

Dr. Howell sent me to the duplicating room to pick up a copy of an article for a course I was in. When I got there, no one was around, so I went in to find the article myself. While I was looking for the article, I found a copy of the test I was going to take the next day. I had been studying for that test for a week, and I was really worried about it. I just impulsively picked up the test and walked out with it.

Following this description of the hearing, each subject juror was asked to fill out a four-item questionnaire concerning his opinions about the case. The first item asked the subject to rate the degree of certainty with which he felt the defendant to be guilty. This item was in the form of a 7-point scale, ranging from "I feel that the defendant is definitely guilty" (scored as 7) to "I feel that the defendant is definitely not guilty" (scored as 1). Following the ratings of the defendant's guilt, each subject was asked to give his recommended punishment for the defendant. The nine possible punishments were dismissal of the case (scored as 1), warning, reprimand, social probation, 1-week suspension, 1-month suspension, semester suspension, year suspension, and permanent expulsion (scored as 2-9 respectively).[1] After determining the severity of punishment, each subject was asked to indicate how he felt personally about the defendant. This information was assessed on a 14-point scale, ranging from "extremely negative" (scored as 1) to "extremely positive" (scored as 14). This scale was used as a measure of the subject's attraction toward the defendant. Finally, the subject jurors were asked to evaluate the defendant's morality. This evaluation was made on a 7-point scale ranging from "highly immoral" (scored as 1) to "highly moral" (scored as 7).

After completing the experiment, the subjects were given a 22-item acquiescence-free version of the authoritarianism scale, as used by Byrne and Lamberth (1971). This scale was administered by the subjects' instructors during the week following the experiment. The subjects were not aware, at the time of administration, of the relationship between this scale and the jury simulation experiment. After the authoritarianism data were collected, the experimenter discussed the study with the subjects, explaining its purpose.

In addition to the two levels of attitude similarity, the subjects were dichotomized into authoritarian ($M = 84.97$) and egalitarian ($M = 60.42$) subgroups by division at the F scale sample mean of 72.22. Thus, there was a 2×2 factorial design, with cell sizes ranging from 31 to 39.

TABLE 1.1
Mean Responses of Authoritarian and Egalitarian Jurors on Certainty of Guilt, Severity of Punishment, Attraction, and Morality toward a Defendant with Similar or Dissimilar Attitudes

	Proportion of Similar Attitudes	
Variable	.00	1.00
Certainty of guilt		
Authoritarians	6.08	5.55
Egalitarians	5.81	6.28
Severity of punishment		
Authoritarians	5.13	3.58
Egalitarians	3.84	3.69
Attraction		
Authoritarians	5.74	8.42
Egalitarians	8.26	9.58
Morality		
Authoritarians	3.33	4.91
Egalitarians	3.97	4.89

RESULTS

The means of the four dependent variables are shown in Table 1.1; an analysis of variance was computed for each. With respect to certainty of the defendant's guilt, neither main effect was significant, but there was a highly significant interaction between similarity and authoritarianism ($F = 8.54$, $df = 1/135$, $p < .004$). Tests of simple main effects, using the Newman-Keuls procedure (Winer, 1971), were applied to the data in order to describe the interaction more accurately. It was found that in the similar attitude condition the authoritarians were less certain of the defendant's guilt than were the egalitarians ($p < .05$).

The subjects' recommended severity of punishment yielded significant effects for attitude similarity ($F = 7.68$, $df = 1/135$, $p < .007$), authoritarianism ($F = 3.66$, $df = 1/135$, $p = .054$), and the interaction ($F = 5.29$, $df = 1/135$, $p < .02$). Post hoc comparisons of cell means revealed that the authoritarians in the dissimilar condition recommended more severe punishment for the defendant than did the subjects in the remaining three conditions ($p < .01$).

On the attraction variable, both attitude similarity ($F = 26.30$, $df = 1/135$, $p < .0001$) and authoritarianism ($F = 22.19$, $df = 1/135$, $p < .0001$) yielded significant effects, while the interaction failed to do so.

Only attitude similarity ($F = 51.44$, $df = 1/135$, $p < .0001$) had a significant effect on morality ratings. Authoritarianism ($p < .08$) and the interaction ($p < .06$) only approached significance.

DISCUSSION

The effects of attitude similarity and authoritarianism on judicial decisions were found to be more complex than originally hypothesized. There
was an interactive effect of these two variables on both certainty of guilt
and severity of punishment. Since the defendant in this case clearly admits
his guilt, any response other than that which indicates the defendant as
definitely guilty must be considered as a deviation from the facts. It
appears that an authoritarian presented with a similar, and therefore
better liked, defendant shows a bias in the defendant's favor. An
egalitarian in the identical situation fails to show this bias. The influence
of the irrelevant factor of attitudes on the judgments of authoritarians is
even more salient with respect to recommended punishments than with
decisions about guilt. Both main effects were significant, but further
analysis indicated that the major contributors were the authoritarians in
the dissimilar condition; they were significantly more severe in their
recommended punishments than were the subjects in the other three
conditions. Compared to egalitarians, then, authoritarians are less inclined to judge a similar defendant as guilty and more inclined to punish a
dissimilar defendant severely.

The indicated differences between authoritarians and egalitarians are
even more striking when the relationships among the dependent variables
are examined. Table 1.2 shows the intercorrelations of the four dependent
variables separately for the high and low authoritarian subjects. The coefficients were computed *within* attitude similarity conditions and then
averaged.[2] For the authoritarian subjects, attraction and their evaluations
of the defendant's morality are significantly related to both the guilt and

TABLE 1.2
Intercorrelations of the Four Dependent Variables for
Authoritarians and Egalitarians

Group	Certainty of Guilt	Severity of Punishment	Attraction
Authoritarians[a]			
Severity of punishment	.27*		
Attraction	—.37***	—.32***	
Morality	—.29**	—.33***	.63***
Egalitarians[b]			
Severity of punishment	.15		
Attraction	—.09	—.18	
Morality	.08	—.11	.53***

[a] $n = 72$.
[b] $n = 67$.
* $p < .05$.
** $p < .01$.
*** $p < .005$.

punishment variables. In contrast, for the egalitarians, neither attraction nor morality was significantly related to either of the judicial decisions. Thus, in both groups, attitude similarity was found to affect evaluative responses, but the egalitarians did not allow this reaction to influence their judicial decisions.

Despite the fact that 44 different attitudinal descriptions of the defendant were employed in order to match each subject to the defendant in perfect agreement or disagreement of these five topics, some descriptions were used more often than others. In fact, because of their commonality, 3 of the descriptions were employed for 49 of the 139 subjects. In order to assure that the subjects were responding to attitudinal similarity-dissimilarity and not the commonality versus deviancy of the defendant's opinions, these descriptions were separated from the less common descriptions and analyzed for their effect on each of the four dependent measures. If subject jurors were responding to commonality versus deviancy of the defendant's opinions, one would expect greater perceived guilt and harsher punishments for those defendants disagreeing with commonly held views than for those disagreeing with less common opinions.[3] The analyses of all four dependent measures indicated no effect of agreement or disagreement with common or uncommon attitudinal positions ascribed to the defendant ($F < 1$ in all cases).

The effect of attitude similarity on attraction was, not surprisingly, highly significant. The effect of authoritarianism on attraction was, however, a considerable surprise considering earlier findings of no relationship between the two variables (Byrne, 1965) even when authoritarian-relevant attitudes are used (Sheffield & Byrne, 1967). How can one account for these contradictory findings? The possibility was raised that authoritarians do, in fact, respond more strongly to attitude similarity-dissimilarity than egalitarians; the previous findings were collected over half a decade ago at the University of Texas and may not be generalizable to the present time or place. It would be extremely interesting if there have been sufficient societal changes in polarization since the earlier research to bring about a new relationship between liberalism-conservatism and the similarity-attraction relationship. In any event, a study was undertaken to test this possibility. The same 22-item balanced F scale and a 48-item attitude scale were administered to several sections of the introductory psychology course at Purdue University. Two months later, 57 subjects (38 males, 19 females) took part in a standard similarity-attraction experiment (Byrne, 1969) in which they were exposed to a 48-item attitude scale (purportedly filled out by another student) simulated at .20, .50, or .80 proportion of similar attitudes. The subjects were further divided into authoritarians ($M = 87.37$) and egalitarians ($M = 60.96$). The similarity variable once again was found to have a significant ($p < .02$) effect on attraction, but neither authoritarianism nor the Similarity x Authoritarianism interaction approached significance. Thus, the Texas findings were replicated, and a different explanation for the inconsistent findings were necessarily sought.

A more probable explanation would seem to be that the effects of authoritarianism on evaluative responses are elicited only by specific situations, and that broad transituational generality should not be expected (Byrne, 1974; Mischel, 1968; Sarason & Smith, 1971). The trial setting with a socially acceptable target plus the affect-eliciting attitudinal information evoke quite different responses in authoritarians and egalitarians, whereas a simple attitude-attraction task does not. One question raised by this conceptualization is whether the trial situation alone is sufficient to bring about authoritarianism effects. To answer this question, another study was conducted in which the procedures of the original experiment were replicated, except that the attitudinal information was omitted. A group of 64 introductory psychology students (37 males, 27 females) at Purdue University took part in the simulated trial experiment. They were again dichotomized into authoritarians ($M = 84.08$) and egalitarians ($M = 60.08$). Analysis of variance indicated no effect of authoritarianism on any of the four dependent variables ($F < 1$ in each case). Thus, neither the manipulation of attitude similarity alone nor the trial situation alone is sufficient to evoke the authoritarian reaction which is found to be quite strong when the two are combined. It is interesting to speculate that had the authoritarianism-trial experiment been conducted first, it is unlikely that this particular personality variable would have been included in the original authoritarianism-attitudes-trial experiment. There would seem to be danger in extrapolating from one simple experimental situation to a more complex experimental situation with respect to the effects of personality variables. This series of experiments points not only to the futility of conceptualizing personality traits as broadly transituational and general in nature, but they also demonstrate the ease with which seemingly general trait consistent behaviors disappear when rather simple changes in the situation occur.

Obviously, the simulated jury technique employed in this investigation is not an exact duplication of the situation in which genuine jurors are involved in actual trials. Some comfort about the comparability of the laboratory and the "real world" is provided by the correspondence between experimental findings and the correlational and descriptive data gathered in legal settings. One procedural difference that might be noted is that our subject jurors were not permitted to interact and deliberate before reaching their decisions. The gravity of such a limitation is reduced by the findings of Kalven and Zeisel (1966). They reported in an extensive study of over 3,500 cases in the Chicago Jury Project that 90% of these cases are decided by the members of the jury *before* they deliberate.

The results of the present study, and of others reported here, could have important implications for the legal system. Most notably, the constitutional guarantee of trial by a jury of peers takes on added importance. Attitudes have long been recognized to be relatively homogeneous within class strata. The relationship between economic status, occupation, and demographic variables and attitude homogeneity has also been firmly established. Considering the findings of the present research, trial by a jury of attitudinally similar peers versus attitudinally dissimilar nonpeers could well result in quite different verdicts. Peership may require narrow and specific definition. It is impossible to imagine a trial, from a simple traffic violation to the dramatic case of the Chicago Seven, in which there is not an expression of the defendant's attitudes or in which attitudes could not be inferred from variables such as dress, age, sex, race, manner of speech, or whatever. The fact that some jurors, such as the egalitarians in our experiment, are more immune than others to legally irrelevant information might point the way toward a means whereby the legal system could attain greater objectivity.

REFERENCES

Adorno, T. W., Frenkel-Brunswik, E., Levinson, D. J., & Sanford, R. N. *The authoritarian personality.* New York: Harper, 1950.

Berkowitz, L., & Walker, N. Laws and moral judgments. *Sociometry,* 1967, *30,* 410-422.

Broeder, D. W. Plaintiff's family status as affecting juror behavior. *Journal of Public Law,* 1965, *14,* 131-143.

Bullock, R. Significance of the racial factor in the length of prison sentences. *Journal of Criminal Law,* 1961, *52,* 411-415.

Byrne, D. Interpersonal attraction and attitude similarity. *Journal of Abnormal and Social Psychology,* 1961, *62,* 713-715.

Byrne, D. Authoritarianism and response to attitude similarity-dissimilarity. *Journal of Social Psychology,* 1965, *66,* 251-256.

Byrne, D. Attitudes and attraction. In L. Berkowitz (Ed.), *Advances in experimental social psychology.* Vol. 4. New York: Academic Press, 1969.

Byrne, D. *The attraction paradigm.* New York: Academic Press, 1971.

Byrne, D. *An introduction to personality: Research, theory, and applications.* (2nd ed.) Englewood Cliffs, N.J.: Prentice-Hall, 1974.

Byrne, D., Bond, M. H., & Diamond, M. J. Response to political candidates as a function of attitude similarity. *Human Relations,* 1969, *22,* 251-262.

Byrne, D., & Clore, G. L. Effectance arousal and attraction. *Journal of Personality and Social Psychology,* 1967, *6* (4, Whole No. 638).

Byrne, D., & Clore, G. L. A reinforcement model of evaluative responses. *Personality: An International Journal,* 1970, *1,* 103-128.

Byrne, D., & Ervin, C. R. Attraction toward a Negro stranger as a function of prejudice, attitude similarity, and the stranger's evaluation of the subject. *Human Relations,* 1969, *22,* 397-404.

Byrne, D., Ervin, C. R., & Lamberth, J. Continuity between the experimental study of attraction and real-life computer dating. *Journal of Personality and Social Psychology,* 1970, *16,* 157-165.

Byrne, D., & Lamberth, J. *The effect of erotic stimuli on sex arousal, evaluative responses, and subsequent behavior.* (Tech. Rep. of the Commission on Obscenity and Pornography, Vol. 8). Washington, D.C.: United States Government Printing Office, 1971.

Chambers v. Florida, *United States Supreme Court Reports,* 1940, *309* (227), 241.

Epstein, R. Authoritarianism, displaced aggression, and social status of the target. *Journal of Personality and Social Psychology,* 1965, *2,* 585-589.

Epstein, R. Aggression toward outgroups as a function of authoritarianism and imitation of aggressive models. *Journal of Personality and Social Psychology,* 1966, *3,* 574-579.

Frank, J. *Courts on trial.* Princeton, N.J.: Princeton University Press, 1950.

Gouaux, C. Induced affective states and interpersonal attraction. *Journal of Personality and Social Psychology,* 1971, *20,* 37-43.

Griffitt, W. Environmental effects on interpersonal affective behavior: Ambient effective temperature and attraction. *Journal of Personality and Social Psychology,* 1970, *15,* 240-244.

Griffitt, W., & Guay, P. "Object" evaluation and conditioned affect. *Journal of Experimental Research in Personality,* 1969, *4,* 1-8.

Griffitt, W., & Jackson, T. The influence of ability and nonability information on personnel selection decisions. *Psychological Reports,* 1970, *27,* 959-962.

Griffitt, W., & Veitch, R. Hot and crowded: Influences of population density and temperature on interpersonal affective behavior. *Journal of Personality and Social Psychology,* 1971, *17,* 92-98.

Hatton, D. E., Snortum, J. R., & Oskamp, S. The effects of biasing information and dogmatism upon witness testimony. *Psychonomic Science,* 1971, *23,* 425-427.

Kalven, H., Jr., & Zeisel, H. *The American jury.* Boston: Little, Brown, 1966.

Lake, L. W. *How to win lawsuits before juries.* Englewood Cliffs, N.J.: Prentice-Hall, 1954.

Landy, D., & Aronson, E. The influence of the character of the criminal and victim on the decisions of simulated jurors. *Journal of Experimental Social Psychology,* 1969, *5,* 141-152.

Lipsitt, P. D., & Strodtbeck, F. L. Defensiveness in decision making as a function of sex-role identification. *Journal of Personality and Social Psychology,* 1967, *6,* 10-15.

Merritt, D. L. The relationships between qualifications and attitudes in a teacher selection situation. Unpublished doctoral dissertation, Syracuse University, 1970.

Mischel, W. *Personality and assessment.* New York: Wiley, 1968.

Nagel, S. S. *The legal process from a behavioral perspective.* Homewood, Ill.: Dorsey Press, 1969.

Roberts, A. H., & Jessor, R. Authoritarianism, punitiveness, and perceived social status. *Journal of Abnormal and Social Psychology,* 1958, *56,* 311-314.

Sarason, I. G., & Smith, R. E. Personality. In P. H. Mussen & M. R. Rosenzweig (Eds.), *Annual review of psychology.* Vol. 22. Palo Alto, Calif.: Annual Reviews, 1971.

Sears, D. O., & Freedman, J. L. Effects of expected familiarity with arguments upon opinion change and selective exposure. *Journal of Personality and Social Psychology,* 1965, *2,* 420-426.

Sheffield, J., & Byrne, D. Attitude similarity-dissimilarity, authoritarianism, and interpersonal attraction. *Journal of Social Psychology,* 1967, *71,* 117-123.

Sherwood, J. J. Authoritarianism, moral realism, and President Kennedy's death. *British Journal of Social and Clinical Psychology,* 1966, *5,* 264-269.

Strodtbeck, F. L., James, R. M., & Hawkins, C. Social status in jury deliberations. *American Sociology Review,* 1957, *22,* 713-721.

Sutherland, E. *Principles of criminology.* Philadelphia: J. B. Lippincott Co., 1966.

Thibaut, J. W., & Riecken, H. W. Authoritarianism, status, and communication of aggression. *Human Relations,* 1955, *8,* 95-120.

Walster, E. Assignment of responsibility for an accident. *Journal of Personality and Social Psychology,* 1966, *3,* 73-79.

Weld, H. P., & Danzig, E. R. A study of the way in which a verdict is reached by a jury. *American Journal of Psychology,* 1940, *53,* 518-536.

Winer, B. J. *Statistical principles in experimental design.* New York: McGraw-Hill, 1971.

NOTES

1. These nine possible punishments were developed from a list of 11 disciplinary judgments used by universities in such hearings. The original 11 dispositions were ranked by 60 undergraduates; the items "monetary fine" and "academic probation" were excluded from the alternatives because of their high variance among the undergraduate judges.

2. This procedure eliminates the effects of the attitude similarity variable on each response and permits a non-confounded examination of the effects of authoritarianism on the interrelationships.

3. While such differential judicial decisions might have served to weaken the theoretical interpretation of these results, it would not lessen the importance of the findings in terms of their significance for the legal system. A judicial decision based on such factors as perceived deviancy (or dissimilarity) is in direct violation of the constitutional guarantees of "due process" and "equal protection of the law" as stated in the Fourteenth Amendment. These rights, according to Supreme Court Justice Black (Chambers v. Florida, 1940), are "planned and inscribed for the benefit of every human being subject to our Constitution—of whatever race, creed, or persuasion."

2

PAUL D. CHERULNIK and MURRAY M. CITRIN

Individual Difference in Psychological Reactance: The Interaction between Locus of Control and Mode of Elimination of Freedom

One hundred and eight male and female college students served as subjects in an experiment designed to investigate individual differences in psychological reactance. Equal numbers of subjects designated as internals and externals on the basis of their pretest scores on Rotter's Internal-External scale were asked to indicate their liking for each of four posters. Two days after being told that they would be given the poster of their choice, two groups of subjects learned that the poster to which they had given their third-highest rating would be unavailable to them, one group for reasons that were personal and the other for reasons that were impersonal. A third group, the control, simply rerated the posters after an equivalent time period. A significant Locus of Control x Mode of Elimination of Freedom interaction was observed. It was found, as predicted, that (a) internals showed greater reactance, that is, reported greater liking for the initially third-rated poster, following personal elimination of freedom; (b) externals showed greater reactance following impersonal elimination of freedom; and (c) the control group's ratings did not change. These findings were discussed primarily in terms of the relationship between the concepts of control over reinforcement and elimination of freedom.

In his theory of psychological reactance, Brehm (1966) proposed that the elimination or threatened elimination of the freedom to engage in an available alternative behavior results in a motivational arousal to recover that freedom. He labeled that consequent motivational arousal reactance. Research by Brehm and Cole (1966), Brehm, Stires, Sensenig, and Shaban (1966), Burton (1962), Hammock and Brehm (1966), and others has confirmed the occurrence of this effect. In that research, reactance was measured principally as the increase in the reported desirability of a behavioral alternative following its elimination or threatened elimination.

Source: Paul D. Cherulnik and Murray M. Citrin, "Individual Difference in Psychological Reactance: The Interaction between Locus of Control and Mode of Elimination of Freedom," *Journal of Personality and Social Psychology,* 1974, *29,* 398-404. Copyright 1974 by the American Psychological Association. Reprinted by permission.
The data on which the present article is based were collected by the second author in the course of thesis research for the master's degree at the University of Maine, Orono.

Brehm (1966) considered two basic modes of elimination of freedom—the personal and the impersonal. He defined the elimination of freedom as personal "when one of a person's free behaviors is eliminated and he can perceive or easily imagine that the elimination was intentionally aimed at him [p. 38]." The elimination of freedom is impersonal when "an individual cannot easily perceive it as having been *directed* at himself [p. 17]" and "his loss of freedom could just as well have happened to someone else [p. 17)." In his original exposition of the theory, Brehm (1966) treated these as alternative and equivalent in their capability for arousing reactance.

Brehm's treatment of reactance implies that conditions attending the act of eliminating a behavioral freedom are the crucial determinants of the arousal and the effects of reactance, to the exclusion of the characteristics of the individual whose freedoms are at stake. On its face, in light of the vast literature dealing with cognitively based individual differences, such a state of affairs appears unlikely to exist. It seems probable that the conditions attending reactance arousal are not perceived identically by all of the individuals exposed to them.

To this point, however, the question of individual differences in response to the elimination of specific behavioral freedoms has been given very little attention. Two studies have been published that include post hoc analyses of relationships between personality variables and reactance arousal. Jones (1970) found no strong or consistent correlations between a number of personality measures, including locus of control and self-esteem, and a measure of reactance. No theoretical rationale was provided by which such relationships were to be expected, nor were any specific predictions made. Grabitz-Gniech (1971) found that an impersonal elimination of freedom aroused somewhat less ($p < .10$) reactance in subjects who expressed strong feelings of inadequacy.

The present investigation represents an extension of this line of research to the prediction of such a relationship. One might proceed by attempting to link a personality variable to a variable of reactance theory. Individuals might be expected to differ with regard to whether or not they felt they had a particular freedom, how important a particular freedom was to them, how they expressed reactance arousal, and the like. The present study is concerned with individual differences in the magnitude of reactance aroused by alternative means of eliminating a behavior freedom. It had its source in the appearance to the authors of a conceptual relationship between Brehm's (1966) differentiation of personal and impersonal modes of elimination of behavioral freedom and Rotter's (1966) distinction between internal and external modes of perception of locus of control of reinforcement.

On the basis of Rotter's (1966) Internal-External scale, it is possible to assess the extent to which individuals perceive reinforcements they receive to be consequences of their own behaviors or relatively permanent attributes of themselves (e.g., abilities, aptitudes) or, alternatively, the extent to which those reinforcements are perceived as being under the control of luck, fate, or powerful others (individuals, institutions, etc.). Individuals to whom the former description may be applied were termed by Rotter, internals, and those fitting the latter description, externals. A very small sample of the existing literature should suffice to illustrate the behavioral concomitants of an individual's perception of the locus of control, as expressed verbally on Rotter's scale. Internals perform better on tasks in which success is dependent on skill, while externals perform better on tasks whose outcome is controlled by chance (Petzel & Gynther, 1970; Watson & Baumal, 1967). Internals can be expected to seek and find more information relevant to control over situations in which they find themselves than do externals (Seeman, 1963; Seeman & Evans, 1962) and to initiate more controlling action in those situations (Gore & Rotter, 1963; Strickland, 1965). Internal locus of control is associated with greater academic achievement than is external (Coleman, Campbell, Hobson, McPartland, Mood, Weinfeld, & York, 1966). In short, considerable evidence exists for the predictive validity of the locus of control concept. Internals behave as though they believe that they themselves bear the primary responsibility for what happens to them, while externals behave as though they believe that control rests in the hands of fate or others.

The parallel between personal and impersonal modes of elimination of freedom and internal and external modes of perceiving the locus of control is sharpened by the consideration of operational definitions of the modes of elimination of freedom. A personal elimination of freedom may be accomplished by creating a situation in which the target person perceives the unavailability of a previously available behavioral alternative to be based on some action or personal characteristic of his own. In such a case, he would be expected to perceive the elimination of freedom to be aimed intentionally at him, meeting Brehm's (1966) criterion. An impersonal elimination of freedom, by contrast, might be characterized by the target person's attribution of his loss of the behavioral freedom in question to conditions for which he is not personally responsible, such as chance, fate, or the action of another over which he has no control. Such an agent would be unlikely to appear to be acting exclusively or directly toward him. Brehm et al. (1966) have, in fact, used an impersonal elimination manipulation that fits this description.

The rationale underlying specific predictions of individual differences in the magnitude of arousal of the reactance motive in the present study is based, then, on an analogy between personal and impersonal modes of elimination of freedom and internal and external modes of perceiving the locus of control of reinforcement. It was reasoned that the condition of whether the responsibility for the elimination of an individual's behavioral freedom was attributable to him or to outside forces constituted the perceived locus of control over rewards that were associated with that behavioral freedom. Thus, the elimination of a behavioral freedom that an individual perceives he has is held to be equivalent to the exercise of control over the potential rewards which are associated with that freedom. This is particularly clear in the experimental paradigm that Brehm and his colleagues have typically employed. There the behavioral freedom that is eliminated is the individual's freedom to choose and thereby acquire an object of some tangible value.

From the point of view of the target of an elimination of freedom, it follows that the conditions that he is able to identify as controlling the availability of a given behavioral alternative may be expected to determine the extent to which he perceives that alternative as, in Brehm's terms, a behavioral freedom. And the character of this perception would be expected to be a function of his perception of the locus of control. Rotter's internal person, who feels that the outcomes of his behavior are contingent primarily upon his own actions or attributes, would be expected to react strongly against being deprived of a behavioral freedom, that is, the opportunity to gain a worthwhile reward, if that deprivation appeared to be based on an action or attribute of his own. He would perceive such a deprivation as an exception to his normal feeling of control. The external, on the other hand, who perceives fate or the actions of others to be the predominant determinant of the outcomes of his behaviors, would react strongly against being deprived of a behavioral freedom by such forces, which he sees as the normal providers of his rewards. The internal, by the same token, would be less likely to see as a freedom a behavioral alternative under the control of an external force. He does not expect such forces to reward him. And an external who perceives that the availability of a behavioral alternative is contingent upon one of his own actions or attributes is less likely to experience reactance arousal as a consequence of its being denied to him, since he does not expect such factors to be influential in controlling his reinforcements.

On the basis of the preceding rationale, it was predicted that internals would exhibit greater reactance, in the form of reporting an increase in the desirability of the eliminated freedoms, to the elimination of freedom in the personal than in the impersonal mode, while the relative magnitude of the effects of the two modes of elimination would be reversed for externals.

METHOD

Subjects

One hundred and eight male and female undergraduates enrolled in three psychology courses participated in a study of "aesthetic judgments." Participation was required by their instructors. All of the students (approximately 200) enrolled in the three courses were administered Rotter's (1966) Internal-External scale at least one week prior to the experiment. Those students identified as extreme scorers were chosen from each class, and the remaining students were excused. Internal-external scores for the original pretest group were distributed around a mean of 10.42 with a standard deviation of 3.98. The subjects who obtained scores of 9 or below were classified as internals, and those with scores of 13 and above were classified as externals. Scores for the internal group had a mean of 6.46 with a standard deviation of 2.24, while the externals' scores had a mean of 14.80 with a standard deviation of 1.75. The subjects were not divided according to sex, since sex has not been found to be related to the effects of either of the independent variables in the present study—locus of control or elimination of freedom.

Materials

Ten contemporary posters of the sort available in almost any college bookstore were shown to approximately 100 students in classes other than those from which the subjects for the actual experiment were drawn. These students were asked to rate each for attractiveness on a scale consisting of a 100-millimeter line by placing a vertical mark through the line at a point representing their ratings. The words "not very much" appeared 10 millimeters from the left end of each line, the words "more or less" at the midpoint, and "very much" 10 millimeters from the right end. All of the ratings throughout the experiment were made on identical scales. The posters were labeled by letters of the alphabet A-J, and the rating scales were labeled correspondingly. From the original group of 10, 4 posters were chosen for use in the experiment on the basis of having received approximately equal and highly positive ratings.

Overview

The plan for this experiment was very similar to those of previous studies of reactance (e.g., Brehm et al., 1966). Three equivalent groups of subjects made up of equal numbers of internals and externals rated four posters. One, the control group, merely rated them again after an interval of 48 hours. The two remaining groups were told that two days later they would be allowed to choose one poster as a reward for their participation. At that time they were told that one poster (for each subject the one originally rated third-highest) was unavailable. The reason given to one group was loss in transit (the impersonal elimination), and to the other some unspecified personal characteristic (the personal elimination). Both elimination groups were then asked to rate all four posters a second time.

Procedure

The experiment was conducted in two sessions 48 hours apart during the subjects' normal class periods. The two mode of elimination manipulations and the control condition were administered to three separate groups of subjects. Those members of three similar classes who had been selected on the basis of their pretest scores as internals and externals were used. Since the poster to be eliminated for each subject in the experimental groups depended on his initial ratings, instructions other than those introducing the experiment needed to be individualized and therefore were distributed in written form. Since the subjects were seated near one another, it was necessary that their instructions appear to be similar. It was decided for that reason not to mix the three treatments, personal, impersonal, and control, within classes. As a result, the subjects' instructions differed by only the one letter designating the unavailable poster, minimizing the likelihood that differences would be detected and suspicion thereby engendered.

The smallest group of internals or externals in any of the three classes was 18. Therefore, 1-4 subjects were randomly eliminated from each of the other groups after the experiment in order to simplify the data analysis. This was not done at the outset in order to guard against possible attrition from the first session to the second.

At the beginning of the first session, the experiment was orally described to all of the subjects as a study of the processes underlying personal preferences for artistic products. The subjects were then asked to rate the four posters presented to them. Members of the control group were asked to reexamine and rerate the posters. They were then excused. No debriefing was undertaken with this group, since the description that they had been given of their part in the experiment was substantially straightforward.

Members of both elimination of freedom groups were told at the close of the first session after they had rated the posters that each would be given a complimentary copy of the poster of his choice as a reward for his participation in the study. They were asked to return in two days, when a shipment from the poster manufacturer was expected to arrive, to choose and receive their gifts.

During the second session for the subjects in the two experimental groups, instructions were distributed in printed form for reasons explained above. All of these subjects were asked to reexamine and rerate the four posters, and each was informed that one of the posters was unavailable to him—the reactance induction. The poster so identified was in each case the one that the subject had given his third-highest rating during the first session. This poster was chosen, following Brehm's (1966) rationale, to eliminate any possibility that frustration would be aroused. The personal and impersonal elimination of freedom conditions were differentiated on the basis of the rationale given the subjects for the unavailability of this poster. The subjects in the impersonal group were informed that the expected copies of one of the posters had simply not arrived in the shipment and that poster was thus unavailable to be chosen. The personal instructions stated that the shipment of posters that was received was inadequate to permit the subjects a free choice among the four and therefore the experimenters had evaluated each subject's scholas-

TABLE 2.1
Summary of Analysis of Variance

Source	SS	df	MS	F
Locus of control (A)	.46	1	.46	.001
Mode of elimination of freedom (B)	436.51	2	218.25	.421
A X B	323.51	2	161.75	.312
Error	52874.80	102	518.38	
Repeated measures (C)	468.17	1	468.17	4.315**
A X C	6.69	1	6.69	.062
B X C	573.69	2	286.85	2.644*
A X B X C	688.40	2	344.20	3.172**
Error	11067.00	102	108.50	
Total	66439.30	215		

*$p < .10$.
**$p < .05$.

TABLE 2.2
Comparisons of Pre- and Postinduction Ratings of
Poster Initially Ranked Third

Experimental Conditions	Preinduction Mean	Postinduction Mean	Mean Pre-Post Change
Internal-personal	42.78	50.17	7.39*
Internal-impersonal	49.00	51.28	2.28
Internal-control	50.50	48.61	—1.89
External-personal	49.11	48.11	—1.00
External-impersonal	45.56	56.89	11.33*
External-control	46.28	45.83	— .45

Note: All of the means are based on a sample size of 18.
*$p < .05$, Duncan's multiple-range test.

tic and personal school records and had on that basis decided that one
poster would not be "meaningful" to him. Therefore, the instructions
went on, he would be required to choose only among the remaining three.

After reading their instructions, the subjects in both experimental
groups completed their ratings of the posters. They were then thoroughly
debriefed, thanked, and excused.

RESULTS

The subjects' ratings of the critical poster were subjected to analysis of
variance. Comparisons were made for two between-subjects variables,
locus of control and mode of elimination of freedom, and one within-
subjects variable, the two repeated measures of the attractiveness of the
critical poster (Winer, 1971, pp. 559-571). A summary of this analysis is
presented in Table 2.1.

A direct test of the experimental hypothesis was provided by the F ratio
for the Locus of Control x Mode of Elimination of Freedom x Repeated
Measures interaction, which was found to be statistically significant ($F =$
3.172, $p < .05$). The hypothesis appears to have been quite clearly supported by the data. Internals responded more strongly to the personal
than to the impersonal elimination of freedom manipulation, while
externals exhibited the reverse pattern of response. As expected, the
subjects in the control condition did not change their ratings from the first
to the second session.

A further examination of the change from pre- to postinduction in the
ratings of the critical poster was carried out using the Duncan multiple-
range test. These comparisons, shown in Table 2.2, revealed that the pre-
to postinduction increase in favorability of the unavailable poster, the
reactance effect, was statistically significant only for internals in the
personal elimination of freedom condition and externals in the impersonal
elimination of freedom condition. Thus, internals and externals differed
not only in the relative magnitude of their responses to the two modes of
elimination of freedom but in the presence or absence of any reliable
response to those modes.

Pre- and postinduction ratings of the three posters that were not
eliminated were also analyzed. Since these ratings were not found to be
significantly affected by the independent variables, either singly or in
combination, these analyses are not presented here.

DISCUSSION

At the outset, one feature of the experimental procedure deserves discussion. The personal elimination of freedom manipulation was accom-

plished through the use of instructions that contained a veiled attack on the subject's status as well as the implication of an invasion of his privacy. It is possible that this message had connotations for at least some subjects that were irrelevant to its intended meaning. It might, for example, have been taken for a threat to other freedoms by virtue of its implication that the subject was vulnerable to exposure in ways he may not have thought possible. In devising this particular manipulation, virtually no guidance was available to the authors from previous research. Only an experiment by Jones (1972) had used a personal elimination manipulation that precisely fit the working definition proposed above, and it was employed in a rather unique experiment in which freedom was eliminated by flattery. It is our conviction that while the manipulation used here may have had undesirable side effects, especially in its implied derogation of subjects, there is no basis for considering them a threat to the validity of the experiment as a test of its stated hypotheses.

The differential responsivity of internals and externals to the personal and impersonal elimination of freedom inductions may be dealt with conceptually in a number of related ways. As described above, this effect was predicted on the basis of the presumed expectancies of internals and externals for control over their rewards. It was argued that the individual's perception of the operation of forces that he normally expects to control his reinforcements would have a greater effect on his behavior than would the perceived operation of forces not normally expected by him to be important determinants of his reinforcements. It might similarly be argued that internals and externals have become differentially sensitized to modes of control. Rotter (1966) proposed that individuals' expectancies for the locus of control, as reflected in their scores on the Internal-External scale, represent generalizations of their perceptions of past occurrences of control over the outcomes of their own behaviors. Some past occurrences of control over one's behavior can be assumed to be equivalent to past eliminations of one's behavioral freedoms. Locus of control could therefore be expected to affect the magnitude of reactance aroused in an individual by influencing the extent to which he feels free to perform a particular behavioral act. Brehm (1966) stressed quite strongly that the arousal of reactance is dependent on subjective feelings of freedom on the part of the individual toward the behavioral alternative that is eliminated or threatened with elimination. An internal may feel, for example, that fate, in the form of a parcel being lost or delayed in the mails, does not play a significant part in determining his reinforcements. Therefore, he would not really feel that the chance occurrence of an unfavorable event, which resulted in the elimination of an opportunity to perform a goal-directed act, is an abridgement of one of his personal freedoms. In the same way an external who does not feel that control is contingent upon his own acts or attributes would not consider the elimination of a behavioral opportunity a restriction of his own personal freedom if it were based on an act or attribute of his. Thus, it might be hypothesized that individuals attend more to conditions of control in the modes whose influence they perceive to be dominant or are more sensitive to cues in modes where they expect control to take place.

Alternatively, it is possible to maintain that the level of one's motivation to recover a behavioral freedom that has been eliminated is a function of the subjective probability of successfully recovering that freedom. In the case where the basis for the elimination lies within an area in which one normally expects to have control, it might be expected that a high level of reactance arousal would be observed. Such a state would be experienced by the internal when he feels that his own behaviors or attributes are responsible for the elimination of his freedom, and by the external when another's behavior or forces such as chance or fate are implicated. In each case, the individual would feel more confident about his chances of success when he is dealing with reinforcement-controlling forces from which he has become accustomed to receiving rewards.

It is important to note here that Rotter's (1966) original exposition of the concept of locus of control made no mention of a difference between internals and externals in the frequency with which they are rewarded in their environments. It is consistent with Rotter's conceptualization to maintain that internals and externals both expect to be rewarded at a rate which is independent of their perception of the locus of control but differ in their perceptions of the agents responsible for their receiving those rewards. Some investigators (e.g., Ransford, 1968) have referred to the external's orientation as a feeling of powerlessness, implying that externals receive fewer rewards than internals due to their perceptions that their own efforts lack efficacy. This position might lead one to expect that externals would exhibit chronically low levels or reactance arousal. However, recent work by Gurin, Gurin, Lao, and Beattie (1969), Forward and Williams (1970), and others has called into question this interpretation of locus of control. This recent work supports the more complex differentiation of internals and externals that we feel is explanatory of the results of the present experiment. Different assumptions would understandably lead to different explanations. However, it is felt that the explanation advanced by the present authors has the advantages of requiring fewer assumptions beyond Rotter, having been successful in predicting the results of the present experiment, and being consistent with the findings of the present experiment and those of Jones (1970) that externals exhibit at least as much reactance following the elimination of one of their behavioral freedoms as do internals, other things being equal.

It is also interesting that our position would imply the nonutility of Jones's and any other similar attempt to correlate reactance arousal with locus of control across a number of experimental threatment groups. Although Jones did not elaborate, it is possible that his effort was based on the assumption that externals would consistently show less reactance arousal than internals because they felt powerless or felt that they had few freedoms. Solar and Bruehl's (1971) finding that externals score higher on Machiavellianism than internals reinforces the notion that externals do not feel powerless but simply pursue rewards in different avenues from those preferred by internals.

In summary, the findings of the present experiment may be construed as a contribution toward the validation of both the reactance and locus of control constructs. In each case, they add to an already substantial body of evidence, yet they constitute a valuable increment. It has been shown once again that the elimination of a behavioral freedom elicits behavior whose antecedent conditions can reasonably be assumed to include the motivational state that Brehm has termed reactance. Further, the reactance effect has been shown to be sufficiently robust to allow the observation of variability associated with the personal characteristics of the individual whose freedom is eliminated. In addition, yet another set of situational conditions has been delineated in which locus of control is a powerful predictor of behavior.

Finally, we would like to state our belief that psychological reactance shows promise of being an important concept on a number of levels: as an empirical phenomenon, in light of the current outbreak of the continuing philosophical debate concerning the capability of the individual to preserve control over his own destiny, and, relatedly, as a manifestation of the reciprocality of the social influence process. It appears certain that research which will contribute to the explication of its antecedents, the process by which it occurs, and its consequences will continue to be carried out.

REFERENCES

Brehm, J. W. *A theory of psychological reactance.* New York: Academic Press, 1966.

Brehm, J. W., & Cole, A. Effect of a favor which reduces freedom. *Journal of Personality and Social Psychology,* 1966, *3,* 420-426.

Brehm, J. W., Stires, L. K., Sensenig, J., & Shaban, J. The attractiveness of an eliminated choice alternative. *Journal of Experimental Social Psychology,* 1966, *2,* 301-313.

Burton, B. L. Reactance to attempted reduction of degree of choice. Unpublished undergraduate honors thesis, Duke University, 1962. Cited in J. W. Brehm,

A theory of psychological reactance. New York: Academic Press, 1966. Pp. 55-57.

Coleman, J. S., Campbell, E. Q., Hobson, C. J., McPartland, J., Mood, A. M., Weinfeld, F. D., & York, R. L. *Equality of educational opportunity.* Washington, D.C.: U.S. Government Printing Office, 1966.

Forward, J. R., & Williams, J. R. Internal-external control and black militancy. *Journal of Social Issues,* 1970, *26*(1), 75-92.

Gore, P. M., & Rotter, J. B. A personality correlate of social action. *Journal of Personality,* 1963, *31,* 58-64.

Grabitz-Gniech, G. Some restrictive conditions for the occurrence of psychological reactance. *Journal of Personality and Social Psychology,* 1971, *19,* 188-196.

Gurin, P., Gurin, G., Lao, R. C., & Beattie, M. Internal-external control in the motivational dynamics of Negro youth. *Journal of Social Issues,* 1969, *25* (3), 29-53.

Hammock, T., & Brehm, J. W. The attractiveness of choice alternative when freedom to choose is eliminated by a social agent. *Journal of Personality,* 1966, *34,* 545-554.

Jones, R. A. Volunteering to help: The effects of choice, dependence, and anticipated dependence. *Journal of Personality and Social Psychology,* 1970, *14,* 121-129.

Jones, R. A. Modesty as a reactance phenomenon. Paper presented at the meeting of the Eastern Psychological Association, Boston, April 1972.

Petzel, T. P., & Gynther, M. D. Effects of internal-external locus of control and skill or chance instructional sets on task performance. *Journal of General Psychology,* 1970, *82,* 87-93.

Ransford, H. E. Isolation, powerlessness, and violence: A study of attitudes and participation in the Watts riot. *American Journal of Sociology,* 1968, *73,* 581-591.

Rotter, J. B. Generalized expectancies for internal versus external control of reinforcement. *Psychological Monographs,* 1966, *80*(1, Whole No. 609).

Seeman, M. Alienation and social learning in a reformatory. *American Journal of Sociology,* 1963, *69,* 270-289.

Seeman, M., & Evans, J. W. Alienation and learning in a hospital setting. *American Sociological Review,* 1962, *27,* 772-783.

Solar, D., & Bruehl, D. Machiavellianism and locus of control: Two conceptions of interpersonal power. *Psychological Reports,* 1971, *29,* 1079-1082.

Strickland, B. R. The prediction of social action from a dimension of internal-external control. *Journal of Social Psychology,* 1965, *66,* 353-358.

Watson, D., & Baumal, E. Effects of locus of control and expectation of future control upon present performances. *Journal of Personality and Social Psychology,* 1967, *6,* 212-215.

Winer, B. J. *Statistical principles in experimental design.* (2nd ed.) New York: McGraw-Hill, 1971.

3

HENRY L. KAPLOWITZ

Machiavellianism and Forming Impressions of Others

One by-product of our recent national immersion into the Watergate affair has been the renaissance of the term "Machiavellian." Regardless of their political orientation most newspaper columnists have seen fit to decry *Machiavellian* plots hatched by certain *Machiavellian* leaders. What exactly does this term connote? *Webster's New Collegiate Dictionary* defines Machiavellianism as "the political theory of Machiavelli; esp: the view that politics is amoral and that any means however unscrupulous can justifiably be used in achieving political power." What can be said psychologically about those who hold this point of view?

After some years of experience with departmental chairpersons, deans, and college presidents, Richard Christie (1970b), a social psychologist at Columbia University, realized that successful manipulators are not limited to the political arena. In fact, he hypothesized that it would be possible to predict a person's success at manipulating others by assessing their agreement on a paper-and-pencil attitude scale with statements derived from Machiavelli's writings. Ideally, the true Machiavellian would be someone who maintains a cool detachment in interpersonal relationships looking for the most rational strategy to advance his interests and not being concerned with accepted moral values. Even though his view of human nature may be quite cynical, he should not display any symptoms of psychopathology.

In developing the scale Christie culled Machiavelli's works for pertinent statements, rephrased them when necessary to make them more contemporaneous, and added some new statements congruent with Machiavelli's philosophy. In order to control for aquiescence response bias—the tendency for some people to agree with statements of opinion, regardless of content—a number of items were reversed. After testing the reliability of these items on different samples, Christie put together a 20-item scale with strong internal consistency. His only problem was that his scale strongly correlated in a negative direction with scales of social desirability. Thus a subject who agreed with Machiavelli would have to endorse notions that are considered undesirable in our society. Perhaps an experienced

Source: Prepared especially for this volume.

manipulator would be wary of describing his feelings in such unflattering terms.

To control for social desirability Christie used an ingenious technique adapted from Heineman's (1953) revision of the Taylor Manifest Anxiety Scale. Subjects were presented with three items and asked to choose which one they agreed with most and which one they agreed with least. The three items consisted of a statement relating to Machiavellianism, a nonrelated statement of equal social desirability, and a third buffer item that was high in social desirability if the other two were low, or low in social desirability if the other two were high.

An example is the following set of items (Christie, 1970a, p. 25):

1. People who talk about abstract problems usually don't know what they are talking about.
2. Anyone who completely trusts anyone else is asking for trouble.
3. It is essential for the functioning of a democracy that everyone vote.

Item 2 is in agreement with Machiavelli. Item 1 is not related to Machiavellianism but is matched with 2 for low social desirability, and item 3 is the buffer item of opposite social desirability—in this case it is high. Thus, a subject who is attempting to respond in the most favorable light will endorse the buffer item and then have to choose which of the equally undesirable statements he disagrees with most. The belief is that a person with a Machiavellian orientation will be more prone to reject the non-Machiavellian statement, since his biases are in accord with the Mach item.

This forced-choice form of the scale, which was Christie's fifth revision, is aptly called the Mach V Scale. It successfully managed to control for social desirability and acquiescence response bias, while maintaining acceptable levels of reliability. Then the paramount question of validity came up: Did the scale in fact successfully predict manipulative behavior?

Christie and Geis (1970a) reviewed 50 experiments involving the personality trait of Machiavellianism. They concluded that in almost all experimental situations that involved face to face interaction, provided a latitude for improvisation, and promoted some level of irrelevant affect, the outcome was dramatically in favor of the high Mach.

One interesting example of the high Mach's manipulative ability was evidenced in the "Ten Dollar Game" experiment by Christie and Geis (1970b). Three male subjects who scored high, medium, and low, respectively, on the Mach scale were seated around a table with 10 $1 bills on it. The experimenter instructed them that any two of the three participants could divide the money as soon as they reached a final agreement on the split. The third participant would be excluded from sharing the money.

While it is conceivable in this game for the bargaining to go on endlessly with the excluded participant offering a better deal to one of the partners in the hope of making a new agreement, it turned out that final agreements were reached relatively quickly. The high Machs were included in every pair of winners. The low Machs, on the other hand, were included in the winning coalitions less frequently than one would expect by chance alone.

In another study it was shown that when given the role of experimenter and allowed to deceive subjects taking a personality test, high Machs manipulated their subjects more often and in more creative ways than low Mach student experimenters did (Geis, Christie, & Nelson, 1970). Also, when induced to cheat in an experiment by a confederate and then accused by the experimenter of cheating, high Machs denied their cheating longer than low Machs. During their denial they looked their accuser directly in the eye for a greater proportion of the time than low Machs did (Exline, Thibaut, Rickey, & Gumpert, 1970).

It does appear, then, that subjects who score high on a scale of Machiavellian attitudes not only endorse the use of manipulation and deceit but are quite adept at applying these tactics. Christie and Lehmann (1970) factor analyzed the responses of 1,782 college students to the Mach IV and Mach V scales. In addition to a duplicity factor, which deals with statements relating to manipulative interpersonal tactics, they found two other factors, labeled "Affirmative Negativism" and "Disbelief in People." These factors relate to high scorers agreeing with negative statements about society and having a cynical view about the nature of man. It might be expected then, that the negative view of others expressed on the Mach scales would also show up in measures of person perception.

Harris (1966) found that high Machs consistently rated others with whom they had interacted on a difficult task more negatively than low Machs did. In his experiment, each subject had the opportunity to interact with one high Mach and one low Mach subject separately. After completing the task, subjects rated their partners on a scale consisting of 20 pairs of bipolar descriptions. Regardless of their partners' Mach orientation, high Machs rated them more negatively than low Machs did.

Inasmuch as Harris' experiment involved interaction on a difficult task, it is possible that the behavior of the high Machs brought out more negative reciprocating behaviors from their partners. Thus, the differences in perception that Harris found may have been due to changes in the object of perception (the partner) that were caused by the rater's behavior. In the study reported below, I attempted to control for the possibility that the subjects would influence the object of perception by using a standard stimulus—a film.

Another point of interest in this investigation was whether judgmental distortions by high and low Machs are related to certain qualities of the stimulus. Sherif and Hovland (1961) note that one's own attitude establishes an internal anchor which affects the judgment of a stimulus, when the attitude is salient. Perhaps the low Mach who endorses those items on the scale about the goodness of man uses this internal anchor of expectancy to judge the behaviors of others. Those social stimuli that fall around this anchor may be judged accurately, those slightly removed from the anchor may be assimilated, and those falling some distance from the low Mach's own attitude may be contrasted. Thus, a person behaving very positively may be perceived accurately whereas the judgment of a person behaving negatively may be distorted such that he is seen as extremely negative, while an ambiguous behavior may be assimilated to the positive side of the scale. Likewise, a high Mach may be expected to show a contrast distortion when judging social stimuli that fall on the positive side of the scale, assimilate ambiguous social stimuli, and accurately judge negative behaviors in keeping with his cynical attitudes.

In the research reported below, both positive and negative social stimuli were used to assess whether a contrast distortion would occur with extreme stimuli. It was hypothesized that: (1) low Machs would judge a negative stimulus as more negative than high Machs, and (2) high Machs would judge a positive stimulus as more positive than low Machs. Although no directional hypothesis was stated, it was decided to treat sex as an independent variable, inasmuch as Christie and Geis (1968) note that most of the behavioral correlates of Machiavellianism are found only among males.

METHOD

Design. A 2x2x2 factorial design was employed. The three factors were sex, Machiavellianism level (high or low), and stimulus film presented (positive or negative).

Subjects. The subjects were 44 males and 44 females who had scored above and below the median for their respective sex on the Mach V scale and were present in their general psychology classes at Kean College when the experiment was run.

Negative Film Condition. One group was shown a ten-minute film depicting a man at home in the morning and later at his office. At home, the character acts detached from his family while reading his paper, argues with his wife, and becomes enraged when he steps on his child's toy left by the door. The office sequence shows his interacting with his boss, secretary, and co-workers in a more neutral manner. This film was used in a study on impression formation by Hershkowitz (1954) in which the character had been rated as having traits that were primarily negative.

Positive Film Condition.   Another group was shown a ten-minute film which depicts the same man at home and in the office, but in this condition his behavior at home is attentive and affectionate. The neutral office sequence remains the same as in the negative film. Subjects in Hershkowitz's study rated the character in this film as having primarily positive traits.

After viewing the film the subjects wrote a description of the character and checked off traits they believed applied to him from a 43-item checklist developed by Hershkowitz from descriptions generated by other viewers. The checklist data were transformed into an average rating for each subject. This was done by having 20 judges rate each of the 43 items on a seven-point scale, the end points of which were labeled "extremely positive" and "extremely negative." The average value for each item was found, and an individual subject's score was attained by summing the value of each trait checked and dividing by the number of traits checked.

RESULTS

The mean value of traits assigned to the film stimulus in each condition is shown in Table 3.1. A $2 \times 2 \times 2$ analysis of variance was conducted on the data (see Table 3.2).

TABLE 3.1
Mean Value of Traits Assigned to Character in Positive and Negative Film

Group	Positive Film	Negative Film
High Machs		
Males	2.24	4.51
Females	2.84	4.68
Low Machs		
Males	2.99	5.03
Females	2.64	4.98

Note: 1 = extremely positive, 7 = extremely negative.
$n = 11$ per cell.

TABLE 3.2
Analysis of Variance on the Mean Value of Traits Assigned to Film Character

Source	df	MS	F
Film (A)	1	99.52	234.72**
Mach Level (B)	1	2.59	6.11*
Sex (C)	1	.19	<1
A X B	1	.10	<1
A X C	1	.02	<1
B X C	1	1.86	4.39*
A X B X C	1	.73	1.72
Error	80	.42	

*$p < .05$.
**$p < .001$.

The filmed stimuli used in this experiment clearly were perceived appropriately as being positive or negative, as evidenced by the significant main effect for film: $F = 234.72$, $p < .001$. The Machiavellian orientation of the subjects also significantly influenced their judgments of the character, $F = 6.11$, $p < .05$. The means associated with the Mach main effect indicate that, as hypothesized, high Machs perceived the character more positively than low Machs did.

A significant interaction was also found between Mach level and sex ($F = 4.39$, $p < .05$). An inspection of the cell means when both film conditions are combined shows that the difference between the mean ratings of high vs. low Mach males is .63, whereas the difference between high vs. low Mach females is only .05. This would indicate that the main effect for Mach level reported above is attributable primarily to the judgmental distortions of male subjects rather than females. This finding is consistent with Christie and Geis's (1968) conclusion that Mach scale scores rarely relate to behaviors of female subjects.

DISCUSSION

The differences in person perception reported here are contrary to the findings of Harris (1966) that high Machs consistently judge others more negatively, while low Machs are Pollyannas who distort their perceptions to fit their positive illusions. It is the belief of this writer that this difference is attributable to the extreme nature of the stimuli used in this study. It is also possible, however, that the usual effects of Machiavellianism only become evident in face-to-face interactions where the low Mach becomes emotionally involved with his co-actors, while the high Mach remains detached and cool. Christie and Geis (1970a) believe this to be a necessary condition for manipulative differences to occur. Perhaps the presentation of a live negative model that the subjects could interact with would produce a distortion that is the reverse of that reported here.

The most appropriate explanation for the findings reported appears to be assimilation-contrast theory (Sherif & Hovland), 1961). The own-attitudes of the high and low Mach form internal anchors against which social stimuli are judged. Very distant stimuli may be contrasted and judged to be further than their actual position on the scale. Thus, low Machs may perceive the negative film character as being extremely negative, while high Machs view his negative behaviors with more detachment.

In line with this theory a neutral stimulus would be assimilated toward the own-attitude of the judge. With regard to Machiavellianism, a high Mach would be prone to judge a neutral stimulus as being more negative, while a low Mach would judge the same stimulus as being more positive.

Thus, the differences in judgments found in the Harris study may be explained as assimilation effects.

The results of this study emphasize the need for a more thorough investigation of the effects of personality traits such as Machiavellianism on impression formation. It would appear that when a complete range of stimuli is judged, personality-related distortions usually found with neutral stimuli may be reversed when extreme stimuli are presented. The question of whether interaction of the Machs with the person to be judged produces results different from the judgment of filmed stimuli also remains to be answered.

REFERENCES

Christie, R. Scale construction. In R. Christie & F. Geis (Eds.), *Studies in Machiavellianism.* New York: Academic Press, 1970 (a).

Christie, R. Why Machiavelli? In R. Christie & F. Geis (Eds.), *Studies in Machiavellianism.* New York: Academic Press, 1970 (b).

Christie, R., & Geis, F. Some consequences of taking Machiavelli seriously. In E. F. Borgata & W. W. Lambert (Eds.), *Handbook of personality theory and research.* Chicago: Rand McNally, 1968.

Christie, R., & Geis, F. Overview of experimental research. In R. Christie & F. Geis (Eds.), *Studies in Machiavellianism.* New York: Academic Press, 1970 (a).

Christie, R., & Geis, F. The ten dollar game. In R. Christie & F. Geis (Eds.), *Studies in Machiavellianism.* New York: Academic Press, 1970 (b).

Christie, R., & Lehmann, S. The structure of Machiavellian orientations. In R. Christie & F. Geis (Eds.), *Studies in Machiavellianism.* New York: Academic Press, 1970.

Exline, R., Thibaut, J., Hickey, C., & Gumpert, P. Visual interaction in relation to Machiavellianism and an unethical act. In R. Christie & F. Geis (Eds.), *Studies in Machiavellianism.* New York: Academic Press, 1970.

Geis, F., Christie, R., & Nelson, C. In search of the Machiavel. In R. Christie & F. Geis (Eds.), *Studies in Machiavellianism.* New York: Academic Press, 1970.

Harris, T. Machiavellianism, judgment, independence and attitudes toward teammate in a cooperative judgment task (Doctoral dissertation, Columbia University, 1966). *Dissertation Abstracts,* 1967, *27,* 3935-A. (University Microfilms No. 67-5782)

Heineman, C. A forced-choice form of the Taylor anxiety Scale. *Journal of Counseling Psychology,* 1953, *17,* 447-454.

Hershkowitz, A. *Forming impressions of personality.* Unpublished master's thesis, The New School for Social Research, 1954.

Sherif, M., & Hovland, C. *Social judgment.* New Haven: Yale University Press, 1961.

4

RONALD GOLDMAN, MELVYN JAFFA, and STANLEY SCHACHTER

Yom Kippur, Air France, Dormitory Food, and the Eating Behavior of Obese and Normal Persons

Three field studies, designed to test the generalizability of experimental findings on the eating behavior of obese and normal Ss, are presented. These studies examine the relationship of weight deviation to fasting on Yom Kippur, toleration of institutional food, and adjustment to time-zone changes. Conforming to laboratory-generated expectations, fat Jews prove to be more likely to fast on Yom Kippur, fat students to be more intolerant of dormitory food, and fat fliers to more easily adjust to time-zone changes than do their normal counterparts.

The results of recent studies of the eating behavior of obese and normal subjects indicate that: (*a*) Physiological correlates of food deprivation such as gastric motility and hypoglycemia are directly related to eating and to the reported experience of hunger in normal-size subjects but unrelated in obese subjects (Schachter, Goldman, & Gordon, 1968; Stunkard & Koch, 1964); and (*b*) external or nonvisceral cues such as smell, taste, the sight of other people eating, the passage of time, etc., stimulate eating behavior in obese subjects to a greater extent than in normal subjects (Nisbett, 1968; Schachter & Gross, 1968). This paper will examine implications of these relationships in a variety of nonlaboratory settings—specifically, religious fasting, tolerance of institutional food, and the effects of time-zone changes on eating behavior.

WHO FASTS ON YOM KIPPUR?

Evidence indicates that for obese subjects the impulse to eat is triggered by an external, food-relevant cue. In contrast, the impulse to eat for normal individuals appears to be stimulated by the set of physiological cues consequent on food deprivation. Assuming that blocking this impulse by doing without food is an irritating or painful state, it should follow that

Source: Ronald Goldman, Melvyn Jaffa, and Stanley Schachter, "Yom Kippur, Air France, Dormitory Food, and the Eating Behavior of Obese and Normal Persons," *Journal of Personality and Social Psychology*, 1968, *10*, 117-123. Copyright 1968 by the American Psychological Association. Reprinted by permission.

These studies were supported by National Science Foundation Grant GS732.

in circumstances where food-relevant external cues are sparse, or, where the individual can successfully distract himself from such external cues, the obese person should have a considerably easier time fasting or doing without food than should normal size persons. The Schachter and Gross (1968) findings that the obese rarely eat breakfast or, on weekends, lunch can be construed as consistent with this expectation.

In order to test directly this expectation and some of its corollaries the relationship of overweight to fasting on Yom Kippur was studied. Yom Kippur, the Jewish Day of Atonement, is the most sacred of Jewish holy days and the only one for which fasting is commanded by Biblical Law. The traditional Jew begins his fast on the evening of Yom Kippur and does without food or water for 24 hours. Except when sleeping, he spends virtually all of his time in prayer in a synagogue, a physical environment notoriously barren of graven images, let alone food-related cues; a ritual conducted in Aramaic and Hebrew whose chief direct reference to food is passing mention of a scapegoat. Almost certainly informal conversations within the synagogue at this time must to some degree be concerned with the fast; but the ritual proper and the physical surroundings are virtually devoid of food-relevant cues.

Among contemporary Jews, observance of Yom Kippur ranges from those who meticulously adhere to every detail described to those who are only vaguely aware that there is such a day. Between these extremes lies every variation of token or partial observance—people who will spend only an hour or two in synagogue, Jews who do without regular meals but sneak half a sandwich and a sip of celery tonic, and so on.

Given this characterization of Yom Kippur, if these speculations about obesity and fasting are correct, it should follow among Jews for whom the day has any meaning that (a) Fat Jews will be more likely to fast than normally built Jews; (b) the difficulty of fasting will, for obese Jews, depend upon the abundance of food-related cues in their immediate environment, while for normal Jews these two variables will be unrelated. Thus it should be anticipated that fat, fasting Jews who spend a great deal of time in synagogue will suffer less from fasting than fat, fasting Jews who spend little time in synagogue and there will be no such relationship for normal, fasting Jews. Plausibly, there will be far fewer food-related cues in the synagogue than on the street or at home. The likelihood, therefore, that the impulse to eat will be triggered is greater out of synagogue than in. For normal Jews, this distinction is of less importance. In or out of synagogue, stomach pangs are still stomach pangs.

In order to test these expectations, a few days after Yom Kippur, 1965, a questionnaire was administered to all of the students in several classes in introductory social science and psychology at the City University of New

York and at New York University. The questionnaire was anonymous and designed to learn from Jewish respondents their sex, height, and weight, whether or not they had fasted on Yom Kippur, how unpleasant they had found the fast, and a variety of other information relevant to how religious they were and their experiences during Yom Kippur.

Since these hypotheses are irrelevant to Jews who are totally irreligious and only dimly aware of the holiday and its proscriptions, our sample for analysis is limited to those Jews who gave some indication of being religious. The criterion is simple and derives from answers to the question, "Approximately how many times have you been to synagogue in the last year?" Any Jew who had been to synagogue at least once during the past year, for some reason other than a wedding or a bar mitzvah, was considered a religious Jew. Of a total of 748 questionnaires, 456 were from Jewish respondents (247 men, 209 women). Of these, 296 respondents (160 men, 136 women) are, by this criterion, religious Jews.[1]

The basic data on obesity and fasting are presented in Table 4.1. Whether or not a subject fasted was determined by his answer to the question, "Did you attempt to fast last Wednesday for the Yom Kippur holiday?" Anyone who answered "Yes" is classified as a faster. The Metropolitan Life Insurance Company (1959) norms for height and weight were used to calculate weight deviations. Subjects were classified as obese if their weight deviations fell among the top 20% of all subjects of their own sex, a cutoff point used in the three studies described in this paper. In this sample, any male who was 15.4% overweight or more is classified as obese. For females, a 20% cutoff point includes girls who, from their answers to the questions about weight and height, are as little as 4.8% overweight. Despite the fact that one would hardly consider a woman, truly of this slight weight deviation, as obese, we have, for consistency's sake, employed the 20% cutoff point for both males and females in all of the studies described in this paper. Not wishing to debate the pros and cons of this procedure we note simply that in the two studies in this paper involving females, employing a higher cutoff point for females tends to strengthen the main effects.

The data in Table 4.1 are clearly consistent with expectations. Among fat religious Jews 83.1% fasted on Yum Kippur. In comparison, 68.8% of

TABLE 4.1
Obesity and Fasting on Yom Kippur

	Obese Jews	Normal Jews
Fasters	49	163
Non-fasters	10	74

Note: $x^2 = 4.75$, $p < .05$.

normal Jews fasted. Obesity does play a part in determining who fasts on Yom Kippur.[2]

Let us examine next the impact of those factors presumed to differentially affect the difficulty of fasting for normal and obese subjects. In keeping with our general scheme, we have assumed that the presence or absence of food-relevant cues directly affects the ease with which an obese person fasts and has less impact on a normal person. If one accepts our characterization of the synagogue on Yom Kippur as devoid of food-related cues, it should be anticipated that for obese fasters answers to the question "For how many hours did you attend religious services this Yom Kippur?" will be negatively related to ratings of fasting unpleasantness as measured by a scale headed, "Insofar as you did fast this Yom Kippur, how unpleasant an experience was it?" The more hours in synagogue, the less exposure to food-relevant cues and the less unpleasant should fasting be for the externally controlled obese person. For the normal faster, attuned to his viscera, there should be little relationship.

The data are consistent with these expectations. For the obese, the correlation between hours in synagogue and unpleasantness is —.50. For normals, the correlation is only —.18. Testing the difference between these correlations, $z = 2.19$, which is significant at the 0.3 level. For the obese the more time in synagogue the less of an ordeal is fasting; for normals, hours in synagogue have little to do with the difficulty of the fast.

WHO EATS DORMITORY FOOD?

The taste or quality of food can be considered an external determinant of eating behavior. As such, food quality should have more of an effect on obese than on nonobese eaters. In an experiment designed to test this hypothesis Nisbett (1968) found that when the available food was generally rated as good, obese subjects ate more than did normals, who ate more than did skinny subjects. When the food was considered bad, this trend tended to reverse with skinny subjects eating more than either normal or obese subjects. Generalizing from these findings, it seems reasonable to assume that taste will not only have an effect on how much fat, as compared with normal, subjects eat, but on where they eat. It seems a plausible guess that the obese will be more drawn to good restaurants and more repelled by bad ones than with normal subjects.

At Columbia, students have the option of eating in the university dining halls or in any of the swarm of more or less exotic restaurants and delicatessens that surround this metropolitan campus. It is probably small surprise to the reader to learn that typical campus opinion of dormitory food is unfavorable. Student-conducted surveys document widespread dissatisfaction with the university dining halls, enumerating complaints about cold food, poor service, stale desserts, etc., etc. (University Dormitory Council, 1964).

If an undergraduate elects to eat in a dormitory dining hall, he may if he chooses join a prepay food plan at the beginning of the school year. For $500 he purchases a meal contract which entitles him to a weekly meal ticket worth $16.25 with which he can pay for food at the university dining hall or snack bar. Anytime after November 1, the student may cancel his food contract by paying a penalty of $15, and the remainder of his money is refunded. If general campus opinion of dormitory food is at all realistically based, those for whom taste or food quality is most important should be most likely to discontinue their food contracts. Obese students should be more likely to drop out of the food plan than normal students.

The sample for this study is the entire body of freshmen entering Columbia in 1965 who signed up for the food plan on first entering the college. There were 698 students in this freshman class, 211 of whom signed food contracts. This sample is limited to freshmen first because they constitute the bulk of meal-plan subscribers and second because the noncommuters among them are required to live in dormitories during their entire first academic year. Thus, their decision to leave the plan could not be affected by moving out of the dormitories as it could for upperclassmen. All freshmen fraternity pledges (five obese and 16 normal students) are also eliminated from the sample, for pledges automatically, and without penalty, switch to eating at their fraternity houses when they pledge.

Weight deviations were computed from records in the Dean of Students' office using the Metropolitan Life Insurance Company (1959) norms.[3] As in the other studies in this report, the top 20% of the weight-deviation distribution is classified as obese. For this sample, this includes all students who were 11.3% overweight or more.

TABLE 4.2
Relationship of Obesity to Renewing Meal Contracts

	Obese	Normal
Dropped meal contract	32	100
Renewed meal contract	5	49

Note: $x^2 = 5.40$, $p < .05$.

The basic data are presented in Table 4.2 where it can be seen that expectancies are confirmed. Some 86.5% of fat freshmen let their contracts expire as compared with the 67.1% of normal students who dropped out of the meal plan. Obesity does, to some extent, predict who chooses to subsist on institutional food.

ADJUSTING TO TIME ZONE CHANGES

There are occasions when there is a marked discrepancy or opposition between external cues relevant to eating and the internal, physiological correlates of food deprivation or satiation, for example, being served a gorgeous dessert after consumption of a mammoth meal or confronted with some nauseating, rudely prepared concoction after a period of starvation. Our line of thought leads to the expectation that the obese will be relatively more affected by the external cue than will the normal subject, that is, he will eat more of the dessert and less of the mess. Studies by Hashim and Van Itallie (1965) and Nisbett (1968) do, in good part, support these expectations.

A more subtle instance of this opposition of cues is represented by the Schachter and Gross (1968) study in which, by means of doctored clocks, subjects were manipulated into believing that the time was later or earlier than the true time. If we assume that the intensity of gastric motility, etc., is a function of true time (i.e., hours since last meal), then this clock manipulation can create circumstances in which external and internal cues are, to some degree, in opposition. For example, a subject may be under the clock-produced impression that it is after his usual dinner time while in actuality it is before this time. In such circumstances, Schachter and Gross found that the manipulated external cue almost entirely determined how much obese subjects ate and did not similarly affect normal subjects.

Long-distance East-West travel creates a state which is, in a way, a real life analogue of this time-manipulation experiment. Given time-zone changes, the traveler, biologically more than ready to eat, may arrive at his destination at a local time still hours away from routine eating times and from the barrage of food-related external cues invariably synchronized with culturally routinized meal times. A jet flight leaving Paris at 12:00 noon requires 8 hours to reach New York, where on arrival the local time is 2:00 P.M. If the passenger has eaten an early lunch on the plane and no dinner, he is, on arrival, physiologically more than ready for a full meal but still 4 or 5 hours away from local dinner hours. Whatever mode he chooses of coping with his situation, eating a full meal on arrival, snacking, or putting off a meal until local dinner time, his situation is for a time an uncomfortable one, characterized by a marked discrepancy between his physiological state and locally acceptable eating hours and he must, in short order, adjust to an entirely new eating schedule. A prediction is by no means unequivocal, but from the variety of facts already presented it seems an intuitively sound guess that the obese will have an easier time in this situation than will normal travelers.

Thanks to the good offices of the Medical Department of Air France we have had access to data which to some extent permit evaluation of this hypothesis. Concerned with medical and psychological effects of time-zone changes, Air France studied a sample of flight crew members assigned to transatlantic routes (Lavernhe, Lafontaine, & Laplane, 1965). The subjects of this inquiry were 194 male and 42 female personnel regularly flying the Paris-New York and Paris-Montreal routes. On the East to West journey these flights are scheduled to leave Paris roughly around noon, French time, fly for approximately 8 hours, and land in North America sometime in the early afternoon, Eastern time. Flight crew members eat lunch shortly after takeoff and, being occupied with landing preparations and servicing passenger needs, are not served another meal during the flight. They land in North America some 7 hours after their last

FIGURE 4.1
Relationship of Weight Deviation to Complaining about the Effects of Time-Zone Changes on Eating

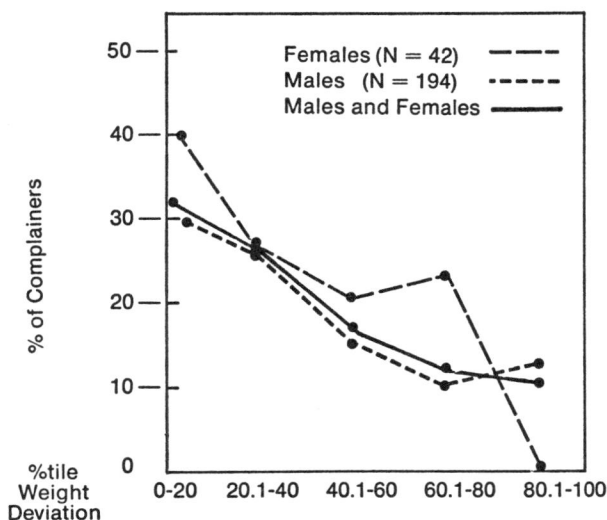

Range of Weight Deviation:
Males (−20.7% to −9.2%)(−9.1% to −3.4%) (−3.1% to +1.7%) (+1.9% to 9.0%) (+9.8% to +29.2%)
Females (−21.5% to −12.5%) (−10.7% to 7.5%) (−6.9% to −4.1%) (−3.8% to 0.5%) (+.06% to +11.4%)

meal at a time that is generally past the local lunch hour and well before local dinner time.

The Air France study was *not* directly concerned with reports of hunger or eating behavior, but the investigators systematically noted all individuals who volunteered that they "suffered from the discordance between their physiological state and meal time in America."[4] This coding appears to apply chiefly to fliers who complain about the fact that they either do without food or make do with a snack until local dinner time.

The basic data are presented in Figure 4.1, which plots the proportion of complainers at each quintile of the weight-deviation distribution of this group of flying personnel. Because of the stringent physical requirements involved in air crew selection there are, of course, relatively few really obese people in this sample. Despite this fact, it is evident that there is a consistent relation between the extent of weight deviation and the likelihood of spontaneously mentioning difficulties in adjusting to the discrepancy between physiological state and local meal times. The more overweight the French flier, the less likely he is to be troubled by this discrepancy. The linear nature of the relationship is consistent with the results of Nisbett's (1968) experiment. Comparing groups of extremely skinny, fat, and normal subjects, Nisbett demonstrated that the impact of the external cue, taste, on eating behavior was a direct function of the degree of overweight.

Testing the significance of the differences in these data by the procedure employed in the two previous studies, we find $x^2 = 2.93$ ($p < .10$) for the heaviest quintile of French fliers compared with the remainder of the sample. If we compare all of those flying personnel who are overweight (.1% to 29.9 % overweight) with all of those who are not overweight (0% to 21.5% underweight) the data distribute as in Table 4.3, where it can be seen that 11.9% of the overweight complain as compared with 25.2% of the nonoverweight ($x^2 = 6.52$, $p < .02$). Apparently fatter, flying Frenchmen are less likely to be troubled by the effects of time changes on eating.

TABLE 4.3
Relationship of Weight Deviation to Complaining about the Effects of Time-Zone Changes on Eating Beharior

	Subjects who are:	
Subjects who:	Overweight	Not overweight
Complain	12	34
Don't complain	89	101

Note: $x^2 = 6.52$, $p < .02$.

DISCUSSION

From these three studies we know the following facts: (a) Fat Jews are more likely to fast on Yom Kippur than normal Jews; (b) for fat, fasting Jews there is an inverse relationship between the "unpleasantness" of fasting and the number of hours spent in synagogue on Yom Kippur. There is no such relationship for normally built Jews who fast; (c) fat freshmen are more likely to drop university meal plan contracts than are normal freshmen; (d) fatter French fliers are less likely to be troubled by the effects of time-zone changes on eating routine than are thinner French fliers.

We have chosen to interpret these facts in terms of a conceptual scheme involving assumptions about the relationship between weight deviation and the relative potency of external and internal stimulants to eating. These three studies were designed to test specific implications of this schema in appropriate field settings. As with any field research, alternative explanations of these findings are legion and, within the context of any specific study, impossible to overrule. Except for the most obvious alternatives, we have chosen to avoid the tedium of listing and feebly feuding with more or less plausible alternative interpretations—a procedure whose chief virtue would be the demonstration that we are aware of our interpretive problems even if we can do nothing about them.

There is, however, one alternative interpretation cogent not only to the present studies but to some of the findings in our various laboratory experiments. Two of these field studies, Yom Kippur and Air France, are concerned with some aspect of fasting behavior and the ease with which the obese can do without food[5]—a finding deriving from and related to the laboratory demonstration that manipulated food deprivation has no effect on the eating of the obese. Rather than the interpretation we have elected, which rests on the assumption that the obese do not label the physiological correlates of food deprivation as hunger, one could suggest that the obese are, after all, overweight, that they have large stores of body fat and, within the time limits of these studies, that they actually do not experience such states as gastric motility and hypoglycemia. Though a plausible hypothesis, the available evidence suggests that for gastric motility, at least, the hypothesis is not correct. The Stunkard and Koch (1964) study of gastric contractions and self-reports of hunger was in essence conducted under fasting conditions. Subjects ate their regular dinners, ate no breakfast, and at 9:00 A.M. came to the laboratory where, having swallowed a gastric balloon, they remained for 4 hours. During this period the extent of gastric motility was much the same for obese and normal subjects. The obese simply did not coordinate the statement, "I feel hungry" with periods of gastric motility while normal subjects did.[6]

One final point in defense of our general schema. It is the case that nonobvious derivations do plausibly follow from this formulation of the interrelationships of external and internal determinants of eating behavior. For example, the negative correlation between hours in synagogue and the unpleasantness of fasting for the obese and the lack of such correlation for normal subjects must follow from this set of ideas and we can conceive of no alternative conceptualization of this entire body of data which would lead to this prediction. In any case, whatever the eventual interpretation of the three studies, if one permutes these facts, the implications are unassailable: fasting, fat, French freshmen fly farther for fine food.

REFERENCES

Brown, J. D., & Pulsifer, D. H. Outpatient starvation in normal and obese subjects. *Aerospace Medicine,* March 1965, 267-269.

Duncan, G., Jinson, W., Fraser, R., & Christori, F. Correction and control of intractable obesity. *Journal of the American Medical Association,* 1962, *181,* 309-312.

Hashim, S. A., & Van Itallie, T. B. Studies on normal and obese subjects with a monitored food dispensing device. *Annals of the New York Academy of Sciences,* 1965, *131,* 654-661.

Lavernhe, J., Lafontaine, E., & Laplane, R. An investigation on the subjective effects of time changes on flying staff in civil aviation. Air France Medical Department paper delivered before the Aerospace Medical Association, April, 1965. (Mimeo)

Metropolitan Life Insurance Company. New weight standards for men and women. *Statistical Bulletin,* 1959, *40,* 1-4.

Nisbett, R. E. Taste, deprivation, and weight determinants of eating behavior. *Journal of Personality and Social Psychology,* 1968, *10,* 107-116.

Schachter, S., Goldman, R., & Gordon, A. The effects of fear, food deprivation, and obesity on eating. *Journal of Personality and Social Psychology,* 1968, *10,* 91-97.

Schachter, S., & Gross, L. Manipulated time and eating behavior. *Journal of Personality and Social Psychology,* 1968, *10,* 98-106.

Stunkard, A., & Koch, C. The interpretation of gastric motility: I. Apparent bias in the report of hunger by obese persons. *Archives of General Psychiatry,* 1964, *11,* 74-82.

University Dormitory Council. Report on food services at Columbia University. *Columbia Spectator,* March 9, 1964, p. 1.

NOTES

1. Included in this group of religious Jews are 25 respondents who had not been to synagogue during the past year but who had fasted on Yom Kippur. In puzzling

over just how to classify such respondents, it seemed to us that undertaking the Yom Kippur fast was, at least, as good an indication of religiousness as attending synagogue once or twice during the year. These non-synagogue-going fasters, are, then, classified as religious. It should be noted, however, that the main effects of the study (and the statistical levels of confidence involved) remain much the same whether or not this subgroup is treated as religious.

2. There is a tendency for obese respondents to be slightly more religious than normal subjects, that is, to attend synagogue slightly more during the year. Though this is a nonsignificant difference, it is troubling, for obviously the more religious are more likely to fast. In order to check on this alternative interpretation, the proportion of fasters among obese and normal respondents of various degrees of religiosity (as measured by the amount of synagogue going) was compared. At every point of comparison from slightly religious (one or two visits to synagogue) to extremely religious (20 or more visits), the obese are more likely to fast.

3. For 25 of the 211 freshmen who signed food contracts, the existing records were incomplete or unavailable so that it was impossible to determine weight deviation. Table 4.2 includes the 186 cases for whom the data are complete.

4. J. Lavernhe and E. Lafontaine, personal communication, 1966.

5. Other investigators who have noted this phemomenon in various contexts are Brown and Pulsifer (1965) and Duncan, Jinson, Fraser, and Christori (1962).

6. One final datum from our own studies also suggests that this alternative interpretation is incorrect. If it is correct that the intensity of the physiological correlates of food deprivation is, within time limits, less for the obese than for normal subjects it should follow that, under any conditions, obese subjects will find it easier to fast. The data on the relation of hours in synagogue to self-ratings of fasting difficulty in the Yom Kippur study indicate, however, that this is not the case. Obese subjects who spend most of the day in synagogue (8 or more hours) do suffer considerably less from fasting than do normal subjects who spend the same amount of time in synagogue. However, among those who spend little time in synagogue (2 hours or less), the obese report more difficulty with the fast than do normals. It would appear that the obese have an easier time doing without food than do normals in the absence of external, food-relevant cues but a more difficult time in the presence of such cues.

CHAPTER IX

Communication:
Verbal and Nonverbal

1. Joshua A. Fishman, "Interactional Sociolinguistics: Micro and Macro"
2. Jonathan C. Finkelstein, "The Experimenter Expectancy Effect: Cues and Clues"
3. Aaron Hershkowitz, "Naturalistic Observations on Chronically Hospitalized Patients: I. The Effects of 'Strangers'"
4. Michael G. Efran and J. Allan Cheyne, "Affective Concomitants of the Invasion of Shared Space: Behavioral, Physiological, and Verbal Indicators"

The Klan, deciding to harass Mr. Levine, who ran a tailor shop in a hamlet in Mississippi, told the school children to stand in front of the shop every afternoon and shout, *"Yid, Yid!"*

The children set to their work with enthusiasm. Out came Mr. Levine. "Thank you, thank you," he said. "If you'll come back and do that tomorrow, I'll give each of you a dime."

The next day the children came back—with reinforcements; and after the hooting began, Mr. Levine distributed dimes to each *kleine* Klanner.

The following day—more children, more catcalls. But this time Mr. Levine only distributed nickels.

On the morrow the children returned, but got not a penny. "What's the idea?" they wanted to know.

396

"I'm sorry, kids, but I can't afford any more advertising,"
sighed Mr. Levine.
The children never came back.

In the days of the Tsar, Koplinski fell off a bridge and
proceeded to drown—threshing around and shouting for
help at the top of his lungs.
Two Tsarist policemen heard his cries and ran to the rail,
but when they saw it was a Jew in the water, they simply
laughed.
"Help! Help!" cried Koplinski. "I'm drowning!"
"So drown, *Zhid* (*Yid*)!"
And just as Koplinski started under for the proverbial
third time, he had an inspiration: "Down with the Tsar!" he
shouted.
At once, the policemen jumped into the water, pulled
Koplinski out, and arrested him for sedition.

From The Joys of Yiddish by Leo Rosten.
Copyright © 1968 by Leo Rosten.
Used with permission of McGraw-Hill Book Company.

Commentary

Communication is the process which enables man to be a
social being. It is through the process of communication that
man influences others and is influenced by others. The selections in this chapter explore the various channels of communication—verbal and nonverbal—that play a role in social interaction.

The first selection ("Interactional Sociolinguistics: Micro and
Macro," by Fishman) indicates the usefulness of the concepts
and approaches of sociolinguistics for an understanding of the
interdependence of the characteristics of language and the interpersonal context within which it is used.

While the first selection focuses on aspects of verbal communication, the remaining selections deal with nonverbal communication. The growing interest in nonverbal communication
as a topic of study is evidenced by the increasing number of
publications, both scholarly and popular, that are appearing
(Harrison, Cohen, Crouch, Genova, & Steinberg, 1972). Why
study nonverbal communication? One reason is that it can play

an important role in social interaction due to the characteristics that distinguish it from verbal communication. Although there may be as many specific reasons for studying nonverbal communication as there are investigators, a brief mention of some distinctive features of nonverbal communication can point up its potential interest for the student of social behavior. Verbal communication in social interaction leaves relatively little room for ambiguity, due to the high degree of shared meaning which language provides for its users. On the other hand, various dimensions of nonverbal communication, because they do not have explicitly stated shared meanings, allow them to be used when the sender or receiver of a communication wants to maintain ambiguity of intent, to be dissociated completely from the message, or to take the focus off the message itself. These considerations may play a role in potentially embarrassing situations or those in which explicit communication of intent may be threatening. Another important use of nonverbal communication is in situations where verbal communication is not physically feasible. An example of the latter is given by Goffman (1971) in discussing how vehicles and pedestrians avoid collisions:

By the term "externalization," or "body gloss," I refer to the process whereby an individual pointedly uses over-all body gesture to make otherwise unavailable facts about his situation gleanable. Thus, in driving and walking the individual conducts himself—or rather his vehicular shell—so that the direction, rate, and resoluteness of his proposed course will be readable. In ethological terms, he provides an "intention display." By providing this gestural prefigurement and committing himself to what it foretells, the individual makes himself into something that others can read and predict from; by employing this device at proper strategic junctures—ones where his indicated course will be perceived as a promise or warning or threat but not as a challenge—he becomes something to which they can adapt without loss of self-respect (p. 11).

Nonverbal communication can be divided into the following three main dimensions or channels:

1. *Paralanguage.* This refers to various nonlexical features of vocal expression, such as pitch, hesitations, stress, rate, and nonfluencies.
2. *Proxemics.* This refers to the use of space, location, and interpersonal distance.

3. *Body movement, or kinesics.* This refers to movement of hands, head, feet, or other parts of the body, as well as postural changes involving the whole body. Facial expression and eye contact can also be included under the broad category of body movement, although these are often discussed separately because they have each developed research traditions of their own.

The last three readings in this chapter tap these three main dimensions of nonverbal communication. Selection 2 ("The Experimenter Expectancy Effect: Cues and Clues," by Finkelstein) describes how nonverbal cues can play a role in an experimenter's communication to his subjects of his expectancies concerning the outcome of his experiment. If the researcher's expectancies become salient to his subjects, a potential source of error is introduced into his experiment, and he cannot be sure that the results are due to the effects of his treatments or were obtained because subjects behaved in a manner that would help confirm his hypothesis. The phenomenon of experimenter expectancy effects has been studied in detail by Rosenthal (1963). Finkelstein's article surveys the evidence for, and provides a useful conceptualization of, the role of nonverbal factors—especially paralanguage—in the mediation of experimenter expectancies.

The third selection in this chapter used the method of naturalistic observation to learn about the accommodative strategies used by psychiatric patients in response to strangers entering their dayroom. In Selection 3 ("Naturalistic Observations on Chronically Hospitalized Patients: I. The Effects of 'Strangers'") Aaron Hershkowitz reports observing systematic changes in the proxemic behaviors of the patients over time which could be understood in terms of their increasing accommodation to the presence of strangers (the observers) in their midst. When observers first entered the dayroom, patients invariably headed toward a "way station" such as the ping-pong table. As the patients got used to the presence of the strangers, their way-station behaviors gradually decreased. This study demonstrates the possibility of making meaningful inferences about behavior based upon systematic observations of ongoing behavior in field settings.

The final selection in this chapter ("Affective Concomitants of the Invasion of Shared Space," by Efran and Cheyne) reports an experiment designed to test the hypothesis that intrusion into the personal space of another would result in the arousal of unpleasant affect in the intruder. Measures of various kinesic behaviors (such as mouth gestures), as well as heart rate and mood, were obtained from subjects who had to walk between two people who were conversing, or walked past the conversants, or did not meet any people en route from one part of the lab to the other. With the exception of the heart rate measure, the findings generally supported the hypothesis.

REFERENCES

Goffman, E. *Relations in Public: Microstudies of the Public Order.* New York: Basic Books, 1971.

Harrison, R. P., Cohen, A. A., Crouch, W. W., Genova, B. K. L., & Steinberg, M. The nonverbal communication literature. *The Journal of Communication,* 1972, *22,* 460-476.

Rosenthal, R. On the social psychology of the psychological experiment: The experimenter's hypothesis as unintended determinant of experimental results. *American Scientist,* 1963, *51,* 268-283.

1

JOSHUA A. FISHMAN

Interactional Sociolinguistics: Micro and Macro

Boss	Carmen, do you have a minute?
Secretary	Yes, Mr. Gonzalez.
Boss	I have a letter to dictate to you.
Secretary	Fine, Let me get my pen and pad. I'll be right back.
Boss	Okay.
Secretary	Okay.
Boss	Okay, this is addressed to Mr. William Bolger.
Secretary	That's B-o-r-g-e-r?
Boss	B-o-l
Secretary	Oh, oh, I see.
Boss	Okay. His address is in the files.
Secretary	Okay.
Boss	Okay. Dear Bill, Many thanks for telling me about your work with the Science Research Project. The information you gave me ought to prove most helpful.
Secretary	That was "The information you gave me ought to prove most helpful?"
Boss	Correct.
Secretary	Okay.
Boss	Okay, ah. I very much appreciate the time you gave me. Never mind, strike that out. Ah, enclosed are two of the forms that you let me borrow. I'll be sending back the data sheets very soon. Thanks again, I hope that your hospital stay will be as pleasant as possible and that your back will be soon in top shape. Will soon be in top shape. It was nice seeing you again. Sincerely, Louis Gonzalez.
Secretary	Do you have the enclosures for the letter, Mr. Gonzalez?
Boss	Oh yes, here they are.
Secretary	Okay.
Boss	Ah, this man William Bolger got his organization to contribute a lot of money to the Puerto Rican parade. He's very much for it. Tú fuiste a la parada? (Did you go to the parade?)

Source: From Joshua A. Fishman, *The Sociology of Language* (Rowley, Mass.: Newbury House Publishers, 1972), pp. 29-54. Reprinted with permission from Newbury House Publishers Inc., Rowley, Massachusetts 01969.

Secretary   Sí, yo fuí.
             (Yes, I went.)
Boss   ¿Sí?
             (Yes?)
Secretary   Uh huh.
Boss   ¿Y ćomo te estuvo?
             (And how did you like it?)
Secretary   Ay, lo más bonita.
             (Oh, very pretty.)
Boss   Sí, porque yo fuí y yo nunca había participado en la parada y
             (Yes, because I went and I had never participated in the parade and

             este año me dió curiosidad por ir a ver como era y estuvo eso
             this year I became curious to go and see how it was and that was

             fenómeno. Fuí con mi señora y con mis nenes y a ellos tambíen
             a phenomenon. I went with my wife and my children and they

             le gustó mucho. Eh, y tuve día bien agradable. Ahora lo que
             also liked it very much. And I had a pleasant day. Now

             me moldesta a mi es que las personas cuando viene una cosa así,
             what bothers me is that people when something like this comes along,

             la parada Puertorriqueña o la fiesta de San Juan, corren de la
             the Puerto Rican parade, or the festival of San Juan they run from

             casa a participar porque es una actividad festiva, alegre, y sin
             the house to participate because it is a festive activity, happy, and

             embargo, cuando tienen que ir a la iglesia, o la misa para pedirle . . .
             then, when they have to go to church or to mass, to ask . . .)
Secretary   (Laughter)
Boss   A Diós entonce no van.
             (God then they don't go.)
Secretary   Sí, entonces no van.
             (Yes, then they don't go.)
Boss   Pero, así es la vida, caramba.
             (But that's life, you know.) Do you think that you could get this letter
             out today?
Secretary   Oh yes, I'll have it this afternoon for you.
Boss   Okay, good, fine then.
Secretary   Okay.
Boss   Okay.

If we carefully consider the above conversation it becomes evident that it
reveals considerable internal variation. Speaker A does not always speak
in the same way nor does his interlocutor, Speaker B. Were it possible for
us to listen to the original tapes of this conversation, several *kinds* of variation within each of them would become evident to us: variations in speed

of speaking, variations in the extent to which Spanish phonology creeps into English discourse and vice versa, variations in the extent to which English phonology creeps into the Spanish discourse, etc. However, even from the conventionally (orthographically) rendered transcription just presented one kind of variation remains exceedingly clear: that from Spanish to English or from English to Spanish for each speaker. It is precisely because bilingual code switching is often more noticeable than other kinds of sociolinguistic variation that bilingualism is so commonly examined in sociolinguistic theory and research. However, the concepts and findings that derive from such examinations must be provocative and illuminating for the sociology of language more generally. And, indeed, that *is* the case, for the societal patterning of bilingual interaction is merely an instance (hopefully, a more obvious and, therefore, pedagogically useful instance) of the vastly more general phenomenon of societal patterning of variation in verbal interaction.

How shall we describe or measure the phenomenon of interest to us: societal patterning of variation in verbal interaction? Usefully accurate description or measurement is certainly the basic problem of every scientific field of endeavor. Most of mankind has constantly been immersed in a veritable ocean of crosscurrents of talk. Nevertheless, as with most other aspects of everyday social behavior, it is only in very recent days that man has begun to recognize the latent order and regularity in the manifest chaos of verbal interaction that surrounds him.

HOW SHOULD TALK BE DESCRIBED CONTEXTUALLY?

How should "talk" be contextually described in order to best reveal or discover its social systemization (assuming that its "basic" linguistic description is already available)? Let us begin with some passages of actual "talk," making sure to preserve its verbatim form (preferably, by utilizing sensitive audio and visual recording equipment) rather than merely summarizing the content of such talk. The smallest sociolinguistic unit that will be of interest to us is a *speech act:* a joke, an interjection, an opening remark (Schegloff, 1968), a question, in general—a segment of talk that is also societally recognizable and reoccurring. Speech acts are normally parts of somewhat larger *speech events,* such as conversations, introductions, lectures, prayers, arguments, etc. (Hymes, 1967), which, of course, must also be societally recognizable and reoccurring.

If we note that a switch has occurred from variety *a* to variety *b*—perhaps from a kind of Spanish to a kind of English, or from more formal English to less formal English, or from regionally neutral, informal Spanish to Jíbaro (rural) informal Spanish—the first question that presents itself is whether one variety tends to be used (or used more often) in certain kinds of speech acts or events, whereas the other tends to be used (or used more often) in others. Thus, were we aware of the speech acts recognized by bilingual Puerto Rican youngsters in New York, we might venture to explain a switch such as the following:

First Girl	Yes, and don't tell me that the United States is the only one that has been able to in Puerto Rico. . . .
Boy	Okay so you have a couple of people like Moscoso and Luís Ferrer.
First Girl	¡Un momento!
Boy	¡Bueno!
First Girl	¡Un momento!
Boy	Have you got people capable of starting something like . . . like General Motors?

as being related to the act of interruption or disagreement in the midst of a somewhat specialized argument. There may be a problem, however, when testing this interpretation, in determining the speech acts and speech events that are to be recognized within a speech community.

Certainly, it is not appropriate to simply apply the system of acts and events that has been determined for one speech community in the study of another, without first determining its appropriateness in the second community. Similarly, it is not sufficient for the investigator, no matter how much experience he has had with the verbal behavior of a particular speech community, merely to devise as detailed a listing of speech acts and events as he can. Such a list runs the decided risk of being *etic* rather than *emic,* i.e., of making far too many, as well as behaviorally inconsequential, differentiations, just as was often the case with phon*etic* vs. phon*emic* analysis in linguistics proper. An *emic* set of speech acts and events must be one that is validated as meaningful via final recourse to the native members of a speech community rather than via appeal to the investigator's ingenuity or intuition alone.

An *emic* set of speech acts and speech events is best approximated, perhaps along a never-ending asymptote, by playing back recorded samples of "talk" to native speakers and by encouraging them to react to and comment upon the reasons for the use of variety *a* "here" as contrasted with the use of variety *b* "there." The more the sensitive investigator observes the speech community that he seeks to describe sociolinguistically the more hunches he will have concerning functionally different speech acts and speech events. However, even the best hunches require verification *from within the speech community.* Such verification may take various shapes. The views of both naïve and skilled informants may be cited and tabulated as they comment upon recorded instances of variation in "talk" and as they reply to the investigator's patient probes and queries as to "Why didn't he say 'Just a minute!' instead of '¡Momento!'? Would it have meant something different if he *had* said that instead? When is it appropriate to say '¡Momento!' and when is it appropriate to say 'Just a minute!' (assuming that the persons involved know both languages equally well)?", etc. Once the investigator has *demonstrated* (not merely assumed or argued) the validity of his sets of functionally different speech acts and events, he may then proceed to utilize them in the collection and analysis of samples of talk which are *independent* of those already utilized for validational purposes. Such, at least, is the rationale of research procedure at this microlevel of sociolinguistic analysis, although the field itself is still too young and too linguistically oriented to have produced many instances of such cross-validation of its *social* units selected for purposes of *socio*linguistic analysis.

MICRO-LEVEL ANALYSIS IN THE SOCIOLOGY OF LANGUAGE

Sociolinguistic description may merely begin—rather than end—with the specification and the utilization of speech acts and events, depending on the purpose of a particular research enterprise. The more linguistically oriented a particular study may be, the more likely it is to remain content with microlevel analysis, since the microlevel in the sociology of language is already a much higher (i.e., a more contextual and complicated) level of analysis than that traditionally employed within linguistics proper. However, the more societally oriented a particular sociolinguistic study may be, the more concerned with investigating social processes and societal organization per se, the more likely it is to seek successively more macro-level analyses. Microlevel sociology of language (sometimes referred to as ethnomethodological) constitutes one of the levels within sociolinguistic inquiry (Garfinkel, 1967; Garfinkel & Sachs, in press). The various levels do not differ in the degree to which they are correct or accurate. They differ in purpose, and therefore in method. We can trace only a few of the successive levels in this Section, primarily in order to demonstrate their similarities and their differences.

One of the awarenesses to which an investigator may come after pondering a mountain of sociolinguistic data at the level of speech acts and events is that variation in "talk" is more common and differently proportioned or distributed between certain interlocutors than it is between others (Schegloff, 1968). Thus, whereas either the boy or the girl in Conversation 2 may initiate the switch from one language to another, it may seem from Conversation 1 that the boss is the initiator of switching far more frequently than is the secretary. Therefore, while a great deal of switching is functionally *metaphorical,* i.e., it indicates a contrast in emphasis (from humor to seriousness, from agreement to disagreement, from the inessential or secondary to the essential or primary, in any interchange already underway in a particular language variety), interlocutors may vary in the extent to which they may appropriately initiate or engage in such switching, depending on their *role-relationship* to each other. Note, however, that it is necessary for a certain appropriateness to exist between a variety and certain characteristics of the social setting before it is possible to utilize another variety for metaphorical or contrastive purposes.

ROLE-RELATIONSHIPS

Any two interlocutors within a given speech community (or, more narrowly, within a given speech network within a speech community) must recognize the role-relationship that exists between them at any particular time. Such recognition is part of the communality of norms and behaviors upon which the existence of speech communities depends. Father-son, husband-wife, teacher-pupil, clergyman-layman, employer-employee, friend-friend: these are but some examples of the role relationships that may exist in various (but not in all) speech communities (Goodenough, 1965). Role relationships are implicitly recognized and accepted sets of mutual rights and obligations between members of the same sociocultural system. One of the ways in which members reveal such common membership to each other, as well as their recognition of the rights and obligations that they owe toward each other, is via appropriate variation (which, of course, may include appropriate nonvariation) of the way(s) they talk to each other. Perhaps children should generally be seen and not heard, but when they *are* heard most societies insist that they talk differently to their parents than they do to their friends (Fischer, 1958). One of the frequent comments about American travelers abroad is that they know (*at most*) only one variety of the language of the country they are visiting. As a result, they speak in the same way to a child, a professor, a bootblack, and a shopkeeper, thus revealing not only their foreignness, but also their ignorance of the appropriate ways of signaling local role relationships.

It is probably not necessary, at this point, to dwell upon the kinds of variation in talk that may be required (or prohibited) by certain role-relationships. In addition, and this too should require no extensive discussion at this point, whether the variation required is from one language to another or from one geographic, social, or occupational variety to another, the functionally differential role relationships must be *emically* validated rather than merely *etically* enumerated. There are certainly sociolinguistic allo* roles in most speech communities. However, two

---

* Functionally equivalent—Ed.

other characterizations of role-relationships do merit mention at this point, particularly because they have proved to be useful in sociolinguistic description and analysis.

Role-relationships vary in the extent to which their mutual rights and obligations must or must not be *continually stressed.* The king-subject role-relationship may retain more invariant stress than the shopkeeper-customer relationship. If shopkeepers and their customers may also interact with each other as friends, as relatives, as members of the same political party, etc., whereas kings and their subjects (in the same speech community) may not experience a similar degree of role change, access, and fluidity *vis-à-vis each other,* then we would expect to encounter more variation in the "talk" of two individuals who encounter each other as shopkeeper and customer than we would expect between two individuals who encounter each other as king and subject. In addition, a shopkeeper and his customer may be able to set aside their roles entirely and interact entirely on the basis of their individual and momentary needs and inclinations. This may not be permissible for the king and his subjects. Thus, we should say that a shopkeeper and his customer may engage in both *personal* and *transactional* interactions (Gumperz, 1964), whereas the king and his subjects engage only in transactional interactions. Transactional interactions are those which stress the mutual rights and obligations of their participants. Personal interactions are more informal, more fluid, more varied.

In part, speech acts and events are differentially distributed throughout various role relationships because personal and transactional interactions are differentially permitted in various role relationships. The sociology of language is necessarily of interest to those investigators who are concerned with determining the functionally different role relationships that exist within a given community. Microlevel sociology of language, at least, is concerned with the validation of such relationships, via demonstration of differential role access, role range, and role fluidity, as well as via the demonstration of differential proportions of personal and transactional interaction, through the data of "talk." Role-relationships may be used as data-organizing units both with respect to variation in talk as well as with respect to other variations in interpersonal behavior. That is the reason why role-relations are so frequently examined in the sociology of language.

THE SITUATION: CONGRUENT AND INCONGRUENT

It has probably occurred to the reader that if the shopkeeper and his customer are not to interact only as such, but rather also as friends, lovers, relatives, or party members, that more than their roles are likely to change. After all, neither the *time* nor the *place* of the storekeeper-customer role-relationship is really ideal for any of the other relationships mentioned. Lovers require a time and a place of their own, and the same is true—or, at least, is typical—for other role relationships as well. These three ingredients (the *implementation* of the rights and duties of a particular role-relationship, in the *place* (locale) most appropriate or most typical for that relationship, and at the *time* societally defined as appropriate for that relationship), taken together, constitute a construct that has proven itself to be of great value in the sociology of language: the *social situation* (Bock, 1964).

The simplest type of social situation for microlevel sociology of language to describe and analyze is the congruent situation in which all three ingredients "go-together" in the culturally accepted way. This is not to say that the investigator may assume that there is only one place and one time appropriate for the realization of a particular role-relationship. Quite the contrary. As with the wakes studied by Bock on a Micmac Indian Reserve, there may be various times and various places for the appropriate realization of particular role-relationships. Nevertheless, the total number of permissible combinations is likely to be small, and small or not, there is likely to be little ambiguity among members of the society or culture under study as to what the situation in question is and what its requirements are with respect to their participation in it. As a result, if there are language usage norms with respect to situations these are likely to be most clearly and uniformly realized in avowedly congruent situations.

However, lovers quarrel. Although they meet in the proper time and place, they do not invariably behave toward each other as lovers should. Similarly, if a secretary and a boss are required to meet in the office at 3:00 A.M. in order to complete an emergency report, it may well be difficult for them to maintain the usual secretary-boss relationship. Finally, if priest and parishioner meet at the Yonkers Raceway during the time normally set aside for confessions, this must have some impact on the normal priest-parishioner role relationship. However, in all such instances of initial incongruency (wrong behavior, wrong time, or wrong place) the resulting interaction—whether sociolinguistic or otherwise—is normally far from random or chaotic. One party to the interaction of another, if not both, reinterprets the seeming incongruency so as to yield a congruent situation, at least phenomenologically, for that particular encounter, where one does not exist socioculturally.

Because of incongruent behavior toward each other lovers may reinterpret each other as employer and employee and the date situation is reinterpreted as a dispassionate work situation. Because of the incongruent time, secretary and boss may view the work situation as more akin to a date than is their usual custom. Because of the incongruent place priest and parishioner may pretend not to recognize each other, or to treat each other as "old pals." In short, after a bit of "fumbling around" in which various and varying tentative redefinitions may be tried out, a new congruent situation is interpreted as existing and *its* behavioral and sociolinguistic requirements are implemented (Blom & Gumperz, 1972; Fishman, 1968). Thus, whereas bilingual Puerto Rican parents and their children in New York are most likely to talk to each other in Spanish at home when conversing about family matters, they will probably speak in English to each other in the public school building (Fishman, Cooper, & Ma, 1968). As far as they are concerned these are two different situations, perhaps calling for two different role relationships and requiring the utilization of two different languages or varieties.

Situational contrasts need not be as discontinuous as most of our examples have thus far implied. Furthermore, within a basically Spanish-speaking situation one or another member of a bilingual speech community may still switch to English (or, in Paraguay, to Guarani) in the midst of a speech event for purely metaphorical (i.e., for emphatic or contrastive) purposes. Such *metaphorical switching* would not be possible, however, if there were no general norm assigning the particular situation, as one of a class of such situations, to one language rather than to the other. However, in contrast to the frequently unilateral and fluid back-and-forth nature of metaphorical switching (perhaps to indicate a personal interlude in a basically transactional interaction) there stands the frequently more reciprocal and undirectional nature of *situational* switching.

More generally put, *situational switching is governed by common allocation,* i.e., by widespread normative views and regulations that commonly allocate a particular variety to a particular cluster of topics, places, persons, and purposes. *Metaphorical switching, on the other hand, is governed by uncommon or contrastive allocation.* It is operative as a departure from the common allocations that are normally operative. Without well-established normative views and regulations relative to the functional allocation of varieties within the repertoire of a speech community neither situational nor metaphorical switching could effectively obtain. A switch to cockney where Received Pronunciation (and grammar) is called for may elicit a brief raising of eyebrows or a pause in the conversation—until it is clear from the speaker's demeanor and from the fact that he has reverted to *RP* that no change in situation was intended. However, such metaphorical switching can be risky. Someone might feel that for the situation at hand cockney is in poor taste. Metaphorical switching is a luxury that can be afforded only by those that comfortably share not only the same *set* of situational norms but also *the same view as to their inviolability.* Since most of us are members of several speech networks, each with somewhat different sociolinguistic norms, the chances that situational shifting and metaphorical switching will be misunderstood and conflicted—particularly where the norms pertaining to variety selection have few or insufficiently powerful guardians—are obviously great.

THE TRANSITION TO MACRO-LEVEL SOCIOLOGY OF LANGUAGE

The situational analysis of language and behavior represents the boundary area between microlevel and macrolevel sociology of language. The very fact that a baseball conversation "belongs" to one speech variety and an electrical engineering lecture "belongs" to another speech variety is a major key to an even more generalized description of sociolinguistic variation. The very fact that humor during a formal lecture is realized through a metaphorical switch to another variety must be indicative of an underlying sociolinguistic regularity, perhaps of the view that lecturelike or formal situations are generally associated with one language or variety whereas levity or intimacy is tied to another (Joos, 1959). The large-scale aggregative regularities that obtain between varieties and societally recognized functions are examined via the construct termed *domain* (Fishman, 1965; Fishman, 1972).

Sociolinguistic domains are societal constructs derived from painstaking analysis and summarization of patently congruent situations (see Fishman, Cooper, & Ma, 1968, for many examples of the extraction of *emic* domains via factor analysis as well as for examples of the validation of initially *etic* domains). The macrosociologist or social psychologist may well inquire: What is the significance of the fact that school situations and "schoolish" situations (the latter being initially incongruent situations reinterpreted in the direction of their most salient component) are related to variety *a*? Frequently, it is helpful to recognize a number of behaviorally separate domains (behaviorally separate in that they are derived from discontinuous social situations), all of which are commonly associated with a particular variety or language. Thus, in many bilingual speech communities such domains as school, church, professional work sphere, and government have been verified and found to be congruent with a language or variety that we will refer to as *H* (although for purely labeling purposes we might refer to it as *a* or *X* or *1*). Similarly, such domains as family, neighborhood, and lower work sphere have been validated and found to be congruent with a language or variety that we will refer to as *L* (or *b*, or *Y* or *2*). All in all, the fact that a complex speech community contains various superposed varieties—in some cases, various languages, and in others, various varieties of the same language—is now well documented. The existence of complementary varieties for intragroup purposes is known as *diglossia* (Ferguson, 1959) and the communities in which diglossia is encountered are referred to as *diglossic*. Domains are particularly useful constructs for the macrolevel (i.e., community-wide) functional description of societally patterned variation in "talk" within large and complex diglossic speech communities.

Some members of diglossic speech communities can verbalize the relationship between certain broad categories of behavior and certain broad categories of "talk." More educated and verbally fluent members of speech communities can tell an investigator about such relationships at great length and in great detail. Less educated and verbally limited members can only grope to express a regularity which they vaguely realize to exist. However, the fact that the formulation of a regular association between language (variety) and large-scale situational behaviors may be difficult to come by is no more indicative of a dubious relationship than the fact that grammatical regularities can rarely be explicitly formulated by native speakers is to be considered as calling the abstracted rules themselves into question.

As with all constructs (including situations, role-relationships, and speech events), domains originate in the integrative intuition of the investigator. If the investigator notes that student-teacher interactions in classrooms, school corridors, school auditoriums, and school laboratories of elementary schools, high schools, colleges, and universities are all realized via H as long as these interactions are focused upon educational technicality and specialization, he may begin to suspect that these hypothetically congruent situations all belong to a single (educational) domain. If he further finds that hypothetically incongruent situations involving an educational and a noneducational ingredient are, by and large, predictably resolved in terms of H rather than L if the third ingredient is an educational time, place, or role relationship, he may feel further justified in positing an educational domain. Finally, if informants tell him that the predicted language or variety would be appropriate in all of the examples he can think of that derive from his notion of the educational domain, whereas they proclaim that it would not be appropriate for examples that he draws from a contrasted domain, then the construct is as usefully validated as is that of situation or event—with one major difference.

Whereas particular speech acts (and speech excerpts of an even briefer nature) can be apportioned to the speech events and social situations in which they occurred, the same cannot be done with respect to such acts or excerpts in relationship to societal domains. Domains are extrapolated from the *data* of "talk" rather than being an actual component of the *process* of talk. However, domains are as real as the very social institutions of a speech community, and indeed they show a marked paralleling with such major social institutions (Barker, 1947). There is an undeniable difference between the social institution, "the family," and any particular family, but there is no doubt that the societal norms concerning the former must be derived from data on many instances of the latter. Once such societal norms are formulated they can be utilized to test predictions concerning the distributions of societally patterned variations in talk across all instances of one domain vs. all instances of another.

Thus, domains and social situations reveal the links that exist between microlevel and macrolevel sociology of language. The members of diglossic speech communities can come to have certain views concerning their varieties or languages because these varieties are associated (in behavior and in attitude) with particular domains. The *H* variety (or language) is considered to reflect certain values and relationships within the speech community, whereas the *L* variety is considered to reflect others. Certain individuals and groups may come to advocate the expansion of the functions of *L* into additional domains. Others may advocate the displacement of *L* entirely and the use of *H* solely. Neither of these revisionist views could be held or advocated without recognition of the reality of domains of language-and-behavior in the existing norms of communicative appropriateness. The high culture values with which certain varieties are associated and the intimacy and folksiness values with which others are congruent are both derivable from domain-appropriate norms governing characteristic verbal interaction.

ON THE REALITY OF SOCIOLINGUISTIC COMPOSITING

So little (if, indeed, any) microsociolinguistic data has been subjected to rigorous quantitative analysis or obtained via experimentally controlled variation that it is fitting that we pause to examine a study that has attempted to do so, even if it deals only with sociolinguistic normative views and claims. The study in question (Fishman & Greenfield, 1970) is concerned with the relative importance of persons, places, and topics in the perception of congruent and incongruent situations and with the impact of perceived congruence or incongruence on claimed language use in different domains. Since domains are a higher order generalization from *congruent situations* (i.e., from situations in which individuals interact in appropriate role relationships with each other, in the appropriate locales for these role relationships, and discuss topics appropriate to their role relationships) it was first necessary to test intuitive and rather clinical estimates of the widespread congruences that were felt to obtain. After more than a year of participant observation and other data-gathering experiences it seemed to Greenfield (1968) that five domains could be generalized from the innumerable situations that he had encountered. He tentatively labeled these "family," "friendship," "religion," "education," and "employment" and proceeded to determine whether a typical *situation* could be presented for each domain as a means of collecting self-report data on language choice. As indicated below each domain was represented by a congruent person (interlocutor), place, and topic in the self-report instrument that Greenfield constructed for high school students.

Domain	Interlocutor	Place	Topic
Family	Parent	Home	How to be a good son or daughter
Friendship	Friend	Beach	How to play a certain game
Religion	Priest	Church	How to be a good Christian
Education	Teacher	School	How to solve an algebra problem
Employment	Employer	Workplace	How to do your job more efficiently

Greenfield's hypothesis was that within the Puerto Rican speech community, among individuals who knew Spanish and English equally well, Spanish was primarily associated with family and with friendship (the two, family and friendship constituting the intimacy value cluster), while English was primarily associated with religion, work, and education (the three constituting the status-stressing value cluster). In order to test this hypothesis he first presented two seemingly congruent situational components and requested his subjects (a) to select a third component in order to complete the situation, as well as (b) to indicate their likelihood of using Spanish or English if they were involved in such a situation and if they and their Puerto Rican interlocutors knew Spanish and English equally well. Section I of Table 1.1 shows that Greenfield's predictions were uniformly confirmed among those subjects who selected congruent third components. Spanish was decreasingly reported for family, friendship, religion, employment, and education, regardless of whether the third component selected was a person, place, or topic.

However, as Blom and Gumperz (1972), Fishman (1968), and others have indicated, seemingly incongruent situations frequently occur and are rendered understandable and acceptable (just as are the seemingly ungrammatical sentences that we hear in most spontaneous speech). Interlocutors reinterpret incongruences in order to salvage some semblance of the congruency in terms of which they understand and function within their social order. Were this not the case then no seemingly congruent

TABLE 1.1
Spanish and English Usage Self-Ratings in Various Situations for Components Selected

I. *Congruent Situations:* Two "congruent" components presented; S selects third congruent component and language appropriate to situation. 1 = all Spanish, 5 = all English.

CONGRUENT PERSONS SELECTED

	Parent	Friend	Total		Priest	Teacher	Em-ployer	Total
Mean	2.77	3.60	3.27		4.69	4.92	4.79	4.81
S.D.	1.48	1.20	1.12		.61	.27	.41	.34
N	13	15	15		13	13	14	15

CONGRUENT PLACES SELECTED

	Home	Beach	Total		Church	School	Work-place	Total
Mean	2.33	3.50	2.60		3.80	4.79	4.27	4.27
S.D.	1.07	1.26	1.10		1.51	.58	1.34	.94
N	15	6	15		15	14	15	15

CONGRUENT TOPICS SELECTED

	Family	Friend-ship	Total		Reli-gion	Edu-cation	Employ-ment	Total
Mean	1.69	3.30	2.64		3.80	4.78	4.44	4.38
S.D.	.92	1.20	.95		1.47	1.53	1.12	.73
N	16	18	18		15	18	18	18

II. *Incongruent Situations:* Two "incongruent" components presented; S selects third component and language appropriate to situation. 1 = all Spanish, 5 = all English.

PERSONS SELECTED

	Parent	Friend	Total		Priest	Teacher	Em-ployer	Total
Mean	2.90	3.92	3.60		4.68	4.77	4.44	4.70
S.D.	1.20	.64	.70		.59	.48	.68	.52
N	16	16	16		14	15	9	15

PLACES SELECTED

	Home	Beach	Total		Church	School	Work-place	Total
Mean	2.63	3.86	2.77		3.71	4.39	4.42	4.10
S.D.	.77	.94	.70		1.32	1.90	.96	.82
N	15	5	15		15	15	15	15

TOPICS SELECTED

	Family	Friend-ship	Total		Reli-gion	Edu-cation	Employ-ment	Total
Mean	2.83	3.81	3.26		3.07	3.66	3.81	3.49
S.D.	1.04	1.13	1.02		1.00	1.20	.85	.76
N	18	16	18		18	17	18	18

domains could arise and be maintained out of the incongruences of daily life. In order to test this assumption Greenfield proceeded to present his subjects with two incongruent components (e.g., with a person from one hypothetical domain and with a place from another hypothetical domain) and asked them to select a third component in order to complete the situation as well as to indicate their likelihood of using Spanish or English in a situation so constituted. Greenfield found that the third component was overwhelmingly selected from either one or the other of any two domains from which he had selected the first two components. Furthermore, in their attempts to render a seemingly incongruous situation somewhat more congruent his subject's language preferences left the relationship between domains and language choice substantially unaltered (directionally), regardless of whether persons, places, or topics were involved. Nevertheless, all domains became somewhat less different from each other than they had been in the fully congruent situations. Apparently, both individual indecisiveness as well as sociolinguistic norms governing domain regularity must be combined and compromised when incongruences appear. Language choice is much more clear-cut and polarized in "usual" situations governed neatly by sociolinguistic norms of communicative appropriateness than they are in "unusual" situations which must be resolved by individual interpretation.

Yet another (and for this presentation, final) indication of the construct validity of domains as analytic parameters for the study of large-scale sociolinguistic patterns is yielded by Edelman's data (Edelman, Cooper & Fishman, 1968). Here we note that when the word-naming responses of bilingual Puerto Rican children in Jersey City were analyzed in accord with the domains derived from Greenfield's and Fishman's data reported

TABLE 1.2
Mean Number of Words Named by Young Schoolchildren
(N = 34)

Age	Language	Family	Education	Domain Religion	Friendship	Total
6-8	English	6.2	8.2	6.6	8.3	7.3
	Spanish	7.6	6.2	5.8	6.4	6.5
	Total	6.9	7.2	6.2	7.4	6.9
9-11	English	11.7	12.8	8.7	10.9	11.0
	Spanish	10.5	9.4	7.2	9.7	9.2
	Total	11.1	11.1	7.9	10.3	10.1
Total	English	9.0	10.5	7.7	9.6	9.2
	Spanish	9.0	7.8	6.5	8.0	7.8
	Total	9.0	9.1	7.1	9.0	8.5

TABLE 1.3
Analysis of Variance of Young Schoolchildren's Word-Naming Scores

Source	Sum of Squares	df	Mean Square	F	F95	F99
Between Subjects	1844.12	33				
C (age)	689.30	1	689.30	19.67*	4.17	7.56
D (sex)	15.54	1	15.54	.44	4.17	7.56
CD	87.87	1	87.87	2.51	4.17	7.56
error (b)	1051.41	30	35.05			
Within Subjects	1795.88	238				
A (language)	123.13	1	123.13	9.73*	4.17	7.56
B (domain)	192.54	3	64.18	8.51*	2.71	4.00
AB	65.12	3	21.71	11.67*	2.71	4.00
AC	16.50	1	16.50	1.30	4.17	7.56
AD	42.08	1	42.08	3.32	4.17	7.56
BC	61.54	3	20.51	2.72	2.71	4.00
BD	2.89	3	.96	.13	2.71	4.00
ABC	23.99	3	8.00	4.30*	2.71	4.00
ABD	6.70	3	2.23	1.20	2.71	4.00
ACD	14.62	1	14.62	1.15	4.17	7.56
BCD	13.53	3	4.51	.60	2.71	4.00
ABCD	7.98	3	2.66	1.43	2.71	4.00
error (w)	1225.26	210				
error$_1$ (w)	379.88	30	12.66			
error$_2$ (w)	678.31	90	7.54			
error$_3$ (w)	167.07	90	1.86			
Total	3640.00	271				

*Significant at or above the .01 level.

above significant and instructive findings were obtained. The most Spanish domain for all children was "family" (Table 1.2). The most English domain for all children was "education." The analysis of variance (Table 1.3) indicates that not only did the children's responses differ significantly by age (older children giving more responses in both languages than did younger children), by language (English yielding more responses than does Spanish), and by domain (church yielding fewer responses than does any other domain), but that these three variables *interact significantly* as well. This means that one language is much more associated with certain domains than is the other and that this is differentially so by age. This is exactly the kind of findings for which domain analysis is particularly suited. Its utility for intersociety comparisons and for gauging language shift would seem to be quite promising, but its major value should be in describing and demonstrating the dependence of communicative appropriateness on the compositing appropriateness of members of speech communities, whether monolingual or bilingual.

One thing appears to be clear from the theoretical and empirical work cited: there are classes of events recognized by each speech network or community in which several seemingly different situations are classed as being of the same kind. No speech network has a linguistic repertoire that is as differentiated as the complete list of apparently different role relations, topics, and locales in which its members are involved. Just *where the boundaries come* that do differentiate between the *class of situations* generally requiring one variety and another class of situations generally requiring another variety must be empirically determined by the investigator, and constitutes one of the major tasks of descriptive sociology of language. The various domains and the appropriate usage in each domain must be discovered from the data of numerous discrete situations and the shifting or nonshifting which they reveal. This is a central task of descriptive sociology of language, and it can only be accomplished by painstaking research—utilizing *all* the available social science methods: participant observation, interviews, surveys, and experiments too. The compositing concerns of some researchers in the sociology of language are thus far from being research strategies alone. Ultimately they also seek to reveal the behavioral parsimony of members of speech communities, all of whom inevitably come to rely on a relatively functional sociolinguistic typology to guide them through the infinite encounters of daily interaction.

SOCIOLOGY OF LANGUAGE: MULTILEVEL AND MULTIMETHOD

The list of constructs utilized in the sociolinguistic description and analysis of samples of "talk" is far from exhausted. We have not mentioned several of the social units long advocated by Hymes (1962), such as

FIGURE 1.1
Components of Speech Events: A Heuristic Schema

(S) SETTING or SCENE: time and place; also, psychological setting and cultural definition as a *type* of scene

(P) PARTICIPANTS or PERSONNEL: e.g., addressor-addressee-audience

(E) ENDS: ends in view (goals, purposes) and ends as outcomes

(A) ART CHARACTERISTICS: the form *and* the content of what is said

(K) KEY: the tone, manner or spirit in which an act is done

(I) INSTRUMENTALITIES: channel (the choice of oral, written, telegraphic, or other medium) and code (Spanish, English, etc.) or subcode (dialect, sociolect)

(N) NORMS OF INTERACTION and of INTERPRETATION: specific behaviors and properties that may accompany acts of speech, as well as shared rules for understanding what occurs in speech acts

(G) GENRES: categories or types of speech acts and speech events: e.g., conversation, curse, prayer, lecture, etc.

participant vs. audience roles, the purposes and the outcomes of speech events, the tone or manner of communication, the channel of communication employed (oral, written, telegraphic), or all the various parameters and components for the analysis of talk data that he has more recently advanced (Hymes, 1967; see Figure 1.1); we have not discussed such social psychological parameters as the saliency of individual vs. collective needs

FIGURE 1.2
Relationships among Some Constructs Employed in Sociolinguistic Analysis

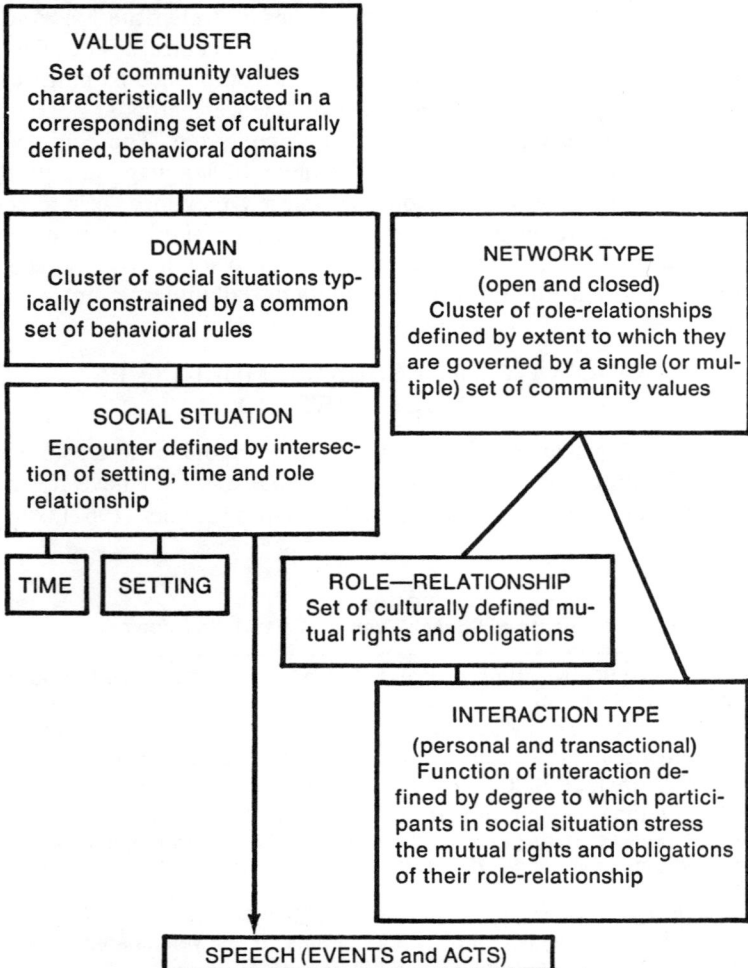

From: Robert L. Cooper, "How Can We Measure the Roles Which a Bilingual's Languages Play in His Everyday Behavior?", in L. G. Kelly (ed.), *The Description and Measurement of Bilingualism* (Toronto University Press, Toronto, 1969), p. 202.

(Herman, 1961), or the several functions of speech so revealingly discussed by Ervin-Tripp. Suffice it to say that there are several levels and approaches to sociolinguistic description and a host of linguistic, sociopsychological, and societal constructs within each (see Figure 1.2). One's choice from among them depends on the particular problem at hand (Ervin-Tripp, 1964). This is necessarily so. The sociology of language is of interest to students of small societies as well as to students of national and international integration. It must help clarify the change from one face-to-face situation to another. It must also help clarify the different language-related beliefs and behaviors of entire social sectors and classes. In some cases the variation between closely related varieties must be highlighted. In other cases the variation between obviously unrelated languages is of concern.

It would be foolhardy to demand that one and the same method of data collection and data analysis be utilized for such a variety of problems and purposes. It is one of the hallmarks of scientific social inquiry that methods are selected as a *result* of problem specifications rather than independently of them. The sociology of language is neither methodologically nor theoretically uniform. Nevertheless, it is gratifying to note that for those who seek such ties the links between micro- and macroconstructs and methods exist (as do a number of constructs and methods that have wide applicability through the entire range of the sociology of language). Just as there is no societally unencumbered verbal interaction, so are there no large-scale relationships between language and society that do not depend on individual interaction for their realization. Although there is no mechanical part-whole relationship between them, microlevel and macrolevel sociology of language are both conceptually and methodologically complementary.

REFERENCES

Barker, George C. "Social Functions of Language in a Mexican-American Community," *Acta Americana*, V (1947), 185-202.

Blom, Jan Peter, and John J. Gumperz. "Some Social Determinants of Verbal Behavior," in John J. Gumperz and Dell Hymes (eds.), *Directions in Sociolinguistics: The Ethnography of Communication.* Holt, New York, 1972.

Bock, Philip K. "Social Structure and Language Structure," *Southwestern Journal of Anthropology,* XX (1964), 393-403; also in J. A. Fishman (ed.), *Readings in the Sociology of Language.* Mouton, The Hague, 1968, 212-222.

Edelman, Martin, Robert L. Cooper, and Joshua A. Fishman. "The Contextualization of Schoolchildren's Bilingualism," *Irish Journal of Education,* II (1968), 106-111.

Ervin-Tripp, Susan. "An Analysis of the Interaction of Language, Topic and Listener," *American Anthropologist,* LXVI, ii (1964), 86-102; also in J. A. Fishman (ed.), *Readings in the Sociology of Language,* Mouton, The Hague, 1968, pp. 192-211.

Ferguson, Charles A. "Diglossia," *Word,* XV (1959), 325-340.

Fischer, John L. "Social Influences in the Choice of a Linguistic Variant," *Word,* XIV (1958), 47-56.

Fishman, Joshua A. "Who Speaks What Language to Whom and When?" *Linguistique,* II (1965), 67-88.

Fishman, Joshua A. "Sociolinguistic Perspective on the Study of Bilingualism," *Linguistics,* XXXIX (1968), 21-50.

Fishman, Joshua A. "The Links between Micro- and Macro-sociolinguistics in the Study of Who Speaks What Language to Whom and When," in Dell Hymes and John J. Gumperz (eds.), *Directions in Sociolinguistics: The Ethnography of Communication.* Holt, New York, 1972, also in J. A. Fishman, R. L. Cooper, and Roxana Ma, et al. *Bilingualism in the Barrio.* Bloomington (Ind.) Language Sciences Series, 1971.

Fishman, Joshua A., Robert C. Cooper, Roxana Ma, et al. *Bilingualism in the Barrio.* Final Report on contract OEC-1-7-062817-0297 to DHEW. New York, Yeshiva University, 1968; also Bloomington (Ind.) Language Sciences Series, 1971.

Fishman, Joshua A., and Lawrence Greenfield. "Situational Measures of Normative Language Views in Relation to Person, Place and Topic among Puerto Rican Bilinguals," *Anthropos,* 1970; also in J. A. Fishman (ed.), *Advances in the Sociology of Language II,* Mouton, The Hague, 1972.

Garfinkel, Harold. *Studies in Ethnomethodology.* Prentice-Hall, Englewood Cliffs, N.J., 1967.

Garfinkel, Harold, and H. Sachs (eds.). *Contributions in Ethnomethodology.* Indiana University Press, Bloomington, in press.

Goodenough, Ward H. "Rethinking Status and Role: Toward a General Model of the Cultural Organization of Social Relationships," in M. Banton (ed.), *The Relevance of Models for Social Anthropology.* Praeger, New York, 1965, pp. 1-24.

Greenfield, Lawrence. "Situational Measures of Language Use in Relation to Person, Place and Topic among Puerto Rican Bilinguals, *Bilingualism in the Barrio.* Final Report to DHEW re Contract No. OEC-1-7-062817-0297. Yeshiva University, New York, 1968.

Gumperz, John J. "Linguistic and Social Interaction in Two Communities," *American Anthropologist,* LXVI, ii (1964), 37-53.

Herman, Simon N. "Explorations in the Social Psychology of Language Choice," *Human Relations,* XIV (1961), 149-164; also in J. A. Fishman (ed.), *Readings in the Sociology of Language.* Mouton, The Hague, 1968, pp. 492-511.

Hofman, John E. "Models of Interaction of Language and Social Setting," *Journal of Social Issues,* XXXIII, ii (1967), 8-28.

Hymes, Dell H. "The Ethnography of Speaking," in T. Gladwin and W. C. Sturtevant (ed.), *Anthropology and Human Behavior.* Anthropology Society of Washington, Washington, D.C., 1962, pp. 13-53; also in J. A. Fishman (ed.), *Readings in the Sociology of Language.* Mouton, The Hague, 1968, pp. 99-138.

Joos, Martin. "The Isolation of Styles," *Monograph Series on Languages and Linguistics (Georgetown University),* XII (1959), 107-113. (Also in J. A. Fishman [ed.], *Readings,* pp. 185-191.)

Schegloff, Emanuel A. "Sequencing in Conversational Openings," *American Anthropologist,* LXX (1968), 1075-1095; also in J. A. Fishman (ed.), *Advances in the Sociology of Language.* Mouton, The Hague, 1971.

2

JONATHAN C. FINKELSTEIN

The Experimenter Expectancy Effect: Cues and Clues

Perhaps as part of a course requirement in your psychology class, or out of sheer curiosity, you have volunteered to participate in a study entitled "person perception" or "photo rating." When you report to the laboratory, you are ushered into a small room. The experimenter, sitting at a table, greets you and asks you to have a seat across from him. He then begins to explain what will be happening.

I am going to read you some instructions. I am not permitted to say anything which is not in the instructions nor can I answer any questions about this experiment. OK?

We are in the process of developing a test of empathy. This test is designed to show how well a person is able to put himself into someone else's place. I will show you a series of photographs. For each one I want you to judge whether the person pictured has been experiencing success or failure. To help you make more exact judgments you are to use this rating scale.

The experimenter places a sheet of paper containing the following scale in front of you and continues his explanation.

The Empathy Test Rating Scale

Extreme Failure	Moderate Failure	Mild Failure	Mild Success	Moderate Success	Extreme Success
−10 −9 −8	−7 −6 −5 −4	−3 −2 −1	+1 +2 +3	+4 +5 +6	+7 +8 +9 +10

As you can see the scale runs from −10 to +10. A rating of −10 means that you judge the person to have experienced extreme failure. A rating of +10 means that you judge the person to have experienced extreme success. A rating of −1 means that you judge the person to have experienced mild failure, while a rating of +1 means that you judge the person to have experienced mild success. You are to rate each photo as accurately as you can. Just tell me the rating you assign to each photo. All ready? Here is the first photo. (Rosenthal, 1966, p. 144)

The experimenter then positions the first photo for you to observe. After five seconds he places the photo face down and you are to give your rating. The wallet-size photos mounted on index cards show male faces. This first photo, and the ones remaining are quite unremarkable. What at first may have appeared to be a simple perception task, to judge the pictured per-

---

Source: Prepared especially for this volume.

son's success or failure, has suddenly become almost impossible. Yet you must give a rating, so you rate the first photo +5, moderate success.

Let's go back a bit to the point when the experimenter arrived at the laboratory. He too was met and greeted by an experimenter, the designer of the study, and he received the following information.

You have been asked to participate in a research project developing a test of empathy. The reason for your participation in this project is to standardize results of experiments of this type. There is the problem in psychological research of different experimenters getting somewhat different data on the same tests as a function of individual differences. Therefore, to standardize the tests it is better methodological procedure to use groups of experimenters. You will now be asked to run a series of Ss and obtain from each ratings of photographs. The experimental procedure has been typed out for you and is self-explanatory. According to preceding research of this nature, the type of subjects that you will be using have averaged a +5 rating. Therefore, the Ss you are running should also average about a +5 rating.

Just read the instructions to the Ss. Say nothing else to them except hello and goodbye. If for any reason you should say anything to an S other than that which is written in your instructions, please write down the exact words you used and the situation which forced you to say them. (Rosenthal, 1963, p. 282).

Other experimenters in the study were given the same instructions, except that they were led to expect that their participants would average about a −5 rating. Next, the main experimenter wished your experimenter good luck and gave him a copy of the procedure he was to follow.

In front of you, you will find the instructions you are to read to your Ss, a sheet of paper for recording each S's rating for each photo and a set of . . . numbered photos.

After recording background data from each subject at the top of the recording sheet and reading instructions to the S, you are ready to begin.

Take photo #1 and say: "This is photo #1" and hold it in front of the S until he tells you his rating, which you write down on the recording sheet. Continue this procedure through the . . . photos. Do not let any S see any photo for longer than 5 seconds. After each subject, total the ratings of the . . . photos and find the average (mean). (Rosenthal, 1963, pp. 282-283.)

The major purpose of the experimental procedure I have just described was not to standardize an empathy test. In fact, the photos compiled for the experiment were chosen because they had been rated, as a set, near zero on success-failure. In other words, they were neutral or ambiguous stimuli which did not tend to evoke extreme judgments. These photos did not comprise a test; there were no "good" or "bad," "right" or "wrong" rating responses.

The actual purpose of the experiment was to demonstrate that how an experimenter expects his participants to perform can have an effect on how they in fact perform. To put it more formally, in research—especially social science research—the process itself of collecting data (i.e., systematically observing, doing experiments, conducting interviews etc.) can alter or bias the phenomenon being studied (Orne, 1962, 1969; Rosenberg, 1965, 1969; Rosenthal, 1966, 1969). One major element in all psychological experiments is the experimenter, who thinks up hypotheses, plans and designs studies and experiments, and often administers the procedures to the persons who participate. Can the experimenter's expectations (hypotheses) about how participants will respond affect their responses? How is this effect brought about? That is, what does the experimenter do, even unintentionally, that communicates his expectancy (cues), and what leads participants to use this information, perhaps without awareness, to guide their responses (clues)?

Research over the past 15 years has demonstrated the existence of the experimenter expectancy affect (Rosenthal, 1966, 1969; Timaeus, 1973), although its potency has been questioned (Barber & Silver, 1968). Given that an experimenter's expectations can affect participants' responses in a systematic way, what is of interest is how this effect is brought about. In what ways does an experimenter who expects his participants to rate photos positively behave differently from an experimenter who expects his participants to rate the same photos negatively?

EXPERIMENTER BEHAVIOR: CUES

Perhaps what the experimenter is unintentionally doing to bring about the expectancy effect is apparent. Each participant sees and rates ten or more photos, and the experimenter usually hears and records each of the participants' responses. If the experimenter expects positive success ratings and the participant emits such responses, the experimenter might reinforce those responses verbally, perhaps with "Good," "Uhhuh," or a smile or a glance (Rosenthal, 1969; Timaeus, 1973). Should the participant begin emitting counterexpectancy responses, the experimenter might withhold reinforcement or apply some type of punishment, perhaps a frown.

Although there is some evidence that such operant conditioning practices are used by naive experimenters, inspection of data from a number of experiments argues against this being the mechanism involved in mediating expectancy effects. If conditioning were the usual practice we would expect participants' responses to fall increasingly into line with the experimenter's expectation over the course of the ten photo presentations. A participant's ratings might start out being near neutral and then become more extreme in the direction of the experimenter's expectation with each successive picture. However, experiments reviewed by Rosenthal (1966, 1969) indicate significant expectancy effects as early as the first photo. Analyses of ratings of photos presented later in the series often show a reduction in the magnitude of the experimenter expectancy effect. Further, expectancy effects have been found when participants recorded their ratings privately and when the experimental instructions were delivered by tape recordings (Adair & Epstein, 1968; Duncan, Rosenberg, & Finkelstein, 1969; Rosenthal, 1969).

If experimenters are not unintentionally conditioning their participants' responses, what possibilities remain? Perhaps the experimenter's demeanor, the tone or mood he sets, affects the participants' responses. There is evidence that visual interaction seems to affect the participant's mood, which he may then "project" into the photo-rating stimuli. In an experiment by Jones and Cooper (1971) experimenters' eye-contact glances at their participants were manipulated. One-half of the experimenters were instructed to maintain high eye contact (30.1 actual glances) during instruction reading, while the other half were instructed to almost never look at their participants. The results of this procedure indicated that participants who were glanced at more frequently felt more positively about themselves and rated the pictured persons as being more successful. Although in this study experimenters were given no expectation regarding each participant's performance, perhaps experimenters who are set to expect positive success ratings engage in more visual interaction with their participants than those expecting negative ratings.

An early experiment by Rosenthal and Fode (1963) hints at another possibility. In this experiment there was an attempt to isolate the contributions of visual and auditory cues to the expectancy effect. Experimenters were randomly assigned to one of four conditions. In two of the conditions, positive (+5) and negative (−5) control, the usual procedures were employed, except that the photographs were numbered and mounted on a large sheet of cardboard rather than being displayed one at a time. In both of the remaining conditions the photos were also displayed on the cardboard sheet, but in one—the nonvisual (+5) condition—the experimenter and the participant were separated by an opaque screen so that visual communication was cut off. In the other, nonverbal condition, the

TABLE 2.1
Unweighted Mean Photo Ratings by Condition

−5 Control	+5 Control	+5 Nonvisual	+5 Nonverbal
0.48	2.27	1.32	0.41

Source: Adapted from R. Rosenthal and K. L. Fode, "Psychology of the Scientist: Three Experiments in Experimenter Bias," *Psychological Reports*, 1963, *12*, 491-511, Experiment 2.

experimenter and participant were face to face, but the experimenter remained silent after greeting the participant and handing his written instructions. Table 2.1 presents the mean photo rating obtained in each of these conditions.

Statistical analyses of these findings indicate that the +5 and —5 control conditions are significantly different, thus demonstrating the basic experimenter expectancy effect. Furthermore, the removal of visual cues significantly decreased the expectancy effect as compared to the +5 control condition. However, this restriction of visual cues did not remove the effect; the +5 nonvisual condition is significantly more positive than the —5 control. Since all of the experimenters in the control and nonvisual conditions read the same instructions to their participants, these findings suggest an important role for noncontent aspects of speech as a source of expectancy cues. In contrast, in the +5 nonverbal condition, where verbal interaction between the experimenter and the participant was cut off, the effect of the experimenter's +5 expectancy disappeared. In fact, the similarity of the averages of the +5 nonverbal and —5 control conditions suggests almost a reverse effect of the +5 expectancy when the experimenter was silent. While the nonverbal condition, being a rather unusual and perhaps a tension-arousing situation, does not really tell us much about the role of visual cues, the overall findings emphasize the potency of nonverbal vocal cues in conveying the experimenter's expectation.

The importance of nonverbal vocal cues is again seen in an experiment by Adair and Epstein (1968) which involved the basic procedures of the person perception task, with experimenters expecting either positive or negative ratings. In addition, the instructions were tape-recorded as they were being read to the participants by the experimenters. These tape-recordings were then used in a second experiment as "substitutes" for live experimenters. In both experiments significant experimenter expectancy effects were found. The tape-recorded renditions of the experimental instructions appeared to contain enough cues to convey the experimenters' expectations. But where and what are these nonverbal vocal cues? They must be somewhere in the instructions the experimenter reads to the participant, somewhere between, "I am going to read you some instructions" and "Here is the first photo."

What these vocal cues to the experimenter's expectation are has been suggested by Duncan and Rosenthal (1968). Again, since all experimenters in a given study use the same words in delivering instructions to their participants, the cues must arise from how the experimenters say them. The paralinguistic aspects of speech—the stress, pitch and juncture of vocalization, its intensity, tempo, and hesitancy—are features of speech which may serve as cues to the experimenter's hypothesis. To examine this possibility, the readings of the section of the instructions dealing with the scaled response alternatives available to the participant (see page 421) by three experimenters were recorded, and differences in these features were analyzed by Duncan. A differential emphasis score indicative of the relatively greater stress on the reading of the success vs. failure side of the scale in the instructions was calculated for each recording. When these scores were correlated with participants' average photo ratings, the correlation was found to be $+.72$. The experimenters' relative stress of the success vs. failure side of the rating scale in delivering the instructions was thus found to be a fairly good predictor of how participants would rate the photos. Vocal cues, as the studies presented indicated, appear to provide information that may influence participants' responses.

One question posed in the preceding section asked in what ways experimenters' expectations affected their interpersonal behavior with participants. We have seen evidence suggesting that experimenters' expectations are reflected in their visual and vocal behavior, and these behaviors can serve to communicate the experimenters' hypotheses to participants. The studies reviewed also pointed to possibly two different functions of the experimenters' expectancy-relevant behavior; affective, setting a mood, and cognitive, conveying expectancy information. The experimenter's visual and nonverbal vocal behavior may lead the participant to "feel" more positive or negative, or these same behaviors of the experimenter may convey information regarding the experimenter's expectation. Determining the primary functions of visual and nonverbal vocal cues involves knotty problems. I would hazard the guess from the available evidence that nonverbal vocal cues seem to provide expectancy-relevant information, while visual cues, such as glancing, may primarily affect the tone of the experimental interaction and the participant's mood. Clearly, more research into the capacities and functions of these channels of experimenter-participant communication is needed for a better understanding of the experimenter expectancy effect, and perhaps subtle communication phenomena in general.

FROM CUES TO CLUES

If experimenters can emit cues systematically related to their hypotheses, and participants can be sensitive to these cues, why are participants' responses affected by them? Why are the cues that are emitted by experimenters turned by the participant into clues to the experimenters' hypotheses? And why do participants use these clues to guide their responses? If you will again put yourself into the place of a participant in the person perception experiment, you will appreciate the difficulty of the photo-rating task. The photos themselves provide almost no cues on which to base a judgment; they are neutral, ambiguous stimuli. Nevertheless, you must come up with a rating and report it to the experimenter. It should not be surprising that participants might search for and be sensitive to cues beyond the photos, but why do they use these cues, even without awareness, in constructing their responses? Why not simply give relatively neutral +1 and —1 responses, perhaps on a random basis? One reason might be that participants would probably view such a tactic as inappropriate, since they are in an experiment which is presumably designed to "show" something. More importantly, this experiment may be viewed by participants as more than an academically interesting exercise. Remember, they had been told: "We are in the process of developing a test of empathy . . . how well a person is able to put himself into someone else's place." Empathy, or interpersonal sensitivity, may be regarded as an important ability characteristic by most persons. The photo-rating "test" purports to measure just this characteristic in an objective, standardized manner. Being able to rate the photos in an other than neutral fashion would serve to substantiate the participant's own empathetic ability and to reflect this to the experimenter. In other words, the participant has a stake in the "test" and in the experiment. To obtain a positive evaluation, to do well, to appear "good," "sensitive," and "empathic" may well be a participant's main concern in the person perception experiment (Rosenberg, 1965, 1969).

How could we see whether this concern of participants affects their utilization of any cues emitted by the experimenter? Minor (1970) designed a study in which experimenters were led to expect either success (+5) or failure (—5) photo ratings. Several participants were randomly assigned to each experimenter, but certain background information was systematically varied across participants. In an effort to reduce concerns about how they would do on the photo-rating task, some participants were told that the experiment was being conducted to gain baseline data, that all participants' ratings would be averaged, that no one individual's scores would be examined, and that they were in a control group for later studies to be conducted on the effects of practice, fatigue, and so on in person perception. This was the low evaluation apprehension manipulation. Minor attempted to increase the evaluation apprehension of another group of participants by informing them that the photo-rating task was an effective measure of psychological abnormality and that persons who cannot judge how others are feeling are often found clinically to be psychologically maladjusted. Experimenters with each expectancy administered the photo-rating task to both low and high evaluation apprehension participants.

COMMUNICATION: VERBAL AND NONVERBAL

TABLE 2.2
Mean Photo Ratings for the +5 and −5 Expectancy Conditions
by Evaluation Apprehension Level

	Expectancy	
Evaluation Apprehension	*+5*	*−5*
High	+.16	−1.06
Low	−.78	− .59

Source: Adapted from M. W. Minor, "Experimenter-Expectancy Effect as a Function of Evaluation Apprehension," *Journal of Personality and Social Psychology*, 1970, *15*, 326-332.

The results, presented in Table 2.2, indicate clearly that an expectancy effect is found only under the high evaluation apprehension condition. When evaluation apprehension was suppressed, when participants' concerns about what the "test" might reveal were reduced, there was no difference between the +5 and −5 expectancy conditions. A cue, or a set of cues, becomes a clue and a basis for responding when a participant's evaluation apprehension is aroused, that is, when the cues have relevance and meaning of a personal sort for participants' self-conceptions and self-presentations.

The experimenter expectancy effect was shown in Minor's experiment to be a product of both the experimenter's behavior and the participant's evaluation apprehension. We saw earlier that nonverbal vocal behaviors might serve as cues and affect participants' responses (Duncan and Rosenthal, 1968). Would the evaluation apprehension level of participants affect their utilization of these particular vocal cues? This question was addressed in an experiment by Duncan, Rosenberg, and Finkelstein (1969). Rather than inducing expectations in experimenters, tape recordings of readings of the instructions were analyzed. Instruction tape recordings coded as having positive or negative biases in the reading of the response scale alternatives were chosen and used in the experiment. The photo-rating task was administered to groups of participants by making the photos into slides and projecting them onto a large screen. Each participant was seated in an individual booth and received the tape-recorded instructions through a headphone. Two-thirds of the participants were

TABLE 2.3
Mean Photo Ratings under Conditions of Differential Vocal
Cues and Evaluation Apprehension

Evaluation Apprehension	*Differential Vocal Cues*	
	Positive	*Negative*
Low	.07	.42
Control	.57	−.20
High	.84	−.39

Source: Adapted from S. D. Duncan, Jr., M. J. Rosenberg, and J. Finkelstein, "The Paralanguage of Experimenter Bias," *Sociometry*, 1969, *33*, 207-219.

randomly assigned written background information sheets. The background information sheets were adapted from Minor (1970) and served to suppress or enhance evaluation apprehension. One third of the participants received no background information sheet, to yield a "control" evaluation apprehension condition. Participants privately wrote their ratings of the photos on individual recording sheets. The six conditions and results of this experiment are presented in Table 2.3.

Participants' average ratings of the photos were found to be a joint function of the experimenters' differential vocal cues and the participants' level of evaluation apprehension. When participants were relatively unconcerned about appearing empathic, in the low evaluation apprehension conditions, the biases of the recordings had no significant effect on their ratings. When evaluation apprehension was not manipulated, that is, when it was left at a level induced only by the situation and the usual task instructions, the biases effectively swayed participants' responses. This effect was magnified for both the positively and negatively biased recordings when evaluation apprehension was experimentally increased. The findings of Minor and of Duncan, Rosenberg, and Finkelstein point up the basic social-psychological or interactive nature of the experimenter expectancy effect. It is a phenomenon which is responsive to conditions affecting both the experimenter and the participant.

THE EXPERIMENTER EXPECTANCY EFFECT AS A METHODOLOGICAL ISSUE

Interest in the experimenter expectancy effect grew because of the possibility that experimenters' expectations in many types of studies might bias responses and results. An experimenter who expected greater conformity in one treatment group than in another, or more attitude change in one than another, or less experience of pain in one than another, or greater improvement in emotional adjustment in one group than in another might obtain a statistically significant predicted difference not because of the treatment's effectiveness but because his prediction led him to unintentionally behave differently with different groups of participants. The experimenter expectancy effect, in this sense, is an issue in the control of "extraneous variables" in experimental research.

To exemplify this methodological issue, imagine a physician conducting an experiment to determine the effectiveness of two pain-reducing drugs. He dispenses, in a random fashion, drug X and drug Y to a random sample of patients. Perhaps the doctor has heard good things about the efficacy of drug Y; perhaps in a few nonrandom cases his patients have extolled the drug's relief-giving powers. The doctor has an expectation hypothesis that patients given drug Y will respond better than patients given drug X. Furthermore, he knows which patients have received which drug and has entered this information on the patient's records. (To keep matters relatively uncomplicated we will assume that both drugs look exactly alike, taste and smell alike, and have the same "side-effects.") While the patient sample has been randomly selected, the drugs dispensed in a random fashion and made to appear virtually identical, the experimenter (the doctor) has an expectation about each drug's performance and knows who is getting which drug. As a result of this expectation, the doctor's behavior in dispensing drug X and drug Y might differ. Differential eye contact, differential nonverbal vocalizations, perhaps even other behaviors which differentially arouse evaluation apprehension in each group of patients could lead patients to report, and even experience, greater pain relief with drug Y than drug X.

How might the effects of the doctor's, or any experimenter's, expectations be controlled? The answer is rather simple, although it may be difficult to implement fully in particular experiments. We cannot tell the doctor to stop having his expectation; even if we did, I doubt that that would help in controlling its effect. We can, however, deprive him of the knowledge about which patients are receiving which drug. We can "blind" him to the drug treatment condition of his patients until he has collected all of his data. While he will still have his hypothesis about the drugs' effects, he will have no effective expectation as to how any particular patient will respond. If he unwittingly behaves differently toward patients, his behavior will be unrelated to which drug was dispensed. To accomplish this control we might have each patient go to a given druggist who dispenses the drug and records who gets what. Only when the experiment is over does the druggist release this information to the doctor. Similar and alternative procedures having the same effect can be devised for social-psychological experiments to control for experimenter expectancy effects (Rosenthal, 1966; Timaeus, 1973).

THE EXPERIMENTER EFFECT AS AN INTERPERSONAL INFLUENCE PHENOMENON

While interest in and controversy about the experimenter expectancy effect arose and was maintained because of its implications for experimental methodology, currently its relevance to the study of interpersonal influence is receiving emphasis. Interpersonal influence is a very broad area of study which refers to the phenomenon of the behavior of one person or group affecting the behavior of others. Such topics as conformity, obedience, social facilitation, persuasion, attitude change, and compliance are a few which comprise the study of interpersonal influence. Some of these phenomena involve one person or a group intentionally trying to induce another to behave in a particular way, such as persuasion. Others involve unintentional influence, such as social facilitation phenomena. Nevertheless, there may be unintentional components to even intentional influence attempts. The experimenter expectancy paradigm can serve as a vehicle to point up and investigate subtle forms of unintended communication that may underlie many forms of interpersonal influence.

Research on questions regarding the experimenter expectancy effect can also be informed by conceptualizations and findings from the broader interpersonal influence area. In discussing attitude change produced by persuasive communications, McGuire (1969) analyzed the change process into a set of successive, mediational steps. For attitude, and behavioral, change to occur, McGuire suggested that the listener must (1) pay attention to the communication, (2) comprehend its arguments, (3) yield to its conclusions, (4) remember the conclusion and his yielding to it, and (5) engage in attitude-relevant behavior. Variables which facilitate attention, comprehension, yielding, retention, and action should facilitate or increase the likelihood of attitude and behavior change. But a given variable, for example the listener's anxiety, might function to facilitate some steps and hinder others. Attention and comprehension (message reception) might decrease as the listener's anxiety increased. Yielding, however, might be related in a direct way to anxiety; the more anxious the listener, the less critical and resistant he might be. This scheme of mediational steps, although developed for analysis of one form of intentional influence, might profitably be employed to investigate and organize the effects of variables on the experimenter expectancy effect. Not only the experimenter's behavior, but "structural" aspects of the experimenter (e.g., sex, status, chronic anxiety) and of the laboratory situation (e.g., orderliness, comfort), as well as conditions and characteristics of the participants, have all been found to affect the magnitude and direction of the experimenter expectancy effect. For example, experimenters rated higher in "dominance" and "professionalism" have been found to obtain greater expectancy effects than those rated lower on these characteristics (Rosenthal, 1966, 1969). Application of McGuire's scheme would lead us to ask which particular mediational steps in the influence process are facilitated by the experimenter's dominance and professionalism. Similar questions could be posed with regard to conditions and characteristics of the participants. Does evaluation apprehension function to increase attention to cues; or does it primarily facilitate yielding? Or is its enhancement of the experimenter expectancy effect a product of both increased attention and increased yielding?

Of perhaps greater value would be using the multiple-step scheme to consider why variables that one might hypothesize would have an effect on the experimenter expectancy effect do not. For example, Rosenthal (1966) reports that across a number of experiments, participants' "need for social approval" (Crowne and Marlowe, 1960) has been found to be unrelated to participants' susceptibility to experimenter expectancy influence. Yet need for social approval, as a characteristic of participants, has been found to be related to yielding to other forms of interpersonal influence, particularly those of an intentional nature. Why the discrepancy? Perhaps a person with a greater need for social approval is not as sensitive to the major sources of cues that convey an experimenter's expectation (attention). Or he may be less able to decode the clue value of the cues, even if he can pay attention to them (comprehension). We saw that nonverbal vocal cues were very important in communicating the experimenter's expectation. A participant with a high need for social approval may be much more sensitive to the visual channel and thus miss what are perhaps more subtle vocal cues. Whatever may be the case, applying ideas and findings from the broader interpersonal influence literature would open new questions for investigations and perhaps lead to more precise understanding. It seems worthwhile at this time for those interested in interpersonal influence phenomena and those pursuing an understanding of the mechanisms and processes involved in the experimenter expectancy effect to attempt greater integration and coordination of their findings and research endeavors.

REFERENCES

Adair, J. G., & Epstein, J. S. Verbal cues in the mediation of experimenter bias. *Psychological Reports*, 1968, *22*, 1045-1053.

Barber, T. X. & Silver, M. J. Fact, fiction, and the experimenter bias effect. *Psychological Bulletin Monograph*, 1968, *70*(2), 1-29.

Crowne, D. P., and Marlowe, D. A new scale of social desirability independent of psychopathology. *Journal of Consulting Psychology*, 1960, *24*, 349-354.

Duncan, S. D., Jr., Rosenberg, M. J., & Finkelstein, J. The paralanguage of experimenter bias. *Sociometry*, 1969, *33*, 207-219.

Duncan, S. D., Jr., & Rosenthal, R. Vocal emphasis in experimenters' instruction reading as unintended determinants of subjects' responses. *Language and Speech*, 1968, *11*, 20-26.

Jones, R. A., & Cooper, J. Mediation of experimenter effects. *Journal of Personality and Social Psychology*, 1971, *20*, 70-74.

McGuire, W. J. The nature of attitudes and attitude change. In G. Lindzey & E. Aronson (Eds.), *The handbook of social psychology* (2nd ed.; vol. 3). Reading, Mass.: Addison-Wesley, 1969. Pp. 136-314.

Minor, M. W. Experimenter-expectancy effect as a function of evaluation apprehension. *Journal of Personality and Social Psychology*, 1970, *15*, 326-332.

Orne, M. T. On the social psychology of the psychological experiment: With particular reference to demand characteristics and their implications. *American Psychologist,* 1962, *17,* 776-783.

Orne, M. T. Demand characteristics and the concept of quasi-controls. In R. Rosenthal & R. L. Rosnow (Ed.), *Artifact in behavioral research.* New York: Academic Press, 1969. Pp. 143-179.

Rosenberg, M. J. When dissonance fails: On eliminating evaluation apprehension from attitude measurement. *Journal of Personality and Social Psychology,* 1965, *1,* 18-42.

Rosenberg, M. J. The conditions and consequences of evaluation apprehension. In R. Rosenthal & R. L. Rosnow (Eds.), *Artifact in behavioral research.* New York: Academic Press, 1969. Pp. 279-349.

Rosenthal, R. On the social psychology of the psychological experiment: The experimenter's hypothesis as unintended determinant of experimental results. *American Scientist,* 1963, *51*(2), 268-283.

Rosenthal, R. *Experimental effects in behavioral research.* New York: Appleton-Century-Crofts, 1966.

Rosenthal, R. Interpersonal expectations: Effects of the experimenter's hypotheses. In R. Rosenthal & R. L. Rosnow (Eds.), *Artifact in behavioral research.* New York: Academic Press, 1969. Pp. 181-277.

Rosenthal, R. & Fode, K. L. Psychology of the scientist: V. Three experiments in experimenter bias. *Psychological Reports,* 1963, *12,* 491-511.

Timaeus, E. Some non-verbal and paralinguistic cues as mediators of experimenter expectancy effects. In M. Von Cranach & I. Vine (Eds.), *Social communication and movement.* New York: Academic Press, 1973. Pp. 445-464.

3

AARON HERSHKOWITZ

Naturalistic Observations on Chronically Hospitalized Patients: I. The Effects of "Strangers"

INTRODUCTION

Despite a great deal of interest and speculation about the nature of the chronically hospitalized mental patient, very little systematic or theoretical information is available about him. There are many reasons for this. In the first place, the emphasis of research in this area has usually been on diagnostic categories, *i.e.,* schizophrenia, organic brain syndrome (11, 12). Actually, as is well known, no group of long-term hospitalized patients is homogeneous with respect to these classifications. Moreover, most investigators, when they deal with so-called "chronics" do so with an interest in individual patients on a testing and/or therapeutic level. Their immediate clinical and practical concern is to understand a single patient, or at best a small group of them, rather than the activity of the group as a whole (6). Some investigators who have studied the chronic population have used pre-categorized rating scales or judgments to compare patients under different conditions (1, 4). Such a procedure, useful as it is, has made for only limited descriptive material and only touched on some narrow aspects of "chronicity." It has left out, for the most part, the larger context of the patients' behavior (8).

One of the main stumbling blocks in the investigation and understanding of such patients is the fact that a large majority of them are non-testable and non-verbal—in short, they can be termed non-social or non-communicative. Very little is known about the overt behavior of chronically hospitalized patients on a day-to-day basis; scant attention has been paid to describing the setting and stimulus conditions which instigate such behavior; and few attempts have been made to manipulate experimentally relevant variables in an on-going context. In other areas with a large gap in social communication, for example, with animals and children, there

Source: From Aaron Hershkowitz, "Naturalistic Observations on Chronically Hospitalized Patients: I. The Effects of 'Strangers,'" *Journal of Nervous and Mental Disease,* 135, 258-64. Copyright 1962, The Williams & Wilkins Co. Reproduced by permission.

This study was supported by Grant M-4625 of the National Institute of Public Health, U.S. Public Health Service. Part of the paper was read at the XIV International Congress of Applied Psychology, Copenhagen, August 19, 1961.

has been a large amount of descriptive data gleaned by careful and intense observations (2, 5, 9).

In those fields, observation in a natural setting has become a recognized and important technique which has yielded encouraging and worthwhile results (2, 5, 7). The present investigator believes that it can be an equally profitable procedure for other populations. In the specific case of the long-term mental patient, it is quite obvious that descriptive observational material is absolutely necessary both practically and theoretically. Practically, because if such patients are to be more than just management or custodial problems, more information—sheer information as such—is needed. Unfortunately, the usual psychological procedures have not yielded much information. Many patients in the sample in this study had not been tested or interviewed for periods ranging from five to 15 years. Some records of the chronic population do not contain anything new, of psychological import, since the original admission.

On the theoretical level as well, such naturalistic data merit attention. A good case in point is the lack of systematic information on such a relevant variable as the regularized or so-called stereotyped behavior pattern that seems to characterize the long-term mental patient. The concept of rigidity has often been invoked to "explain" such behavior (3, 10). Although it has had considerable influence on the theoretical level, no effort has been made to determine under what conditions and how frequently behavior that could be called "rigid" actually occurs in a naturalistic setting. This has restricted our understanding of such behavior, most particularly with non-verbal patients. Moreover, it obscures the relation of such behaviors to similar activities which might occur in other groups which, under ordinary circumstances, are not considered "abnormal." For example, in everyday life there are numerous routinized, repetitive or regularized activities which do not appear mysterious or atypical, i.e., they do not merit being classified as "rigid." It is clear that naturalistic observations can thus serve both as an avenue of understanding these patients, and a necessary requisite for subsequent experimental manipulation. This is the rationale of the research here reported. It is also the background for the techniques utilized.

STATEMENT OF THE PROBLEM

The initial task was to investigate the general activities and behavior patterns of chronically hospitalized patients. As such, the research was not designed to focus upon any one kind of behavior or any one type of patient. Rather, its aim was to capture, in a descriptive-observational way, as much as possible of the on-going behavior of a person or persons in an on-going setting. Two levels of observations were utilized. First, minute-by-minute detailed recordings of the behavior of single patients in many settings over the entire waking day were obtained. Second, intense observations of groups of patients in a single setting for periods varying from 30 to 90 minutes were made. The method of observation, which will be dealt with in more detail below, was "naturalistic" and non-focused. The observers were instructed—indeed they had to be trained—to describe what they saw directly, without recourse to pre-established psychological categories and without any pre-biasing theoretical assumptions.

OBSERVATIONAL PROCEDURES AND CHARACTERISTICS OF THE WARD POPULATION

The first problem emerging from an observational study was, of course, the effect of the observers themselves. An immediate analysis of the records brought this out directly. What is important here is one of the effects, *i.e.*, that of the observers being considered as "strangers" or "intruders" in the setting. In order to assess the influence of the observers on

FIGURE 3.1
Schematic Outline of Dayroom

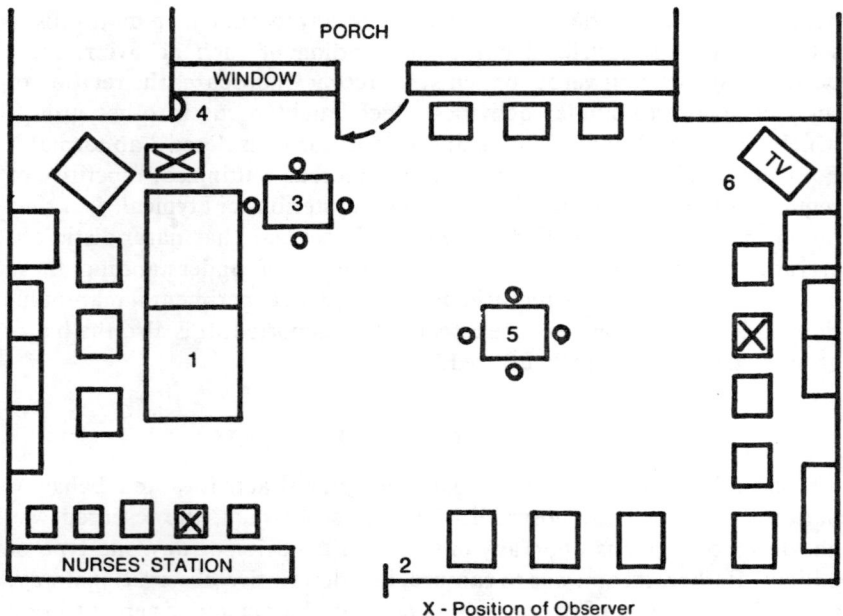

X - Position of Observer

this level, the first six behavior records of patients in one setting (the day-room) were analyzed. Certain highly routinized behavior patterns emerged, which served as a basis for speculation. These, in turn, led to further detailed observation.

The observations took place on a chronic closed neuropsychiatric ward of a Veterans Administration General Medical and Surgical Hospital. There were 29 service-connected patients on this ward, who carried diagnoses ranging from brain damage to chronic schizophrenia. Their age varied from 26 to 75 years (median: 42). Length of hospitalization ranged from two to 35 years; the median length of hospitalization was 14.5 years. The patients came from a wide variety of ethnic, religious and socioeconomic backgrounds.[1] A full-time psychologist was in charge of the ward and under him were six psychiatric residents in training at the Yale Medical School. A full-time nurse and two aides were available to service the ward. The ward itself was chosen because it was a closed ward which lent itself practically and efficiently to intense observational procedures. More importantly, the patients on this ward were, for the most part, those considered to be non-verbal and non-testable. For reasons already mentioned, they represented a most interesting and valuable group for full-time observational methods.

Three observers, seated at different and strategic parts of the dayroom (see Figure 3.1) recorded on a minute-by-minute basis everything that occurred in that setting. Each observation lasted 30 to 45 minutes. Observers were instructed to record descriptively, and in simple language, everything that they could perceive directly and immediately. At a later time, opportunity was given to insert parenthetically into the record all material that the observer felt was of interest, but which was not immediately perceived. These included judgments, inferences and imputations about behavior related to things outside the setting as well as interpretations of directly perceived actions.

In order to facilitate the descriptions, a schematic diagram of the dayroom was made. The room was subdivided so that each observer was assigned responsibility for activity in a limited sector or sub-section of the setting. Areas and prominent objects, such as furniture, etc., were further symbolized and coded to ease the recording of patient activities.

Figure 3.1 is a schematic outline of this dayroom together with its relevant objects, furniture and equipment. It should be noted that, for the most part, the chairs were arranged around the perimeter of the room; the entrances from the corridor and the exits to the porch were arranged at opposite ends of the room. Most important for the present purpose, it should be pointed out that there was a bulletin board on the right hand side of the entrance (2 in Figure 3.1); that a ping-pong table took up the

largest portion of the left side of the room (1 in Figure 3.1); and that a
water fountain was located at the extreme left corner of the dayroom (4 in
Figure 3.1).

The observers sat on three different sides of the dayroom: one on the
immediate left on the entrance side; one on the opposite side of the room;
and the third on the right side in the middle of the side wall (see X's in
Figure 3.1). Observation positions were selected so that each recorder had
an unrestricted view of the entire dayroom and, most particularly, was in a
position to cover a specific portion of it.

Immediately after the observation, the three separate records were co-
ordinated into a single unitary, overall setting description. In this way all
the behavior of each patient in the dayroom could be accounted for. It was
therefore possible to trace the behavior of any single patient from the start
to the finish of the recording period. It was at this time that the paren-
thetical remarks mentioned above were made on the record.

RESULTS

A first look at the records indicated a striking regularity in the entering
behavior of the patients. This led to an examination of the behavior pattern of each patient coming into the dayroom and to note: (1) which place
the patient went to upon entering; (2) how long he stayed there; (3) what
he did there; and (4) what place he went to next. The first six consecutive
observations (over a period of two and one-half weeks) were taken as a
basis for describing patients' entering activity.

Table 3.1 presents a breakdown of the three main places that patients
went to upon entering the dayroom. It will be noted that at the first session
patients almost invariably went to one of three places: the ping-pong
table, the bulletin board or the water fountain. It may also be seen that
this kind of behavior showed a marked decrease at each subsequent

TABLE 3.1
Percentage Breakdown of First Contact upon Entering
Dayroom (First Six Observations)

Number of Entrances in Dayroom	First Contact upon Entering			
	Ping-Pong Table	Bulletin Board	Water Fountain	Others
28	50%	35%	12%	4%
36	41	33	17	9
30	40	27	16	16
27	27	14	22	37
31	13	13	13	61
24	17	8	17	58

FIGURE 3.2
Percentage of "Way Station" Behavior upon Entering Dayroom

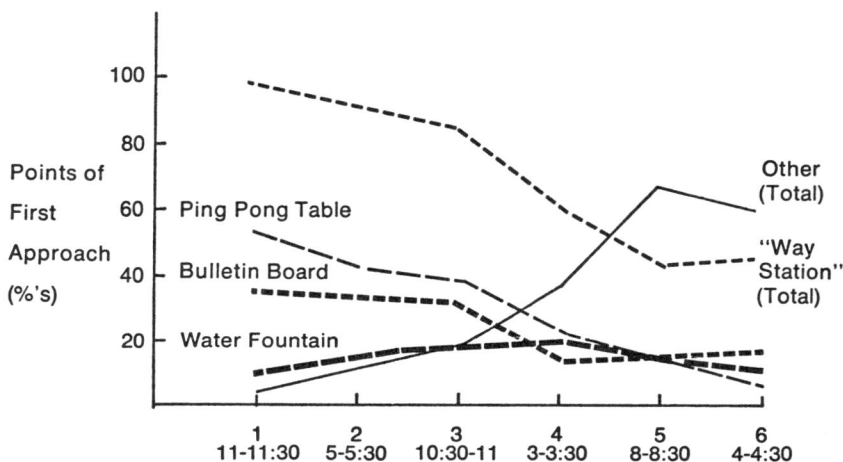

observation. The total amount of behavior at these three places decreased from 96 per cent at the first observation to 42 per cent at the sixth observation. A chi-square test indicates that this decrease is significant ($p <$ .001).

Figure 3.2 shows the behavior in a more dramatic way. Under the heading of "others" are included such places and objects as the table in the middle of the room, the televison area, the nurses' station, various chairs and the like. In general there were twenty other places at which a patient could stop.

An analysis of patient behavior at this particular sensitive spot further revealed that he did not perform any meaningful or functional act in that locale. At the ping-pong table, for example, the patient would move an ashtray or re-arrange a newspaper; often he merely touched the table and went away. Few, if any, of the patients actually looked at the bulletin board directly. Indeed there was rarely anything on it. With respect to the water fountain some of the patients (50 per cent) did, in fact, drink. The remaining half merely jiggled the faucet or touched it before leaving the area.

A similar picture emerges if the time spent in each area is examined. It was quite minimal. Frequently it was a mere hesitation, ordinarily noted in the records as a spot where a shift of the direction of motion or activity occurred. At other times, there was an actual pause and a slight "wait." The records are clear that at no time was there more than a minute spent lingering in these areas. Not infrequently the time was less than 15 seconds.[2]

What the patients did next was equally of interest. In the first place, the subsequent move and stop was always one which lasted a relatively long period of time. It was at this time that a patient often found his seat. In the second place, it was noted that the direction in which the patient went was invariably away from the nearest observer. In the first three observations, for example, of the initial contacts with the ping-pong table, 86 per cent subsequently came to rest in the upper right quadrant of the dayroom. That is, they were always picked up on the observer's records of that area. From the bulletin board, 76 per cent of the patients went next to the right side—the only side not immediately occupied by an observer. From the water fountain, 83 per cent of the patients exited to the porch. This put them out of the range of observation altogether. Finally, it should be mentioned that the subsequent move was, by and large, functionally oriented, *e.g.*, the patient found a seat, obtained a cigarette, looked at television.

The findings with respect to the water fountain are of special interest, since there appears to be no difference between the first and sixth observation. In fact, the activity to and from the water fountain appears to be constant. In this connection it should be pointed out that there was a window next to the water fountain which gave the patient a view of the porch. The records clearly show that the patients used the window to look out to the porch. As indicated, 83 per cent of the patients ended up on the porch after being at the water fountain. However, the water fountain was functionally used half of the time, *i.e.*, for drinking. It could not be clearly stated, therefore, that the water fountain was not an endpoint in the behavior. It should be noted that at the end of the sixth observation 50 per cent of the patients still utilized the water fountain functionally. But it was of special interest that of these none went out on the porch. Although the numbers involved here are too small to make any conclusive generalizations, it tends to indicate that for half of the patients, at least originally, the water fountain was used for something other than drinking.

We may summarize the results by noting that the stereotyped entering behavior dropped considerably over six observations; that the absolute number of places to which patients initially went increased; that these places could be considered functionally useful to them. In what follows some tentative generalizations will be offered to account for these findings.

DISCUSSION AND CONCLUSIONS

The most striking aspect of the first three observational sessions was the stereotyped and rigid "place" behavior. This led to the following hypothesis. Upon entering the dayroom and perceiving strangers (*i.e.*, the observers) most patients seemed to orient themselves so as to avoid, or in some way to disengage themselves from what was strange in the room. The points toward which they gravitated functioned as "way stations." They served as places from which the patient could best judge who was in the dayroom, what could be done about it and where the next safe step could be made. One may speculate about the reasons for this apparent stereotyped behavior and the subsequent changes in time. The "way station" may be utilized as a place from which the patient can plan his next move so he can be most comfortable in what he considers a threatening situation. This information, for the most part, leads him to an action which goes in the direction away from the source of the perceived disturbance.

In order to test the above hypothesis more actively, subsequent observations were made when an additional strange person was present in the dayroom. These took place at the twelfth observational session, approximately thirteen days after the last observational session shown in Table 3.1 [above]. This stranger, who had not been in the dayroom before and was not known to the patients, caused a dramatic rise in "way station" behavior. From the previous 42 per cent—which could be considered to be a chance expectation—it rose to 85 per cent. Moreover, the patients avoided the side of the room where the stranger was. In fact, the patients seemed to have an imaginary line separating them from the stranger. It is also noteworthy that the absolute number of entries into the dayroom decreased. However, this was not statistically significant.

On a qualitative level it is obvious that the behavior of patients in the "way station" is, in a sense, indirect behavior. The patient does not come into the dayroom looking around, making obvious and deliberate efforts to get away from the stranger. Rather, he acts as if he was not interested or not directly involved in the affair. That is, the patient comes in ostensibly to go somewhere, *i.e.*, the ping-pong table, the bulletin board, the water fountain. Actually, the presence of observers seem to make him unsure of where he wants to go. He then has to determine where to go, all the while maintaining the appearance that he is disinterested in the observer and that he knows what he is up to. In other words, the use of the "way station" stop enables the patient to deal with the disturbance as if there were no disturbance, *i.e.*, to get away from the "intruder" without showing any reaction to his presence.

This type of behavior is not unlike that occurring in some everyday non-institutional situations—*i.e.*, when one comes into a crowded room and is uncertain about who is there or what he wants to do. One way to deal with this is to act as if one has, in fact, a mission or knows the place. One does not ordinarily act as if one is lost or afraid or disturbed. This analogy between the routinized behavior of the patients and the common, everyday situation should not be drawn too strictly. There are some differences between them. The patients act very much more indirectly. They also seem to be more intent in getting away from any potentially unpredictable or unknown social interactions. Moreover, this behavior can be evoked in a setting very familiar to them. That such a setting can be turned into a strange place by the intrusion of another person is quite striking. One can imagine what it would be like for them to meet a stranger in a novel place under new conditions. Another difference which is important is the fact that the threshold and sensitivity of "strangeness" is very different for the chronic patient. A wide array of objects and/or people may induce the stereotyped behavior described above. All of these points merit further investigation.

The finding that the effects of strangeness are reduced over a period of time is significant. It indicates that the patients can, in fact, adjust over a period of time to newcomers. It also indicates that the chronic patient is not completely unaware of his surroundings, that he reacts to them and adjusts to them, albeit indirectly. At the same time, it is the indirection that makes it difficult for the investigator to become aware of the disturbance and subsequent accommodation.

In conclusion, some directions for further investigation in this area may be mentioned. It would be interesting to determine the range of people and objects toward which a "strangeness reaction" can occur. Further investigation is also needed to trace the patients' accommodation toward different people in different settings. One possible reason for the relative rapidity of the accommodations to strangers presented here is that during these sessions the observers sat at the same position over a relatively long period of time. If the observers had changed their seats, if the locale or the observers were changed frequently and unpredictably, in all probability there would have been more "way station" behavior. Finally, more observational studies in a naturalistic setting are required to establish in what way patients chose "way stations" and how these are related to the physical setting and routine of the ward.

REFERENCES

Ameen, L. and Laffal, J. The response of locked ward patients to the change of doctors in a residency program. *Diseases of the Nervous System, 21,* 1-3, 1960.

Barker, R. G. and Wright, H. F. *Midwest and its children.* Row Peterson, Evanston, Illinois, 1954.

Goldstein, K. Concerning rigidity. *Character and Personality, 11,* 209-226, 1943.

Laffal, J., Sarason, I. G., Ameen, L. and Stern, A. Individuals in groups: A behavior rating technique. *International Journal of Social Psychiatry, 11,* 254-262, 1957.

Lorenz, K. *King Solomon's Ring.* Translated by M. K. Wilson. Crowell, New York, 1952.

Pace, R. E. Situational therapy. *Journal of Personality, 25,* 578-588, 1957.

Scott, J. The place of observation in biological and psychological science. *American Psychologist, 10,* 61-63, 1955.

Stanton, A. H. and Schwartz, M. S. *The mental hospital.* Basic Books, New York, 1954.

Tinbergen, N. *The study of instincts.* Clarendon Press, Oxford, 1951.

Werner, H. *Comparative psychology of mental development.* Revised ed. Follett, Chicago, 1948.

Wittenborn, J. Symptom patterns in a group of mental hospital patients. *Journal of Consulting Psychology, 15,* 290-302, 1951.

Wittenborn, J. The behavioral symptoms of certain organic psychoses. *Journal of Consulting Psychology, 16,* 104-106, 1952.

NOTES

1. An analysis of social class, religion, etc. did not show any relationship to the behavior involved in this report.

2. The observational record was performed at one-minute intervals and shorter intervals than these were not directly obtainable.

4

MICHAEL G. EFRAN and J. ALLAN CHEYNE

Affective Concomitants of the Invasion of Shared Space: Behavioral, Physiological, and Verbal Indicators

An experiment was conducted in which subjects were required to intrude on the shared space of two conversing confederates. It was hypothesized that these subjects would experience greater affective arousal and display more agonistic gestures than would control subjects who were not forced to intrude on the space of others. As predicted, subjects in the intrusion conditions displayed more agonistic facial responses and later reported less positive mood ratings than did the control subjects. Differences which had been predicted in cardiovascular activity were not obtained. The interrelations between nonverbal agonistic displays, stress, and human territorial behavior were discussed with special reference to the effects of high population density.

Two complementary and active research areas with both human and nonhuman subjects are the study of proxemic behavior in general and the more restricted study of the effects of population density and over-crowdedness. A consistent finding in the animal literature is that conditions of high population density are associated with the development of physiological anomalies in individual animals which collectively tend to suppress the group's continued growth and to threaten its adaptability. These conditions have been observed in detail both in the laboratory (e.g., Calhoun, 1971; Thiessen, 1964) and in the field (e.g., Christian, Flyger, & Davis, 1960; Deevey, 1966). Many of the commonly observed reactions, such as adrenal hypertrophy (Christian, 1963; Christian & Davis, 1966; Deevey, 1966; Rodgers & Thiessen, 1964), suggest that animals experience increased stress. However, relatively little has been done to examine the nature of the specific social and behavioral acts which vary as a func-

Source: Michael G. Efran and J. Allan Cheyne, "Affective Concomitants of the Invasion of Shared Space: Behavioral, Physiological, and Verbal Indicators," *Journal of Personality and Social Psychology*, 1974, *29*, 219-226. Copyright 1974 by the American Psychological Association. Reprinted by permission.

This research was supported by Canada Council Grant S70-0342.

The authors wish to express their gratitude to P. Wright who served as the first experimenter in this project, to R. Rigelhof and the Scarborough College graphics unit for their technical assistance and advice, to the Superintendent of Scarborough College and his staff for the physical modifications to the laboratory which were required, and to the many others who assisted in conducting this experiment.

tion of population density and which ultimately are responsible for stress reactions under these conditions (Stokols, 1972).

The literature on personal space and interaction distance is not specifically concerned with overcrowding but does often deal with the social psychology of stress. Agonistic behaviors and the means by which animals communicate status, threat, and submission are interwoven with the distance maintained between animals. The traditional concept of dominance hierarchies in social groups, for example, is now commonly associated with territorial and proxemic behavior. Dominance hierarchies are often reflected in the distances maintained between members of social groups (Chance, 1967; Leyhausen, 1971; Madge & Madge, 1965; McBride, James, & Shoffner, 1963). Furthermore, the reactions elicited in spatial confrontations often consist of aggressive displays which precede actual attack behavior, as well as signs of submission which serve to resolve disputes nonviolently. For example, Chance (1962) has discussed the role of staring and gaze avoidance in structuring agonistic encounters in nonhuman primates. Ellsworth, Carlsmith, and Henson (1972) have examined related phenomena with human subjects.

Under crowded conditions the opportunity for personal space violations and other nonviolent dominance-related confrontations increases. These encounters involve spatial parameters and nonverbal acts through which conflicts are conveyed, provoked, avoided, or resolved. An underlying theme in the present research is that it may be useful to consider the cumulative reaction to these numerous nonviolent, perhaps even individually trivial, encounters as a critical factor mediating the negative effects of crowdedness.

While the nonverbal communication literature and the personal space literature have not focused on the issue of crowdedness, the results of the few available studies are consistent with the results of investigations with nonhuman primates and other animals. Griffitt and Veitch (1971), for example, found that people experienced negative affective consequences when exposed to high population densities. Freedman, Levy, Buchanan, and Price (1972) also found negative affective consequences under some conditions of high density. Studies of proximity and nonverbal communication have consistently shown how nonverbal cues, affective arousal, and interpersonal spacing are interrelated. Decreased interpersonal distance, for example, has been found to be associated with the amount of eye contact engaged in by two people (Argyle & Dean, 1965). Similarly, distance has been found to influence the number of emitted self-manipulative gestures (Kleck, 1970) which are indicative of negative affect (Freedman, 1972; Grant, 1968; McGrew, 1972; Rosenfeld, 1966). People also interpose less distance between themselves and others that they like than others that they dislike (Allgeier & Byrne, 1973; Hall, 1959; Little, 1965). Data collected by McBride, King, and James (1965) even suggest that changes in galvanic skin response (GSR) accompany encroachment of the subject's personal space by the experimenter.

The thesis being developed here is that overcrowding represents an end point on a continuum. The dramatic effects observed in extremely crowded conditions may in large measure be the product of reactions to mundane interpersonal encounters which are engaged in on an everyday basis. It remains to be demonstrated that these mundane everyday interactions arouse negative affect in the individuals experiencing them. The study reported here tested the general hypothesis that behaviors which have been considered under the rubric of personal space and nonverbal communication may also usefully be construed as confrontations which occasion negative affective arousal and which may be related to the more dramatic consequences of high population density.

In two previous studies (Cheyne & Efran, 1972; Efran & Cheyne, 1973) it was demonstrated that when two conversants are separated by distances of up to 48 inches, people are reluctant to walk between them, even when to walk around them entails some inconvenience. It was suggested that by conversing, two people exercise an implicit territorial claim to the space between them which others are reluctant to violate and that encounters of this variety represent minimal confrontations of the type previously discussed.

In the present experiment, nonverbal acts, physiological reactions, and subjective mood ratings were recorded for subjects who either walked between two conversants, past (but not between) two conversants, or down a vacant corridor. It was predicted that subjects who violated two conversants' shared space would show more negative affect, as reflected in physiological arousal, nonverbal signs of agonistic behavior, and lower subjective mood scale ratings, than would subjects who walked down a vacant corridor. Subjects who walked past (but not between) two conversants were expected to show an intermediate level of affective arousal since walking in close proximity to two conversants (i.e., within earshot) may also be interpreted in some sense as a violation of their privacy.

METHOD

Subjects

The subjects for this experiment were 39 male students at Scarborough College of the University of Toronto.[1] They participated in partial fulfillment of an introductory psychology course requirement.

Procedure

A cover story was used to justify the physiological recording procedure and to permit observation in a context which the subject was not likely to view as part of the experiment. Each subject was given a scheduled time to arrive at the laboratory and was tested individually.

When the subject arrived, he was admitted to the laboratory suite by the first experimenter (a graduate research assistant), who explained that he would conduct the experiment for a member of the psychology faculty (the first author was identified in this role and served as the second experimenter). The experiment was described as one concerned with the physiological correlates of perception. It was explained that after the experimental session, each subject would be briefly interviewed by the senior investigator to be certain that everything had gone as planned. The research assistant pointed to a door within the suite and told the subject that the faculty member was currently working in the room indicated. Following the experiment the subject was told to go there to meet with him. The subject and the first experimenter then entered another room, where a bogus task was described and conducted. In this room the subject was shown a pursuit rotor, as well as an array of clocks, counters, and other paraphernalia. It was explained that the subject's heart rate was to be monitored while he simultaneously tracked a moving light source with one hand and used his other hand to depress a button signaling detection of an auditory tone. Two recording electrodes were placed under the subject's shirt and attached to a small FM transmitter which was contained in a vinyl belt which the subject wore. The subject was shown a sample of his electrocardiogram (EKG) record as it was received and plotted by a recorder in the same room. It was explained that telemetry was being used since it permitted maximum mobility during the tracing task. Each subject was then engaged in six trials of a bogus task designed to look impressively scientific and important. During this time the experimenter recorded some of the changing values on the numerous clocks and counters.

Following completion of the bogus task, the subject was asked to sit as relaxed and quiet as possible so that a base-line record of heart rate activity could be obtained. The experimenter said that during this time he would bring the perceptual task data to the senior investigator, who would make a preliminary examination of it to determine whether additional tracking trials would be necessary. The experimenter then explained that after the data had been examined and after sufficient EKG base-line information had been recorded, the subject would be called on the intercom system. It was explained that at that time he should go directly to the room which had earlier been indicated. The subject was asked to leave the electrodes in place in case additional trials were necessary. Finally the experimenter thanked the subject for his participation and left the room, closing the door behind him.

Following the rest period, the subject was called on the intercom by the senior investigator who again asked the subject to walk to the room earlier indicated so they could meet for a few minutes. As the subject left the room to comply with the instructions, he encountered the actual independent variable manipulation. The position of two confederates in the hall ensured that depending on the condition the subject was assigned to, he either had to walk between two conversants (violation condition), past but not between them (minimum violation condition), or down a corridor in which the confederates were replaced by inanimate objects (no-violation condition) to reach his destination. A hidden motion picture camera with telephoto zoom lens was used to record the subject's facial expressions as he walked down the corridor. Door switches activated an event recorder channel on the EKG to designate that portion of the record obtained while the subject was in the corridor.

After entering the interview room, the subject was asked to return to the first room to pick up a file folder with his name on it which, it was explained, had inadvertently been left behind. This procedure was followed in order to expose the subject to the independent variable manipulation two more times.

When the subject returned with the folder, he was told that no additional trials would be necessary and was asked to complete a mood scale. This was justified to him by indicating that mood is an important determinant of physiological responding which other investigators often failed to take into account.

FIGURE 4.1
Laboratory Suite and Positions A, B, and C of Confederates

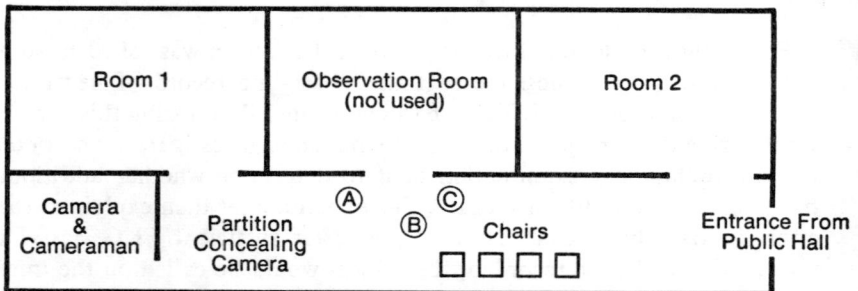

Independent Variable

Figure 4.1 represents the laboratory suite. The corridor was 6 feet wide and 27 feet long with 18 feet between the doors to Room 1 and Room 2. In the violation condition the first experimenter stood in Position A and a female confederate stood in Position B. In the minimum violation condition the first experimenter stood in Position A and the female confederate stood in Position C. In both of these conditions the experimenter wore a white laboratory coat and the female wore casual but tidy attire. They spoke in normal conversational tones and kept their own gestural behavior to a minimum. As the subject approached, they momentarily paused in their conversation, the confederate in Position A glanced at him, and then the conversation proceeded. The conversants were instructed not to emit any nonverbal cues which the subject might regard as a "signal of passage." In the no-violation condition a tripod-mounted television camera (with lens capped and aimed at the floor) was placed by itself in Position B.

Dependent Variables

Heart Rate.   Frontal-plane EKG measurements were taken with chest-placed electrodes to minimize muscle noise. EKG telemetry was accomplished with an Onyx biomedical FM transmitter, a specially adapted Sony FM receiver, a Brush EKG preamplifier, and a Brush 200 general purpose recorder.

Expressive Behavior.   A Bolex 16-millimeter motion picture camera with telephoto zoom lens was used to record the subject's expressive behavior. The laboratory had been equipped with additional built-in fluorescent lighting fixtures which permitted filming in ambient light. High-speed film was used, and the corridor did not appear unusually bright to the casual observer. The camera and cameramen were concealed behind a plywood partition. Additional lenses protruding through holes cut in the partition, and aimed in obviously nonfunctional directions, as well as a television monitor and tripod-mounted camera placed in front of the partition, created the impression that the photographic equipment was in a state of storage rather than use.

The motion pictures were analyzed with an Athena 224 stop-motion film analyzer. This projector permits frame by frame viewing, as well as a variety of slow-motion presentation rates.

Mood Scale.   This scale consisted of self-rated mood on six of the evaluative scales from the semantic differential (Osgood, Suci, & Tannenbaum, 1957). The scales were represented by the bipolar adjective pairs of good-bad, high-low, pleasant-unpleasant, comfortable-uncomfortable, happy-sad, and warm-cold. Instructions given prior to completion of this scale focused the subject's attention on how he felt while in the corridor. He was told that the experimenter was interested in the most precise measure of mood possible and that previous experience had shown that the best way to obtain this was to recall a specific and delimited time span which could be mentally reconstructed. The subject was then asked to recall and indicate exactly how he felt during the time between the moment he was called on the intercom and the moment he entered the interviewing room for the second time (i.e., the time corresponding to his walk in the hall).

RESULTS

Expressive Behavior

Predictions relating nonverbal signs of arousal to territorial violations had been made with reference to three specific categories of nonverbal behavior: the subject's pattern of eye closures, gaze and head direction, and expressive mouth gestures. The motion pictures were submitted to a frame by frame analysis and transcribed to yield simultaneous measures of these behaviors.

It was predicted that subjects who were exposed to violation conditions would experience the most affective arousal and would therefore reduce

TABLE 4.1
Mean Proportion of Frequency and Duration of Expressive Behaviors

Behavior	Violation (n = 13)	Minimum Violation (n = 11)	No Violation (n = 10)	F
Frequency of head and gaze down and eyes closed[a]	.44	.23	.08	9.83*****
Duration of head and gaze down and eyes closed[b]	.12	.06	.02	5.71***
Frequency of partial eye closure[b]	.14	.10	.04	4.96**
Duration of partial eye closure	.36	.25	.23	2.57*
Frequency of negative mouth gestures[a]	.86	.25	.09	9.61*****
Duration of negative mouth gestures	.17	.05	.02	7.12****

Note: $N = 34$. Five subjects were excluded from these analyses because complete film records were unavailable for them due to technical difficulties.
[a]Proportions reported have been multiplied by 100 to facilitate presentation.
[b]Proportions reported have been multiplied by 10 to facilitate presentation.
*$p < .10$.
**$p < .025$.
***$p < .01$.
****$p < .005$.
*****$p < .001$.

direct confrontation by closing their eyes or by displaying a submissive posture by directing their gaze downward or bowing their head (Chance, 1962; Grant, 1969; McGrew, 1972). Violation subjects were also expected to display the greatest amount of partial eye closure. This category of behavior may result from either an assertive frown posture (Blurton-Jones, 1971; Brannigan & Humphries, 1972; Grant, 1969; McGrew, 1972) or from the lowered eyelids associated with looking down. It was expected that subjects in the no-violation condition would show the fewest and shortest duration of these behaviors, subjects in the violation condition the most and longest durations of these behaviors, and subjects in the minimum violation condition an intermediate amount of this type of behavior. Similarly, it was expected that the number and duration of agonistic-related or arousal-related mouth gestures would vary as a function of territorial encroachment. The specific gestures recorded in the last category of behavior were tongue out, lips in, tight lips, mouth corners back, pursed mouth, and twist. These gestures have been described in detail elsewhere (Blurton-Jones, 1972; Grant, 1969; McGrew, 1972).

The relative frequency and duration for each category of expressive behavior are given in Table 4.1. Subjects varied in the amount of time they took to walk from one room to the other. Therefore, the absolute frequency and duration of nonverbal gestures were transformed to a proportion for each subject by dividing them by the total number of film frames recorded. The mouth gesture analyses were based on film records obtained during both walks from the experimental room to the interview room. Analyses of other gestures were limited to film obtained only on the first walk. It was necessary to exclude the second walk from the analyses of these gestures because the empty folder which the subjects carried became the target of considerable visual inspection, making the significance of gaze, head, and eye movements unclear. It can be seen from Table 4.1 that the predictions were supported by all of the comparisons except that for the total duration of partial eye closure which only approached significance. Each of the significance levels reported in Table 4.1 is based on an independent simple analysis of variance. The obtained value of F ($df = 2/31$) for each analysis is also given in Table 4.1. Multiple comparisons were evaluated at the .05 level of significance with Duncan's new multiple-range test. The violation group and minimum violation group were found to differ in mean frequency of head and gaze down and eyes closed, duration of head and gaze down and eyes closed, as well as frequency of negative mouth gestures. The minimum violation group and no-violation group differed in frequency of head and gaze down and eyes closed. The violation group and no-violation group differed in all analyses for which a significant main effect was reported.

In addition to the greater incidence of agonistic mouth gestures in the violation condition, those subjects who were expected to show the most arousal also showed the greatest variety of elicited agonistic mouth gestures. A mean of 1.62 different gestures was observed for subjects in the violation condition, .73 in the minimum violation condition, and .40 in the control no-violation condition ($F = 4.28$, $df = 2/31$, $p < .05$). In contrast to the large number of agonistic gestures observed, only 12 smiles were recorded. These consisted of simple, upper, and wide smiles (Grant, 1969) and were displayed by four subjects in the violation condition, three subjects in the minimum violation condition, and one subject in the no-violation condition.

Although subjects varied considerably in the amount of time required to walk between rooms, there were no systematic differences associated with the experimental manipulation.

Heart Rate

Each subject's heart rate during the rest period and during his first walk between the two rooms was calculated. Analysis of variance was used to assess these data with the treatment effect serving as a between-groups variable and the time of measurement (i.e., before or during the walk) serving as a within-group variable. The results of this analysis indicated a very significant overall heart rate increase ($F = 312$, $df = 2/24$, $p < .001$) but no other significant effects. Heart rate increases were observed for all subjects with a mean increase of 42%. The number of subjects represented in this analysis was slightly decreased due to record loss because of technical difficulties in telemetry. Inspection of the data failed to show any consistent pattern of heart rate change associated with the independent variable.

Mood Scale

Each of the six mood scale items were scored from $+3$ to -3 with a score of zero assigned to the neutral point on the scale. The item scores were summed to provide a mood rating for each subject. As hypothesized, subjects in the violation group expressed the least positive mood evaluation, subjects in the minimum violation group produced mood ratings of intermediate value, and subjects in the no-violation control group expressed the most positive moods. The mean mood rating obtained from each of these groups was 3.00, 4.27, and 9.20, respectively ($F = 6.30$, $df = 2/31$, $p < .01$). Duncan multiple-range tests indicated that the violation group and the minimum violation group each differed significantly from the control no-violation group ($p < .05$). The difference between the mean mood score for the violation condition and the minimum violation condition was not significant.

DISCUSSION

In the introduction it was argued that seemingly trivial social encounters may usefully be construed as potential interpersonal disputes. Handling these disputes was hypothesized to entail a state of negative affective arousal and was expected to produce the type of gestural behavior usually observed in agonistic interactions. Three parallel components of this hypothetical emotional state were operationally defined with reference to a microanalysis of nonverbal expressive behavior, a measure of cardiovascular activity, and a subjective mood scale. The hypothesis was strongly supported when affective arousal was identified by a microanalysis of nonverbal gestures. The results did not support the hypothesis when the emotional response was equated to changes in cardiovascular activity. The hypothesis also received strong support when arousal was defined by the individual's report of how he felt.

Subjects reported less positive moods under the violation condition than under the no-violation condition. Following the experiment, subjects were asked if they recalled meeting the first experimenter in the corridor and what their response to him had been. All subjects remembered him. Some subjects said that they could not recall any noticeable response. The recorded comments made by other subjects, however, were quite consistent with the hypotheses. The following comments are among those made by subjects in the violation condition:

I felt I wanted to walk around them but I couldn't.
[I felt] I had to excuse myself.
I was the outsider and walking by makes you sort of uncomfortable.
It was rude to walk between them.
I said hello as a way of distracting them . . . so that walking through was not an intrusion.

In describing their feelings subjects used words such as awkward, embarrassed, unpleasant, and uncomfortable. These ratings and verbal reports of negative affect generated by a brief, almost momentary encounter are consistent with reports given following protracted crowding (e.g., Griffitt & Veitch, 1971; Smith & Haythorn, 1972). It is important to note that while subjects described the encounter in these terms, their other comments indicated that they had not construed the confederates as unusually rude or hostile or the situation as anything other than commonplace. Collectively, the subjects' comments suggested that these were common reactions to a common situation.

The failure to show differential heart rate changes may have been influenced by the high arousal level which all subjects showed. Any changes that might have resulted from the territorial infringements manipulated here would have been superimposed on those that were evoked when the subject was notified that it was time to be interviewed by the experimenter. This event was more provoking than had been anticipated and may well have masked any treatment effects (i.e., via a ceiling effect that reduced the sensitivity of the heart rate index of arousal).

Many of the nonverbal acts which are associated with the type of territorial challenges discussed here are often explained by reference to good manners and polite behaviors. Within the present framework, these acts serve as one of the principal mechanisms of social intercourse. A prolonged stare may be impolite, but it is also a potent determinant of behavior in man as well as other animals (Chance, 1962; Ellsworth et al., 1972).

In the present study those subjects who were expected to experience the most negative affective arousal also displayed the greatest amount of agonistic expressive behavior. Many of the nonverbal gestures recorded in this study find remarkably close parallels in agonistic encounters in nonhuman primates (e.g., Andrew, 1963; Chance, 1962; Darwin, 1872; Hass, 1970; Jolly, 1972; van Hoof, 1962, 1967; Vine, 1970). In monkeys and apes these gestures communicate status regarding both territory and dominance relationships. These behaviors have a spontaneity which makes it appear as if they function at the periphery of awareness and volitional control. Furthermore, there is some evidence which suggests that their locus of control is in the limbic area of the brain rather than in the cortical regions which control human speech and higher mental functioning (e.g., MacLean, 1958; Ploog & Melnechuk, 1969). The similarity found between the way these gestures are elicited in both human and nonhuman primates implies two complementary ideas. The first is consistent with current trends in primate research and suggests that primate societies are more complicated than has previously been fashionable to suppose. The second is that human society may operate through mechanisms which are less uniquely human than is currently fashionable to suggest.

Given that brief encounters between strangers occasion a variety of agonistic displays and negative affective reactions, it appears that the mundane encounters which we all experience each day constitute unpleasant, even stressful, events, The ubiquity of these events may make them more potent contributors to the "stress of modern life" than has previously been assumed.

REFERENCES

Allgeier, A. R., & Byrne, D. Attraction toward the opposite sex as a determinant of physical proximity. *Journal of Social Psychology,* 1973, *90,* 213-219.

Andrew, R. J. The origin and evolution of the calls and facial expressions of the primates. *Behavior,* 1963, *20,* 1-109.

Argyle, M., & Dean, J. Eye-contact, distance, and affiliation. *Sociometry,* 1965, *29,* 289-304.

Blurton-Jones, N. G. Criteria for use in describing facial expressions in children. *Human Biology,* 1971, *43,* 365-413.

Blurton-Jones, N. G. (Ed.) *Ethological studies of child behaviour.* London: Cambridge University Press, 1972.

Brannigan, C. R., & Humphries, D. A. Human nonverbal behaviour: A means of communication. In N. G. Blurton-Jones (Ed.), *Ethological studies of child behaviour.* London: Cambridge University Press, 1972.

Calhoun, J. B. Space and the strategy of life. In A. H. Esser (Ed.), *Behavior and environment.* New York: Plenum, 1971.

Chance, M. R. A. An interpretation of some agonistic postures: The role of "cut-off" acts and postures. *Symposia of the Zoological Society of London,* 1962, *8,* 71-89.

Chance, M. R. A. Attention structure as the basis of primate rank orders. *Man,* 1967, *2,* 503-518.

Cheyne, J. A., & Efran, M. G. The effect of spatial and interpersonal variables on the invasion of group controlled territories. *Sociometry,* 1972, *35,* 477-489.

Christian, J. J. The pathology of overpopulation. *Military Medicine,* 1963, *128,* 571-603.

Christian, J. J., & Davis, D. E. Adrenal glands in female voles (microtus pennsylvanicus) as related to reproduction and population size. *Journal of Mammalogy,* 1966, *47,* 1-18.

Christian, J. J., Flyger, V., & Davis, D. E. Factors in the mass mortality of a herd of Sika deer, *Cervus nippon. Chesapeake Science,* 1960, *1,* 79-95.

Darwin, C. *The expression of the emotions in man and animals.* London: Murray, 1872.

Deevey, E. S. The hare and the haruspex. In R. Haber (Ed.), *Current research in motivation.* New York: Holt, Rinehart & Winston, 1966.

Efran, M. G., & Cheyne, J. A. Shared space: The cooperative control of spatial areas by two interacting individuals. *Canadian Journal of Behavioural Science,* 1973, *5,* 201-210.

Ellsworth, P. C., Carlsmith, J. M., & Henson, A. The stare as a stimulus to flight in human subjects: A series of field experiments. *Journal of Personality and Social Psychology,* 1972, *21,* 302-311.

Freedman, J. L., Levy, A. S., Buchanan, R. W., & Price, J. Crowding and human aggressiveness. *Journal of Experimental Social Psychology,* 1972, *8,* 528-548.

Freedman, N. The analysis of movement behavior during the clinical interview. In A. W. Siegman & B. Pope (Eds.), *Studies in dyadic communication.* New York: Pergamon, 1972.

Grant, E. C. An ethological description of nonverbal behaviour during interviews. *British Journal of Medical Psychology,* 1968, *41,* 177-184.

Grant, E. C. Human facial expression. *Man,* 1969, *4,* 525-536.

Griffitt, W., & Veitch, R. Hot and crowded: Influences of population density and temperature on interpersonal affective behavior. *Journal of Personality and Social Psychology*, 1971, *17*, 92-98.

Hall, E. T. *The silent language.* Greenwich, Conn.: Fawcett, 1959.

Hass, H. *The human animal: The mystery of man's behavior.* New York: Dell, 1970.

Jolly, A. *The evolution of primate behavior.* London: Macmillan, 1972.

Kleck, R. E. Interaction distance and nonverbal agreeing responses. *British Journal of Social and Clinical Psychology*, 1970, *9*, 180-182.

Leyhausen, P. Dominance and territoriality as complemented in mammalian social structure. In A. H. Esser (Ed.), *Behavior and environment.* New York: Plenum, 1971.

Little, K. B. Personal space. *Journal of Experimental Social Psychology*, 1965, *1*, 237-247.

MacLean, P. D. The limbic system with respect to self preservation and the preservation of the species. *Journal of Nervous and Mental Deficiencies*, 1958, *127*, 1-11.

Madge, J., & Madge, J. *Survey of new army married quarters.* London: Ministry of Public Building and Works, 1965. Cited by R. Sommer, Naturalistic social research. In A. H. Esser (Ed.), *Behavior and environment.* New York: Plenum, 1971.

McBride, G., James, J. W., & Shoffner, R. N. Social forces determining spacing and head orientation in a flock of domestic hens. *Nature*, 1963, *197*, 1272-1273.

McBride, G., King, M. G., & James, J. W. Social proximity effects of galvanic skin responsiveness in adult humans. *Journal of Psychology*, 1965, *61*, 153-157.

McGrew, W. C. *An ethological study of children's behavior.* New York: Academic Press, 1972.

Osgood, C. E., Suci, G., & Tannenbaum, P. *The measurement of meaning.* Urbana: University of Illinois Press, 1957.

Ploog, D., & Melnechuk, T. Primate communication. *Neurosciences Research Program Bulletin*, 1969, *7*, 419-490.

Rodgers, D. A., & Thiessen, D. D. Effects of population density on adrenal size, behavioral arousal and alcohol preference in inbred mice. *Quarterly Journal of Studies on Alcohol*, 1964, *25*, 240-247.

Rosenfeld, H. M. Instrumental affiliative functions of facial and gestural expressions. *Journal of Personality and Social Psychology*, 1966, *4*, 65-72.

Smith, S., & Haythorn, W. W. Effects of compatibility, crowding, group size, and leadership seniority on stress, anxiety, hostility, and annoyance in isolated groups. *Journal of Personality and Social Psychology*, 1972, *22*, 67-79.

Stokols, D. On the distinction between density and crowding: Some implications for future research. *Psychological Review*, 1972, *79*, 275-277.

Thiessen, D. D. Population density and behavior: A review of theoretical and physiological contributions. *Texas Reports on Biology and Medicine*, 1964, *22*, 266-314.

van Hooff, J. A. R. A. M. Facial expressions in higher primates. *Symposium of the Zoological Society of London*, 1962, *8*, 97-125.

van Hooff, J. A. R. A. M. The facial displays of the catarrhine monkeys and apes. In D. Morris (Ed.), *Primate ethology.* London: Weidenfeld & Nicolson, 1967.

Vine, I. Communication by facial-visual signals. In J. M. Crook (Ed.), *Social behavior in birds and mammals*. London: Academic Press, 1970.

NOTES

1. A total of 45 subjects participated in this study, but data for 6 of these were excluded from the analyses because these subjects either were suspicious of deception or failed to comply with the instructions. The remaining 39 subjects left 15 in violation condition, 14 in the minimum violation condition, and 10 in the no-violation condition.

Name Index

Subject Index

Action, distortion of, 151

Adrian College, 112

Aggression, 187–216; annoyance, effect on, 203–211; behavioral consequences of, 188; catharsis, 187, 201–211; decreasing levels, 203–204; energy, 187, 195–196; hydraulic model of, 187; reinforcement, 197–199; rewarding, 197–198; TV violence, 188–191; ventilation therapy, 194–197, 199–200; verbal, 198–199

Altruism, 218, 219; models, 220, 233–245; self-attribution, 248

Ambiguity of intent, 398

Annoyance effect on aggression, 203–211

Antisemitism, 131, 134

Anxiety state, 51–52

Apathy, 219

Arousal, 38–51; attribution theory, 39–41, 43–52; dissonance theory, 329–339; drug-produced, 38–51, 329–339; naturally–occuring, 39; proxemic behavior, 450; reactance to freedom elimination, 367, 375

Asch conformity paradigm, 150, 161

Assimilation–contrast theory, 383

Attitude, 17, 111–112, 119, 120, 123, 124, 302–308; behavior, 303–308, 310–317, 319–327; laboratory induced change, 319–327; measures, 311, 313–314, 317; similarity effects on judicial decisions, 358, 360; verbal, 310–311

Attraction, *see* Interpersonal attraction

Attributional bias, 27–36

Attribution theory, 1, 5–6; arousal, 38–41, 337–338; biased, 28–36; causal, 39–47

Authoritarianism, 351, 354–363; effect on judicial decisions, 360

Authority; compliance with, 179; defiance, 178, 179, 183; loss of responsibility, 181; personality, 351; philosophy of obedience, 176

Balance theory, 4; belief congruence, 67; common enemy, 85, 86, 92; interpersonal attraction, 66

Banality of evil, 179

Barber hypnotic induction procedure, 170

Barber Suggestibility Scale, 171

Barber task motivation instructions, 171

Behavior, 2; actual vs expressed intent, 109; attitude, influence on, 303–308, 310–317; commitment, 314, 315; conformity, 152; consequential vs inconsequential, 108,

THE BOOK MANUFACTURE

Contemporary Social Psychology: Representative Readings was typeset at Fox Valley Typesetting. Printing and binding were by R. R. Donnelley. Cover design was by Don Dickerson. The typefaces used are Helvetica and Times Roman.